WORLD MILITARY LEADERS

A Biographical Dictionary

WORLD MILITARY LEADERS

A Biographical Dictionary

Mark Grossman

An imprint of Infobase Publishing

World Military Leaders: A Biographical Dictionary

Facts On File, Inc.
An imprint of Infobase Publishing
132 West 31st Street
New York NY 10001

ISBN-10: 0-8160-4732-4
ISBN-13: 978-0-8160-4732-1

Library of Congress Cataloging-in-Publication Data

Grossman, Mark.
  World military leaders : a biographical dictionary / by Mark Grossman.
    p.   cm.
  Includes bibliographical references and index.
  ISBN 0-8160-4732-4 (hardcover : alk. paper) 1. Military biography—Dictionaries.
I. Title.
  U51.G76 2005
  355'.0092'2—dc22   2005008908

Facts On File books are available at special discounts when purchased in bulk quantities for businesses, associations, institutions or sales promotions. Please call our Special Sales Department in New York at (212) 967-8800 or (800) 322-8755.

You can find Facts On File on the World Wide Web at http://www.factsonfile.com

Text design by Joan M. McEvoy
Cover design by Cathy Rincon

Printed in the United States of America

VB FOF 10 9 8 7 6 5 4 3 2 1

This book is printed on acid-free paper.

This book is dedicated to my good friends Carol Hoffman,
Paula Herbst, and Audrey and Alan Taylor,
without whose incredible support this volume
would not have been completed;
and to my niece Julie Grossman
and my nephew Bradley Grossman,
who wanted to see their name in print
and finally get the chance.

Breathes There the Man
Sir Walter Scott

Breathes there the man with soul so dead
Who never to himself hath said,
This is my own, my native land!
Whose heart hath ne'er within him burned,
As home his footsteps he hath turned
From wandering on a foreign strand?
If such there breathe, go, mark him well;
For him no minstrel raptures swell;
High though his titles, proud his name,
Boundless his wealth as wish can claim,
Despite those titles, power, and pelf,
The wretch, concentrated all in self,
Living, shall forfeit fair renown,
And, doubly dying, shall go down
To the vile dust from whence he sprung,
Unwept, unhonored, and unsung.

CONTENTS

LIST OF ENTRIES

Kluge, Hans Günther von
Kublai Khan
Kuropatkin, Alexei Nikolaevich
Kutuzov, Mikhail Illarionovich Golenishchev
Lafayette, Marie-Joseph-Paul-Yves Roch-Gilbert du Motier, marquis de
Lambert, John
Lannes, Jean, duc de Montebello
Lee, Robert Edward
Leslie, Alexander, first earl of Leven
Leslie, Sir David, first baron Newark
Lincoln, Benjamin
Lucan, George Charles Bingham, third earl of
MacArthur, Douglas
Macbeth
MacMahon, Marie-Edmé-Patrice-Maurice de, duc de Magenta
Makharoff, Stepan Osipovich
Marion, Francis
Masséna, André, duc de Rivoli
Maurice, prince of Orange and count of Nassau
McClellan, George Brinton
Mehmet II
Miltiades
Moltke, Helmuth Johannes Ludwig, count von Moltke
Moltke, Helmuth Karl Bernard, count von Moltke
Monash, Sir John
Monck, George, duke of Albemarle
Monmouth, James Scott, duke of
Montagu, Edward, second earl of Manchester
Montcalm de Saint-Véran, Louis-Joseph de Montcalm, marquis de
Montfort, Simon de, earl of Leicester
Montgomery, Bernard Law, first viscount Montgomery of Alamein
Montrose, James Graham, first marquis of
Moore, Sir John
Murat, Joachim
Napier, Sir Charles
Napier, Sir Charles James
Napoleon Bonaparte
Narses
Nebuchadnezzar
Nelson, Horatio, Viscount Nelson

Nevsky, Alexander, Saint
Newcastle, William Cavendish, duke of
Ney, Michel, duc d'Elchigen, prince of the Moskowa
Nimitz, Chester William
Nivelle, Robert-Georges
Nogi, Maresuke, Kiten
Norfolk, Thomas Howard, second duke of
Nur-ad-Din
Oda, Nobunaga
Oudinot, Nicolas Charles, duc de Reggio
Oxford, John de Vere, 13th earl of
Paskevich, Ivan Fedorovich
Patton, George Smith, Jr.
Paullus Macedonicus, Lucius Aemilius
Paulus, Friedrich Wilhelm Ernst
Penn, Sir William
Perry, Oliver Hazard
Pershing, John Joseph
Pétain, Henri-Philippe-Benoni-Omer-Joseph
Philip II
Philip VI
Phocion
Plumer of Messines, Herbert Charles Onslow Plumer, first viscount
Pompey
Radetzky, Joseph Wenzel Anton Franz Karl, count Radetzky von Radetz
Raglan, FitzRoy James Henry Somerset, first baron
Ramses II
Rennenkampf, Pavel-Georges Karlovich von
Richard I the Lion-Hearted
Richard III
Ridgway, Matthew Bunker
Roberts, Frederick Sleigh, first earl Roberts of Kandahar
Robert the Bruce
Rodney, George Brydges, first baron Rodney of Stoke-Rodney
Rokossovsky, Konstantin Konstantinovich
Rommel, Erwin Johannes Eugen
Rooke, Sir George
Rosecrans, William Starke
Rupert, Prince
Saladin

INTRODUCTION

It is well that war is so terrible, lest we grow too fond of it.

—Robert E. Lee

The history of warfare can be considered the history of humankind. But stories behind the wars—behind the leaders who led soldiers into battle—are equally important. This is not a work on why battles are fought, or their ultimate disposition. This is a review of the lives and actions of those who commanded armies, some vast and some small, in battle.

At Adrianople in Thrace, August 378, the Eastern Roman emperor Valens took on the Goths, led by Fritigern. Historians believe, through histories written at the time and other evidence, that Valens commanded 20,000 men, while Fritigern had about 100,000 behind him. Valens and nearly the entire Roman army was massacred, one of the worst military defeats of ancient times. However, the Roman historian Ammianus's epic tale of the clash survives even today: "Dust rose in such clouds as to hide the sky, which rang with fearful shouts. In consequence, it was impossible to see the enemy's missiles in flight and dodge them . . . all found their mark, and [these] darts brought death on every side. The barbarians poured on in huge columns, trampling down horse and man and crushing our ranks so to make ordinary retreat impossible." Nearly 1,700 years later, warfare is still part of our lives. As American and other coalition forces fight in Afghanistan and Iraq, tales of battles fought are being written for future historians—and another leader, Tommy Franks, takes his place among those who have held the title *general.*

In the midst of the buildup of American and British troops to invade Afghanistan in October 2001, journalist David White wrote in the *Financial Times:* "No one starts a war—or rather no one in his right senses should do so—without being clear in his mind what he intends to achieve by that war and how he intends to conduct it." The history of warfare—and humans' role in it—has been studied over the centuries through writings, reminiscences, and strategies. The character, responsibilities, and service of these soldiers, from the earliest of times to the present, are all examined in this work. The forces they led and the battles they fought are all observed and considered.

In his *Military Dictionary* (1810), Charles James observes:

> The best modern generals have never lost sight of the brilliant examples that they have been left; they have never ceased to call into practice the tactics of the ancients, as far as the difference of arms and a change of manners would allow. To those who peruse the histories of the 17th and 18th centuries and read over the actions of the most celebrated generals this observation will appear peculiarly apposite. It is justified in the uniform conduct of the great Condé, Prince Eugène, Turenne, Marlborough, Marshal Saxe and Frederick the Great. . . . Impressed as it were by the result of cumulative reflection they overlook immediate occurrences, plunge into futurity and snatch out of the womb of time the ultimate issue of events.

But James wrote this at the dawn of the 19th century. Over the period of human history, writers have studied the inner workings of the military and military science. In the sixth century B.C., Sunzi (Sun Tzu) wrote, "An Army should always be ready but never used." Napoleon Bonaparte allegedly stated, "Victory belongs to the most persevering." A commander, be it of a land or sea force, stands above all as the leader, the chief officer of his force, the chief strategist, the chief inspiration for those who follow him. A leader has to embody the virtues of wisdom, sincerity, benevolence, courage, and strictness. As armies have gained in their abilities to fight differing kinds of wars, these responsibilities and virtues have grown. From the beginning of human history, when troops marched into battle with spears and knives, to today's airborne missiles and machine guns, this role has expanded. This work examines how these leaders used the tools given them.

While such words as *commander* or *leader* are universally understood, the terms *general* and *admiral* have only come into use within the last 500 years. Thus, such leaders as Nebuchadnezzar, Belisarius, Mark Anthony, Julius Caesar, Gnaeus Pompeius, Nur-ad-Din, Richard Neville, and Alexander Nevsky are included in this book though none was termed admiral or general. The custom of so naming commanders of armed forces became common in Europe in the 16th century, and over time, certain terminology became standard.

The basic fighting unit, a regiment or battalion, was led by a lieutenant colonel or colonel. Two or more regiments were called a brigade, commanded by a brigadier general (one star), while two or more brigades formed a division, commanded by a major general (two stars). Two or more divisions formed an army corps under a lieutenant general (three stars), while two or more corps became an army under a general (four stars). As armies and navies became ever larger, a five-star rank became necessary for commanders in chief with several armies under their command. In the United States, this officer is titled General of the Army, although in some nations the much older term *field marshal* is used. The same general principle applies to naval officers who may lead a flotilla, then a squadron, then a fleet, and then fleets; the highest rank is Fleet Admiral (Admiral of the Fleet in Great Britain).

The granting of such titles has often been merely an honor, a token of gratitude from a nation. Frequent reference is made in this book to commanders being given the rank of field marshal for a notable victory, even though they only led a division in the battle concerned. Thus, Congress specifically created the six-star rank of General of the Armies for John J. Pershing (though he never wore the insignia). George C. Marshall was awarded the rank of five-star general, but he was not a commander in the field, and for this reason he was excluded from consideration in this book.

It should also be remembered that when a country sends an army to fight with an ally, the army commanders may be of equal rank, but one will have authority over the other, with government agreement; Eisenhower and Montgomery in the Second World War are typical examples. In this book, I have used commonly understood terms for clarity wherever possible.

I set out at the start with a list of some 1,000 names of military leaders I hoped to examine. The one main objective was to focus on those generals and admirals who had fought at least one major battle—on sea or land—which was important to history. With this key goal in mind, the list was whittled down to the entries that comprise this work. Any errors of fact or other errors are entirely mine. Finally, the reader should note that all dates are rendered in the European—and military—style of day-month-year.

I would like to thank the following people and institutions, without whose help this work would never have been completed: The staff of the British Library, London, where much of this book was written; the staff of the New York Public Library, who aided in finding some important material not found anywhere else; the staff of the Hayden Library of Arizona State University, Tempe, Arizona, where much of the research for this work was conducted; and the staff of the Maricopa County Library, Phoenix, who ably retrieved for me many books via interlibrary loan.

—Mark Grossman

Abbas I (Abbas the Great) (1571–1629) *shah of Persia*

Abbas the Great (ruled 1587–1629), known for his military exploits in the Persian Gulf and in what is now modern-day Iraq, was the grandson of Shah Tahmasp and the son of Shah Mohammed Mirza Khudabanda (d. 1595). Abbas may have been named after Abbas (d. 653), the uncle of Mohammed and of Caliph Ali. Abbas I was named as ruler of Khurasan (now modern Khorasan, Iran) in 1581, and six years later, he succeeded his father as shah when Mohammed abdicated.

As he took the throne of Persia (now Iran), Abbas's reign was challenged by a revolt in Persia and the threat of an invasion by forces of the Ottoman Empire (centered in what is now modern Turkey). Abbas paid tribute to the Ottomans to forge a peace and end the threat of incursion; he was then given a free hand to turn on the rebellious forces within his country and defeat them. A military campaign against rebelling Uzbeks (now part of Uzbekistan) in Khurasan was also successful. In 1598, after a lengthy and protracted war, he ended the threat from the Uzbeks when his forces took control of the city of Moshad (now one of Iran's major cities). As the first of the Safavid leaders, Abbas helped establish modern Persia—later renamed Iran—as a single state, and his advocacy of a single language—in this case, Farsi—unified that nation.

With internal dissent and rebellion crushed, Abbas turned back to the potential external enemy: the Ottoman Empire. He opened his attack in 1601, with his forces taking the city of Tabriz (now the capital of East Azerbaijan province, Iran) in 1604. The mountainous area in what is now known as the Caucasus also fell to Abbas's forces, most notably Georgia and Shirvan. Although Abbas's military exploits in this area were largely successful, Ottoman resistance caused the conflict to last until the end of his reign.

In 1606, Abbas fought off a major offensive by the Ottoman Turks under Sultan Ahmed II, including a significant clash at Sis, where 20,000 Turks were killed in a single battle. Although Turkey sued for peace, they continued to fight Abbas and his empire in various clashes. However, for many years there was relative peace in his kingdom. It was not until 1616 that Abbas again moved against the Turks, fighting a two-year war that culminated in a major victory in 1618. In 1622, Abbas's army marched on the island of Hormuz, in the Strait of Hormuz, and, with the assistance of the English East India Company, threw out the Portuguese merchants who controlled that island's trade. Abbas then moved the center of trading activity to the city of Gombroon (now in Iran), renamed it Bandar Abbas, and established a foothold in the major markets of the Persian Gulf. In 1623, Abbas's forces took Baghdad, now in modern

Iraq, but when they tried to extend their hold on Mosul (in modern northern Iraq) and Basra (in modern southern Iraq, near the Persian Gulf), his troops were thrown back and could not hold either city. In another clash, he took the city of Kandahar (also Qandahar, in modern Afghanistan), but it was lost to the Uzbeks in 1630, a year after Abbas's death.

During his reign, Abbas was also known for his numerous public works projects, most notably at the Persian capital of Esfahan. He died in 1629 at the age of either 58 or 59. His tomb at Kashan, located in the Shrine of Habib ibn-Musa, is considered one of the marvels of that age.

Modern historians remember Abbas not only for his unification of Persia but for his skillful use of the military to crush internal rebellion and meet external threats. His drafting of two English brothers, the mercenaries Sir Robert and Sir Anthony Sherley, to train the Persian army in modern fighting methods unknown to most of the Middle Eastern world, rank him as one of the lesser-known but more important military leaders in world history. Historian Tom Magnusson writes: "A remarkable monarch, Abbas was intelligent and farsighted but sometimes cruel and harsh; he was a skillful and energetic administrator and general, and his reform of the Persian army made it very nearly the equal of the Ottoman army."

References: Keegan, John, and Andrew Wheatcroft, "Abbas," in *Who's Who in Military History from 1453 to the Present Day* (London: Routledge, 1996), 1–2; Monshi, Eskandar Beg, *History of Shah 'Abbas the Great—Tarike 'alam ar aye 'Abbas I,* translated by Roger M. Savory (Boulder, Colo.: Westview Press, 1978); Sherley, Sir Anthony, *His Relation of his travels into Persia: . . .* (London: Printed [by Nicholas Okes] for Nathaniell Butter, and Joseph Bagfet, 1613); Magnusson, Tom, "Abbas I the Great," in *The Encyclopedia of Military Biography,* edited by Trevor N. Dupuy, Curt Johnson, and David L. Bongard (London: I. B. Taurus, 1992), 2.

Abercromby, Sir Ralph (1734–1801) *British general*

Sir Ralph Abercromby's several important military victories were matched by his command of the British army, in which he restored discipline and morale. Historians Martin Windrow and Francis K. Mason write: "Although his career was crowned by several notable victories, Abercromby is remembered more as the restorer of high professional standards in the British Army than as a master of tactics."

Abercromby was born in the village of Tullibody, in Clackmannanshire, Scotland, on 7 October 1734, the eldest son of George Abercromby. He was educated at the prestigious Rugby school and later studied law at the University of Leipzig and Edinburgh University. Entering into a military career, he was offered a cornet's commission in the 3rd Dragoon Guards in March 1756. He saw action with this unit in the Seven Years' War (1756–63) and rose to become a lieutenant colonel in 1773 and brevet colonel in 1780. In 1781, he was named a colonel in the King's Irish Regiment. However, because he sympathized with the American colonists fighting for independence, he felt it better to leave the military than continue and possibly be forced to fight in a war in which he did not believe. He retired in 1783.

Abercromby decided to enter the political realm: He was elected to a seat in Parliament from Clackmannan, Scotland, but he quickly tired of his duties and left office; he was succeeded by his brother Robert (1740–1827), who also later served as a general in the British army. When France declared war on England in 1793, Ralph Abercromby again took up arms for England and was named as commander of a brigade under the duke of York, second son of George III. Serving for a time in Holland, he saw action at La Cateau (16 April 1794) and was wounded at Nijmwegen. He was in charge of the British withdrawal from Holland in the winter of 1794 and conducted this duty so well that he was honored with a Knighthood of the order of the Bath. In 1795, the king named him to succeed Sir Charles Grey as commander in chief of British forces in the West Indies.

In 1796, Abercromby once again went into battle, seizing the islands of Grenada, Trinidad, St. Lucia, St. Vincent, and the then-French settlements of Demerara and Essequibo. He was then recalled to England, where in 1797 he was appointed as head of the English army in Ireland. However, the Irish government blocked his efforts to reform the army. Abercromby resigned his commission after less than a year in office. That same year, 1797, he was made second in command to the duke of York, with whom he had previously served, in the English drive to retake Holland, which ended in disaster and failure.

In 1801, Abercromby was sent to Egypt to help drive the French out of that country. When the English army landed at Aboukir Bay on 2 March 1801, 5,000 English soldiers faced a large French force under the command of General Louis Friant. Historian George Bruce writes: "The landing [of the English] was effected under a heavy musketry and artillery fire, which cost the assailants 1,100 killed and wounded. The French were driven from their positions with a loss of 500 men."

Aboukir is known to historians as an important English military victory. After this success, Abercromby advanced to the important French threshold of Alexandria. In the midst of the battle on 21 March 1801, Abercromby was hit in the thigh by a rifle ball. He was taken from the field and placed on the English flagship *Foudroyant,* but surgeons were unable to remove the ball. As Abercromby lay dying, according to one account, one of his men placed a blanket under his head. "What is it you have placed under my head?" he inquired. When told it was a soldier's blanket, he replied, "Only a soldier's blanket? Make haste and return it to him at once!"

Seven days after being shot, Abercromby succumbed to his wound at the age of 66. His body was moved to Malta, and he was laid to rest there. The battle of Alexandria, where he lost his life, was a significant one for the French, who found the English troops to be their equal and whose casualties were extremely heavy. The English lost 1,464 men, including Abercromby.

A wave of sympathy for the dead general swept over England, and the House of Commons voted to erect a memorial in his honor in St. Paul's Cathedral in London. His widow was made Baroness Abercromby of Aboukir and Tullibody, given a pension of £2,000 a year, and allowed to keep the title in her family for two additional generations. A memoir of the later years of Abercromby's life (1793–1801) by his third son, James (who was Speaker of the House of Commons, 1835–39, and became Lord Dunfermline), was published in 1861.

References: Dunfermline, James Abercromby, Lord, *Lieutenant-General Sir Ralph Abercromby, K.B., 1793–1801: a Memoir by his son James Lord Dunfermline* (Edinburgh, Scotland: Edmonston and Douglas, 1861); Rough, Sir William, *Lines on the Death of the Late Sir Ralph Abercromby.* (London: J. Bell, 1801); Windrow, Martin, and Francis K. Mason, "Abercromby, Sir Ralph," in *The Wordsworth Dictionary of Military Biography* (Hertford-shire, U.K.: Wordsworth Editions Ltd., 1997), 3–4; Bruce, George, "Abukir II," in *Collins Dictionary of Wars* (Glasgow, Scotland: HarperCollins Publishers, 1995), 1.

Abrantes, duc de *See* JUNOT, JEAN-ANDOCHE ALEXANDRE, DUC D'ABRANTES.

Æthelstan (Athelstan) (ca. 894–95–939) *English king*
Crowned on the King's Stone at Kingston-upon-Thames (with a claim to be the first undisputed king of all England), Æthelstan is most remembered for his warfare against the Scots and Welsh. According to several sources, he was born in either 894 or 895, the son of Edward the Elder (870–924), who served as king of England from 899 to 924, and Edward's wife Egwina (or Ecgwyn). Edward's father was Alfred the Great (ca. 849–899), the great Saxon king whose battles to save England from Danish invasions culminated in the capture of London and victory at the battle of Edington (878). When Edward the Elder died, his son Æthelstan succeeded on 4 September 924, and he was crowned at Kingston-upon-Thames shortly afterward. A year later, the new monarch signed a treaty with Sihtric of York, to avoid warfare for Northumbria. However, when Sihtric died in 927, Æthelstan expelled Sihtric's brother, Guthfrith, and as his forces moved into Northumbria. He met with several tribes, including the Northumbrians and Strathclyde Britons, who agreed to allow him to take control, the first southern English king to do so. Thereafter he called himself *rex totius Britanniae* (king of all Britain).

In 934, Æthelstan's forces invaded Scotland by land and sea; his land forces quickly moved as far north as Dunottar, while the navy seized Caithness. He took control over Scotland, but three years later a mighty confederation formed by King Constantine III of Scotland, the Welsh of Strathclyde, Owen of Cumberland, and two Norwegian leaders, Anlaf Godfredsson and Anlaf Sihtricsson, set out to end his reign. These forces confronted Æthelstan's army—which was supported by his half brother Edmund—at Brunanburh. Since the 12th century, historians have tried to locate the exact site of the battle, to no avail; many historians believe it was fought in either northwestern England or southwestern Scotland, near the Solway Firth. What little information that exists comes from the *Anglo-Saxon Chronicle* for 937:

> In this year King Aethelstan, Lord of warriors,
> ring-giver to men, and his brother also,
> Prince Eadmund, won eternal glory
> in battle with sword edges
> around Brunanburh. They split the shield-wall,
> they hewed battle shields with
> the remnants of hammers.
> The sons of Eadweard, it was only befitting
> their noble descent
> from their ancestors that they should often
> defend their land in battle against
> each hostile people,
> horde and home. The enemy perished,
> Scots men and seamen,
> fated they fell. The field flowed
> with blood of warriors, from sun up
> in the morning, when the glorious star
> glided over the earth, God's bright candle,
> eternal lord, till that noble creation
> sank to its seat. There lay many a warrior
> by spears destroyed;
> Northern men
> shot over shield, likewise Scottish as well,
> weary, war sated.

It remains unknown whether this "account" was written by an observer or a mere writer wishing to catalog this great battle. Few historians mention the casualties inflicted at Brunanburh; historian George Bruce reports that there was "great slaughter." In any event, Æthelstan prevailed.

Æthelstan lived for two years following his great victory at Brunanburh. He died on 27 October 939, was buried at Malmesbury Abbey, just south of Wiltshire, and was succeeded by his half brother Edmund. His reign had lasted a short 15 years, but in that time he established himself as a significant figure in English history. Æthelstan was the first English king to develop relations with other European rulers, and his half sisters married into the royal families of France and the Holy Roman Empire.

References: Hilliam, David, "Athelstan," in *Kings, Queens, Bones and Bastards: Who's Who in the English Monarchy from Egbert to Elizabeth II* (Phoenix Mill, Thrupp, Stroud, U.K.: Sutton Publishing Limited, 2000), 17; Attenborough, F. L., ed. and trans., *The Laws of the Earliest English Kings.* (New York: Russell & Russell, 1963); Garnett, James Mercer, *Elene; Judith; Æthelstan, or, The Fight at Brunanburh; Byrthnoth, or, The Fight at Maldon; and The Dream of the Rood: Anglo-Saxon Poems.* Translated by James Mercer Garnett (Boston: Ginn & Company, 1901); Philpotts, Robert, *What Happened at Maldon? The Story of the Battle of Maldon, August 991* (London: Blackwater Books, 1991); Macrae-Gibson, O. D., "How Historical Is the Battle of Maldon?," *Medium Ævum*, 39, no. 2 (1970): 89–107; Dumville, David N. "Between Alfred the Great and Edgar the Peacemaker: Æthelstan, First King of England," in *Wessex and England from Alfred to Edgar: Six Essays on Political, Cultural, and Ecclesiastical Revival* (Woodbridge, U.K.: Boydell Press, 1992), 141–171.

Aetius, Flavius (Aëtius) (ca. 390–454) *Roman general*

Noted chiefly for having defeated ATTILA and the Huns in what was the last major military victory for the Roman Empire before it fell, Flavius Aetius was born at Dorostolus, in the province of Moesia (now near the Black Sea in the Balkans). He was the son of Gaudentius, who is identified simply as a master-general in the Roman army cavalry, later to become master of the horse and count of Africa. Moesia was a Roman stronghold in the Balkan area when Aetius was born. At some point in his youth, he was kidnapped by barbarians and raised as one of them, first by the Goths and later by the Huns; he was raised personally by Rhuas, the king of the Huns. Aetius acquired the knowledge of barbarian tactics, and in 424 he commanded a force of some 60,000 barbarians into what is now Italy.

Following the death of the Roman emperor Honorius on 15 August 423, there was a fierce struggle to succeed him. Although Honorius's relative Valentinian had positioned himself to become emperor, the throne was seized by Ioannes (also called Johannes), the *primicerius notatiorum* (chief notary), who was backed by ambassadors Aetius and the Huns. The Eastern Roman emperor Theodosius II sent ambassadors to Rome, and they persuaded some of Ioannes's aides to betray him; he was arrested, taken to a small village, and executed. When word of Ioannes's arrest (but not his execution) arrived at the Huns' camp, Aetius set out with a force to rescue him. Valentinian, taking control of Rome, offered Aetius a pardon and named him the count of Italy in exchange for his ending any war against Ioannes's killers. Aetius accepted this offer, which led to his becoming one of the most important generals in the Western Roman Empire. In 429, he was named a *magister utriusque militum* (master of the soldiers).

One of Aetius's chief rivals for power was Count Bonifacius (Boniface), the *comes* (count) of Africa, who, siding with the Vandals in Africa, marched on Rome to end Aetius's influence. When the Hunnic and Vandal armies met in battle at Rimini (432), Aetius killed Bonifacius with his own javelin.

From 433, Aetius was involved in the Roman wars in Gaul (modern France) against many of the barbarian tribes there, including the Visigoths and Franks. However, few of his military accomplishments are noted by historians. In 436, Aetius and a Hunnic army defeated the Burgundians, a group of East Germanic tribesmen, after they had invaded Upper Belgica (now north and east of the River Loire in modern France). Aetius's victory against this tribe was so complete—more than 20,000 Burgundians died in battle, as opposed to few Romans and Huns—that the clash is remembered in history in *The Nibelungenlied,* an epic poem written in Middle High German around 1200.

Aetius's greatest military victory is that of Châlons-sur-Marne, also called the battle of Maurica or Campus Mauriacus, or the battle of the Catalunian Plains. On 20 September 451, Aetius, commanding groups of barbarian soldiers, including Visigoths and Burgundians—both of whom he had previously defeated—faced Attila and the Huns, Aetius's former allies. Attila had turned against the Roman Empire to rampage across Rome-controlled Europe, devastating the Balkans and exacting tribute from the Eastern Roman Empire. When the Huns turned on Gaul, Western Roman emperor Marcian called on Aetius to defeat his former allies. At Châlons-sur-Marne, Attila gathered the forces of many barbarian tribes, including the Ostrogoths, the Gepids, the Thuringians, and the Franks. To start the battle, Aetius dispatched Thorismund, the son of King Theodoric of the Visigoths, and his forces to seize an area that overlooked the whole field; Thorismund battled back the Hunnic forces to take the area. The Huns joined the Ostrogoths to assault the main Visigothic regiment, but the Visigoths held despite the death of King Theodoric. A contingent of Gepids attacked a position held by Romans and Franks, but they, too, could not break through.

The battle lasted throughout the day; it is estimated that perhaps 300,000 men died, although many historians dispute this number. The end of the fight came when, in the darkness, Thorismund and his men charged down the hill from the heights he had seized and drove the Huns and Ostrogoths into flight.

Edward Creasy, who named Châlons as one of the 15 most decisive battles in world history, writes: "But when the morning broke and revealed the extent of the carnage with which the plains were heaped for miles, the successful allies saw also and respected the resolute attitude of their antagonist. Neither were any measures taken to blockade him in his camp, and so to extort by famine that submission which it was too plainly perilous to enforce with the sword. Attila was allowed to march back the remnants of his army without molestation, and even with the semblance of success." The battle was critically important in the history of Europe since it halted the advancement of the Huns to France and broke the hitherto unstoppable Attila, who died two years later. As a result, the Huns were never the power they had been before Châlons-sur-Marne.

Aetius's dreams of victory were short-lived. In September 454, he was about to marry one of his sons to the daughter of Roman emperor Valentinian III. However, during an argument over whether Aetius's son could become emperor, Valentinian drew a dagger and murdered the general. The foul deed would cost the Roman Empire its very existence: Lacking a reliable military commander to stave off outside threats, Rome would be invaded and destroyed in two decades' time. Aetius's death was avenged when one of his friends accosted Valentinian at the Campus Martius in Rome and stabbed him to death.

References: Gwatkin, H. M., et al., eds., *The Cambridge Mediaeval History,* 8 vols. (Cambridge, U.K.: Cambridge University Press, 1911–36), I:418–419; Hodgkin, Thomas, *Italy and Her Invaders,* 6 vols. (Oxford, U.K.: Clarendon Press, 1880–89); Mócsy, András, *Pannonia and Upper Moesia: A History of the Middle Danube Provinces of the Roman Empire* (London: Routledge & K. Paul, 1974); "Challons, Battle of," in *The Hutchinson Dictionary of Ancient and Medieval Warfare* (Oxford, U.K.: Helicon Publishing, Ltd., 1998), 64–65; "Flavius Aetius," in *Command: From Alexander the Great to Zhukov—The Greatest Commanders of World History,* edited by James Lucas (London: Bloomsbury Publishing, 1988), 39–40.

Agricola, Gnaeus Julius (37–93) *Roman general*
Although Gnaeus Agricola is remembered for his conquests of the British Isles, most of the information on him comes from notes taken by his son-in-law, the famed Roman historian Tacitus, which appeared in the work *Agricola.* He was born on 13 June A.D. 37 in Forum Julii, in the province of Gallia Narbonensis (now Fréjus, in the area of Provence, France), the son of Julius Graecinus, a praetor (a magistrate with judicial duties). When he was 18, he was made a *tribunus laticlavius* (military tribune) on the military staff of Gaius Suetonius Paulinus, who served as governor of Britain from A.D. 58 to 61. He also served on the staff of Paulinus's successor, Publius Petronius Turpilianus. After marrying, Agricola was made a quaestor (a magistrate with financial powers), considered the first step in a career in the Roman governmental hierarchy. In 66 he was advanced to the office of people's tribune, and two years later he became a *praetor peregrinus* (a judicial magistrate who decided cases between foreigners).

In A.D. 69, when a civil war broke out in Rome, Agricola sided with Vespasian against the Emperor Vitellius. Vespasian was victorious, and he rewarded Agricola by naming him *legatus legionis* (commander of a legion [today's general]). He commanded the 20th Legion in Britain, serving under the governor Quintus Petillius Cerialis. Agricola was given the status of a patrician when he returned to Rome in 73 and served for a short time as governor of Aquitania (A.D. 74–77). In 77, he was named a consul as well as *legatus augusti pro-praetore,* or governor, of Britain. It was during this period that Agricola rose to become a major military leader. From 78 until 84, he fought numerous tribes in England and Wales. In 78, Roman forces decisively defeated the Ordovices tribe in northern Wales and routed the Druids on the island of Ynys Môn (today's Anglesey) off the northwestern coast of Wales. Using these victories, Agricola colonized England with a series of garrisons. Marching northward and westward into Scotland and Wales, his forces took more territory under their control, and he established a frontier of posts between the firths of Clota and Bodotria (now the Clyde and Forth rivers). In 83, the Caledonians tried to destroy Roman forces, but the Romans crossed the Forth and Agricola defeated them at Mons Graupius (now Ardock) in 84. A legacy of Agricola's campaign is the Roman fortress at Inchtuthil (near Dunkeld), built that year.

It was at this time that the new Roman emperor, Domitian, recalled Agricola to Rome, probably out of jealously of Agricola's conquest of the British islands. Agricola was offered the proconsulship of Asia (today's western Turkey), but he refused and instead retired to his family home in Gallia Narbonensis (today's southern France), where he died on 23 August 93 at the age of 53.

References: Tacitus, Cornelius, *The Agricola,* edited by Duane Reed Stuart (New York: Macmillan, 1924); Hanson, W. S., *Agricola and the Conquest of the North* (Totowa, N.J.: Barnes and Noble, 1987); Charlesworth, Martin Percival, *Five Men: Character Studies from the Roman Empire* (Cambridge, Mass.: Harvard University Press, 1936).

Agrippa, Marcus Vipsanius (63–12 B.C.)
Roman general and statesman
Little is known of Marcus Agrippa's beginnings. He was born in 63 B.C. to parents of a lower class, although some historians doubt this; his schooling and upbringing remain unknown. At some point in his life he became friends with Octavian (later AUGUSTUS), whose uncle, Julius CAESAR, became the great Roman general and statesman. Agrippa was at Octavian's side when the latter was informed in March 44 B.C. that Caesar had been assassinated in Rome, and Agrippa went with him to Rome to claim the throne of the Roman Empire. When Caesar's enemies blocked Octavian, Agrippa aided his friend in forming a private army to fight them. Although the two were close during this period, no mention of Agrippa is made in any of the histories of the famous battles between Octavian and his enemies, most notably Philippi (42 B.C.). However, during the so-called War of Perusia (40 B.C.), a year-long siege of what is today Perugia, Agrippa took a leading role, and Octavian rewarded him by naming him governor of Gaul (modern France).

In 38 B.C., while still governor of Gaul, Agrippa led an army to annihilate a force of rebel tribes from Aquitane; he followed this victory by crossing the Rhine River in a punitive expedition against the German tribes, a service for which he was named consul. At the same time, Octavian had been defeated by Sextus Pompeius, the son of the famed Roman general POMPEY, at the battle of Cumæ (38 B.C.). Agrippa took control of Octavian's army in what is known as the War of the Second Triumvirate. At Naucholus on 3 September 36

Marcus Agrippa

the Roman Senate and had the power to veto senatorial legislation. His two sons, Gaius and Lucius, were named as possible successors to Emperor Augustus. Agrippa was sent to the eastern part of the Roman Empire to oversee the defense of the eastern provinces, and he stayed there from 17 to 13 B.C. He returned to lead the Roman armies in a bloodless suppression of a Pannonian insurrection in Illyricum. However, he became ill and returned to Rome, where he died sometime in 12 B.C. Little known today, Agrippa helped to lay firm foundations for the Roman Empire. His descendants included the emperors Nero and Caligula.

References: Reinhold, Meyer, *Marcus Agrippa: A Biography* (Geneva: N.Y.: W. F. Humphrey Press, 1933); Wright, Frederick Adam, *Marcus Agrippa: Organizer of Victory* (London: G. Routledge & Sons, 1937); Lewis, Charles Lee, *Famous Old-World Sea Fighters* (London: G. G. Harrap, 1929); Shipley, Frederick W., *Agrippa's Building Activities in Rome* (St. Louis, Mo.: Washington University Press, 1933); Bruce, George, "Mylex" and "Naulochus," in *Collins Dictionary of Wars* (Glasgow, Scotland: Harper-Collins Publishers, 1995), 171, 174.

B.C., Agrippa and some 300 ships met Sextus Pompeius with a navy of equal strength. Agrippa won a decisive victory, and Pompeius fled after losing more than 380 of his ships. That same year, in a second battle at Mylae (no exact date), Agrippa again defeated Pompeius's forces; Sextus Pompeius was captured and, a year later, put to death. These victories aided Octavian in taking power, and he made peace with his enemies, most notably Mark ANTONY. Eventually, however, this peace broke down, and the two parties went to war. Augustus put Agrippa in charge of his fleet, and the defeat of Antony at Actium (2 September 31 B.C.) made Octavian ruler of the entire Roman Empire. For this service Agrippa was again made a consul, and when Octavian—now called Augustus—consolidated his rule in Rome, Agrippa became the emperor's deputy in all but name. When Marcellus, Augustus's nephew, died, the emperor gave the hand of his widow, Julia, to his friend and closest adviser, Agrippa.

In 19 B.C., Agrippa put down a rising in Spain. The following year, he was named *tribunicia potestas* (tribune of the plebs), an official who oversaw the workings of

Ahenobarbus, Cnaeus Domitius (?–31 B.C.)
Roman general
Little is known of Cnaeus Domitius Ahenobarbus, including his exact birth date. What is known is that he was the scion of a family of distinguished Roman citizens; historian William Smith outlined his genealogical chart in his famed *Dictionary of Greek and Roman Mythology* (1844). According to Smith, Ahenobarbus was a direct descendant great-grandson of the first Cnaeus Domitius Ahenobarbus (?–196 B.C.), a Roman consul and legate to SCIPIO AFRICANUS in the war against Antiochus the Great. His father, Lucius Domitius Ahenobarbus, took his son to the battle at Pharsalia (better known as the battle of Pharsalus, 48 B.C.), and it appears that they sided with the forces of the Roman general Gnaeus Pompeius Magnus, better known as POMPEY. Pompey was defeated at Pharsalia by Julius CAESAR, and Lucius Ahenobarbus was killed in flight after the battle. Cnaeus Ahenobarbus survived, though he could not return to his native Italy until he was pardoned by Caesar in 46 B.C.

Two years later, on 15 March 44 B.C., Caesar was murdered by a group of conspirators, including his own adopted son, Marcus Junius Brutus. Some historians believe that Ahenobarbus, seeking revenge for Pompey's defeat, was one of the conspirators, but the evidence is conflicting, and he was not one of the assassins. However, once the murder had been committed, Ahenobarbus left Rome and followed Brutus when the latter fled to what is now Macedonia. Rome then began to hunt down the assassins and conspirators. In 42 B.C., when the Roman Domitius Calvinus tried to sail his fleet from Brundisium (modern Brindisi, southern Italy), Ahenobarbus, commanding some 50 ships in the Ionian Sea, met and defeated him. However, on land at Philippi (in Macedonia, northwest of Mount Pangea, near the Aegean Sea), 100,000 men under Brutus and Cassius fought the Roman legions under Octavian (later AUGUSTUS) and Mark ANTONY, with the Roman army victorious. Brutus committed suicide following the defeat, and Ahenobarbus became a pirate, plundering the coast of the Ionian Sea.

In 40 B.C., Mark Antony agreed to pardon Ahenobarbus, naming him as the governor of Bithynia (now in modern Turkey), where he took part in Antony's Parthian campaign. He was given the title of consul in 32 B.C. That same year, though, Octavius and Antony severed all ties and became sworn enemies. Ahenobarbus sided with Antony, who was having an affair with Cleopatra. Because of that affair, many of Antony's officers felt he should step aside and allow Ahenobarbus to command them. Instead, Ahenobarbus crossed over to Octavian, who destroyed Antony's forces at the battle of Actium. Ahenobarbus was not involved in that battle, having died mysteriously days before it happened. The exact date and manner of his death, as well as his place of burial, remain a mystery. His great-grandson, Nero Claudius Drusus Germanicus (A.D. 37–68) became Nero, emperor of Rome.

References: "Ahenobarbus," in *Dictionary of Greek and Roman Biography and Mythology,* 3 vols., edited by William Smith (London: Taylor and Walton, 1844), I:83–86; Bruce, George, "Philippi," in *Collins Dictionary of Wars* (Glasgow, Scotland: HarperCollins Publishers, 1995), 194.

Alaric I (ca. 370–410) *Visigoth military leader*
Alaric was born the son of a nobleman about A.D. 370 on Peuce Island, an island in the delta of the Danube

River now in Romania. Although it is unknown exactly when he became the leader of the Visigothic tribe, for some time he served as the chief of Gothic forces serving in the Roman army. In 394, it was first noted that he was named as a military leader of the *fœderati* (Visigoth regular troops), and in this capacity he fought for the emperor Theodosius I in crushing the forces of Eugenius, a usurper to the Roman throne, at the battle of the Frigidus (394). However, following the death of Theodosius in 395, Alaric left the service of Rome and shortly thereafter was named as head of the Visigoths. Almost immediately, Alaric turned on his old employer. Charging that Rome had failed to pay the Goths for serving the emperor, he decided to exact tribute by capturing Roman property and marched with the Visigothic army toward Constantinople, then the capital of the Eastern Roman Empire. When Roman forces in that city seemed ready to overwhelm him, he turned south, marching into Greece, sacking the Piraeus at Athens, and striking the cities of Argos, Megara, and the former capital of Sparta. In 396, however, Flavius Stilicho, a Roman general, succeeded in trapping Alaric's force in Greece, though Alaric himself escaped. In a surprising turn of fortune, Alaric regained power when the Eastern Roman emperor Arcadius, probably fearful of the growing influence of the Western Empire based in Rome, made him governor of Illyria (part of today's Yugoslavia), and named him *magister militum* (master of soldiers).

After gathering troops and weapons, Alaric turned his army west and invaded Italy, where he was again met and defeated by the Roman general Stilicho at Pollentia (now Pollenza, Italy) on 6 April 402. Alaric subsequently attempted a second invasion of Italy but again met with defeat. It was not until after Flavius Stilicho was murdered in 408 and many Roman troops defected to Alaric's side that the tide turned. By this time tired of warfare, Alaric offered peace to the Western Roman emperor Flavius Honorius, but the emperor refused, and in 408 Alaric marched on Rome. This time he could not be stopped, and he laid siege to the city until the Roman Senate agreed to his request for land and tribute. However, Honorius held his position, and in 409 Alaric again invaded Italy and surrounded Rome. When Honorius again refused to meet his demands, Alaric named Attalus, a Roman noble, as the western emperor, in exchange for which Attalus appointed Alaric as *magister utriusque militum* (literally, "master of both services").

However, when Attalus refused to let Alaric move his army into Africa, Alaric again besieged Rome, deposing Attalus, whose enemies opened Rome's gates to him. When Alaric marched in on 24 August 410, he became the first foreign military leader to occupy that city in over 800 years.

Alaric was now free to march into Africa, whose corn both Rome and Alaric badly needed, but he was seriously ill. The Visigoths left Rome and marched north through Italy, and he died at Cosentia, Bruttium (modern-day Cosenza, Italy). He was buried by his comrades, but his grave is now lost.

Sources on the life of Alaric are scant; the chief authorities for any information are the historians Orosius and the poet Claudian, whose contemporary works have been studied thoroughly. Jordanes, a Visigothic historian who lived in the A.D. sixth century, wrote a history of the Visigoths and included information on Alaric not seen in other publications.

References: Brion, Marcel, *Alaric the Goth,* translated by Frederick H. Martens (London: Thornton Butterworth Limited, 1932); Stevens, F. P., *From Constantine to Alaric* (Liphook, Hants., U.K.: Privately published, 1984).

Albemarle, duke of *See* MONCK, GEORGE, DUKE OF ALBEMARLE.

Albert, archduke of Austria (Friedrich Rudolf Albrecht Habsburg-Lorraine) (1817–1895)
Austrian field marshal
Born Friedrich Rudolf Albrecht Habsburg-Lorraine in Vienna, Austria, on 3 August 1817, Albert was the eldest of four sons of Archduke CHARLES of Austria (1771–1847), the younger brother of Emperor Francis I of Austria-Hungary. Archduke Charles was himself a military leader, fighting for France at the battles of Jemappes (6 November 1792) and Neerwinden (18 March 1793) before siding with the European powers against NAPOLEON, when he was defeated by the French leader at Wagram (6 July 1809). Albert was educated under his father's tutelage before he entered the Austrian military in 1837 with the rank of colonel of infantry. He studied the art of war under Count Karl RADETZKY, the Austrian general whose numerous victories had gained him a reputation in military history. In 1848, when Italian par-

tisans started nationalistic uprisings in Austria, Radetzky, backed by his aide Albert, crushed the opposition at the battles of Pastrengo, Santa Lucia, and Custozza. Because of his service, Albert was named as commander of a division in the II Corps under General Constantin D'Aspre. Albert's service at the battle of Novara (23 March 1849) led to his being made a full general. In 1850, he became a general of cavalry. A year later, he was named the military and civil governor of Hungary, a part of the Austro-Hungarian Empire, where he served until he was relieved at his own request in 1860.

Soon after returning to Vienna, Albert was named to succeed Count Radetzky as the commander in chief of Austrian forces in Italy. In 1863, he was promoted to field marshal. As the threat of war with Prussia and Italy increased, Albert took command of the field army in Italy. On 18 June 1866, Italy declared war on Austria, and Albert moved his troops to fight the Italian forces; his victory at Custozza (23 June 1866) crowned their defeat. Historian George Bruce writes of this battle as the encounter "between 74,000 Austrians under the Archduke Albert and 80,000 Italians under General [Alfonso Ferrero, Marchese Della] La Marmora. . . . La Marmora crossed the Mincio [River] and advanced against the Archduke, who was covering Verona. The Italians, having to pass through a hilly country, the columns were much broken up, and as they debouched [marched from a confined area into the open] into the plain of Custozza, they were beaten in detail, and driven back by the Austrians, who gained a signal victory. The Austrians lost 4,650 killed and wounded; the Italians 720 killed, 3,112 wounded, and 4,315 prisoners. La Marmora was compelled to recross the Mincio." Because of his victory at Custozza, Albert was able to reinforce Bohemian troops who, in aiding the Austrian side, were beaten back themselves by Prussian forces. An Austrian naval victory at Lissa on 20 July confirmed the Austrian success. Albert went back to Vienna to defend the capital against attack by Prussia, but peace came before a final offensive could take place.

At the end of the Italian War in 1866, Albert, now nearly 50 years old, was called upon as inspector general to reorganize the Austrian army. He spent the remainder of his life in this endeavor, transforming the Austrian military into a more efficient fighting machine. Albert attempted to sign a military alliance with France in 1870, but the Franco-Prussian War interrupted the negotiations, and the treaty was never signed.

In early 1894, Albert caught a cold while attending the funeral of his nephew Francis II (1836–94), the former king of Naples (ruled 1859–61). He died in Arco, in South Tirol, then in Austria-Hungary, on 18 February 1895 at the age of 78. Although barely remembered today, he was a worthy successor to Radetzky and did much to improve the Austrian armed forces.

References: Wawro, Geoffrey, *The Austro-Prussian War: Austria's War with Prussia and Italy in 1866* (Cambridge, U.K.: Cambridge University Press, 1996); Bruce, George, "Custoza," in *Collins Dictionary of Wars* (Glasgow, Scotland: HarperCollins Publishers, 1995), 68.

Albufera, duc de *See* SUCHET, LOUIS-GABRIEL, DUC D'ALBUFERA DA VALENCIA.

Alexander, Sir Harold Rupert Leofric George, first earl Alexander of Tunis (1891–1969)
British general

Harold Alexander was born in London on 10 December 1891, the third son of the fourth earl of Caledon, who died in 1897. He spent much of his childhood on his family estate at Caledon in County Tyrone, Ireland, and was educated at Harrow School and the Royal Military Academy at Sandhurst. In 1911, he was commissioned into the Irish Guards. He saw action in the First World War, during which he was wounded twice and decorated with the Distinguished Service Order, Military Cross, and the Legion of Honor. After the war, he was placed in command of troops sent to northern Russia to fight the communists, and by the early 1920s he had risen to the rank of brigadier general. In the period between the two world wars, Alexander was commander of the Irish Guards (1928–30), served with General Claude Auchinleck in the Northwest Frontier in India, and was the commander of the Nowshera Brigade in the Northern Command in India. In 1937, at the age of 45, he became the youngest major general in the British Army.

Returning to the United Kingdom when the Second World War began, Alexander took charge of the evacuation of some 500,000 Allied troops from Dunkirk (May–June 1940). Named general officer commanding in chief for the Southern Command of the United Kingdom in 1940, Alexander was later sent to help in the retreat of Allied troops from Burma in early 1942.

In August 1942, he and General Bernard Law MONTGOMERY were sent to the Middle East as commander in chief and commander of the Eighth Army, respectively, to drive German troops from North Africa. In February 1943, Alexander was named deputy commander in chief of Allied troops in North Africa and commander in chief of the 18th Army Group in Tunisia. The editors of the *The Wordsworth Dictionary of Military Biography* write: "After the Anglo-American landings in Algeria under General [Dwight D.] Eisenhower, Alexander was directly responsible for the coordination of the simultaneous convergence from east and west on the Axis forces withdrawing into Tunisia. Following a setback suffered by the American forces attacking from the west (for which Eisenhower must take some responsibility, since he had become embroiled in Franco-American political turmoil), all Allied ground forces in Tunisia were grouped into the 18th Army Group under Alexander's command." Alexander coordinated the eastern and western forces against the Germans under General Jürgen von Arnim, forcing the Axis forces into the northeastern portion of Tunisia and their ultimate surrender on 13 May 1943. Alexander cabled British prime minister Winston Churchill: "Sir: It is my duty to report that the Tunisian campaign is over. All enemy resistance has ceased. We are masters of the North African shores."

Alexander became Supreme Allied Commander of Allied Armies in Italy; under his command, the Allied forces invaded Sicily and then southwestern Italy. The Americans of General George PATTON's Seventh Army and the British of General Montgomery's Eighth Army fought their way up Italy to break the Axis resistance. Alexander moved into Rome on 4 June 1944 and was promoted to field marshal, the highest rank in the British army. On 29 April 1945, he received the unconditional surrender of all German forces in Italy. This was followed a few days later by the surrender of all German armies in Europe.

In 1946, Alexander was created viscount Alexander of Tunis and made a Knight of the Garter. That same year, he was named governor-general of Canada, a post he held until his retirement in 1952, when he became Earl Alexander of Tunis and Errigal. He was then named defense secretary to Prime Minister Winston Churchill, serving until 1954. In 1959, Alexander was awarded the Order of Merit.

Alexander died of heart failure at the Wexham Park Hospital in Slough on 16 July 1969 at the age of 76; he was buried at Tyttenhanger, Hertfordshire. Despite having been overlooked by most historians for his role in fighting the Second World War, he remains perhaps one of the most revered military leaders in British history. As historians Martin Windrow and Francis K. Mason have written, "Unquestionably the greatest British field commander of the Second World War, Alexander played the leading role in almost every campaign in which British troops were involved, displaying a unique tactical and strategic aptitude in defeat as well as in victory."

References: Nicolson, Nigel, *Alex: The Life of Field Marshal Earl Alexander of Tunis* (London: Weidenfeld and Nicholson, 1973); Jackson, William Godfrey Fothergill, *Alexander of Tunis as Military Commander* (London: Batsford, 1971); Alexander, Harold Rupert Leofric George Alexander, earl Alexander of Tunis, *The Alexander Memoirs, 1940–1945,* edited by John North (London: Cassell, 1962); Windrow, Martin, and Francis K. Mason, "Alexander, Harold Rupert Leofric George, 1st Earl Alexander

of Tunis," in *The Wordsworth Dictionary of Military Biography* (Hertfordshire, U.K.: Wordsworth Editions Ltd., 1997), 8–11; Alexander, Harold Rupert Leofric George Alexander, earl Alexander of Tunis, *The Battle of Tunis* (Sheffield, U.K.: J. W. Northend, 1957).

Alexander the Great (Alexander III) (356–323

B.C.) *king of Macedon and military leader*
The son of Philip II of Macedon and his wife Olympias, an Epirote princess, Alexander III, known better as Alexander the Great, was born at Pella in 356 B.C., possibly in October. To discuss Alexander without mentioning the impact of his father, Philip, is to ignore history, since it bears strongly on why Alexander became, on his own, a far greater warrior than his father. When Alexander was just a child, his father was making Macedon (now Macedonia in northern Greece) into one of the greatest Greek city-states, as well as the dominant power in the Balkans.

Alexander the Great having Homer's books buried under Darius's tomb. Engraving by Marcantonio Raimondi, ca. 1480, after a fresco in the Vatican by Raphael

A diplomat and master strategist, Philip II was most notable for his development of the Macedonian army, in particular its infantry, which he armed with sarissas and which his son Alexander would employ in his conquest of the Persian Empire. (The sarissa is a 14-foot pike used by specifically trained troops known as pikemen.)

Alexander enjoyed all the privileges of a prince. As a youngster, he was tutored by Aristotle, the great Greek orator and educator, whom Philip called to Pella. His father schooled him in the art of war, and by age 16 Alexander was commanding troops in battle. He was intimately involved in the victory of the Macedonian armies at Chaeronea (338 B.C.), a triumph that gave Macedon control over Greece. In 336 B.C., when Alexander was 20, Philip—then preparing to invade Anatolia—was murdered by one of his bodyguards at Aegae during his daughter's marriage to the son of Alexander I of Epirus.

Alexander took his father's place and pushed aside any opposition to his total and complete rule; this included ordering the murder of Philip's son with his second wife, Cleopatra (also known as Eurydice). As soon as his control was confirmed, Alexander gathered together his father's army, made up of some 30,000 well-armed and well-trained troops, and marched toward Asia Minor to put into action his father's scheme to control that portion of the world. In 335 B.C., Alexander marched north toward the Balkans, vanquishing the tribe known as the Triballians and crossing the Danube River to destroy the settlement of Getae. He was then informed that the Illyrians had seized Pelion, an important tactical vantage point that enabled them to control the northern passes. Returning at once to his homeland, Alexander defeated the Illyrians and subsequently put down a revolution in Thebes, destroying that city.

In 334 B.C., Alexander's armies crossed into Asia Minor at Arisbe in what is now modern Turkey. Alexander met the first contingent of the Persian armies under Darius III on the shores of the Granicus River, where 35,000 Macedonians defeated some 40,000 Persians and Greek sympathizers under Memnon of Rhodes. Historian George Bruce writes: "Alexander crossed the Granicus in the face of the Persian army, leading the way himself at the head of the heavy cavalry, and having dispersed the Persian light horse, he brought up the phalanx, which fell upon and routed the Greek mercenaries. The Persians lost heavily, while the Macedonians' loss was very slight." Alexander was then free to march onto

the Persian capital, encountering little resistance; there was fighting at Melitus, but it fell quickly to Alexander's forces. Memnon of Rhodes made a last stand at Halicarnassus (334 B.C.), but, facing complete disaster, he and his troops fled the city. Alexander then marched south to conquer Egypt and Syria before defeating the Persians at Issus (333 B.C.), and at the battle of Arbela (331 B.C.) (more properly the battle of Gaugamela). (Issus and Arbela are both in today's Turkey.) Backed by nearly 50,000 troops, he again defeated Darius III of the Persian Empire. This is considered by historian Edward Creasy to have been one of the most important battles in history, as it helped to spread Greek culture to the Indian subcontinent. During his retreat, Darius was murdered by Bessus, one of his generals.

Alexander began marching eastward toward what is now modern-day Iran. He moved farther east into the Kabul Valley into what is now Afghanistan, and by the winter of 330–329 B.C., he had moved into the Hindu Kush, where he remained for more than a year. In spring 328 B.C., his forces crossed the Hindu Kush into Bactria to fight Bessus, Darius's murderer and successor. Several battles ensued, and Bessus was captured and put to death. In summer 328, Alexander and his army crossed the Jaxartes River and moved into the steppes of Asia; a year later, they crossed back over the Hindu Kush and into what is now India. There, in November 326 B.C., a victory at the River Hydaspes (now Jhelum, in modern Pakistan) over the Indian king Porus (who was captured but allowed to rule with Alexander's consent) was followed by a mutiny of soldiers who had been away from home for nearly a decade. The mutiny was suppressed, and Alexander marched south toward the Indus delta, reaching that waterway in the summer of 325 B.C. He assumed, when seeing the Indus, that this river linked India with the rest of the world.

Acknowledging that he and his men needed to return home, Alexander began the march back to Macedon in 325 B.C. He never reached it. In June 323 B.C., while in Babylon, he came down with what historians believe was a case of malaria; he died on 13 June 323 B.C., at the age of only 33. Because he had considered himself divine and immortal, Alexander had never established a successor or a way for a successor to be chosen. Following his death, a group of Macedonian generals began to battle one another for control of his empire. These men—Antigonus Monophthalmus (ca. 382–301 B.C.), his son Demetrius Poloiorcetes (336–283 B.C.),

Cassander (?–287 B.C.), Seleucus Nicator (ca. 358–281 B.C.), Ptolemy Soter, Eumenes of Cardia (ca. 361–316 B.C.), and Lysimachus (ca. 355–281 B.C.)—were collectively known as *Diadochi* (Greek for "successors"). Antigonus Monophthalmus, also known as Antogonus Cyclops, was a one-eyed general who named himself king of Macedon, but he was defeated by Seleucus Nicator at Ipsus (306 B.C.). Alexander's son, Alexander Aegus, was eventually captured by Cassander, the son of Antipater and king of Macedonia, and put to death. Within 20 years of Alexander's death, his empire had completely fallen apart. But the remarkable conquest of such a vast area in such a short time, from Greece in the west to north India in the east, from the Black Sea to the Arabian gulf, is still a feat to be wondered at.

Historian David Rooney writes of Alexander's impact on history: "Alexander, with his belief in his link to Zeus, the Father of the Gods, constantly attempted to match the achievements of antiquity. He is justly regarded as an outstanding and inspiring military leader in every aspect of war. As a tactician he was unrivaled—in direct leadership in battle, in the development of new weapons both for sieges and for battles, of the direct control of troops in battle, and in the speed of movement. All these attributes would have come to nothing if he had not organized the most remarkable logistic system to support his armies across most of the then known world."

References: Hogarth, David George, *Philip and Alexander of Macedon. Two Essays in Biography* (London: J. Murray, 1897); "Philip (II) of Macedon," in *The Hutchinson Dictionary of Ancient and Medieval Warfare* (Oxford, U.K.: Helicon Publishing, Ltd., 1998), 251; "Alexander the Great and Heroic Leadership," in John Keegan, *The Mask of Command* (New York: Viking/Elisabeth Sifton Books, 1987), 13–91; Lanning, Michael Lee, "Alexander the Great," in *The Military 100: A Ranking of the Most Influential Military Leaders of All Time* (New York: Barnes and Noble Books, 1996), 14–17; Bruce, George, "Granicus" in *Collins Dictionary of Wars* (Glasgow, Scotland: HarperCollins Publishers, 1995), 101; "Alexander the Great," in *Command: From Alexander the Great to Zhukov—The Greatest Commanders of World History,* edited by James Lucas (London: Bloomsbury Publishing, 1988), 30–31; Rooney, David, "Alexander the Great," in *Military Mavericks: Extraordinary Men of Battle* (London: Cassell & Co., 1999), 31–33.

Alfred the Great (Ælfred) (849–899) *Anglo-Saxon king*

Known for his lifelong struggle to defend southern England against Danish incursions and for his efforts to lay the foundations of an English nation, Alfred the Great was born Ælfred sometime in 849. He was the fourth son of Æthelwulf, the king of Wessex, and his wife, Queen Osburh. Æthelwulf died in 858 and was succeeded in turn by his three eldest sons: Æthelbald, Æthelbert, and Æthelred (or Ethelred). On the accession of Æthelred in 866, Alfred began his public life when he was formally appointed as Æthelred's heir. In 871, at the age of 22, Alfred succeeded Æthelred as king of Wessex. In the years before he became king, he married and also fought the invading Danish forces alongside the West Saxons and Mercians. He fought battles at Engelfield (31 December 870), which ended in victory, and at Reading (4 January 871), which was a defeat. On 8 January 871, he fought at Ashdown, followed by battles on 22 January at Boring on Basing and finally on 22 March 871 at Marton, where Alfred was defeated by the combined English-Danish forces to end what has been dubbed by historians as "Alfred's year of battles." In April 871, Æthelred died, leaving Alfred in control of Wessex, and this part of England enjoyed relative calm until 875, when the Danes again invaded England. Alfred led forces against this and similar invasions in 876 and 877, repelling all of them until the great invasion of 878, when the Danes were led by Guthrum.

In January 878, when the Danes swept secretly into Chippenham soon after the new year, Alfred was celebrating Christmas. His forces were surprised by the attack, and as the *Anglo-Saxon Chronicles* stated, "most of the people they reduced except the King Alfred, and he with a little band made his way . . . by wood and swamp, and after Easter he . . . made a fort at Athelney, and from that fort kept fighting against the foe." In May 878, Alfred and his renewed forces swept out of Athelney and defeated the Danes at Edington in Wiltshire. Guthrum and 29 of his chiefs accepted Christian baptism as well as Alfred's rule in what has been called the Peace of Wedmore (878), establishing theoretical English authority over an area called the Danelaw and placing Wessex and Mercia under Alfred's control.

Content to allow the Danelaw borders to remain in place, Alfred set about to construct a series of fortifications at this border called "burhs" to defend his kingdom. At least 33 of these were completed, according to the "Burghal Hidage," a document that dates from the reign of Alfred's son Edward. These places grew into towns, many of which took the word *burh* in their name, later modernized to *bury* and *borough.* However, in either late 892 or early 893 (historians disagree about the exact date), another Danish invasion took place. More than 330 ships landed, in one wave at Appledore and another under Hæsten at Milton in Kent. While Alfred began to negotiate with Hæsten to surrender, the other force at Appledore moved north; at Farnham they were attacked by Alfred's son Edward, who defeated them and forced them to flee. In 893, defeated again at Benfleet or Bemfleet, they joined forces with Hæsten's troops and marched to the Thames Valley, where they were met at Buttington and defeated by forces under the earls of Mercia, Somersetshire, and Wiltshire. A series of small skirmishes continued, but for the Danes the war was effectively over. It ended in either 896 or 897 with the Danes simply ending the fight.

Alfred turned to administrative and scholarly pursuits. Along with creating the "burhs" to defend his kingdom, he also formed a naval force, the beginnings of the English navy. He was also a noted scholar: From 892 until his death seven years later, Alfred translated at least five Latin works into English, including Pope Gregory the Great's *Cura Pastoralis* (Pastoral Care), *The Universal History of Orosius,* and Bede's *Historia Ecclesiastica* (Ecclesiastical History), among others. He wrote the preface for *Dialogues of Gregory,* which was translated by his friend Werferth, bishop of Worcester.

Alfred died on or about 26 October 899, although the year is uncertain. Much of his life would remain a mystery were it not for the writers of Asser (Asserius Menevensis, d. 910), his main biographer, and the *Anglo-Saxon Chronicles,* many of which describe in glowing terms his numerous military victories. One of the most important of the English kings, he is the only one to bear the title "the Great." Historian John Peddie writes in his life of Alfred: "Afflicted by poor health for most of his life, Alfred nonetheless showed unflagging energy as a warrior, administrator, scholar and educator. He was remarkable for both his extraordinary range of interests and his wisdom. In battle he was faced by the Danish invaders and the real threat of Viking supremacy in England. With the help of the first Royal Navy, which he founded with minimal resources, the invaders were eventually repelled. Anglo-Saxon hegemony was was preserved—for a while—and Alfred survived to found

an English monarchy which, under his son and grandson, saw most of modern England united under one crown." His son Edward, known as Edward the Elder, succeeded him to the throne.

References: Peddie, John, *Alfred: Warrior King* (Gloucestershire, U.K.: Sutton Publishing, 1999); Keynes, Simon, and Michael Lapidge, trans., *Alfred the Great: Asser's Life of King Alfred and Other Contemporary Sources* (London: Penguin Books, 1983); "Extracts from King Alfred's Works," in *English Historical Documents, ca. 500–1042,* edited by Dorothy Whitelock (London: Eyre & Spottiswoode, 1955), 844–46.

Allenby, Edmund Henry Hynman, first viscount Allenby of Megiddo (1861–1936)
British field marshal

Born on 23 April 1861 in the village of Felixstowe, England, at Brackenhurst, his grandfather's estate, Edmund Allenby was educated at Haileybury College, north of London, and at the Royal Military College at Sandhurst. He was then sent to serve with the Inniskilling Dragoons, stationed in what are now modern-day Botswana and South Africa, and saw action with British troops during the Boer War (1899–1902). He subsequently moved on to various cavalry commands before he was named inspector of cavalry in 1910.

When the First World War broke out in 1914, Allenby commanded a cavalry division of the British Expeditionary Force (BEF) on the western front in France. Following the first battle of Ypres (14 October–11 November 1915), he was promoted to commander of the Third British Army, which, in April 1917, played a key role in the battle of Arras (4–11 April 1917). That same year, Allenby showed great military skill at the second battle of Leper, as well as at the taking of Vimy Ridge, and he was promoted to the rank of general.

In June 1917, the British, in an attempt to control the Middle East, sent Allenby to what was then Palestine (now modern Israel). A series of skirmishes against the Turkish forces occupying the area had been unsuccessful, and Allenby was sent to command British forces to end the Turkish occupation. He arrived in Egypt, where, he stated, he would "take Jerusalem by Christmas." Replacing Sir Archibald Murray, Allenby found the British forces in a state of disarray. He immediately set about reorganizing the troops into an army composed of some

Sir Edmund Allenby

88,000 men arranged into seven divisions and a Desert Mounted Corps consisting of camel- and horse-mounted soldiers.

Allenby took command of this force and marched to Beersheba, initiating a surprise attack on the Turks on 31 October 1917. Historian George Bruce writes that Allenby's troops "assaulted the 30-mile Turkish Gaza-Beersheba line at Beersheba, in the western foothills of the Judaean Hills, and forced the Turkish 7th Army back to Tel el Sheria. The heavily fortified line was finally reduced after a week's fighting. Gaza fell on November 6–7, Askalon on the 9th, [and] Jaffa on the 16th. Allenby then swung to the east and outflanked Jerusalem from the north. Turkish resistance to the northwest of it, on the Nebi Samwil ridge, was overcome by 9 December and Jerusalem surrendered." Two days after Jerusalem fell to the Allies, Allenby entered the city as a hero, having liberated it from the Muslims. His first order of business was to guarantee that all of the historic holy places

and shrines would be open to all faiths. This was the end of Muslim control and the beginning of Christian control of the holy sites in Jerusalem, a period that lasted until the creation of the state of Israel in 1947.

In early 1918, many of Allenby's troops were sent back to France to meet the crisis there, and the summer was spent training their replacements from India. On 19 September 1918, after a diversionary attack in the eastern section of Palestine, which drew off Turkish forces, Allenby launched a combined force of British, French, Indian, and Arab troops—some 70,000 men—against 11 Turkish divisions at Damascus, now the capital of Syria. Twelve days later his men entered Damascus; on 8 October, Beirut (now in Lebanon) fell to the allied forces, and on 18 October, Tripoli was taken. Aleppo, the last jewel in the crown that was the Turkish-controlled Middle East, was occupied on 25 October. The Damascus/Beirut/Tripoli offensive was the final set back in the Ottoman Empire's chances of aiding Germany against the Allies. Within weeks of the fall of Tripoli, the Turks sued for peace, signing the armistice at Mudros on 30 October 1918 and ending the war in the Middle East. In 16 months, Allenby's forces had completely changed the direction of the war and killed over 80,000 Turkish soldiers while losing less than 900. For this service to his nation, he was promoted to field marshal in 1919 and given the peerage of Viscount Allenby of Megiddo.

Following the end of the First World War, Allenby was named high commissioner of Egypt, serving from 1919 to 1925. Although he was considered a moderate leader, he took strong measures against radical elements in Egyptian society following the assassination of Sir Oliver Lee Stack, the Egyptian army's sirdar, or commander in chief. In 1925, Allenby retired from the military to serve as rector of Edinburgh University in Scotland.

Viscount Allenby, known as "Bull," died in London on 14 May 1936, three weeks after his 75th birthday. He was buried with full military honors in Westminster Abbey in London.

References: Falls, Cyril, "Allenby, Edmund Henry Hynman, First Viscount Allenby of Megiddo," in *The Dictionary of National Biography* 22 vols., 8 supps., edited by Sir Leslie Stephen and Sir Sidney Lee, et al. (London: Oxford University Press, 1931–40), I:7–12; Dupuy, Arnold C., "Allenby, Edmund Henry Hynman," in *Brassey's Encyclopedia of Military History and Biography,* edited by Col.

Franklin D. Margiotta (Washington, D.C.: Brassey's, 1994), 47–50; Hughes, Matthew D., *General Allenby and the Campaign of the E.E.F. in Palestine, 1917–18* (Ph.D. dissertation, University of London, 1995); Spach, John Thom, "Allenby and the Last Crusade," *Military History* 12, no. 7 (March 1996), 26–32; Bruce, George, "Damascus III," "Gaza IV," and "Gaza V," in *Collins Dictionary of Wars* (Glasgow, Scotland: HarperCollins Publishers, 1995), 70–71, 95–96.

Alp-Arslan (Mohammed Ibn Da'ud) (ca. 1029/30–1072) *second sultan of the Seljuk dynasty of Persia*

Alp-Arslan was born Mohammed Mohammed Ibn Da'ud in 1029 or 1030 (some historians also report 1032); his Turkish name *Alp-Arslan* means "the lion hero" or "valiant lion." The great-grandson of Seljuk, the founder of the dynasty and empire that bore his name, Alp-Arslan was the son of Da'ud Chagri Beg of Khurasan. In 1059, he succeeded his father as the ruler of Khurasan, and five years later he superseded his uncle Toghrul Beg as the sultan of Oran, becoming the ruler of what is today Iran and Iraq.

Almost from the beginning of his reign until its end, Alp-Arslan was a warrior figure, fighting to keep control over his empire. When his father's cousin, Kutulmish, tried to revolt in Khurasan to the north, Alp-Arslan put the insurrection down on his own. In 1064, he headed a powerful army that moved into Armenia and took control of the land lying between the Caspian and Black Seas, neighboring today's Georgia.

During Alp-Arslan's fight for control of Armenia and parts of what is now Georgia, the Byzantine emperor Romanus Diogenes was dealing with bands of invading Turkomen into areas in Asia Minor controlled by Byzantium. After defeating these bands in three wars—one of which was fought by his chief general, Manuel Comnenus—Romanus decided to challenge the Seljuk control of Armenia. In 1071, with an army of some 100,000 men, Romanus moved into Armenia.

Alp-Arslan, who had started to invade parts of what is now Syria, headed home to fight off Romanus's attack on his rule of Armenia. On 26 August 1071, his army met Romanus at Manzikert, or Malazgird (now in modern Turkey). Alp-Arslan wanted to avoid the battle and offered peace to Romanus, who refused even though his alliance with Norman mercenaries was shaky. Alp-Arslan controlled more than 15,000 heavily armed

cavalry against Romanus's 60,000 troops, commanded by his general Sav-Tengi (Taranges). However, the main Byzantine force was left with little support, and when Alp-Arslan's troops moved against the Byzantine wings, Romanus was captured. The Byzantine losses were light—approximately 2,000 men. Alp-Arslan treated Romanus kindly and sent him back home bearing gifts.

Alp-Arslan now prepared to invade Turkistan, the home of his ancestors, and marched his army to the Oxus River. His troops had captured a Turkomen fortification, and Alp-Arslan asked to have the commander brought before him. The man, Yusuf al-Khwarizmi, took out a dagger and stabbed Alp-Arslan, who died just a few hours later, on 24 November 1072. His burial site is unknown. In his life, though, Alp-Arslan had set in train a series of Suljuk conquests that led to the beginning of the Ottoman Empire.

References: Windrow, Martin, and Francis K. Mason, "Alp-Arslan," *The Wordsworth Dictionary of Military Biography* (Hertfordshire, U.K.: Wordsworth Editions Ltd., 1997), 13–14; France, John, *Victory in the East: A Military History of the First Crusade* (Cambridge, U.K.: Cambridge University Press, 1994), 147; Friendly, Alfred, *The Dreadful Day: The Battle of Manzikert, 1071* (London: Hutchinson, 1981).

Alva, Fernando Álvarez de Toledo, duke of (duke of Alba) (1507–1582) *Spanish general*

Perhaps the most successful military officer of the Holy Roman Empire, the duke of Alva was born in the village of Piedrahita, Spain, on 29 October 1507, the scion of a wealthy family. In 1524, when only 17, he joined the imperial army of the Holy Roman Empire and, while fighting against the French at Pavia (1525) and at Fuenterrabia (1526), showed himself to be an excellent military officer. For his service in this engagement and in expeditions to Tunis and Algiers, Alva was made a general by the age of 26, and he commanded an army by 30.

In 1546, the imperial forces in Germany were put under Alva's command in the war against the Schmalkaldic League. This was an alliance formed by Protestant princes at Schmalkalden in 1531 when Charles V, the Holy Roman Emperor, threatened to resist the rise of Lutheranism in the empire. Charles V was at the head of the force against the league, but Alva commanded the troops in battle. On the opposing side were Philip of Hesse and John Frederick I, the elector of Saxony. Alva and Charles met the league's forces at Mühlberg on 24 April 1547. Historian George Bruce describes Mühlberg as a clash "between the German Protestants, 9,000 strong, under the Elector Frederick of Saxony and the Landgrave of Hesse, and the Imperial army, together 3,500 Papal troops, 13,000 in all, under Charles V. The Protestants were totally defeated, and their two leaders taken prisoners. The Imperialists lost 50 [men] only." This battle is known for being the first to see the use of cavalry with pistols. Charles then called together the Diet of Augsburg (1547), a meeting that acceded to the incorporation of the Netherlands into Charles's empire.

Charles's abdication in 1556 and the succession of Spain's Philip II as Holy Roman Emperor changed Alva's life for the worse. Philip did not hold the general in the same high regard as did Charles, and Alva was sent to the Netherlands in 1568 to put down a revolt against Habsburg rule. Named captain general of the Netherlands, he established the Council of Blood, or the Council of Troubles, to put down the insurrection. In the next few months, more than 18,000 people were arrested and executed for conspiring against the crown; their property was confiscated by Alva and given to Philip II. Among those who met their fate under the council's dictates were Lamoral, Count Egmont (1522–68), a Flemish general who had fought under Charles V and won important victories for him at Saint Quentin (1557) and Gravelines (1558) before he was arrested for protesting against Alva's excesses; and Admiral Philippe de Montmorency, Count Horn (1518–68). Both were beheaded on 5 June 1568, and their deaths, as well as an appearance before the council by William of Orange, precipitated a civil war. Led by William, an army of Belgians met Alva's forces at Jemmingen on 21 July 1568; Alva was victorious, William fled, and the "war" concluded when Alva entered Brussels on 22 December 1568. However, this victory did not end Belgian resistance, and increased fighting, particularly at Haarlem (11 July 1573), led Philip to recall Alva in 1573.

In 1580, Philip sent Alva to Portugal after that country's king, Henry, died without an heir; Philip intended to secure the throne for himself. Alva's forces met a ragtag band of citizens, backing the rival claim of Dom Antonio de Crato, at Alcântara on the Tagus River on 25 August 1580. With little experience and few weapons, the citizens were routed by Alva's forces, and he marched into Lisbon, taking it for Spain. Portugal would be ruled by Spain for the next 60 years.

Despite this last victory for Philip, Alva fell into disfavor with the king, and he remained in Lisbon without any power or recognition. He died in Lisbon on 11 December 1582 at the age of 75.

References: Maltby, William S., *Alba: A Biography of Fernando Alvarez de Toledo, Third Duke of Alba, 1507–1582* (Berkeley: University of California Press, 1983); Windrow, Martin, and Francis K. Mason, "Alvarez de Toledo, Fernando, Duke of Alva," in *The Wordsworth Dictionary of Military Biography* (Hertfordshire, U.K.: Wordsworth Editions Ltd., 1997), 14–16; Bruce, George, "Alcántara I" and "Mühlberg," in *Collins Dictionary of Wars* (Glasgow, Scotland: HarperCollins Publishers, 1995), 8, 169; Fitzjames Stuart y Falcó, Jacobo Maria Carlos Manuel, duke de Berwick y de Alba, *The Great Duke of Alba as a Public Servant* (London: G. Cumberlege, 1947).

Amherst, Jeffrey, Baron Amherst of Montreal

(1717–1797)   *British general*

Born at Sevenoaks, in Kent, England, on 29 January 1717, Jeffrey Amherst was his father's namesake and the scion of an ancient Kentish family. He began his career as a page to the duke of Dorset. In 1731, at the age of 14, he joined the English army, rising to become aide-de-camp to General John Ligonier and seeing action during the War of the Austrian Succession (1740–48) at several engagements, including Dettingen, Fontenoy, and Roucoux. By the end of that conflict, he had been promoted to serving on the staff of William, the duke of Cumberland, and he saw additional action at Hastenbeck and Lauffeld. Both Ligonier and Cumberland saw something in the young officer, and he was promoted rapidly, attaining the rank of lieutenant general by 1756.

Two years later, William Pitt, the prime minister of Great Britain, made Amherst the commander of a force sent to Canada to capture French Canada for England, despite his lack of seniority. Amherst's goal was to end the French command of parts of North America and make Canada a British colony. His force sailed from Portsmouth and landed at the French fortress at Louisbourg, which, after a short siege, surrendered on 26 July 1758. For this quick victory, Amherst was promoted to commander in chief of all British forces in North America, succeeding James Abercromby.

To conquer the French and the main concentration of their forces at Montreal, Amherst realized he would have to proceed cautiously rather than risk a full head-on assault. To this end, in July 1759 he attacked Fort Niagara, which severed French general Louis-Joseph, marquis de MONTCALM DE SAINT-VÉRAN's access to communication and supplies in French Louisiana. With 11,000 men in his command, Amherst then launched an attack against Fort Ticonderoga, capturing it without a shot on 26 July 1759. Amherst's forces also took Crown Point (August 1759), and General James WOLFE was sent to Quebec, which was taken in September 1759. These three armies, having cut off the French in several areas and denied them a cohesive defense, now marched on Montreal. Realizing that surrender was the only possibility, the French gave up the city in September 1760. Amherst, having accomplished the Pitt government's dream in one short year, was named governor-general of what was called British North America.

Congratulated by Parliament for his service, Amherst was made a Knight Commander of the Order of Bath (KCB), and he seemed to have become a great military commander. However, while the French had collapsed before his forces, another enemy put up a far more aggressive defense: the American Indians under Chief Pontiac. Pontiac saw the British victory over the French as a threat to his own tribe, the Ottawa, whom he led into a revolt in 1763. Amherst tried to put down the uprising with regular military methods, but the Indians' use of hit-and-run and other tactics frustrated the British. What Amherst finally did has become highly controversial: Many historians agree that the British commander used smallpox to murder the Indians, perhaps the first use of biological agents in warfare. Historian John Cuthbert Long, in his 1933 biography of Amherst, quotes one letter that the British commander wrote: "Could it not be contrived to send a smallpox . . . I will try to infect them with some blankets . . ." He sent a similar message to Colonel Henry Bouquet on 16 July 1763: "You will do well to try to inoculate the Indians by means of blankets, as well as to try every other method that can serve to extirpate this execrable race." It appears that this and other methods that Amherst utilized all failed, because the British government recalled him in late 1763. However, the Treaty of Paris, signed that same year, confirmed England's gains, ending French rule in North America and consolidating the British position.

To soften the blow of being recalled, Parliament appointed Amherst as governor of the Virginia colony in 1768 and, two years later, as governor of Guernsey. In 1772, he was made a privy councillor and lieutenant general of the Ordnance. From 1778 to 1795, with a break of one year, he served as commander in chief. In 1776, he was styled as Baron Amherst, and he was given the title of field marshal in 1796. He died at Sevenoaks in Kent, on 31 August 1797 at the age of 80. Lord Walpole said of him, "[He] was a man of indomitable perseverance and courage, but slow and methodical in his movements. Provident, conciliating and cool, Amherst disposed his operations with steadiness, neither precipitating nor delaying beyond the due point, and comprehending the whole under a due authority which he knew how to assume." However, one biographer, Henry Morse Stephens, has noted that "Lord Amherst's great military services were all performed in the years 1758, 1759, and 1760, when he proved himself worthy of high command by his quiet self-control and skillful combinations. His failure with the Indians was not strange, for he committed the great fault of despising his enemy . . . He was by no means a good commander-in-chief, and allowed innumerable abuses to grow up in the army. Yet, though not a great man, he deserves a very honorable position amongst English soldiers and statesmen of the last century."

Amherst's brother John (ca. 1718–78) was a British admiral, as was his brother William (1732–81), who served with Jeffrey at Louisburg and Montreal. Amherst College in Massachusetts was named in Jeffrey Amherst's honor.

References: Mayo, Lawrence Shaw, *Jeffrey Amherst: A Biography* (New York: Longmans, Green & Co., 1916); Long, John Cuthbert, *Lord Jeffery Amherst: A Soldier of the King* (New York: Macmillan, 1933); Stephens, Henry Morse, "Amherst, Jeffrey, Baron Amherst," in *The Dictionary of National Biography*, 22 vols., 8 supps., edited by Sir Leslie Stephen and Sir Sidney Lee, et al. (London: Oxford University Press, 1921–22), I:357–359.

Anson, George, Baron Anson of Soberton (1697–1762) *English admiral*

Born in the village of Shugborough, Staffordshire, on 23 April 1697, George Anson was the nephew of Lord Macclesfield, chief justice of England from 1710 to 1718 and lord chancellor of England from 1718 to

1725. According to the biography by Sir John Barrow, Anson entered the English navy in February 1712 and quickly rose through a series of promotions, rising to become commander of a sloop by 1722.

In 1740, Great Britain prepared to go to war against Spain. Anson, then only 43, was named commander of the HMS *Centurion,* the flagship of a force sent to attack Spanish possessions in South America. The squadron left England in 1740, but the lateness of the start meant they met foul weather while rounding Cape Horn. Anson reached his intended target, the island of Juan Fernández, in June 1741, although three of the six ships in the squadron had been lost; of the original 961 men on the three ships that did make it, only 335 survived. Anson wrote in his diary that "as we did not get to land till the middle of June, the mortality went on increasing, and the disease extended itself so prodigously, that, after the loss of above two hundred men, we could not at last muster more than six foremast-men in a watch capable of duty." Despite being low on men—many of whom were sick—Anson and his ships were able to wage a limited war on Spanish forces along the coast of what is now Chile, capturing the town of Paita on 15 November 1741 after a three-day battle.

At last Anson was forced to gather all the surviving sailors onto his own remaining ship, the *Centurion,* and he sailed to Macao in China. From Macao, he sailed back across the Pacific and captured the *Nuestra Señora de Covadonga,* a Spanish galleon, off Cape Espiritu Santo on 20 June 1743. After relieving the ship of its gold, he again sailed to Macao and sold its trade cargo for £400,000 but kept the vast amount of gold. He then sailed back to England via the Cape of Good Hope, returning home on 15 June 1744. British historian N. A. M. Rodger writes: "Anson's voyage is remembered as a classic tale of fortitude and leadership in the face of fearful disasters, but to the British public of 1744 it was the treasure of the galleon, triumphantly paraded through the streets of London, which mattered. The war against Spain had yielded few of the expected easy victories, and now France had entered the war. Anson's triumph showed that the heirs of Drake were not altogether unworthy of him. The commodore himself was the hero of the hour, and every political group was anxious to recruit him." However, because Anson had not had any major victories during the voyage, the Admiralty refused to promote him to captain. He resigned his commission in anger.

Anson joined a group of Whigs opposed to the government of Prime Minister Thomas Pelham-Holles, the first duke of Newcastle, and the lord of the Admiralty, the earl of Winchelsea, who had passed Anson over for a promotion. In December 1744, this group of Whigs was brought into the government, and John Russell, the duke of Bedford (1710–71), a friend of Anson's, was named to replace Winchelsea; he immediately confirmed Anson's promotion. Anson was elected to the House of Commons as a member of Parliament (MP) from Hedon. In 1745, the duke of Bedford resigned his office, and Anson worked with his replacement, the earl of Sandwich.

Anson's naval career, however, was not over. While remaining a member of the Board of Admiralty, he was named as commander of a fleet to fight the French and sent to intercept French ships off the coast of Spain near Cape Finisterre. According to historian George Bruce, in the battle of 23 May 1747, the French, with 38 ships under the command of Jacques-Pierre de Jonquière, marquis de la Jonquière (1685–1752) against a fleet of just 16 ships under Anson, were "completely defeated," losing 10 ships and nearly 3,000 prisoners. Jonquière was captured and spent two years in an English prison before being released. Anson again returned home as a hero, and for his service in this conflict he was promoted to vice admiral and raised to the peerage as Baron Anson of Soberton, a title that died with him.

In 1748, Anson was promoted to full admiral, and in 1751 he became first lord of the Admiralty. With Bedford's and Sandwich's assistance, he moved on a series of reforms to improve and correct serious problems and deficiencies in the British navy, including a lack of discipline. He pushed the passage of a revised Navy Discipline Act (1749) and advocated the creation of a corps of marines (1755) as well as a sound system of courtsmartial. Inspections of naval dockyards and other facilities were also given a high priority. Because of Anson's work, the British navy started to become the finest fleet in the world. Fired by Prime Minister William Pitt in 1756, he was recalled to the Admiralty a year later and served as first lord from 1757 until his death. In 1761, a year before he died, he was given the title Admiral of the Fleet, the highest rank in the British navy.

George Anson, perhaps one of the finest military minds of the British navy, died at Moor Park in Hertfordshire on 6 June 1762 at age 65. Historian N. A. M. Rodgers, summing up Anson's career and service, writes:

"Both as a sea commander and as a statesman, Anson triumphed over adversity by courage and determination. Flexible and pragmatic at a tactical level both at sea and ashore, he kept his ultimate goal clearly in view. He was an outstanding judge of men, which served him well both in the navy and in politics. His professional legacy was above all a tradition of devotion to duty, of aggressive attack and of taking his subordinates into his confidence which was transmitted through his followers to future generations."

References: Anson, Walter Vernon, *The Life of Admiral Lord Anson, the Father of the British Navy, 1697–1762* (London: John Murray, 1912); Barrow, Sir John, *The Life of George, Lord Anson, Admiral of the Fleet, Vice-Admiral of Great Britain, and First Lord Commissioner of the Admiralty, Previous to, and During, the Seven Years' War* (London: John Murray, 1839); Rodger, N. A. M., "George, Lord Anson," in *Precursors of Nelson: British Admirals of the Eighteenth Century,* edited by Peter Le Fevre and Richard Harding (London: Chatham Publishing, 2000), 176–199; "*Memorandum by Thomas Pelham-Holles, 1st Duke of Newcastle under Lyne, Newcastle House—London; 4 June 1757* [Ne C 3158, 4.6.1757]," in *Letters of and Relating to Thomas Pelham-Holles, 1st Duke of Newcastle under Lyne* (Newcastle, U.K.: University of Nottingham Library, 1725–1771).

Antony, Mark (Marcus Antonius, Mark Anthony)

(82/83–30 B.C.) *Roman general*

Mark Antony was born in 82 B.C. (although some sources list his date of birth as 83 B.C.) in Rome, the son of Marcus Antonius (known as Creticus, ?–71 B.C.), a Roman military leader and praetor (magistrate) who lost a major battle to the Cretans. His paternal grandfather was Marcus Antonius (143–87 B.C.), one of the best known of the Roman orators, who also served as a consul and censor; his maternal grandfather was Julius CAESAR's uncle Lucius. Antony is first noted in Roman histories in 54 B.C., when he was 28 and serving with Julius Caesar in Gaul (now modern France). Caesar was Antony's main influence, both as a father figure—his father died when Antony was only 11—and as a military figure. Antony rose in rank from quaestor (financial official) to tribune, and in 49 B.C. he was put in command of Roman forces that drove POMPEY from Italy. That same year, Caesar put Antony in charge as deputy gov-

ernor of Italy while Caesar was in Spain. Antony was at Caesar's side at the battle of Pharsalus (48 B.C.), and in 47 B.C. he again served as deputy governor of Italy while the Roman leader was in Africa.

Although some historians believe that Antony may have had something to do with Caesar's assassination on 15 March 44 B.C., there has never been firm proof, and Antony was not one of Caesar's murderers. Following the assassination, Antony strove to become Rome's ruler, and though he did not arrest Caesar's killers, he did publish his mentor's will. His stunning eulogy at Caesar's funeral brought the ire of the Roman people on the assassins, forcing them to flee. One of them, Decimus Junius Brutus, held the province of Cisalpine Gaul; Antony got the Roman Senate to transfer control of the territory to him, and when Brutus refused to hand it over, Antony assembled an army and marched to seize it.

The Senate, however—urged by Caesar's heir, Octavian, who was to become the Roman emperor AUGUSTUS—claimed the land for Rome. Antony was denounced as a traitor to Rome, Octavian moved to fight him, and their armies met at Mutina (now Modena, Italy) (14–27 April 43 B.C.). Historian George Bruce writes: "[Mutina] was between the adherents of Antony, and three Consular armies under Hirtius, Octavius [Octavian], and Vibius Pansa. Antony, who was besieging Mutina, was attacked simultaneously by the three armies. That of Pansa was routed and Pansa slain, but Octavius and Hirtius gained some small success. Antony, however, was undefeated, and continued the siege. On the 27th Octavius and Hirtius made a combined attack on his lines and succeeded in forcing their way through into the town, though Hirtius fell in the action." Although they were victorious, Antony and his men raised the siege of Mutina, and he retreated to Gaul, where he combined his forces with the Roman consul Marcus Aemilius Lepidus (?–13 B.C.) and then marched on Rome. Octavian, unable to defend the city, instead made a truce with Antony, who would no longer be a public enemy: Under the *Triumviri Republicae Constituendae* (Republican Constitutional Triumvirate), also called the Second Triumvirate, Antony, Octavian, and Lepidus united to create a powerful army, and Antony was given control of all of Gaul.

The triumvirate marched against the conspirators who murdered Julius Caesar, and in two battles at Philippi (42 B.C.), Antony and Octavian took on Marcus Brutus and Gaius Cassius. The first clash brought no victor, but in the second the triumvirs destroyed the conspirators and their armies. The writers of *The Hutchinson Dictionary of Ancient and Medieval Warfare* say of the two battles:

> The Republicans mustered 19 legions and 20,000 cavalry plus light infantry, while the triumvirs fielded 19 rather stronger legions and 13,000 cavalry. In the first battle, Antony, who was in overall charge, routed Cassius' legions on the left flank, capturing his camp. In despair, Cassius committed suicide, unaware that the right wing, under Brutus, had enjoyed great success against Octavian's troops, inflicting heavy losses. After a 3-week break, the triumvirs outmaneuvered Brutus and forced him to offer battle. The clash between the main infantry lines was hard fought, but Octavian's infantry pushed back Brutus' troops. The second and third lines failed to stop the enemy's advance, and the whole army was put to flight. Brutus committed suicide soon afterwards.

Following this victory, Antony moved to Greece and Asia Minor. In 41 B.C., he went to Egypt, where he met and fell in love with the Egyptian queen Cleopatra, an affair that would be his undoing. Although he renewed the triumvirate with Octavian, his popularity was slipping.

In 34 B.C. Antony conducted a successful military campaign in Armenia. After he returned to Egypt, he proclaimed Cleopatra as the "queen of kings" and named her son Caesarion (whose father was Julius Caesar) the "king of kings." Antony completed the break with Octavian and Rome when he divorced Octavian's sister, whom he had married just a few years earlier. Octavian therefore declared war, and the Roman fleet moved against Antony, meeting his forces on 2 September 31 B.C. at Actium (now Akri in western Greece). Antony controlled some 480 galleys, while Octavian had 400 at his disposal, but Octavian's were much lighter and much faster. These ships were commanded by the Roman general Marcus AGRIPPA, who cut off Antony's supplies from the land. When Antony's forces panicked and fled, Antony wanted to retreat by land, but Cleopatra demanded that they go back to Egypt by ship. In the midst of their escape, their ships were destroyed, though

they evaded capture and returned to Egypt, pursued by Octavian. In 30 B.C., Octavian's forces stormed Alexandria, cutting Antony off. Faced with surrender and certain execution, he chose to commit suicide in the belief that Cleopatra had already done so. In fact, she had not, but she took her own life when it was confirmed that Antony was already dead.

Although not considered a major military figure, Mark Antony was nonetheless an important strategist and commander in some of Rome's conflicts. Unfortunately, he is better remembered for his ill-fated romance with Cleopatra than for any of his military service.

References: Pelling, C. B. R., *Life of Antony* (Cambridge, U.K.: Cambridge University Press, 1988); Huzar, Eleanor Goltz, *Mark Antony: A Biography* (London: Croon Helm, 1978); Bruce, George, "Mutina" and "Philippi," in *Collins Dictionary of Wars* (Glasgow, Scotland: HarperCollins Publishers, 1995), 171, 194; "Actium, Battle of," in *The Hutchinson Dictionary of Ancient and Medieval Warfare* (Oxford, U.K.: Helicon Publishing, Ltd., 1998), 1.

Astley, Jacob, Baron Astley (1579–1652)
English Royalist commander

Despite his noted service at the battles of Edgehill (1642), Arundel (1644), and Gosworth Bridge (1644), Jacob Astley remains one of the least known of the commanders who fought on the side of King Charles I during the first English Civil War. He was born in 1579, a member of a family from Norfolk; one of his ancestors, Thomas Lord Astley, was killed at the battle of Evesham (1265). In 1598, when he was 19, Astley went to the Netherlands, where he fought for Henry of Orange, and some time later he went to Germany to fight in the Thirty Years' War (1618–48) under GUSTAV II. When he returned to England, he was so well thought of that King Charles I appointed him to various military offices.

When the so-called First Bishops' War broke out in 1639 in an effort to enforce Charles I's control of Scotland, the king named Astley as his sergeant major general (major general) of the infantry. Astley discovered that the English army was ill-equipped for battle, and he was not responsible for the defeat the English forces suffered at the hands of Alexander LESLIE and MONTROSE. A truce ended the conflict for a time, but then the Second Bishops' War broke out in 1640. Charles sent a force under the command of Astley and Edward

Conway, Lord Conway, to the River Tyne in control of some 26,000 troops. At the battle of Newburn on 28 August 1640, Astley and Conway were hopelessly outnumbered by the Scottish Covenanter forces, and both men were forced to flee as the Scots took Newcastle. Because of this defeat and the threat of further reverses, Charles signed the Treaty of Ripon on 14 October 1640. Astley, despite his failures on the battlefield, remained a favorite of the king.

Charles's battles continued during his struggle with Parliament for control of the English government. When the first English Civil War began in 1642, he named Astley major general of the foot, one of his leading commanders of the Royalist cause. The first major battle of this conflict was on 23 October 1642 at Edgehill, in Warwickshire. Prior to the start of the engagement, Astley prayed for victory—a prayer that has become famous: "O Lord, Thou knowest how busy I must be this day. If I forget Thee, do not Thou forget me." There was no victor at Edgehill, but Charles failed to follow up his chance to defeat the rebellious forces. At the siege of Gloucester (10 August–5 September 1643), Astley commanded a division, and at the first battle of Newbury (20 September 1643), he led royal infantry troops. He served under Sir Ralph Hopton at Arundel (9 December 1643) and Cheriton (29 March 1644). At the second battle of Newbury (27 October 1644), he ably defended Shaw House, but the royalist forces were routed, and Charles was forced to flee. At Naseby (14 June 1645), Astley commanded the infantry under Prince Rupert, but once again the royalist forces were defeated, making victory in the Civil War an impossibility. He moved his force of some 1,500 men west, and on 21 March 1646, he entered into battle against Colonel Thomas Morgan and Sir William BRERETON at Stow-on-the-Wold, where he was captured by the Parliamentary forces. To his captors Astley stated, "You have now done your work and may go and play, unless you will fall out amongst yourselves." He was sent into imprisonment at Warwick, until the Royalist forces surrendered in June 1646, after which he was allowed to go home.

Astley died at his home in February 1652. Historian Peter Young writes of him: "He was a little taciturn, silver-haired veteran of the Dutch Service, who thoroughly understood his profession, and had the added advantage that he got on well with Prince Rupert. If the old Royalist foot regiments had become formidable, we may attribute it to the skill and discipline of honest old Astley who had commanded them at Edgehill, Gloucester, Newbury, Cropredy Bridge and Losteithiel."

References: Browne, Richard Charles, "Astley, Sir Jacob, Baron Astley," in *The Dictionary of National Biography*, 22 vols., 8 supps., edited by Sir Leslie Stephen and Sir Sidney Lee, et al. (London: Oxford University Press, 1921–22), I:677–678; Fissel, Mark Charles, *The Bishops' Wars: Charles I's Campaigns Against Scotland, 1638–1640* (Cambridge, U.K.: Cambridge University Press, 1994); Young, Peter, *Naseby 1645: The Campaign and the Battle* (London: Century Publishing, 1985), 31.

Attila the Hun (Etzel, Ethele) (ca. 406–453)
king of the Huns

Attila the Hun, also known as Etzel in German histories and Ethele by the Hungarians, is probably the best-known invader of the Middle Ages as well as a participant in one of the greatest battles in world history. Little is known of his life, except that he was a member of the Huns, a nomadic central European tribe of the Caspian steppes that moved westward to attack the forces of the

Attila the Hun

Roman Empire. In 433, Attila succeeded his uncle, Roas the Hun, who had been exacting tribute from the Romans as a payoff for not harassing the Roman forces. In 447, Attila refused the Roman tribute and moved his forces through southern Europe, conquering the area between the Black Sea and the Mediterranean Sea.

In 442, Attila advanced on Constantinople, but his army was halted and defeated in Thrace by Aspar, the general for the Roman emperor Theodosius II. Attila then turned south and ravaged Greece with such ferocity that Theodosius was forced to seek terms, offering greater tribute than before—2,100 pounds of gold. Nevertheless, Attila's forces went on a killing spree, sacking villages and churches until blood ran in the streets. The savagery earned Attila the sobriquet of "The Scourge of God."

In 451, Attila turned to Gaul (now modern France), where the Hunnish tribe met the forces of the Romans under AETIUS and the Visigoths under Theodoric and Thorismond. Attila was allied with Genseric, the king of the Vandals, and the two great forces met at Châlons. More than 300,000 men were probably killed at this engagement. Though the Visigothic leader Theodoric was killed, Attila and the Hunnish troops withdrew over the Rhine, unable to defeat the Roman forces. Edward Creasy, in his famed work on the most decisive battles in human history, lists Châlons as one of the 15 most important; most historians agree.

Frustrated in his hope of conquering Gaul, Attila turned south toward Italy, besieging and destroying several major cities, including Aquileia, Padua, and Milan. However, in Mantua a delegation from Rome, which included Pope Leo I, persuaded Attila not to attack that city. Attila withdrew, but in 453 he changed his mind and again moved to invade Italy. It was during this period that he suffered a brain hemorrhage and died, perhaps saving western civilization; his burial site remains unknown. After his death, the Huns could not achieve the power and prestige they had had under Attila.

Although the best-known of the Hunnish military leaders, Atilla remains an obscure figure. Sources on his life include the *Historia Miscella* of Jordanes Priscus, and written accounts by Gregory of Tours. Edward Gibbon, in *The Rise and Fall of the Roman Empire*, writes of Attila:

> His features, according to the observation of a Gothic historian, bore the stamp of his national origin . . . a large head, a swarthy complexion, small, deep-seated eyes, a flat nose, a few hairs in the place of a beard, broad shoulders, and a short square body, of a nervous strength, though of a disproportioned form. The haughty step and demeanour of the king of the Huns expressed the consciousness of his superiority above the rest of mankind; and he had a custom of fiercely rolling his eyes, as if he wished to enjoy the terror which he inspired. . . . He delighted in war; but, after he had ascended the throne in a mature age, his head, rather than his hand, achieved the conquest of the North; and the fame of an adventurous soldier was usefully exchanged for that of a prudent and successful general.

References: Herbert, William, *Attila, King of the Huns* (London: H. G. Bohn, 1838); Howarth, Patrick, *Attila, King of the Huns: Man and Myth* (London: Constable, 1994); Thompson, E. A., *A History of Attila and the Huns* (Oxford, U.K.: Clarendon Press, 1948); Creasy, Edward Shepherd, "The Battle of Chalons," in *Decisive Battles of the World* (London: The Colonial Press, 1899), 141–156.

Augereau, Pierre-François-Charles, duc de Castiglione (Pierre-François-Charles Augerau)

(1757–1816) *French general, marshal of France*

Pierre-François-Charles Augereau was one of NAPOLEON's great military commanders, but his name is little known today. The son of a domestic servant, Augereau (also spelled Augerau) was born in Paris in 1757. He joined the Prussian army in 1774 at the age of 17, rising to the rank of colonel in 1793; prior to the French Revolution, he joined the Neapolitan army and settled in Naples. When the revolution began in 1789, he returned to his native land and joined the French army with the rank of private. By 1793 he had become a major general.

In April 1796, Augereau commanded French soldiers in seizing the castle of Cosseria and the camp at Ceva, and the following month he led troops to victory at Lodi (10 May 1796). He then served under Napoleon's command and was put in charge of the assault on Castiglione (3 August 1796). Although not credited with any major work, he was a key participant at the battle of Arcola (15–17 November 1796) between the French under Napoleon and the Austrians under Marshal Alvinzi, who had defeated Augereau and André Messéna at Caldiero on 12 November. Napoleon wrote of Augereau that he ". . . has plenty of character, courage, firmness, activity; is inured to war; is well liked by the soldiery; is fortunate in his operations."

Napoleon sent Augereau to Paris in late 1797 to aid in the coup of 18 Fructidor (4 September 1797) that overthrew the revolutionary government. After Napoleon took power in France, Augereau was honored with the title of marshal of France on 19 May 1804 and awarded the Grand Eagle of the Legion of Honor in 1805. With this rank, he was placed in command of the VII Corps of the French army, and in 1806 he saw action at Konstanz (Constance) and Bregenz. That same year, in two separate battles at Auerstädt and Jena, Napoleon's armies crushed Prussian troops and took control of Prussia. At the battle of Jena (14 October 1806), Augereau's forces crushed the troops under the command of Prussian general Ernst von Rüchel (also Ruechel). On 8 February 1807, Augereau suffered one of his few military defeats at Eylau when, with their general ill and strapped to his horse, his troops rushed the center of the Russian army in a snowstorm and were badly defeated. Wounded in his arm, Augereau was evacuated back to France, where he was awarded the title of the duc de Castiglione (duke of Castiglione). Transferred to Spain, Augereau was put in charge of the VII Corps of the French army in Spain, and though he was again victorious, particularly at the siege of Gerona (4 June–10 December 1809), he was criticized for excessive cruelty.

Following this action, Augereau did not serve again until 1812, when Napoleon marched into Russia. However, in this campaign and that of 1813, Augereau had clearly lost much of his dash and vigor, and Napoleon criticized his performance. Prior to the battle of Leipzig (16–19 October 1813), Augereau told Napoleon that he could become the military leader of old: "[G]ive me back the old soldiers of Italy, and I will show you that I am." In 1814, after Napoleon was overthrown, Augereau went to serve King Louis XVIII, but after Napoleon's escape from Elba, he returned to his old commander; his service, however, was rejected. Napoleon's attempt lasted only 100 days, ending at Waterloo. With Louis XVIII back in power, Augereau was stripped of his pension and titles, the final blow. Confined to his estate at La Housaye, he died there of heart failure on 12 June 1816. Despite his long and distinguished record of service, his part in Napoleon's wars is nearly forgotten.

References: Durant, Will, and Ariel Durant, *The Age of Napoleon: A History of European Civilization from 1789 to 1815* (New York: Simon and Schuster, 1975); Bruce, George, "Eylau" and "Jena," in *Collins Dictionary of Wars* (Glasgow, Scotland: HarperCollins Publishers, 1995), 85, 118–119.

Augustus (Gaius Octavius, Octavian) (63 B.C.– A.D. 14) *Roman emperor*

Augustus was born Gaius Octavius—better known as Octavian—in Rome on 23 September 63 B.C., the son of Gaius Octavius, a Roman senator who died when Octavian was four years old; through his mother he was a great-nephew of Julius CAESAR. Because of his status as a patrician, he enjoyed the privileges and education of that class, and he was named as a pontifex, or priest, when he was only 15. From an early age, Octavian was involved with his great-uncle Julius Caesar in a number of military expeditions, and in 46 B.C. he served at Caesar's side in fighting in Africa. In 44 B.C., although he was only 18, he was named as master of the horse.

Octavian was in Apollonia in Illyria (modern Yugoslavia) when he learned that Caesar had been assassinated in Rome. Returning there, he discovered that Caesar's will named Octavian as his heir. Mark ANTONY, Caesar's friend who had taken control of the city following the killing, dissuaded Octavian from avenging Caesar's murder. However, there were many in Rome, including a majority of the Roman Senate, who like Octavian, wanted to punish Caesar's killers. Octavian was given a Senate seat, and he participated in the formation of a demand that Antony release Caesar's wealth, over which he had assumed control. When Antony gathered Roman troops in northern Italy, Cicero and the other senators gave their approval for Octavian to raise an army and fight him there.

Marching north with the consuls Hirtius and Pansa, Octavian fought and, in 43 B.C., defeated Antony at Mutina (now Modena, Italy), forcing the latter's withdrawal into Gaul (now present-day France). However, Hirtius and Pansa were killed, and these two men had been the Roman Senate's only control on Octavian, who met with Antony and his co-consul Lepidus in Bologna. In 43 B.C., the three men agreed to form a coalition, called the second Triumvirate, with their main goal being to defeat Caesar's murderers, the consuls Marcus Junius Brutus and Gaius Cassius Longinus. In 42 B.C., at Philippi in northern Greece, the triumvirate was victorius in one of the most noted battles in Roman history. Historian George Bruce writes:

> [The battle was] between the Republicans under Brutus and Cassius, 100,000 strong, and the army of the Triumvirs, about equal in numbers, under Octavius and Mark Antony. Brutus on the right repulsed the legions of Octavius and penetrated into his camp. Cassius however was overthrown by Antony and would have been overwhelmed but for the arrival of aid from the successful right wing. The action was renewed on the second day, when the Triumvirs were completely victorious and the Republican army dispersed. Brutus committed suicide on the field of battle. These two battles decided that Rome would be ruled by an autocracy.

After Philippi, Octavian and Mark Antony, in what has come to be known as the Treaty of Brundisium (40 B.C.), reached agreement to split up the Roman Empire under their exclusive control; Lepidus was given a province in Africa. Antony married Octavian's sister Octavia, but he later formed an alliance with Queen Cleopatra in Egypt, which would become a scandalous love affair. Octavian, meanwhile, began a series of military expeditions on the coast of Dalmatia on the Adriatic Sea, but returned home to quell the threat of civil war hanging over Rome. He took on one rival for power, Sextus Pompeius, a son of the famed Roman general POMPEY, and defeated him in 36 B.C. with the assistance of Marcus AGRIPPA in a massive naval battle at Mylae.

An extension of the Treaty of Brundisium, agreed at Tarentum in 36 B.C., was finished by 32 B.C., when Octavian received information that Antony was having an adulterous affair with Cleopatra. After Antony divorced his wife, Octavian received a copy of Antony's will and read the document in public; a codicil gave large amounts of money to Antony's illegitimate children with Cleopatra. Using this, Octavian persuaded the Roman Senate to declare war against Antony. The opposing forces met at Actium, off the western coast of Greece, on 2 September 31 B.C. While Antony's land troops were far superior in numbers to Octavian's, Marcus Agrippa's naval force cut off his supplies, despite the Romans having only 400 ships to Antony's 500. Antony and Cleopatra attempted to return to Egypt by sea, but they were defeated in battle and escaped with only a por-

tion of their force. Octavian chased them to Egypt and cornered them in Alexandria, where both Antony and Cleopatra committed suicide. To avoid any challenge to his leadership, Octavian had Caesarion, Julius Caesar's illegitimate child with Cleopatra, put to death.

Octavian was now the unchallenged leader of the world. He was given the titles of imperator (commander) and princeps, or "first citizen of Rome." He asked that the Senate control Rome, in his program known as the First Settlement of 27 B.C. Theoretically, Octavian ceded all power and allowed Rome to remain a Republic; in exchange, the Senate gave him the name *Augustus,* meaning "revered one" or "sacred one." He also retained the role of commander of the Roman armies. From this point on, Augustus ruled as the first Roman emperor.

Following these changes, Augustus launched a series of wars across Europe, fighting in Spain and Gaul, although after Actium he only commanded the army himself in the so-called Cantabrian war in Spain (26–25 B.C.). With the death of Lepidus in 12 B.C., his title of *pontifex maximus* was granted to Augustus; in 2 B.C., the Roman Senate granted Augustus the title of *pater patriæ,* or "father of the country."

In A.D. 14, after a lengthy reign, Augustus decided to withdraw from public life and go to Beneventum to retire. However, on the way, he fell ill in Capri, and after returning to the Italian mainland, he died in the village of Nola on 19 August A.D. 14, one month shy of his 77th birthday. His body was returned to Rome, where he was cremated and given his own mausoleum.

Two thousand years later, Caesar Augustus is second only to his great-uncle Julius Caesar in the popular memory of Roman leaders. While Julius Caesar's statesmanship and military skill established him as dictator of Rome, Augustus went on to even greater things. The first of the Roman emperors, he extended Rome's authority around the Mediterranean, put an end to the civil war, and laid the foundations of an empire that was to last until Constantinople fell in 1453.

References: Buchan, John, *Augustus* (Boston: Houghton Mifflin, 1937); Green, Peter, *Alexander to Actium; The Historical Evolution of the Hellenistic Age* (Berkeley: The University of California Press, 1990); Bruce, George, "Philippi," in *Collins Dictionary of Wars* (Glasgow, Scotland: HarperCollins Publishers, 1995), 194; Baker, George Philip, *Augustus: The Golden Age of Rome* (New York: Dodd, Mead & Company, 1937); Del Mar, Alexander, *The Worship of Augustus Caesar, Derived from a Study of Old Coins, Monuments, Calendars, Aeras, and Astronomical and Astrological Cycles, the Whole Establishing a New Chronology and Survey of History and Religion* (New York: Cambridge University Press, 1900); Rawson, Edward Kirk, *Twenty Famous Naval Battles, Salamis to Santiago* (New York: T. Y. Crowell & Company, 1899); "Actium, Battle of," in *The Hutchinson Dictionary of Ancient and Medieval Warfare* (Oxford, U.K.: Helicon Publishing, Ltd., 1998), 1; Shuckburgh, Evelyn S., *A History of Rome to the Battle of Actium* (New York: Macmillan and Company, 1894).

B

Bagration, Prince Pyotr Ivanovich (Petr Ivanovitsch Bagration, Peter Bagration) (1765–1812) *Russian general*

Born in Kizlyar, Georgia, sometime in 1765, Prince Pyotr Ivanovich Bagration was the scion of a famed Georgian family; he was distantly related to King David IV of Georgia. His grandfather, Aleksander Bagration, was a noted military officer, as was his father, Ivan Bagration. Pyotr (also Peter or Petr) Bagration entered the Russian army in 1782 when he was 17; he served for several years in the Caucasus region of Russia, fighting forces of the Ottoman Empire trying to control the region. In 1788, he saw major military action when he participated in the Russo-Turkish War of 1787–88 and, under the command of the Russian generals Gregory Potyemkin and Aleksander Suvorov, assisted in the attack on the Turkish fort Ochakov on the coast of the Black Sea. He then returned to the Caucusus, where he served until 1794, rising to the rank of premier major.

In 1794, Bagration was transferred to the Sofia Carabineers Regiment, and during the Russo-Polish War of 1792–94 he was present at the capture of Warsaw and promoted to the rank of lieutenant colonel. In 1798, he was promoted to colonel and placed in charge of the 6th Russian regiment. In 1799, he served under Suvorov in Italy against the French, leading the attack on Brescia (10 April 1799), at Milan (16 April 1799), and at Lecco (26–28 April 1799), where he was wounded in the leg.

When Napoleon and the French army invaded Austria in 1805, Bagration proved himself to be even more of a key commander for the allied Russian army. To protect the army's retreat, he fought a series of battles to slow down the French advance. These included actions at Amshteten and Krems, but the most notable was against Jean Lannes at Oberlollabrünn (16 November 1805), a disastrous defeat that cost Bagration some 3,500 men—half his force of 7,000. The sacrifice achieved its purpose, however, as it enabled the mainforce under Mikhail KUTUZOV to withdraw unharmed. For his "defeat" at Oberlollabrünn (now Hollabrünn), Bagration was promoted to lieutenant general. He joined forces with Kutuzov and, being able to push back the French on the way to Austerlitz, defeated them in two battles at Wischau (25 November 1805) and Raustnitsa (December 1805). The two armies met at Austerlitz on 2 December 1805, when 60,000 Russians and 25,000 Austrians faced 73,000 French under Napoleon. Historian George Bruce writes of the clash: "An attempt to turn the French flank failed, and led to the allies' left being cut off from their center. Their left and center were thus beaten in detail, and the right, which had at first held its own, was surrounded, and driven in disorder across a partially frozen lake, where many perished. The allies lost 27,000 killed, wounded, and prisoners, and a large number of guns. The French lost about 8,000."

Bagration put up persistent resistance against the French at Eylau (now Bagrationovsk, Russia) on 8 February 1807 and at Friedland (now Pravdinsk) on 14 June 1807. In 1808, he marched his troops across the frozen Gulf of Finland to capture the Åland Islands in the war against Sweden, winning a crucial victory at Artchio on 15–16 February 1808, and in 1809 he fought the Turks at Machin (18 August), Fursov (22 August), and Rossevat (4 September).

In 1812, Bagration was once again sent to fight the French, commanding the Second Army of the West; he was defeated by a French force at Mogilev on 23 July 1812. At Borodino on 7 September 1812, he headed the left wing of the Russian army, commanded by Mikhail BARCLAY DE TOLLY. During the battle, Bagration received a wound that proved mortal; he lingered for 17 days, succumbing on 24 September 1812. Czar Nicholas I later erected a monument in his honor at Borodino.

References: Golubov, Sergei Nikolaevich, *No Easy Victories: A Novel of General Bagration and the Campaign of 1812,* translated by J. Fineberg (London: Hutchinson International Authors Ltd., 1945); Keegan, John, and Andrew Wheatcroft, "Bagration, Prince Petr Ivanovich," in *Who's Who in Military History from 1453 to the Present Day* (London: Routledge, 1996), 18; "Austerlitz," in Bruce, George, *Collins Dictionary of Wars* (Glasgow, Scotland: HarperCollins, 1995), 25.

Baird, Sir David (1757–1829) *British general*
Born in Newbyth, East Lothian, Scotland, on 6 December 1757, David Baird was commissioned in the 2nd Regiment of Foot and entered the British army in 1772 (some sources report the year as 1773), joining his regiment in Gibraltar. In 1779, he was transferred to India, where, as a captain in the 73rd Highlanders, he served under Colonel Baillie. When Baillie's troops were taken prisoner in 1780 by Hyder Ali (the Indian warrior also known as Haider Ali), Baird was incarcerated with his fellow soldiers and spent four years in captivity at Seringapatam. Released in 1784, he remained in India, not returning home to England until 1789. Two years later he went back to India, breaking his journey to serve in South Africa.

In India, Baird took up arms against Tipu (also Tippoo) Sahib and was promoted to the rank of major general. He saw action at the first battle of Seringapatam (5–6 February 1792), where some 22,000 British and Indian troops, under Lord CORNWALLIS went against a Mysore fortification under Tipu Sahib. Baird led a second assault on Seringapatam (6 April–3 May 1799), earning high praise for his bravery. Because of his services to the British army, he fully expected to be named commander of the British forces in India, and when he was passed over for Arthur Wellesley (later the duke of WELLINGTON), he resigned his commission in a fit of anger. He reentered the British army in 1801.

From 1801 to 1802, Baird served in Egypt against the French, and in 1805 he was created Knight Commander of the Order of Bath (KCB) and promoted to lieutenant general. That year he was given command of an expedition against the Dutch at the Cape of Good Hope; he received the surrender of the Dutch forces the following year, bringing the area under British control. In 1807, Baird commanded a division at the siege of Copenhagen, and in 1808 he was sent to Spain as second in command of the British army. When General Sir John MOORE was mortally wounded at the Battle of La Coruña on 16 January 1809, Baird became the commander in chief, but he also was wounded and lost his left arm. Because of this, he was given no further command, but he received the thanks of Parliament and was created a baronet for his services (1809). In 1814, he was promoted to the rank of full general, and from 1820 to 1822 he served as commander of British forces in Ireland. In 1829, he became the governor of Fort George in his native Scotland, where he died on 29 August 1829 at the age of 72.

Baird biographer Henry Morse Stephens writes: "If Baird was not a very great soldier, he was certainly a gallant soldier, and the prisoner of Hydar Ali, the stormer of Seringapatam, and the general of the march across the desert, will deservedly remain a popular hero. There was a chivalrous gallantry in his nature which made the old pun, 'Not Baird, but Bayard,' particularly applicable to him."

References: Stephens, Henry Morse, "Baird, Sir David," in *The Dictionary of National Biography,* 22 vols., 8 supps., edited by Sir Leslie Stephen and Sir Sidney Lee, et al. (London: Oxford University Press, 1921–22), I:914–917; Wilkin, Walter Harold, *The Life of Sir David Baird* (London: George Allen & Co., 1912); Gore, Montague, *Character of Sir David Baird* (London: James Ridgway, 1833); Investigator, "Letters commenting upon Mr. Theodore Hook's Memoir of the Life of Sir David Baird," *The Asiatic Journal* (1834), 1–30; Bruce, George, "Seringapatam I" and "Seringapatam II," in *Collins Dictionary of Wars* (Glasgow, Scotland: HarperCollins Publishers, 1995), 225.

Barclay de Tolly, Mikhail Bogdanovich, Prince (1761–1818) *Russian general*

Despite his Russian name, Mikhail Barclay de Tolly, born in Luhde-Grosshof, Livonia, on 27 December 1761, was the scion of a Scottish family who had moved to Russia sometime in the 17th century. In 1776, when he was only 15, he enlisted in the Pskov regiment, earning an officer's commission within two years and rising to the rank of captain in 1788. That same year he fought against the Turks in the Russo-Turkish War (1787–91), in which he saw action at the siege of Ochakov (1788) and at Kaushany, Akkerman, and Bendery (all 1789). Transferred to Finland in 1790, he fought against Swedish forces and took part in the attack on the Kerkinossky fortress (19 April 1790). In 1792, he was sent to Poland, where he helped put down an insurrection at Vilno (1794). For this service he was awarded the Order of St. Vladimir and named a major general.

In the wars against NAPOLEON, Barclay de Tolly fought for the Russian army against the French forces that tried to subjugate Europe. Serving under the Russian commander Levin August Theophil Bennigsen, he showed his military capabilities at the battle of Pultusk (26 December 1806), when 60,000 Russians faced some 35,000 French under Marshal Jean LANNES. Despite their overwhelming advantage, the Russians lost the struggle and left some 3,500 dead on the battlefield. (Russian histories claim 8,000 French were killed, but historians figure the number to be about 1,500.) At Eylau on 8 February 1807, Barclay de Tolly once again served with distinction, and he was promoted to the rank of lieutenant general. In 1808, when Russia went to war against Sweden, he took the lead in marching with his fellow Russian general, Prince Pyotr BAGRATION, to capture Sweden's Åland Islands. In 1810, he was made minister of war.

When Napoleon invaded Russia in 1812, Barclay de Tolly joined with the rest of his countrymen in opposing the aggression, and he was given command of one of the Russian armies. Russia was unprepared to fight such a war, especially against an opponent as experienced and strong as Napoleon, and this was shown in the massive Russian defeat at Smolensk (16–17 August 1812). Barclay de Tolly took the blame for the defeat and resigned his command to General Mikhail KUTUZOV. He then took to the field with the Russian army at Borodino (7 September 1812), where Napoleon won a tactical victory and Prince Bagration suffered a mortal wound. Napoleon marched into Moscow, but Kutuzov was able to evacuate some 90,000 Russian troops, saving them from slaughter at the hands of the French. Again, Barclay de Tolly took the blame for the defeat at Borodino—despite the fact that many historians credit him for actually cutting Russian losses—and resigned his commission. He did not return to the battlefield until the following year, when, in dire need of leadership, Czar Nicholas I named him commander of the Russian armies again. In 1813, Barclay de Tolly saw major action at Dresden (26–27 August), Kulm (29–30 August), and Leipzig (16–18 October). The 1813 campaign reversed Napoleon's victories and forced the French army westward toward France, owing to decisive leadership from generals such as Barclay de Tolly. He led Russian troops in the two advances into France that ended Napoleon's reign of terror on the European continent, after which he retired. He was made field marshal in 1814 and given the title of prince in 1815.

Barclay de Tolly died in Insterburg (now in modern Poland), on 26 May 1818 at the age of 56. Historians John Keegan and Andrew Wheatcraft write: "Though posterity denied him the status according Kutozov or Suvorov, he deserved well of his country for his work as minister and his rescue of the Russian army from decay and inanition."

References: Josselson, Michael, *The Commander: A Life of Barclay de Tolly* (Oxford, U.K.: Oxford University Press, 1980); Keegan, John, and Andrew Wheatcroft, "Barclay de Tolly, (Prince) Bogdanovich," in *Who's Who in Military History from 1453 to the Present Day* (London: Routledge, 1996), 20–21.

Basil II (Bulgaroctonus, "Slayer of the Bulgars") (ca. 958–1025) *Byzantine emperor*

The great-great-grandson of Basil I (for whom he was named) and the son of Romanus II, both Byzantine emperors, Basil II was born around 958. In 963, Romanus died, and Basil was co-crowned as emperor, sharing the title with his brother Constantine. Since Basil and Constantine were minors, their stepfather, Nicephorus II Phocas, ruled as emperor (regent). When Nicephorus died in 969, John I Tzimisces took his place, and when John died on 10 January 976, Basil and Constantine became co-rulers, although Constantine played very little part. Almost immediately, Basil showed his ruthless side by crushing two generals who had opposed his leadership, Bardas Phocas and Bardas Sclerus; they went to war against Basil but were defeated in 979 and 987. Meanwhile, the practical administration was carried out by the boys' great-uncle, Basil Paracoemonenus, whose overthrow Basil engineered in 985.

Basil's reign as Byzantine emperor was marked by a series of wars against numerous opponents. Starting with the warlords of Asia Minor, whose large estates he seized, his armies marched to annex parts of Armenia to provide for an entrenched border against the Seljuk Turks. In 996, he invaded Bulgaria, whose leader, Tsar Samuel, had extended his borders to the edge of the Balkans, a move Basil saw as a threat. This lengthy war lasted until 1014 and saw Basil exhibit extreme brutality against the Bulgars, earning his nickname as Bulgaroctonus, or "Slayer of the Bulgars." After the battle of Kleidion (or Belasitsa), in which some 15,000 Bulgars were captured, Basil had them blinded and sent back to Tsar Samuel, who fainted at the appearance of the men and died soon afterward. Over the next four years, Basil won complete control over the Bulgars, but he allowed them some autonomy with ultimate control held by Byzantium.

In 1025, Basil began setting up a military force to move toward Sicily to retake it from the Arabs, but he died suddenly in December that year. His brother Constantine took power as Constantine VIII, ruling from 1025 to 1028 and sharing power with his daughter Zoe.

Although histories of the Byzantine Empire note Basil's reign for its military victories and cruelty against its enemies, his regime did mark the last major military conquest of the empire before its slow collapse.

References: Charanis, Peter, "The Monastic Properties and the State in the Byzantine Empire" in *Dumbarton Oaks Papers, number 4* (Cambridge, Mass.: Harvard University Press, 1948), 51–118; Ostrogorsky, George, *History of the Byzantine State,* translated by Joan Hussey (New Brunswick, N.J.: Rutgers University Press, 1969), 300.

Bazaine, François-Achille (1811–1888) *French marshal*

Born at Versailles, France, on 13 February 1811, François-Achille Bazaine entered the French army in 1831; some sources report that he enlisted as a private soldier. Two years later, he received a commission, and subsequently he saw action in the lengthy French campaign in Algeria, in the Crimean War (1854–56), in the French action against rebels in Lombardy in 1859, and in support of Emperor Maximilian in Mexico from 1862 to 1867. For his service in Mexico, Bazaine was promoted to the rank of marshal in 1864. In this role he aided in the evacuation of French troops as the rule of the Emperor Maximilian, whom France had placed on the Mexican throne, collapsed. (Maximilian was captured and executed by the Mexicans.)

In 1870, three years after the Mexican campaign ended, Bazaine took part in the Franco-Prussian War, commanding the III Corps of the Army of the Rhine, one of eight French formations on the Franco-Prussian frontier. Bazaine immediately moved his forces toward Metz. At Colombey on 14 August 1870, Bazaine's forces faced the Prussians under General Karl Friedrich von Steinmetz. The battle was indecisive: The French lost some 7,000 men, while the Prussians lost about 5,000; Bazaine received a nonfatal wound. This was a sign of things to come, because Bazaine found the French army ill-fed and ill-equipped for war, especially unable to fight a force as well trained and equipped as the Prussians. However, he pushed on, taking on the Prussians at Mars-la-Tour on 16 August 1870; the inconclusive result forced Bazaine to retreat to Metz. The two sides then clashed at Gravelotte (18 August 1870), where the French, backed by forces numbering some 113,000, faced a Prussian army under the command of William of Prussia (later Kaiser Wilhelm) of 187,000 men. Historian George Bruce writes: "The battle was most hotly contested, but while the French held their ground in the neighborhood of Gravelotte, the Prussians, under General [Helmuth Karl Bernhard] von Moltke, turned their right flank at St. Privat, and they were eventually obliged to abandon all their positions, and retire into Metz, where they were subsequently blockaded. The Prussian losses amounted to 899 officers and 19,260 men killed and wounded. The French losses were somewhat less. This battle is also known as the battle of St. Privat. The Prussians were now able to destroy the French at Sedan."

As the Prussians moved on Metz, Bazaine and the French army tried to cut them off at Bellevue (18 October 1870). The French were driven back with heavy casualties, approximately 1,200 men. They took shelter in the fortress at Metz, holding out from the end of the battle at Bellevue until 26 October 1870. On that day, facing the reality of the situation, which was compounded by the French disasters at Gravelotte and Sedan (1 September 1870), Bazaine surrendered his army to Prince Frederick Charles—a total of three marshals, 6,000 officers, and nearly 175,000 men. The loss to the French was fatal, and the war would soon end in the French defeat.

Bazaine, released by the Prussians, returned to France and was reviled as a traitor. He demanded an official inquiry to investigate the reasons behind the loss at Sedan and Gravelotte that forced his surrender. The inquiry was carried out and, in 1872, concluded that Bazaine was to blame for the disasters; he was also held accountable for several factors over which he had no control, including administrative matters that had left his army improperly fed. Bazaine rejected the report and demanded that he be court-martialed so that he could clear his name. This exercise backfired: Bazaine was convicted of treason and sentenced to death on 10 December 1873. His old friend Patrice de MacMahon, now the president of France, commuted the old soldier's sentence to life in prison. Bazaine was sent to the island of Île Sainte-Marguerite in the Mediterranean and allowed to have his wife and children live with him. On 9 August 1874, with the aid of his wife, Bazaine escaped from the island fortress and fled first to Italy and then to Spain, settling in Madrid under the protection of King Alfonso XII of Spain. Bazaine died in Madrid on 23 September 1888 at the age of 77. In his final years, he wrote his memoirs, *Épisodes de la Guerre de 1870* (published 1888).

References: Windrow, Martin, and Francis K. Mason, "Bazaine, François-Achille," in *The Wordsworth Dictionary of Military Biography* (Hertfordshire, U.K.: Wordsworth Editions Ltd., 1997), 22–24; Guedalla, Philip, *The Two Marshals: Bazaine, Pétain* (New York: Reynal & Hitchcock, 1943); Wylly, Harold Carmichael, *The*

Campaign of Magenta and Solferino, 1859 (London: Swan Sonnenschein & Co., 1907); Bruce, George, "Bellevue," "Gravelotte," and "Metz," in *Collins Dictionary of Wars* (Glasgow, Scotland: HarperCollins Publishers, 1995), 33, 101, 161.

Beatty, David, first earl Beatty, Viscount Borodale of Wexford, Baron Beatty of the North Sea and of Brooksby (1871–1936) *British admiral*

Born in the village of Howbeck Lodge, Stapeley, near Nantwich in Cheshire, England, on 17 January 1871, David Beatty was the son of Captain David Longfield Beatty. He entered the British navy in 1884, when he began training as a cadet on the HMS *Britannia*. Beatty's first service to his nation was in Egypt and the Sudan from 1896 until 1898 when, with the rank of lieutenant, he served under Lord KITCHENER along the Nile. He first showed the signs of his military prowess when, with his commander wounded, he assumed control and helped take Dongola (June 1896). He also served as the second in command of a gunboat flotilla that engaged Muslim rebels at their fortress in Hafir (19–26 September 1896). He finished his service in Africa with the taking of Khartoum on 2 September 1898. At the end of the war, Beatty was promoted to commander, and in 1900 he was sent to China, where once again he showed his courage and ability, at Tientsin, where he was wounded twice. This service earned him promotion to the rank of captain. In 1905, he was appointed MVO (member of the Royal Victorian Order), and in 1910 he became a rear admiral.

In 1911 (or 1912, according to some sources), Winston Churchill, at that time first lord of the Admiralty, named Beatty as the naval secretary. Beatty served in this position until 1913, when he was named commander of the First Battle Cruiser Squadron. In August 1914, he was promoted to acting vice admiral one day before the British declared war on Germany, setting off the World War I.

Beatty's first service in the war was his assault on the German forces at the Heligoland Bight, a small island off Germany's northwest coast that had been captured by Admiral Thomas Russell in the Napoleonic Wars on 31 August 1807. Here, almost 107 years later to the day (27–28 August 1914), Beatty fought one of the first battles of the First World War. The British fleet lured the Germans into the area and sank three cruisers and one destroyer without any British losses. On 24 January 1915, Beatty fought an even more famous battle at Dogger Bank, an island in the North Sea. There, he intercepted four German heavy cruisers and destroyers commanded by Admiral Franz Von Hipper. This fleet had intended to shell towns on the British coast, but Beatty surprised them 60 miles east of England. During the clash, the German cruiser *Blücher* was sunk by Beatty's flagship, the HMS *Lion.* However, just as the *Lion* swung out to face more ships, she too was hit and disabled; the battle was cut short with minimal British losses.

On 30 May 1916, Beatty fought in one of the most important naval encounters in world history: the battle of Jutland in the North Sea. Once again, Beatty's fleet faced that of the German Admiral Von Hipper, this time teamed with Admiral Reinhard SCHEER's High Seas Fleet. Beatty's smaller force deliberately tempted the Germans to attack, as he and his superior, John JEL-LICOE, had planned, so that Jellicoe's Grand Fleet could defeat them. Beatty fought this battle as he waited for Jellicoe's fleet to arrive, and during the fight, the HMS *Queen Mary* and the HMS *Indefatigable* were sunk, with massive losses; more than 1,000 sailors died on the *Inde-fatigable.* However, Beatty did slow down the Germans and forced equally devastating losses on them. Jellicoe, in overall command of the Jutland action, was blamed for the German fleet's escape, and Beatty replaced him as commander of the British Grand Fleet on 29 November 1916. Because there were several British naval officers of higher rank and with more seniority than Beatty, his promotion was quite controversial.

Beatty's "loss" at Jutland in fact was a victory, because it showed the ultimate weakness of the German ability to defeat the English fleet. Due to this, the Germans never again challenged British control of the seas, and Jutland was his last major battle. He accepted the surrender of the German navy at the Firth of Forth (Scotland) on 21 November 1918. On that day he stated, "The German flag will be hauled down at sunset today and will not be hoisted again without permission." For his services during the First World War, Beatty was given the title of Earl Beatty of the North Sea and Brooksby, promoted to Admiral of the Fleet, and given a grant of £100,000.

Beatty remained as head of the British navy until his retirement in 1927. During this period, he oversaw

the decommissioning of his beloved navy during the period of peace following the end of the war. In 1921, he served as a British delegate to the Washington Naval Conference in the United States (1921–22). He died in London on 11 March 1936 at the age of 65 and was laid to rest in Saint Paul's Cathedral in London next to John Jellicoe. His gravestone reads simply "Beatty" and the date MDCCCLXXI.

References: Rawson, Geoffrey, *Earl Beatty: Admiral of the Fleet: Viscount Borodale and Baron Beatty of the North Sea and of Brooksby* (London: Jarrolds, 1930); Rosskill, Stephen Wentworth, *Admiral of the Fleet Earl Beatty: The Last Naval Hero: An Intimate Biography* (London: Collins, 1980); Chalmers, William Scott, *The Life and Letters of David, Earl Beatty, Admiral of the Fleet . . .* (London: Hodder and Stoughton, 1951); Hunter, Francis T., *Beatty, Jellicoe, Sims and Rodman: Yankee Gobs and British Tars as Seen by an "Anglomanic"* (Garden City, N.Y.: Doubleday, Page & Company, 1919).

Belisarius (ca. 505–565) *Byzantine general*

Historians agree that Belisarius was one of the greatest military commanders of his time. Perhaps one of the finest works on him is *The Life of Belavius* (1829) by Lord Mahon, who writes:

> Belisarius . . . was born at Germania, on the confines of Thrace and Illyria. . . . The exact age of Belisarius is not recorded; but in his first military enterprise, which took place about two years before the accession of Justinian, we find him termed, by Procopius, a lately-bearded stripling. The same expression is applied by the same historian to Photius at his departure for the Gothic war. Now the mother of Photius was then 36 years of age, and her son could, therefore, hardly have exceeded twenty. If we suppose this to have been the age of Belisarius at his earliest exploit, and fix his birth at twenty years before, we shall, I think, approach as nearly to the truth as our imperfect information will allow.

Belisarius first appears in histories of the Byzantine period as a bodyguard to the Emperor Justinian I, who soon made him commander of the Byzantine army of some 25,000 men. Starting in 530, Belisarius took part in a series of wars that helped establish him as one of history's greatest generals. He fought against the Saddanids of Persia (now modern Iran) and quickly defeated that army despite being vastly outnumbered. His key victory in this war was at Daras (530). However, in 531, he was defeated by the Saddanids at Callinicum, the only battle he would lose in his long career. Recalled by Justinian, he redeemed himself when he aided in the suppression of the so-called Nika revolt (532) and saved the emperor's throne. In response to this service, Justinian once again placed Belisarius in charge of the Byzantine army and sent him to north Africa to fight the Vandals.

At Carthage on 14 September 533, Belisarius faced a Vandal army of some 160,000 men; historians agree that the Byzantine forces were far inferior in numbers. The Vandals, commanded by Gelimer, divided into three wings and hastily attacked the main Byzantine army. Belisarius used this moment to launch an assault on Gelimer and forced the Vandals to flee, resulting in Carthage's surrender. He took Gelimer as his prisoner and returned to Byzantium in triumph.

In 535, Justinian dispatched Belisarius to Italy to fight the Goths and defend Rome. He first invaded Sicily and then moved on to Naples. Finally he reached Rome, where, in two battles nine years apart, he demonstrated his military genius and shielded the city from tribal enemies. In the first battle in March 537, a Gothic army of 30,000 men under the Vandal king Vitiges marched on Rome and faced Belisarius's troops (whose numbers are unknown). The Byzantines' fierce resistance forced Vitiges to raise the siege in March 538 after a year of fighting. Vitiges was captured in 540 when Belisarius defeated the Vandals at Ravenna in a rout for the Byzantine forces.

With the Goths defeated, Justinian recalled Belisarius and sent him back to Persia, where another force under King Chosroes I was threatening the Byzantine Empire. Belisarius fought the Persians from 541 to 544, but when the Goths restarted their war in Italy, he was forced to return there, leading to the second battle of Rome in May 546. In this battle, Totila, the king of Italy, besieged Rome and forced the city's surrender. Belisarius then marched on the city and rescued it for a short period until Totila retook it later.

Despite Belisarius's numerous victories for Justinian, the emperor was jealous of his general, and in 548 he named Belisarius's rival, Narses, as the new head of the Byzantine army. Despite this slight, Belisarius re-mained in Italy, fighting off tribal forces with inadequate resources until his recall to Byzantium in 549. He then retired for a decade, only to be recalled back into service in 559 when an army of Bulgars advanced to the walls of Constantinople; he successfully repelled the attempted invasion, again demonstrating his military genius. Yet despite this service, Justinian still regarded Belisarius with suspicion; he was arrested on charges of conspiring to remove the emperor, and his property was confiscated. Some historians have claimed that Belisarius was reduced to begging in the streets of Constantinople; another writer claims that Justinian had Belisarius's eyes put out. These stories are unproven; a 12th-century painting by the famed artist Gérard shows a blind Belisarius, but it is not believed to be based on any actual history. In any event, Justinian finally became convinced of Belisarius's innocence and restored his property and good name in 563, two years before his death on 13 March 565.

References: Lord Mahon, *The Life of Belisarius,* 2d ed. (London: John Murray, Albemarle Street, 1848); Oldmixon, John, *The Life and History of Belisarius, Who Conquer'd Africa and Italy . . .* (London: A. Baldwin, 1713); Marmontel, Jean François, *The History of Belisarius, The Heroick and Humane Roman general . . .* (Philadelphia: J. Crukshank, 1770); "Belisarius," in *Command: From Alexander the Great to Zhukov—The Greatest Commanders of World History,* edited by James Lucas (London: Bloomsbury Publishing, 1988), 31–32; Bury, J. B., "The Reconquest of Italy," in *History of the Later Roman Empire From the Death of Theodosius I to the Death of Justinian,* 2 vols. (London: Macmillan and Co., 1923), II:226–249; Bruce, George, "Carthage II," "Rome IV," "Rome V," and "Tricameron," in *Collins Dictionary of Wars* (Glasgow, Scotland: HarperCollins Publishers, 1995), 52, 212, 251.

Benbow, John (1653–1702) *British admiral*

John Benbow was probably born in Shrewsbury, Shropshire, where his father, a burgess, owned a tannery house, on 10 March 1653. In 1678, he entered the English navy (some sources put him in the merchant marines), rising to the rank of captain in 1689. He served under the British admiral Edward Russell and saw action at the battle of La Hogue (19–20 May 1692), when a combined British and Dutch fleet, under the command of Russell and Admiral Philips Van Almonde, defeated a French fleet under the command of Admiral Anne-Hilarion de Cotentin, comte de Tourville. Many historians agree that Benbow played an important role in the French defeat. A year later, he commanded a squadron in the bombardment of St. Malo, in November 1693.

Benbow went on to serve in the West Indies from 1698 to 1700. In 1702, he returned to the area as commander in chief. On 19 August, while commanding a British squadron, he sighted four French ships off the coast of South America at Santa-Maria (now in modern Colombia), all commanded by J. B. Ducasse. Benbow chased the ships for five days in his flagship, the *Breda,* leaving the rest of his fleet behind, unguarded. When he caught up with the French, he and his men were alone and outnumbered. The French ships opened fire on the *Breda,* and one of the shots hit Benbow in his right leg, shattering it. Despite this life-threatening wound, he remained in full command on deck, but because of the damage to his ship, he was forced to back off the engagement. He evacuated to Jamaica, where he succumbed to his wounds on 4 November 1702. Only 49 years old, Benbow was buried in Kingston. Two commanders of ships that had refused to come to his aid were court-martialed for insubordination and shot.

References: Laughton, John Knox, "Benbow, John," in *The Dictionary of National Biography,* 22 vols., 8 supps., edited by Sir Leslie Stephen and Sir Sidney Lee, et al. (London: Oxford University Press, 1921–22), II:207–211; Campbell, John, *Lives of the Admirals, and Other Eminent British Seamen . . . , 4 vols.* (London: Applebee, 1742–44), I:25–40; Bruce, George, "La Hogue," in *Collins Dictionary of Wars* (Glasgow, Scotland: HarperCollins Publishers, 1995), 134–135.

Beresford, William Carr, Viscount Beresford
(1768–1854)   *British general*
Of Portuguese descent, William Carr Beresford was born on 2 October 1768, the illegitimate son of the marquis of Waterford. In 1785, at age 17, he entered the British army, serving in 1786 in Nova Scotia, where he lost the sight in one eye during a training accident. In 1793, Beresford saw his first action at Toulon after he was transferred to Corsica, serving under Sir Ralph Abernathy from 1795 to 1796. In 1795, he was given the command of the 88th Regiment, the Connaught

Rangers. From 1799 to 1803, while serving under the command of Sir David BAIRD, Beresford saw action in Egypt and later in South Africa. In 1806, he involved in the capture of Cape Town when the Dutch surrendered control of that city to British authority.

That same year, Beresford was named to command a land force sent to South America to capture Buenos Aires for the British. Although his forces easily took the city, they could not hold it against an insurrection by locals who despised British rule, led by a Frenchman, the chevalier de Tiniers. During the insurrection, Beresford was captured and held prisoner for six months until he escaped. He reached England in 1807 and was immediately sent to the Continent to fight in the Peninsular War. He helped invade the island of Madeira, holding it for the king of Portugal and serving as governor for six months, until he was ordered to Portugal to serve with Sir Arthur Wellesley (later the duke of WELLINGTON). He marched with Sir John MOORE during Moore's famed expedition into Spain, and he showed great valor at the battle of Corunna on 16 January 1809. For his services to the nation, Portugal's king named Beresford conde (count) de Trancoso, and bestowed a knighthood of the Tower and Sword of Portugal. Beresford undertook the reorganization of the Portuguese army with such success that Wellington incorporated many of the Portuguese troops into his own command, and they saw battle at Busaco (27 September 1810).

In 1811, Wellington sent Beresford to take over a force of troops formerly under the command of Lord Hill, who had returned to England due to illness. While Beresford was a more than competent commander, these new troops did not take to him, and at the battle of Campo Maior (or Mayor) on 25 March 1811, they disregarded his orders, and many were massacred. Beresford did lead his men to victory at La Albuera (16 May 1811) and Badajoz (16 March 1812), but historians usually credit Sir Henry Hardinge, and not Beresford, for these achievements. Beresford was severely wounded at the battle of Salamanca (22 July 1812), but he later recovered. He was present at the battle of Vitoria (21 June 1813) and at the battles of the Pyrenees (25 July–1 August 1813), commanded the British center at Nive (9–13 December 1813) and Orthez (27 February 1814), and led his men in the battle of Toulouse (10 April 1814). At the end of the Peninsular War, he was bestowed with the title of Baron Beresford of Albuera and Cappoquin and given a lifetime pension of £2,000 per year.

In 1819, following the revolution in Portugal, all British officers in the government's employ were dismissed, and Beresford returned to England, where he became a member of the Conservative Party. Four years later, in 1823, Beresford's barony was made a viscountcy. When his friend the duke of Wellington became prime minister and formed his cabinet in 1828, he named Beresford as master general of the ordnance, a role in which Beresford served until his retirement in 1830. He died at Bedgebury, Kent, on 8 January 1854 at the age of 85. Although not a spectacular military commander, he was well thought of by his peers: Wellington once remarked that in the event of his death in battle, he desired that Beresford be his sole replacement as head of the British armies on the European continent.

References: Stephens, Henry Morse, *Beresford, William Carr, Viscount Beresford* in *The Dictionary of National Biography*, 22 vols., 8 supps., edited by Sir Leslie Stephen and Sir Sidney Lee, et al. (London: Oxford University Press, 1921–22), II:330–335; Shand, Alexander Innes, *Wellington's Lieutenants* (London: Smith, Elder, & Co., 1902); Halliday, Sir Andrew, *Observations on the Present State of the Portuguese Army* (London: Printed for J. Murray, 1811); "Extract from a Memoir by Colonel Money," in Napier, W. F. P., *History of the War in the Peninsula and in the South of France from the Year 1807 to the Year 1814,* 6 vols. (London: Thomas & William Boone, 1836), V:585–586.

Bernadotte, Jean-Baptiste Jules, prince de Pontecorvo (Charles XIV John) (1763–1844)

French general, king of Sweden and Norway

Jean-Baptiste Jules Bernadotte was probably one of NAPOLEON's finest generals, famed for his military strategy. Born in Pau, France, on 26 January 1763, he was the son of a lawyer (though some sources report that his father was a tailor). When Bernadotte was 17, he entered into the French army, rising to the rank of adjutant in 1790. France was then in the midst of the French Revolution, but Bernadotte seemed to avoid its pitfalls. He saw action at the battle of Fleurus (25 June 1794) under General Jean-Baptiste Jourdan, and for this service he was promoted to the rank of general. Two years later, in 1796, when Napoleon Bonaparte became the head of the French army in Italy, Bernadotte served with him. During that campaign (1796–97), the French army won numerous victories over the Italians, Austrians, and Sardinians. In July 1799, Bernadotte was named minister of war, and he was later appointed French ambassador to Vienna. When Napoleon took power in a coup d'état on 10 November 1799, overthrowing the Directory (the interim French government established after the execution of King Louis XVI), Bernadotte took no part. However, when it appeared Napoleon would consolidate his power, Bernadotte sided with him and subsequently strengthened his position when he married the sister-in-law of Joseph Bonaparte, Napoleon's brother.

For two years Bernadotte served as councillor of state, and in 1802 he was once again given a command in the French army. In January 1803, Napoleon named him as the new minister to the United States, but rumors of war with Britain led him to delay his voyage until 1804. On 18 May 1804, Napoleon proclaimed the French Empire and was crowned its emperor. Bernadotte, one of his chief supporters, was named one of the new emperor's marshals and, the following month, governor of the electorate of Hanover, a portion of what is now modern Germany, captured by the French.

In 1805, war broke out between the French and Austrians, and Bernadotte became commander of the First French Corps. Perhaps his single greatest victory came during this conflict: At Austerlitz on 2 December 1805, he played a minor, albeit important, role in the victory of the French over a combined Russian-Austrian force under General Mikhail KUTUZOV. Napoleon sent Bernadotte to occupy Ansbach in Prussia (now modern Germany) prior to the battle, cutting off any aid from the Prussians to the Russians. Because they were separated from the main Grand Armée of France, Bernadotte and his troops did not see action at the dual battles of Jena and Auerstädt on 14 October 1806; however, Napoleon rewarded Bernadotte for his services by naming him prince of Pontecorvo (also called Ponte-Corvo).

Bernadotte was sent to Poland to fight the Prussians, who had sent reinforcements for the Russians. At Mohrungen on 25 January 1807, Bernadotte and a force of some 17,500 men defeated the Russians. This victory gave Napoleon the chance to take on a force of 75,000 Russians and Prussians under General Leonti Leontyevich Benningsen at Eylau (now in modern Russia). The battle on 7–8 February 1807 ended in a deadlock, with the French suffering 10,000 dead and the Russians, who were forced to withdraw, some 25,000 casualties.

Napoleon wanted to send Bernadotte to fight against Sweden, but this was postponed to enable him to go against the Austrians instead. At the battle of Fried-land (14 June 1807), Bernadotte, aided by Marshal Jean LANNES, occupied a position with 17,000 French troops as 61,000 Russians under Benningsen led a full assault. However, when Napoleon entered the fray with an additional 80,000 French soldiers, the Russians retreated with over 20,000 casualties.

In 1809, Napoleon put Bernadotte in command of the French army's IX Corps, also known as the Saxon Corps. At Wagram on 5–6 July 1809, he made a key mistake when his forces were attacked by Archduke CHARLES of Austria, losing the area of Anderklaa. Napoleon, furious that this setback cost him nearly 40,000 men overall, fired Bernadotte on the spot. The emperor later relented and, after Bernadotte had returned to Paris, put him in charge of defending the Netherlands from a potential British invasion. Bernadotte handled this position well, but it was not appropriate service for a field general, and he returned to France.

In 1810, Charles XIII of Sweden and Norway adopted Bernadotte as his official heir to the throne, since the crown prince chosen by Parliament had died in 1810, leaving no heir. Historians believe that Charles had been impressed by Bernadotte's service in northern Germany and with his conduct on the field of battle. It is also believed that Charles desired an alliance with Napoleon against the Russians. Once Napoleon gave his blessing, Bernadotte was named as crown prince of Sweden in 1810, taking the name Charles John.

Bernadotte subsequently changed from an obedient and loyal French military officer backing Napoleon to an angry Swedish prince who decided to lead his newly adopted land against France. In 1812, he entered into an alliance with his former enemy, Russian czar Alexander I, and the following year Sweden joined Russia in its war against France. Taking to the field, Bernadotte commanded an army of some 30,000 men used in several battles against his homeland's forces. These included actions at Gross-Beeren (23 August 1813) against General Nicholas Charles OUDINOT and Dennewitz (6 September 1813) against Marshal Peter NEY. At Leipzig on 16–18 October 1813, with 300,000 Russian, Prussian, and Austrian forces, he confronted and defeated Napoleon himself, leaving more than 50,000 French dead. This was a major setback for Napoleon.

Bernadotte now went to war against the Danes to consolidate Sweden's power in Scandinavia. In January 1814, he forced King Frederick VI of Denmark to sign the Treaty of Kiel, which ceded authority over Norway, formerly controlled by Denmark, to Sweden. That same year, following Napoleon's defeat and exile to the island of Elba, Bernadotte returned to France in a bid to become king of France and to establish a grand alliance of Sweden and France. However, finding his fellow Frenchmen bitter that he had turned against his homeland, he left France, never to return.

Returning to Sweden, Bernadotte discovered that the Norwegian people had refused to accept the Treaty of Kiel, and he went to war against them in July 1814. After just a month, the Norwegians were defeated, and they were forced to sign the Convention of Moss on 14 August, joining the two nations into one.

On 5 February 1818, Charles XIII died, and Bernadotte was crowned King Charles XIV John of Sweden and Norway. He sat on the throne of these two countries for 26 years, although he never learned to speak Swedish. His alliance with Russia resulted in increased trade, and he pushed the construction of Sweden's Göta Canal. His intolerance for a free press and some infringements on liberties led to demonstrations against him and calls for his abdication in the 1830s. However, he remained on the throne until his death in Stockholm on 8 March 1844; he was succeeded by his son Oscar I. The current Swedish monarch, King Carl XVI Gustaf (Charles XVI in English), is a direct descendent of Bernadotte. Another descendant was Count Folke Bernadotte (1895–1948), the UN representative in Israel who was murdered while trying to reach a truce between the Jews and Arabs.

References: Wencker, Friedrich, *Bernadotte, A Biography,* translated by Kenneth Kirkness (London: Jarrolds, 1936); Barton, Sir Dunbar Plunkett, *The Amazing Career of Bernadotte, 1763–1844* (London: John Murray, 1929); Palmer, Alan Warwick, *Bernadotte: Napoleon's Marshal, Sweden's King* (London: John Murray, 1990); Bruce, George, "Austerlitz" and "Eylau," in *Collins Dictionary of Wars* (Glasgow, Scotland: HarperCollins Publishers, 1995), 25, 85.

Berwick, James FitzJames, first duke of (earl of Teignmouth, Baron Bosworth, duc de FitzJames)

(1670–1734) *marshal of France*

James FitzJames was born in Moulins, France, on 21 August 1670, the illegitimate son of James of York (1633–1701), later James II of England, and his mistress Arabella Churchill, the sister of James Churchill, the duke of Marlborough. He spent very little of his life in his father and mother's native country; educated in France, he attended the Colleges of Juilly, du Plessis, La Flesche, and Paris. His first military service was fighting in Hungary under the command of Charles of Lorraine, and he was present at the battle of Buda (now Budapest, 1686). In 1687, when James was 17, his father created him duke of Berwick-upon-Tweed, usually styled as the duke of Berwick, earl of Teignmouth, and Baron Bosworth. In 1688, his father named him governor of Portsmouth and lord lieutenant of Hampshire. In 1688, James, a Catholic who was not popular in Protestant England, fled the nation when William of Orange, James's Protestant son-in-law, invaded England at the invitation of Parliament and took the throne as William III. James, duke of Berwick, also fled to France.

While in France, Berwick formed an army of Jacobites (supporters of James) and invaded Ireland, seeing action at Derry, Enniskillen, and Donegal. He also fought at the Battle of the Boyne (1 July 1690), where, under the command of Frederick Herman Schomberg, the Jacobites were decisively defeated by the forces of William III, though Schomberg was killed in the battle. James II fled again to France, but he left Berwick behind to continue to fight for control of Ireland. After a series of minor battles in which Berwick tried to hold off William III's forces, England finally won control of Ireland, and Berwick returned to his father in France. He then joined the French army, seeing action almost immediately at the seige of Mons and the battle of Lueze (19 September 1691). He also fought at the battles of Steinkirk (3 August 1692) and Neerwinden (29 July 1693; also called the battle of Landen, which was near Neerwinden). At the latter siege, Berwick was taken prisoner by his uncle, General Charles Churchill, brother to his mother Arabella and to James CHURCHILL, duke of Marlborough. He was taken before King William III of England, but he escaped punishment when he was exchanged for the duke of Ormonde.

Returning to service in the French army, Berwick served under François de Neufville, duc de Villeroi. In 1696, he once again tried to restore his father to the throne of England, even traveling to London in disguise, but he was unable to raise support. After seeing action in Spain, he was later naturalized as a French citizen (17 December 1703). In 1704, he was named as head of the French army in Spain but was soon replaced and sent on an expedition to Nice. His success there saw him promoted to marshal of France (15 February 1706) and given the official title of duc de Fitzjames. At the side of King Philip V of Spain he returned to fight the allied army of the English, Portuguese, and Austrians at Almansa (25 April 1707), where his army, though hopelessly outnumbered, defeated Henri de Ruvigny, the earl of Galway. When Galway moved into Madrid, Berwick's forces, joined by King Philip, took them on and defeated them.

From 1709 to 1712, he conducted a series of campaigns defending the southeast frontier of France, and then returned to command French forces in Spain. This led later to another great victory for him at Barcelona (11 September 1714), in which his forces stormed the city in the last battle of the War of the Spanish Succession. For his service to Spain, Philip V granted Berwick a pension and in April 1717 named him as governor of Guienne.

In 1733, after several years in the service of the French and Spanish forces, Berwick, at age 63, commanded another French army in a battle against Austria in the War of the Polish Succession. Marching to the Rhine River on 12 June 1734, he faced the Austrian forces at the battle of Philipsbourg (also Philipsburg), near Württemberg (now in Germany). During the battle—there is conflict as to the true story—a cannon shot from either the French or Austrian side hit Berwick and took off his head. Berwick's biographer, Sir Charles Petrie, writes:

> At the beginning of June the investment of Philipsburg began, and as was his custom Berwick personally inspected the trenches every morning. On June 12th he did this in company with his [second] son, the Duke of FitzJames, and in the course of his inspection he reached an advanced point where several French soldiers had been killed by their own artillery. A sentry had in consequence been placed near the spot to warn people of the danger, but he does not appear to have done so in the case of Berwick. The guns on both sides opened fire, and a ball carried off the Marshal's head, but from which side it came was never established.

Berwick was 64 years old. His body was returned to Strasbourg, France, and, after being embalmed, was buried in the cathedral there. Berwick had asked that his body be eventually removed to the Rue Saint Jacques in Paris, to be buried next to his eldest son, James Francis, the duke of FitzJames and marquis of Teignmouth, who had predeceased him in 1721 and was considered by some to be the heir to the throne of England. Berwick's memoirs were published in 1778.

References: Stephens, Henry Morse, "Fitzjames, James, Duke of Berwick," in *The Dictionary of National Biography,* 22 vols., 8 supps., edited by Sir Leslie Stephen and Sir Sidney Lee, et al. (London: Oxford University Press, 1921–22), VII:178–179; Petrie, Sir Charles, *The Marshal Duke of Berwick: The Picture of an Age* (London: Eyre & Spottiswoode, 1953); Berwick, James Fitzjames, duke of Berwick, *Memoirs of the Marshal Duke of Berwick* (London: T. Cadell, 1779).

Bingham, George Charles *See* LUCAN, GEORGE CHARLES BINGHAM, THIRD EARL OF.

Birdwood, Sir William Riddell, Baron Birdwood of Anzac and Totnes (1865–1951)
British general

Despite his great defeat at Gallipoli, Sir William Riddel Birdwood was perhaps one of the few officers to escape from that military disaster with his reputation intact. He went on to a distinguished military career thereafter, including his participation in several important battles on the western front in the First World War. He was born on 13 September 1865 at Kirkee, near Bombay, India, where his father was serving in the Indian Civil Service. As a boy, Birdwood returned to his native land and attended Clifton College in Bristol, then the Royal Military College at Sandhurst. In 1883, he was assigned to the Royal Scots Fusiliers. Three years later, he was transferred to the Indian staff corps, serving as a cavalry officer in the 12th Lancers, the 11th Bengal Lancers, and the Viceroy's Bodyguard from 1886 to 1899. During the Boer War (1899–1902), he served in South Africa and was a member of the staff of General Horatio Herbert KITCHENER. In 1911, he was promoted to major general, and from 1912 to 1914 he served as secretary of the Indian Army Department.

In November 1914, following the outbreak of the First World War, Lord Kitchener, now serving as sec-

Sir William Birdwood

retary of state, selected Birdwood to command a combined force of British, French, Australian, New Zealand troops (the latter two designated the Australia-New Zealand Army Corps, or ANZAC). After several months of training, in March 1915 Birdwood prepared his forces to land in the Dardanelles. The aim of this mission was to capture Istanbul, the Turkish capital, and thus aid Russian forces against the Germans and Austrians from the east. The main landing site was at the peninsula of Gallipoli. This expedition would become one of the worst tragedies of modern military fighting. Although Kitchener had confidence in Birdwood's strategy to take the area, a more senior officer, Sir Ian HAMILTON, was sent to command the operation. Birdwood took this in his stride and went to work forming a plan to invade at Gallipoli.

On paper, Birdwood's plan—to land at dawn at a spot where Turkish resistance was thought to be light—seemed a perfect strategy. However, there were serious flaws, many owing not to him but to his superiors. First, he was given a force of men inexperienced in warfare;

second, he was given only 13 divisions—some 490,000 men—to the Turks' 20 divisions, led by General Liman von Sanders. An initial bombardment by British and allied ships on Gallipoli and the other Turkish holdings did not dislodge the enemy, and the landing went ahead. Historian George Bruce writes:

> Eventually, on 25 April [1915], some 75,000 men were landed on the Peninsula's southern tip, another 35,000 at Cape Helles plus 35,000 ANZACs further up the west coast, but the Turks held their main positions and under Colonel Kemal (later Kemal Ataturk), counter-attacked. By 8 May Hamilton had lost about a third of his men in fierce fighting and there were signs of a stalemate, but resisting calls for evacuation he ordered his army to dig in. Another landing of 25,000 men at Sulva Bay on 6 August 1915 failed largely owing to the apathy of General [Sir Frederick] Stopford, who slept on a ship at the critical time. A stalemate like that of the western front developed. Hamilton was replaced on 22 November by General [Charles] Munro, and finally the Cabinet in London agreed to withdrawal. Suvla Bay and Anzac Cove were evacuated by the Navy on 20 December and Cape Helles on 9–10 January, after another general action, but no lives were lost in the skilful withdrawal, the only success in the entire campaign. British and French casualties were about 250,000 and those of Turkey probably about the same.

Birdwood had opposed the Gallipoli campaign's continuation once he saw it was to be a failure, but he was overruled. On 19 November 1915, he took command of the Gallipoli force, replacing General Munro. Many historians credit Birdwood for the evacuation and withdrawal from the Dardanelles, and it is for this reason that his military career was not adversely affected by the horrific loss at Gallipoli.

Birdwood then served as commander of the Australian forces on Europe's western front from September 1916 until the end of the war in November 1918. He clashed repeatedly with his superiors, Sir Douglas HAIG, commander of British forces in France, and Sir Hubert Gough, commander of the British Fifth Army. Once again, despite his warnings and protestations, Birdwood's forces were sent into several battles he felt were unnec-

essary, including the ones at Pozieres Ridge (23 July–4 August 1916) and Fromelles (19–20 July 1916), both of which proved to be disastrous for the Allied forces. At the Somme (1 July–18 November 1916), he moved his men into battle despite his misgivings; the loss was more than 6,300 killed and wounded. When Gough moved his men under his immediate command to that of Sir Herbert PLUMER's, Birdwood felt his views should be taken into account. In the third battle of Ypres (17 June 1917), his advice was accepted, but even so, the British lost more than 250,000 dead and wounded, with negligible land gains.

On 23 October 1917, Birdwood was promoted to general. In the final push of the war, starting in April 1918 at the Somme, his cautious leadership helped gain territory for the Allies. On 31 May 1918, he was promoted to commander of the British Fifth Army, succeeding Plumer. However, in the final battles of the war, he was passed over by his superiors and did not take an active role in the final offensive that ended the conflict in November 1918.

Following the war, Birdwood went to Australia with the men he commanded and was widely acclaimed; he was made a baronet in 1919. In 1920 he was named commander of the northern army of India, where he served until 1924, after which he was promoted to the rank of field marshal and placed in command of all forces in India. He retired from the army in 1930.

In 1931, when John Lawrence Baird, first baron of Stonehaven, retired as governor-general of Australia (at that time a part of the British Commonwealth), Birdwood hoped to succeed him. However, Australian prime minister James Henry Scullin wanted an Australian for the post, and Sir Isaac Alfred Isaacs was named instead. Birdwood returned to England, where he was made Baron Birdwood of Anzac and Totnes in 1938. He wrote two books of memoirs: *Khaki and Gown: An Autobiography* (1941) and *In My Time* (1946). He died in Cambridge on 17 May 1951.

References: Birdwood, Field Marshal Lord Birdwood of Anzac and Totnes, *In My Time: Recollections and Anecdotes* (London: Skeffington & Son, Ltd., 1946); Hudson, Derek, "Birdwood, William Riddell, first Baron Birdwood," in *The Dictionary of National Biography*, 22 vols., 8 supps., edited by Sir Leslie Stephen and Sir Sidney Lee, et al. (London: Oxford University Press, 1951–60), II:112–114; Bruce, George, "Gallipoli," in *Collins Dic-*

tionary of Wars (Glasgow, Scotland: HarperCollins Publishers, 1995), 94–95.

Blake, Robert (1599–1657) *English general and admiral*

Noted for his services to the Parliamentarian forces during the English Civil Wars and the best English naval commander of his day, Robert Blake was born in Bridgwater, Somersetshire, the son of Humphrey Blake, a well-to-do merchant. He began his studies at St. Alban Hall, Oxford, in 1615, and moved to Wadham Hall (now Wadham College) two years later. He abandoned his studies in 1625, when his father died, and returned to Somerset to run the family business.

In 1640, Blake was elected as a member of Parliament (MP) for Bridgwater. This parliamentary session is known in history as the Short Parliament, cut short due to arguments over policy with King Charles I, which would eventually force a civil war. Blake lost his seat in the next election in 1641; some historians speculate that he may have foreseen the coming of civil war and went to the Netherlands to get military training.

When the first English Civil War broke out in 1642, Blake, who sided with the Parliamentary forces, was made a general and placed in command of troops. On 26 July 1643, he and his army, with Colonel Nathaniel Fiennes, moved to Bristol to defend it from Prince Rupert, a Royalist general, but Blake and Fiennes were defeated. Blake then went to Lyme Regis, Dorset, to which Prince Maurice, Prince Rupert's brother, laid siege in March and April 1644. Blake was able to hold Lyme Regis until the garrison could be relieved by Robert Devereux, third earl of ESSEX, in June. In July, Blake and his forces marched from Lyme to Taunton, a critical center of operations for the Royalist army. The parliamentarians took Taunton easily and, though attacked by Royalists three times, held the city for a year until troops led by General Sir Thomas FAIRFAX arrived to relieve them in May 1645.

Blake was a popular commander amongst the parliamentary forces, and in 1645 he was elected to Parliament as a member from Bridgwater, suspending his military service. He returned to active duty in 1648, when, in the Second Civil War, he organized forces in the Somerset region. In February 1649, he was named with two other so-called generals at sea, Richard Deane and Edward Popham, as "commissioner to command

the fleet" of Parliament. His first battle in this capacity was at Kinsale (April 1649). Facing Prince Rupert's fleet off the southern coast of Ireland, Blake was able to blockade them for a period of six months. On 20 October, after Blake had been forced to lift the blockade due to bad weather, Rupert sailed with seven warships to Lisbon, Portugal. Blake pursued the prince, but the king of Portugal, John IV, refused him entry into the Tagus River to attack Rupert. A fleet under the command of Edward Popham sailed from England to join Blake, and both men warned John that if Rupert were protected, Portuguese trade would be attacked. The king, however, held firm.

Rupert twice tried to escape, but Blake contained him. On 14 September, Blake attacked a Portuguese fleet returning from Brazil loaded with treasure; he sank one ship, emptied 13 others of their booty, and returned to England with the treasure. He then returned to fight Rupert, whom he trailed to the coast of Spain and defeated him at Cartagena (6 November 1650), destroying the royalist fleet. For this action, Blake was thanked by Parliament and given a prize of £1,000. His next service was in conjunction with Sir George Ayscue in 1651, when the two men captured and destroyed a Royalist base in the Scilly Islands as well as a similar one in the Channel Islands. He spent the remainder of 1651 patrolling the English Channel for any naval challenges to Parliamentary rule.

When the Anglo-Dutch War broke out in 1652, Blake was placed in command of the fleet in the English Channel. Even before war had been declared, he moved with 20 warships on a fleet of 42 Dutch warships commanded by Admiral Maarten Harpertszoon TROMP that was sailing near the coast of Dover. Because their countries were technically at peace, Blake demanded that Tromp salute the English fleet; when Tromp refused, Blake, though woefully outgunned, fired on the Dutch, sank two of their ships, and forced them to retreat. When war was declared that July, Blake set out to capture the Dutch fleet or destroy it. On 28 September, he and William Penn (father of the William Penn who founded the Pennsylvania colony in America), pitted their 68 warships against a Dutch fleet of 59 ships commanded by Michael de Ruyter and Witte Corneliszoon De Witt off the Kentish Knock in the North Sea. After a furious three-hour fight, Blake's forces captured two Dutch ships and wrecked several others.

At Dungeness on 29–30 November 1652, Blake and 40 English ships, took on Tromp and 95 Dutch ships. Blake's forces suffered a serious loss, with six ships sunk and two captured, and they were forced to withdraw into the Thames River, allowing the Dutch control of the English Channel. Blake rebuilt his fleet, and at Portland (18–20 February 1653), also called the Three Days Battle, Blake suffered a serious leg wound but defeated Tromp and the Dutch and reestablished English control over the Channel. When General George MONCK and Richard Deane faced Tromp at North Foreland (2–3 June 1653), Deane was killed but Blake came to the aid of the English forces and defeated Tromp. Ill health from his wound forced Blake to return to England, and he did not participate further in the war, which ended with the battle of Scheveningen on 31 July 1653.

Blake went into retirement, although he did serve for a time as a member of Parliament from Bridgwater in what was called the Barebones Parliament. This was named after Nicholas Barbon, who led parliamentary criticism of the lord protector, Oliver CROMWELL, who in turn dismissed Parliament. When Cromwell went to war with the French and Spanish, Blake was called back into service. Given command of an English fleet of 24 warships, he attacked the fort at Porto Fariña in Tunis (now Tunisia) to discourage Barbary pirates threatening English shipping, and these firm measures were successful. Blake then moved to the coast of Spain off Cádiz, threatening to capture Gibraltar, and it was at this point that his finest victory came. At Tenerife (Canary Islands) on 20 April 1657, he attacked the Spanish and destroyed or captured their entire fleet with the loss of only one English ship.

Ill health forced Blake to sail for England. He was nearly home when he succumbed to his war wounds on 17 August 1657 at the age of only 58. He was buried in Westminster Abbey, but, following the restoration of Charles I's son, Charles II, his body was removed from the abbey and thrown into a pit near the abbey. It was recovered and reburied in the churchyard of St. Margaret's Church in London.

Historian C. R. B. Barrett, in his 1917 treatise on "the missing years" of Blake's early life (1625–1640), sums up his life and his career: "It must . . . in fairness be stated that no one really satisfactory account of Blake exists as a whole. Of his parliamentary career, which began in 1640, little is told us. His military exploits, which began in 1642, are worthy of far more atten-tion than has been bestowed on then, and to this day, as a commander of land forces, he has been neglected by military historians. His naval exploits have, however, been adequately treated and his distinguished services as Admiral and General at Sea have been recorded at length and in detail."

References: Laughton, John Knox, "Blake, Robert," in *The Dictionary of National Biography,* 22 vols., 8 supps., edited by Sir Leslie Stephen and Sir Sidney Lee, et al. (London: Oxford University Press, 1921–22), II:632–641; Beadon, Roger, *Robert Blake: Sometime Commanding All the Fleets and Naval Forces of England* (London: Edward Arnold & Co., 1935); Vere, Francis, *Salt in Their Blood: The Lives of the Famous Dutch Admirals* (London: Cassell & Company, Ltd., 1955); Barrett, C. R. B., "The Missing Fifteen Years (1625–1640) in the Life of Robert Blake, Admiral and General at Sea," *The Journal of the Royal United Science Institution* 62 (1917): 98–110; *A Great Victory Obtained by His Excellency the Lord General Blake* . . . (London: Printed for George Horton, 1652); Bruce, George, "Dover" and "Portland," in *Collins Dictionary of Wars* (Glasgow, Scotland: HarperCollins Publishers, 1995), 76, 200.

Blücher, Gebhard Leberecht von (1742–1819)
Prussian general

Born in Rostock, Mecklenburg-Schwerin (now in Germany), on 16 December 1742, Gebhard Leberecht von Blücher did not consider a military career until he visited the Swedish island of Rügen, where he saw Swedish hussars training. He then joined the Swedish army as a cornet (junior officer). Coincidentally, the first action he saw was against his native Prussia; taken prisoner (ironically, by the same regiment he later commanded), Blücher was persuaded to join the Prussian army. He was given the rank of lieutenant in the regiment that had captured him; however, he soon became aggrieved by what he felt was the unworthy promotions of other men, and he left the army in 1772, retiring to his family's estate in Pomerania.

In 1787, following the death of Prussian king Frederick II, Blücher was induced to return to the army, this time with the rank of major, and he commanded his old regiment when it was sent into battle in Holland. When Prussia went to war against France, he saw major action at the battles of Orchies (1793), Frankenstein (1793), and Oppenheim (16 January 1794). In 1793, he was promoted to the rank of colonel, the following year to the rank of major-general, and in 1801 he was made a lieutenant general.

When the French leader NAPOLEON began his second war of conquest of Europe in 1803, Blücher became a constant opponent to his aims. The Prussian leader's first major clash against French forces under the French commander Marshal Louis-Nicholas DAVOUT was at Auerstädt (also called Jena, 14 October 1806). The Prussians lost some 22,000 men in their defeat to the French, who suffered 11,000 casualties. Blücher then withdrew his troops to Pomerania. When part of the Prussian army under the Prince of Hohenlohe was cut off and forced to surrender, Blücher joined the army of Prince William of Brunswick-Oels at Mecklenburg. To cut off the French, he moved onto the city of Lübeck, but the French fought him near there and forced his surrender at Ratkau on 6 November 1806. He was subsequently exchanged for the French general Claude Victor Perrin and returned to the Prussian ranks, where he was put in charge of the defense of Pomerania's Coastline. It was not until 1813 that he was placed back in command of regular troops.

Following Napoleon's disastrous withdrawal from Russia in early 1813, Blücher again fought the French general. At Lützen (2 May 1813) and Bautzen (20 May 1813), he lost to Napoleon's forces; however, at Katzbach on 26 August 1813, he defeated French General Étienne MacDonald, and at Leipzig on 16–18 October 1813, he defeated Napoleon himself. For this battle, Blücher was promoted to the rank of field marshal. He led the advance into France, crossing the Rhine River and winning a decisive victory at La Rothière on 1 February 1814, but a series of small defeats pushed him back to Châlons. On 9–10 March 1814, Blücher defeated Napoleon at Laon, with the French losing some 6,000 dead and wounded. Blücher and his army marched into Paris on 31 March, and Frederick William III of Prussia styled Blücher as the prince of Wahlstadt for his services to the nation.

Napoleon was exiled to the island of Elba, but he escaped in 1815, returned to France, took power a second time, and went on the offensive once again. Blücher went back into action as commander of the Army of the Lower Rhine. In June 1815, Blücher, commanding an army of some 124,000 Prussians, marched to join Arthur Wellesley, duke of WELLINGTON, and his force of 95,000 English and Dutch troops, but was attacked

by Napoleon on the way. The writers of *The Wordsworth Dictionary of Military Biography* write:

Although taken by surprise, Blücher reacted promptly, and by the evening of 15 June had positioned part of his forces at Sombreffe, while Wellington was concentrated fifteen miles to the west. The key point linking was the small crossroads village of Quatre Bras. On the following day Napoleon fell on Blücher at Ligny, rocking him back; believing that [Marshal Peter] Ney had captured Quatre Bras, he ordered him to strike Blücher's right flank and thereby complete the victory. But following a gallant defense by a British brigade and procrastination by the French marshals, the center of the Allied line was temporarily held. Blücher, initially defeated and himself wounded, retreated north to Wavre, but the French commander, [Emmanuel] Grouchy, failed to maintain contact with the retreating Prussians and gave Blücher time to reorganize his forces.

Blücher's march back into the battle (for which he earned the nickname "Marshal Vorwärts" or "Marshal Forwards") finally turned the tide for the duke of Wellington at the Battle of Waterloo, completing the allied victory and Napoleon's final defeat. The Frenchman was forced into exile at St. Helena, where he died a few years later. Blücher again marched into Paris and was rewarded with the Grand Cross of the Order of the Iron Cross. He retired to an estate in Prussia.

Blücher died in Krieblowitz, Prussia (now Katy Wroclawskie, Poland), on 12 September 1819 at the age of 76. Historian Michael Lanning writes: "Blücher, never a master of tactics or strategy, was unsurpassed in his personal bravery. What he lacked in finesse and refinement he compensated for in his ability to motivate his soldiers, who admired his excessive indulgences in alcohol, tobacco, and other vices. At times, Blücher's allies as well as his enemies doubted the field marshal's sanity because of his strange actions, including claims at one time that he was pregnant with an elephant. Regardless of whether his erratic behavior resulted from real mental instability, heavy consumption of gin, or his own misguided sense of humor, Blücher's reputation as a fighter could strike fear into his opponents by his mere appearance on the battlefield."

References: Windrow, Martin, and Francis K. Mason, "Blücher, Gebhard Leberecht von, Prince of Wahlstadt," in *The Wordsworth Dictionary of Military Biography* (Hertfordshire, U.K.: Wordsworth Editions Ltd., 1997), 28–31; Henderson, Ernest F., *Blücher and the Uprising of Prussia against Napoleon, 1806–16* (New York: G. P. Putnam's Sons, 1911); "Blücher, Gebhard," in *Command: From Alexander the Great to Zhukov—The Greatest Commanders of World History,* edited by James Lucas (London: Bloomsbury Publishing, 1988), 68–69; Lanning, Michael Lee, "Gebhard Leberecht von Blücher," in *The Military 100: A Ranking of the Most Influential Military Leaders of All Time* (New York: Barnes and Noble Books, 1996), 231–233.

Boadicea   *See* BOUDICCA.

Boscawen, Edward   (1711–1761)
British admiral

Edward Boscawen was born on 19 August 1711, the third of five sons of Hugh Boscawen, first viscount Falmouth, and his wife Charlotte, who was the niece of John CHURCHILL, duke of Marlborough. Boscawen entered the British navy at 15 and was assigned to the warship *Superbe,* setting sail for the West Indies in April 1726. He served on her for three years and then saw service on several other ships in the Mediterranean and in British waters.

In 1732, Boscawen was promoted to the rank of lieutenant. Five years later, he was given the command of the *Shoreham,* a 20-gun warship. When war began with Spain the following year, he was ordered to the West Indies in the *Shoreham.* While en route, it ran aground on the western end of the island of Cuba, and Boscawen and his crew were forced to abandon the ship. He joined the famed British admiral Edward VERNON, who was sailing to attack the Spanish at Port Bello. The attack was successful, and Boscawen helped to destroy the Spanish fort's defenses.

For the next year or so, following the recovery and repair of the *Shoreham,* Boscawen and his crew cruised the Caribbean between what is now Cuba and Florida, attacking and capturing Spanish vessels. In 1741, he was reassigned to Vernon's squadron and saw action at Cartagena (in today's Colombia), where he led a raiding party that took a battery of 15 cannons (24-pounders). In a

letter to the governor of Jamaica, Vernon later wrote, "Captain Boscawen, all say made a prudent general in the disposing his men landing in as good order as could be expected for night work in an unknown country." Vernon then placed Boscawen in charge of destroying the defenses of the fort at Boca Chica, farther along the coast.

Because of his service, Boscawen was promoted to the rank of captain, and he succeeded Lord Aubrey Beauclerk as commander of the 70-gun warship *Prince Frederick.* He sailed this ship back to England for new orders, but when he arrived in May 1742 he was placed in command of the warship *Dreadnought,* which he sailed to the Azores off Spain. There he spent much of 1742 and 1743 intercepting Spanish ships.

In 1742, Boscawen was elected to a seat in the House of Commons from Truro, but he did not formally sit in the Commons for nearly 20 years, instead concentrating on his military career. In late 1743, he was recalled and assigned to the Home Fleet under Sir John Norris, a force whose main goal was to defend the English isles. The first major threat during Boscawen's time in the Home Fleet came in early 1744, when a French armada under Admiral Jacques Aymar, comte de Roquefeuil, sailed into the English Channel to assist in a French invasion of England. Norris initially tried to fight the French with Boscawen's assistance, but strong weather drove the fleets apart, and the invasion was cancelled. In April 1744, Boscawen was assigned to a squadron commanded by Sir Charles Hardy escorting ships to the Mediterranean. On 24 April, Boscawen's ship sighted the French 26-gun frigate *Medée* southwest of Ushant. He gave chase, and after several hours the French ship was captured (later to become the English privateer *Boscawen*). Boscawen later fought a limited battle with French forces (July 1744), but he was able to escape without being captured. In the next several years, he commanded other ships in the Home Fleet, defending England against invasion.

In 1746, as commander of the *Namur,* Boscawen was assigned to the western squadron under George ANSON. During the latter part of that year, he helped capture the French hospital ship the *Mercure.* In May 1747, the first major sea battle of the War of the Austrian Succession took place off Cape Finisterre, Spain. The French, under Admiral Jacques-Pierre de la Jonquière, were escorting a convoy of merchant ships. Anson was victorious and captured 10 French ships. According to

Boscawen, the *Namur* "came very near three or four of them where we were warmly engaged on both sides for about three-quarters of an hour. We then shot ahead and about half past four engaged the *Sérieux* [the French flagship]." The English victory of 3 May 1747 was a severe blow to the French; for his part in this battle, Anson was raised to first lord of the Admiralty and to the peerage as Baron Anson.

Boscawen, shot in the shoulder during the fight, was promoted to rear admiral and placed in command of a fleet sent to India. He was warned before arriving there that the French had constructed defenses at Pondicherry. Due to faulty intelligence, his initial attack in August 1748 suffered numerous casualties, and the onset of bad weather forced him to withdraw. Although a peace treaty had been negotiated between Britain and France before the battle, Boscawen received orders to remain on station until the peace terms were implemented and he formally accepted control of Madras from the French. On 12 April 1749, while waiting for further word, a hurricane hit the area, sinking the *Namur* with all hands on board. Boscawen, who was onshore with some of his aides at the time, survived the disaster. He sailed back to England on another ship, arriving in April 1750, and was named a commissioner of the Admiralty on 22 June 1751. In February 1755 he was promoted to the rank of vice admiral.

In 1755, relations between Britain and France once again declined, and Boscawen, among other military figures, prepared again for war (the Seven Years' War, 1756–63). He was given charge of a secret mission to intercept a French fleet sent to reinforce French forces in Canada against the British. Commanding the warship *Torbay,* Boscawen sailed under the command of Lord HOWE (later Baron Howe of Langar). The three French ships were sighted, and Howe demanded that they surrender. The *Torbay* came up beside them, and when the French resisted, Boscawen ordered that they be fired upon. After a two-hour battle, one of the ships escaped, but two were captured, including the *Alcide.* Remarkably, Boscawen had captured the captain of this ship, Hocquart, following the battle at Cape Finisterre in 1747, and Hocquart had been commander of the *Medée* when Boscawen had captured that ship in 1744; so he was now taken by the British admiral for the third time.

Given command of the 74-gun warship *Invincible,* Boscawen joined Sir Edward HAWKE's fleet off Ushant. For a period of time, there were no battles, and Boscawen illustrated the mood in a letter home to his wife: "We are at this minute practising firing, it being calm and many of the fellows hit the mark, note nobody is firing at them." In late July 1756, Boscawen was given command of the 100-gun warship *Royal George.* Two years later, in February 1758, he was made an admiral of the blue and given command of the fleet sent to Canada to capture the city of Louisbourg preparatory to taking Quebec from the French. The trip took 11 weeks due to bad weather, and the fleet arrived at the end of May 1758. Finding the harbor blocked by the French ships, Boscawen ordered a landing south of Louisbourg at Gabarus Bay. In coordination with the British army, including the commanders James WOLFE and Jeffrey AMHERST, the entire French force was assaulted. This synchronized attack led to a swift reduction in French resistance, which by the end of June was near collapse. Consequently, the destruction of the French ships at Louisbourg ultimately ended the struggle. Wolfe and Amherst wanted to move on Quebec, but Boscawen resisted, calling attention to diminishing supplies and inclement weather due to the lateness of the year. His influence was such that Wolfe and Amherst relented, and the attack on Quebec was put off until 1759. Returning to England, Boscawen stumbled upon a French ship attempting to flee from the Canadian battlefront, but in a quick action he captured the prize.

In April 1759, Boscawen sailed from England with a new mission. Once again aboard the *Namur,* he was sent to the Mediterranean, where he took command of the fleet off Toulon to stop attempts by the French to coordinate an invasion of England. When he sailed into Gibraltar to pick up supplies, the French, under Admiral de la Clue, attempted to break out of Toulon. Boscawen followed, and the British fleet encountered the French near Lagos, Portugal, on 17 August 1759. When his flagship was hit, Boscawen transferred the flag to the *Newark.* De la Clue tried to escape into Lagos Bay, but two of his four remaining ships were set afire, with de la Clue's ship, the *Ocean,* running ashore. After this signal victory, destroying and dispersing the French fleet, Boscawen brought his squadron back, anchoring at Spithead on 1 September 1759. His heroism at Lagos earned him promotion to general of marines.

Returning home, Boscawen resumed his seat in Parliament, which he had held since 1742. Although he was a military hero, his involvement in the election of 1761 brought controversy, as the Tories had put forward a candidate of their own that year. In late 1760, he was asked to withdraw his candidacy, but he refused. However, the matter was settled when Boscawen caught a fever his men had suffered from during the attack on Lagos and afterward. He died at his home at the Hatchlands, near Guildford, on 10 January 1761 at the age of 49, and he was buried at the church of St. Michael Penkevil in Cornwall.

Boscawen's death cost his nation a brilliant naval officer. His actions at Cape Finesterre and Lagos, among others, had led some to claim that he was one of England's five greatest naval commanders, ranking him with Howe and perhaps even Horatio NELSON. One historian wrote: "There is no exaggeration in the statement on his monument that 'with the highest exertions of military greatness he united the gentlest offices of humanity; his concern for the interest, and wearied attention to the health, of all under his command, softened the necessary exactions of duty and rigours of discipline.'" Boscawen's daughter Elizabeth married Henry Somerset, fifth duke of Beaufort, and their son, FitzRoy James Henry Somerset, also known as Baron RAGLAN, served as the commander of British forces in the Crimea during the war there in the 1850s.

References: "Boscawen, Edward," in *The Dictionary of National Biography,* 22 vols., 8 supps., edited by Sir Leslie Stephen and Sir Sidney Lee, et al. (London: Oxford University Press, 1921–22), II:877–881; Charnock, John, "Boscawen, Edward," in *Biographia Navalis; or, Impartial Memoirs of the Lives and Characters of Officers of the Navy of Great Britain . . . ,* 4 vols. (London: Printed for R. Faulder, Bond-Street 1794–98), IV:310; letter from Vernon, in *The Vernon Papers,* edited by Bryan McLean Ranft (London: Publications of the Navy Records Society, 1958), 195–196; Richmond, H. W., *The Navy in the War of 1739–48,* 3 vols. (Cambridge, U.K.: The University Press, 1920), III:92; Kemp, Peter K., ed., "Boscawen's Letters to His Wife, 1755–1756," in *The Naval Miscellany,* 4 vols., edited by Christopher Lloyd (London: Navy Records Society, 1952), IV:229.

Boudicca (Boudica, Boadicea, Bonduca) (ca.
A.D. 30–62) *British warrior queen*
Boudicca was, according to legend, the daughter of a minor chief of the Iceni, a British tribe occupying the area now known as the counties of Norfolk and Suffolk. In A.D. 48, she became the wife of Prasutagus, king of the Iceni, and had two daughters by him. Prasutagus had submitted when the Romans invaded in A.D. 43 and ruled as a vassal-king under Roman control. When he died in A.D. 60, his will left half his personal wealth to the Roman emperor and the remainder to his wife and daughters. The Roman authorities in Britain annexed Prasutagus's kingdom, disputed the will, and claimed all Prasutagus's wealth. When Boudicca protested, they arrested her and her daughters. According to some accounts, she was whipped and her daughters were ravished before being released. Whatever the truth of the matter, the insult to their queen triggered a revolt among the Iceni, who were already embittered by their land being taken and given to ex-Roman soldiers, a common practice in the Roman colonies. (The bestowing of land rewarded legionaries who had completed their military service, created Roman settlements in the colony, and provided a ready source of veterans to help in putting down rebellion if necessary.)

The Iceni were soon joined by the Trinobantes, and Boudicca led her army across the southeast of England, quickly overcoming the small Roman garrisons nearby and capturing and destroying the Roman settlements at Camulodunum (Colchester); Verulamium (St. Albans); and Londinium (London), where the ashes of the fire with which she destroyed the city are still to be seen when foundations are dug for new office buildings. A large Roman force, comprising much of the Ninth Legion from Lincoln, was routed and every Roman sympathizer was slaughtered, but the return of the Roman governor Suetonius Paulinus from North Wales with the Twentieth Legion saw an end to Boudicca's campaign in A.D. 62. In a battle in the Midlands, now believed to be near today's Coventry, Paulinus positioned his force with a wood at his back and his cavalry on a hillside on either side. Boudicca's force had no plan of attack and rushed forward, relying on their numbers to overwhelm the legionaries in front of them. The steadiness of the legionaries first held and then repulsed the disorganized Britons, who at last turned and ran; thousands were cut to pieces by the Roman cavalry as they fled. Boudicca escaped, but, knowing her cause was now hopeless, she took poison rather than risk capture. It was long believed that her body was buried on the site now occupied by King's Cross Station in London, but historians now think it more likely she lies somewhere near the battlefield in the Midlands. A memorial to Boudicca, showing her in a chariot leading her followers into battle, stands beside Westminster Bridge in London.

Although her rebellion against the Romans occurred nearly 2,000 years ago, Boudicca is still remembered as Britain's warrior queen who led her troops into battle against a foreign invader.

References: Francis John Haverfield, "Boadicea," in *Encyclopaedia Britannica,* 14th ed., 24 vols. (London: Encyclopaedia Britannica Co., Ltd., 1929), III:759–760; Rankov, N. Bins, "Boudicca," in *The Oxford Companion to Military History,* edited by Richard Holmes (New York: Oxford University Press, 2001), 143; Webster, Graham, *Boudicca: The British Revolt against Rome A.D. 60,* rev. ed. (London: Batsford, 1993); Matthews, John, *Boadicea: Warrior Queen of the Celts* (Poole, U.K.: Firebird, 1988); Collingridge, Vanessa, *Boudica* (London: Ebury Press), 2005.

Braddock, Edward (1695–1755) *British general*
Edward Braddock was born in Perthshire, Scotland, in 1695, the son of Major General Edward Braddock, an English military officer. The younger Braddock entered the British army in 1710, joining his father's old regiment, the Coldstream Guards, and rising to the rank of lieutenant by 1716. Although he served in this regiment for many years, he did not see action until he was sent to the Netherlands as a lieutenant colonel in 1747 and fought at the siege of Bergen-op-Zoom under William, Prince of Orange. In 1753, he was transferred to the 14th Regiment of Foot and promoted to colonel.

On 29 March 1754, Braddock was promoted to major general and given the command of British troops in North America, fighting the French and their Native American allies. His official appointment proclaimed that he was to be the "general and commander-in-chief of all our troops and forces yt [yet] are in North America or yt shall be sent or rais'd [sic] there to vindicate our rights and possessions." However, Braddock was in fact commanding an army confused in its mission and woefully lacking in resources to fight the skillful French and Indian forces. Historian Henry Chichester writes in the *Dictionary of National Biography* that when Braddock arrived in the colonies, "He found everything in the utmost confusion. The colonies were at variance; everywhere the pettiest jealousies were rife; no magazines had

been collected, the promised provincial troops had not even been raised, and the few regulars already there were of the worst description."

Despite these handicaps, after convening a council and spending some months training new soldiers (a young Virginian named George WASHINGTON, acted as aide-de-camp) and gathering more supplies, Braddock set out to attack and hold Fort Duquesne (now Pittsburgh, Pennsylvania). Moving westward from Cumberland, Maryland, he and his force of 2,100 men, including some 1,400 British troops, were ambushed on the march on 9 July 1755 at Monongahela, about eight miles from Fort Duquesne. A combined French and Indian force of only 800 men attacked the English in a wooded ravine, and surrounding the British column and slaughtering them. In total, nearly 900 English were killed, including 63 officers; the French lost only 16 men. In the melee, Braddock, who had several horses shot out from under him, was mortally wounded by a bullet that hit his arm and went through his body. Carried from the field, he lingered for four days until he died from his wounds on 13 July 1755. One of his last requests was that his horse and his manservant be given to his chief aide, Washington. Braddock's men, anxious that the French not find his body, buried him in an unmarked grave and rolled vehicles over it to disguise it. Some years later, some bones from the site were dug up and removed; the remainder were lost. In 1913, historian Andrew Stewart wrote an article for *The New York Times* entitled "Was General Braddock Shot Down By One of His Own Army?" which theorized that Braddock was the victim of a friendly-fire accident.

No painting or drawing of Braddock exists; a crude drawing of his alleged burial circulated for many years. Because his sole military command ended so badly, he has been largely forgotten, except for the fact that his protégé, George Washington, later commanded the American army against British forces in North America.

References: Chichester, Henry Manners, "Braddock, Edward," in *The Dictionary of National Biography,* 22 vols. 8 supps., edited by Sir Leslie Stephen and Sir Sidney Lee, et al. (London: Oxford University Press, 1921–22), II:1061–1063; McCardell, Lee, *Ill-Starred General: Braddock of the Coldstream Guards* (Pittsburgh: University of Pittsburgh Press, 1958); Kopperman, Paul E., *Braddock at the Monongahela* (Pittsburgh: University of Pittsburgh

Press, 1977); Stewart, Andrew, "Was Gen. Braddock Shot Down by One of His Own Army?," *The New York Times,* Magazine sect., 19 October 1913, 5.

Bradley, Omar Nelson (1893–1981) *American general*

Along with Generals Dwight D. EISENHOWER and George S. PATTON, Omar Bradley is considered one of the major Second World War American commanders. Born in Clark, Missouri, on 12 February 1893, he was the son of a schoolteacher father who died young. His mother worked as a seamstress to support the family and send her son to the U.S. Military Academy at West Point, from which he graduated in 1915. He served on the Mexican border, was then posted to Montana, and was disappointed that the 1918 armistice ending World War I arrived before he could serve in Europe. Following the end of the war, Bradley lectured in mathematics at West Point. He attended the general staff school in 1929 and the Army War College in 1934. In 1941, he served as an infantry instructor at Fort Benning, Georgia. He was promoted to the rank of brigadier general in 1941.

When the United States entered the Second World War after the Japanese attack on the naval base at Pearl Harbor in Hawaii, Bradley was named as the commander of the 82nd Infantry Division; later, he was appointed to command the 28th Infantry Division. Early in 1943, he was sent to North Africa, succeeding General George S. Patton as commander of the United States' II Corps, which he led through the defeat of the Germans in North Africa and the allied invasion of Sicily. He played a key part in the defeat of the Germans on 7–9 May 1943 at Tunis and Bizerte (also called Bizerta), part of the dual American and British action called Operation Torch.

For his service in North Africa, Bradley was promoted to lieutenant general in June 1943 and awarded the Distinguished Service Medal. In autumn 1943, he was transferred to London and named by the Allied commander General Dwight D. Eisenhower to become commander of U.S. ground forces in Europe. His first practical test in this role came on 6 June 1944, when American, British, and other Allied troops stormed the beaches of Normandy, France, in Operation Overlord, better known as D-Day. Bradley's troops landed on the beaches codenamed Omaha and Utah. When the attack on Omaha beach became bogged down with terrible

American casualties, Bradley briefly considered withdrawal, but his men held their ground and eventually achieved their objectives, making the landings a tremendous success. Bradley's leadership of the First Army is widely considered to have made the difference in the successful Allied advance toward the east from northern France. The inclusion of troops from Patton's Third Army allowed Bradley to form the 12th Army Group, of which he became commander, and he was present when American forces liberated Paris on 25 August 1944.

On 12 March 1945, shortly before the end of the war, Bradley was given a fourth star. He was one of the leaders who coordinated the allied rout of the German army, crossing the Rhine River at the captured bridge at Remagen and eventually halting at Pilsen in Czechoslovakia as the war ended. Historians speculate that Bradley, in command of some 1.2 million troops, could have taken Berlin had the Soviet army not done so first.

From 1945 until 1947, Bradley acted as the interim administrator of the Veterans Administration, later to become the cabinet-level Department of Veterans Affairs. On 7 February 1948, he succeeded Eisenhower as chief of staff of the U.S. Army, serving until 16 August 1949. On that same day, he was named chairman of the Joint Chiefs of Staff, the head of all U.S. armed services. He also served as the first chairman of the Military Committee of the North Atlantic Treaty Organization (NATO) from 1949 to 1950. Bradley was given a fifth star in September 1950, earning the title General of the Army. His memoirs, *A Soldier's Story,* were published in 1951. He retired from active duty in August 1953, going to work for the Bulova Watch Company and rising to become chairman of the board in 1958. After his death in New York City on 8 April 1981, age 88, he was laid to rest with full military honors in Arlington National Cemetery in Virginia. His stone simply reads: "Omar Nelson Bradley. General of the Army."

Historians contrast Bradley's mild demeanor with that of his fellow American, George S. Patton. Historian James Lucas writes, "Bradley was a quiet spoken, well-mannered man, who, having given an order, expected it to be carried out thoroughly and swiftly without his interference. Nor did he welcome interference from his superiors. Once he had been given a job, he would carry it out. He needed no supervision. Because of his reluctance to interfere with a subordinate's operations, he at times seemed not to exercise sufficient control over Patton—but that was Bradley's way. His aim was to teach by example, a reflection of the early days when he lectured at West Point. Quiet, dependable, an excellent administrator and a sound tactician—this was Omar Bradley."

References: Bradley, Omar Nelson, *A General's Life: An Autobiography* (New York: Simon and Schuster, 1983); "Bradley, Omar N.," in *Command: From Alexander the Great to Zhukov—The Greatest Commanders of World History,* edited by James Lucas (London: Bloomsbury Publishing, 1988), 194–195; Windrow, Martin, and Francis K. Mason, "Bradley, Omar," in *The Wordsworth Dictionary of Military Biography* (Hertfordshire, U.K.: Wordsworth Editions Ltd., 1997), 36–37; North Brace, "Bradley, Omar Nelson," in *Encyclopedia of American War Heroes* (New York: Checkmark Books, 2002), 25.

Brauchitsch, Heinrich Alfred Hermann Walther von (1881–1948) *German general*

Born in Berlin, Germany, on 4 October 1881, Walther von Brauchitsch joined the German army unit called the Third Garde Grenadiers when he was 19. Starting as a lieutenant, he rapidly moved up through the ranks, and when the First World War broke out, he was a major. Brauchitsch saw action on the western front, and after the war ended, he remained in the army, becoming the commander of a regiment of artillery in 1925.

Brauchitsch seems to have remained outside the politics engulfing Germany following the end of the First World War, and he continued his rise in the military, earning promotion to major general in 1930 and two years later becoming inspector of artillery. In 1932, he rose to become chief of the artillery wing of the Reichswehr, also known as the German Defense Force. The following year, when Nazi leader Adolf Hitler became the leader of Germany, Brauchitsch was named commander of the East Prussian military area, also called the First Army military area.

Although he was to rise through the German military ranks, Brauchitsch was himself not a Nazi and did not sympathize with the Nazis' program. Because he was not a party loyalist, he frequently clashed with many of his fellow officers. However, Hitler saw Brauchitsch's value, retained him as one of his commanders, and, in 1937, promoted him to general of artillery. A year later, Hitler dismissed General Werner von Fitsch as commander of the Wehrmacht (the Germany army), replacing him with Brauchitsch. At the same time, Brauchitsch

ceded much of his authority as commander to Hitler, a move that infuriated his fellow officers. However, Brauchitsch did not support the German invasion of Austria and Czechoslovakia (1938), agreeing with many of his officers' misgivings that such a move was certain to spark a war in Europe for which Germany was unprepared. He was aware of a 1938 plot by several German officers to unseat Hitler in a coup but did nothing to stop it or encourage it. He is quoted as saying, "I myself won't do anything, but I won't stop anyone else from acting."

In 1939, when the German invasion of Poland began the Second World War, Brauchitsch directed the army in carrying out the offensive. The following year, Germany invaded France, and Brauchitsch was one of 12 field marshals named by Hitler. In 1941, he was one of the leaders in the planning of Operation Barbarossa, Hitler's Napoleonic-like invasion of Russia. Although he had tried to convince Hitler that such an action would be nothing short of disastrous, Brauchitsch launched the invasion of Russia in June 1941. Enforcing Hitler's Order for Guerilla Warfare, he participated in the mass slaughter of tens of thousands of Soviet prisoners of war, an act that would make him a war criminal. His plan was to take Moscow quickly; however, when Hitler ordered him to change the plan, move troops and supplies toward Leningrad, and secure the Caucasus, Brauchitsch realized this diversion would cost them the advantage the rapid initial advance had gained them and involve the Wehrmacht in a long, debilitating war. He warned Hitler about the cost of the diversion, but to no avail. When two separate elements of the army became trapped in fighting for every inch of ground, and Moscow's capture became less of a reality, Hitler blamed Brauchitsch for the failure. Brauchitsch's health suffered, and on 19 December 1941, just a few months into Barbarossa, he was removed from command, and Hitler took direct control of the German army.

Brauchitsch took no part in the war thereafter. At the war's conclusion, he was arrested by the Allies and placed on trial with the Nazi hierarchy at Nuremberg in 1946. Charged with crimes against humanity, as well as complicity in the Nazi plan to take over Europe, he pled innocent, declaring that he was unaware of any war crimes and even denying that he signed the order for the extermination of Soviet guerillas. Because his crimes were considered less than those of other German military leaders, Brauchitsch was separated from the others and sent to a prison in Wales. In 1948, he was returned to Germany to stand trial, but by then his health was in complete decline. He died in Hamburg, Germany, on 18 October 1948, before his trial could begin. He was just two weeks past his 67th birthday.

References: Keegan, John, and Andrew Wheatcroft, "Brauchitsch, Walther von," in *Who's Who in Military History from 1453 to the Present Day* (London: Routledge, 1996), 39; Hart, W. E., *Hitler's Generals* (Garden City, N.Y.: Doubleday, Doran & Co., 1944); Dutch, Oswald, *Hitler's 12 Apostles* (New York: R. M. McBride & Company, 1940).

Brereton, Sir William (1604–1661) *English general*

Sir William Brereton was born in 1604, the son of William Brereton of Handforth, Cheshire, and baptized at Manchester; he was six when his father died. He attended Brasenose College, Oxford, in 1621, but apparently never graduated. In 1627, he was created a baronet due to his family's wealth and standing. That same year, he won a seat in Parliament from Cheshire, but he only served a short time before he gave it up. In 1634 and 1635, he traveled around England, Ireland, and Holland, and kept a diary of his travels. In 1640, having returned to England, he was elected again to Parliament and this time served in the two sessions of the House of Commons known as the Short and Long Parliaments because of their length of session.

A strong critic of the government of Charles I, Brereton became a leader of Parliamentarian force beginning to rise against the king. In 1642, the leaders of the House of Commons appointed him one of the parliamentary deputies. When war finally broke out, Brereton was named as commander in chief of the troops in the Cheshire area. At Nantwich on 28 January 1643, he defeated the Royalist army under Sir Thomas Acton, a victory that made Nantwich the capital of the Parliamentary forces. In March, he marched on Middlewich, where he inflicted another serious defeat on Acton (12 March 1643); however, when Royalist reinforcements arrived, Brereton's forces were forced to retreat.

In summer 1643, Brereton's troops captured the towns of Stafford, Whitechurch, and Wolverhampton. During this period of activity, Nantwich, his headquarters, was placed under siege by Lord Byron. Brereton, with the assistance of Parliamentarian commander Sir Thomas FAIRFAX, attacked Byron's forces on 14 February 1644, forcing the surrender of a number of royalist troops. Marching toward Cheshire, Brereton defeated Prince RUPERT at Tarvin (August 1644). His victories against the Royalists at Rowton Heath (September 1645) and Denbigh (1 November 1645, defeating the Royalist general Sir William Vaughan), helped to weaken the Royalist armies, as did his successful 12-month siege of Chester in 1644–45. Brereton's victory over Lord Ashley at Stow-in-the-Wold on 22 May 1646 was the last major fight against the Royalists in the first English Civil War. His successes were an important factor in the Parliamentary victory.

Retiring at the end of the conflict, Brereton may have served as a judge in the trial of Charles I, who was executed in January 1649, but this is unconfirmed. He died in Croydon, near London, on 7 April 1661, and his body was taken north to Cheadle. Although there is a legend that Brereton's coffin was lost in a flood, his family believes he lies in the family vault in Cheadle. Despite being mentioned often in histories of the English Civil War, Brereton's name is largely forgotten today.

References: Henderson, Thomas Finlayson, "Brereton, Sir William," in *The Dictionary of National Biography*, 22 vols., 8 supps., edited by Sir Leslie Stephen and Sir Sidney Lee, et al. (London: Oxford University Press, 1921–22), II:1179–1180; Stoye, John, *English Travellers Abroad, 1604–1667: Their Influence in English Society and Politics* (London: Jonathan Cape, 1952), 174; *A True and Fuller Relation of the Battell [sic] Fought at Stow in the Would [sic], March. 21. 1645. Between the Forces under Sir William Brereton, Coll: Morgan, and the Lord Ashley....* (London: Printed for Tho. Underhill, 1646), 1–3; Brereton, William, Sir, *The Letter Books of Sir William Brereton*, 2 vols., edited by R. N. Dore (Chester, U.K.: Record Society of Lancashire and Cheshire, 1984–90), II:220–400.

Brock, Sir Isaac (1769–1812) *British general*

Sir Isaac Brock was born at Guernsey, in the Channel Islands, on 6 October 1769, the scion of a wealthy family. Historian David Breakenridge Read, in his 1894 biography of Brock, writes: "Major-General Sir Isaac Brock was of the very reputable family of Brock of Guernsey, one of the Channel Islands. There was, indeed, a Sir Hugh Brock, an English knight, who, in the reign of Edward

II, was a keeper of a castle in Brittany, then an English duchy, but which was overrun by the French about the middle of the fourteenth century, the English driven out, and the French made masters of the principality."

Brock received his education at Southampton and Rotterdam, entering the British army in 1785 with the rank of ensign in the 8th Regiment, also known as the King's Regiment. By the age of 27, he held the rank of lieutenant colonel in the 49th Regiment of Foot. He was sent to Holland in 1799, where, serving under Sir John MOORE, he was wounded at the battle of Egmont-op-Zee. In 1801, when British forces under Lord NELSON attacked Denmark, Brock was one of those seeing action. A year later, he was sent to Canada to guard that country's border against a possible invasion by the United States.

For three years, 1802–05, Brock served at various military posts from Montreal to York (now Toronto) and Quebec while transforming the 49th Regiment of Foot into one of Britain's best regimental units. He was recalled to London but in 1806 was transferred back to Canada when war with the United States appeared imminent. The British navy's impressment, or kidnapping, of American sailors from U.S. ships had led to increased tension between the two countries. When, in 1807, the British attacked an American warship, the *Chesapeake,* and dragged four British deserters from the vessel, armed conflict moved closer, although it would not break out for another five years. In 1810, Brock became commander of all troops in Upper Canada; a year later, he was named lieutenant governor of Canada, in effect becoming both the civil and military leader.

In 1812, with the imminent outbreak of war between the United States and Great Britain, Brock prepared for an invasion of Canada by fortifying defenses and arming citizens and soldiers. However, he had not received the supplies from London that he needed, and when war was declared he had only about 4,000 soldiers fully equipped to fight. On 12 July 1812, American general William Hull crossed into Canada from what is now Detroit, Michigan, with 2,200 men. Marching on the city of Sandwich (now Windsor), Hull hesitated before attacking Brock's main force. This mistake allowed Brock to go on the offense. British troops arrived at the American base of Michilimackinac and took control, cutting Hull off from further supplies and reinforcements. He withdrew south to Fort Detroit, back over the border. Brock then joined with American Indians,

including those under the command of the Shawnee chief Tecumseh, and marched toward Detroit with 730 men and 600 Indian fighters. Brock anticipated a long siege at Detroit, and when he arrived there he demanded Hull's surrender but was refused. With more than 2,500 troops, Hull had a 2-to-1 advantage over Brock, but what Brock did not know was that the Americans were ill prepared to fight, and future reinforcements were not coming. On 16 August 1812, Hull surrendered his entire force and the fort, stunning both his officers and Brock himself. Although barely a shot had been fired, except for some cannons by the British, Brock was lauded for his "victory." He was eventually knighted and hailed as "the hero of Upper Canada."

Brock did not stop at Detroit; he moved his troops into a defensive position near the Niagara River near the village of Queenstown (also Queenston). On 13 October 1812, General Stephen Van Rensselaer and his force crossed the Niagara with some 3,000 troops and easily captured the heights surrounding Queenstown. Brock moved troops to oppose them. Brock biographer Read writes:

> In the struggle which ensued, [Captain] Wool's men were driven to the edge of the high bank of the Niagara River. Here the Americans, with the storming foe before them, a precipice of 180 feet behind, and the roaring Niagara beneath, found themselves in an extremely perilous position. An attempt was made by some of the American officers to raise the white flag, with an intention to surrender, but Captain Wool tore it down and trampled it under foot. Reinforcements coming to their aid, the regulars opening a scathing fire of musketry. Brock, always in the front, roused beyond himself, conspicuous by his height, dress, gesture and undaunted bearing, was pointing to the hill, when he was struck by a ball in the right breast, which passed through his left side. He reeled and fell. His attendant officers rushed to his side, but saw at once that their brave commander was mortally stricken. He lived only long enough after receiving the fatal bullet to request that his fall might not be noticed, or prevent the advance of his brave troops, adding a wish, which could not be distinctly understood, that some token of remembrance should be transmitted to his sister.

Brock's body was first interred at Fort George and later removed to a monument built in his honor at Queenstown Heights. However, in 1840, an Irishman blew it up to protest English rule over Ireland. The monument was replaced, and it now stands at Queenstown Heights with a statue of Brock topping it. Another memorial was erected at St. Paul's Cathedral in London.

References: Eayrs, Hugh S., *Sir Isaac Brock* (Toronto: The Macmillan Company of Canada, 1918); Read, David Breakinridge, *Life and Times of Major-General Sir Isaac Brock* (Toronto: William Briggs, 1894); Nursey, Walter R., *The Story of Isaac Brock, Hero, Defender and Saviour of Upper Canada, 1812* (Toronto: William Briggs, 1908); Symons, John, *The Battle of Queenston Heights: Being a Narrative of the Opening of the War of 1812, with Notices of the Life of Major-General Sir Isaac Brock, K.B., and a Description of the Monument Erected to his Memory* (Toronto: Thompson & Co., Printers, 1859); Brock, Sir Isaac, *The Life and Correspondence of Major-General Sir Isaac Brock, K.B. . . .*, edited by Ferdinand Brock Tupper. (London: Simpkin, Marshall, 1845).

Bruce, Robert the   *See* ROBERT THE BRUCE.

Brusilov, Alexei Alexseievich   (1853–1926)
Russian general

Born in Tbilisi, Georgia, in 1853, Alexei Alexseievich Brusilov was the son of an aristocrat and received an excellent education. He was enrolled in His Majesty's Imperial Corps of Pages, a regimental school for military training in St. Petersburg founded by Russian emperor Alexander I in 1802. After finishing his training, Brusilov was sent to the Caucusus region, where he started his career in the Russian army as a cavalry officer. In 1877, when he was just 24, he distinguished himself in the Russo-Turkish War of 1877–78. Although little is known of his career after this period, he must have made an impression on his superiors because he was promoted steadily, reaching the rank of general in 1906.

In 1914, Europe was ripe for conflict. Serious social conditions, nationalist rebellions, belligerent leaders, and an expansive arms race gave rise to the war that became one of the deadliest in world history. Following Russian entry into the First World War, Brusilov was given command of the Russian Eighth Army in Galicia.

By September 1915, his troops had marched westward and taken control of Rovno (now in the Ukraine) and were near Lutsk (also Luck) on the Styr River (now in Poland) on 4–6 June 1916.

On 14 April 1916, Czar Nicholas II ordered that Brusilov replace the elderly and infirm general Nikolai Yudovich IVANOV as commander of the combined 7th, 8th, 9th and 11th Russian divisions. It was at this time that Brusilov pushed his idea for a major offensive against the Austro-Hungarian army. Although the other Russian generals disagreed and felt a more defensive posture was a better plan for action, the czar agreed with Brusilov and gave his permission for the movement, which became known as the Brusilov Offensive. Its key component was a massive drive to force the Austro-Hungarians to move troops to meet the Russian advance, thus relieving Italian forces in the south. The attack began on 4 June 1916: Three large Russian armies, all under Brusilov's command, attacked the Austro-Hungarian Fourth and Seventh Army lines and broke through, utilizing the element of surprise to gain important ground and capture the key city of Lutsk. However, a second wave of attack, with men under the command of General Alexei Evert, was delayed, and Brusilov could not follow up his apparent victory. The Germans, under General Erich Ludendorff, pushed reinforcements toward the Russian line, and the key Russian goal of taking the city of Kovel was finished. The offensive ground on, but it became a stalemate rather than a victory for either side. In the end, the Austrians lost some 1.5 million men, with over 1.1 million dead and wounded; Russian losses were estimated at nearly 500,000. Even though the Russians had not won a clear-cut victory, the offensive had destroyed any chance the Austro-Hungarians had to end the war in the East quickly, and it forced the Germans to fight the war on two fronts. Romania, having sat on the sidelines between the two powers, entered the war on the side of the Allies on 27 August 1916.

On 20 June 1916, an interview with Brusilov by Stanley Washburn, correspondent for *The Times* of London, appeared in that paper. In it, the Russian commander noted that "the Russian success is due to the absolute co-ordination of all the armies involved, the carefully planned cooperation of all branches of the service, and, most important of all, the fact that over the whole front the attack began at the same hour." Though Brusilov was vain about his "successes," his words appeared to be motivating to the Russian troops:

The sweeping successes attained by my armies are not the product of chance, or of Austrian weakness, but represent the application of all the lessons which we have learnt in two years of bitter warfare against the Germans. In every movement, great or small, that we have made this winter we have been studying the best methods of handling the new problems which modern warfare presents. . . . At the beginning of the war, and especially last summer, we lacked the preparations which the Germans have been making for the past 50 years. Personally I was not discouraged, for my faith in Russian troops and Russian character is an enduring one. I was convinced that, given the munitions, we should do exactly as we have done in the past two weeks.

Historians believe that General Evert's delay in reinforcing Brusilov led to the stalemate in the East and, ultimately, the Russian Revolution. When the revolution occurred, in February 1917, Brusilov supported the czar's abdication, and he was rewarded when Alexander Kerensky, head of the provisional government now controlling Russia, named him commander in chief of the entire Russian army in July 1917. In this role, Brusilov led the so-called Kerensky Offensive (July 1917), which, like the Brusilov Offensive, was initially successful but stalemated because of a lack of reinforcements and supplies. As a result of his failure in the Kerensky Offensive, Brusilov was replaced as commander in chief by General Lavr Kornilov on 1 August 1917.

With the Bolsheviks' assumption of power in 1918, as well as the end of the First World War, Brusilov's military career appeared to be over. It was not until 1920, when the Bolsheviks had destroyed all internal opposition, that he sided with them. In return for his support, he was named as a commander in the new Red Army, and, with the Russo-Polish War of 1920, sent to Warsaw. However, he was not involved in fighting, serving as a consultant to the army and as an inspector of the Russian cavalry until his retirement in 1924. Brusilov died in Moscow on 17 March 1926. His memoirs were translated into English and published in the United States as *A Soldier's Note-Book, 1914–1918* in 1930.

References: Brusilov, Aleksei Alekseevich, *A Soldier's Note-Book, 1914–1918* (Westport, Conn.: Greenwood Press, 1971); Washburn, Stanley, "The Russian Victories:

Gen. Brusiloff on the Campaign," *The Times* (London), 20 June 1916, 8.

Budenny, Semyon Mikhailovich (Simeon Mikhailevich Budenny) (1883–1973)
Soviet marshal

Born in Rostov-na-Donu (Rostov-on-Don) in southern Russia on 12 April 1883 (or 25 April 1883 [N.S.]; some sources list his date of birth as 1876), Semyon Mikhailovich Budenny was the son of a peasant family. He entered the Russian army in 1903 when he was 20 and rose to become a sergeant major in the czarist cavalry, serving in the First World War. However, he was a staunch left-winger, and in 1917 he helped to form, and was elected president of, a divisional soviet (council) in the Caucusus, where he was stationed. In 1919, Budenny joined the Communist Party, and he served in the Russian Civil War, utilizing his cavalry skills to conduct a guerilla war against the anticommunist or White forces. After the war's end, he was asked to form the Red Cavalry and became the first commander of that force.

In 1935, Budenny became a marshal of the Soviet Union, one of its leading military figures. Five years later, when the USSR declared war on Finland, he commanded the Russian forces, and for his services he was named deputy commissar for defense. When Germany invaded the Soviet Union in 1941, Budenny was given command of the southwest wing of the Red Army and put in charge of defending Kiev from the Nazi assault. When he saw that Kiev was lost, he asked Soviet leader Joseph Stalin for permission to withdraw his army, but Stalin refused, telling him to remain in defense of the city and fight to the death. However, the Nazi tanks were moving on Kiev, and before he was finally forced to withdraw, Budenny lost some 350,000 Soviet soldiers killed and an additional 600,000 taken prisoner by the Germans. As one magazine of the time stated, "Defeated in the Ukraine campaign of 1941, he resigned active command, but as Inspector General of Cavalry reshaped tactics and regained the cavalry a place in modern battle."

Budenny's career as a soldier was over. He spent the remainder of the Second World War as a general with no command, and in 1946 he was elected to the Presidium of the Supreme Soviet. He became Inspector General of Cavalry in 1953.

Semyon Budenny died in Moscow on 17 October 1973. He was one of the last of the original marshals of the Soviet Union, and although he suffered a severe defeat at Kiev, he was given the Hero of the Soviet Union award.

References: Windrow, Martin, and Francis K. Mason, "Buddeny, Semyon," in *The Wordsworth Dictionary of Military Biography* (Hertfordshire, U.K.: Wordsworth Editions Ltd., 1997), 38–39; "The Men Who Are Winning the Race to Germany," *Picture Post* (U.K.) 24, no. 5 (29 July 1944), 7–9; Budenny, S. M., *Proidennyi Put* (The Path of Valour) (Moscow: Progress Publishers, 1972).

Buller, Sir Redvers Henry (1839–1908) *British general*

Sir Redvers Buller remains almost a controversial figure, praised by some but blamed by others for defeats in the Second Boer War. Born in Devonshire, England, on 7 December 1839, Buller received his education at Eton, the best-known English private school. He entered the British army in 1858 and saw action in China in 1860. Ten years later, he was promoted to the rank of captain and commissioned in the King's Royal Rifle Corps. He served in the First Ashanti War (1873–74), the Kaffir War (1878–79), and the Zulu War of 1879. Following the retreat of British troops from Inhlobane on 29 March 1879, he received the Victoria Cross for bravery.

In 1881, Buller was sent to southern Africa to fight in the First Boer War, serving as chief of staff for Sir Evelyn Wood. In 1882, he was sent to Egypt, where, under Sir Garnet Wolseley, first viscount Wolseley, he fought at Tamai (13 March 1884) in the First Sudan War. In this action, British troops under Lieutenant General Gerald Graham (1831–99) attacked and defeated the Mahdists under Osman Digna, suffering 214 casualties to more than 2,000 for the Mahdists. In 1885, Buller served as chief of staff to Wolseley. It was in the Sudan that he exhibited great bravery, noted especially during the retreat of the British army from Gabat to Korti, as well as during his victory at Abu Klea (16–17 February 1885). For this service, he was awarded the Knight Commander of the Order of Bath (KCB). He returned to England and, on 15 October 1887, was named quartermaster general at the War Office. After several years of service there, he was promoted to full general in 1896.

From October 1898 to October 1899, Buller was the general officer commanding at Aldershot, the senior field command in the United Kingdom. In 1899, the Second African War, or Second Boer War, broke out, and Buller was named to command the British troops there. On 31 October 1899, he arrived in Capetown to take control of that city and to aid the 13,000 British troops whom the Boers held under siege at Ladysmith. His first attempt to bring relief to Ladysmith was repelled on 15 December 1899 at the battle of Colenso. Historian George Bruce writes: "Buller attempted to carry by a frontal attack the Boer position on the opposite side of the Tugela [River] and, notwithstanding the gallantry of the troops, was compelled to retire, with a loss of 71 officers and 1,055 rank and file." Buller launched a second attempt to relieve Ladysmith on 10 January 1900, which also ended in failure 17 days later. A third effort, begun on 5 February and lasting until 7 February, ended at Vaalkranz, again unsuccessful, but he eventually liberated Ladysmith on 28 February.

Although he was ultimately successful, Buller's repeated failures caused the British government to lose confidence in him, and he was removed from command, to be replaced by Lord ROBERTS. Buller's tactical inefficiency had been signaled by his conduct of military training back in Britain. As historian Geoffrey Regan writes: "In the 1899 military manoeuvres [training exercises] at Aldershot, Buller, who had not commanded troops for twelve years, ordered his men to make a full frontal assault against an equal number of defenders. His men had just finished a fourteen-mile march and were in no condition for attacking anybody. Not surprisingly, the manoeuvres had to be abandoned. Buller's conduct of the manoeuvres was comically inept: no trenches were dug for fear of damaging the countryside, no man was allowed to dive for cover lest he damage his uniform, and the soldiers eventually had to resort to volley firing at each other in the open and at ranges of less than a hundred metres."

Buller returned to England and was given the title of Knight Grand Cross of the Most Distinguished Order of St. Michael and St. George (GCMG) despite mistakes that had cost the lives of thousands of men and earned him the nickname "Reverse" Buller. When he returned to Aldershot in January 1901, he was criticized in the English press. Buller answered his critics in a speech on 10 October 1901, but the British high command found this to be a breach of military discipline and placed him on half-pay. Buller never recovered from the scandal, and he retired to his home in Devon, where he died on 2 June 1908 at the age of 68.

Sir Redvers Buller is the subject of much argument in the history of the British military. Many historians consider him a good staff officer who was a poor tactician; others write glowingly of his overall career. Winston Churchill described him as "a characteristic British personality. He looked stolid. He said little, and what he said was obscure. He was not the kind of man who could explain things, and he never tried to do so. He usually grunted, or nodded, or shook his head, in serious discussions; and shop of all kinds was sedulously excluded from his ordinary conversation."

References: Buller, Sir Redvers Henry, *The Life and Campaigns of Sir Redvers H. Buller, V.C.* (London: George Newnes Limited, 1900); Bruce, George, "Colenso" and "Tamai," in *Collins Dictionary of Wars* (Glasgow, Scotland: HarperCollins Publishers, 1995), 61, 242; Powell, Geoffrey, *Buller—A Scapegoat?: A Life of General Sir Redvers Buller, 1839–1908* (London: Leo Cooper, 1994); Regan, Geoffrey, "Sir Reverse Buller," in *Geoffrey Regan's Book of Military Blunders* (London: André Deutsch, 2001), 26–29.

Burgoyne, John (1722–1792) *British general*

John Burgoyne was born in London in 1722, the son of Captain John Burgoyne, a British military officer. Educated at Westminster School, he was a close friend of the son of the 11th earl of Derby. In 1740, at age 18, Burgoyne joined the British army by purchasing a cornet's commission in the 13th Dragoons. He married Lord Derby's daughter in 1743, but was forced to move to France to avoid paying a number of debts he owed.

In 1756, through his father-in-law's influence, Burgoyne returned to England, where he rejoined the army. He saw action during the Seven Years' War (1756–63) as a member of first the 11th Dragoons and later the Coldstream Guards, after which he returned to England and was elected to a seat in Parliament representing first, Midhurst (1761) and then, seven years later, Preston (1768). In 1773, he called for an investigation into the finances of the British East India Company.

Although Burgoyne is best known as a military officer, it was during this period that he became a writer, penning a series of plays, including *The Maid of the Oaks*

(1775), which was produced for the English stage by famed stage actor and manager David Garrick. He rose to the rank of major general, and in 1775 he was sent to North America to aid General Thomas Gage in putting down the revolt in the English colonies. Landing at Boston in May 1775, he was informed of the skirmishes at Lexington and Concord that sparked what became the American Revolutionary War. Burgoyne slowly became disgusted with the attitude of the British authorities in prosecuting the war. He returned home to England after the Battle of Bunker Hill (17 June 1775), which, though a British victory, saw 1,054 British soldiers killed or wounded, with very few American losses.

In 1776, Burgoyne was sent back to North America, this time to fight in Canada under Sir Guy Carleton, the commander in chief of British forces in Canada. Setting out for Lake Champlain, they seized Crown Point and laid siege to Fort Ticonderoga. Once again, however, Burgoyne was irritated by what he felt were several errors on Carleton's part, and once again he departed his command and returned to England. This time, Prime Minister Frederick North, Lord North, heard his concerns and asked that Burgoyne draw up a battle plan. The proposed scheme laid out a march of the 12,000 men under Carleton's command to the south to join Sir William Howe near New York. Impressed, Lord North sent Burgoyne back to Canada, this time as commander in chief.

In June 1777, Burgoyne led some 7,000 men south, once again taking Crown Point and, on 6 July 1777, retaking Fort Ticonderoga. However, the key to his plan was the meeting with the forces under Sir William Howe. When Howe did not send reinforcements, and another army under Colonel Barry St. Leger was defeated by the colonists, Burgoyne was trapped without supplies and support. On 24 September, he attempted to break through the American lines at Bemis Heights with only 5,000 men to the Americans' 20,000. The attack failed, and Burgoyne was forced to retreat and then, facing reality, to surrender. His capitulation was accepted by General Horatio GATES at Saratoga on 17 October 1777. Historians Martin Windrow and Francis K. Mason write: "He was by no means the worst of Britain's commanders in the War of American Independence and his famous capitulation at Saratoga was neither premature nor avoidable."

Nevertheless, this was the end of Burgoyne's military career. Chastened by his defeat, he returned to England, where he was harshly criticized for the disastrous campaign. In his final years, he spent much of his time writing more plays, including *The Heiress,* which appeared on the London stage in 1786. He died in London on 4 August 1792 and was buried in Westminster Abbey.

References: Stephens, Henry Morse, "Burgoyne, Sir John," in *The Dictionary of National Biography,* 22 vols., 8 supps., edited by Sir Leslie Stephen and Sir Sidney Lee, et al. (London: Oxford University Press, 1921–22), III:340–342; Windrow, Martin, and Francis K. Mason, "Burgoyne, John," in *The Wordsworth Dictionary of Military Biography* (Cumberland House, Hertfordshire, U.K.: Wordsworth Editions Ltd., 1997), 41; Howson, Gerald, *Burgoyne of Saratoga: A Biography* (New York: Times Books, 1979); Mintz, Max M., *The Generals of Saratoga: John Burgoyne and Horatio Gates* (New Haven, Conn.: Yale University Press, 1990); "Extract of a Letter from General Gates, dated camp at Saratoga, October 18, 1777: 'Sir, I have the Satisfaction to Present your Excellency with the Convention of Saratoga, by which His Excellency Lieutenant General Burgoyne has Surrendered Himself,'" (Lancaster, Pa.: Printed by Francis Bailey, 1777).

C

Caesar, Julius Gaius (ca. 100/102–44 B.C.)
Roman statesman and general

Julius Caesar was not just a leader of Rome: He was a soldier-statesman, one of the first in world history to combine the running of government with the management of the military. Although historians dispute the exact date of his birth, he was probably born about 100 or 102 B.C. into a patrician family with deep and historic ties to Rome; one of his alleged ancestors was the mythological Iulus, the grandson of Anchises and Venus. Because of this bond, his family was known as the Iulus Caesares. Caesar's own father served as a praetor (judicial magistrate), and his uncle was a consul. Another uncle was the famed Roman general Marius, the husband of his mother's sister.

When Caesar won election as a Roman consul in 60 B.C., it appeared that his life would be one of a political figure. However, he sensed a power vacuum in the leadership of Rome, and he worked with several other political leaders to reduce the power of the Roman Senate. Toward that end, in 59 B.C. he formed and alliance with his fellow consuls Gnaeus Pompeus (POMPEY) and Marcus Licinius CRASSUS; this was the so-called First Triumvirate, in which each man would handle a specific portion of the Roman government. Caesar was granted control of the areas of Cisalpine Gaul, or northern Italy; Narbonese Gaul, or southern France; and

Illyricum, or the present-day Balkans. He was also given the command of an army of approximately 20,000 men, which he used to consolidate Roman power over Gaul, or what is now France. He also dealt with a threat from a nomadic group called the Helvetii: When these tribes moved from their home in what is now Switzerland into central Gaul, he moved his army before them and, in a major clash at Bibracte (58 B.C.), forced them to return back home. Historian Frank Abbott writes:

> Caesar's achievements in the West between 58 and the outbreak of the Civil war in 49 were as noteworthy as those of Pompey in the East. When he went north in the spring of 58 to take charge of the three provinces, Cisalpine Gaul, Illyricum, and Transalpine Gaul, he found two very serious questions facing him: For nearly three years the Helvetii had been preparing to leave their old home and migrate westward into Gaul. In the early part of 58 their arrangements were complete, and the migration began. They had intended to go through the Roman province, but by a rapid march northward Caesar closed this route, forced them to pass through the territory of the Sequani, ultimately inflicted a crushing defeat on them near Bibracte, and forced the remainder . . . to return to its own country.

Seeking to secure his strength amongst the Gallic population, Caesar then marched against the tribal leader Ariovistus, chief of the clan known as the Suebi. Although Ariovistus had been an ally of Gaul, his power threatened Roman control of the area. In 58 B.C., in a huge battle, apparently fought somewhere in what is now in the region of Upper Alsace in France, Caesar and the Romans defeated the Subei and ended their threat. Over the next several years, he went to war with the tribes of Gaul, and although his Roman forces were vastly outnumbered, the Gallic armies never consolidated and did not present the threat to the Romans that they could have. Caesar later wrote of these battles in his landmark work *De Bellum Gallico* (Commentaries on the Gallic War), one of the earliest books on military history. Writing in the third person, he penned details on battles which otherwise would be lost to history, described how he had defeated the Belgae, and told of how he had sent Marcus Crassus to fight the tribes called Armorica in what is now Normandy in northwestern France.

Following the murder of Marcus Crassus after his disastrous defeat at the battle of Carrhae in 53 B.C., jealousy and hatred spread amongst the followers of Rome's other commander, Gnaeus Pompeus, also known as POMPEY. Pompey feared that Caesar, with his military victories and growing popularity, would become a dictator if not opposed, and Pompey therefore allied himself with Caesar's opponents in the Roman Senate. Upon his recommendation, in 49 B.C. the Senate ordered Caesar to return home. Caesar thereupon marched his armies back toward Rome, crossing the Rubicon river in northern Italy and setting off a massive civil war. In what could only be called an enormous demonstration of military power, he pursued Pompey's small army down to the southern Italian city of Brundisium, but they escaped to Greece.

Rather than following Pompey, Caesar marched back through northern Italy and into Spain to attack Pompey's supporters there; he defeated them at the battle of Illerda (49 B.C.). Then, armed with warships, he sailed to the west coast of Greece to attack Pompey unsuccessfully at his base at Dyrrhachium. Despite this, Caesar advanced further into Greece, pursued by Pompey, as per his plan. At Pharsalus (9 August 48 B.C.), a city in Thessaly, Greece, Caesar won a key victory. Historian George Bruce writes: "The Pompeian cavalry drove back that of Caesar, but following in pursuit were thrown into confusion by the legionaries, whereupon they turned and fled from the field; the infantry followed and the battle became a rout in which 8,000 Pompeians and only 200 Caesarians fell. After the battle 20,000 Pompeians surrendered."

Pompey and some of his remaining army escaped to Egypt, where he asked the Egyptian king Ptolemy for asylum. Upon being brought ashore, however, he was murdered and his head removed, on Ptolemy's orders. When Caesar came to Egypt to confront Pompey again, instead he was presented with his opponent's head. He continued to fight with Pompey's legions, clashing with them at Thapsus in northern Africa (46 B.C.) and at Munda in Spain (45 B.C.).

Following these triumphs, Caesar began to make peace with his opponents and political enemies, includ-

Julius Caesar

ing two leading Roman senators, Cassius Longinus and Marcus Brutus. In February 44 B.C., the Roman Senate, bowing to Caesar's strength and power, voted to make him dictator for life. A group of senators, led by several who were extremely close to Caesar, concluded that he needed to be stopped, and they planned to assassinate him. On 15 March 44 B.C.—known as the Ides of March—Caesar went to the Roman Senate to preside over that body. As he entered the building, one of the assassination conspirators, Casca, approached him with a document to read. As Caesar studied it, the others came forward, drew knives, and attacked the Roman leader. As Brutus plunged the knife into Caesar, the Roman leader allegedly cried, "Et tu, Brute?" ("You, too, Brutus?"). However, historians now believe that he actually said, in Greek, "Kai su, Technon?" ("You, too, my child?")—acknowledging that Brutus was Caesar's illegitimate child from his mistress Servilia. The assassins fled from the Senate, believing their act to be heroic. Instead, they were hunted down and murdered.

Caesar's assassination at the hands of men who were his friends has been depicted in the play *Julius Caesar* by William Shakespeare, although historians have recently questioned the conventional view of the assassination, based on newly discovered evidence.

In March 2003, historian Richard Girling pushed his thesis in *The Sunday Times Magazine* (London) that Caesar well may have staged his own assassination—a form of what is now called assisted suicide. Girling explains: "Why would Caesar want to kill himself? He is the most glorious personage on Earth, able freely to help himself to anything he fancies, from a peeled grape to an entire country. Who in his right mind would put an end to such a life? In searching for the answer we need to consider both Caesar's age (at 56 he is, by contemporary standards, an old man) and his state of health. Ancient texts make it clear that Caesar is by now suffering grievously from epilepsy—a discovery that . . . supplies a crucial link in the evidence chain." Girling believes that Caesar probably suffered from temporal-lobe epilepsy, which explains some of the irrational actions he took during his life, as well as from reported illnesses that included suffering from severe fainting fits and bouts of diarrhea.

Whatever the theories of Julius Caesar's death, 15 March 44 B.C. saw the end of a man whose name still rings through history. A superb politician, statesman, and strategist, he laid the foundations for his nephew Octavian (Caesar AUGUSTUS) to build an empire whose influence is still felt today in literature, law, and architecture as well as the machinery of democratic government.

References: Balsdon, John Percy Vyvian Dacre, *Julius Caesar: A Political Biography* (New York: Atheneum, 1967); Fuller, John Frederick Charles, *Julius Caesar: Man, Soldier, and Tyrant* (New Brunswick, N.J.: Rutgers University Press, 1965); Caesar, Julius Gaius, *The Commentaries of C. Julius Caesar, of his Wars in Gallia, and the Civil Wars betwixt him and Pompey* (London: Tho. Newcomb, 1677); Abbott, Frank Frost, *A History and Description of Roman Political Institutions* (Boston: Ginn & Company, 1907), 119–122; "Caesar," in *Command: From Alexander the Great to Zhukov—The Greatest Commanders of World History,* edited by James Lucas (London: Bloomsbury Publishing, 1988), 32–33; Bruce, George, "Pharsalus I," in *Collins Dictionary of Wars* (Glasgow, Scotland: HarperCollins Publishers, 1995), 193; Dodge, Theodore Ayrault, *Cæsar: A History of the Art of War Among the Romans Down to the End of the Roman Empire* (Boston: Houghton, Mifflin and Company, 1892); Clarke, Samuel, *The Life & Death of Julius Caesar, the First Founder of the Roman Empire* . . . (London: Printed for William Miller, 1665); Girling, Richard, "Et Tu Julius? A New Investigation Has Yielded a Startling Verdict on History's Most Infamous Murder," *The Sunday Times Magazine* (London), 9 March 2003, 48–55.

Campbell, Sir Colin, Baron Clyde (Colin Macliver) (1792–1863) *British general*

Despite being one of the leaders of the British forces in the Crimea, Sir Colin Campbell is sometimes forgotten next to the more dominant figure of Fitzroy Somerset, Baron RAGLAN. Nonetheless, in historical context, Campbell's contributions in the Crimea and in a series of campaigns around the world make him an important military leader in British history.

Campbell was born in Glasgow, Scotland, on 20 October 1792, the illegitimate son of a carpenter named Macliver and his mistress Agnes Campbell. He escaped these humble circumstances by being taken under the wing of his maternal uncle, Colonel John Campbell, who in 1807 obtained for his charge a meeting with the duke of York. The duke became interested in the 15-year-old and granted him a commission but put his name forward not as Macliver but as Campbell. He was known as Campbell for the rest of his life.

Starting as an ensign in the 9th Foot in 1808, Campbell was sent to Portugal and saw action in the Peninsular War (1808–13) under Sir John MOORE. His services at the battles of Rolica (17 August 1808) and Vimiero (21 August 1808) as well as during the retreat of British troops from Corunna (16 January 1809) made him eligible for quick promotion. In 1809, while serving at Walcheren in the Netherlands, he came down with a fever that plagued him for the remainder of his life.

In 1810, Campbell went to Gibraltar, and on 5 March 1811 he participated in the battle of Barossa. Sent to Spain, he fought at the battles of Tarifa, now called Punta de Tarifa, in southern Spain (December 1811–January 1812) and Vittoria (21 June 1813). He was the commander of the right wing of the regiment that attacked San Sebastian on 17 July 1813. Following this clash, the noted British general Sir Charles James NAPIER wrote, "It was in vain that Lieutenant Campbell, breaking through that tumultuous crowd with the survivors of his chosen detachment, mounted the ruins—twice he ascended, twice he was wounded, and all around him died."

Upon his return to England, Campbell was posted with the 7th Battalion, 60th Rifle Regiment. He saw action in America in 1814 and in Demerara in 1823; he was promoted to lieutenant colonel in 1832. After he returned to active duty, Campbell participated in the Opium War in China (1841–43), serving under Sir Hugh Gough and seeing action in 1842 at Hong Kong, Chinkiangfu (Chin-kiang-foo), and Nanjing (Nanking). His services in that conflict led to his promotion to colonel. He was subsequently made a Companion of the Order of Bath and, in 1844, promoted to brigadier general.

In 1846, Campbell was sent to China a second time, succeeding Major General Sir James Schoedde. He sailed from Chusan in July 1846, arrived in Calcutta, India, that October, and was made commander of his brigade in Lahore (now in Pakistan). He recommended direct action against the Moolraj, an Indian rebel who had attacked Mooltan, but this was rejected by his superiors. During the second Sikh War (1848–49), he served under Lord Gough, who, after the battle of Chilianwala (14 January 1849), asked him, "Can you hold your ground?" Campbell replied, "My Lord, I have been performing the duties of a Brigadier, and know noth-

ing about the rest of the army, but I have two regiments which can do anything, and another which is getting into order—nothing can hurt me now!" For his services, Campbell was knighted in 1849. That year, writing that "I am growing old and only fit for retirement," he asked for a posting in England, but he stayed in India until 1853.

In February 1854, Campbell was placed in command of the Highland Brigade in the Crimea in southern Russia. His actions at Varna (June 1854) resulted in his promotion to major general, and he again distinguished himself at Alma (20 September 1854) when the allied armies of Britain and France, backed by the Turkish—some 63,000 troops under Lord Raglan—fought the Russians under Prince Aleksandr Menshikov. Historian Henry Morse Stephens writes: "He led his brigade steadily against the redoubt which had been retaken by the enemy after being carried by the light division; and with his Highlanders in line overthrew the last compact columns of the Russians. His horse had been shot under him, and he had won the victory, but the only reward he asked was leave to wear the highland bonnet instead of the cocked hat of a general officer." The Russians lost more than 1,800 men, while the allies lost a combined 420.

At Balaklava (also Balaclava, 25 October 1854), Campbell commanded the 93rd Highlanders, rallying his men when attacked by Russian cavalry with the words: "Remember there is no retreat from here, men! You must die where you stand!" His men yelled back, "Ay, ay, Sir Colin; we'll do that!" The Russians fled in the face of the determined British resistance, leading journalist William H. ("Bull Run") Russell, covering the war for *The Times* of London, to call Campbell's men "the thin red line." Their stand became a legend in histories of the Crimean War.

Soon after Balaklava, Campbell returned home a hero in November 1855. Promoted to lieutenant general in June 1856, he was sent back to the Crimea, but when he was given the post of inspector general of infantry, he returned to London. Following the Sepoy Rebellion in India (also known as the Indian Mutiny), Campbell was sent there to succeed Lord ANSON, who had died as commander in chief, and Campbell reinforced the British garrison at Cawnpore. On 9 November 1857, he marched his men to relieve the British garrison at Lucknow, from which he saved hundreds of women and children and wounded. In 1858, he initiated a series of operations that ended the Indian Mutiny and brought peace to northern India. In May 1858, he was promoted to general, and two months later he was raised to the peerage, becoming Baron Clyde. He remained in India until June 1860 when, beset by ill health, he returned to England for the final time. In 1862, his final honor came when he was elevated to the rank of field marshal.

Baron Clyde died at his home at Chatham on 14 August 1863 at the age of 70. Remembrances soon flooded in for this son of Scotland born in poverty who rose to become one of England's finest field generals. Lord Granville wrote in a personal letter: "I received her Majesty's order to express to the Duke of Cambridge her Majesty's grief, and to say that the great military services of Lord Clyde in difficult parts of the world, the success with which in most trying circumstances he restored peace to her Majesty's empire in India, and the personal regard which the Queen and her beloved Consort [Prince Albert] entertained for his high and honourable character, make her Majesty deeply deplore the loss which the Queen, in common with her Majesty's subjects, has sustained."

References: Stephens, Henry Morse, "Campbell, Sir Colin, Baron Clyde," in *The Dictionary of National Biography*, 22 vols., 8 supps., edited by Sir Leslie Stephen and Sir Sidney Lee, et al. (London: Oxford University Press, 1921–22), III:803–807; Shadwell, Lieutenant General Lawrence, *The Life of Colin Campbell, Lord Clyde, Illustrated by Extracts From His Diary and Correspondence* (Edinburgh and London: William Blackwood and Sons, 1881); Forbes, Archibald, *Colin Campbell, Lord Clyde* (London: Macmillan and Company, 1895); Windrow, Martin, and Francis K. Mason, "Campbell, Colin, Baron Clyde of Clydesdale," in *The Wordsworth Dictionary of Military Biography* (Cumberland House, Hertfordshire, U.K.: Wordsworth Editions Ltd., 1997), 42–44; Bruce, George, "Alma" and "Balaclava," in *Collins Dictionary of Wars* (Glasgow, Scotland: HarperCollins Publishers, 1995), 12, 27; "Campbell, Sir Colin," in *Command: From Alexander the Great to Zhukov—The Greatest Commanders of World History*, edited by James Lucas (London: Bloomsbury Publishing, 1988), 69–70; Campbell, Sir Colin, *Memorandum of the Part Taken by the Third Division of the Army of the Punjaub, at the Battle of Chillianwala* (London: James Ridgway, Piccadilly, 1851); Deakin, T. J., "Tactical Triumph at the Alma," *Military History* 12, no. 7 (March 1996): 42–49.

Castiglione, duc de *See* AUGEREAU, PIERRE-FRANÇOIS-CHARLES, DUC DE CASTIGLIONE.

Cavendish, William *See* NEWCASTLE, WILLIAM CAVENDISH, DUKE OF.

Charles XII (Karl XII) (1682–1718) *king of Sweden*

Charles XII (also known as Karl XII) lived to be only 36, dying in the war against Norway in 1718. He was the son of Charles XI of Sweden and his wife Ulrike Eleanora. Charles XI reigned from his father's death in 1660 until his own death in 1697, when his son, only 15 years old, became king of Sweden. Charles XII's inexperience in the ways of running a country encouraged Norway's neighbors, Russia, Poland, and Denmark, to form an alliance to attack Sweden and annex that country into their own. This was led by Russia's Czar Peter I (better known as Peter the Great), along with King Frederick VI of Denmark and Augustus II the Strong, king of Poland and elector of Saxony. Charles decided to launch a preemptive attack against these three nations in what would be called the Great Northern War. Starting with Denmark, the Swedish forces, backed by English troops, moved to counter the Danish invasion of Schleswig. With the aid of the English and Dutch—led by Sir George ROOKE—the Swedes invaded Denmark on 4 August 1700 and attacked Copenhagen. The Danes quickly collapsed and sued for peace, signing the Treaty of Travendal on 18 August 1700 and agreeing to pull out of the alliance.

Sweden's quick defeat of the Danes led King Augustus and Czar Peter to fear that the Scandinavian country would expand beyond her borders. Russia immediately marched troops into the Swedish territories of Estonia and Livonia. Charles XII then marched to the Russian fortress at Narva, where a major battle took place on 20 November 1700. Historian George Bruce writes: "8,000 Swedes under Charles XII and 50,000 Russians under General [Prince Basil Vassilyevich] Dolgorouky [met]. The Russians were besieging Narva, but driving in two large bodies who occupied advancing positions, Charles boldly attacked their entrenched camp. Following a brief cannonade, the Swedes stormed the trenches, and though the Russian artillerymen stood to their guns, after three hours' hard fighting the defenders were driven out in disorder, having lost 10,000 in the trenches, while many more fell in the fight. The Swedes lost 600 only."

Fleeing from the battle, the Russian troops ran through the ice-filled Narva River, only to crack the ice and drown in untold thousands. The battle was a disaster for Peter and Russia, and, having dealt them such a huge defeat, Charles turned against Poland and Augustus. Marching into Livonia, he defeated the Poles at Riga on 17 June 1701. The following month, he invaded Poland and defeated a Russian-Saxon army at Dunamunde on 9 July 1701. On 14 May 1702, he moved into Warsaw, and his armies marched to Klezow (also Klissow), where Charles fought against a joint Polish-Saxon army and defeated them (9 July 1702), allowing him to march into Krakow. A further defeat of a Saxon army at Pultusk (21 April 1703) led to Augustus's removal from the Polish throne. Charles replaced him with his own appointee, Stanislas Leszcynski.

While Charles was in Poland, Russia's Peter the Great recovered from his defeat at Narva and moved his army into Livonia a second time. Instead of heading to Livonia to again take on Peter's forces, Charles made the fateful decision to invade Russia instead. Like Napoleon a century later and Hitler two centuries later, Charles learned the hazards of the Russian winter. When his troops finally reached the Ukraine on 27 June 1709, he stopped at Poltava on the Vorskla River. There, Peter's forces, some 25,000 men, met Charles's troops, estimated at 40,000 strong but tired and hungry from marching with few supplies. A Swedish attack failed to push the Russians back; the counterattack by the Russians led to a bloody battle. Charles, wounded, fled with his chief officers south toward Turkey; the Swedish army he left behind surrendered two days after the battle began, having lost nearly 10,000 dead and wounded. The Turks imprisoned Charles for a short time but ultimately released him. Russia, unopposed, moved into Finland, and Augustus was placed back onto the Polish throne. Charles then spent the next four years in Turkey in an unsuccessful attempt to persuade them to attack Russia.

Angered by the defeat, Charles traveled back home in 1714 to prepare his forces for another fight. In 1716, he repelled an invasion of Sweden by a Danish-Norwegian army at Scania (also Scane). He then advanced into Norway. On 30 November 1718, while leading his troops at Frederickshald, he was shot in the head and killed instantly; he was only 36 years old. Sweden lost

the war with Norway and was forced to sign the Treaty of Nystad (1721), by which it ceded Livonia and its Baltic possessions to Norway. With Charles's death, his sister, Ulrike Eleanora, became the queen, serving for one year until her husband Frederick I of the House of Hesse took the throne.

Samuel Johnson, in his 1748 work *The Vanity of Human Wishes,* wrote of Charles:

His fall was destined to a barren strand,
A petty fortress, and a dubious hand;
He left the name, at which the world grew pale,
To point a moral, or adorn a tale.

References: Bengtsson, Frans Gunnar, *The Sword Does Not Jest: The Heroic Life of King Charles XII of Sweden* (New York: St. Martin's Press, 1960); Hatton, Ragnhild Marie, *Charles XII of Sweden* (New York: Weybright and Talley, 1968); Windrow, Martin, and Francis K. Mason, "Charles XII, King of Sweden," in *The Wordsworth Dictionary of Military Biography* (Hertfordshire, U.K.: Wordsworth Editions Ltd., 1997), 47–48; Latimer, Jon, "Storm of Snow and Steel at Narva, Military History" 17, no. 5 (December 2000): 58–64; Bruce, George, "Narva," in *Collins Dictionary of Wars* (Glasgow, Scotland: HarperCollins Publishers, 1995), 174; Johnson, Samuel, *The Vanity of Human Wishes. The Tenth Satire of Juvenal, Imitated by Samuel Johnson* (London: R. Dodsley, 1748), 219.

Charles XIV John   *See* BERNADOTTE, JEAN BAPTISTE JULES, PRINCE DE PONTECORVO.

Charles, archduke of Austria (Charles Louis Habsburg) (1771–1847) *Austrian general*

An epileptic, Charles Louis Habsburg was born in 1771, the fifth child of the Holy Roman Emperor Leopold II and the brother of Francis II (also Franz II). Although Charles was sickly for his entire life, he learned military strategy from a former adjutant of FREDERICK II (the Great), and at age 21 he entered the Austrian army with the rank of major general. He saw action against France in the revolutionary war, including at the battle of Jemappes (6 November 1792). Named governor-general of the Netherlands, he fought and defeated the French at Neerwinden (18 March 1793) in an effort to end the French invasion of that nation. However, he lost to the

French under General Jean-Baptiste Jourdan at Fleurus (26 June 1793).

The French defeat of Austria led to Charles being named commander of the Army of the Rhine in 1796. Immediately, he marched his troops into action, winning battles at Rastadt (5 July), Amberg (24 August), and Würzburg (3 September). During what was called the War of the Second Coalition, Charles again took on Jourdan and defeated him at Stockach (25 March 1799). However, when his efforts to work in an alliance with the Russian marshal Aleksandr Vasilyevich Suvorov ended in failure, Charles was relieved of his command in February 1800. After the calamitous Allied defeat at Hohenlinden on 3 December 1800, when the Austrians lost 7,000 killed and wounded and 12,000 were taken prisoner, he was reinstated. The defeat was so horrific, however, that the Austrians soon sued for peace.

In the following years, Charles was named minister of war and later governor of Bohemia, after which he headed up the Austrian military in its attempt to reform itself structurally. He helped form the brigade of soldiers called Jäger, or light infantry corps.

When Austria joined Russia in a second war against France in 1805, Charles opposed the conflict but fought anyway. Sent to Italy, he led the Austrians to victory at Caldiero on 29–31 October 1805. Another period of peace allowed him several years to implement reforms of the military, and when Austria went to war against France for a third time in 1809, he was placed in command of his country's forces. He was defeated by NAPOLEON at Eckmuhl (22 April), but at Aspern-Essling (21–22 May), he commanded some 80,000 troops against 90,000 French and Bavarians, handing the French leader his first major defeat. Napoleon avenged his loss by defeating Charles at Wagram on 5–6 July 1809. This final defeat led to Charles's resignation from command, and he never saw military action again.

Despite being an invalid for most of his life, Charles lived to be 67, dying in 1847. Many historians cite him not for his military victories and defeats on the field of battle but for his reforms of the Austrian army and his numerous writings on military strategy.

References: "Charles, Archduke," in *Command: From Alexander the Great to Zhukov—The Greatest Commanders of World History,* edited by James Lucas (London: Bloomsbury Publishing, 1988), 70; Rothenberg, Gunther Erich, *Napoleon's Great Adversaries: The Archduke Charles and the Austrian Army, 1792–1814* (London: Batsford, 1982); Petre, Francis Loraine, *Napoleon & the Archduke Charles: A History of the Franco-Austrian Campaign in the Valley of the Danube in 1809* (New York: J. Lane, 1909); Eysturlid, Lee, *The Formative Influences, Theories, and Campaigns of the Archduke Carl of Austria* (Westport, Conn.: Greenwood Press, 2000).

Charles Martel (Charles the Hammer) (686–741) *military leader of the Franks*

Charles Martel was born on 26 August 686 in Herstal (today's Wallonia, Belgium), the illegitimate son of Pippin the Middle, mayor of the palace of Austrasia, and his concubine Alpaida. As a result of the invasion of Europe by the Goths and Vandals from Asia in the third and fourth centuries, the Roman Empire had rapidly declined, and the area now called France was under the control of the Franks. Over time, their tribal rulers had consolidated their authority into four regions: Austrasia (northeast France and Belgium), Neustria (northwest and central France), Aquitaine (southwest France), and Burgundy (southeast France). Although the four regions were ruled by a king, his authority had been so weakened that he had become a nominal figurehead, and the real power was exercised by his mayors of the palace. This post was similar to that of vizier in the Islamic caliphates or chancellor in medieval England—that is, an official who was responsible for administration and government. In the four Frankish territories, the post had become hereditary, and the family of Pippin the Middle had been hereditary mayors of the palace of Austrasia from 615 onward. A man of immense wealth and influence, Pippin had defended Austrasia's eastern border against the Frisians, the Alammani, and the Bavarians and had secured a position of such importance that the title of king was well within his grasp, if he had sought to obtain it.

At the insistence of his wife Plectrude, Pippin had nominated his grandson Grimoald as his heir, but because Grimoald was only eight years old when Pippin died in 714, there was protest against his accession. Plectrude imprisoned Charles, the obvious rival to Grimoald, and although this served to prevent an uprising in Austrasia, neighboring Neustria, which Pippin had brought under Austrasian control, saw its opportunity and made preparations to seek revenge. Charles escaped from prison and was promptly installed as mayor of the palace by the Austrasian nobles who were looking for a military leader to counter the Neustrian advance.

In 716, the Neustrians, joined by the Frisians from the north, fought Charles's Neustrian army near Cologne. Having had little time to gather his troops, Charles was defeated and forced to take flight; he hid in the Eifel mountains. The Neustrians celebrated their victory by taking Cologne and installing the Neustrian king as ruler. On their return home, however, Charles took them by surprise and defeated them at the Battle of Amblève (716). He defeated them again at Vincy, near Cambrai, the following year. He then returned to Cologne and dealt with the forces still loyal to Plectrude before turning north and sending the Neustrians' allies, the Frisians, back to their coastal territory (today's north Holland). He completed the security of Austrasia's frontiers by forcing the Saxons back east over the river Weser.

In 718, worried about Charles's increasing authority, the Neustrians allied themselves to Aquitaine, and their combined forces met and were defeated by Charles at Soissons. The result was that Charles was now acknowledged as mayor of the palace over all the Frankish kingdoms—but not as king.

From 718 to 732, Charles's power grew through a series of victories over the tribes and peoples on the Frankish frontiers. He attacked and ravaged the lands of the Saxons as far east as the Weser, the Lippe, and the Teutoburg Forest. In 719, he occupied West Frisia, introducing Christianity to that country, and then turned south to invade Bavaria. Further campaigns there in 725 and 728 consolidated Frankish control, and victory over the Allemani in 730 meant that most of today's Germany was also brought under his control. It was now that Charles prepared for the great battle he had long expected to fight—the battle for which he is still remembered.

In the century since the death of Muhammed, his followers had conquered much of the Middle East, swept west right across North Africa, and taken Spain. The forces of the emir of Córdoba had invaded France from the south in 721 and besieged Toulouse, the major city of Aquitaine. They had eventually been defeated by Odo, duke of Aquitaine, and retreated back to the Pyrenees, but Charles was sure they would return. In order to meet them, he reintroduced a system last used by the Romans: a standing army of regular troops. It had become the practice in Europe simply to gather such soldiers as one could for a single campaign and then let them return home once it was over. Knowing he needed trained, experienced troops to withstand the Muslim cavalry, Charles recruited soldiers to serve on a full-time basis. When the emir again marched north into France, Odo of Aquitaine met them at the Garonne river but was decisively defeated. The triumphant Arab forces advanced north and, somewhere between Tours and Poitiers, met Charles, who had carefully selected the ground on which his army would fight.

Charles had positioned his army on a hill with a wood behind them and formed them into a tight square, similar to the phalanx developed by ALEXANDER THE GREAT a thousand years before. On 10 October 732, assaulted repeatedly by the emir's heavy cavalry, his trained infantry resisted all assaults from the Arabs until Charles sent some scouts around them to free prisoners in the Arab campsite. Fearing the loss of the loot they had taken, many of the Arabs withdrew to safeguard their belongings. While attempting to rally them, the Arab commander was killed, and his troops fled in disorder. Without cavalry and without bows and arrows, Charles's infantry had defeated an armored cavalry force that far outnumbered them. After the battle of Tours, it would be another thousand years before the forces of Islam would be so dangerous a threat to Europe (and would be thwarted by JOHN III SOBIESKI).

Historians now believe that Charles Martel's victory at Tours was due largely to the failure of the Muslim commanders to realize that they were not facing the untrained, tribal forces they had overcome so easily in the past. They also had not realized that Aquitaine was no longer just another province to be overrun but part of a new growing empire with a leader ready to defend it. Nonetheless, although the emir of Córdoba's assault on France had been halted, his forces were still a threat, and in 736 his army landed on the south coast of France and proceeded to capture and then fortify towns in Provence. In 737, Charles—who had strengthened his authority by occupying Burgundy and subjugating the Frisians, who had again risen against him—came south to deal once again with the Arab incursion. Once again the emir's generals had underestimated him. In the five years since the Battle of Tours, Charles had formed a heavy cavalry force that he had trained to work in close cooperation with his foot soldiers. The combination was too much for the emir's forces, who lost town after town and eventually were defeated in a decisive battle at Narbonne.

In the last four years of his life, Charles encouraged the spread of Christianity and made Boniface archbishop of Germany east of the Rhine. He died at Quierzy-sur-Oise on 22 October 741 and was buried in the Saint Denis Basilica in Paris. His immediate legacy was an empire that would be inherited by his grandson Charles—who became known as Charlemagne, the first Holy Roman Emperor. His longer-term legacy was the firm establishment of Christianity in Germany and the Netherlands and the fusion of the dukedoms, provinces, and fiefdoms of the Frankish kingdom into the entity known today as France. It would be nearly a thousand years before it was truly unified, but Charles Martel began the process. He did so by reintroducing the system of a regular army and by the development of trained and armored cavalry. He can be said to have pulled Europe out of the Dark Ages into the Middle Ages—and to have saved western Europe from Arab conquest.

References: Costanbeys, Marios, "Martel, Charles," in *The Oxford Companion to Military History,* edited by Richard Holmes (New York: Oxford University Press, 2001), 391–392; Dupuy, Ernest R., and Trevor N. Dupuy, "Decline of the Merovingians, 600–731" and "Campaign and Battle of Tours, 732," in *The Encyclopedia of Military History,* 2d rev. ed. (London: Jane's, 1986), 203–206; Deviosse, Jean, *Charles Martel* (Paris: Librairie Jules Tallandier, 1978); Fouracres, Paul, *The Age of Charles Martel* (New York: Longman, 2000).

Chinggis Khan   *See* GENGHIS KHAN.

Churchill, John, first duke of Marlborough
(1650–1722)   *English field marshal*
John Churchill, first duke of Marlborough, was the scion of a famed English family. Born at Ashe, Devon, on 24 June 1650, he was the son of Sir Winston Churchill, a member of Parliament and adviser to King Charles II of England, and his wife Elizabeth Drake. The Churchill family can be traced back to the 11th century. Historian William Coxe, writing in his landmark work *Memoirs of John Duke of Marlborough* (1818–19), says, "[Marlborough] was descended from Roger de Courcil, or Courselle, one of the Coursils of Poitou, who was a Norman baron, and accompanied William [the Conqueror] in 1066."

In 1667, when he was 17, John Churchill received a commission in the Foot Guards and was sent to Tangier (now Algeria) in northern Africa, fighting the Moors there for a period of two years. In 1672, he saw action in the Third Dutch War (1672–74), especially on 28 May 1672 at the battle of Sole Bay (also called Southwold), where a combined English and French fleet of ships, under the command of James, duke of York (later King James II of England) fought the Dutch under Admiral Michel de Ruyter in an indecisive battle. Churchill was subsequently promoted to captain and fought with English forces sent to France to help King Louis XIV against the Dutch; at Nijmegen and Maastricht (1673), he showed the first signs of the leadership he would display so well later. Promoted to command a regiment, he served with distinction at Enzheim on 4 October 1674.

In 1685, James II ascended to the throne and employed Churchill on a special mission to France. For this service, he was rewarded with a promotion to major general and given a barony. However, three years later, when James, a Catholic, was expelled in favor of the Protestant William of Orange, later William III of England, Churchill sided with William, for which he was

John Churchill, duke of Marlborough

created earl of Marlborough. From 1689 to 1691, he commanded a series of minor military expeditions in Flanders, Belgium, and Ireland.

In 1692, after letters he had written to James II in exile were uncovered, Churchill was stripped of his titles and imprisoned in the Tower of London, accused of working to reinstate the former king to the English throne. He was soon released, and William III restored his titles and rank in the army, but Churchill remained under suspicion for some years.

In 1702, William died, and Anne, his wife Mary's sister—a close friend of Churchill's wife—ascended the throne of England. The death of King Charles II of Spain, who left no heir, set off a conflict in Europe known as the War of the Spanish Succession (1701–14), fought between France and Spain, and England, Austria, and the Netherlands. Churchill, having once fought on the side of France, now fought against her, as England saw a French king on Spain's throne as a threat to its security. After the allied forces had taken several French garrisons, Churchill, now created duke of Marlborough, joined with the Austrian general EUGÈNE, prince de Savoie, in a series of battles against the French. At Schellenberg on 2 July 1704, Marlborough won the first major battle of this conflict. In his *Chronicles of an Old Campaigner, 1692–1717* (published 1904), a French officer, Jean-Martin de la Colonie, writes of this battle:

> The English infantry led this attack with the greatest intrepidity, right up to our parapet, but there they were opposed with a courage at least equal to their own. Rage, fury, and desperation were manifested to both sides, with the more obstinacy as the assailants and assailed were perhaps the greatest soldiers in the world. The little parapet which separated the two forces became the scene of the bloodiest struggle that could be conceived. Thirteen hundred of grenadiers, of whom seven hundred belonged to the Elector's Guards, and six hundred who were left under my command, bore the brunt of the enemy's attack at the forefront of the Bavarian infantry. . . . At last the enemy, after losing more than eight thousand men in this first onslaught, were obliged to relax their hold, and they fell back for shelter to the dip in the slope, where we could not harm them. A sudden calm now reigned amongst us, our people were recovering their breath, and seemed

more determined even than they were before the conflict. The ground around our parapet was covered with dead and dying, in heaps almost as high as our fascines, but our whole attention was fixed on the enemy and his movements; we noticed that the tops of his standards showed at about the same place as that from which they had made their charge in the first instance, leaving little doubt that they were reforming before returning to the assault.

The most important battle of the early part of the war was at Blenheim on 12 August 1704, when Marlborough and Eugène commanded some 52,000 troops against the French and Bavarians under Marshals Camille d'Houston, duke of Tallard; Ferdinand, Count Marsin; and their ally, Maximilian Emmanuel of Wittelsbach, the elector of Bavaria. An attack by Marlborough, followed by an assault by Eugène, aided the Allies in a victory. The English and Austrians lost about 12,000 killed and wounded, while the French casualties were upwards of 40,000, and Tallard was captured. Following the victory, a grateful Parliament and Queen Anne bestowed on this military hero a 2,000-acre estate near Oxford that was dubbed Blenheim. The massive home, designed by the playwright Sir John Vanbrugh, was built from 1705 to 1722 and is one of the most spectacular examples of English baroque architecture.

Marlborough's own victory at Ramillies (23 May 1706) was a mastery of strategy that forced a complete French withdrawal from the Low Countries. A further victory with Eugène at Oudenaarde (11 July 1708), when Marlborough faced overwhelming French forces but fought them off, confirmed his preeminence as one of the finest military commander of his age.

Marlborough's final military victory came at Malplaquet on 11 September 1709; however, it was a Pyrrhic victory, as the Tories in Parliament, opposed to his command of the army, used the high number of British casualties at Malplaquet to try forcing Marlborough from power as commander. Nonetheless, the House of Commons, under the Whigs, had passed a resolution earlier that year: "The astounding progress of Her Majesty's arms under the Earl of Marlborough has brilliantly restored the honour of the English nation." Marlborough continued to win battles against the French, including breaking their defensive lines in 1711.

With the rise of the Tories to power, Marlborough was accused of embezzling money to finish his estate home at Blenheim. In fact, Marlborough had gone into debt building the house and was forced to finish it without his general's salary; it is estimated that he spent some £45,000 overall. In 1712, to avoid the harassment of the allegations against him, he and his wife left England for Holland. Three years later, George I assumed the throne, and the monarch restored Marlborough's military rank and pay. However, due to declining health, Marlborough could not return to service, but he did return to England, where he remained until his death. After a series of strokes, John Churchill, first duke of Marlborough, died at Blenheim on 16 June 1722, eight days shy of his 72nd birthday.

Blenheim is now a major tourist attraction. The home was also the birthplace of the duke's descendant, Sir Winston Churchill, prime minister of Great Britain, on 30 November 1874.

Historian Michael Lee Lanning writes: "John Churchill established himself as one of the premier leaders of the eighteenth century by exhibiting superior tactical and strategic abilities while coordinating a vast allied army from divergent nations. Justifiably criticized for ambition and opportunism, Churchill mastered an ever-changing political arena and loyally represented whoever was in power during internal strife over the crown of England. In doing so, he not only secured his own military career but also elevated Britain from a minor island nation to a great European power."

References: Stephen, Leslie, "Churchill, John, First Duke of Marlborough," in *The Dictionary of National Biography*, 22 vols., 8 supps., edited by Sir Leslie Stephen and Sir Sidney Lee, et al. (London: Oxford University Press, 1921–22), IV:315–341; Coxe, William, *Memoirs of John Duke of Marlborough . . .* , 3 vols. (London: Printed for Longman, Hurst, Rees, Orme, and Brown, 1818–19); Bradlaugh, Charles, *John Churchill, Duke of Marlborough* (London: Freethought Publishing Company, 1884); Chandler, David G., *Marlborough as Military Commander* (London: Batsford, 1973); Taylor, Frank, *The Wars of Marlborough, 1702–1709* (Oxford, U.K.: B. Blackwell, 1921); La Colonie, Jean-Martin de *Chronicles of an Old Campaigner, 1692–1717*. Translated by Walter C. Horsley (London: John Murray, 1904), 182–192; Bruce, George, "Blenheim," "Oudenarde," and "Ramillies," in *Collins Dictionary of Wars* (Glasgow, Scotland: HarperCollins

Publishers, 1995), 37–38, 186, 206; Lanning, Michael Lee, "John Churchill (Duke of Marlborough)," in *The Military 100: A Ranking of the Most Influential Military Leaders of All Time* (New York: Barnes and Noble Books, 1996), 119–122.

Clare, Richard FitzGilbert de, second earl of Pembroke (Strongbow, Richard Strongbow) (ca. 1130/1135–1176) *Anglo-Norman military leader*

Born sometime around 1130–35, Richard FitzGilbert de Clare was the son of Gilbert FitzGilbert de Clare, later first earl of Pembroke and lord of Orbec. His mother was Isabel de Beaumont, sister of Robert, earl of Leicester. At the time Richard de Clare (known as Strongbow) was born, England was ruled by the fourth and youngest son of WILLIAM I (the Conqueror), Henry I, who reigned from 1100 to 1135. Henry had a son and daughter by his marriage to Edith-Matilda, daughter of the king of Scotland, but the death of his son William Aetheling meant his direct heir was his daughter Matilda, who had married the German emperor Henry V. After the emperor died, Matilda married Geoffrey, count of Anjou, in 1131, and Henry twice brought her to London, where she was acknowledged by the assembled barons as his heir. Despite this formal acceptance of her, though, many nobles were reluctant to have a woman ruling the kingdom and favored Matilda's cousin, Stephen, who was also a grandson of William I through the Conqueror's daughter Adela.

When Henry I died in 1135 and Stephen was crowned king, many barons supported Matilda and took up arms on her behalf. The ensuing conflict throughout Stephen's reign (1135–54) and the continual changes of support among the barons meant that Stephen's reign has become known as "the Anarchy." Richard de Clare's father supported Stephen and was rewarded for his loyalty in 1138 with the earldom of Pembroke and lands on the Welsh border. He continued to support Stephen until 1146, when Stephen took a Clare relative hostage as security for the good behavior of the hostage's uncle, upon which Gilbert de Clare and his son changed sides and supported Matilda.

In 1148, after Gilbert de Clare died, Richard inherited his father's lands in England and Normandy in France and took the title earl of Pembroke. In 1153, however, Stephen named as his heir Matilda's son Henry, who, on Stephen's death in 1154, succeeded as Henry

II. Probably because of Gilbert de Clare's support for Stephen, Henry refused to confirm Richard's right to his father's lands and title, though he was able to keep some of his property.

In 1168, Dermot MacMurchada, king of Leinster in Ireland, was deposed and came to England seeking assistance from Henry II. Henry was already involved in a struggle to keep his territories in France but gave permission for Dermot to seek help from among the English barons. Dermot at once approached Richard de Clare and offered him his daughter Aoife in marriage as well as succession to the Leinster throne. Clare agreed and set about forming an army, the first contingent of which he sent to Ireland in May 1169. This force met with the soldiers Dermot had gathered and went on to capture the city of Wexford. A year later, in August 1170, they were reinforced by Clare, who brought over another 200 foot soldiers and 1,000 archers. Under his leadership, this army then took Waterford (28 August 1170), where Clare and Aoife were married. The army then moved north to besiege Dublin, which soon fell to them.

Henry II, probably suspicious of Clare's success or anxious to assert his authority, then issued an order that Clare and his soldiers were to return to England by Easter (28 March) 1171 or their lands would be forfeit. Clare did not obey the order, and when Dermot Mac-Murchada died in May 1171, he declared himself king of Leinster. Outraged by this action, three Irish chieftains joined forces to besiege Dublin but were repulsed. On the advice of his uncle, Clare then returned to England to make his peace with Henry, to whom he gave up Dublin and other major cities. Henry, in turn, acknowledged Clare's right to hold the other Irish lands he had taken and also granted him the title of earl—though not the earldom of Pembroke.

In October 1171, Henry landed at Waterford in Ireland with an army, large enough to persuade many of the Irish chieftains to swear allegiance to him, and went north to occupy Dublin. Once established there, he put his own followers in command of the major English garrisons in Waterford, Wexford, and Dublin, thereby ensuring Clare would be unable to win them back by force. In April 1173, however, Henry's sons raised a rebellion against their father in France, and Henry called on Clare to fight for his cause. Clare defended Gisors in Normandy and took part in the relief of Verneuil in Au-

gust. At Rouen, Henry rewarded Clare by naming him governor of Ireland and giving him the city of Wexford.

In 1174, there was a major uprising by Irish chiefs that led to Clare's forces being evicted from the county of Limerick, but this was soon regained. In 1176, other uprisings took place, and it was during this campaign that de Clare died of an infection of his foot on 20 April 1176. He was buried in the Holy Trinity church in Dublin. His son Gilbert died childless about 1189, but Henry II ensured that Clare's daughter Isabel retained her father's landholdings in England and Wales. When she married William Marshal in 1189, the king made her husband earl of Pembroke, the title which he had long refused her father.

Richard FitzGilbert de Clare played a vital role in the survival of the Crown under the Normans as well as the first English invasion of Ireland, an event that still has repercussions to this day. The noted early English historian Giraldus Cambrensis (ca. 1146–ca. 1223), known as Gerald of Wales, wrote in his famed work *Expugnatio Hibernica* (The conquest of Ireland): "In war Strongbow was more of a leader than a soldier . . . When he took up his position in the midst of battle, he stood firm as an immovable standard around which his men could re-group and take refuge. In war he remained steadfast and reliable in good fortune and bad alike."

References: Altchscul, Michael, *A Baronial Family in Medieval England: The Clares, 1217–1314* (Baltimore, Md.: The Johns Hopkins Press, 1965); Barnard, Francis Pierrepont, *Strongbow's Conquest of Ireland* (New York: G. P. Putnam's Sons, 1888); Cambrensis, Giraldus, *Expugnatio Hibernica: The Conquest of Ireland by Giraldus Cambrensis,* translated by A. B. Scott and F. X. Martin. (Dublin, Ireland: The Royal Irish Academy, 1978).

Clark, Mark Wayne (1896–1984) *American general*

Mark Wayne Clark was born on 1 May 1896 at the Madison Barracks in Sackets Harbor, New York, where his father, a military officer, was serving in the United States Army. He graduated from the U.S. Military Academy at West Point in 1917 and was assigned to the army's 5th Division. Sent to France as a member of the American Expeditionary Force (AEF), the American component in the First World War, he was wounded in battle on his

General Mark Clark reviewing the troops in World War II

first day in France and did not see any further combat in that conflict. During the years between the two world wars, Clark served in various Department of War assignments, and by the beginning of the Second World War he held the rank of major.

The American entry into the war in late 1941 gave Clark the opportunity for promotion: He was advanced to the rank of major general and named as chief of staff of the Army Ground Forces. In 1942, General George Marshall sent Clark to England, where he met Prime Minister Winston Churchill, who nicknamed him "the American eagle." He was then selected to lead a covert mission to the French colonies in North Africa to gather intelligence for a potential Allied invasion of North Africa, which would eventually lead to an invasion of southern Europe. Upon his return to the United States, Clark was named by General Dwight D. EISENHOWER as deputy supreme commander of the North Africa invasion, codenamed Operation Torch. When it took place,

Clark commanded II Corps, and after an initial severe setback, the Germans were defeated.

Following this operation, Clark was promoted to lieutenant general (the youngest in U.S. history) and named commander of the U.S. Fifth Army, a combined American and British force that invaded Italy at Salerno on 9 September 1943. A history of the battle, released by the U.S. Department of War (the precursor of the Department of Defense), reported: "Under orders from General Clark, the VI Corps and, in turn, the 36th Division had prepared landing plans. The 141st and 142nd Regimental Combat Teams (36th Division) were to land as assault forces, in six waves on the Paestum beaches, advance to the railroad about 2,500 yards inland, reorganize in assembly areas, then move on to their objectives—the hills 10 miles distant. Once established on the hills, they would control the entire southern half of the Salerno plain." However "easy" this initial landing was, writes historian James Lucas, "the advance up the

Italian peninsula was bitterly contested at every river crossing and mountain pass by an enemy intent on holding the allies south of Rome." Clark's forces saw battle at the Rapido River (14 January 1944), at Anzio Beach (22–29 January 1944), against the fortress at Monte Cassino (January—May 1944), and in the assault on and surrender of Rome (4 June 1944). However, they incurred severe casualties in several of these clashes, American bombers completely destroyed the abbey at Monte Cassino, and Clark was widely criticized for concentrating on taking Rome and therefore allowing the German Tenth Army to escape. When the war ended, Clark was still in Italy, mopping up remaining German resistance. In the years after the war, he served as the U.S. high commissioner in Austria from 1945 to 1947. He then served as commander of the Sixth Army at Fort Monroe, Virginia.

On 28 April 1952, President Harry S. Truman put Clark in charge of the United Nations command in Korea, replacing General Matthew B. RIDGWAY, who had succeeded Eisenhower as allied supreme commander in Japan and the Far East Command. Clark controlled all allied forces fighting in Korea from May 1952 until the end of the war in July 1953. He retired formally from the army in October 1953, upon which he served as president of The Citadel, a military college in Charleston, South Carolina. Clark's memoirs appeared in two separate volumes: *Calculated Risk* (1950) and *From the Danube to the Yalu* (1954). He died in Charleston on 17 April 1984, two weeks before his 88th birthday.

References: Blumenson, Martin, *Mark Clark* (New York: Congdon & Weed, 1984); Nicholson, Dennis Dewitt, *A History of the Citadel: The Years of Summerall and Clark* (Charleston, South Carolina: The Citadel, 1994); Mathews, Sidney T., *General Clark's Decision to Drive to Rome* (Washington, D.C.: Department of the Army, Office of Military History, 1960; Washington, D.C.: Center of Military History, U.S. Army, 1990); Clark, Mark W., *Calculated Risk* (New York: Harper, 1950); "Clark, Mark W.," in *Command: From Alexander the Great to Zhukov—The Greatest Commanders of World History,* edited by James Lucas (London: Bloomsbury Publishing, 1988), 197; *Salerno* (Washington, D.C.: Historical Division, War Department, for the American Forces in Action series, 1944), 17; D'Este, Carlo, *Fatal Decision: Anzio and the Battle for Rome* (New York: HarperCollins, 1991).

Clinton, Sir Henry (1738–1795) *British general*

The youngest son of George Clinton, the royal governor of Newfoundland and New York who was himself the younger son of the sixth earl of Lincoln, Henry Clinton was either born in New York or went there with his father; historians disagree on the details. As a boy, he entered the New York militia with the rank of captain lieutenant, and after returning to England, in 1751 he entered the British army at the age of 13 as a lieutenant in the 2nd Regiment, or the Coldstream Guards.

In 1758, Clinton was promoted to the 1st Regiment, or the Grenadier Guards, with the rank of lieutenant colonel. He was attached to a brigade of guards serving under Prince Ferdinand and later served as an aide-de-camp to Charles, prince of Brunswick, both in the Seven Years' War (1756–63). His service in this conflict earned him a promotion to colonel in 1762, and he was made a major general in 1772. That same year, he was elected to the House of Commons, but he did not take his seat due to his wife's death in childbirth.

In 1775, when the American colonists revolted against British rule, Clinton was sent to America, where he served under General Thomas Gage and with Sir William Howe and Lord CORNWALLIS. Their first major battle was on 17 June 1775 at Bunker Hill (actually at nearby Breed's Hill). Historian Richard M. Ketchum, in a 1962 article for *American Heritage,* writes: "Gage immediately held a council of war with the three major officers who had recently been sent from England to help him quell the rebellion, Major Generals William Howe, Henry Clinton, and John Burgoyne. Clinton sensibly favored an attack on the narrow and unprotected neck of the Charlestown peninsula, just behind Bunker Hill, which would thus cut off the main American force. Gage overruled him. Whether out of pride in their crack regiments (which had been treated roughly in the retreat from Lexington and Concord) or contempt for the Provincial troops, the British high command decided instead to make a frontal assault on Breed's Hill."

The battle went badly for the British: They suffered some 1,054 casualties, of which 226 had been killed, while colonial losses were 450 dead and wounded. Gage was removed from command and recalled to London; Howe was named as commander in chief of all British forces in the colonies, with Clinton appointed as his second in command because his service at Bunker's Hill had been meritorious.

Howe and his forces became pinned down in Boston when the colonists, under George WASHINGTON, seized the heights at Dorchester. Howe was therefore forced to evacuate British troops from the city on 17 March 1776. Clinton then went to Charleston, South Carolina, where he commanded an expedition that resulted in a British defeat at Fort Sullivan (28 June 1776). Clinton served under Howe in the battle of Long Island (27 August 1776) and in the taking of New York (15 September 1776), for which he was knighted in 1777. When Howe was recalled to London, Clinton replaced him as commander in chief of British troops on 21 March 1778. However, by this time the Americans had taken control of the conflict, and Clinton's leadership could not stop the ultimate outcome. Although his tenure as commander was marked by the British defeat of Washington at Monmouth Courthouse in New Jersey (28 June 1778) and his taking Charleston in May 1780, British rule in America was ending. Clinton was on his way from New York when Lieutenant General Charles Lord CORNWALLIS surrendered at Yorktown (12 October 1781). Held to blame for his failure to aid Cornwallis, he resigned his command on 26 March 1782 and turned it over to Sir Guy Carleton.

Clinton returned to England, where he was reelected to the House of Commons in 1790. Promoted to the rank of full general in October 1793, he was named governor of Gibraltar in July 1794, but illness did not allow him to take the post. His last years were marked not so much by service to country as by an unending campaign, with the backing of supporters, to clear his name as to the full blame for the British loss at Yorktown, which he claimed belonged solely to Cornwallis. But, whereas Cornwallis was given additional commands—most notably in India—Clinton was appointed to insignificant posts. He died in Cornwall on 23 December 1795. His son, Sir Henry Clinton (1771–1829), was also a distinguished British military officer, serving in the Corunna campaign (1808–09) in the Peninsular War and commanding a regiment at Waterloo (1815).

Clinton's memoirs were printed as *A Narrative of the Campaign in 1781 in North America* (1783). His letters and papers, remaining in his family's possession for more than 160 years, were published as *The American Rebellion* (1954), which argued that he was completely blameless for the disaster in the colonies. Historian and editor William L. Wilcox writes that Clinton's tome was an "apologia for a career that failed. But the failure, in the

last analysis, came from a cause that he would have died rather than admit. His nemesis was himself." Many historians have now come to believe that Clinton was correct in blaming Cornwallis for the defeat at Yorktown.

References: Clinton, Sir Henry, *The American Rebellion: Sir Henry Clinton's Narrative of His Campaigns, 1775–1782, with an Appendix of Original Documents,* edited by William B. Willcox (New Haven, Conn.: Yale University Press, 1954); Willcox, William B., *Portrait of a General: Sir Henry Clinton in the War of Independence* (New York: Alfred A. Knopf, 1964); Ketchum, Richard M., "The Decisive Day is Come," *American Heritage* 13, no. 5 (August 1962): 80–93; Clinton, Sir Henry, *The Narrative of Lieutenant-General Sir Henry Clinton, K.B., Relative to His Conduct During Part of His Command of the King's Troops in North America, . . .* (London: Printed for J. Debrett, 1783); Patterson, J., *State of the Troops, British and German, under the Command of Lieutenant-General Sir Henry Clinton, at New-York, and Posts Depending, October 1, 1777* (New York[?], 1777).

Clive, Robert Clive, Baron (1725–1774)
British general

The son of a lawyer, Robert Clive was born at his family's estate, Styche, in the parish of Moreton Say, near Market Drayton, Shropshire, on 29 September 1725. The family, having originated with the name Clyve, had held the estate of Styche since the reign of Henry II; one of Clive's ancestors served as a member of Parliament during the Long Parliament (1640–60). In 1743, when Clive was 18, he became a writer, or clerk, for the British East India Company and was sent to Madras, India; he arrived in 1744.

In 1746, as part of the ongoing conflict between Great Britain and France, the French captured Madras, and Clive was taken prisoner. However, he escaped his captors and made his way to British lines, where he was drafted into the army with the rank of ensign. Immediately, he displayed great courage and so impressed his superiors that he was given a command and took part in three battles. Promoted to captain, in August 1751 he led a contingent of men to Arcot, near Bellore, about 65 miles west of Madras. Historian George Bruce writes:

This fortress was captured by ensign [Clive had in fact already been promoted to captain] Robert

Clive, with a force of 200 Europeans and 300 Sepoys . . . The garrison, 1,100 strong, offered no resistance, but marched out on Clive's approach. In the course of the autumn Arcot was beleaguered by an army of 10,000 Indians and 150 French under Chunda Sahib, the French nominee for the Nawabship of Arcot. Against this overwhelming force, Clive, whose garrison had been reduced by sickness to 120 Europeans and less than 200 Sepoys, held out for seven weeks, until the approach of a Marantha army forced Chunda Sahib to raise the siege. The garrison had 45 Europeans and 30 Sepoys killed. French advance in India was checked.

Because the French had to move their troops to Arcot to head off the siege there, their siege of the British-held town of Trichinopoly (now Tiruchirappalli) was lifted, making Clive's victory all the more important. As Bruce indicates, his triumphs helped end any chance the French had to conquer the British in India.

In 1753, Clive returned to England, where he was feted as a hero. He returned to India three years later, this time as governor of Fort Saint David near Madras. There, he assembled a large force against the nawab of Bengal, Siraj-ud-Daula or Suraj-ud-Dowlah (?–1757), who was challenging British rule in India and who had captured Calcutta. (It was here that the famed "Black Hole of Calcutta" outrage against British citizens was committed.) Clive marched his troops to Calcutta and, in a stunning victory (January 1757), he recaptured the city and forced the Nawab to flee. Clive chased him to Plassey in West Bengal state, and the battle that took place there on 23 June 1757 was one of the most decisive in the history of India. In a letter to the archbishop of Canterbury, as well as one to William Pitt, later the prime minister, Clive wrote of the clash:

The 22nd, in the evening, we crossed the river, and landing on the island, marched straight for Plassey Grove, where we arrived by one in the morning.

At daybreak we discovered the Nawab's army moving towards us, consisting, as we since found, of about fifteen thousand horse and thirty-five thousand foot, with upwards of forty pieces of cannon. They approached apace, and by six began to attack with a number of heavy cannon, supported by the whole army, and continued to play on us very briskly for several hours, during which our situation was of the utmost service to us, being lodged in a large grove with good mud banks. To succeed in an attempt on their cannon was next to impossible, as they were planted in a manner round us, and at considerable distances from each other. We therefore remained quiet in our post.

About noon the enemy drew off their artillery, and retired to their camp. We immediately sent a detachment, accompanied by two field-pieces, to take possession of a tank with high banks, which was advanced about three hundred yards above our grove, and from which the enemy had considerably annoyed us with some cannon managed by Frenchmen. This motion brought them out a second time; but on finding them make no great effort to dislodge us, we proceeded to take possession of one or two more eminences lying very near an angle of their camp. They made several attempts to bring out their cannon, but our advance field-pieces played so warmly and so well upon them that they were always driven back. Their horse exposing themselves a good deal on this occasion, many of them were killed, and among the rest four or five officers of the first distinction, by which the whole army being visibly dispirited and thrown into some confusion, we were encouraged to storm both the eminence and the angle of their camp, which were carried at the same instant, with little or no loss. On this a general rout ensued; and we pursued the enemy six miles, passing upwards of forty pieces of cannon they had abandoned, with an infinite number of carriages filled with baggage of all kinds. It is computed there are killed of the enemy about five hundred. Our loss amounted to only twenty-two killed and fifty wounded, and those chiefly sepoys.

The nawab, Suraj-ud-Dowlah, fled to Rajmahal, where he was taken captive by followers of his uncle and leading commander, Mir Jafar Ali Khan, who had gone over to the British. By the order of Jafar Ali Khan, the nawab was put to death on 4 July 1757 at his capital at Murshidabad. Jafar Ali Khan was installed by the British as the new nawab, and Clive became the governor of Bengal.

Clive's work in India was not through. He led a victory over the Dutch at Biderra (November 1759), where he avenged the Dutch massacre of British forces at Amboyna; it was at this clash that he wrote his famed message to one of his commanders: "Dear Forde, fight them immediately; I will send you the order of council tomorrow." Clive remained in India until 1760, when his health declined, after which he returned to England. One writer at the time said of Clive's departure, "It appeared as if the soul was departing the Government of Bengal." In 1762, he was created Baron Clive.

Following a series of internal scandals and claims of financial irregularities, the officers of the British East India Company asked Clive to return to Caluctta to serve as governor of the company. He arrived there in 1765 and proceeded to reform the enterprise's finances, end corruption, and repair the company's administrative foundations. However, he also had taken funds from the nawab's fortune, using them as the basis of the "Clive Fund" for the invalided soldiers in his command and their widows. Historians believe that he never benefited personally from this fund, but following Clive's return to England in 1767, General John BURGOYNE, who later served in the American Revolution, claimed in the House of Commons that Clive should be impeached for peculation, the crime of embezzlement. The House held that while "Robert, Lord Clive, did . . . render great and meritorious services to his country," nonetheless he "did obtain and possess [for] himself a total of £234,000 from the Nawab's fund." Clive went to the Commons and, in a reply to Lord North, the Prime Minister, stated, "My situation, sir, has not been an easy one for these past 12 months past, and though my conscience could never accuse me, yet I felt for my friends who were involved in the same censure as myself. . . . I have been examined by the select committee more like a sheep-stealer than a member of this House."

By this time, because of ill health, Clive was taking laudanum, a form of opium, then used as a painkiller. Although in 1773 the House of Commons ultimately cleared him of all charges, the strain of the accusations had taken too heavy of a toll. He died on 22 November 1774; his death is listed as a suicide from an overdose of laudanum. Clive's body was later taken by his family from London, where it had been buried without ceremony, to a small churchyard at his birth home of Moreton Say. A plaque over his grave reads: "Sacred to the Memory of Robert Lord Clive KB Buried within the walls of this church Born Sep 29 1725 Died Nov 22 1774 Primus in Indis." Ronald Colman played Clive in the 1935 film *Clive of India*.

References: Edwardes, Michael, *Clive: The Heaven-Born General* (London: Hart-Davis, MacGibbon, 1977); Caraccioli, Charles, *The Life of Robert Lord Clive, Baron Plassey. . . .*, 4 vols. (London: T. Bell ca. 1775); Bruce, George, "Arcot," in *Collins Dictionary of Wars* (Glasgow, Scotland: HarperCollins Publishers, 1995), 18; "Speech by Lord Clive in the House of Commons in defence of his conduct and that of the Company's servants in Bengal, 30 March 1772," *English Historical Documents, 1714–1783,* edited by D. B. Horn and Mary Ransome (London: Eyre and Spottiswoode, 1957), 808–811.

Condé, Louis II de Bourbon, prince de (Great Condé, duc d'Enghien) (1621–1686) *French general*

Louis, prince de Condé, known as the Great Condé, was born on 8 September 1621 in Paris, the son of Henri de Bourbon, prince de Condé, and Charlotte de Montmorency. He was the great-grandson of the prince de Condé who had led the French Protestant Huguenots in the wars of religion that had torn France apart in the middle of the 16th century. Educated by the Jesuits at Bourges from 1630 to 1636, he entered the royal military school in Paris, and in 1640, as the duc d'Enghien, he joined the French army of Picardy. He saw action at the siege of Arras in July of that year and fought again at Perpignan in 1642. On his return, he married Claire-Clémence de Maillé-Brézé, a niece of Cardinal Richelieu, but the marriage was not a happy one.

At Rocroi (19 May 1643), d'Enghien led the French army in their first decisive victory against Spain in many years and followed up his success with further victories at Thionville (10 August 1643) and Sierck (8 Sept 1643). With Henri de TURENNE, he won further victories over the Bavarians at Freiburg (3–9 August 1644), Mainz (17 September 1644), and Nordlingen (3 August 1645), and in 1646 he led a successful campaign in Flanders and took Dunkerque. On the death of his father on 26 December 1646, d'Enghien became prince de Condé and inherited vast wealth and estates that included most of Burgundy. Sent to Catalonia in Spain, he was defeated at Lérida (18 June 1647) but was recalled to lead the French army fighting in the Netherlands. He subsequently won an important victory at Lens (19–20 August 1648), which led to the Treaty of Munster that ended the Thirty Years' War (1618–48).

It was soon after this that the intermittent French civil wars known as the Fronde broke out. The king, Louis XIV, was an infant, and France was effectively ruled by Cardinal Mazarin, who had succeeded Cardinal Richelieu. Mazarin's autocratic government on behalf of the young king had made him very unpopular, and many French nobles sought to evict Mazarin and take his place. (This was a situation similar to the Wars of the Roses in England 200 years before.) In the first war of the Fronde, the nobles concerned were originally united in their enmity toward Mazarin, but they soon split as they put their personal ambition before the common cause. The result was that some fought for other nations against France since they saw the French government as their enemy.

In January–March 1649, on behalf of the king, Condé successfully besieged Paris, which had rebelled, but he then behaved with such arrogance that Mazarin had him arrested on 18 January 1650 and kept him confined for over a year. Condé's friends and allies then launched the second Fronde, which secured his release as well as Mazarin's temporary exile. Once again, however, his arrogance and assumption of authority caused antagonism, and the Queen Regent, Mazarin's ally, turned against him. Condé then started a rebellion in the south in September 1651, formed an alliance with his former enemy Spain, and advanced on Paris. At Faubourg St. Antoine, his forces were met by those of his cousin and erstwhile colleague on the battlefield, Turenne, and Condé's army escaped by taking refuge in Paris. The subsequent siege of Paris by Turenne only ended when Condé fled in October 1652 and offered his services to Spain, whose king made him commander in chief. On 25 November 1654, the French declared him a rebel and condemned him to death.

Condé led the Spanish forces against France with little success, mainly because he found the Spanish army's tactics and training inadequate against their French counterparts. Finally his army was decisively beaten at the battle of the Dunes (14 June 1658) near Dunkerque, and Spain and France signed a treaty, the Peace of the Pyrenees, in 1659. Condé then sought to make his peace with the young Louis XIV and was received back into favor at a formal meeting on 27 January 1660. Despite this, the king was reluctant to give Condé a military command, and it was not until 1668 that he again saw service when he fought the Spanish and took four of their towns in Franche-Comté in 15 days. In 1672, he joined Turenne in an invasion of the Protestant-held Netherlands and was wounded in a clash while crossing the Rhine at Tollhuis (12 June 1672). He then defended Alsace successfully against invasion, checked the army of the prince of Orange at Seneff (11 August 1674) in a

battle during which Condé had three horses killed under him, and raised the siege of Oudenarde. A year later, he led the French army into Alsace again to meet the Austrians and forced them to withdraw.

Ill health and age now forced Condé to retire from service, and he lived the last years of his life at Chantilly, where he died on 11 November 1686. An arrogant, self-willed man, he had distinguished himself on the battlefield by great physical courage, excellent tactical judgment, and skillful handling and deployment of his forces.

References: Francis John Haverfield, "Condé, Louis II, de Bourbon, Prince of" in *Encyclopaedia Britannica*, 14th ed., 24 vols. (London: Encyclopaedia Britannica Co., Ltd., 1929), VI:214–215; Cust, Edward, *The Campaigns of the Great Condé (1621–1686)* (Tonbridge, U.K.: G. Simon, 1990); FitzPatrick, Walter, *The Great Condé and the Period of the Fronde: A Historical Sketch* (London: TC Newby, 1873); Godley, Eveline Charlotte, *The Great Condé: A Life of Louis II Bourbon, Prince of Condé* (London: J. Murray, 1915); Windrow, Martin, and Francis K. Mason, "Condé, Louis II de Bourbon, Prince de," in *The Wordsworth Dictionary of Military Biography* (Hertfordshire, U.K.: Wordsworth Editions Ltd., 1997), 54–56.

Coote, Sir Eyre (1726–1783) *British general*

Born in Kilmallock, in County Limerick, Ireland, in 1726, Eyre Coote was the son of a clergyman. He joined the British army as a member of the 27th Regiment, and in 1745 he saw service during the Jacobite uprising. In 1754, as a member of the 39th Regiment, he was sent to India, the first British military contingent to be sent there. He was promoted to captain in 1755 and was part of a regiment sent to fight under Robert CLIVE at Calcutta (January 1757). Following the landmark battle of Plassey (23 June 1757), Coote, now a major, was sent to pursue French troops, which he did for 400 miles. His service earned him high praise as well as a promotion to lieutenant colonel and the command of the 84th Regiment.

When a second war between England and France in India broke out in 1760, Coote was one of the leaders of the British military forces. At Wandiwash on 22 January 1760, 1,900 British and 3,350 Indian troops under Coote faced a French force of some 2,250 French and 1,300 Indians under Thomas-Arthur, comte de Lally-Tollendal. Historian George Bruce writes of this battle: "The French army was accompanied by 3,000 Marantha horse [troops] who took no part in the action. After severe fighting Lally was defeated with a loss of 600 [French] besides Indians, the British losing 190 only." (Following the defeat, the comte de Lally was sent back to France, where he was executed on 9 May 1766 for his capitulation.)

At the siege of Pondicherry (15 January 1761), Coote supported Sir William Monson in defeating the remnants of Lally's army. For his role in this conflict, Coote was named commander of the British East India Company's offices and forces in Bengal. He returned to England in 1762 and was granted a jeweled sword from the company as a gift for his services.

Made a Knight of the Order of the Bath (KB) in 1771, Coote returned to India in 1779 with as a lieutenant general and commander of all British forces in India. The intrigues of Hyder Ali (also Haider Ali), the commander of the Mysore forces, led Coote to march his army to Chelambakam, where the Mysore force defeated the British on 16 June 1781. However, he continued the hunt to Porto Novo (also Portonovo), where, on 1 July 1781, some 8,500 troops under Coote faced 65,000 fortified Mysoris under Hyder Ali. What appeared to be the makings of a rout of the British in fact turned out to be a gallant day for Coote's forces: While losing only 306 men, the British inflicted upward of 10,000 casualties on the Mysoris—making Porto Novo one of the most one-sided victories in military history. Coote chased Hyder Ali to Pollilur, where again he inflicted a huge defeat on the Mysoris (27 August 1781). This was followed up by a third defeat of the Mysore forces at Sholingarh in September 1781.

Due to declining health, Coote returned to Madras, where he died on 28 April 1783. His body was returned to England, where he was buried in the Rockburne Church in Hampshire. Lieutenant Colonel Mark Wiljs, in his early 19th century work *Historical Sketches of the South of India,* writes:

> Nature had given to Colonel Coote all that nature can confer in the formation of a soldier: and the regular study of every branch of his profession, and experience in most of them, had formed an accomplished officer. A bodily frame of unusual vigor and activity, and mental energy always awake, were restrained from excessive action by a patience and temper which never allowed the spirit of enterprise to outmarch the dictates of prudence. Daring valour and cool reflection strove for the mastery in the composition of this great man. The conception and execution of his designs equally commanded the confidence of his officers; and a master at once of human nature and of the sciences of war, his rigid discipline was tempered with an unaffected kindness and consideration for the wants and even the prejudices of the European soldiers, and render him the idol of the native troops.

One of Coote's descendants is General Colin Powell, former chair of the Joint Chiefs of Staff (1989–93) and secretary of state (2001–05) in the administration of President George W. Bush. He is descended from Coote, his great-great-great grandfather, through a liaison of Coote's son with a woman in Jamaica.

References: Wylly, Harold Carmichael, *A Life of Lieutenant-General Sir Eyre Coote, K.B., compiled by Colonel H. C. Wylly, C. B., with an introduction by General Sir Charles Monro, Bart.* (Oxford, U.K.: The Clarendon Press, 1922); Sheppard, Eric William, *Coote Bahadur: A Life of Lieutenant-General Sir Eyre Coote* (London: W. Laurie, 1956); Winser, Andrew, "Lieut. General Sir Eyre Coote, 1726–1783," *The Hatcher Review* 2, no. 15 (1983): 218–227; Bruce, George, "Wandiwash II," in *Collins Dictionary of Wars* (Glasgow, Scotland: HarperCollins Publishers, 1995), 265; Wilks, Mark, *Historical Sketches of the South of India, in an Attempt to Trace the History of Mysoor . . . ,* 3 vols. (London: Longman, Hurst, Rees, and Orme, 1810–17), I:251–52.

Cornwallis, Charles, first marquis and second earl Cornwallis, Viscount Brome, Baron Cornwallis of Eye (1738–1805)
British general
Born on 31 December 1738, Charles Cornwallis was the son of Charles, the first earl Cornwallis. According to historian and biographer Charles Ross, the family came from Cornwallys, or Cornwaleys, in Ireland during the reign of Edward III. One ancestor, Thomas Cornwallis, became the sheriff of London in 1378, and another, Frederick Cornwallis, fought for Charles I in the Royalist army during the English Civil War. Charles Cornwallis was educated at Eton—the most prestigious of English private schools—and Clare College, Cambridge, whence he entered the British army as an ensign in the 1st Guards, also known as the Grenadiers. He then went

to Turin, Italy, where he attended a military academy. Thereafter, he served in Germany during the Seven Years' War (1756–63), rising to the rank of lieutenant colonel. In 1762, with his father's death, he was styled as the second earl Cornwallis. He took his seat in the House of Lords as a Whig, and when Charles Watson-Wentworth, the second marquess Rockingham, became prime minister in 1765, Cornwallis was named lord of the bedchamber.

Cornwallis served in the House of Lords as an aide-de-camp to King George III, as chief justice in Eyre, south of the Trent River, and as the joint vice treasurer of Ireland. He opposed the Tory program in the American colonies, and, sympathetic to the aims of the colonists, he voted against the Declaratory Act in 1766. However, when war broke out against the British in the colonies, Cornwallis accepted the command of British troops. He sailed from England on 10 February 1776 in command of seven British regiments. Prior to Cornwallis's arrival, Lord William Howe, the commander of all British forces in North America, had evacuated Boston (17 March 1776) under threat of a siege and had withdrawn to Halifax in Canada. Cornwallis brought reinforcements to Howe, and their combined army marched back into the colonies, seeing action at Staten Island (July 1776) and New York (15 September). After the battle at White Plains (1 November 1776), Cornwallis seized Fort Lee on 16 November. He pursued General George WASHINGTON toward Trenton, but on 26 December, Washington crossed back over the Delaware River and inflicted a severe blow on Cornwallis's forces. On 3 January 1777, he struck again at Princeton. Cornwallis did win a victory for the British at Brandywine, Pennsylvania (11 September 1777), and took control of Philadelphia on 28 September 1777. He also won a decisive victory over General Horatio GATES at Camden, South Carolina (16 August 1780).

The remainder of the war would not go so well for Cornwallis. After Camden, he marched north and set up his headquarters at Yorktown, a seaport in Virginia, where he won a quick battle against General Nathanael GREENE and seized the Americans' cannons. In a letter to a General William Phillips, Cornwallis wrote:

> I have had the most difficult and dangerous campaign, and was obliged to fight a battle two hundred miles from my communication, against an enemy seven times my number. The fate of it was long doubtful. We had not a regiment or corps that did not at some time give way. It ended, however, happily, in our completely routing the enemy and taking their cannon. . . . I last night heard of your arrival in the Chesapeake. Now, my dear friend, what is our plan? If we mean an offensive war in America, we must abandon New York, and bring our whole force into Virginia; we then have a stake to fight for, and a successful battle may give us America. If our plan is defensive, mixed with desultory expeditions, let us quit the Carolinas (which cannot be held defensively while Virginia can be so easily armed against us), and stick to our salt pork at New York, sending now and then a detachment to steal tobacco, &c.

At Yorktown, the Americans under General Washington, combined with French soldiers under Jean-Baptiste Donatien de Vimeur, comte de Rochambeau, encircled Cornwallis's regiments and laid siege to them. On 14 October 1781, the outer portions of the English fortifications were breached, and five days later Cornwallis was forced to surrender his entire army. Sir Henry CLINTON had left New York for Yorktown with reinforcements, but arrived too late to change history. The treaty signed two years later in Paris (November 1783) ended the war. Although Cornwallis is widely blamed by historians for his conduct in fighting the war, he returned home and remained a hero to the British people. (Clinton received the majority of blame for not reinforcing Cornwallis soon enough.)

In 1785, Cornwallis was named as the English envoy to the court of FREDERICK II (the Great) of Prussia. On 23 February 1786, he was named governor-general of India, where he served until August 1793. His series of reforms of British rule in India, known as the Cornwallis Code, aided in the administrative control of that country. After the Third Mysore War broke out in 1790, Cornwallis was named commander of British troops in India on 29 January 1791. In a series of battles, including Bangalore (21 March 1791) and Seringapatam (5 February 1792), he defeated the Mysoris, under Tipu (also Tippoo) Sahib, and Tipu sued for peace, signing the Treaty of Seringapatam in March 1792. For his services in this conflict, Cornwallis was made Marquis Cornwallis of Eye.

Cornwallis served two additional tours overseas: as viceroy of Ireland (1798–1801), when he worked to end strife between Protestants and Roman Catholics; and, again, as governor-general of India (1805). He also aided in finalizing the signing of the Peace Treaty of Amiens (1802), a short-lived truce in the war between France and England. His health began to fail when he sailed for India in 1805, and he died on 5 October at Ghazipur (now Uttar Pradesh) soon after arriving. He was laid to rest in Ghazipur, and a memorial was installed over his grave.

References: Seton-Kerr, Walter Scott, *The Marquess Cornwallis* (Oxford, U.K.: Clarendon Press, 1890); Wickwire, Franklin B., and Mary Wickwire, *Cornwallis: The American Adventure* (Boston: Houghton Mifflin, 1970); Ross, Charles, ed., *Correspondence of Charles, First Marquis Cornwallis*, 3 vols. (London: John Murray, 1859); Reese, George Henkle, comp., *The Cornwallis Papers,* 2 vols. (Charlottesville: University of Virginia Press, 1970); Aspinall, Arthur, *Cornwallis in Bengal: The Administrative and Judicial Reforms of Lord Cornwallis in Bengal . . .* (Manchester, U.K.: Manchester University Press, 1931).

Crassus, Marcus Licinius (ca. 115–53 B.C.)
Roman general

The son of the consul and censor Publius Licinius Crassus, who served as the Roman governor of Spain, Marcus Crassus was born about 115 B.C. The elder Crassus was killed—some historians claim he committed suicide—following the victory of the Roman generals Marius and Cinna at Rome (87 B.C.) over the Roman general Lucius Cornelius Sulla (138–78 B.C.); his eldest son, Publius Crassus, was also killed in the clash, leaving Marcus Crassus to escape to Spain with some of his father's supporters. There he hid in a cave for eight months to avoid capture. When Cinna was killed, his assistant Carbo took power, and Sulla aimed to take control of Rome. Crassus raised an army of about 2,500 soldiers and joined Sulla, who told him, "I give you an escort—your father, your brother, your friends, and your relations who have been put to death without law or justice, and whose murderers I am going to punish." It was during Sulla's wars against the powers of Rome that Crassus served with another military commander, Gnaeus Pompeius, better known as POMPEY the Great.

Crassus rose to become one of Sulla's most important generals. He led Roman troops in action at Colline Gate (November 82 B.C.), and many historians credit Crassus,

as the commander of Sulla's right wing, of making moves decisive to Sulla's victory. However, Pompey was handed the task of finishing the war against Mithridates. Sulla's complete control over Rome allowed Crassus to use his family's wealth to buy up large estates of those whom Sulla had murdered. He then turned to politics, using his influence to get certain people elected to the Roman Senate, while he was made a praetor (governor).

In 73 B.C., the Roman slave Spartacus led a revolt against the slaveholders of Rome. Sulla sent a praetor, Claudius Glaber Clodius, to crush the insurrection; instead, Spartacus's forces conquered the Romans. Within a year, some 100,000 slaves had joined Spartacus, and he went on to defeat several small Roman armies in northern Italy led by L. Gellius Publicola and Gnaeus Cornelius Lentulus Clodianus. Because Pompey was in Spain, the Roman Senate gave Crassus the title of commander imperium to fight Spartacus, and he was given six legions of troops. In their first battle, Spartacus won a spectacular victory against two legions of Crassus's army; however, Crassus used the tactic of decimation—killing every 10th man in his army as a punishment for defeat—as an incentive for his troops to fight better. He then won the next battle, forcing Spartacus to withdraw to the area of Rhegium in southern Italy. Boxed in, he could not move to Sicily. Pompey was recalled from Spain and sent against Spartacus as well as an army under Marcus Licinius Lucullus from Macedonia. At the Siler (now Petelia) River (71 B.C.), Crassus met Spartacus's force and crushed them; Spartacus is alleged to have died in the battle, even though his body was never found. Crassus crucified the survivors of Spartacus's army along the Appian Way, hanging some 6,000 of them, and returned home to accolades. One of his aides was a young military officer named Julius CAESAR.

For putting down the slave revolt, Crassus was elected as a consul along with Pompey (in 70 B.C.), although Pompey was the senior because of his military victory in Spain. Crassus returned to his former work in political circles, serving as a censor in 65 B.C. and working for land reform and decreased taxes.

Following his military victories in Gaul (now modern France), Caesar returned to Rome and formed the so-called First Triumvirate with Pompey and Crassus. In effect, however, Caesar was the real power, with Pompey getting land for his soldiers and Crassus the decreased-tax program he desired. By this time, Crassus and Pompey were in opposition: Pompey supported the tribune

Publius Clodius, while Crassus was a member of the group who opposed Clodius. Caesar returned to Gaul, where he served as governor. He met Crassus at Ravenna (Italy) in 56 B.C. in an attempt to soothe the latter's worries over the leadership of Rome. As appeasement, Crassus was appointed governor of Syria.

As Syria's governor, Crassus decided to crush an enemy of Rome, Parthia. This nation (in today's Turkey) once dominated what is now the Middle East and was a leading opponent to Rome's ambitions for power in the area. In 55 B.C., working with his son Publius Licinius Crassus, who had served under Caesar in Gaul, Crassus assembled a huge force of some 30,000 men. He crossed the Euphrates River, and, in 53 B.C., met the Parthian army under Surena (some historians report his name as Sillaces) at Carrhae. An Arab chieftain, Ariamnes, convinced Crassus that the Parthian army was small; actually, Ariamnes was in the Parthians' employ and had duped Crassus. The battle turned out to be a disaster for the Romans, as historian George Bruce writes: "[T]he Parthians, entirely cavalry, adopted their usual tactics of retiring and drawing their foes in pursuit. As the heavily armed legionaires became strung out across the plain, they turned upon them and cut them down in detail, 500 Romans being made prisoners and the rest . . . killed." Crassus's son Publius was one of the casualties on the battlefield. Crassus was captured; the Parthian king, Horodes (also Orodes), ordered his head cut off and molten gold poured into it. Horodes allegedly said as the gold was poured into Crassus's severed head, "Now sate thyself with the metal of which thou wert so greedy when alive."

References: Adcock, Frank E., *Marcus Crassus, Millionaire* (Cambridge, U.K.: Heffer, 1966); Ward, Allen Mason, *Marcus Crassus and the Late Roman Republic* (Columbia: University of Missouri Press, 1977); Bruce, George, "Carrhae," in *Collins Dictionary of Wars* (Glasgow, Scotland: HarperCollins Publishers, 1995), 51.

Cromwell, Oliver (1599–1658) *English military commander, lord protector of England*

Oliver Cromwell was born the son of a small landowner on 25 April 1599 in Huntingdon, Huntingdonshire, near Cambridge, England. One of his ancestors, Thomas Cromwell, served as a minister to King Henry VIII. Cromwell received his education at Sidney Sussex College, Cambridge University, where he went through a religious conversion, leaving him with Puritan beliefs. He also studied at Lincoln's Inn, one of the four Inns of Court of English law. However, he did not become a lawyer, instead returning to his small estate in Cambridge. In 1628, he was elected to the House of Commons for Huntingdon, and he later served in the Short Parliament (April 1640), known for its brief duration. During this time in the Commons, Cromwell sided with the Scots in opposing King Charles I's call for raising funds to restore the episcopacy to Scotland. In the Long Parliament (August 1640 through April 1660), Cromwell—reelected to the House of Commons from Cambridge—became an outspoken critic of the king, calling for increased constitutional safeguards against monarchial powers and for the Parliament, not the king, to name military commanders.

In 1642, years of disputes between Parliamentary leaders and the king exploded in what has been called the first English Civil War. Cromwell resigned his seat in the Commons and took a commission as a captain of horse, in charge of a cavalry regiment later to be called the Ironsides. Though he did not have any military experience, he immediately showed innate skill, taking control of his alma mater, Cambridge, before it could be seized by royalist forces. At Edgehill on 23 October 1642, he fought under Robert Devereux, third earl of ESSEX. He wrote to the Parliamentarian John Hampden that "old decayed serving men, and tapsters, and such kind of fellows" would never fight "gentlemen that have honour and courage and resolution in them. . . . You must get men of spirit . . . that [are] likely to go as far as gentlemen will do, or else you will be beaten still." At Grantham on 13 May 1643, Cromwell first displayed his gift for leadership, defeating a Royalist force. At Gainsborough on 24 July 1643, he seized the town after it had been lost by the Parliamentarian Lord Willoughby eight days earlier. On 11 October 1643, he was joined by General Lord Thomas FAIRFAX in crushing a Royalist force at Winceby. By now his services were so exemplary that he was recognized with two appointments: to a parliamentary committee of the kingdoms of England and Scotland, established on 16 February 1644 to handle war matters, and to serve as the second in command to Edward MONTAGU, Lord Manchester.

Cromwell's efforts for Parliament continued: Lord Newcastle, the Royalist general, took refuge in the city of York, where he was besieged first by Fairfax and Lord Leven (commanding a Scottish force), then by Cromwell. The Royalist Prince RUPERT relieved Newcastle but was forced to face the parliamentary forces at Marston Moor (2 July 1644). Cromwell's Ironsides regiment of cavalry broke Rupert's horsemen, forcing his army to compensate at the left and center, which were also broken. The Royalists left some 4,000 dead and wounded on the field, and the Parliamentarians won control of the north of England. In a letter to his brother-in-law after his victory at Marston Moor, Cromwell wrote, "Truly England and the Church of God hath had a great favour from the Lord, in this great victory given unto us, such as the like never was since this war began. It had all the evidences of an absolute victory obtained by the Lord's blessing upon the Godly Party principally. We never charged but we routed the enemy. The Left Wing, which I commanded, being our own horse, saving a few Scots in our rear, beat all of the Prince's horse. God made them as stubble to our swords. We charged their regiments of foot with our horse, and routed all as we charged. The particulars I cannot relate now; but I believe, of twenty thousand the Prince hath not four thousand left. Give glory, all the glory, to God."

Several mistakes by Lord Manchester led Cromwell to believe the army should be reorganized under one commander. As the army's leaders, Fairfax and Cromwell led Parliamentarian forces to victory at Naseby (14 June 1645), following which Cromwell wrote to the Speaker of the House of Commons, Sir John Glanville: "Honest men served you faithfully in this action . . . He that ventures his life for the liberty of his country, I wish he trust God for the liberty of his conscience, and you for the liberty he fights for." Appointed to the rank of lieutenant general of the horse in the so-called New Model Army, Cromwell succeeded in ending the Royalist threat in a number of small battles, most notably at Exeter (9–13 April 1646) and Oxford (24 June 1646). The king surrendered in May 1646, was handed over to Parliament for trial, and, on 30 January 1649, was beheaded.

Cromwell also dealt with purges of dissent within his ranks, crushing the Levellers, a radical element of the New Model Army, and prosecuting their leader, John Lilburne. He marched into Ireland and ferociously put down two uprisings, one at Drogheda and another at Wexford, writing after these slaughters: "I am persuaded that this is a righteous judgment of God upon these bar-

barous wretches, who have imbrued their hands in so much innocent blood."

When Charles II, son of the executed king, made his way to Edinburgh and proclaimed himself king of England, Cromwell led a new army as lord general (since Fairfax had resigned) and marched north. Initially he could not get the Scottish commander, Sir David LESLIE, to meet him in open battle, so he retired to the city of Dunbar. Here, on 3 September 1650, some 11,000 Parliamentary forces faced 22,000 Scottish Royalists. Although Leslie's forces were on a hill overlooking Dunbar, Cromwell's troops marched to their right, surprising them and forcing a massive withdrawal in which some 3,000 Scots were killed and 10,000 taken prisoner, while Cromwell lost a total of 30 men. This was followed by a similar victory over Charles II at Worcester on 3 September 1651. General George MONCK mopped up any resistance to Cromwell's reign, and the wars against him were over.

Infuriated by criticisms against him in Parliament, Cromwell dissolved it and replaced it with a group of 140 allies (ironically called "saints"). The Barebones Parliament, as it was called, first met in July 1653. When Parliamentary leader John Bradshaw criticized Cromwell for his dissolution of the Long Parliament, Bradshaw was dismissed. In December 1653, the Barebones Parliament dissolved itself and named Cromwell lord protector of England. An Instrument of Government was drawn up, confirming Cromwell in his role as leader of the government, with advice given by a Council of State. He was installed as lord protector at Westminster Hall on 16 December 1653.

Over the next five years, Cromwell ended the first Anglo-Dutch War (1652–54) and initiated the Anglo-Spanish War (1654–60). A Royalist uprising in March 1655—called Pedruddock's Rising—led Cromwell to institute military law over the nation. Like Charles I, he found that he needed Parliament to finance military operations, and a second Protectorate Parliament was called in September 1656. The following February, this Parliament drew up a document called The Humble Petition and Advice, in which they offered to have Cromwell crowned as king of England. However, Cromwell refused, telling the meeting, "I will not build Jericho again." He did accept another term as lord protector and agreed that he could name those sitting in the House of Lords. When his choices became controversial, members of Parliament spoke out, and Cromwell dissolved the body on 4 February 1658. However, following this move, his health declined, and he died suddenly on 3 September 1658.

Cromwell was buried in Westminster Abbey, but when Charles II took power in 1661, the body was disinterred, beheaded, and thrown into the Thames River. Cromwell's head, placed on a spike on the Tower Bridge, was recovered years later by his daughter and buried in the 20th century at Cambridge University, his alma mater.

One of his intimates wrote of Cromwell: "His body was wel [sic] compact and strong, his stature under 6 foote (I beleeve [sic] about 2 inches)[,] his head a storehouse and shop both of vast treasury of natural parts. His temper exceeding fyery [sic] . . . but the flame of it kept down . . . yet did he exceed in tenderness towards sufferers . . . A larger soul, I thinke [sic], hath seldome [sic] dwelt in a house of clay than his was."

References: Cromwell, Oliver, *The Very Interesting Life of the Famous Oliver Cromwell, With Accounts of the Civil Wars in Those Kingdoms, to Which are Added, Memoirs of major Desborough, and Henry Ireton* (Manchester, U.K.: William Wills, 1840); Bruce, George, "Marston Moor," in *Collins Dictionary of Wars* (Glasgow, Scotland: HarperCollins Publishers, 1995), 157; *The Overthrow of the Scottish Army: Or, a Letter Sent from Lieutenant General Cromwell, to the Committee of Lancashire sitting at Manchester, shewing the utter Routing of the Scottish Forces* (London: Printed for John Bellamy, 1648); "Oliver Cromwell Writes to his Brother-in-Law after the Battle of Marston Moor, 2 July 1644," in *Eyewitness to History,* edited by John Carey (Cambridge, Mass.: Harvard University Press, 1987), 177–178.

Cyrus the Great (Kuru-sh, Kurash) (ca. 590/585–529 B.C.) *Persian king*

Much of Cyrus's life is clothed in mystery and, as historians have found, myth. Born between 590 and 585 B.C. in what is now Persis, Iran, he was the son of Cambyses I of the clan of the Achaemenidae, the predominate clan of the Persian Pasargadae tribe. In either 559 or 558 B.C., Cyrus rose to become the king of the Persians when his father died.

Soon after taking power, Cyrus went to war against the Medes, in another part of Persia, and took captive their king, Astyages; in 550 B.C., he incorporated the Median Empire into his own, then proclaimed himself the king of all Persians. This upset the Babylonians, who shared a border with Persia, and they joined with the Lydians and Spartans to fight him. In 546 B.C., Cyrus marched on Lydia and took control of it, and he fought and defeated Babylon in 539 B.C. In 11 short years, Cyrus had conquered three of the mightiest powers in the world at that time. After he defeated Babylon, he issued his *Charter of the Rights of Nations,* in which he laid out a plan for respecting human rights, the first such declaration in the history of man. In it, he explained, "When my soldiers in great numbers peacefully entered Babylon . . . I did not allow anyone to terrorize the people. . . . I kept in view the needs of people and all its sanctuaries to promote their well-being. . . . [I] freed all the slaves. I put an end to their misfortune and slavery." Cyrus also allowed the Jews to return from their exile in Babylon to their homes in what is now Israel. He was now master of an empire that extended from the Mediterranean to the Hindu Kush and from the Black Sea to the Persian Gulf.

In 529 B.C., while fighting the Massagetae, a tribe from near the Caspian Sea, Cyrus was killed; his son, Cambyses II, succeeded him. After defeating the Massagetae, Cambyses II took his father's body back to Persis and buried it at Pasargadae, formerly the capital of Persia and now the city of Murghab in modern Iran.

References: Abbott, Jacob, *Cyrus the Great* (New York: Harper & Brothers, 1900); Xenophon, *The Story of Cyrus, Adapted from Xenophon's Cyclopaedia,* translated by Clarence W. Gleason (New York: American Book Company, 1900); Clarke, Samuel, *The Life & Death of Nebuchadnezzar, the Great, the first Founder of the Babylonian Empire, represented by the Golden Head of that Image, Dan. 2.32, and by the Lion with Eagles Wings, Dan. 7.4.: As also of Cyrus, the Great, the first Founder of the Empire of Medes and Persians, Represented by the Breast, and Arms of Silver in that Image, Dan 2.32, and by a Bear, Dan 7. by Sa[muel] Clarke . . .* (London: Printed for William Miller, 1664); "Cyrus the Great," in *Command: From Alexander the Great to Zhukov—The Greatest Commanders of World History,* edited by James Lucas (London: Bloomsbury Publishing, 1988), 35–36.

D

Darius I (Darius the Great, Darivaush, Darius Hystaspis) (ca. 550–486 B.C.) *king of Persia*

Also called Darivaush or Darius Hystaspis, Darius I, perhaps better known as Darius the Great, was a distant cousin of CYRUS THE GREAT. What is known about him comes from inscriptions on stones and other evidence discovered in Persia, now modern Iran; any contemporary histories have been lost. The writings at Behistun, in the Zargos mountains in northwestern Iran, were commissioned by Darius in 515 B.C. and document his accomplishments, a sort of memorial. Another source of information is the so-called Cylinder of Cyrus, discovered in an archaeological excavation in Babylon, a city-state conquered by Darius in 539 B.C. The inscription on the stone reads: "I [am] Cyrus, the King of the World, the King of Babylon, the King of Shumer and Akkad, the king of the four regions."

From these sources and others, historians have ascertained that Darius was part of the royal family of the Achaemenidae. When Cambyses II, son of Cyrus the Great, was killed during a military expedition in Syria in 522 B.C., the empire was ruled for a time by the fakir Gaumata, who took the name Smerdis and claimed to be of Cambyses' family. Darius intended to take back the empire in his family's name, and, joined by "six noble Persians" whose names are listed on the Behistun tablet,

he marched on the fortress where Gaumata was hiding and murdered him.

As king, Darius soon faced a series of insurrections in portions of the Persian Empire, most notably in Babylon, Media, Persia, Sagartia, and Susiana. In each of these uprisings, men claiming to be directly related to Cambyses rose up to declare Darius a usurper, including one, Vahyazdata in Persia, who aimed to avenge the death of Gaumata. Darius assembled an army of Persians and some Medians and marched on each of these rebellions, putting them all down by 519 B.C. These wars established Darius as the unchallenged ruler of Persia and also warned external enemies of his power and influence. He fought the tribes of the Caucasus to the east of Persia, and his administration of these areas and others were documented by the historian Herodotus.

In addition to being a warrior, Darius is also known for his civil rule of the areas he conquered, establishing local governments and minting coinage—including, for the first time, gold coins called *darics,* or "gold" in Persian. He also saw the importance of exploration and sent out several expeditions, including one down the Indus River, to search out new territories, trading partners, and commerce. (At what is now the Suez Canal, excavators found a stone with a hieroglyphic reference to the voyages of one of his ships on the Nile River.) Temples dedicated to Darius were built in Memphis and other sites in Egypt, where he ruled from afar as a pharaoh during the 27th dynasty with the name Setut-re. He also began the construction of a water canal from the Nile to the Red Sea, the first attempt to build what is now the Suez Canal.

Although Darius may have been the first major administrative leader in world history, he is best known for his armed conflicts and for his military reforms. In 512, he began a war against the Scythians to the north, sending his forces across the Bosporus strait and the Danube River. However, when the army marched into what are now the steppes of the Ukraine, they met fierce resistance and withdrew. Unfortunately for historians, the story of this conflict, chiseled into the rock at Behistun, has been nearly obliterated by time and wear, so its full details will probably never be known. When the Greeks supported Greek colonies in Asia rebelling against Darius's rule, he sent his fleet to punish them, but it was destroyed by a storm at Mt. Athos. He then sent an army and fought the Greeks at Marathon (September 490 B.C.). With a force of 60,000 Persians against just 10,000 Athenian hoplites (infantry men), his forces nonetheless suffered one of the most one-sided defeats in history: Some 6,500 Persians were slaughtered, with a loss of only 192 Athenians.

Darius was readying a third attempt to invade Greece when he died in 486 B.C. He was succeeded as the head of Persia by his son XERXES. He is considered one of the greater of the earliest military commanders, despite his loss at Marathon, which historian Edward Creasy named as one of the 10 most important battles in world history. Further, in additon to consolidating many parts of the Persian Empire, Darius is known for the systematic program of running local governments through satraps, or local governors or viceroys, a system held in such high regard that ALEXANDER THE GREAT utilized it when he conquered and controlled numerous foreign lands.

References: Abbott, Jacob, *History of Darius the Great* (London: Thomas Allman, 1850); "Darius the Great," in *The Hutchinson Dictionary of Ancient and Medieval Warfare* (Oxford, U.K.: Helicon Publishing, Ltd., 1998), 92; Grundy, George Beardoe, *The Great Persian War and its Preliminaries: A Study of the Evidence, Literary and Topographical* (New York: Scribner, 1901), 48–64; Bury, John B., "The European Expedition of Darius," *The Classical Review II,* no. 6 (July 1897): 277–282; Bruce, George, "Marathon," in *Collins Dictionary of Wars* (Glasgow, Scotland: HarperCollins Publishers, 1995), 154; Stirling, William Alexander, earl of Stirling, *The Tragedie of Darius* (Edinburgh: Printed by Robert Walde-graue, 1603).

Davout, Louis-Nicolas (Louis Davoût, Louis Davoust, duc d'Auerstadt, prince d'Eckmühl)
(1770–1823) *French marshal*

Although Louis-Nicolas Davout played an important part in NAPOLEON BONAPARTE's numerous military successes, most Napoleonic histories hardly mention him, if at all, and he remains a shadowy and obscure figure; sources on his life list his name as Davoût and even Davoust. He was born in the French village of Annoux on 10 May 1770 and joined the French army in 1788, when he was about 18 years old. In 1791, he became part of the volunteer corps of the Yonne in the Army of Belgium. During the Wars of the French Revolution, he distinguished himself at the major battle of Neerwinden (18 March 1793), when the Austrian army, under the command of General Prince Frederick of Saxe-Coburg-Gotha, defeated a French-Belgian force and compelled the French to withdraw from Belgium.

Davout was promoted to the rank of brigadier general, but he was struck from the officers' roll when it was discovered he was of noble birth and unable to serve in the rank he held. Despite this, he remained in the military, seeing action in the French campaigns on the Rhine River from 1794 to 1797. When Napoleon went to Egypt, Davout served there under Chevalier Louis-Charles-Antoine Desaix de Veygoux, his close friend, who brought him to Napoleon's attention. Davout's service in Egypt impressed Napoleon: On 10 October 1798, he wrote, "The commanding general wishes to give General of Brigade Davout a testimony of the satisfaction of the government for the service which he has rendered to the armies of the Republic."

Despite this commendation, when Napoleon returned to France he did not select Davout to accompany him, and when Davout was recalled to Paris in 1800, he was not immediately given a command. Some historians have questioned Napoleon's motives for this. Perhaps a reason can be found in a letter written by General Jean-Andoche JUNOT, a friend to both Napoleon and

Davout: "The First Consul [Napoleon] does not like Davoust, because when in Egypt he associated with all of those who made a point of being hostile to Bonaparte. I do not know that Davoust can be justly ranked among the First Consul's enemies; but it is certain that he has inspired him with an antipathy as complete as one man can entertain for another. I am the more sorry for this, inasmuch as Davoust is my comrade and a clever man."

Nevertheless, soon after Davout's return to Europe, Napoleon made him a general of division, and he saw action at Marengo (14 June 1800), where his good friend Desaix was killed on the field of battle. In 1800, Davout refused to sign a letter against Napoleon during the latter's absence from Paris. For this sign of loyalty, Napoleon promoted him to major general (3 July 1800), and he was given command of the cavalry division of the French army in Italy, commanded by General Marshal Guillaume Marie Anne Brune. In 1801, Davout married Napoleon's sister Pauline's sister-in-law. He was promoted to the rank of marshal in 1804, when Napoleon became emperor of the French, and named commander of the III Corps of the French army, the left wing and an integral part of France's Grande Armée. Davout became one of the leaders of Napoleon's campaign against Austria, seeing action at Austerlitz (2 December 1805), when he and his troops force-marched for 36 hours to reinforce the left flank of Napoleon's army and hold off a Russian attack that helped the French attain victory. Historian George Bruce writes that "the allies lost 27,000 killed, wounded, and prisoners, and a large number of guns. The French lost about 8,000 [soldiers]." For his service in this battle, Davout was awarded the Legion d'Honneur (Legion of Honor) and named as colonel general of the Imperial Guard.

Still commander of the III Corps, on 14 October 1806 Davout defeated the duke of Brunswick and his Austrian army at Auerstadt, despite being outnumbered three to one in troops. Although Napoleon, who was fighting at Jena that same day, initially dismissed Davout's victory at Auerstadt, he realized its importance and allowed Davout to enter Berlin as the leader of the armies on 27 October 1806. For this important military triumph, Davout was styled as the duc d'Auerstadt (duke of Auerstadt) in 1808. He was also named as an administrator of the Duchy of Warsaw (1807–09).

Davout proved himself to be one of Napoleon's most important commanders: At Eylau on 8 February 1807, leading some 14,000 troops into battle at the last moment, he again forced defeat on the Russians; at Eckmühl on 22 April 1809, he held Prince Charles and his Austrian forces off until Napoleon could deliver reinforcements, then turned on the Austrians to deliver victory for the French; and at Wagram on 6 July 1809, he again defeated the Austrians. Styled as the prince d'Eckmühl, he was named as commander in chief of the French army in Germany on 1 January 1810, overseeing the administration of the occupied territory until 1812. In this position he promoted Napoleon's Continental System for governing those conquered European states. He later served as the administrator for Hamburg (1813–14).

Following Napoleon's exile to Elba and his subsequent return to power—a period known as "The Hundred Days" for its length—Davout served as minister of war. He was the only one of Napoleon's generals not to have sided with the returned monarch King Louis XVII, and because of his loyalty to Napoleon, he was once again made one of his leading advisers, this time helping to reestablish the Napoleonic army, although not as a commander. This force met a devastating defeat at Waterloo on 18 June 1815, and Davout, in Paris, realized that Napoleon was finished. The new French government asked him to ask the emperor to leave Paris, after which Napoleon was arrested by the British and exiled a final time to the island of St. Helena. On 3 July 1815, Davout, representing Napoleon's government, signed the treaty of surrender and armistice with the coalition that defeated him. He packed his belongings and left Paris.

Davout's last years were painful and without the former glory of his days under Napoleon. Deprived of a military pension, it took him two years of fighting with the new French government to reclaim all of his official titles, including those of the duc d'Auerstadt and the prince d'Eckmühl. In 1819, he was admitted as a member of the French House of Peers, a chamber similar to England's House of Lords. He died in Paris on 1 June 1823. Despite his loyalty to his commander and military record, Louis Nicolas Davout has been largely forgotten except by Napoleonic historians.

References: Gallaher, John G., *The Iron Marshal: A Biography of Louis N. Davout* (Edwardsville, Ill.: Southern Illinois University Press, 1976); De Ségur, Count Philippe-Paul, *Napoleon's Russian Campaign* (Alexandria, Va.: Time/Life Books, 1980); Palmer, Alan, *Napoleon in Russia* (New York: Simon and Schuster, 1967); Bruce, George, "Austerlitz" and "Jena," in *Collins Dictionary of Wars* (Glasgow, Scotland: HarperCollins Publishers, 1995), 25, 118–119; Croly, George, *The Year of Liberation: A Journal of the Defence of Hamburgh against the French Army under Marshal Davoust [sic], in 1813,* 2 vols. (London: James Duncan, 1832); Hawkins, Victor B., "Davout, Louis Nicolas, Duke of Auerstädt, Prince of Eckmühl," in *The Encyclopedia of Military Biography,* edited by Trevor N. Dupuy, Curt Johnson, and David L. Bongard (London: I. B. Taurus & Co., Ltd., 1992), 210.

Dayan, Moshe (1915–1981) *Israeli military commander*

The son of Ukrainian emigrants to Palestine (now modern Israel), Moshe Dayan was born in the kibbutz of Deganyah Alef on 4 May 1915. This village was the first in what became Israel and is known as the "mother of all kibbutzim." Dayan's father, Shmuel, was a dedicated Zionist who spent much of his time fighting local Arabs who attacked the kibbutz's residents. As he grew up, Moshe Dayan served as a kibbutz guard, and when he was only 14 he joined the Haganah, the Jewish underground (and illegal) defense force formed to fight the Arabs who were constantly attacking the Jewish settlers. One of his teachers was Captain Charles Orde Wingate, a British military officer who was trying to keep the Jews and Arabs separated. During a series of riots by Arabs against Jewish settlers, Dayan served with the special Jewish police forces in the Galilee and the Jezreel Valley. In 1938, he became the commander of a series of field units known as the *pluggot sadeh.*

In 1939, Dayan was arrested for being a Haganah member; tried in 1940, he was found guilty and sentenced to 10 years in prison. However, he was released in an amnesty in 1941 in exchange for joining the British army, then fighting in the Middle East against the Germans in Lebanon and Syria. During one battle, he was struck in the face by gunfire and subsequently lost his left eye; he later became well known for the eyepatch he wore. He nonetheless remained a key member of the Haganah while serving with British intelligence and then after the war.

In 1948, Israeli became an independent state, and in the war against Arabs who invaded Israel, Dayan commanded troops in defense of Jewish settlements in the Jordan valley, which included his own kibbutz of Deganyah Alef. Promoted to major, he was given command

of the 89th Battalion. When Egypt attacked the newly founded Jewish state, Dayan led an offensive against them in the city of Lydda and stopped any Egyptian advance. In August 1948, he was promoted to lieutenant colonel and appointed commander of the Etzioni Brigade, Israeli troops fighting for Jerusalem. He was one of the key leaders in helping to push for a cease-fire in July 1949. Because of this, he was one of the Israelis who participated in talks in Rhodes to end the war between Israel and Jordan.

In October 1949, Dayan was promoted to the rank of major general and placed in command of the Israeli Southern Command, located in Beersheba. He oversaw the period of retraining of the infant Israeli army into the modern Israeli Defense Force (IDF), also known as Zahal, making it one of the finest military forces in the world despite its small size. Dayan saw that despite a cease-fire with the Arab states surrounding Israel, they were continuing a military buildup supporting Palestinian terrorists. He felt that Israeli policy should be immediate retaliation for any terrorist attacks, and he directed several operations in what is now the Gaza Strip.

Dayan served as the commander in chief of the Israeli army from December 1953 until January 1958. On 29 October 1956, he led Israeli forces in the invasion of the Sinai Peninsula, destroying Egyptian military forces there. Historians Martin Windrow and Francis K. Mason write: "The Sinai Campaign of October–November 1956, which coincided with the Anglo-French invasion of the Suez Canal Zone, was a complete vindication of Dayan's philosophy that the whole of Zahal should be able to operate at the level of commando units of other nations. Speed, surprise, and determination were the keynotes, together with a through understanding of the enemy. Dayan took risks which would have been unforgivable against a European enemy, but which paid off handsomely in practice."

In 1958, Dayan retired from the Israeli army, and the following year he was elected to the Israeli Knesset (Parliament) as a member of the Mapai Party. In the cabinet of Prime Minister David Ben-Gurion, he took the position of minister of agriculture, serving from 1959 to 1963 and from 1963 to 1964 in the same position in Prime Minister Levi Eshkol's cabinet; however, he resigned following a disagreement with Eshkol over policy. Dayan then joined the retired Ben-Gurion to form the Rafi Party, also known as the Alliance of Israel's Workers Party. In 1965, he was elected again to the Knesset as a member of the Rafi Party, which eventually merged with the Labor Party.

Dayan, however, was outside politics, and when another Arab-Israeli war threatened in 1967, Eshkol named him as minister of defense. Dayan had barely taken office when, following a series of attacks by Syria on northern Israel, he and Eshkol agreed that a full-scale assault on several Arab nations—Syria, Jordan, and Egypt—was necessary. This offensive began on 5 June 1967; the Arabs, taken completely by surprise, could not muster any kind of defense, and within six days they were suing for peace. Israel's victory in the Six-Day War was complete: The small nation captured the West Bank and eastern Jerusalem from Jordan, the Golan Heights from Syria, and the Gaza Strip and the entire Sinai Peninsula from Egypt. Under Dayan, Israel had risen to become a respected recognized nation after one of the most dramatic fast-moving campaigns the world had ever seen.

In 1969, following Eshkol's death, Golda Meir became the first female prime minister of Israel, and she retained Dayan as defense minister. He continued Israel's buildup of control over areas it had captured, but he did not foresee a lightning attack from Egypt, which began on 6 October 1973, the Yom Kippur holiday. Egyptian forces crossed the Suez Canal and took Israeli troops completely by surprise; by 22 October, Israel and Egypt had negotiated a cease-fire. Despite Dayan's years of service, the entire military disaster was blamed on him, and there were calls for his resignation. A commission established to investigate the failure placed the blame on several field officers rather than Dayan, but his usefulness to Meir was finished. He resigned his portfolio in June 1974, two months after she resigned as prime minister.

Although it appeared that his career in the military and Israeli politics was over, Dayan remained a respected figure. In 1977, Menachem Begin, a member of the Likud Party, was elected prime minister, and he named Dayan, a member of the opposition Labor Party, as foreign minister. Despite the fact that he was a lifelong warrior who had spent much of his life fighting Arab enemies of his homeland, he took the position with an eye toward finding peace with these adversaries. Taking office, he began negotiations with his archenemies the Egyptians and eventually reached a compromise in which Egypt agreed to recognize Israeli control over the West Bank and the Gaza Strip in exchange for the return of the Sinai Peninsula to Egypt. In landmark talks that

eventually brought together Prime Minister Begin and Egyptian president Anwar Sadat at Camp David under the auspices of U.S. president Jimmy Carter, the agreement was signed in September 1978. Dayan the warrior had worked to bring peace to Israel.

In 1979, Dayan discovered he was suffering from inoperable colon cancer. Resigning from government in a disagreement with Begin, he spent his final months writing his memoirs. He founded a new political party, Telem, which advocated full sovereignty for the Palestinians and Israeli withdrawal from the West Bank and Gaza Strip. In 1980, he was elected to the Knesset as a member of Telem (which later went out of existence). Dayan died in Tel Aviv on 16 October 1981 at the age of 66 and was buried with full military honors. He was the author of four books, including *Moshe Dayan: Story of My Life* (1976) and *Breakthrough: A Personal Account of the Egypt-Israel Peace Negotiations* (1981).

Historian Michael Lee Lanning writes of Dayan's legacy: "The achievements of Dayan are extensive yet simple: the state of Israel, despite wholesale enemies, continues to exist. Dayan is remarkable not only for his feats but also for his innate abilities to train and lead men. His military education came not from academies or service school but from the kibbutz and the battlefield. Dayan's professional skills in training his army and his aggressiveness and flexibility on the battlefield made the IDF one of the world's most efficient, effective fighting forces of all time."

References: Lau-Lavie, Naphtali, *Moshe Dayan: A Biography* (London: Vallentine, Mitchell, 1968); Dayan, Moshe, *Moshe Dayan: Story of My Life* (New York: Morrow, 1976); Slater, Robert, *Warrior Statesman: The Life of Moshe Dayan* (New York: St. Martin's Press, 1991); Windrow, Martin, and Francis K. Mason. "Dayan, Moshe," in *The Wordsworth Dictionary of Military Biography*, (Hertfordshire, U.K.: Wordsworth Editions Ltd., 1997), 74–78; Lanning, Michael Lee, "Moshe Dayan," *The Military 100: A Ranking of the Most Influential Military Leaders of All Time* (New York: Barnes and Noble Books, 1996), 255–258.

Decatur, Stephen (1779–1820) *American naval officer*

Born at Sinnepuxent, Maryland, on 5 January 1779, Stephen Decatur was the son of a merchant ship captain and naval officer of French descent. He received his education at the University of Pennsylvania, but he was forced to enter the military after being tried and acquitted for murdering a prostitute in Philadelphia. He joined the United States Navy on 20 April 1798, when it was first formed, with the rank of midshipman; he was promoted to the rank of lieutenant on 21 May 1799, serving on the USS *United States.*

Decatur first saw action during the naval war with France (1798–1800), when his quick temper also resulted in several duels. After being promoted in 1799, he was given command of the USS *Argus.* It was while serving in the Tripolitan War (1801–05), a conflict with pirates in the Mediterranean, that Decatur earned his place in history. A number of small city-states on the shores of northern Africa—situated in what is now present-day Libya—had long preyed on ships in the Mediterranean. Reassigned as the commander of the USS *Enterprise,* one of the ships in the fleet under the command of Commodore Edward Preble, Decatur captured a pirate ship, the *Mastico,* which he renamed the USS *Intrepid.* After the pirates captured the USS *Philadelphia,* Decatur led a small group of American sailors into Tripoli harbor on 16 February 1804 and burned the ship to keep it from it being used in the pirate fleet. Later that same year, he led another group of sailors into Tripoli harbor and defeated a Tripolitan force in a landmark battle. For these actions, he was promoted to the rank of captain on 16 February 1804.

For the next decade, Decatur was the commander of several warships, including the USS *Constitution* and the USS *Chespeake.* In 1807, he served as a judge on the court-martial of Captain James Barron, who had fought a battle against a British warship. The court finding that Barron was guilty caused increased bitterness between the two men, an anger that would lead to tragedy.

During the War of 1812 with Great Britain, Decatur again distinguished himself, capturing the HMS *Macedonian* on 25 October 1812. On 15 January 1815, as the commander of the USS *President,* he was forced to concede defeat against several British warships in New York harbor, although the HMS *Endymion* was destroyed. Captured, Decatur was imprisoned in Bermuda for several weeks until he was paroled. A naval board of inquiry cleared him of any bad judgment. When the war ended, Decatur served as commander of the U.S. Mediterranean Squadron so effectively that the dey of Algiers signed a peace treaty to avoid another conflict. It was at a dinner during these negotiations that Decatur

Stephen Decatur

gave his famous toast to America: "Our country! In her intercourse with foreign nations may she always be in the right; but our country right or wrong!"

Returning to the United States, Decatur served on the Board of Navy Commissioners, an oversight committee for the U.S. Navy, and this led to his tragic death. When his old enemy James Barron asked for his reinstatement to the navy, a move that could only be sanctioned by the board, Decatur led the way in refusing the request. Because of this stand, Barron challenged Decatur to a duel, and the two men met in Bladensburg, Maryland, on 22 March 1820. In deference to the older Barron, Decatur demanded a shorter length between the two men and told people beforehand that he would not shoot to kill. When the time came, Decatur fired a shot that hit Barron in the thigh; Barron, however, shot Decatur in the chest, a mortal wound. He died in agony 12 hours later. He was initially buried in the tomb of a friend, Joel Barlow, in Washington, but his remains were removed to Philadelphia and laid to rest there.

References: Mackenzie, Alexander Slidell, *Life of Decatur, a Commodore in the Navy of the United States* (Boston: C. C. Little and J. Brown, 1846); Crompton, Samuel Willard, "Decatur, Stephen," in *American National Biography,* 24 vols., edited by John A. Garraty and Mark C. Carnes (New York: Oxford University Press, 1999), 6:325–326; Lewis, Charles Lee, *The Romantic Decatur* (Philadelphia: University of Pennsylvania Press, 1937); Dunne, William M. P., "Pistols and Honor: The James Barron-Stephen Decatur Conflict, 1798–1807," *American Neptune* 50, no. 4 (1990): 245–259; *Correspondence, between the Late Commodore Stephen Decatur and Commodore James Barron, which led to the Unfortunate Meeting of the Twenty Second of March* (Boston: Russell & Gardner, 1820).

Decius, Gaius Messius Quintus Traianus (ca. 201–251) *Roman emperor*

It is possible that his short reign as emperor, combined with his death in battle, accounts for why so little is known of Gaius Decius. A Pannonian, he was apparently born around A.D. 201 at Budalia, near Sirmium (in, roughly, today's Hungary; described by historian William Hazlitt as "A city of Pannonia . . . on Savus flumen ["a flowing stream"], at its confluence with Bacuntius"). He had most likely been a member of the Roman Senate for some time when, in 245, Emperor Philip gave him the command of a military expedition to the Danube. About 248 or 249, his troops, who loved him, proclaimed him emperor against Philip, who, when the news reached Rome, gathered his own military force to end Decius's "reign." In 249, the two armies met near Verona, in Italy, where Decius's troops were victorious and Philip was slain.

At the same time that he was ending Philip's reign, Decius was forced to deal with several rebellious threats from outside forces. The most serious of these was from the Goths, who marched westward on Rome. The details of the encounter are unfortunately lost to history. It is known that Decius's army faced the Goths at Abrittus, near Dobruja, on the border of today's Romania

and Bulgaria, in June 251. During the battle, Decius and his son, Gaius Valens Hostilianus Messius Quintus (called Herennius in one source), were both slain, and the Goths overran the Roman army.

Decius was forgotten almost as soon as his death was confirmed. Even his intended successor, Publius Licinius Valerianus (Valerian), was tossed aside for another, although later he served as Roman emperor from 253 to 260.

References: Hazlitt, William, "Sirmium," in *The Classical Gazetteer: A Dictionary of Ancient Geography, Sacred and Profane* (London: Whittaker & Son, 1851), 321; "Decius," in *The Penguin Dictionary of Ancient History,* edited by Graham Speake (London: Penguin Books, 1995), 192–193; Wolfram, Herwig, *History of the Goths* (Berkeley: University of California Press, 1988); Bradley, Henry, *The Story of the Goths, from the Earliest Times to the End of the Gothic Dominion in Spain* (New York: G. P. Putnam's Sons, 1888).

de Clare, Richard FitzGilbert *See* CLARE, RICHARD FITZGILBERT DE, SECOND EARL OF PEMBROKE.

Denikin, Anton Ivanovich (1872–1947) *Russian general*

Born near Warsaw, Poland, then under Russian rule, on 16 December 1872 (or 4 December 1872 [O.S.]) Anton Ivanovich Denikin was the son of a serf. He entered military service in the Czar's army, attending the Junker School in Kiev and the Academy of the General Staff, both important Russian military academies, and rose rapidly from the rank of captain to colonel. He saw service during the Russo-Japanese War (1904–05), a disastrous campaign for the Russians, but he was considered a rising star in the Russian military. In 1914, when the First World War broke out, Denikin, then serving as chief of staff of the Kiev military district, was named deputy chief of staff under General Alexei Alexseievich BRUSILOV's Eighth Army. A month after the war began, he was made commander of the 4th Russian Rifle Brigade and sent to Galicia in Poland. He subsequently became the commander of the Russian VIII Corps and served under Brusilov during the Brusilov Offensive against Austrian troops in June 1916. Because of his ser-

General Anton Denikin

vice during this campaign, Denikin was named chief of staff of the southwestern front.

Following the war's end, Denikin returned to Russia, where Czar Nicholas, the head of the Romanov dynasty, had been overthrown in a bloodless coup in February 1917—the February Revolution—and a government under Alexander Kerensky had been established. Although Denikin had served the czar faithfully for more than a decade, he was a strong supporter of Nicholas's removal from power. His shifting loyalties allowed him to work under successive regimes, and he served as chief of staff to Generals Brusilov, Mikhail Alexeyev, and Lavr Kornilov. When Kornilov attempted a military coup to bring a military government to Russia, Denikin supported him, but the coup plot collapsed and both men were arrested and taken to the city of

Bykova. The two men escaped together when Vladimir Lenin and the Bolsheviks seized power in October 1917. Denikin joined with Kornilov and Alexeyev to form the nucleus of what was to become the anti-Bolshevik, or White, army; Alexeyev established a military force in Rostov and Novocherkassk on the Don River. On 13 April 1918, Kornilov died, and Denikin succeeded him as commander of the Whites, while Alexeyev served as the political leader of the ragtag army.

Working with other dissident groups, including the Don Cossacks under General Petr Krasnov and czarist troops under General Nikolai Drozdovsky, Denikin began a campaign against the Bolsheviks (also called the Reds) in the Caucasus mountains (June 1918). Within three months, a rapid series of victories against the Reds led to an increase in the numbers of Denikin's forces from 9,000 to over 40,000. Assistance from the allied countries, including the United States, aided the Whites' cause. By February 1919, Denikin's army had faced down more than 150,000 trained Bolshevist troops and pushed the Reds to near surrender. General Alexeyev died on 25 September 1918, and Denikin became the commander in chief of the armed forces of Southern Russia.

By the middle of 1919, Denikin was on the verge of defeating the Bolsheviks and bringing an end to Communist rule in Russia. His force had grown to over 150,000 well-trained troops, and they were marching across southern Russia unopposed. He had seized the cities of Odessa, Kiev, Poltava, Kharkov, and controlled more than 400,000 square miles of territory. It appeared that with some military assistance from the Allies, Denikin would move onto the Bolshevists and defeat them once and for all. In May 1919, he launched a huge offensive against the Reds. Denikin's rapid victories allowed his army to move through the Ukraine and north toward Moscow. However, he did not know that the Communist government in Moscow had strengthened its front-line troops, which held him off.

In October 1919, Denikin's White forces were defeated at Oryol, and the following month General Semyon BUDENNY's Red forces met Denikin's troops at Kupyansk and broke through the White lines, forcing a retreat. In March 1920, Bolshevist forces retook Rostov, and Denikin evacuated his forces to the Crimea. These reverses were the end of his leadership: In April 1920, he reluctantly handed over control of the White armies to General Peter Nikolayevich Wrangel and left for exile in France. In 1946, he moved to the United States and settled in Ann Arbor, Michigan, where he died on 8 August 1947 at the age of 74. Despite having desired that his body be returned to Russia, he was laid to rest in a Russian cemetery in Jackson, New Jersey.

In 1994, following the end of Communist rule in Russia, a monument was erected at the All Saints Church in Sokol in Russia; titled "Reconciliation of the Peoples Who Fought in the First and Second Wars, and the Civil War," it was dedicated in Denikin's name. On 8 August 2002, on the 55th anniversary of Denikin's death, a memorial was held in Moscow to honor his life.

References: Denikin, Anton Ivanovich, *The Career of a Tsarist Officer: Memoirs, 1872–1916,* translated by Margaret Patoski (Minneapolis: University of Minneapolis Press, 1975); Lehovich, Dimitry V., *White Against Red: The Life of General Anton Denikin* (New York: Norton, 1974); Hodgson, John Ernest, *With Denikin's Armies: Being a Description of the Cossack Counter-Revolution in South Russia, 1918–1920* (London: L. Williams, Temple Bar Publishing Company, 1932); Rosenberg, William G., *A. I. Denikin and the anti-Bolshevik Movement in South Russia* (Amherst, Mass.: Amherst College Press, 1961).

de Wet, Christiaan Rudolf de   *See* WET, CHRISTIAAN RUDOLF DE.

Dewey, George   (1837–1917)   *American admiral*
George Dewey was born in Montpelier, Vermont, on 26 December 1837, the son of a local physician who was founder of the National Life Insurance Company, where two of his sons joined him. For George Dewey, however, a naval career was his only goal, and he began on this road in 1852 when, at the age of 15, he enrolled in Norwich University, a military academy in Hanover, New Hampshire. After two years in that institution, he received an appointment to the United States Naval Academy at Annapolis, Maryland. Graduating fifth in his class from Annapolis in 1858, Dewey was commissioned a lieutenant in 1861 when the U.S. Civil War began.

Dewey was assigned to the *Mississippi,* an old steam frigate that participated in the Union blockade of southern ports during the war. In 1862, he was promoted to executive officer of the *Mississippi,* and he saw action at the battle of New Orleans (24–25 April 1862). At the battle of Port Hudson, Louisiana (14 March 1863), the *Mississippi* caught fire and sank. Dewey was then transferred to become executive officer of the *Monongahela,* the flagship of Admiral David FARRAGUT's naval force in the Mississippi River region. By the end of the Civil War, he had been promoted to the rank of lieutenant commander and was serving as executive officer of the *Kearsarge.*

Following the war, Dewey was posted as an instructor at Annapolis for three years. In 1870, he was put in command of the sloop *Narragansett;* however, when that ship needed repairs, he was transferred to the store ship *Supply,* and, in 1871, was ordered to sail to France to bring food and other supplies to war victims of the Franco-Prussian War. By the time he reached Cherbourg, the war had ended, and Dewey instead left the supplies in London before sailing home. In 1872, he was promoted to the rank of commander and assigned to a torpedo station in Newport, Rhode Island.

When his wife died in childbirth, Dewey asked to be relieved of duty in Rhode Island and was placed in command of the *Narragansett* a second time. This time the ship was sent to the Pacific Ocean to survey the

Admiral George Dewey

lower part of California and a portion of the Mexican coast. In 1875, tired of this duty, Dewey was relieved of command and allowed to serve as a lighthouse inspector in Boston. In 1878, he was named by Secretary of the Navy Richard W. Thompson to the Lighthouse Board in Washington, where he served until 1882. Two years later, he was promoted to the full rank of captain, and, in 1896, to commodore.

In 1897, Dewey was named commander of the Asiatic squadron of the United States Navy, succeeding Admiral Frederick G. McNair, and placed in command of the USS *Olympia,* the flagship of the Asiatic fleet. On 15 February 1898, the USS *Maine* exploded in Havana harbor in Cuba, then ruled by Spain. When an investigative body of the Department of the Navy held that an outside source—probably Spanish provocatives—had blown the ship up, the United States declared war on Spain. Dewey, who had sailed to Hong Kong four days before the *Maine* was destroyed, was ordered to sail to the Philippines, a Spanish possession in the Pacific Ocean; the telegram, from Assistant Secretary of the Navy Theodore Roosevelt, instructed him: "Proceed at once to the Philippine Islands. Commence operations . . . against Spanish fleet. You must capture Spanish vessels or destroy."

The *Olympia* and Dewey's squadron of four cruisers, two gunboats, and one revenue cutter reached Manila Bay on 30 April 1898. They faced a fleet of seven Spanish warships, part of a navy considered to be the best in the world at the time. Dewey therefore planned a night attack in the harbor rather than face the Spanish in the open sea. At 5:40 A.M. on May 1, the Americans began to attack the Spanish ships anchored at Cavite Point in Manila Bay. Just before the attack, Dewey issued what is probably the most famous order in American naval warfare, telling the captain of his flagship: "You may fire when you are ready, Gridley." The Spanish squadron was commanded by Rear Admiral Patricio Montojo y Pasarón, who led with the cruiser *Reina Cristina.* Dewey's early move sealed the fate of the Spanish when they were hemmed into between Cavite and Sangley Point, and the seven Spanish ships were soon sunk or rendered useless. The Spanish lost 323 men killed and 151 wounded; the Americans lost just one man due to heat prostration. Dewey's victory rates as a decisive American naval victory, even though it was later learned that the Spanish ships were in fact in poor condition and the troops demoralized.

The United States Congress passed a resolution thanking Dewey for his service, as well as the officers and men in his command, and authorized the secretary of the navy to "present a sword of honor to Commodore George Dewey, and cause to be struck bronze medals commemorating the battle of Manila Bay . . ." Nine days after the battle, Dewey was promoted to rear admiral, and on 3 March 1899, he was promoted to the rank of admiral—only the third American naval officer to be so honored (the other two were David Farragut and David Dixon Porter). Returning to the United States, Dewey was given a hero's parade in New York City.

Despite his victory, Dewey never served again in a military capacity. He attempted a run for the U.S. presidency in 1900 but withdrew after a few days. That same year, President William McKinley named him president of the General Board of the Navy, assisting in transforming the 19th-century American navy into a 20th-century fighting force. He later served on two other commissions; as chair of the court of inquiry that investigated the conduct of Rear Admiral Winfield Scott Schley during the American occupation of the Philippines, and as chair of the joint army-navy board that examined better cooperation between the services. He published his memoirs in 1913.

George Dewey died in Washington, D.C., on 16 January 1917. As he lay dying, his last words were: "Gentlemen, the battle is done . . . the victory . . . is ours!" He was laid to rest initially in Arlington National Cemetery, but in 1925 his remains were moved to the National Cathedral in Washington, D.C.

References: Spector, Ronald H., *Admiral of the New Empire: The Life and Career of George Dewey* (Baton Rouge: Louisiana State University Press, 1974); Ellis, Edward Sylvester, *Dewey and Other Naval Commanders* (New York: Hovendon & Company, 1899); West, Richard S., *Admirals of American Empire: The Combined Story of George Dewey, Alfred Thayer Mahan, Winfield Scott Schley, and William Thomas Sampson* (Indianapolis: Bobbs-Merrill, 1948); Lanning, Michael Lee, "George Dewey," in *The Military 100: A Ranking of the Most Influential Military Leaders of All Time* (New York: Barnes and Noble Books, 1996), 335–337; Conroy, Robert, *The Battle of Manila Bay: The Spanish-American War in the Philippines* (New York: The Macmillan Company, 1968).

Don John of Austria *See* JOHN OF AUSTRIA.

Drake, Sir Francis (ca. 1540–1596) *English sailor*
Francis Drake was born about 1540, although his exact date of birth is unknown, near Tavistock in Devonshire, southwestern England. When he was a child, Drake and his family were forced to move to Kent because of his father Robert's Protestantism in a Catholic area. The few facts known of his early life come from a 1626 work by his nephew, also named Sir Francis Drake, entitled *Drake Revisited.* Historians disagree about how he began his life at sea: One source in the archives of Venice reports that he was a page to King Philip of Spain in England, although he never spoke Spanish and the evidence is thin at best. Some historians claim that he was probably apprenticed as a sailor on a small vessel owned by an old man into whose care Drake was put. When the man died, he left the ship to Drake, who used it for trading purposes for some time. However, about 1565 he joined a small group of ships under Captain John Lovell to sail to Guinea in trade there, even though this was against Spanish policy. In 1567, he took command of the *Judith,* a commercial ship on which sailed his kinsman Sir John HAWKINS, who also became one of England's great naval heroes in his time. Other ships in this expedition to San Juan de Lua were destroyed by the Spanish navy, but the *Judith* and another ship returned to England, and Drake was applauded as a hero.

Drake spent the next year unsuccessfully suing the Spanish government for his losses, so he again sailed ships to the West Indies in 1570 and 1571 to try and recoup there. After returning to England a second time in 1571, Drake recruited a number of English seamen to sail to the New World, including ports in the Caribbean, "with intent to land at Nombre de Dios . . . [and] the granary of the West Indies, wherein the golden harvest brought from Peru and Mexico to Panama was hoarded up till it could be conveyed to Spain." Sailing from Plymouth in May 1572, the ships reached the Caribbean in July 1572. There, they attacked various Spanish fortifications and took control of Spanish ships and stores of supplies, most notably at the Isle of Pines (now in Cuba). Landing at Nombre de Dios, Drake and his forces marched onto the Spanish town and after a pitched battle—during which he was wounded in the thigh—the English won a quick victory. They then moved into the Isthmus of Panama, to a point where Drake saw the Pacific Ocean for the first time.

In 1573, Drake and his men returned to England as heroes. One source noted that "the news of Drake's return did so speedily pass over all the church and surpass their minds with desire and delight to see him, that very few or none remained with the preacher, all hastening to see the evidence of God's love and blessing towards our gracious queen and country." He met with Queen Elizabeth and soon received from her a commission to continue his activities with the Crown's authority; this amounted to a declaration of war against Spain.

Drake assembled a squadron of five ships, including his own ship the *Pelican,* and in December 1577 this expedition sailed from Plymouth toward the coast of South America. Bad weather caused the destruction of two of the ships, but the *Pelican* and two others arrived at South America in April 1578. There, crossing through the Straits of Magellan, Drake renamed his ship *The Golden Hind.* Storms in the straits sank one ship with all on board, and the other ship, crippled, turned back and reached England in June 1579. Drake and his single ship reached the Pacific Ocean in October 1578, and he used *The Golden Hind* to plunder various Spanish settlements on the coasts of what are now Chile and Peru. Among other adventures, his men were attacked by Indians (who shot Drake in the face with an arrow). In March 1579, they captured the *Cacafeugo,* a Spanish ship carrying incredible amounts of gold and other treasure. *The Golden Hind* moved up the coast of the Americas, stopping somewhere near either northern Mexico or what is now southern California for repairs. Drake then sailed across the Pacific, through the Indian Ocean, and around the southern tip of Africa before he returned to England in September 1580 to a hero's welcome. It is said that his ship was "very richly fraught with gold, silver, silk, pearls, and precious stones." In April 1581, Queen Elizabeth visited Drake on board his ship and knighted him for his service to England and for circumnavigating the globe. The treasure he had brought back was estimated in value at a million and a half pounds, and with his share of this, Drake purchased a home, Buckland Abbey, near Plymouth.

In 1585, when England declared war on Spain following an embargo placed on English shipping by the Spanish king, Queen Elizabeth offered to the sailing men of her nation 25 ships "to revenge the wrongs offered her, and to resist the king of Spain's preparations." Drake was made the head of this fleet, commanding in the ship *Elizabethan Bonaventure.* It sailed from Plymouth on 14 September 1585 with Martin Frobisher as vice admiral. When they arrived in this Caribbean, Drake's force raided the island of Vigo, the village of St. Iago (which they burnt down), and landed on Hispaniola, where land forces under Sir Christopher Carleill took the towns of San Domingo (now in the Dominican Republic), and, later, Cartagena.

Two years later, in 1587, Drake led an important raid on the port of Cádiz, Spain, sinking a reported 33 Spanish ships. This delayed the Spanish Armada, a feared fleet of warships, from sailing to invade England, which allowed the English to prepare superior sea forces. In the newspaper *The English Mercurie,* printed in July 1588, the following appeared:

> Earlie this Morninge arrived a Messenger at Sir *Francis Walsingham*'s Office, with Letters of the 22d [of July] from the Lorde High Admirall [Lord Howard] on board the *Ark-Royal,* containinge the followinge materiall Advices.
>
> On the 20th of the Instant Capt. *Fleming,* who had beene ordered to cruize in the Chops of the Channell, for Discoverie, brought Advice into Plymouth, that he had descried the Spanish Armado near the Lizard, making for the Entrance of the Channell with a favourable Gale. Though this Intelligence was not received till near foure in the Afternoone, and the Winde at that time blew hard into the Sound, yet by the indefatigable Care and Dilligence of the Lord High Admiral, the *Ark-Royal,* with five of the largest Frigates, anchored out of the Harbour that very Eveninge. The next Morninge, the greatest part of her Maiestie's Fleet gott out to them. They made in all about eight Sail, divided into four Squadrons, commanded by his Lordship in Person, Sir Francis Drake Vice-Admiral, and the Rear-Admirals Hawkins and Frobisher. But about one in the Afternoone, they came in Sighte of the Spanish Armado two Leagues to the Westward of the Eddistone, failing in the Form of a half-Moon, the Points whereof were seven Leagues asunder . . . The Lord High Admirall observing his generall Alacritic, after a Council of War had beene held, directed the Signall of Battle to be hung out. We

attacked the Enemy's Reare with the Advantage of the Winde . . . In the meane tyme, Sir Francis Drake and the two Rear-Admirals Hawkins and Frobisher, vigorously broadsided the Enemies sternmost Ships commanded by Vice-Admiral Recalde, which were forced to retreat much shattered to the main Body of their Fleet. . . .

The victory of Howard, Drake, Hawkins, and Frobisher over the Spanish was one of the turning points in English history.

Drake returned home, again as a hero, and temporarily settled into a quiet life at his home near Plymouth. However, in 1595 he was again called upon to go to sea and attack the Spanish in the Caribbean, where, commanding the *Defiance,* he raided Spanish forts in what is now Panama. However, after the start of the new year, 1596, he came down with a disease most historians feel was probably yellow fever (although William Laird Clowes, in a history of the English Royal Navy, says it was dysentery). He took to bed on his ship, where he succumbed on 28 January 1596 (a few days following the death of Hawkins). His remains were placed in a lead coffin, and he was buried in the sea off the coast of Panama.

The place of Sir Francis Drake in the history of England is secure, although his circumnavigation of the world is perhaps better known than his service in the defense of his homeland. In his work on the history of commanders in world history, historian James Lucas wrote of Drake: "The revolution in naval warfare of the 16th century meant that new tactics and strategies had to be devised to make full use of the new technology. Francis Drake was one of the seamen who grasped this idea wholeheartedly, with a full tactical and strategical understanding of the new power the galleon and the cannon would provide in combination."

References: Bell, Douglas Herbert, *Drake* (London: Duckworth, 1935); Sugden, John, *Sir Francis Drake* (New York: Holt, 1990); Corbett, Sir Julian Stafford, *Drake and the Tudor Navy; With a History of the Rise of England as a Maritime Power* (London: Longmans, Green, 1898); *The English Hero: Or, Sir Fran. Drake Reviv'd. Being a Full Account of the Dangerous Voyages, Admirable Adventures, Notable Discoveries, and Magnanimous Achievements of that valiant and Renowned Commander . . .* (London: Printed for N. Crouch, 1698); Drake, Sir Francis, Bart., *The World Encompassed by Sir Francis Drake, being his next voyage to* *that to Nombre de Dios formerly imprinted . . .* (London: Printed for Nicholas Bourne, 1628); "Some New Spanish Documents Dealing with Drake," *The English Historical Review* 193 (January 1934): 14–31; *The English Mercurie. Published by Authoritie. For the Prevention of False Reportes* (London: Printed by C. Barker, 1588), 1–4; Maynarde, Thomas, *Sir Francis Drake his Voyage, 1595 . . .* (London: Hakluyt Society, 1849); "Drake, Sir Francis," in *Command: From Alexander the Great to Zhukov—The Greatest Commanders of World History,* edited by James Lucas. (London: Bloomsbury Publishing, 1988), 36–37; Clowes, William Laird, *The Royal Navy: A History From the Earliest Times to the Present* (London: Sampson Low, Marston and Company, 1897).

E

Early, Jubal Anderson (1816–1894) *Confederate general*

Born in Franklin County, Virginia, on 3 November 1816, Early entered the U.S. Military Academy at West Point, graduating in 1837. He saw his first action in the Second Seminole War (1835–42), fighting the Seminole in Florida, but after in 1838 he resigned his commission to return home and begin practicing law. He sat as a member of the Virginia legislature in 1841 and 1842, and served as commonwealth attorney from 1842 to 1852. During the Mexican-American War (1846–48), he was a member of the Virginia Volunteers with the rank of major (1847–48).

In 1861, following the election of Republican Abraham Lincoln as president of the United States, several southern slave states held conventions to vote on seceding from the American union. Early was a delegate to the Virginia Convention, and although he had been opposed to secession, the bitter hatred of Lincoln expressed by others at the parley changed his mind, and he ultimately backed Virginia's leaving the Union. With the formation of the Confederate States of America and an army to defend the South, Early was commissioned a colonel in the 24th regiment of the Virginia Infantry. On 21 July 1861, he led the right flank of Confederate forces in the defeat of Union troops at Manassas Junction, or First Bull Run. For his service in this action,

Early was promoted to brigadier general, and after seeing additional action in 1861 and 1862, he was promoted to major general in January 1863. He led sections of Confederate forces at Antietam (17 September 1862), Fredericksburg (11–15 December 1862), Chancellorsville (1–3 May 1863), Gettysburg (1–3 July 1863), and the Wilderness (5–7 May 1864).

As the tide of the war turned against the Confederacy, Early took command of the Valley District of the Department of Northern Virginia, later commanding the III Corps of the Army of Northern Virginia. In May 1864, he was promoted to the rank of lieutenant general, and the following month he defeated Union forces in the Shenandoah Valley. At the Monocacy River on 9 July 1864, Early's troops, numbering some 14,000, routed approximately 6,000 Union forces under Major General Lewis Wallace, leaving nearly 1,900 Union and 700 Confederate casualties. However, his battle with Wallace gave the Union commander, General Ulysses S. GRANT, the time to send reinforcements to Washington, D.C., ending any chance of a Confederate attack on the Union capital. (Nonetheless, Early's men had advanced to within a few hundred yards of the White House.) Seeing Early as a threat, Grant, sent an enormous force order General Philip SHERIDAN against the southern officer, forcing Early's army to stand heroically at Fisher's Hill (21–22 September 1864), where he was defeated, and at Cedar

95

Jubal Anderson Early

Creek (19 October 1864), where he should have won a brilliant victory but lost. He staged a final resistance at Waynesboro (2 March 1865) and won the battle, but for Early and the Southern cause it was too late.

With the end of the war, Early went to Texas, then to Mexico, and finally to exile in Canada. In 1869, when the threat of prosecution for treason had passed, he returned to Virginia, where he resumed his law practice. He published his memoirs, *Autobiographical Sketch and Narrative,* in 1866 and *A Memoir of the Last Year of the War* in 1867. Early served as president of the Southern Historical Association, helping to preserve and advance the reputations of such Confederate leaders as Robert E. LEE, Thomas "Stonewall" JACKSON, and others. In his later years, he moved to New Orleans, Louisiana, where he retired and also worked with former Confederate general P. G. T. Beauregard on the Louisiana lottery. He died in Lynchburg, Virginia, on 2 March 1894 at the age of 77.

References: Early, Jubal, *Jubal Early's Memoirs: Autobiographical Sketch and Narrative of the War Between the*

States (Baltimore, Md.: Nautical & Aviation Publishing Company of America, 1989); Bushong, Millard Kessler, *Old Jube: A Biography of General Jubal A. Early* (Boyce, Va.: Carr Publishing Company, 1955); Gallagher, Gary W., *Jubal A. Early, the Lost Cause, and Civil War History: A Persistent Legacy* (Milwaukee, Wis.: Marquette University Press, 1995); Mahr, Theodore C., *The Battle of Cedar Creek: Showdown in the Shenandoah, October 1–30, 1864: Early's Valley Campaign* (Lynchburg, Va.: H. E. Howard, 1992).

Edmund II Ironside (ca. 980–1016) *English king*
Born about 980 or 981, Edmund was the son of King Ethelred the Unready (reigned 978–1016). Ethelred died on 22 April 1016, and his son was crowned king of England at St. Paul's Cathedral in London the following day. The year before, he had defied his father and married Ealdgith, the widow of a Danish lord, one of many who had invaded England.

After the Dane Cnut Sveinsson—better known today as Canute—invaded England in 1015, Edmund raised a small army to resist him. In 1016, Edmund fought four major battles against Canute's forces, including at Penselwood and Sherston, and Edmund turned back to defeat Canute's siege of London. However, on 18 October 1016 at Assandun (now Ashingdon, in Essex), Edmund and his forces suffered a devastating defeat when the Mercians, one of the clans in his force, refused to fight. Canute decided to meet Edmund at a summit at Deerhurst, an island in the River Seven, where the two men reached an agreement to divide the English kingdom between them.

Edmund—who had earned the nickname "Ironside" from wearing armor in battle—died mysteriously on 30 November 1016, having either been murdered or succumbed to disease; he was buried in the Glastonbury Abbey. Canute then took control of all of England, reigning until his own death in 1035.

References: Hunt, William, "Edmund or Eadmund, called Ironside," in *The Dictionary of National Biography,* 22 vols., edited by Sir Leslie Stephen and Sir Sidney Lee, et al. (London: Oxford University Press, 1921–22), VI:403–405; Hilliam, David, "Edmund II (Ironside)," in *Kings, Queens, Bones and Bastards: Who's Who in the English Monarchy from Egbert to Elizabeth II* (Thrupp, Stroud, Gloucestershire, U.K.: Sutton Publishing, 1998), 20–21;

Boswell, E., ed., *Edmond Ironside; or, War Hath made All Friends* (London: Oxford University Press, 1928).

Edward I (1239–1307) *English king*

Edward I, the eldest son of King Henry III (1207–72) and Eleanor of Provence, was born at Westminster, London, on 17 June 1239. It is said that when presented with this heir to the throne, Henry named him Edward "after the glorious king and confessor [Edward the Confessor], whose body rests in the Church of St. Peter." In 1254, when Edward was 15, his father gave him grants of land and numerous titles, paving the way for his ascension to the English throne. That same year, he was sent by arrangement to Castile, Spain, where he married Eleanor, the half sister of King Alfonso X of Spain. Edward was close to his maternal uncle, Simon de MONTFORT, earl of Leicester, who argued with Henry about the Provisions of Westminster (1259), a piece of legislation that, like the Provisions of Oxford the year before, reduced the king's control over government appointments. When Edward sided not with his father but with de Montfort, there ensued a period of estrangement that ended with Henry's forgiveness of Edward in May 1260. Foreseeing a possible fight between the Crown and England's barons, Henry then sent Edward to Gascony, where he stayed for three years.

In 1262, after Henry had renounced the Provisions of Oxford and Westminster, a war broke out between the king and the barons under de Montfort. Edward returned from Gascony and took up arms for his father and the Crown. At Lewes on 14 May 1264, Henry was captured; Edward surrendered to de Montfort, but he escaped in May 1265. Leading the Royalist forces, Edward defeated de Montfort at Newport on 8 July 1265, driving the barons into Wales. A branch baron army under de Montfort's son, Simon the Younger, sprang up, but Edward met them at Kenilworth and defeated them there on 1 August 1265. Edward then turned back on Leicester, attacking and killing him at Evesham (4 August 1265) while also rescuing his father from imprisonment. Before the battle, de Montfort had predicted his own defeat and death, writing that he and his men should "let us commend our souls to God, because our bodies are theirs . . . they are approaching wisely, they learned this from me." Edward's harsh retaliation against the barons after his victory at Evesham set the stage for more than a year of resistance before they sued for peace

in 1266. Under the Statute of Marlborough (1267), full royal authority was restored to the throne.

Following this momentous victory, Edward decided to lead a Crusade to the Holy Land, although due to several difficulties he could not start his journey until 1270, following the death of King Louis IX of France. That year, Edward arrived at Acre (now in Lebanon) and led an army against Muslim forces near Jerusalem. Although he gained no substantial land, he did strengthen his standing as a warrior.

Edward was returning to England in 1272 when he learned of his father's death; he was crowned king of England on 19 August 1274. Almost from the start of his reign, he was at war—first against the Welsh, starting in 1277, to end border disputes. He launched a major offensive and defeated the Welsh prince Llyewelyn ap Gruffydd in November 1277. However, Gruffydd and his brother David viewed the Treaty of Conway, which ended the conflict, as a temporary measure rather than permanent peace. In 1282, following the abduction of England's representative in Wales, Edward assembled a large force and invaded Wales, killing Gruffydd, whose brother David was captured and later executed by the English. Edward then built a series of castles to confirm his hold on Wales, and despite a number of minor revolts, Wales was never again a threat to England: Under the Statute of Wales (1284), it was made an integral part of the English kingdom, whose shire system was extended to Wales.

Edward next turned his sights on Scotland. In 1290, when Margaret of Norway, the last heir to the Scottish throne, died, Scottish noblemen asked Edward to name a successor. In November 1292, Edward chose John of Balliol over Edward Bruce, but Balliol was still a Scot who resented Edward's claim to be "overlord." When war broke out between England and France in 1294, Balliol lost most of his authority as the Scottish nobles entered into an alliance with the French in October 1295. Outraged by this betrayal, Edward assembled an army and invaded Scotland in March 1296.

To pay for his fighting force, the king brought together a group of men in a parley (meeting) to pass laws for taxes. This eventually became a constant parley, or parliament. At the same time that he was turning on Scotland, Edward asked the parliament to fund a war against France following King Philip's seizure of the English territory of Gascony. Known as the Model Parliament because it represented a major cross-section of

English landowners, barons, clergy, knights, and others, this became the exemplar of future parliaments.

The English army moved into Scotland and laid siege to the city of Berwick on the River Tweed. A month later, Balliol denounced Edward openly, calling attention to the English monarch's alleged "grievous and intolerable injuries . . . for instance by summoning us outside [of] our realm . . . as you own whim dictated . . . and so . . . we recounce [sic] the fealty and homage which we have done to you." The English met the Scottish, under the earl of Athol, at Dunbar on 27 April 1296, a battle in which the Scottish lost 10,000 dead and wounded. Emboldened, Edward's army raced toward Moray Firth, laying waste to Scottish castles and seizing important treasures such as the Stone of Scone (pronounced "scoon"), a rock on which Scottish kings had been crowned. (Edward placed it in Westminster Abbey; it was not returned to Scotland until 1996.) On 28 August 1296, Edward held a parliamentary meeting at Berwick and invited Scottish landowners and barons. There, more than 2,000 signed a proclamation declaring their allegiance to Edward and against John of Balliol, who fled and spent the remainder of his life in exile.

Sir William WALLACE took Balliol's place as the leader of the Scottish opposition to Edward. In a series of battles, his forces retook control of much of Scotland before Edward again marched an army into Scotland and defeated Wallace's forces at Falkirk on 22 July 1298. Scottish losses were estimated at over 5,000 dead and wounded, compared to 200 English dead. Wallace fled and stayed on the run until 1305, when he was betrayed, taken to London, and brutally executed.

In 1304, tired of fighting Scottish armies, Edward called a parliament, including Scottish members, at which he set out a proposal for a new government in Scotland, autonomous from England. ROBERT THE BRUCE, brother of former Scottish leader Edward Bruce, was a member of the council, but in 1306 he rebelled and was crowned king of Scotland. Despite his advanced age, Edward again summoned an army to march into Scotland, but on the journey north, his health failed. As his army moved toward Burgh-on-Sands, he died on 7 July 1307 at the age of 68. His body was returned to London and given a royal funeral at Westminster Abbey, where he was laid to rest. Although Edward had requested that his bones be disinterred and carried into battle against the Scottish, his body was sealed into its tomb and never again disturbed. In the 17th century, graffiti reading *Pactum serva* (keep truth) and *Scotorum malleus* (hammer of the Scots) was written on the tomb.

Edward left a lasting legacy in English history—not just for his calling of Parliament, which still meets to this day, but for laws that set the groundwork for the English law system. These included the First Statute of Westminster (1275), which listed a series of laws into one model code; the Statute of Gloucester (1278) and Statute of *Quo Warranto* (1290), both of which regulated feudal administration; the Second Statute of Westminster (1285), which confirmed the right of families to hold onto estates; and the Third Statute of Westminster, or *Quia Emptores* (1290), which held that land given by the king could not be rented or sold off, a process called subinfeudation. Historian David Hilliam, in his compendium of biographies of English monarchs, writes of Edward: "What a pity it is that we have no effigy, no picture, no visual record of this great king! Even his tomb in Westminster Abbey is a vast ugly lump, hidden in the shadows, with its famous inscription 'Hammer of the Scots' scrawled in a messy way on the side—just a bit of 17th-century graffiti on a fourteenth-century stone coffin. The result is that many people hardly know or remember one of England's great kings." However, historian James Lucas concludes that "Edward I is generally regarded as the greatest warrior king in medieval England."

References: Seeley, Robert Benton, *The Life and Reign of Edward I* (London: Seeley, Jackson & Halliday, 1872); Salzman, Louis Francis, *Edward I* (London: Praeger, 1968); "Hilliam, David, "Edward I," in *Kings, Queens, Bones and Bastards: Who's Who in the English Monarchy from Egbert to Elizabeth II* (Thrupp, Stroud, Gloucestershire, United Kingdom: Sutton Publishing, 1998), 46–47; Hunt, William, "Edward I," in *The Dictionary of National Biography*, 22 vols., 8 supps., edited by Sir Leslie Stephen and Sir Sidney Lee, et al. (London: Oxford University Press, 1921–22), VI:432–456; Morris, John E., *The Welsh Wars of Edward I: A Contribution to Mediaeval Military History, Based upon Original Documents* (Oxford: Clarendon Press, 1901); Powicke, Sir Frederick, et al., *The Battle of Lewes, 1264* (Lewes, U.K.: Friends of Lewes Society, 1964); *Letter from Sir Joseph de Cancy, Knight of the Hospital of St. John of Jerusalem, to King Edward I. (1281), and Letter from King Edward I. to Sir Joseph (1282). . . .* (London: The Palestine Pilgrims' Text Society, 1890), 14–15; "Edward I," in *Command: From Alexander the Great to*

Zhukov—The Greatest Commanders of World History, edited by James Lucas. (London: Bloomsbury Publishing, 1988), 37.

Edward II (1284–1327) *English king*

Edward II was born at Caernarfon Castle, Wales, on 25 April 1284, the fourth son of EDWARD I and Eleanor of Castile and heir to the English throne since three older brothers had died in infancy. His father was often away fighting the Welsh or the Scottish, and his mother was frequently absent in Europe. He was the first to be named Prince of Wales, a title still given to the eldest son of the ruling monarch. Following his father's death on 7 July 1307, Edward, then just 23 years old, succeeded to the throne; he was crowned in Westminster Abbey in London on 24 April 1308, and married Isabella, the daughter of King Philip IV of France that same year.

Even before his marriage, Edward had showed signs that he was a homosexual. When he left for France to marry Isabella, he left behind his "favorite," Piers Gaveston. From the start of Edward's reign, the barons, who controlled the army, did not trust him because they feared Gaveston's influence. Therefore they used their power to check Edward at every turn and force Gaveston into exile. In 1309, Edward recalled Gaveston and again took up a relationship with him. The barons, upset, demanded Gaveston's exile. Parliaments held in 1310 and 1311 formed a Committee of Lords Ordainers to control Edward and placed his cousin Thomas, earl of Lancaster, in the role of regent to corule. In 1311, Edward was again forced to exile Gaveston, who returned in 1312. This time, the barons kidnapped Gaveston and killed him.

Because of this conflict between the Crown and the barons, the Scottish under ROBERT THE BRUCE reasserted control over their homeland. In 1314, Edward formed an army to put an end to Robert's reign. However, at Bannockburn, near Stirling, his incompetence was demonstrated to a horrific degree on 23 June, when Robert the Bruce stood with some 40,000 troops to Edward's 60,000. As historian George Bruce writes, "Bruce's position was partly covered by a marsh, and further strengthened by pitfalls, in which the English cavalry were entrapped." Clever traps laid by the Scots forced the English cavalry to stumble, rendering them helpless as Scottish arrows laid into them. When the battle was over, some 10,000 English troops lay dead in

the turning point of the English-Scottish wars. Edward I's dream of a united nation lay in ruins because of his son Edward II. It would not be until 1603, when James VI of Scotland became James I of England, that England and Scotland would put aside their differences.

By 1314, Lancaster, Edward's coregent, was openly in defiance of the king; he and three other earls defied a king's summons for military duty to serve against the Scots. With Gaveston gone, Edward had taken up with Sir Hugh Despenser as well as his son, also named Hugh. This affair set off more opposition to Edward's rule, and Lancaster demanded that the Despensers be exiled, which was done in 1321.

By 1322, the barons were in full rebellion against Edward, who had recalled the Despensers. Seeking to put down the insurrection, he formed an army. At Boroughbridge on 16 March 1322, Sir Andrew Harclay defeated Lancaster, dragged him from a church where he had sought sanctuary, and had him beheaded in York. Fearing for her life, Edward's wife Isabella fled to France in 1325 with her son by Edward, but she returned a year later with her lover Roger Mortimer, a baron who opposed Edward. On 24 September 1326, they landed at Suffolk, where barons and others who opposed Edward's rule met Isabella. They joined her cause, captured and hanged the Despensers, and proclaimed her son, "Keeper of the Realm." Edward fled but was captured and forced to abdicate the throne on 25 January 1327 in favor of his son, who was crowned as EDWARD III. Edward II was placed in protective custody by his enemies.

Edward died at Berkeley Castle, Gloucestershire, on 21 September 1327, age 43; historians believe he was murdered by having a red hot poker thrust into his bowels. He was buried in St. Peter's Abbey, now Gloucester Cathedral in Gloucester.

References: Hilliam, David, "Edward II," in *Kings, Queens, Bones and Bastards: Who's Who in the English Monarchy from Egbert to Elizabeth II* (Thrupp, Stroud, Gloucestershire, U.K.: Sutton Publishing, 1998), 47–48; Bruce, George, "Bannockburn," in *Collins Dictionary of Wars* (Glasgow, Scotland: HarperCollins Publishers, 1995), 29; Fryde, Natalie, *The Tyranny and Fall of Edward II* (Cambridge, U.K.: Cambridge University Press, 1979); Haskins, George L., "A Chronicle of the Civil Wars of Edward II," *Speculum: A Journal of Mediaeval Studies* 14, no. 1 (January 1939): 73–75; Baker, Sir Richard, *A Chronicle of the Kings of England from the Time of the Roman Govern-*

ment unto the Death of King James . . . (London: E. Cotes, 1660), 15–18.

Edward III (1312–1377) *English king*

The eldest son of King EDWARD II and his wife Queen Isabella, and the grandson of King EDWARD I, the future Edward III was born at Windsor, now the British royal residence, on 13 November 1312. In 1320, at the age of 8, Edward was summoned to Parliament and given the title of earl of Chester; five years later, he was named duke of Aquitaine. His father, an alleged homosexual who was uninterested in Isabella, surrounded himself with a series of men, including Sir Hugh Despenser. To avoid having her son come under the influence of these men, and because of the conflict between her husband and the English barons, Isabella took her son and fled to her native France in 1325. The following year, at the age of 14, he was betrothed to Philippa of Hainault and then returned to England with his mother and her lover, Roger Mortimer. His father fled but was captured and, in 1327, forced to abdicate in favor of his 14-year-old son, who was crowned in Westminster Abbey on 29 January 1327. Edward III's reign would last for 50 years, one of the longest in English history.

Just six years into his reign, Edward followed the example of his father and grandfather and went to war against the Scots. In 1329, ROBERT THE BRUCE, champion of Scottish independence, died, leaving Scotland without a clear leader. The Scottish barons backed Edward de Balliol, who promptly invaded England in 1332 and won a quick victory against the English at Dupplin Moor on 12 August and was crowned at Scone on 24 September. However, David II, Robert the Bruce's only son, had been crowned on 24 November 1331, and, backed by a group of Scottish barons, he overthrew de Balliol. Despite de Balliol's border incursions, he was backed by Edward III, who assembled an army and marched north to defeat the Scottish forces under David. Edward sacked the border town of Berwick, after which he was attacked at Halidon Hill on 18 July 1333 by a Scottish force led by Archibald Douglas, the Scottish regent, who had been sent south to relieve the town. Historian George Bruce writes that "the Scots were powerless against the English archers, and were defeated with heavy loss, including the Regent, and four Earls." This defeat subjugated the Scots and ended this conflict on Edward's northern border for some years.

Edward's next conflict was with France. In 1337, PHILIP VI of France declared that Gascony (to which the English kings had long claimed sovereignty) belonged entirely to France. Edward negotiated a treaty with Emperor Louis of Bavaria, paving the way for the opening of hostilities that history has labeled the Hundred Years' War (1338–1453). After the siege of Cambrai in 1339 (when cannons were first used), Edward's fleet won the battle of Sluis (or Sluys, 24 June 1340). In this naval conflict, 200 English ships under the command of Sir Robert Morley and Richard Fitzalan defeated a French naval force of 70 ships under Hughes Quieret, destroying the entire French fleet. Edward then invaded France in 1346. He landed near Cherbourg, captured Caen, crossed the Seine and the Somme, and met the French at Crécy-en-Ponthieu, 12 miles north of Abbeville. Here, on 26 August 1346, perhaps one of the most important land battles in the history of England took place. Edward, with 40,000 English soldiers under his command, faced a French force of 100,000 men under the count of Alençon; despite the overwhelming French advantage, Edward's troops used the longbow and cannons to decimate the French lines. Jean Froissart, a French historian, writes:

> This battle between the Broye and Cressy [sic] was very murderous and horrible, and no doubt many great feats of arms were performed which never came to light, for when the battle began it was already very late in the day. This injured the French more than anything else, for many men-at-arms, Knights, and Squires lost their Lords during the night, and wandered about the field meeting with the English at a great disadvantage; and were nearly all killed, for none were ransomed or given quarter, according to an order given in the morning because of the great number of the enemy. The Count Louis de Blois, nephew of King Philip and of the Count d'Alençon, fought very valiantly with his people, as did likewise the Duke of Lorraine. . . . There were many French Knights and Squires, as well as others of Germany and Savoy, who by force of arms broke the array of the English archers, and reached the English men-at-arms and fought valiantly with them, sword in hand. . . . [T]he defeat and loss of the French was so great owing to the number of Dukes, Counts, Barons, and Knights which were left on the field, that the

King Edward III, engraving by George Vertue, ca. 1730

Kingdom itself was greatly enfeebled by the loss of honour, of reputation, and power: and it should be noted that if the English had pursued their enemy as they [did] afterwards at Poitiers, many more would have been killed or taken, including the King of France.

The French army was destroyed at Crécy: Historians believe that some 15,000 French died in the struggle, including John, the king of Bohemia, who was blind but fought for the French, and Philip VI was wounded as he fled. Edward's son Edward, also known as the Black Prince, displayed great courage during the fight, and after the battle he reputedly took the crest of the dead king of Bohemia, three ostrich feathers, as his own (although some historians discount this legend).

Crécy solidified Edward's gains in France, allowing him to move onto and lay siege to the fort at Calais, which held out until its surrender in August 1347. Edward now controlled much of northern France. However, the rigors of warfare and the Black Death that was ravaging both England and Europe affected his army, and financial needs meant he was forced to return home to England to oversee affairs.

Continued battles with the Scottish had led to another war, culminating in the battle of Neville's Cross (17 October 1346), near Dunham, when English forces under Henry Percy and Ralph de Neville, fourth Baron Neville of Raby utilized archers and men at arms (noncavalry infantrymen) to defeat a Scottish force led by David the Bruce, king of Scotland, who was captured.

Edward had left his son Edward in charge of the war in France. The Black Prince would later win a brilliant victory at Poitiers (19 September 1356), in which the French king John II (who had succeeded Philip VI in 1350) was captured; in 1359, John was forced to sign the Treaty of London. When the French rejected the terms of the treaty, Edward again invaded France, besieging the town of Rheims in an attempt to have himself crowned king of France. However, the town held out, and he was forced to sign the Treaty of Calais (1360), renouncing his claims to the French throne. A third English invasion of France in 1369, led by Edward's son John of Gaunt, the duke of Lancaster, led to the Treaty of Bruges, which left only small amounts of France, including Bordeaux and Calais, in English hands.

Two more attacks of the Black Death in England in 1361 and 1369 devastated the country and Edward was forced to deal with extremely difficult economic circumstances. Religious divisions in England were dealt with in several pieces of legislation enacted by Parliament, including the Statutes of Provisors (1351), which controlled the activities of foreign clergy in England. In 1366, Edward resisted papal demands for compulsory financial contributions, a measure that set a precedent for Henry VIII (1507–47). When the Black Prince returned from France in 1371 in ill health, Edward led an army into France in 1372 when he was 60 years old, but strong winds forced his ships to sail back to England.

In 1375, Edward retired to his estate at Richmond, where he died on 21 June 1377 at the age of 62; he was buried in Westminster Abbey. With Edward's death, succession of the English crown passed not to his son the Black Prince, who had died on 8 June 1376, but to his grandson Richard II (ruled 1377–99).

Historian David Bongard sums up Edward's legacy: "Edward III was a ruler of unusual strategy and ability, far closer to his grandfather [Edward I] than to his father [Edward II]. As a general he was a fine tactician but lacked Edward I's strategic insight. In the affairs of his own realm, he strove to be just, open-handed, and kind, although he abdicated many of his responsibilities toward the close of his reign, much to the detriment of his kingdom. Personally brave and an eager soldier, he was at heart a knight."

References: "Edward III," in *Command: From Alexander the Great to Zhukov—The Greatest Commanders of World History,* edited by James Lucas (London: Bloomsbury Publishing, 1988), 37–38; Warburton, Rev. William, *Edward III* (New York: Scribner, 1887); Mackinnon, James, *The History of Edward the Third (1327–1377)* (London: Longmans, Green, 1900); Longman, William, *The History of the Life and Times of Edward the Third* (London: Longmans, Green and Co., 1869); Barnes, Joshua, *The History of that Most Victorious monarch Edward III. King of England and France, and Lord of Ireland . . .* (Cambridge, U.K.: Printed by J. Hayes for the Author, 1688); Nicholson, Ranald, *Edward III and the Scots: The Formative Years of a Military Career, 1327–1335* (Oxford, U.K.: Oxford University Press, 1965); Bruce, George, "Halidon Hill," in *Collins Dictionary of Wars* (Glasgow, Scotland: Harper-Collins Publishers, 1995), 106; Hewitt, H. J., *The Organization of War under Edward III, 1338–62* (Manchester, U.K.: Manchester University Press, 1966); Ayton, Andrew,

Knights and Warhorses: Military Service and the English Aristocracy under Edward III (Woodbridge, Suffolk, U.K.: Boydell Press, 1994); account of Jean Froissart on Crécy in George Wrottesley, *Crécy and Calais, From the Original Records in the Public Record Office* (London: Harrison and Sons, St. Martin's Lane, 1898), 47–48; Adams, William Henry Davenport, and William Pairman, *Great Generals: Charlemagne, Edward the Third, Gustavus Adolphus, the Duke of Marlborough, the Duke of Wellington, Earl Roberts* (London: Gall and Inglis, 1905), 68–69, 130; Bongard, David L., "Edward III," in *Brassey's Encyclopedia of Military History and Biography,* edited by Franklin D. Margiotta (Washington, D.C.: Brassey's, 1994), 293–295.

Eisenhower, Dwight David (1890–1969)
American general, president of the United States

Eisenhower is one of two men (Ulysses S. GRANT is the other) to command American armies and then be elected to two terms as president of the United States. Like Grant, Eisenhower came from common stock. Born in Denison, Texas, on 14 October 1890, he was an infant when his parents moved to Abilene, Kansas; he was later hailed as "the man from Abilene." He graduated from high school and then sought to enter the U.S. Military Academy at West Point as well as the naval academy at Annapolis, Maryland. He was initially accepted to Annapolis, but his age prevented him from attending, so in 1911 he went to West Point, from which he graduated four years later in the same class as fellow Second World War commander Omar BRADLEY. Assigned the rank of lieutenant, Eisenhower was sent to Camp Sam Houston, Texas, and served during the First World War with the 19th Infantry. He later moved to Fort Oglethorpe in Georgia. When the war ended, Eisenhower was transferred to Camp Meade, Maryland, eventually moving on to several other military encampments such as Fort Dix in New Jersey. In 1920, he was promoted twice, to captain and then to major.

During the 1920s, Eisenhower served in the Panama Canal Zone and graduated first in his class from the Command and General Staff School at Fort Leavenworth (1926). As a member of the American Battle Monuments Commission, he wrote the definitive guidebook on battlefields from the First World War. He graduated from the Army War College, Washington, D.C., in 1928, then served on the staff of Assistant Secretary of War General George V. Moseley. From 1932 until 1935,

he was the chief military aide to Army Chief of Staff General Douglas MACARTHUR, and he was promoted to lieutenant colonel in 1936.

When the Japanese attacked Pearl Harbor, Hawaii, on 7 December 1941, bringing America into the Second World War, Eisenhower was serving as the chief of staff to General Walter Kreuger, commander of the Third Army at Fort Sam Houston. He was called to Washington by General George C. Marshall to help to design the American war blueprint, and in May 1942 he was sent on a special mission to London, England, to coordinate cooperation among the Allied forces fighting the Germans and the Japanese. The following month he was designated the commanding officer of American forces in the European Theatre of Operations. In November 1942, he was also named commander in chief of Allied forces in North Africa. Historian Brian Bader writes: "In July 1942 Eisenhower became a lieutenant general and was chosen to head the first major Allied military effort, Operation 'Torch'—the invasion of North Africa. The Allies landed in North Africa in November 1942 and in May 1943 completed the conquest of Tunisia. Throughout the campaign, Eisenhower demonstrated his mastery of coalition warfare, directing and coordinating the efforts of U.S., British, and Free French land, sea, and air forces to drive the Axis powers from North Africa. Promoted to full general in February 1943, he commanded Allied forces in the invasion of Sicily in July-August and the invasion of mainland Italy in September."

As the commander in chief of Allied coalition forces, Eisenhower served as the commanding officer of British generals Bernard Law MONTGOMERY and Harold Rupert ALEXANDER, later the first earl Alexander of Tunisia. Although he is widely credited with helping to defeat German forces in North Africa, he did suffer a defeat at the Kasserine Pass (February 1943) at the hands of the German general Erwin ROMMEL.

In December 1943, Eisenhower was transferred from the command of the Mediterranean Theatre and given command of the Supreme Headquarters of the Allied Expeditionary Force (SHAEF), which was being readied to invade Europe. This invasion, called Operation Overlord, took place on 6 June 1944, when, in a massive, multipart effort, American, British, and Canadian soldiers assaulted several beaches in the Normandy section of northern France and gained a foothold on the European continent by battling back entrenched German forces. As commander in chief, Eisenhower was

In this photo, taken in England a few hours before their jump into France, General Dwight D. Eisenhower urges the men of the U.S. 101st Airborne Division to "Full victory—nothing else."

the chief planner for the entire operation, and its success has helped to make him one of the most important military commanders in world history. Once the Allies had the Germans on the run, Eisenhower implemented a strategy of a comprehensive and broad-based advance, overwhelming the Germans and slowly pushing them back into Germany.

While Eisenhower was directing military strategy, he was also faced with some internal dissent as his numerous subordinates and other commanders all clashed over tactics. General George S. PATTON, for instance, believed that a single thrust against the Germans would work better. Eisenhower did approve a plan proposed

by Montgomery, which became Operation Market Garden, a scheme to drop thousands of Allied troops behind German lines to capture numerous bridges. However, this was a defeat for the Allies that left some 1,500 dead and nearly 7,000 taken prisoner.

On 1 September 1944, after an American army landing in the south of France, Eisenhower was given the command of all Allied operations in that country. On 20 December 1944, he was promoted to General of the Army with five stars, one of only a handful of men to ever hold this honor. He led Allied forces in the Ardennes offensive, a victory that ended any chance that the Germans would reverse Allied gains. His plan to march across the Rhine River and capture western Germany was successful, and Germany surrendered on 8 May 1945.

From July to November 1945, Eisenhower served as the military governor of the American Occupation Zone, headquartered in Frankfurt, Germany. On 19 November 1945, he was named chief of staff of the U.S. Army, and on 11 April 1946 his wartime rank of General of the Army was made permanent as he oversaw the demobilization of American forces in Europe.

Eisenhower retired from the army in 1948 to become the president of Columbia University in New York. However, he was recalled to service only two years later when, on 16 December 1950, President Harry S. Truman named him as supreme allied commander of the North Atlantic Treaty Organization (NATO). He served in this command for two years until he retired on 31 May 1952; he resigned his army commission in July of that same year.

From the end of the war until 1952, Eisenhower was seen as a potential presidential candidate; however, because he was not overtly political, he would not specify whether he was a Republican or a Democrat, and both major American political parties courted him to run in 1948 and 1952. Following his resignation from the army, Eisenhower declared himself on 4 June 1952 to be a candidate for the Republican presidential nomination that year. He won the nomination, was elected overwhelmingly in 1952, and was reelected in 1956. During his two terms as president, Eisenhower oversaw the end of the Korean War and dealt with a wide variety of issues, including the Suez Canal crisis, the invasion of Hungary by the Soviet Union in 1956, the sending of American troops into Lebanon in 1958, increasing tension in Vietnam, and the launching of the Sputnik satellite into Earth orbit by the USSR, the growing debate over civil rights in the United States, and the creation of the Department of Health, Education, and Welfare (HEW) in 1953. He left office widely popular, although his vice president, Richard M. Nixon, failed to succeed him as president.

Eisenhower left Washington on 20 January 1961 and returned to his farm in Gettysburg, Pennsylvania, with his wife Mamie. On 28 March 1969, he died of heart failure at the Walter Reed Army Hospital in Washington, D.C., at the age of 78. Although he was eligible to be buried in Arlington National Cemetery, he was laid to rest instead in the Place of Meditation at the Eisenhower Center in Abilene, Kansas, where his national library is located. In an obituary, *The New York Times* said of him: "Military leadership of the victorious Allied forces in Western Europe during World War II invested Dwight David Eisenhower with an immense popularity, almost amounting to devotion, that twice elected him President of the United States. His enormous political success was largely personal, for he was not basically a politician dealing in partisan issues and party maneuvers. What he possessed was a superb talent for gaining the respect and affection of the voters as the man suited to guide the nation through cold war confrontations with Soviet power around the world and to lead the country to domestic prosperity." Although perhaps better known for his two terms as president of the United States, Eisenhower's service as head of Allied armies in the Second World War serve to make him one of the great commanders in the history of warfare.

References: Kinnard, Douglas, *Eisenhower: Soldier-Statesman of the American Century* (Washington, D.C.: Brassey's, 2002); Hatch, Alden, *General Ike: A Biography of Dwight D. Eisenhower* (New York: Henry Holt and Company, 1944); Parmet, Herbert S., *Eisenhower and the American Crusades* (New York: The Macmillan Company, 1972); Holland, Matthew F., *Eisenhower Between the Wars: The Making of a General and a Statesman* (Westport, Conn.: Praeger, 2001); Bader, Brian R., "Dwight David Eisenhower," in *Brassey's Encyclopedia of Military History and Biography,* edited by Franklin D. Margiotta (Washington, D.C.: Brassey's, 1994), 297; Murray, G. E. Patrick, *Eisenhower versus Montgomery: The Continuing Debate* (Westport, Conn.: Praeger, 1996); "Dwight D. Eisenhower," in *Command: From Alexander the Great to Zhukov—The Greatest Commanders of World History,* edited by James Lucas (London: Bloomsbury Publishing, 1988), 201; "Dwight D. Eisenhower: A Leader in War and Peace," *The New York Times,* 29 March 1969, 1.

Elchingen, duc de *See* NEY, MICHEL, DUC D'ELCHINGEN, PRINCE OF THE MOSKOWA.

Epaminondas (ca. 418/415–362 B.C.) *Theban general*

Although he is barely known today, most historians credit Epaminondas with shaping innovative new ways in combat, including the phalanx, and the use of cavalry. He was born about 418 or 415 B.C. at Thebes, now in Greece, the son of Polymnis, and educated by Lysis of Tarentum, a Pythagorean philosopher. At that time, Sparta, in southern Greece, was the strongest state in the region, while Thebes, farther north, controlled the city-states in Boeotia. In 371, the Spartans called a conference, the Congress at Sparta, at which Epaminondas refused to cede Theban control of Boeotia. Consequently, Agesilaus II of Sparta excluded Thebes from a peace treaty in the Peloponnesian strait, a slight that led to war.

Epaminondas commanded Theban forces against Sparta, and in 371 B.C., the two armies met at Leuctra, a Boeotian city. Fielding a force of some 11,000, the Spartans surrounded the Theban army of approximately 6,000, but the Thebans' larger cavalry force held their ground, and Epaminondas advanced his own forces behind the cavalry. His friend Pelopidas, commanding the forces known as the Sacred Band, delivered the final blow to the Spartans, as the Greek historian Xenophon writes:

> At this juncture there were some Lacedaemonians [Spartan allies], who, looking upon such a disaster as intolerable, maintained that they ought to prevent the enemy from erecting a trophy, and try to recover the dead, not under a flag of truce, but by another battle. The polemarchs [commanders], however, seeing that nearly 1000 of the total Lacedaemonian troops were slain, and seeing, too, that of the 700 regular Spartans who were on the field some 400 lay dead; aware likewise of the despondency which reigned among the allies, and the general disinclination on their part to fight longer—a frame of mind not far from positive satisfaction in some cases at what had happened—under the circumstances, I say, the polemarchs called a council of the ablest representatives of the shattered army, and deliberated on what should be done. Finally, the unanimous opinion was to pick up the dead under a flag of truce, and they sent a herald to treat for terms. The Thebans after that set up a trophy, and gave back the bodies under a truce.

Leuctra was the first recorded Spartan military defeat in over four centuries.

Epaminondas did not hesitate to follow up this victory, returning to Thebes to raise an army of approximately 70,000 men to march on Sparta. In 370 B.C., he defeated Laconia, a Spartan client state, and liberated the citizens under Spartan domination there. In 369 B.C., he marched into Sicyon, where he founded Megalopolis, making it the center of the newly formed (anti-Spartan) Arcadian League. In 366, he again raided Spartan territory, liberating the Achaeans from Spartan control and bringing them into the Arcadian League. In 362 B.C., when Sparta founded the Spartan League to counter the Arcadian League, Epaminondas gathered his army and advanced against the Spartan army at Mantinea. Utilizing his cavalry and phalanx (heavily armed infantry in close formation), he again won a decisive victory against the Spartans. However, he was fatally wounded during the battle and died before his triumph could be savored. Some historians claim that he was killed by Gryllus, the son of Xenophon, but this cannot be confirmed.

Thebes's chances of empire died with Epaminondas. His tactics were later studied and improved by Philip II of Macedon and his son, ALEXANDER THE GREAT. Historian James Lucas sums up Epaminondas's legacy: "Until his defeat of Sparta at Leuctra in 371 B.C., Epaminondas was best known as a private citizen involved in the fringe of Theban politics. After the battle, however, he was recognized as the greatest of Greek generals."

References: "Epaminondas and Leuctra," in *The Penguin Dictionary of Ancient History,* edited by Graham Speake (London: Penguin Books, 1995), 233–234; Cawkwell, George L., "Epaminondas and Thebes," *Classical Quarterly* 66 (1972), 254–278; William Stearns Davis, *Readings in Ancient History: Illustrative Extracts from the Sources,* 2 vols. (Boston: Allyn and Bacon 1912–13), II:279–284; Anderson, John Kinloch, *Military Theory and Practice in the Age of Xenophon* (Berkeley: University of California Press, 1970); "Epaminondas," in *Command: From Alexander the Great to Zhukov—The Greatest Commanders of World History,* edited by James Lucas (London: Bloomsbury Publishing, 1988), 38–39.

Essex, Robert Devereux, third earl of (1591–1646) *English general*

The son and namesake of the second earl of Essex, who was executed for treason in 1601, Robert Devereux was born in London in January 1591. His father's execution when he was just 10 years of age left an emotional scar on him that never healed, and he was forced to apply for a special exemption to allow his father's title to be handed down to him, making him the third earl of Essex in 1604. Following father's example, Essex entered the English military in 1620 when he was 29, and he saw service in the Thirty Years' War (1618–48) in Europe, commanding a regiment in Holland under Sir Horace Vere and leading an ill-fated expedition to Cádiz in Spain in 1625. For his service, he was promoted to the rank of vice admiral, and in 1639, King Charles I appointed him second in command of the army in Scotland during the Second Bishops' War (1639–40). In 1641, the king made him a privy councillor. Nevertheless, Essex supported the parliamentary cause and asked the king to call Parliament into session in 1640 to pay for army expenditures. When Charles refused, Essex turned against him, and when a Parliamentary army was drafted to fight the king, he was named the lord general in July 1642.

When Essex concluded that Charles's forces would march on London to take control of the city, he advanced his own army to head off the king. After capturing Worcester and Hereford (September 1642), he faced Charles at Edgehill on 23 October 1642. According to most historians, this battle was inconclusive, and both armies retreated with no decision. However, a contemporary work from 1642, entitled *A Relation of the Battel [sic] fought between Keynton and Edgehill, by His Majesty's Army and that of the Rebels,* states, with an obvious pro-Royalty bias, that the Parliamentarian forces suffered a terrible loss:

> The King with the whole Body of the Horse, and those of the Foot which were not broken, quartered upon and on one side of the Hill, all that Night; and in the Morning, as soon as it was Day, drew half the Body of the Horse into Battalia, at the Foot of the Hill, and the rest of the Horse and the Foot on the Top of the Hill, where the Standard was placed; and having notice that 3 of the Rebels Cannon were left half way between us and their Quarter, sent out a Body of Horse, and drew them off, they not so much as offering to relieve them: So both Armies, facing one another all day, retired at Night to their former Quarters. . . .
>
> The Rebels in this Battel lost above 70 Colours of Cornets and Ensigns; we 16 Ensigns, but not one Cornet; but our Horse relieved not only the Standard, but divers of our Ensigns. . . .

For the slain on both sides, the Number is uncertain; yet it is most certain that we killed five for one. It is true, that their Chief Officers having fleeter Horses than ours, not so many of their Foot, as ours, were slain and taken Prisoners, to our knowledge as yet; but we lost no Officer of Horse, excepting the Lord Aubigny.

The next Day after the Battel, the Earl of Essex finding his Army extreamly weakened and disheartned by the great Blow they had received by his Majesties Forces, withdrew himself to Warwick Castle; and the same Night the remainder of his Forces went also privately thither much distracted, whereof Prince RUPERT having Notice, the next Morning pursued them, but they were all got into Warwick, or dispersed before he could overtake them; but his Highness took 25 Wagons and Carriages of the Rebels, laden with Ammunition, Medicaments, and other Baggage, whereof he brought away part, and fired the rest.

Following the clash at Edgehill, Essex moved back to Warwick, allowing Charles to move onto London. Charles, however, rested his army, allowing Essex to outflank him and reach London first. At Turnham Green (12 November 1642), Essex established a defensive fortification with some 24,000 men to meet Charles's attack. The Royalists had about half of Essex's force, so this battle was short and led to Charles's withdrawal to Kingston. Having anticipated this move, Essex had established Sir James Ramsey and a force of some 3,000 men to await him, forcing Charles to withdraw to Reading and then Oxford. His chances of taking London were finished.

In 1643, Essex captured Reading and sent a force to relieve Gloucester, two moves that separated the Royalist forces. However, within a year, his fortunes had changed: He relieved Lyme in June 1644, captured Taunton (July 1644), and moved on to Exeter. Charles, whose rest at Oxford had allowed his force to recover, pursued Essex as he himself had been pursued. When Sir William WALLER was defeated at Copredy Bridge (29 June 1644), any chance of relieving Essex's forces was dashed. Essex attempted to march to Falmouth, but this failed, and he fell back to Lostwithiel, where his forces faced Charles on 1 September 1644. Hemmed in at the port of Fowey near Lostwithiel, Essex and his army were cut off. The earl of Warwick attempted a sea rescue, but Royalist forces at Polruan Castle headed this off. Historian George Bruce writes: "The Royalists, 16,000 [strong], took Beacon Hill, the key to Lostwithiel, in the first battle, on 21 August. The remainder of the Roundheads, at first 10,000 [strong], were surrounded and forced to surrender on 2 September at Castle Dore, near Fowey. Not long after this defeat the Roundheads were organized as the New Model Army."

On 1 September, prior to the battle of Lostwithiel, Essex abandoned his forces and escaped by a small boat to the earl of Warwick's ships. He handed the reins of the army to Major General Phillip Skippon, who, facing annihilation, surrendered his force the following day on 2 September. Charles allowed the defeated army to leave provided all of their weapons were relinquished. The 8,000 men marched from Lostwithiel to Portsmouth; along the way, some 4,000 died of exposure and starvation, leaving only 4,000 from the original 10,000 Essex had under his command. Historian F. A. Bates, in his 1927 work *Graves Memoirs of the Civil War,* writes:

Having escaped with the cavalry at Lostwithiel, Colonel Graves joined up with Lord Essex at Portsmouth, and, when the army was ready to take the field again, moved with it to Basingstoke on the 17th October. Some four days later, near Basingstoke, Essex was joined by [Edward MONTAGU, 2nd earl of] Manchester and [Sir William] Waller. The meeting cannot have been a very pleasant one. To the one the disaster appeared solely due to the failure of his friends; to the others it appeared to be the failure of a rash military adventure of which they claimed to have always disapproved. The position as between three independent co-operating generals was clearly intolerable, and the indisposition which had been gradually growing upon him compelled Essex to leave the army and go to Reading, where, on October 26th (the actual date of the battle of Newbury), he is mentioned in a letter to be suffering from fistula.

The loss at Lostwithiel marked the end of Essex's service as commander of the Parliamentarian army. Depressed by his failures, he resigned just before Parliament enacted the Self-Denying Ordinance (3 April 1645), which allowed that no member of Parliament (Essex was in the House of Lords) could hold another public office. Only a year later, on 14 September 1646, Essex died in London and was buried in Westminster Abbey. As he had no sons, the earldom of Essex died with him.

References: Bongard, David L., "Essex, Robert Devereux, 3d Earl of," in *The Encyclopedia of Military Biography,* edited by Trevor N. Dupuy, Curt Johnson, and David L. Bongard (London: I. B. Taurus & Co., Ltd., 1992), 238–239; Devereux, Walter Bourchier, *Lives and Letters of the Devereux, Earls of Essex, 1540–1646,* 2 vols. (London: John Murray, 1853), II:3–9; Snow, Vernon F., *Essex the Rebel: The Life of Robert Devereux, the Third Earl of Essex, 1591–1646* (Lincoln: University of Nebraska Press, 1970); Gardiner, Samuel Rawson, *History of the Great Civil War, 1642–1649,* 4 vols. (London: Longmans, Green, and Co., 1893); Davies, Godfrey, "Documents Illustrating the First Civil War, 1642–45," *The Journal of Modern History* 3, no. 1 (March 1931): 64–71; Davies, Godfrey, "The Parliamentary Army under the Earl of Essex, 1642–5," *English Historical Review* 49 (January 1934): 32–46; *A Relation of the Battel fought between Keynton and Edgehill, by His Majesty's Army and that of the Rebels . . .* (Oxford: Leonard Lichfield, 1642); Bruce, George, "Lostwithiel," in *Collins Dictionary of Wars* (Glasgow, Scotland: HarperCollins Publishers, 1995), 144–145; Bates, F. A., comp., *Graves Memoirs of the Civil War, Compiled from Seventeenth Century Records* (Edinburgh and London: William Blackwood & Sons, 1927); Codrington, Robert, *The Life and Death of the Illustrious Robert Earle of Essex, &c. Containing at large the Wars he Managed, and the Commands he had in Holland, the Palatinate, and in England* (London: [Printed by] F. Leach for L. Chapman, 1646).

Eugène, prince de Savoie-Carignan (Prince Eugene of Savoy) (1663–1736) *Franco-Italian general*

Born in Paris on 18 October 1663, François-Eugène, prince de Savoie-Carignan, was the youngest son of Prince Eugène-Maurice, the head of the House of Savoie-Carignan, and his wife, Olympia Mancini, who was a niece of Cardinal Jules Mazarin. Long time rumor has held that François-Eugène was the illegitimate son of the French king Louis XIV and that Louis's shame over this illicit offspring led him to frustrate his son's military ambitions. When Louis rejected him as an officer, Eugène left France in 1683 and offered his services to Emperor Leopold I of Austria, at that time fighting Turkish forces trying to invade Eastern Europe. Leopold, seeing great promise in this Italian-French soldier, employed him to help relieve Vienna from the Muslims. Eugène was so conspicuous in his victory over the Turks at the battle of Petronell (7 July 1683) and in defense of Vienna (12 September 1683) that Leopold placed him in charge of a regiment of dragoons, an unusual honor for a foreigner. Further action against Muslim forces led to Eugène being wounded at the battle of Buda (3 August 1686) and during the siege of Belgrade (1688), but he served his commanders, Charles V of Lorraine and Louis of Baden, with great distinction.

After Eugène had recovered from his wounds, Leopold sent him on a diplomatic mission to Savoy, the land of his forefathers, where he convinced Duke Victor Amadeus to send assistance to fight the Turks. Eugène rose through the ranks of the Austrian military, gaining the rank of feldmarschall (field marshal) in 1693, when he was only 29 years old. During the War of the Grand Alliance (1688–97), he served as commander in chief of the Austrian imperial army and Austria's allies, known as the League of Augsburg and then the Grand Alliance, against France and her allies. In this conflict, he is best known for his spectacular victory against the Turkish army at Zenta (11 September 1697), frustrating the Ottoman attempt to conquer Hungary.

Returning to Vienna, Eugène served in various political offices, most notably as a member of the Emperor's Privy Council (1700) and as president of the Imperial War Council (1703). During the War of the Spanish Succession (1701–14), he served as a commander of imperial forces, fighting the French generals Nicolas de Catinat and the duc de Villeroi at Carpi (19 July 1701) and Chiari (1 September 1701); in the latter battle, the French lost some 3,000 dead to only 150 Austrians killed. However, at Luzzara on 22 August 1702, Eugène's forces were defeated by the French general Louis Joseph, duc de Vendôme, Eugène's own cousin, who also defeated him at Cassano on 16 August 1705.

In 1704, Eugène joined with the British general John CHURCHILL, duke of Marlborough, to lead allied forces to victory against the combined French and Bavarian army under Count Camille de Tallard and Maximilian II Emmanuel, the elector of Bavaria, at Blenheim

Prince Eugène of Savoy

on 13 August 1704. Historian George Bruce writes of this encounter, one of the major battles of the War of the Spanish Succession:

> With the Danube on its right, the Franco-Bavarian army was deployed for three miles along the top of a rise, from the strongly fortified villages of Blenheim, to Oberglau to Lutzingen, behind marshy land coursed by a stream, the Nebel. It was a strong position, and Marshal Tallard expected the allies to retreat, rather than attack, in [the] face of it . . . but after an overnight surprise march Marlborough and Eugène arrived early before the enemy lines. Eugène then attacked the enemy's far right near Lutzingen, while Marlborough made diversionary attacks on Blenheim and Oberglau to pin down defenders with smaller numbers. . . . Prince Eugène had meanwhile held the attacks of [French General Ferdinand de] Marsin and the Elector and, after Marlborough's charge, he assumed the offensive, routing the French right and center. The Franco-Bavarian army lost about 40,000 [dead and wounded], including 16,000 prisoners, among whom was Marshal Tallard. The allies lost about 12,000. It was the decisive battle of the war.

Eugène was sent back to Italy, where he lost at Cassano (16 August 1705) but won a major victory against the French at Turin (7 September 1706), forcing the French to leave Italy. He rejoined Marlborough and aided in allied victories at Oudenarde (11 July 1708) and Malplaquet (11 September 1709); he was wounded twice at the latter battle. After the Treaty of Utrecht (1713) ended the war between England and France, he continued to fight against French forces, finally settling the Austrian side of the conflict with the Peace of Rastadt (1714).

When war with the Ottoman Empire began again, Eugène led Austrian forces at Petrovaradin (5 August 1716) and helped to end a second siege of Belgrade (1719). With the end of the war, he retired from military service, having spent most of his life in defense of his adopted country. In 1724, he was named as governor of the Austrian Netherlands; he later served as the imperial vicar in Italy. He died in Vienna on 24 April 1736 at the age of 73, assured of his place in military history as one of the great captains of all time and among the greatest of the 18th century.

References: Lugne, Charles Joseph, Prince de Ligne, *The Life of Prince Eugène, of Savoy. . . .* (London: J. Davis, 1812); McKay, Derek, *Prince Eugène of Savoy* (London: Thames and Hudson, 1977); Henderson, Sir Nicholas, *Prince Eugen of Savoy* (London: Weidenfeld and Nicolson, 1964); MacMunn, Sir George Fletcher, *Prince Eugène, Twin Marshal with Marlborough* (London: S. Low, Marston, 1934); *The Life and Military Actions of His Royal Highness Prince Eugène, of Savoy. With an Account of his Death and Funeral* (London, 1739).

F

Fairfax, Sir Thomas, third baron Fairfax, Baron Fairfax of Cameron (1612–1671)

English general

The son of Ferdinando Fairfax, second baron Fairfax of Cameron, Thomas Fairfax was born in Denton, Yorkshire, on 17 January 1612. He attended Cambridge University, after which he fought with the Dutch against the Spanish from 1629 to 1631. From 1639 to 1640, as commander of the Yorkshire Dragoons, he fought in the so-called Bishops' War (a conflict between England and Scotland caused by the English king Charles I's attempt to reform the Scottish church). For his service to the Crown, Fairfax was knighted by King Charles in 1640. Eight years later, in 1648, he succeeded to his father's title as the third baron Fairfax.

When the long struggle between King Charles and Parliament erupted into civil war in 1642, Fairfax joined the Parliamentary cause, taking command of troops in his native Yorkshire. In *An English Garner* (1903), English historian C. H. Firth quotes from manuscripts that Fairfax wrote, which his nephew, Brian Fairfax, published in 1699, although they were overlooked until Firth highlighted them in his work. In one of two papers regarding his actions prior to and during the English Civil War—entitled "A Short Memorial of the Northern Actions, During the War There, From the Year 1642 till the Year 1644"—Fairfax writes, "The first action we had was at Bradford, where we had about 300 men. The Enemy, having about 70 or 800 [probably 700 or 800] pieces of ordnance [cannon], came thither to assault us. We drew out close to the town to receive them. They had advantage of ground, the town being compassed with hills; which made us more exposed to their cannon shot, from which we received some hurt. Yet notwithstanding, our men defended the passages, which they [the Royalist forces] were to descend, so well that they got no ground of us. And now, the day being spent, they drew off; and returned back again to Leeds."

In January 1643, Fairfax marched his men into Leeds and then Wakefield, where he captured 1,500 Royalist troops and their commander, Lord Goring, on 23 January 1643. Despite these victories, his defeat at the hands of William Cavendish, marquis of Newcastle, on 30 June 1643 at Adwalton Moor left all of Yorkshire under Royalist control save for the port of Hull. Assisted by Oliver CROMWELL, Fairfax launched an offensive against the Royalists and won a decisive victory at Winceby (11 October 1643) against Sir John Henderson. At Marston Moor (2 July 1644), he worked with Alexander LESLIE, Lord Leven, and Edward MONTAGUE, second earl of Manchester, to defeat Newcastle and Prince RUPERT. Following the battle at Winceby, Montague wrote that "Sir Thomas Fairfax is a person that exceeds any expressions as a commendation of his resolution and valour." At Helmsley Castle (September 1644), Fairfax was seriously wounded but recovered.

In February 1645, Fairfax was named commander in chief of the New Model Army, the official title of the reformed Parliamentary army. According to Joshua Sprigge in *Anglia Rediviva* (1647), Fairfax's official title was "Captain-General of all the Parliament's Forces in England." As commander, on 14 June 1645 he led some 13,000 forces personally against Prince Rupert, who commanded some 9,000 Royalist troops at Naseby in Northamptonshire, the most decisive battle of the first English Civil War. Historian George Bruce writes: "Prince Rupert's first charge broke the Parliamentary left wing, but as usual the pursuit was carried too far, and before the cavalry returned Cromwell on the right had turned the scale, and the battle was over. The Royalist infantry, overwhelmed by superior numbers, were almost annihilated, 5,000 prisoners and all the artillery being captured." The last Royalist forces were subdued by Fairfax at Langport in July 1645.

King Charles was captured following the defeat at Naseby. When Royalist forces rose up to rescue their sovereign, Fairfax took up arms a second time and led the Parliamentary forces to victory at Maidstone (1 June 1648) and Colchester (13 June 1648). Although he had fought against the king, when Charles was tried and sentenced to death, Fairfax spoke out against the sentence. After the king was beheaded on 30 January 1649, Fairfax agreed to serve as a member of the Council of State, created to establish a new form of government. However, he resigned in protest when his old friend Oliver Cromwell, the new government leader, planned an invasion of Scotland in 1650. Following Cromwell's death in 1658, Fairfax worked with the former Royalist and Parliamentary commander George MONCK to restore the rule of Parliament when its rights were threatened by the military.

In 1660, Fairfax joined with others in inviting Charles II, son of the executed king, to come to England to succeed to the throne, vacant since his father's death 11 years earlier. This, however, was Fairfax's last public service. He retired to his estate at Nunappleton, near Cawood in Yorkshire, where he died on 12 November 1671 at the age of 59.

References: Markham, Clements R., *A Life of the Great Lord Fairfax, Commander-in-Chief of the Army of the Parliament of England* (London: Macmillan and Company, 1870); Gibb, Mildred Ann, *The Lord General, a Life of Thomas Fairfax* (London: L. Drummond, Ltd., 1938); Wilson, John, *Fairfax: A Life of Thomas, Lord Fairfax, Captain-General of all the Parliament's Forces in the English Civil War, Creator & Commander of the New Model Army* (London: John Murray, 1985); *A Perfect Diurnall of Some Passages in Parliament and Daily Proceedings of the Army under His Excellency the Lord Fairfax from Munday the 29 of January till Mund. the 5 of February 1648 [1649 N.S.]: Containing an Account of the Beheading of King Charles the First* (London: Printed for Francis Coles & Lawrence Blacklock, ca. 1649); Sprigge, Joshua, *Anglia Rediviva; England's Recovery: Being the History of the Motions, Actions and Successes of the Army Under the Immediate Conduct of His Excellency Sr. T. Fairfax, Kt., Captain-Gen. of all the Parliaments Forces in England. . . .* (London: Printed for John Partridge, 1647); Young, Peter, *Naseby 1645: The Campaign and the Battle* (London: Century Publishing, 1985), 119–120; Bruce, George, "Naseby," in *Collins Dictionary of Wars* (Glasgow, Scotland: HarperCollins Publishers, 1995), 174.

Farragut, David Glasgow (James Glasgow Farragut) (1801–1870) *American naval officer, first admiral in the United States Navy*

David Farragut was born James Glasgow Farragut at Campbell's Station, near Knoxville, Tennessee, on 6 July 1801. His father, Jorge Farragut, a sailor of Spanish descent, had immigrated to the United States and served in the Revolutionary War; he went on the serve in the War of 1812 before his death in 1817. Through circumstances still unclear, the Farragut family became friends with Commander David Porter of the United States Navy, and Porter offered to take the young James into his care and sponsor him in a naval career. The Farraguts accepted, and on 17 December 1810, at the age of 9½, Farragut was appointed a midshipman, posted to Porter's ship. This was common in navies of the time, and such boys were taught mathematics, navigation, and other academic subjects while learning the practical aspects of seamanship, signaling, and boat handling. It was at about this time that Farragut changed his first name from James to David, as a compliment to his guardian.

Porter's ship, the USS *Essex,* sailed to join a squadron in the West Indies at the start of the War of 1812 but was then sent south to round Cape Horn and cruise the Pacific. Several British prizes were taken in the Pacific, and Farragut saw action at the age of 11. In 1813, he was given command of a British prize and ordered to sail her to Valparaiso. The British captain refused to accept orders from a 12-year-old midshipman and went below for his pistols. Farragut promptly took command, saw his orders obeyed, and took the boat into Valparaiso. On 28 March 1814, he took part in the bloody encounter at Valparaiso between the *Essex* and the *Cherub* and *Phoebe,* and when the wounded were taken back to the United States, he worked ceaselessly as assistant to the surgeon on the long journey home. He then served in the naval force sent to reinforce the American ships fighting the pirates in the Mediterranean, but hostilities had ceased before they got there.

Farragut then pursued the normal career of a naval officer. He served on many ships, helped to put down piracy in the West Indies, was promoted to lieutenant in 1825, built docks for naval vessels, and spent many long months cruising the Gulf of Mexico, an experience that was to prove useful for the two battles that were to make his name in the Civil War (1861–65).

The blockade of the Confederacy proposed by the aged commander in chief General Winfield SCOTT at the start of the conflict had not attracted much public attention. It was seen as a minor issue compared to the battles on land, but President Lincoln had seen the need for a blockade and realized that command of the sea and the taking and neutralization of Confederate ports was an important factor in winning the war. Early in 1862, it was decided to capture one of the South's major ports—New Orleans. The city was an important center, the largest and wealthiest city in the Confederacy, but it lay more than 100 miles from the sea. The difficulty in blockading New Orleans was caused by the Mississippi delta, which meant that Confederate ships had four different channels by which they could reach the open sea, and blockading each channel with Union warships would need an entire fleet. Twenty miles upstream from the junction of the four channels, known as Head of Passes, two strong forts dominated the river, soundly built and with heavy guns that could destroy any ship passing between them. Above that, it was known the Confederates were building ironclad rams and fireships that could easily destroy the ocean-going Union ships unable to maneuver in the narrow river channel. To add to the difficulty, the river changed course so rapidly that what was a clear channel for ocean-going ships one week would be a treacherous sandbar the next.

Farragut, now a captain, had played little part in the conflict so far, but he was chosen for the task because of his reputation as a superb ship handler and for the meticulous preparations he made for any operation he undertook. Although now over 60 years old, he willingly accepted the task and arrived with his force off the Mississippi delta on 22 February 1862. His first obstacle was the shallowness of the channel, which meant reducing the draught of his ships by offloading as many stores as possible from his larger vessels. Even then, it took until 7 April to haul the *Pensacola* and *Mississippi* over the sand banks into the main river channel. Farragut then sent a survey party up the river; they discovered the Confederates had built a boom of logs and chains across it under the guns of two forts dominating the river. On the night of 20 April, a daring raid by two of his gunboats broke the boom, and on the 24th, Farragut took his fleet up-river. Though the two forts' guns inflicted severe damage, Farragut's force got through and promptly found itself facing the fireships and Confederate ram ships that had come downstream to meet them. Farragut's insistence on the intensive training of his crews now earned its reward when his own ship, the *Hartford,* still under the guns of the fort, was set ablaze by a fireship. His men rallied to his commands, put out the fires, and maneuvered their ship out of the shallow waters while still returning enemy fire.

On 25 April, Farragut's fleet steamed into New Orleans and anchored with their great guns dominating the city. (It remained in Union hands till the end of the war.) His success in taking New Orleans was acknowledged by his promotion to the new rank of rear admiral on 16 July 1862. Then, under orders from Washington, and much against his will, Farragut sailed upstream in an attempt to take Vicksburg, the Confederate stronghold. This was unsuccessful, although Farragut sailed his squadron there again the following year to assist General Ulysses GRANT in his attempts to take it. The narrow confines of the river and encounters with Confederate rams built for use on the Mississippi meant that Farragut's ocean-going wooden ships were of little use inland, and at last he was allowed to sail back downriver to the open sea to resume the blockade.

By 1864, the Union blockade had proved so effective that the Confederacy had only three ports open to ships of deep draught: Mobile, Charleston and Wilmington. Farragut, still commanding the Gulf squadron, determined that Mobile should be neutralized, especially as he knew the Confederates were building a massive iron-clad ram ship there whose armor would make her almost invulnerable to the Union fleet. He also knew that Mobile Bay was protected by two heavily gunned forts: Fort Gaines and Fort Morgan, three miles apart with a field of floating mines (known as torpedoes) laid in the waters between them. The only clear channel passed under the guns of Fort Morgan. Reconnaissance by night had revealed that many of the torpedoes had been rendered useless by water seeping into them, but Farragut knew there were still enough active to cripple his fleet.

At 5:30 A.M. on 5 August 1864, Farragut's squadron sailed into the bay in two columns side by side, with Farragut in his flagship, the *Hartford.* As he had done at New Orleans, the 63-year-old climbed up the rigging to see over the smoke of his ship's guns, and his flag captain sent a sailor up behind him to tie the admiral to the shrouds. As the leading Union ship, *Tecumseh,* reached the narrowest part of the channel, its captain altered direction away from Fort Morgan's guns into the minefield and struck a torpedo (mine) a moment later. As the *Tecumseh* sank, the ship behind her, *Brooklyn,* stopped her engines and was swung round by the current, blocking the ships behind her as well as the column to her right. The entire squadron was then at a halt with the guns of Fort Morgan firing at them at close range. Disaster threatened, but Farragut signaled the *Brooklyn* to proceed and ordered the squadron to alter course and sail through the minefield. When someone cried a warning about the "torpedoes," he answered with the shout for which he is still remembered: "Damn the torpedoes. Full speed ahead, Drayton." The whole squadron followed him through the minefield into Mobile Bay with torpedoes bumping against their sides, but not one exploded. Once inside the bay, they made short work of the Confederate warships facing them, though it needed the firepower of the entire squadron to force the massive ironclad *Tennessee* to surrender.

After his victory at Mobile Bay, Farragut resumed his blockade duties in the Gulf, but he was now a tired man and sought to be relieved of duty. He returned to New York, and in December 1864 Congress created the new rank of vice admiral for him. On 25 July 1866, he became the first admiral (four stars) in American history. It was as admiral that he made a goodwill visit to Europe in 1867–68, flying his flag on the USS *Franklin.* He retired shortly afterwards and died at Portsmouth, New Hampshire, on 14 August 1870.

One of the officers who had sailed in Farragut's squadron as he fought his way upriver to New Orleans was Lieutenant George DEWEY. When, as Admiral Dewey, he steamed into Manila Bay nearly 40 years later to face a Spanish fleet far larger his own, he said his plan of attack was based on the simple question: "What would Farragut have done?"

References: Murphy, J. K., *The Lincoln Gunboats* (Marholm, Peterborough, U.K.: Schoolhouse Publishing, 1999); Schneller, Robert John, Jr., *Farragut: America's First Admiral* (Washington, D.C.: Brassey's, 2002); Duffy, James P., *Lincoln's Admiral: The Civil War Campaigns of David Farragut* (New York: Wiley, 1997); Hearn, Chester G., *Admiral David Farragut: The Civil War Years* (Annapolis, Md.: Naval Institute Press, 1998); Martin, Christopher, *Damn the Torpedoes! The Story of America's First Admiral: David Glasgow Farragut* (London and New York: Abelard-Schuman, 1970); Bruce, Anthony, and William Cogar, "Farragut, David Glasgow," in *An Encyclopedia of Naval History* (New York: Checkmark Books, 1999), 132; North, Bruce, "Farragut, David Glasgow," in *Encyclopedia of American War Heroes* (New York: Checkmark Books, 2002), 89–90.

Fisher, John Arbuthnot, Baron Fisher of Kilverstone (1841–1920) *British admiral*

Born into a naval family in Ceylon (now Sri Lanka) on 25 January 1841, John Arbuthnot Fisher joined the Royal Navy in 1854 when he was 13, beginning his service on the HMS *Victory.* His first major military action came during the Crimean War. On 30 October 1874, he was promoted to captain, and he went on to command a series of ships. He was also named to a committee that drafted a revision of *The Gunnery Manual of the Fleet.* On 11 July 1882, while commanding the battleship HMS *Inflexible,* Fisher shelled Alexandria, Egypt, during a minor war with that nation. In 1887, he was named director of naval ordnance, serving until 1890, when he was appointed as Third Sea Lord to the Board of Admiralty. He later served as superintendent of the Portsmouth ship yard, and commander in chief of the North American and West Indies Station, and he commanded the Mediterranean Fleet. Knighted in 1894, he was promoted to Second Sea Lord in 1902. In 1904, he was named to the panel known as Lord Esher's Committee, which examined ways of reforming the War Office Department.

On 21 October 1904 he became First Sea Lord as operational head of the navy. He brought in reforms and modernized a navy that in many ways had changed little since Admiral Horatio NELSON commanded it in 1804. In his six years as First Sea Lord (1903–09), he challenged the naval hierarchy, firing officers he felt were unqualified and incapable of performing their duties, and he began the construction of new *Dreadnought* battleships. On 9 November 1909, Fisher was ennobled as Baron Fisher of Kilverstone. He retired from the Admiralty in January 1910, but he was recalled to active duty by First Lord of the Admiralty Winston Churchill (later prime minister) to replace Prince Louis of Battenburg (whose German name was held against him) as First Sea Lord soon after the beginning of the First World War in 1914. Battenburg's tenure of office during the war's first months had been rocky: Several major British ships, including the HMS *Audacious,* had been sunk; the Germans had defeated two British ships, the HMS *Good Hope* and the HMS *Monmouth,* at the battle of Coronel; and the blockade of German ports was failing. Fisher's first decision was to name Sir John JELLICOE as Admiral of the Grand Fleet. He also assembled a fleet under the command of Sir Frederick Sturdee to hunt down the German force of Maximilian Graf Von Spee in the South Atlantic. Sturdee found and engaged the ships, the German cruisers *Gneisenau* and *Scharnhorst* and their escorts at the battle of the Falkland Islands (8 December 1914), destroying all but one ship.

Lord Fisher clashed with his political master, Winston Churchill, over the Allied expedition to the Dardanelles, also known as Gallipoli, a landing of British, Australian, and New Zealand troops to force Turkey out of the war and deny Germany a southern ally against Russia. Fisher desired a landing in the Baltic, where Allied forces would meet up with czarist Russian troops to open up the eastern front against Germany, but he was overruled by Churchill, and the Gallipoli landings went ahead. The result was a disaster in which thousands of Allied troops died, leaving Turkey virtually untouched and Russia unaided. Fisher, whose advice against the landings had been ignored, made his feelings known at a meeting of the War Council on 14 May 1915, completing the break between him and Churchill. He resigned his post the following day, and Churchill's resignation followed soon after.

Fisher spent his final years in retirement, publishing his memoirs, *Memories and Records,* in 1919. He died in London on 10 July 1920 at the age of 79 and was buried with full honors at Westminster Abbey in London. He was mourned as one of the giants of British naval history. Historian Michael Lee Lanning writes: "With the exception of Horatio Nelson, Fisher is the dominating figure in all of British naval history. Intelligent, innovative, opinionated, and dedicated accurately describe him. His beliefs in placing quality before quantity and his ability to bring his revolutionary ideas to reality greatly strengthened the British navy and served as a benchmark for navies of the world for the following decades."

References: Hough, Richard Alexander, *Admiral of the Fleet: The Life of John Fisher* (New York: Macmillan, 1970); Mackay, Ruddock F., *Fisher of Kilverstone* (Oxford, U.K.: The Clarendon Press, 1973); Marder, Arthur Jacob, *From the Dreadnought to Scapa Flow: The Royal Navy in the Fisher Era, 1904–1919,* 5 vols. (London: Oxford University Press, 1961–70); Fisher, John Arbuthnot, Baron Fisher, *Memories and Records,* 2 vols. (New York: George H. Doran Company 1920); Lanning, Michael Lee, "John Arbuthnot Fisher," *The Military 100: A Ranking of the Most Influential Military Leaders of All Time* (New York: Barnes and Noble Books, 1996), 249–251.

FitzJames, James *See* BERWICK, JAMES FITZJAMES, FIRST DUKE OF.

Fleetwood, Charles (1618–1692) *English general*
Born in Northamptonshire, Charles Fleetwood studied law and was 24 when he joined the Parliamentary forces upon the outbreak of the first English Civil War in 1642. As commander of a cavalry regiment, he served at Naseby (14 June 1645), the battle that finally crippled the Royalist forces of King Charles I. Elected to Parliament the following year, Fleetwood was named governor of the Isle of Wight in 1649. After the second English Civil War broke out, Fleetwood again took up arms against the Royalist forces, commanding a regiment of cavalry as a general of horse at Dunbar (3 September 1650) and Worcester (3 September 1651). He was close to Oliver CROMWELL, the Parliamentary commander who became lord protector of England in place of the monarchy, and he married Cromwell's daughter Bridget.

Fleetwood was named to the House of Lords, later serving as lord deputy, the commander of English troops in Ireland. In 1659, after Cromwell's death, he was named commander in chief of the army. When Charles II, son of the executed King Charles I, returned to England and was restored to the throne in 1660, Fleetwood, who had had no role in the murder of Charles's father, was allowed to retire without being punished. He died in obscurity in Stoke Newington in London on 4 October 1692, the last of the Parliamentary commanders.

References: Marshall, J. A., *The 'Godly Praetorian': The Political Life and Activities of Lieutenant-General Charles Fleetwood in the Destruction of Richard Cromwell's Protectorate and the Demise of the English Republic, September 1658–December 1659,* Master's thesis, University of Lancaster (U.K.), 1985; *An Outcry after the Late Lieutenant General Fleetwood* (London: Hen. Mason, 1660).

Foch, Ferdinand (1851–1929) *marshal of France*

Ferdinand Foch was born the son of parents of Basque heritage in Tarbes, in the Hautes-Pyrénnées region of France on 2 October 1851. When he was 19, he joined the French army to fight in the Franco-Prussian War of 1870, but the war ended before he could be sent to the front. Nevertheless, his limited military experience gave him the impetus to make the army his career. He gained admittance to the École Polytechnique, after which he went to the École d'Application de l'Artillerie (Artillery Training Institute). He received a commission as an artilleryman in 1873.

After an undistinguished career, in 1885 Foch was sent to the École Supériéure de Guerre (War College), completing his training in two years. In 1894, he returned to this institution as an instructor in military history and strategy; his lectures there were published in 1897 as *The Principles of War* (English translation, 1918), and *The Conduct of War* (1899). In 1905, he was made a regimental commander of artillery. In 1907, with the rank of general, he returned to the École de Guerre, where he served as director until 1911.

When the First World War began in August 1914, Foch, as commander of the XX Corps at Nancy, mobilized French forces and helped to halt the German advance at the Marne (20–24 August 1914). Germany sent thousands of its crack soldiers across the Belgian border into France from Amiens to Verdun. As commander of the newly formed French Ninth Army, Foch,

working with General Michel Maunoury's Sixth Army, General Franchet d'Esperey's Fifth Army, and British general Sir John FRENCH's British Expeditionary Force, blocked the Germans, breaking the lines of the German generals Karl von Bülow and Max Clemens von Hausen and leaving some 800,000 German casualties and more than a million combined French and British dead and wounded. The battle would become just the first step in the horrific campaign of trench warfare that was to mark the war on the western front in the next four years of the conflict.

Foch's command of French forces at the first battle of Ypres (14 October–11 November 1915), as well as at the Somme (1 July–18 November 1916), made him the dominant French commander, although he was blamed for the frightful French losses at the latter battle and sent to the Italian front. However, when French general Robert-Georges NIVELLE's haphazard offensive failed in April 1917, he was replaced by General Phillipe PÉTAIN, who named Foch as chief of the French army General Staff. Less than a year later, on 26 March 1918, Foch was named commander in chief of the Allied armies, the combined force of American, British, and French troops in western Europe. He planned a massive counteroffensive to push back the German advance. On 6 August 1918, and in September he directed the Allied counteroffensive. By November 1918, Germany was finished and sued for peace. Historians believe that Foch's 1918 drive against the Germans was responsible for the end of the conflict after four years of bloodletting. For his services, Foch was named marshal of France in 1919.

Returning to Paris as a hero, Foch was given a parade in his honor on 14 July 1919 in which he rode under the Arc de Triomphe de l'Étoile in front of the men he led into battle. Great Britain subsequently also honored him with a field marshal's baton. In 1921, he visited the United States, where he attended the opening of the Washington Conference on Disarmament, held to demobilize the world's armies following the end of the First World War.

Foch died in Paris on 20 March 1929, age 77, and was buried in the Invalides, near the tomb of NAPOLEON, with full military honors. Although he has been praised for his leadership of French and Allied forces in the First World War, British historian Sir James Marshall-Cornwall blames Foch for the massive number of French and British casualties at the Marne, Ypres, and the Somme: "There is little doubt . . . that his doctrine of pursuing a vigorous offensive under all circumstances was largely responsible for the grievous casualties suffered by the French infantry in the opening battles of 1914."

References: Aston, Major-General Sir George, *The Biography of the Late Marshal Foch* (London: Hutchinson & Company, 1929); Liddell Hart, B. H., *Foch: Man of Orléans,* 2 vols. (London: Penguin, 1937); Foch, Ferdinand, *The Principles of War,* translated by Hilaire Belloc (London: Chapman & Hall, 1918); Marshall-Cornwall, Sir James, *Foch as Military Commander* (London: Batsford, 1972); Bruce, George, "Marne I," in *Collins Dictionary of Wars* (Glasgow, Scotland: HarperCollins Publishers, 1995), 156; Gilbert, Martin, *First World War* (London: Weidenfeld & Nicolson, 1994).

Franks, Tommy Ray (1945–   ) *American general*
Little known until the 2001–02 war in Afghanistan, Tommy Franks subsequently achieved worldwide renown. He was born in Wynnewood, Oklahoma, on 17 June 1945 and became the adopted son of Ray and Lorene Franks. Ray Franks worked in such disparate fields as auto mechanics, banking, and farming. In 1954, the Franks family moved from Oklahoma to Midland, Texas, where Tommy Franks grew up. Coincidentally, he went to school with (although did not personally know) a girl named Laura Welch, who would later marry future president George W. Bush.

Entering the U.S. military in 1967, Franks was commissioned as a second lieutenant after he attended the Artillery Officer Candidate School at Fort Sill, Oklahoma; after graduation, he was assigned as an assistant executive officer at the base. He was then posted to the 9th Infantry Division and sent to Vietnam, where he served as a forward observer and aerial observer with the 2nd Battalion, 4th Field Artillery. He also served as fire support officer with the 5th Battalion (mechanized), 60th Infantry, before he left Vietnam in 1968. Returning to Fort Sill, Franks commanded a cannon battery at the Artillery Training Center.

In 1969, Franks was selected to take part in the U.S. Army's "Boot Strap Degree Completion Program," and he was sent to the University of Texas in Arlington, where in 1971 he graduated with a bachelor's degree in business administration. After leaving college, Franks spent time training in the U.S. Army's Artillery

Advanced Course. In 1973, he was assigned to the 2nd Armored Cavalry in West Germany, where he became the commander of the 1st Squadron Howitzer Battery. He later commanded the 84th Armored Engineer Company. After graduating from the Armed Forces Staff College, in 1976 Franks was assigned to the Pentagon in Washington, D.C., where he served in the Department of Defense's Investigations Division as an army inspector general. The following year, he was posted to the Office of the Chief of Staff of the Army, where he served as a member of the Congressional Activities Team, coordinating department policy on Capitol Hill and rising to become executive assistant of the office.

In 1981, after five years in Washington, Franks was reassigned back to West Germany, where he was made commander of the 2nd Battalion, 78th Field Artillery for a period of three years. In 1984, he returned to the United States, where he attended the Army War College at Carlisle, Pennsylvania, and Shippensburg University, earning his M.S. degree in public administration from the latter institution. Assigned to the III Corps at Fort Hood, Texas, Franks served as a deputy assistant G3 until 1987, when he was named commander of the Division Artillery, 1st Cavalry Division.

During Operation Desert Storm, the 1990–91 military operation to eject Iraqi invasion forces from Kuwait, Franks served as assistant division commander (maneuver) of the 1st Cavalry Division. Following the end of the conflict, he was named the assistant commandant of the Field Artillery School at Fort Sill, Oklahoma, where he had begun his military career. In 1992, he was transferred to Fort Monroe, Virginia, where he served as the first director of the Louisiana Maneuvers Task Force, Office of Chief of Staff, U.S. Army, a position he held until 1994. At that time, he was assigned to South Korea, where he became the commander of the Combined Forces Command and U.S. Forces in Korea. From March 1995 to May 1997, he commanded the 2nd Infantry (Warrior) Division in South Korea. On 30 May 1997, he was made commander of the U.S. Third Army/Army Forces Central Command based in Atlanta, Georgia, where he remained until 2000. On 6 July 2000, he was promoted to commander in chief of the United States Central Command (CENTCOM) at Fort MacDill, Florida; he served in this role until his retirement on 7 July 2003.

On 11 September 2001, terrorists from the group known as al-Qaeda ("The Base"), led by Muslim radi-

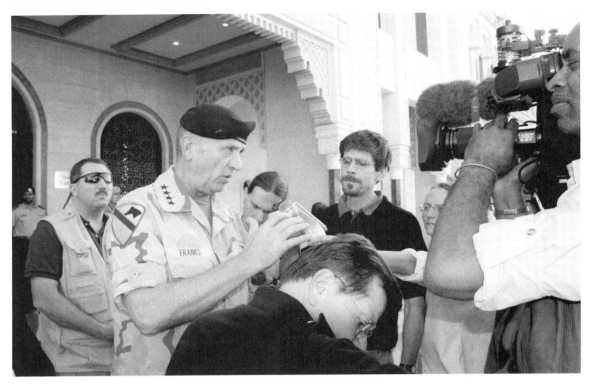

General Tommy Franks speaks with the media during the invasion of Iraq

cal Osama bin Laden, took control of four American aircraft and plunged two of them into the World Trade Center buildings complex in New York City and one into the Pentagon in Washington, D.C.; a fourth was brought down in a field in Pennsylvania when passengers on board attempted to wrest control from the hijackers. Nearly 3,000 people were killed in the worst terrorist attack ever on the American homeland. Bin Laden hid in Afghanistan under the protection of its rulers, a fundamentalist Muslim group known as the Taliban ("Students of Islam"), and their leader, Mullah Mohammad Omar, a radical Islamic scholar. President George W. Bush demanded that bin Laden be turned over to American authorities; when the Taliban refused, he ordered airstrikes on al-Qaeda and Taliban targets inside Afghanistan and initiated Operation Enduring Freedom, the invasion of Afghanistan. Franks, as commander of CENTCOM, became the lead general of the operation, overseeing the complete rout of Taliban

forces, with the assistance of Afghan fighters from the anti-Taliban Northern Alliance troops.

Along with Franks, the war was run by General Richard Myers, chair of the Joint Chiefs of Staff, and Secretary of Defense Donald H. Rumsfeld. Franks's main task was to coordinate the military response, gathering forces in the region and deciding on strategy. Because of computers and satellite technology, he was able to run the operation from Fort MacDill in Florida, although on several occasions he went into the war theater to coordinate maneuvers. Franks became the public face of Operation Enduring Freedom, holding near-daily press conferences to update the world on how the war was going. He had the complete confidence of his superior, Secretary Rumsfeld, who called him "a wise and inspiring commander." Nevertheless, he was criticized in some quarters for his style and compared unfavorably to one of his predecessors as CENTCOM commander, Norman SCHWARZKOPF. But he sidestepped the criticism and went on with his work, trying not to make the same mistakes that had bogged down Soviet forces in Afghanistan for nearly a decade. Afghanistan was unlike any war before it: It was part military operation, part hunt for terrorists, part humanitarian relief. Franks used a delicate touch, relying on Afghan allies to carry out "sensitive" operations, including clashes with al-Qaeda fighters at the Tora Bora mountains.

In late 2002, after he had led the effort that forced the collapse of the Taliban and the flight of al-Qaeda leaders and fighters into neighboring Pakistan, Franks was called upon by the Bush administration to plan an invasion of Iraq. For years since Operation Desert Storm (1990–91), Iraq's tyrannical leader, Saddam Hussein, had managed to circumvent United Nations sanctions, and many believed that he was reconstructing his program of weapons of mass destruction. Though President Bush tried to get a unified front to force Saddam to allow UN inspectors into Iraq, many countries, including France, refused to allow any military action to be pursued. Bush asked Franks to design a war plan for a coalition of several nations, including the United Kingdom and Australia, to carry out an invasion of Iraq. Franks's plan called for invading from Turkey, which did not come off. Nevertheless, after Russian intelligence showed that Saddam was planning a terrorist attack on the United States, an invasion, codenamed Operation Iraqi Freedom, was launched on 20 March 2003. The coalition forces began with an attack—termed *shock and awe*—involving destructive air strikes meant to destroy Saddam's government machinery and at the same time soften up military targets for the ground invasion. Franks's plan of quickly routing the Iraqi Republican Guard, while at the same time speeding his troops northward from Kuwait to the Iraqi capital of Baghdad, worked better than many had expected. On 3 April 2003, just two weeks after the operation began, American forces reached Saddam International Airport, just 10 miles outside of Baghdad. Six days later, on 9 April, American troops moved into Baghdad, took control of the city, and, in a televised celebration, brought down a huge statue of Saddam Hussein. The operation had gone so fast that there were not enough troops in the area to handle the outbreak of looting and civil disorder which gripped the city after Saddam's regime fell. Nonetheless, Franks's plan had worked.

Franks's retirement from the CENTCOM command was announced on 22 May 2003. Secretary of Defense Rumsfeld had offered him the post of army chief of staff, but Franks refused the offer. In 2004, he published his memoirs, *American Soldier,* and campaigned for the reelection of President George W. Bush, who, in December 2004, awarded him the Presidential Medal of Freedom.

During his military career, Franks has earned the Defense Distinguished Medal; twice won the Distinguished Service Medal; four times won the Legion of Merit; and won the Bronze Star for bravery with a "V" for Valor, three Purple Hearts (for wounds suffered in action), the Air Medal, and the Army Commendation Medal, among many other military awards from the United States and other nations around the world. His role in history is still being assessed as the two wars he fought are not yet fully over as of this writing. But his leadership role in two important campaigns means he will be remembered as a commander for some time.

References: Franks, Tommy, *American Soldier* (New York: Regan Books, 2004); Ricks, Thomas E., and Vernon Loeb, "U.S. Commander Shuns Spotlight; Franks Criticized on Pace of War," *The Washington Post,* 9 November 2001, A1; Cornwell, Rupert, "Profile: Tommy Franks," *The Independent* [London], 8 March 2003, 17; McCombs, Phil, "Blood and Guts and Brains and Spirit: After 38 Years, Gen. Tommy Franks is Ready to Take Off His Boots," *The Washington Post,* 23 June 2003, C1; additional Franks biographical information courtesy of the Department of Defense, Washington, D.C.

Frederick II (Frederick the Great) (1712–1786)
king of Prussia

Frederick was born in Berlin on 24 January 1712, the son of the Prussian king Frederick-William I and Sophia-Dorothea, daughter of George I of England. His childhood was unhappy since his father insisted on his undergoing strict military training from his earliest years, combined with a rigid education regime. At age 18, Frederick attempted to escape to England, but he was found out and his father would have executed him on charges of military insubordination if the German emperor, Charles VI, had not intervened on his behalf. Frederick was kept under guard and forced to watch the execution of a young officer friend to whom he had confided his intention to escape.

Realizing his father was inexorable, Frederick resumed his military training and civic duties and, at his father's direction, married Princess Elizabeth of Brunswick-Wolfenbuttel in 1733. For a period (1734–40), he was able to enjoy some leisure at Rheinsberg, studying French literature and music. He corresponded with the philosopher Voltaire and composed several pieces for the flute, an instrument on which he excelled. Following his father's death, he acceded to the throne of Prussia on 31 May 1740.

In October 1740, the German emperor Charles VI died and was succeeded by his daughter Maria Theresa, who inherited Hungary, Bohemia, and Austria as well as other smaller territories on their borders. Frederick revived an old claim on Silesia, lying between Prussia and Austria, and marched his army over its borders in December 1740. He defeated the Austrians at Mollwitz (10 April 1741) and at Chotusitz (17 May 1742), forcing Maria Theresa to cede Upper and Lower Silesia to him by the Peace of Breslau (11 June 1742).

In the Second Silesian War (1744–45), Frederick acquired more of Silesia and then spent 11 years of peace in introducing radical reforms of the Prussian government's administration and improving its finances. The year 1756 saw the start of the Seven Years War in Europe, in which Frederick took the opportunity to fight the Third Silesian War, which won him more territory from the weakened Austrians. When the war ended with the Peace of Hubertushof (15 February 1763), his reputation as a military leader was known across Europe. In 1772, he joined with Russia and Austria in the first partition of Poland, by which he acquired Polish Prussia. This enabled him to join Brandenburg and Pomerania, which Prussia had long ruled, into one territory with Prussia itself. Finally, in 1778 a brief campaign won him more territory around Nuremburg, north of Bavaria, and the Treaty of Teschen gave him the Franconian principalities.

Frederick the Great died at Potsdam on 17 August 1786, having doubled the territory ruled by Prussia and leaving his successor with one of the finest armies in Europe and a full treasury. As good an administrator as he was a military leader, Frederick had fought wars and left Prussia with a large standing army, a sound economy, its treasury full, and its people prosperous. He had raised Prussia from a minor kingdom into a state that challenged Austria as the major Germanic power, a challenge

that would grow until a family descendant (from Frederick's nephew), William I of Prussia, became emperor of Germany in 1871, less than a century later.

References: Bongard, David L., "Frederick II the Great," in *The Encyclopedia of Military Biography*, edited by Trevor N. Dupuy, Curt Johnson, and David L. Bongard (London: I. B. Taurus, 1992), 258–259; Duffy, Christopher, *Frederick the Great: A Military Life* (London: Routledge, 1988); Barker, Thomas M., ed., *Frederick the Great and the Making of Prussia* (New York: Holt, Rinehart and Winston, 1972); McLeod, Toby, "Frederick II 'the Great', King of Prussia," in *The Oxford Companion to Military History*, edited by Richard Holmes (New York: Oxford University Press, 2001), 321–323.

French, Field Marshal Sir John Denton Pinkstone, first earl French of Ypres and High Lake (1852–1925) *British general*

John Denton Pinkstone French was born in Ripple Vale, Kent, England on 28 September 1852, the son of Commander John Tracey William French of the British Royal Navy. He was descended from the French family of French Park, County Roscommon, Ireland. After entering the British navy in 1866, he served as a naval cadet and midshipman but transferred to the army eight years later. He saw military action with the 19th Hussars in the Sudan (1884–85) and served as a commander of the 1st Cavalry Brigade during the Boer War (1899–1902), in which he commanded British forces at the battles of Elandslaagte (21 October 1899), Reitfontein (24 October 1899), Lombard's Kop (30 October 1899), and the capture of Bloemfontein and Pretoria in 1900. He was promoted to general in 1907 and also served as inspector general of the forces from 1907 to 1911, when he was appointed chief of the Imperial General Staff. In 1913, he was promoted to the rank of field marshal.

With the outbreak of the First World War in August 1914, French was named as commander of the British Expeditionary Force (BEF), which was sent to mainland Europe to assist the French army against the invading Germans. (Ironically, his sister, Charlotte French Despard, was one of Britain's leading campaigners against British involvement in the conflict.) French commanded four full British divisions into France and placed them to the left of the French Fifth Army. At Mons (August

1914), British forces repelled the Germans, but the French had begun to withdraw from the area, and therefore the British were forced to do the same. At Le Câteau (August 1914), the British again took on the German First Army; however, once again French suffered a reverse when British general Horace Lockwood Smith-Dorrien held his II Corps forces back, costing the allies a victory; French later fired Smith-Dorrien. Disgusted, French sent a letter to Lord KITCHENER, the secretary of war for England, asking to be relieved of duty rather than continue to send his men needlessly to their deaths. Kitchener met with French in September 1914 and pressured him into agreeing to remain in his position. French commanded British forces at the first battle of Ypres (31 October–17 November 1914), Festuburt (15–25 May 1915), and Loos (25 September–19 October 1915); each of these battles failed to break the German lines. At the outset of the second battle of Ypres, he reported back to London that the Germans were utilizing poison gas. The *Daily Mirror* reported, "Sir John French last night communicated the following, dated yesterday: Yesterday (Thursday) evening the enemy developed an attack on the French troops on our left in the neighbourhood of Bixschoote and Langemarck, on the north east of Ypres salient. This attack was preceded by a heavy bombardment, the enemy at the same time making use of a large number of appliances for the production of asphyxiating gases. The quantity produced indicates long and deliberate preparation for the employment of devices contrary to the terms of the Hague Convention, to which the enemy subscribed."

As the conflict dragged on, French blamed France and his own high command in London for failing to send sufficient equipment to accomplish victory. In December 1915, Lord Kitchener relieved French of his duties, and he was succeeded by his deputy, Sir Douglas HAIG, to effect a closer cooperation with the French and their high command, most notably General Joseph Jacques Césaire JOFFRE. Historian William Philpott writes:

> In August 1914 the British Expeditionary Force (BEF), commanded by Field Marshal Sir John French, had joined their French allies in the field, but the failure to establish a proper chain of command soon caused tensions which were to compromise the cohesion and military effectiveness of the alliance on the battlefield. By the summer of 1915 French's independent demeanour had obliged Kitchener to give in to Joffre's increasingly strident demands for a formal recognition of French authority over the BEF. A similar situation existed in civil-military co-ordination, both in Britain, where Sir John French and Kitchener had long since fallen out over military policy and Kitchener's Cabinet colleagues were increasingly at variance with the Secretary of State's conduct of the war, and in France, where the French opposition were anxious to wrest greater control of the war effort from Joffre and his civilian protector, [Alexandre] Millerand.

Returning to London, French was created Viscount French in honor of his services and became an efficient commander in chief of Home Forces. He was named lord lieutenant of Ireland in 1918, serving until 1921, when he retired and was awarded a grant of £50,000 by the British government. He was also created Earl French of Ypres and High Lake. His only writing is a volume of reminiscences of his command, entitled *1914* (published 1919). His war diaries and addresses were edited by his son, Major Gerald French, and published in 1937. He died in London on 22 May 1925 at the age of 73. Historian James Lucas writes:

> There is no doubt that French was a difficult person, who found it hard to communicate with or trust foreigners. He had been in the Sudan at the time of the Fashoda incident when a French military force had tried to claim British territory. He had also witnessed the pro-Boer sentiments of the French with distaste. He was, thus, an unwilling ally, but once he was totally involved he was absolutely loyal and dependable. He was prickly, being quick to take offense, and was stubborn in defense of his principles. A brave and skilled soldier, he showed himself to be as able to organize and command an expanding British army in France and Flanders as he had been in South Africa. He was given no chance, given the condition of trench warfare, to use the British cavalry in the war which he would have liked. Had he had that opportunity, then he might have scored as complete a victory over the Germans in 1914 as he had over the Boers more than a decade earlier.

References: French, Gerald, *The Life of Field-Marshal Sir John French, First Earl of Ypres, . . .* (London: Cassell and Company, Limited, 1931); Blake, Martin Joseph, "Field-Marshal Sir John French," *The Journal of the Galway Archaeological and Historical Society* 8, no. 4 (1915): 247–251; Napier, Robert M., *Sir John French and Sir John Jellicoe: Their Lives and Careers* (London: The Patriotic Publishing Company, 1914); Goldman, Charles Sydney, *With General French and the Cavalry in South Africa* (London: Macmillan and Co., Limited, 1902); French, John Denton Pinkstone, *Some War Diaries, Addresses, and Correspondence of Field Marshal the Right Honourable, the Earl of Ypres,* edited by Gerald French (London: H. Jenkins, 1937); Wallace, Edgar, *Britain's Great Men: Field Marshal Sir John French and His Campaigns* (London: George Newnes, 1914); "Gas Fumes that Drove Back Our Ally. Sir J French Reports that British Had to Re-adjust Line to New Front," *Daily Mirror,* 24 April 1915, 1; Philpott, William, "Squaring the Circle: The Higher Co-ordination of the Entente in the Winter of 1915–16," *English Historical Review* (September 1999); Cassar, George H., *The Tragedy of Sir John French* (Newark: University of Delaware Press, 1985).

G

Gaiseric (Genseric) (ca. 390–477) *king of the Vandals*

Little is known of Gaiseric, also known in history as Genseric, who was apparently born about A.D. 390. Some sources state that he was the illegitimate son of Godigesel, the leader of the Vandals during their invasion of the Iberian Peninsula (now modern Spain and Portugal), and the brother of Gunderic, the Vandal king and military leader. Historian Poultney Bigelow, writes: "Genseric, the first Prussian Kaiser of Europe, was born about four centuries after Christ in that swamp and sand district of Brandenburg where now stands the palace of Potsdam. History is silent on many details of his life and we must therefore venture a guess now and then after the manner of our scientific colleagues. We select Potsdam as the birthplace of Genseric because of its strategic position between the Baltic and the Elbe, at the centre of waterways admirably suited to commerce or piracy, and therefore marked by Providence as the residence of Prussian or Vandal kings."

In 428, Gaiseric succeeded his brother Gunderic as leader of the Vandals. The following year, when Bonifacius, the Roman governor of (North) Africa, revolted against Rome, he asked the Vandals for military assistance. Gaiseric instead saw an opportunity for the Vandals to win land and treasure. He led the tribe, with an estimated 15,000 troops, from Spain into Africa, where they took advantage of Bonifacius's weakness and proceeded to loot and rob the treasures of Roman Africa in Mauritania and Numidia. Bonifacius tried to hold back the Vandal assault, but he and his supporters were defeated at the city of Hippo Regius in Numidia (431), and Bonifacius fled back to Rome; he would be defeated in 432 at Ravenna by the Roman army under Flavius AETIUS. Their march through Africa unimpeded, the Vandals moved onto Carthage, captured that city on 19 October 439. Now in control of a strategic center and an important port and trading city, Gaiseric proceeded to make Carthage his new capital, the hub of a military empire from which his Vandal ships raided cities around the Mediterranean, including Sicily, Corsica, and areas of southern Europe.

In 455, the widowed Roman empress Licinia Eudoxia (422–462) sent a message to Gaiseric asking for his assistance in fighting Petronius Maximus, who had taken the throne of her murdered husband, the Roman emperor Valentinian III. The Byzantine writer and historian Malchus wrote of this period:

> Around this time, the empress Eudoxia, the widow of the emperor Valentinian and the daughter of the emperor Theodosius and Eudocia, remained unhappily at Rome and, enraged at the tyrant Maximus because of the murder

of her spouse, she summoned the Vandal Gaiseric, king of Africa, against Maximus, who was ruling Rome. He came suddenly to Rome with his forces and captured the city, and having destroyed Maximus and all his forces, he took everything from the palace, even the bronze statues. He even led away as captives surviving senators, accompanied by their wives; along with them he also carried off to Carthage in Africa the empress Eudoxia, who had summoned him; her daughter Placidia, the wife of the patrician Olybrius, who then was staying at Constantinople; and even the maiden Eudocia. After he had returned, Gaiseric gave the younger Eudocia, a maiden, the daughter of the empress Eudoxia, to his son Huneric in marriage, and he held them both, the mother and the daughter, in great honor.

Eudoxia and her daughter were held by Gaiseric at Carthage until 462, a period of seven years, after which they were released when the Eastern Roman emperor Leo I paid Gaiseric and the Vandals a large ransom.

Following the plunder of Rome, Gaiseric's forces moved east, sacking Greece and Dalmatia. Several rulers, including Leo I, the Eastern Roman emperor, and Majorian, the Western Roman emperor, tried to defeat Gaiseric, but they were unsuccessful. (Majorian was murdered in a mutiny by the chief Roman general Ricimer after his failure to defeat Gaiseric.) Leo I's campaign in 468 against Gaiseric and the Vandals led to the battle of Cape Bona, where, historian George Bruce writes, "the Roman fleet of 1,100 galleys and transports under Basiliscus [fought] the fleet of Vandals under Genseric. The Romans were lying at anchor, having landed their troops, and Genseric, taking advantage of a favorable wind, sent in a fleet of fireships following them up by a determined attack. More than half the Roman ships were destroyed." Because of this, the Eastern Roman emperor Zeno was compelled by necessity to sign a treaty of peace with Gaiseric in 476.

Gaiseric died in 477 and was succeded by his son Hunneric. However, without Gaiseric's leadership, the Vandal hold on power waned, and they became a powerless group within a few years. Despite his numerous victories and lengthy rule, Gaiseric remains barely known today. His descendant Gelimer (also known as Geilamir, fl. 530–34), the last king of the Vandals, was defeated by BELISARIUS in 533.

References: Bigelow, Poultney, *Genseric: King of the Vandals and First Prussian Kaiser* (New York: G. P. Putnam's Sons, 1918); "Gaiseric," in *The Hutchinson Dictionary of Ancient and Medieval Warfare* (Oxford, U.K.: Helicon Publishing, Ltd., 1998); Procopius, *History of the Wars, Books I and II,* translated by Henry Bronson Deweing (London: W. Heinemann Ltd., 1914), II:23–73; Gordon, Colin Douglas, *The Age of Atilla: Fifth-Century Byzantium and the Barbarians* (Ann Arbor: University of Michigan Press, 1960); Bruce, George, "Cape Bona," in *Collins Dictionary of Wars* (Glasgow, Scotland: HarperCollins Publishers, 1995), 49.

Gates, Horatio (ca.1728–1806) *American general*

Horatio Gates was born about 1728 (some sources report 1727) in Maldon, Essex, England. Historians have noted the theory that Gates was the illegitimate son of Sir Robert Walpole, prime minister of England (1721–42); this, however, is now commonly discounted. Gates joined the English army and, in 1755, was sent to Halifax, Canada, where he served under Governor-General Edward Braddock, first in Canada and then in Braddock's campaign against Fort Duquesne (now Pittsburgh, Pennsylvania) as part of the French and Indian War (1754–63). During that campaign, Gates was shot and badly wounded, but he recovered after a long rehabilitation. He was then sent to Fort Pitt, where he served as a brigade major under his friend, Brigadier General Robert Monckton. In 1762, he was part of Monckton's successful expedition to the West Indies, resulting in the capture of Martinique. Following this action, Gates returned to England, where he was appointed a major and attempted to purchase a lieutenant colonelcy. Unsuccessful, he returned to America in August 1762, only to find he had lost his commission as a major, whereupon he and his family went back to England. He resigned from the army in 1769 and in 1772 returned to America once more and purchased a plantation in what is now West Virginia.

When the colonies broke off from England in 1775 and declared their independence, Gates offered his services not to his homeland but to his adopted country. In July 1775, he was appointed as adjutant general, and the following year, he was made commander of the northern Continental army. In August 1777, he was named to succeed General Philip Schuyler as commander of the entire Northern Department of the Continental army. Leading his forces into battle, Gates defeated General

Horatio Gates

John BURGOYNE twice at Saratoga (19 September and 7 October 1777), after which Burgoyne surrendered his army to Gates. Historians believe, however, that it was the actions of Gates's subordinates, including Schuyler and Benedict Arnold, that caused Burgoyne's defeat; nevertheless, Congress voted a resolution to congratulate Gates for the victory. For his service, in November 1777 he was named as president of the new Board of War and

Ordnance, a body not unlike the modern Department of Defense.

An intrigue to have Gates replace General George WASHINGTON as commander of the Continental army failed, but Gates remained popular, and on 13 June 1780 he was named commander of the army's Southern Department. His first offensive in this role was on 16 August 1780 against Lord CORNWALLIS, the British commander, at Camden, South Carolina, where the American forces were badly beaten. His superiors questioned his conduct during the battle, and Gates was replaced by General Nathanael GREENE as commander of the Southern Department. Suspended from the service, he was investigated by a military court of inquiry, but it was not until 1782 that the court dismissed all of the charges. By that time, the war was virtually over, and Gates never saw military action again. On 17 August 1782, he wrote to General Washington: "General [Benjamin] LINCOLN has in his letter acquainted me that it is your Excellency's desire to know, if I wish to take Command in in the Army this Campaign. I beg upon your Excellency to believe that I am always ready to obey your Commands, and shall be most happy when I can execute them to your satisfaction; I have but to entreat that no attention to me, or my Rank, may interfere, or break in, upon any part of your Excellency's arrangements . . ." No command was forthcoming.

Gates returned to his lands in Virginia at the end of the American Revolution and remained there until 1790, when he sold the estate and moved to New York City; at the same time, he freed all his slaves and gave financial help to those who needed it. In 1800, he was elected to the New York state legislature, but he resigned soon after taking his seat. He died at his home in New York City on 10 April 1806.

References: Nelson, Paul David, *General Horatio Gates: A Biography* (Baton Rouge: Louisiana State University Press, 1976); Patterson, Samuel White, *Horatio Gates: Defender of American Liberties* (New York: Columbia University Press, 1941); Mintz, Max M., *Generals of Saratoga: John Burgoyne and Horatio Gates* (New Haven, Conn.: Yale University Press, 1990); "Horatio Gates to George Washington, 17 August 1782," George Washington Papers, 1741–1799, Series 4: General Correspondence, 1697–1799, Manuscript Division, Library of Congress, Washington, D.C.; North, Bruce, "Gates, Horatio," in *Encyclopedia of American War Heroes* (New York: Checkmark Books, 2002), 96.

Genghis Khan (Chinggis Khan) (ca. 1162–1227)
Mongol emperor and military leader

Though he became famous for his leadership, military skills, and cruelty, little is known of Genghis Khan's early life. He was born about 1162 in the northern area of what is now Mongolia, into a family that appears to have been of noble origin. However, his life changed when he was nine years old and his father was murdered. It was left to his mother to teach him the ways of becoming a fighter. Before his 20th birthday, around 1180, Genghis assembled a group of men loyal to him; this group was called Nököd. Through a series of marriages, family and tribal ties, and other alliances, by 1206 Genghis had brought together many of the bands of nomadic tribes in what is now Mongolia.

Utilizing the military prowess of some of these fierce warriors, Genghis formed an army. He also claimed that he was of divine parentage, and this was one reason he received obedience from those who served under him. This loyalty became a blood brotherhood known as "anda." However, Genghis Khan also showed that he was completely ruthless: When men were no longer needed, he had them murdered and replaced. This ruthlessness was also applied to those he fought: In Herat, now in modern Afghanistan, he built a tower with the skulls of 20,000 people he had systematically slaughtered.

In 1211, Genghis and his armies marched into northern China, which at that time consisted of three independent empires: the Song (Sung) Empire in the south, the Qin Empire in the north, and the Xi-Xia (Hsi Hsia) Empire in the northwest. In a series of battles, he defeated numerous tribes in the northern area, and by 1217 he controlled most of northern China. (However, the ultimate conquest of "the land of Qin" was not completed until 1234, after Genghis had died.) In 1218, his men moved westward, conquering the area of Qara-Khitai in central Asia. Genghis's forces also took on the Muslim rulers of southeastern Asia, including the empire of the Khwarazm Shah, who controlled what is now Iraq, Iran, Afghanistan, and Turkmenistan. It was during this campaign that Genghis's men slaughtered the populations of Herat, Samarkand, Nishapur, Merv, and Bokhara. According to one historical account: "Genghis' armies were composed of mounted archers, trained from an early age in military techniques largely indistinguishable from what was required of them as hunters and herders. Hence Genghis was able to mobilize an unusually high proportion of the adult male population. As expansion continued, the Mongols secured the services of Chinese and Muslim siege engineers. The army was intensely maneuverable, which may partly explain the (probably misleading) impression of vast numbers. Genghis' practice of warfare had been much admired by such modern authorities as Liddell Hart."

It was during Genghis's push into Central Asia to fight the tribe known as the Tanguts that he suddenly died in August 1227. He was interred by his troops, but his burial place is unknown. Genghis's place in history is assured as perhaps one of the most important warrior/conquerors. Historian E. D. Phillips writes: "As a leader and conqueror Chingis ranks with Alexander and Napoleon, though his methods were those of his fellow nomads ATTILA and TIMUR. His armies were not overwhelmingly numerous, though their mobility often made them appear so. His cruelty had been learnt in a hard school, among peoples whose traditions included tribal massacre after a conclusive victory. His religious vision of destined rule over the world was an extreme example of the belief in historic mission which has been a commonplace even among Christian rulers down to recent times. . . ."

References: "Genghis (Chinggis) Khan" in *The Oxford Companion to Military History,* edited by Richard Holmes (New York: Oxford University Press, 2001), 354; "Khan, Genghis," in *Command: From Alexander the Great to Zhukov—The Greatest Commanders of World History,* edited by James Lucas (London: Bloomsbury Publishing, 1988), 42–43; Edwards, Mike, "Genghis: Lord of the Mongols," *National Geographic* 190, no. 6 (December 1996): 2–37; Phillips, E. D., *The Mongols* (London: Thames and Hudson, 1969), 67.

Genseric *See* GAISERIC.

Giap, Vo Nguyen (1910/1912–) *North Vietnamese military leader*

Despite his lengthy career fighting for the independence of his homeland, Vo remains a shadowy figure. He was born in either 1910 or 1912 in the village of An-Xa, in the Quang Binh province, slightly north of the "partition line" located at the 17th parallel, where the division between North and South Vietnam would be located.

His father, a farmer, had also been involved in the movement for Vietnamese independence, and had taken part in the uprising of 1888. Giap spent much of his youth studying and tending to his rice crop to earn enough to pay for his studies at the University of Hanoi, although one source indicates that he actually attended the National Academy [known as Quoc Hoc] in the southern imperial capital of Hue. He spent much of his youth following his father in agitating for independence, joining the political movement known as the Tan Viet (New Vietnamese Revolutionary Party), which fought for an end to French colonial rule about 1926. In 1930, after joining the Indochinese Communist Party (ICP), he was arrested by the French authorities and sent to prison for three years. Following his release, he restarted his campaign for independence and helped to organize and coordinate student strikes across the country. At the same time, he continued his studies at the University of Hanoi, earning a degree in law in 1937. While in the university he met Dang Xuan Khu, later to become Trung Chinh, with whom Giap coauthored a book, *The Peasant Question (1939).*

In September 1939, hunted by the French, Giap escaped to China, where he met Nguyen Ai Quoc, a shadowy nationalist leader who later took the name of Ho Chi Minh. Ho entered into an alliance with Giap, Chinh, and Pham Van Dong, and in 1941 the four men formed the Vietminh or Viet Minh (Vietnamese Independence League), a revolutionary party modeled on the Soviet Communist Party.

The Second World War afforded great opportunities for the group. The French, fighting off a German invasion and the establishment of the Vichy government in their own country, did not have the resources to rein in the burgeoning Vietnamese independence movement. Giap secretly slipped back into northern Vietnam in 1941, beginning a campaign of disseminating propaganda and serving as Ho Chi Minh's chief lieutenant of the Vietminh movement in northern Indochina. In 1944, Giap was named commander of the Armed Propaganda Brigade, the forerunner of the Vietnamese Liberation Army, later the North Vietnamese Army (NVA).

Giap spent much of his time after the end of the Second World War as a military strategist, utilizing the tactics and system of fighting that Mao Zedong used to bring a communist government to China in 1949. Historian Michael Maclear notes that Giap bombarded the French in Vietnam while the United Nations was fighting in Korea, "Giap, equipped with new heavy mortars from China, targeted a string of French forts in the far north, and one by one they were overwhelmed. Giap then switched to a premature general offensive and sustained several defeats—a setback lasting two years—but the French losses that October (6000 troops killed or captured) were described by Bernard Fall as France's 'greatest colonial defeat since Montcalm died at Quebec.'" After the Geneva agreement of 1954, Giap saw that employing guerilla combat against the American-backed government in Saigon, South Vietnam, would be the best way to overthrow that administration and institute an all-communist state to the entire nation.

Giap rose to become the highest-ranking general in the Quan Doi Nhan Dan Viet Nam (People's Army of Vietnam, or PAVN), in effect in command of all North Vietnamese forces fighting American and South Vietnamese forces. With the formation of the Democratic Republic of Vietnam (DRV) in the north, Giap was named minister of defense, but he remained an integral leader of Ho Chi Minh's fighting force. Because the North Vietnamese Army was not organized like other armies, he did not serve as a field general but rather as a strategist who commanded his men from afar and also supported the Vietcong, communist insurgents in South Vietnam. Ultimately it was his leadership and influence that led the North Vietnamese and their Soviet and Chinese allies to victory despite the fact that they lost battle after battle against the American forces. Giap knew that exerting horrific casualties on the Americans, while at the same time helping to nurture a growing antiwar movement in the United States and around the world, would produce not a decisive military victory but a propaganda triumph that would lead to victory for the North—and he was right.

In 1968, Giap initiated the Tet Offensive on the Vietnamese New Year of Tet, and although his forces were defeated everywhere, the attack served its purposing, creating demoralizing mood against the U.S. government. As the North Vietnamese government in Hanoi opened negotiations with the American government in Paris, and even North Vietnam was subjected to massive casualties and bombings, devastating its economy, Giap continued to carry out regular attacks, which the Americans and their South Vietnamese allies were unable to halt. The attacks finally led the United States to sign a peace treaty in 1973 and carry out a gradual American withdrawal from South Vietnam. Nevertheless, the North Vietnamese continued to aid their Vietcong allies in the south, which resulted in the collapse of the South Vietnamese army by early 1975. That year, Giap was replaced as the chief North Vietnamese strategist by his rival, General Nguyen Chi Trahn. He was therefore not in command when the South Vietnamese government disintegrated, and the North Vietnamese captured Saigon on 30 April 1975, ending a war that had lasted for 40 years.

In the years after the North's victory, Giap was shunted aside and forced from his position as minister of defense. In March 1982, he was removed from the Vietnamese Politburo at the Fifth Communist Party Congress. Despite this, he remained as deputy prime minister until 1991, when he retired. Renowned worldwide for his expertise in guerilla warfare, he is regarded as a national hero.

References: "Vo Nguyen Giap" in *Dictionary of the Vietnam War,* edited by Marc Leepson (New York: Webster, 1999), 435–436; "Giap, Vo Nguyen," in *The Oxford Companion to Military History,* edited by Richard Holmes (New York: Oxford University Press, 2001), 362; Duiker, William J., "People's Army of Vietnam (PAVN)" and "Vo Nguyen Giap" in *Historical Dictionary of Vietnam* (Metuchen, N.J.: The Scarecrow Press, 1989), 138–139, 198–199; Maclear, Michael, *The Ten Thousand Day War: Vietnam: 1945–1975* (New York: Avon Books, 1981).

Golenishchev-Kutuzov, Mikhail See KUTUZOV, MIKHAIL ILLARIONOVICH GOLENISHCHEV.

Gordon, Charles George ("Chinese" Gordon)

(1833–1885) *British general, colonial administrator*
Born in Woolwich, England, on 28 January 1833, Charles Gordon was the fourth son and ninth of 11 children of British general Henry William Gordon. His education was limited: At a young age, he accompanied his family to the island of Corfu, then returned to England and spent some time at Taunton Grammar School before he entered the Royal Military Academy at Woolwich in 1848, when he was 15. After graduation, in June

1852 he was given a commission in the Royal Engineers at the rank of second lieutenant. Initially posted to Chatham, he was transferred to Pembroke Dock in Wales to work on fortifications there.

When the Crimean War began in 1854, Gordon volunteered for service in that conflict. Sent to the region in December 1854, he saw action at Sevastopol and took part in the assault on the Redan (8 September 1855). For his services, Gordon was awarded the French Legion of Honor. In April 1859, he was promoted to the rank of captain and posted to the command of the Royal Engineers at Chatham in England.

When the Second Opium War broke out in 1860, Gordon was sent to Asia, where he served under the command of Sir James Hope Grant, saw action when Beijing (Peking) was seized, and was present when the Chinese emperor's summer palace was burned by the invading forces. For his service in this conflict, Gordon was promoted to brevet major.

When the so-called Taiping (T'aiping) Rebellion broke out in 1851, the ruling Qing (Ch'ing) leader asked Gordon to end the insurrection. Gordon commanded the force to end the uprising, led by the fanatical Tien Wang. Working with American troops under General Frederick Townsend Ward, Gordon and his men protected the city of Shanghai and stormed the city of Singpo (Ts'ing-p'o). When Ward was killed in action, the local Chinese provincial governor asked for a replacement, and Gordon was named. He remained in China, where he helped to establish the "Ever Victorious Army," a mixture of English and Chinese troops. The Taiping Rebellion finally ended when his forces captured the city of Nanking (now Nanjing) in 1864.

Over the next several years, Gordon was promoted to a series of positions, including serving as the governor of Equatoria (Southern Egypt) from 1873 to 1876 and governor general of the Sudan (1877–79). In 1884 the viceroy, or khedive, of Egypt named Gordon as the governor-general of the Sudan for the second time. Gordon's task was to relieve the garrisons under threat from a revolt by the Mahdists, followers of the Mahdi, the leader of the Muslim tribes in the Sudan. Gordon arrived in the Sudan on 18 February 1884 and marched on Khartoum, the capital, rescuing some 2,600 civilians before the Mahdists besieged the city in March. Historian George Bruce writes: "Defended by an Egyptian garrison under General Gordon, this town [Khartoum] was invested by the Mahdi in the early part of 1884, and, after a gallant defence, was stormed [on] 26 January 1885. Gordon was cut down and killed. The forerunners of the relieving force, consisting of the river gunboats under Lord Charles Beresford, arrived off the city on the 28th, two days too late, and after a brief engagement with the Mahdist batteries returned down the river."

Gordon's death has been romanticized: Allegedly, he was caught by several Mahdists and beheaded. Other sources claim that he took his own life, while others say he was wounded and died a slow death. Whatever the cause, Gordon's death came before British forces under Lord Wolseley could relieve the city, a delay caused by the negligence and uncertainty of the British government, which had waited months before dispatching a relief mission. Consequently, Gordon's death played a part in fall of Prime Minister William Gladstone's government.

Gordon's body was never found, but his death took him into the realm of myth. Whatever he was like in real life has been surmounted by his martyrdom, making him larger than life. Gordon was the author of *Reflections in Palestine* (1884).

References: Allen, Bernard Meredith, *Gordon* (London: Duckworth, 1935); Gordon, Henry William, *Events in the Life of Charles George Gordon from Its Beginning to Its End* (London: Kegan Paul, Trench, 1886); Mossman, Samuel, ed., *General Gordon's Private Diary of His Exploits in China* (London: S. Low, Marton, Searle, & Rivington, 1885); Bruce, George, "Khartoum" in *Collins Dictionary of Wars* (Glasgow, Scotland: HarperCollins Publishers, 1995), 126; "Gordon, Maj. Gen Charles George 'Chinese,'" in *The Oxford Companion to Military History*, edited by Richard Holmes (New York: Oxford University Press, 2001), 366; *General Gordon's Mission to the Soudan [sic]. Speech Delivered by the Right Hon. The Marquis of Hartington, M.P., in the House of Commons, on Tuesday, the 13th May 1884, . . .* (London: The National Press Agency, Ltd., 1884); Crabites, Pierre, *Gordon, the Sudan and Slavery* (London: G. Routledge and Sons, Ltd., 1933); Buchan, John, Baron Tweedsmuir, *Gordon at Khartoum* (London: P. Davies, Ltd., 1934).

Graham, James   *See* MONTROSE, JAMES GRAHAM, MARQUIS OF.

Grant, Ulysses Simpson (Hiram Ulysses Grant) (1822–1885) *American general, 18th president of the United States*
Hiram Ulysses Grant was born at Point Pleasant, Clermont County, Ohio, on 27 April 1822, the son of Jesse Grant, a tanner, and Hannah Simpson Grant. In 1823, the year after his son was born, Jesse Grant moved the family to his farm at Georgetown, located about 40 miles from Cincinnati. When Ulysses was of age, his father was able to get him a recommendation from a congressman for an appointment to the U.S. Military Academy at West Point, New York. The congressman, who knew him as Ulysses, added Grant's mother's name, and from West Point onward, he was known as Ulysses Simpson Grant. Grant attended the academy from 1839 to 1843, and although his grades were not great, he did excel in horsemanship. In 1843, he was commissioned into the infantry with the rank of second lieutenant, assigned to the U.S. 4th Regiment, and sent to St. Louis, Missouri.

In 1845, Grant was sent to serve under General Zachary TAYLOR against Mexican forces in Texas. Although Grant was opposed to the war, he fought with honor, seeing action at Monterrey (21–23 September 1846) and at Cerro Gordo (17–18 April 1847), where he took command of a group of fighters. His bravery in action earned him a brevet of first lieutenant following the battle of Molino del Rey (8 September 1847), and he saw additional action at Chapultepec (13–14 September 1847), which resulted in his promotion to captain.

In 1848 following the end of the Mexican War, Grant married Julia Dent. He continued to serve in the army, and in 1851 he was sent to Oregon, but, because of his low pay, he was unable to take his family with him, and he sent them to live in Ohio. While in Oregon, he became lonely and unhappy and began to drink, leading to a severe case of alcoholism. In 1854, this disease impacted on his service, and he was told to sober up or resign his command. Choosing the latter, he returned to his family in Ohio, and for a period of time he worked as a farmer in Ohio. However, finding the work hard and unrewarding, he sold the farm in 1859 and went to St. Louis to find work. There he pursued a series of jobs, including selling real estate and working in his family's leather-goods store in Galena, Illinois, although he failed to gain any satisfaction from these positions.

Although he was not opposed to slavery, Grant did object to the secession of states from the Union.

Ulysses S. Grant

Therefore, when the Civil War broke out in 1861 and President Abraham Lincoln asked for volunteers, Grant responded. After forming a company of volunteers in Galena, he went to the Illinois state capital, Springfield, where he helped to form more companies. In June 1861, Illinois governor Richard Yates gave Grant a commission as colonel of the 21st Regiment of Illinois Volunteers, and in August, at the request of Representative Elihu B. Washburne, President Lincoln commissioned Grant as a brigadier general. He was promptly sent to Camp Girardeau, Missouri, as commander of the District of Southeastern Missouri. There, he having learned the Confederates were moving on Paducah, Kentucky, he forestalled them by occupying the town on 5 September 1861 at the junction of the Mississippi, Ohio, and Tennessee.

In February 1862, Grant seized Forts Donelson and Henry. When Donelson was surrounded, and the Confederate forces refused to surrender, he demanded that it give up without any terms, earning him the nickname "Unconditional Surrender" Grant. For this act, he was promoted to the rank of major general of volunteers and made second in command to General Henry Halleck.

Although most historians consider Grant an exceptional general, he did make several mistakes in the field, most notably at Shiloh, also called Pittsburg Landing, on 6–7 April 1862. Though Halleck had ordered him to move on Confederate forces at Corinth, Mississippi, Grant was surprised by a Confederate attack at Shiloh. The Southerners were forced back to Corinth before Northern reinforcements arrived, but Grant's forces had suffered badly. Halleck, long a critic of Grant, attempted to remove him from command and announced he would take over the governance of the armies of the Tennessee and the Ohio. But then Halleck was posted to Washington in July 1862, and Grant replaced him. He realized that controlling the Mississippi would split the Confederacy, and he resolved to take Vicksburg, "the Fortress of the West." The campaign is still regarded as one of the most tenacious campaigns of the war. After Vicksburg fell on 4 July 1863, Grant was promoted to the rank of major general and made commander of all Union forces west of the Mississippi River. In late 1863, he broke the Confederate lines at Chattanooga, Tennessee, ending southern control of the western theater.

In March 1864, President Lincoln turned to Grant to command all the Union armies and was promoted to lieutenant general on 12 March 1864. Pursuing a campaign of attrition, Grant fought Robert E. LEE's army in Virginia while William SHERMAN, following Grant's strategy, marched his army to the sea, destroying the South's railway system and economic infrastructure as he went. In April 1865, with the South defeated, Grant accepted Lee's surrender at Appomattox Court House, allowing the defeated Southern soldiers to keep their horses and giving them extra rations to take home with them. With the war over, Grant explained to Henry Yates Thompson, a British visitor to the United States, why he was forced to send so many men into the slaughter of battle to win: "My object in war was to exhaust Lee's army. I was obliged to sacrifice men to do it. I have been called a butcher. Well, I never spared men's lives to gain an object; but then I gained it, and I knew it was the only way."

Following Lincoln's assassination in April 1865, Andrew Johnson became president and promoted Grant to full general. Johnson, however, became increasingly unpopular due to his lenient treatment of the former Confederate states. In 1868, Republicans turned to Grant, a man who had never held political office, as their candidate for president. He won the party's nomination and defeated New York governor Horatio Seymour, a Democrat, to become the 18th president of the United States.

In Grant's two terms as president—he was reelected in a landslide in 1872—his administration became known as one of the most corrupt ever, although historians cannot tie any of the corruption to Grant himself. From the "Whiskey Ring" to the "Indian Ring," numerous scandals broke out that soured the nation on its military hero. Nevertheless, Grant did crack down on the Ku Klux Klan and oversaw a mediation that led to payments from the British government for their assistance to the Confederacy during the Civil War. He left office in March 1877, but the Republicans nearly turned to him again three years later, when various party factions at the 1880 Republican Convention wanted to stop Representative James A. Garfield, the eventual party nominee.

Left penniless by a downturn in the economy in 1884, Grant was forced to write his memoirs in an effort to feed his family. When he discovered that he had cancer of the throat, he raced to finish the work, writing the last pages just days before he died on 23 July 1885. He was buried in the huge vault located in New York City that is now called Grant's Tomb.

Historian Michael Lee Lanning writes of Grant's legacy: "Grant—short, stocky and round-shouldered—never impressed anyone with his military bearing. A failure in nearly everything else he attempted, he nevertheless ranks as one of the most influential military leaders in history. His casualty lists were long, and he did indeed drink to excess. However, he won the most divisive and decisive war in U.S. history and ensured that the Union would survive and that slavery would be abolished."

References: McFeeley, William S., Grant: A Biography (New York: Norton, 1981); Coppée, Henry, Grant and His Campaigns: A Military Biography (New York: C. B. Richardson, 1866); Marshall-Cornwall, Sir James Handyside, Grant as Commander (London: Batsford, 1970); John Keegan, "Grant and Unheroic Leadership" in The Mask of Command (Viking/Elisabeth Sifton Books, 1987), 164–234; Thompson, Henry Yates, An Englishman in the American Civil War: The Diaries of Henry Yates Thompson, 1863, edited by Sir Christopher Chancellor (London: Sedgwick and Jackson, 1971); Lanning, Michael Lee, "Ulysses Simpson Grant," in The Military 100: A Ranking of the Most Influential Military Leaders of All Time (New York: Barnes and Noble Books, 1996),127–131.

Greene, Nathanael (1742–1786) American general

Nathanael Greene was born on 7 August 1742 (not 6 June, as reported in some accounts) in the village of Potowomut, near Warwick, Rhode Island, the son of a Quaker farmer. When he was 26, he moved to Coventry, Rhode Island, and was elected to the colonial legislature; he was reelected several times until 1775. In 1774, he joined the Rhode Island militia, but his military activities conflicted with his strict Quaker upbringing, and he was expelled from the Society of Friends.

By 1775, relations between the American colonies and the ruling government in London were at a crisis. Greene was placed in command of a militia unit raised in Rhode Island, and, when the war for independence began, he joined his forces to the colonial army at Cambridge. On 22 June 1775, Greene was appointed a brigadier general by the Continental Congress, and the American commander, General George WASHINGTON, placed him in command of the city of Boston after English forces under Lord William Howe evacuated the city in March 1776. His work in consolidating colonial gains in New England led to his promotion on 9 August 1776 as one of four major generals in the Continental army. Placed in command of American forces on New York's Long Island, Greene became violently ill and could not take part in the battle of Long Island (27 August 1776). He was transferred to take command of Fort Lee, New Jersey, and in October 1776 he succeeded General Israel Putnam as the commander of Fort Washington, New York. Before he arrived there, Fort Washington came under attack by English troops under Lord Howe and the colonial side took heavy losses. Although Greene had not been present when the attack took place, he was widely blamed for the defeat, but Washington, realizing that Greene was blameless, took responsibility for the loss. This confidence in him allowed Greene to command troops in several important battles, most notably at Trenton (26 December 1776), Brandywine (10–11 September 1777), and Germantown (3–4 October 1777).

On the resignation of Thomas Mifflin as quartermaster general, Greene accepted Washington's request to replace him on 2 March 1778 while continuing to command forces on the battlefield. However, in August 1778, after only five months in the post, Greene resigned as quartermaster general when he clashed with the Continental Congress over the rights of a treasury oversight board to interfere with the militia administration.

When General Horatio GATES failed to stop the advances of Lord CORNWALLIS's British forces in South Carolina, Washington again turned to Greene, naming him commander in chief of the southern wing of the Continental army. When Greene arrived in North Carolina in December 1780 to take command, he found an ill-equipped army with low morale facing a vastly superior force under Cornwallis. With tremendous energy, he brought the army into better condition. He then decided to divide his forces and dispersing them around the area, forcing the English to do likewise. At Cowpens, South Carolina, on 17 January 1781, a small American force under General Daniel Morgan defeated an English contingent under Lord Cornwallis. Greene used his dispersed forces to stage a series of hit-and-run attacks on the English, forcing Cornwallis to fight a war for which he was not prepared. Although Greene was defeated at Guilford Court House on 15 March 1781, Cornwallis took so many casualties (548, nearly half his force) that his triumph was a Pyrrhic victory. Unable to pursue

Nathanael Greene

wounded. Once again, however, the English were forced to withdraw to Charleston without following the Americans. Eutaw Springs is generally considered a British victory, but Stuart could not support Cornwallis's troops at Yorktown and remained penned up in Charleston for the rest of the war. This led to Cornwallis's decision to surrender at Yorktown on 19 October 1781, ending the American Revolutionary War.

Although he was a national hero, Greene refused invitations to serve the new government as secretary of War in 1781 and 1784. In recognition of his service, the states of South Carolina and Georgia awarded him land and money. He built an estate on the land in Georgia, naming the property Mulberry Grove, and retired there in 1785. On 19 June 1786, after suffering from sunstroke, Greene died at Mulberry Grove, age 43.

Despite his excellent command of American forces in the war that gave birth to the United States as a nation, Greene's name has been largely forgotten. One biographer, David Paul Nelson, wrote: "The first time [that] Washington met Greene he declared that Greene could be relied upon to assume command of the Continental army should he become incapacitated. Thomas Jefferson asserted long after the war that Greene had no equal as a military thinker among his peers in the officer corps, and Francis Kinloch, a congressman who fought in the war, called him the 'military genius' of the American Revolution. These assessments of Greene are borne out by his military record in both the North and the South, and historians today evaluate his military abilities as highly as did his contemporaries. Few would deny that he deserves to be remembered as the 'strategist of the Revolution.'"

References: Greene, George W., *Life of Nathanael Greene* (New York: G. P. Putnam and Son, 1867–71); Paul, David Nelson, "Greene, Nathanael," in *American National Biography,* edited by John A. Garraty and Mark C. Carnes (New York: Oxford University Press; 24 volumes, 1999), IX:528–30; North, Bruce, "Greene, Nathanael," in *Encyclopedia of American War Heroes* (New York: Checkmark Books, 2002), 102.

Greene or move toward the north, Cornwallis was forced to withdraw to Wilmington and thence to Yorktown. This allowed Greene and his men to gain a much-needed rest. Greene again moved against the British in South Carolina, taking several garrisons and confronting British forces at Orangeburg on 11 May 1781 and at Eutaw Springs on 8 September 1781. Here the British, under Lieutenant Colonel James Stuart, withdrew. However, when Greene's forces stopped to loot the abandoned British camp, Stuart was able to rally his men and return to the field, catching them unprepared and forcing an American evacuation. The British suffered 85 dead and 350 wounded; the Americans had 139 killed and 375

Gustav II (Gustavus Adolphus, Gustavus II, Gustav Adolf the Great) (1594–1632) *king of Sweden*
Gustavus Adolphus was born in Stockholm on 9 December 1594, the son of Charles IX, king of Sweden.

His father prepared him for his role as king by having him taught Latin, Italian, and Dutch by the age of 12 and Spanish, Russian, and Polish later. Introduced into public life early, he was responsible for administering his own estates at 15. When his father died in 1611, Gustavus was, despite his young age, accepted unanimously as the new king, Gustav II.

Gustav began by reorganizing the government and its finances and went on to make peace with Denmark, with whom Sweden had long been at war; this was achieved by the Peace of Knared (28 January 1613). Sweden had also laid claim to and occupied areas across the Baltic Sea to the east, specifically regions of Finland and today's Estonia and Latvia, claims resisted by both Denmark and Poland. He strengthened his hold on these with the treaty of Stolbova (27 February 1617), which excluded the Duchy of Muscovy from access to the Baltic. In 1621, he went to war with Poland and invaded Livonia (today's Latvia), capturing Riga on 13 September 1621. He invaded Lithuania in 1625 and defeated the Polish army at Walhof in January 1626. He then went on to strengthen his hold on the south Baltic by isolating Danzig, but the Polish commander, Stanislaus Koniecpolski, frustrated his efforts, and Gustavus was forced to withdraw after the battle of Stuhm (29 June 1629). He was, however, able to consolidate much of his gains by the six-year truce of Altmark.

Having secured his flanks, Gustav led his army south into Germany in 1630 to aid the Protestant armies fighting against the Catholic League in the Thirty Years War (1618–48). While he overtly declared the reason was to aid the Protestant states of north Germany against the attempts of the Emperor Ferdinand II to restore Catholicism throughout Germany, his real purpose was to ensure that Sweden kept her position of primacy in the Baltic. Imperial success anywhere in the south Baltic could threaten Sweden's commerce, and Gustav was determined that would not happen. He began by landing his army in Pomerania (east Prussia) on 9 June 1630 and promptly attacked and took Stettin, the capital, which he then fortified.

Gustav drove the imperial army out of Pomerania, but while the Swedish army was besieging Spandau and Kustrin, the Catholic forces under the count von TILLY captured Magdeburg, the strongest fortress in north Germany. Gustav now made a treaty with the French (treaty of Barwalde, 13 January 1631), but because of the reluctance of the rulers of Saxony and Brandenburg to join him, he was unable to relieve Magdeburg, which fell on 20 May 1631. On 17 September, however, a combined Saxonian-Swedish army under Gustav's command defeated Tilly at Breitenfeld, just north of Liepzig, and advanced west, occupying the Palatinate and Mainz by the end of 1631.

In April 1632, the Swedes marched east, crossed the Danube, and harried Tilly's forces, pursuing them to the fortress of Ingolstadt, where Tilly died of wounds received. Gustav then advanced and took Munich and would have had a clear road to Vienna itself, if the Holy Roman Emperor Ferdinand had not recalled to service his experienced general Albrecht von Wallenstein (1583–1634), who took up position with his army near Nuremburg. After repulsing Gustav's advance, the Catholic army was forced to retreat into Thuringia, but Wallenstein still had enough troops to challenge Gustavus, and the two armies met again at Lutzen, near Leipzig, on 16 November 1632. The Swedes were initially successful, but Wallenstein pushed back the Swedish center. Gustav, galloping to restore the line, ran into a cavalry detachment of the enemy, was shot several times, and fell mortally wounded. The Swedes, furious at his death, then went on to win the day, but they had lost a great leader.

Gustav's wife, Maria Eleanora of Brandenburg, kept his body in her bedroom until her death. It now lies in the Riddarholmskyrkan in Stockholm.

In his monumental *History of Europe,* H. A. L. Fisher summarizes Gustav's gifts: "In any computation of human excellence, Gustavus Adolphus of Sweden should stand high. A brilliant linguist, for he spoke eight languages, a great soldier and trainer of soldiers . . . Gustavus out-tops the statesmen of his age in energy, simplicity and integrity of character." Fisher goes on to explain some of the reasons for Gustav's military success. Describing his improvements to the Swedish army, Fisher writes that the army was "notable for five characteristics. The men wore uniform. The regiments were small and equipped for speed. A light, mobile field artillery, easy to handle and brilliantly manoeuvered, reinforced the infantry arm. The muskets were of a type superior to that in general use. The cavalry, instead of galloping up to the enemy, discharging their pistols in the Dutch manner, and then turning round and galloping back to reload, charged home with naked steel. To these advantages the quality of the commander supplied an invaluable supplement. Mastering every detail, sharing every hardship, taking every risk, seizing every opportunity, Gustavus inspired his swift and mettlesome warriors to endure, to obey, and if need be, to die."

References: Bongard, David L., "Gustavus Adolphus," in *The Encyclopedia of Military Biography,* edited by Trevor N. Dupuy, Curt Johnson, and David L. Bongard (London: I. B. Taurus, 1992), 303–304; Fletcher, C. R. L., *Gustavus Adolphus and the Thirty Years War* (New York: Capricorn Books, 1963); Ahnlund, Nils, *Gustav Adolf the Great,* translated by Michael Roberts (Westport, Conn.: Greenwood Press, 1983); Roberts, Michael, *Gustavus Adolphus,* 2d ed. (London: Longman, 1992); Bennett, Matthew, "Gustavus Adolphus (correctly Gustav Adolf), King of Sweden," in *The Oxford Companion to Military History,* edited by Richard Holmes (New York: Oxford University Press, 2001), 391–392; Brzezinski, Richard, *The Army of Gustavus Adolphus,* 2 vols. (London: Osprey Military, 1991–93); Fisher, H. A. L., *A History of Europe,* 2 vols. (London: Collins, 1935), 626–627.

H

Habsburg-Lorraine, Friedrich Rudolf *See* ALBERT, ARCHDUKE OF AUSTRIA.

Haig, Douglas, first earl Haig and Baron Haig of Bemersyde (1861–1928) *British general*

Douglas Haig was born in Edinburgh, Scotland, on 19 June 1861, the son of John Haig, a whiskey distiller. He attended school at Clifton College and Brasenose College, Oxford University, and after graduation entered the British Royal Military College at Sandhurst. After a year there, he joined the British army in 1885, serving as an officer of the 7th Hussars. Haig was promoted to the rank of captain in 1891, attended the Military Staff College at Camberley, and then moved to Egypt in 1897. There he was seconded to the Egyptian army during the Omdurman campaign led by British general Sir Horatio KITCHENER to put down the revolt that had followed the 1885 death of General Charles "Chinese" GORDON.

Haig subsequently served during the Boer War in South Africa (1899–1902). When that conflict broke out, he was appointed to the staff of the British commander, Lord ROBERTS, seeing action at the relief of Ladysmith (November 1899–February 1900). During the hostilities, Haig became chief of staff to Sir John FRENCH, later first earl French of Ypres, commander of the cavalry division. In this position, he participated in Lord Roberts' advance from Cape Colony into the Transvaal. For his services in the Boer War, he was promoted to brevet lieutenant colonel.

Following the war in Africa, Haig was decorated with the Companion of the Order of the Bath (CB) and given command of the 17th Lancers for a year. After that service, he was sent to India as an inspector general of cavalry, serving from 1903 to 1906. He was then promoted to major general, and he married the Hon. Dorothy Vivian. Returning to England, he served from 1906 to 1909 as a director of military training in the War Office, helping the first Viscount Haldane of Cloan, the secretary of state, in reorganizing and reforming the British army. In 1907, Haig published *Cavalry Studies,* a work on military reforms. Two years later, he was named chief of staff to the commander in chief of India, General Sir O'Moore Creagh. In 1910, Haig was promoted to lieutenant general, and in 1912 he served as Commander in chief at Aldershot, where he helped to form the 1st and 2nd Cavalry divisions. In 1914, at the outbreak of the First World War, he was named commander of the First Army Corps of the British Expeditionary Force (BEF).

Almost from the beginning of the war, Haig was at the forefront of the British campaign to support French forces on the western front. Because of his skill in conducting the orderly withdrawal of his forces during the early German advance at the battle of Ypres, his former commander, Sir John French, now commanding British forces in France, reorganized the BEF into two armies and named Haig as commander of the First Army. In this role, Haig fought the Germans at Aubers Ridge (9– 17 May 1915), Loos (25 September–19 October 1915), and Neuve Chapelle (10–13 March 1915). For his service, he was honored with the Knight Grand Cross of the Order of the Bath (GCB) by King George V.

Despite their previous close relationship, French and Haig's disagreement on vital matters of coordinating with their French allies, the rising number of casualties, and the stalemate of their armies all led to heightened tension. By December 1915, the British government was questioning French's command of the armies, and Prime Minister Herbert Asquith ordered his resignation. Asquith subsequently wrote to Haig: "Sir John French has placed in my hands his resignation of the office of Command in Chief of the forces in France. Subject to the King's approval, I have the pleasure of proposing to you that you should be his successor."

Haig's new responsibilities were awesome. As a soldier of the 19th century, he had to alter his planning and thinking on the role of cavalry in battle to a new type of conflict in which artillery and machine guns ruled the day. However, he rose to the challenge and led the British forces until the end of the war. In February 1916, the Germans launched a massive offensive on the French at Verdun, which lasted until December. Haig's forces relieved the French in other sectors of the line and, in July 1916, launched an attack to take the pressure off Verdun. The Battle of the Somme saw over 420,000 British troops killed in the four-month campaign, by the end of which only 10 miles of territory had been gained. Blamed by the soldiers for the massive carnage, Haig was criticized as "The Butcher of the Somme." Whether or not he deserved the sobriquet is a matter for debate. Critics point to a statement Haig made just prior to the Somme: "The nation must be taught to bear losses. No amount of skill on the part of the higher commanders, no training, however good, on the part of the officers and men, no superiority of arms and ammunition, however great, will enable victories to be won without the sacrifice of men's lives. The nation must be prepared to see heavy casualty lists." However, he was also being undermined in England: The new prime minister, David Lloyd George, detested Haig and wanted him placed

firmly under the command of Robert NIVELLE, the French commander in chief.

Despite the losses of 1916, Haig convinced his fellow Allied commanders that the German toll had exhausted their army and that a well-placed offensive in 1917 would win the war. He opened this offensive with an Allied victory at Messines (7 June) under General Herbert Plumer, followed by Third Ypres (31 July). The German-Austrian victory over the Italians at Caporetto (23 October 1917) resulted in a unified Supreme War Council being established, and in November there was an Allied victory at Passchendaele.

In early 1918, Haig welcomed the decision to give the command of all Allied forces to Marshal Ferdinand FOCH, the French general. Working with Foch, Haig waited for the German offensive that he knew would be the Germans' last-ditch attempt to break out of the stalemate on the western front and win the war. When it came in mid-1918, his reserve of troops and materiel led to a German withdrawal after heavy losses, followed by a gradual Allied advance and finally, the end of the war on 11 November 1918.

In 1919, Haig was raised to the peerage as first earl Haig and Baron Haig of Bemersyde; he was also awarded the Order of Merit, and Parliament granted him a payment of £100,000. That same year, he was named commander in chief of the British Home Forces, but he left that position in 1921. He spent the remainder of his life in aid of disabled and wounded soldiers from the Great War, toward which end he founded the British Legion in 1921. Serving as president of the organization until his death, he traveled around Britain in fundraising drives for soldiers' relief and medical care and organized the sale of poppies on 11 November, the anniversary of the end of the war. The annual event became known as Poppy Day.

Haig died in London on 28 January 1928 at the age of 66. After a military funeral, he was buried in Dryburgh Abbey, Roxburghshire, south of Edinburgh, next to famed poet and fellow Scotsman Sir Walter Scott. A statue of Haig stands on Whitehall in the center of London; it reads, "Field Marshall Earl Haig. Commander-in-Chief of the British Armies in France, 1915–1918."

Historians still debate Haig's role in the carnage of the First World War. In 1973, his biographer, General Sir James Marshall-Cornwall, wrote: "Haig was truly dedicated to the welfare of his troops, a devotion which he maintained long after hostilities had ceased. . . . In his excellent and perceptive biography of the Field-Marshal, John Terraine drew a comparison between Haig in the Somme battle and Ulysses Grant in the Virginian campaign of 1864. This comparison is of wider application, for Grant and Haig, although so dissimilar in background and upbringing, were by nature very akin. Both men were of shy and withdrawn character, but essentially kindly and humane; they also shared the quality of inflexible determination to reach their appointed goal. Both have been stigmatized as 'bloody butchers.'"

References: De Groot, Gerard J., *Douglas Haig: 1861–1928* (London: Unwin Hyman, 1988); Cooper, Duff, Viscount Norwich, *Haig,* 2 vols. (London: Faber and Faber, 1935–36); Charteris, John, *Field Marshal Earl Haig* (London: Cassell, 1929); Marshall-Cornwall, General Sir James, *Haig as Military Commander* (London: B. T. Batsford Limited, 1973); Haig, Douglas, *Sir Douglas Haig's Despatches* (December 1915–April 1919), edited by John Herbert Boraston (London: J. M. Dent & Sons Ltd., 1919); Winter, Denis, *Haig's Command: A Reassessment* (New York: Viking, 1991).

Halsey, William Frederick, Jr. ("Bull" Halsey)

(1882–1959) *American admiral*

William "Bull" Halsey was born in Elizabeth, New Jersey, on 30 October 1882, and graduated from the U.S. Naval Academy at Annapolis, Maryland, in 1904. In 1907–09, he served on the USS *Kansas,* part of the "Great White Fleet," which was sent around the world by President Theodore Roosevelt in a peaceful and successful demonstration of American naval power. In 1914, during the American invasion and occupation of Veracruz in Mexico, Halsey served on a torpedo boat, and he commanded a destroyer in the Atlantic Ocean during the First World War. He subsequently trained as a pilot, becoming an aviator in the U.S. Navy in 1935. Promoted rapidly, he reached the rank of vice admiral by 1940.

On 7 December 1941, the Japanese attack on the U.S. naval base at Pearl Harbor brought the United States into the Second World War. The assault left Halsey as the commander of the only operational group of American warships in the Pacific Ocean. Under the command of Admiral Chester NIMITZ, Halsey took control of Task Force Sixteen to stage a series of hit-and-run attacks on the Japanese, including the heroic Doolittle

Raid of Tokyo in April 1942. As commander of the aircraft carrier force, he also directed a series of attacks on Japanese targets in the Gilbert and Marshall Islands and planned the critical battle of Midway (4–7 June 1942). As new ships were constructed and added to the fleet, Halsey's command grew, and he used this growing array of ships to attack Japanese targets across the expanse of the Pacific Theater of Operations. He used his ships to attack the Japanese in battles at the Santa Cruz Islands and the battle of Guadalcanal (12–15 November 1942), victories that gave new spirit on the American side. In recognition of his success, Halsey was promoted to the rank of admiral in late 1942.

Through 1943 and into 1944, Halsey was in charge of carrier-borne airforce offensives on the Solomon Islands. On 15 June 1944, he was named as commander of the U.S. Third Fleet. He also directed the American assault on the Philippine islands, a strategic base for hit-and-run attacks against the Japanese homeland. On 20–25 October 1944, with Admiral Thomas Kincaid, commanding the Seventh Fleet, Halsey destroyed the Japanese carrier force in Leyte Gulf so thoroughly that it played little part in the remainder of the war. However, he was not immune from criticism in this victory. Historians Anthony Bruce and William Cogar write: "Controversy surrounds Halsey's role in the battle of Leyte Gulf and specifically as commander of Task Force 38 at the battle of Cape Engaño [25 October 1944]. While he succeeded in sinking all four Japanese carriers, his action nevertheless weakened American naval forces operating against the main Japanese force in the Leyte Gulf. Controversy also surrounded his action in leading his fleet into a typhoon in December 1944, in which three destroyers were lost."

In the final months of the war, Halsey commanded American forces in the fight at Okinawa, near the Japanese islands, from 28 May 1945 until the Japanese surrendered on 2 September 1945. The surrender ceremony was held on the USS *Missouri,* Halsey's flagship. Following the war, he was promoted to the rank of Fleet Admiral on 11 December 1945.

On 1 March 1947, Halsey retired from active service. Thereafter, he became involved in private business, serving as president of International Telecommunications Laboratories from 1951 to 1957. He died on Fishers Island, New York, on 16 August 1959, age 76. His value to the United States during the Second World War is inestimable. General Douglas MACARTHUR called

William "Bull" Halsey "the greatest fighting admiral" of the conflict.

References: Potter, Elmer Belmont, *Bull Halsey: A Biography* (Annapolis, Md.: United States Naval Institute Press, 1985); Merrill, James M., *A Sailor's Admiral: A Biography of William F. Halsey* (New York: Crowell, 1976); Bruce, Anthony, and William Cogar, "Halsey, William Frederick, Jr." in *An Encyclopedia of Naval History* (New York: Checkmark Books, 1999), 168; Watson, Bruce W., "Halsey, William F. ('Bull')," in *Brassey's Encyclopedia of Military History and Biography,* edited by Franklin D. Margiotta (Washington, D.C.: Brassey's, 1994), 421–424.

Hamilcar Barca (Hamilcar Barcas) (ca. 270–229 B.C.) *Carthaginian general*

Although Hamilcar Barca was an important military commander, his son HANNIBAL's historical fame has far surpassed his own, and his name is now forgotten, except among military historians. Born about 270 B.C., Hamilcar's early life is unknown. His first recorded achievement occurred in 247 B.C., when he was approximately 23 years old and took command of Carthage's forces in Sicily, then under almost complete Roman control, during the First Punic War. His forces seized Mt. Ercte (now Monte Pellegrino, near Palermo) and held it against superior Roman forces for five years. When the war ended in 241 B.C. with Carthage's defeat, Hamilcar was allowed to take his forces and leave Sicily with his army intact. Upon his return to Carthage, when Hamilcar was denied any benefits for his service, his men mutinied; it was only through his intervention and by dealing severely with the mutineers that the rising (called by historians "The Truceless War," 238 B.C.), ended. He was then hurriedly reinstated by the government.

Named as the leader of Carthage in 237 B.C., Hamilcar ruled alone as a virtual dictator for the next eight years. Historian Louis P. Rawlings writes: "From 237 until his death in 229 he embarked on a conquest of southern Spain. It appears that he was attempting to build for Carthage an empire to counter that of Rome in Italy. He took with him his three sons, Hannibal, Hasdrubal, and Mago, and reputedly made them swear never to be a friend of Rome." The editors of *The Hutchinson Dictionary of Ancient and Medieval Warfare* write that "[Hamilcar] was appointed to lead an army to the aid of the Sicilian city of Himera, probably because

he was the formal guest-friend (xenos) of Terillus, tyrant of that city."

It was at Himera (229 B.C.) that Hamilcar met his end. Historian George Bruce writes that the clash was "between the Syracusans and Agrigentines, 557,000 strong under Gelon, Tyrant of Syracuse, and the Carthaginians, said to number 300,000, under Hamilcar. The Carthaginians were totally routed, and Hamilcar [was] slain. Syracuse became paramount in Sicily." Historian Lee Sweetapple relates that Hamilcar was drowned at Himera. His legacy, is that he instilled tactical and strategic skills—as well as an undying hatred of Rome—into his famous son Hannibal.

References: Rawlings, Louis P., "Hamilcar Barca," in *The Penguin Dictionary of Ancient History,* edited by Graham Speake (London: Penguin Books, 1995), 298; Delbrück, Hans, *Warfare in Antiquity: History of the Art of War,* vol. I (Lincoln: University of Nebraska Press, 1990), 305, 312; Warmington, Brian Herbert, *Carthage* (Harmondsworth, U.K.: Penguin Books, 1969); "Hamilcar" and "Himera," in *The Hutchinson Dictionary of Ancient and Medieval Warfare* (Oxford, U.K.: Helicon Publishing, Ltd., 1998), 137–138; Bruce, George, "Himera," in *Collins Dictionary of Wars* (Glasgow, Scotland: HarperCollins Publishers, 1995), 110; Sweetapple, Lee A., "Hannibal Barca," in *Brassey's Encyclopedia of Military History and Biography,* edited by Franklin D. Margiotta (Washington, D.C.: Brassey's, 1994), 424.

Hamilton, Sir Ian Standish Monteith (1853–1947) *British general*

Born on the island of Corfu, then under British control, on 16 January 1853, Ian Hamilton accompanied his family back to England and received his education at Wellington College and in Germany. Joining the British army in 1872, he was commissioned into the Gordon Highlanders. He first saw action in the first Afghan War (1878–80) and then in the First Boer War (1881), when he suffered a serious injury at Majuba Hill (27 February 1881), leaving his left arm permanently disabled. He served on the Nile Expedition (1884–85), with the British army in Burma (1886–87), and the North-West Frontier of India, where he commanded a brigade in 1897.

With the outbreak of the Second Boer War (usually known as "the Boer War," 1899–1902), Hamilton was sent to South Africa, serving as commander of a division of mounted infantry under Lord ROBERTS. He saw limited action in this conflict, participating in Roberts's march from Bloemfontein to Pretoria in 1899. In early 1901, Hamilton was brought back to London to serve as military secretary of the War Office. However, later that year he returned to South Africa to serve as the chief of staff to Lord KITCHENER, who had succeeded Roberts as commander of British forces in South Africa in November 1900.

In the next several years, Hamilton served in various capacities: he worked as the chief of the military mission to report on the tactics of the Japanese army during the Russo-Japanese War (1904–05), as adjutant general of the British army (1909–10), and as commander in chief of the Mediterranean Command in Malta (1910–14). His writings on the Japanese army were published as *A Staff Officer's Scrap Book* (two volumes, 1906–07), and in 1910 he published *Compulsory Service,* a work on Lord Roberts's recommendations for mandatory service in the British military forces.

With the outbreak of the First World War in 1914, Hamilton served as commander in chief of the Home Defence forces. In March 1915, he was named commander of the Mediterranean Expeditionary Force, overseeing the dangerous and ill-advised plan to invade the Dardanelles and capture Istanbul. This was meant to force an end to Turkey's challenge to Russia as well as to aid the Russian army on the eastern front against Germany and Austria. Hamilton's forces were repulsed when they tried to pass through the Dardanelles, and although they managed to land at Gallipoli on 25 April, they suffered tremendous casualties. Although London sent more reinforcements, Hamilton saw the Turks slowly grind down his forces, with little chance of relief. By October, after thousands of Allied troops had been killed, Hamilton was consulted by the government of Prime Minister Herbert Asquith and asked to withdraw the Allied forces. He resisted the proposal and was removed from command, to be replaced by General Sir Charles Monro.

Hamilton returned to England under a cloud, his military career over. In his final years, he responded to the official government report of the Dardanelles Commission (1920), and wrote his version of how he saw the campaign in *Gallipoli Diary* (two volumes, 1920), as well as *The Soul and Body of an Army* (1921). He died in London on 12 October 1947 at the age of 94.

References: Hamilton, Ian Bogle Montieth, *The Happy Warrior: A Life of General Sir Ian Hamilton* (London: Cassell, 1966); Lee, John, *A Soldier's Life: General Sir Ian Hamilton, 1853–1947* (London: Macmillan, 2000); Churchill, Sir Winston, *The Boer War: London to Ladysmith via Pretoria: Ian Hamilton's March* (London: Longmans, Green, 1900); Hamilton, Sir Ian, *Listening for the Drums* (London: Faber and Faber, 1944).

Hancock, Winfield Scott (1824–1886)
American general

Named after the famed War of 1812 military hero Winfield Scott, Winfield Hancock was born in Montgomery Square, in Montgomery County, Pennsylvania, on 12 February 1824. He received a local education and then entered a local military academy before graduating from West Point in 1844. He was brevetted as a first lieutenant during service in the Mexican War (1846–48). Promoted to first lieutenant in 1853, he was a captain by November 1855, when he was assigned as assistant quartermaster of the U.S. Army.

With the start of the Civil War in 1861, Hancock asked to be transferred from St. Louis, where he had married, to an eastern command. On 23 September 1861, he was made a brigadier general of volunteers and placed in command of a brigade in the Army of the Potomac. He saw action at Williamsburg (5 May 1862) and at the Peninsula campaign (May–June 1862), earning the praise of Union general George B. MCCLELLAN, who said, "Hancock was superb" in the Williamsburg battle. At the indecisive battle of Antietam (17 September 1862), Hancock took command of the 1st Division of the II Corps when General Israel B. Richardson was killed. In November 1862, he was promoted to major general of volunteers, and by the end of the year he had also been promoted to major in the (regular) U.S. Army.

At Fredericksburg, Virginia (13 December 1862), Hancock led forces that attacked Marye's Heights; his forces lost more than 2,000 men killed and wounded out of a total of 5,000 in his division. At Chancellorsville, Virginia (2–4 May 1863), he was set upon by the main force of the Confederate army under General Robert E. LEE in a victory for the South. Nonetheless, continually hailed as a leading officer for the Union, Hancock was named as commander of the II Corps soon after Chancellorsville.

Hancock's most important campaign was at Gettysburg (1–3 July 1863). On the first day of the battle, after the left flank of the Union army had suffered heavily, and General John F. Reynolds was killed in action, Hancock arrived and had to decide whether the Union force should withdraw or hold their position. He decided to hold his ground on Cemetery Hill and Cemetery Ridge. On the second day, Hancock commanded the center flank of the Union army, taking over the left flank as well after General Dan Sickles was wounded in action. On the third day, Hancock commanded the Union forces, taking the full impact of Pickett's Charge, the Confederates' final desperate attack up the hill when Confederate general George E. Pickett's troops attempted to break through the Union Center. As the Confederate artillery opened fire, Hancock rode along the front of his troops to show he shared the danger with them. In the end, Hancock's forces lost over 4,000 men out of 10,000 troops, but Lee withdrew, defeated. Because of a wound, Hancock went into convalescence for six months before he could return to service. He received the thanks of Congress for his service to the Union.

Hancock returned to service in May 1864 and saw action at Spotsylvania (10–12 May 1864), the follow-up to the battle of the Wilderness. Positioned on the right flank of General Ulysses S. GRANT, he took a leading role in the battle, as historian George Bruce writes: "General Hancock on the right surprised the first line of the Confederate defenses and compelled General [Joseph E.] Johnson and his division to surrender." At Cold Harbor (31 May–3 June 1864), following Grant's orders, Hancock sent his men into a bloody but usuccessful assault. After Cold Harbor, his wound reopened, and he again left the army to convalesce. His return to command was marked by a defeat at Reams' Station (25 August 1864). In November 1864, he again had to give up his command because of his wound and was employed in raising a new corps. He was slated to return to the battlefield when Richmond fell and the war ended.

Following the assassination of President Abraham Lincoln in April 1865, Hancock was placed in command of all troops in the Washington, D.C., area. He also oversaw the military trials of the conspirators in the president's assassination, the execution of some and the imprisonment of the remainder. However, he argued with Washington and urged lenient treatment of the Southern states, now slowly being reintroduced back into the Union under Reconstruction rule. Promoted to major general in the regular army in July 1866, he served in a series of military appointments before retiring.

A lifetime Democrat, Hancock was a candidate for the 1868 presidential nomination, eventually won by New York governor Horatio Seymour. In 1880, he did win the Democratic nomination, with William H. English nominated for vice president, but he was defeated by the Republican James A. Garfield by less than 7,000 votes. (Garfield was assassinated less than a year into his term.) In his final years, Hancock lived on Governor's Island, New York, where he died on 9 February 1886, five days before his 62nd birthday. His body was returned to his native Pennsylvania, and he was laid to rest in the Montgomery Cemetery in Norristown, Pennsylvania.

Hancock was an important member of the Union high command during the Civil War, although some historians overlook his service. Ulysses S. Grant, who clashed with Hancock over strategy, wrote of him: "Hancock stands [as] the most conspicuous figure of all the general officers who did not exercise a separate command. He commanded a corps longer than any other, and his name was never mentioned as having committed in battle a blunder for which he was responsible."

References: Jordan, David M., *Winfield Scott Hancock: A Soldier's Life* (Bloomington: Indiana University Press, 1988); Walker, Francis Amasa, *Hancock in the War of Rebellion* (New York: The Press of G. J. Little & Company, 1891); Gambone, A. M., *Hancock at Gettysburg: And Beyond* (Baltimore: Butternut and Blue, 1997); Bruce, George, "Spotsylvania," in *Collins Dictionary of Wars* (Glasgow, Scotland: HarperCollins Publishers, 1995), 236; Tucker, Glenn, *Hancock the Superb* (Indianapolis, Ind.: Bobbs-Merrill, 1960).

Hannibal (Hanba'al) (247–ca. 183/182 B.C.)
Carthaginian general

Most of the facts of Hannibal's life come not from Carthaginian sources but those of his Roman enemies. The son of HAMILCAR BARCA, another Carthaginian commander whose exploits have been well documented in history, he was born in Carthage, located in what is now modern Tunisia, in 247 B.C., and named Hannibal (properly "Hanba'al" in his native language, meaning "mercy of Ba'al"). At the age of nine, he served at his father's side in campaigns in Spain. Hamilcar's death in 229 B.C. did not deter the 18-year-old Hannibal's desire to become a military commander. Hamilcar's brother-in-law, Hasdrubal, became the Carthage forces' commander, but he was murdered in 222 B.C., and Hannibal, now 25, became commander in chief of the Carthaginian armies fighting in Spain.

Hannibal's military strategy was not unlike his father's: He showed little or no mercy for his enemies. Attacking the Romans in Spain, he captured Salamanca in 220 and in 219 attacked and defeated Saguntum when Rome, busily fighting the Second Illyrian War, could not come to the city's assistance. Hasdrubal had promised Rome he would never attack Saguntum, and angry Romans demanded Hannibal's arrest and extradition. Ignoring them, Hannibal named his brother, also called Hasdrubal, as commander of the Carthaginian armies in Spain, and in 218 B.C. he crossed the River Ebro and advanced into Gaul (today's France). Rome, still angered over the attack on Saguntum, declared all-out war on Carthage, initiating the Second Punic War.

Instead of reinforcing his armies in Spain, Hannibal decided to preempt the Roman assault and move into Italy on his own. With an army of some 40,000 men and, for the first time, 37 elephants used as battering rams and attack mechanisms—almost like modern tanks—he crossed the River Rhône and passed through the Alps and across the River Po near what is now the city of Turin, Italy. Although under the control of Rome, the Po Valley was inhabited by Gauls who had been enslaved by the Romans and welcomed the Carthaginian army. Rome, seeing the danger in Hannibal enlisting the Italian Gauls to his side, sent an army to fight him. At Ticinus in 218 B.C., 26,000 Carthaginians under Hannibal and 25,000 Romans under Publius Cornelius Scipio (better known as SCIPIO AFRICANUS [the Elder]) fought at a river near Turin. The Romans were defeated with heavy casualties, and Scipio was wounded. With this victory, some 14,000 Gauls joined Hannibal's forces.

The Romans again tried to stop Hannibal at Trebbia, near Placentia (what is now Piacenza, Italy). Scipio had retreated south and was joined by two legions commanded by the Roman consul Tiberius Sempronius Gracchus. Adopting the suggestion of his younger brother Mago, Hannibal sent out a small force to make the Romans believe the Carthaginian troops were small in numbers. This diversion force caused Sempronius to move his men across a frozen river, where Mago was hiding with over 2,000 men, split between infantry and cavalry. The Romans were attacked first by Mago's troops, then by thousands of Carthaginian, Spanish, and Gallic light infantry backed by elephants. As the Romans fled, thousands were attacked on the frozen river, into which they fell and drowned in untold numbers. Sempronius retreated with some 10,000 men to Placentia. Roman losses are estimated to be approximately 15,000–20,000, although exact numbers are impossible to calculate. Carthaginian losses were light.

Hannibal marched toward the Apennine Mountains in northern Italy, attacking and ravaging the countryside; during a minor battle, he lost an eye. The Romans again attacked, at Lake Trasimeno (now Trasimene, 217 B.C.). The Romans, 25,000 soldiers under the Roman consul Gaius Flaminius, attacked without support from a larger Roman army under his fellow consul Gnaeus Servilius Geminus. Hannibal set a trap for Flaminius similar to the one he had set for Sempronius: His men lit fires far from his actual camp to make the Romans believe his army was further away than it actually was. Flaminius then marched his men toward Lake Trasimeno, thus sending them into the Carthaginian trap. As they were blocked in on one road, Hannibal's forces swept down on them, forcing the Romans to fight an enemy they could not see. The rear of the Roman army broke quickly, and these men fled into the lake, where they drowned as they were attacked. The center, led by Flaminius, tried to fight, but they were cut down by Gallic cavalry. Only a few Romans escaped through the fog of the early morning; left behind were Flaminius and 15,000 dead Romans.

After this victory, Hannibal expected Rome to surrender, but instead, Quintus Fabius Maximus Verrucosus was named as the new Roman commander, with full dictatorial powers to defeat the Carthaginians. However, Fabius was slow to raise an army, and he was mocked as "cunctator" ("the Delayer"). Consequently, he was removed from power and replaced by Marcus Claudis Marcellus, and a new Roman army was sent to defeat Hannibal. On 2 August 216 B.C. at Cannae on the Aufidus (now the Ofanto) River, Hannibal was confronted by a superior Roman force of some 85,000 under Terentius Varro and Aemilius Paullus, significantly outnumbering his 50,000-man army. Nevertheless, surrounding the Romans with his cavalry, Hannibal's forces cut them down by the thousands, and his infantry finished the job. Some 50,000 Romans lay dead after the battle; Hannibal lost approximately 5,700. This battle, the worst in Roman history, is cited by historians as a classic example of envelopment and the use of numerically inferior forces to defeat a superior army.

Despite his numerous victories, Hannibal was unable to defeat Rome itself because, with the Roman command of the sea, he could not obtain supporting forces from Carthage. Notwithstanding his incredible victories, his army was slowly being bled to death with the constant, slow attrition of his force. By 212 B.C., the Romans had retaken several areas lost to Hannibal, forcing his troops away from Rome. In 207, the death of his brother Hasdrubal at the Metaurus River (now the Metauro River) left Hannibal without one of his great generals. For four years, his army held out in southern Italy, but he was forced to retreat to Carthage when Publius Cornelius Scipio (Scipio Africanus) attacked the city in 203 B.C. On 19 October 202 B.C., Hannibal confronted Scipio in his last major battle at Zama, also known as Naraggara or Margaron and now Saqiyat Sidi Yusuf, Tunisia. Armed with 48,000 troops and elephants, Hannibal tried to use the same techniques he had used in the past, but the Romans had learned his strategy. Although Scipio had only approximately 30,000 troops, he utilized the encirclement movement to attack Hannibal's forces. Scipio's superiority was in cavalry, supplied by Masinissa, the ruler of the North African kingdom of Numidia. The Carthaginians were decisively defeated—some 20,000 were killed in the clash—and Hannibal fled to Carthage. The battle ended the Second Punic War, and in exchange for ending the fighting, Carthage gave up control of Spain to Rome.

In his final years, Hannibal served as a *suffete,* or chief magistrate, of his city-state. His chief task was to raise capital to pay the indemnity Rome had imposed on Carthage after the loss at Zama. However, in 195 B.C., Rome accused him of once again working to defeat Roman rule, and to avoid arrest, Hannibal was forced to flee to what is now Syria. Sheltered by Antiochus III of Syria, he served the Syrian army in its war against Rome. When Syria was defeated at Magnesia in 190 B.C., Hannibal once more fled, this time to Bithynia in Asia Minor, where he was made commander of a fleet of ships. His last battle was against King Eumenes II of Pergamun. His victory came, according to legend, when his forces threw snakes into the enemy ships.

The Bithynians faced defeat when Rome intervened on the side of Eumenes, and Hannibal, unable to flee, realized that he would be handed over to the Romans. Facing torture and execution, he poisoned himself in the Bithynian village of Libyssa (now near modern day Gebze in Turkey) in 183 or 182 B.C. His tomb at Gebze still stands.

Hannibal is considered one of the greatest generals in the history of warfare. Historian J. F. Lazenby, in his massive work on the Second Punic War, explains:

Apart from what we can glean from his actions, we really do not know what sort of a person Hannibal was. Polybius, the nearest in time of the extant sources, says that 'some consider him to have been cruel to excess, some avaricious.' But the Greek historian himself seems to have thought that any cruelty that Hannibal displayed was the result of circumstances, and in his main narrative records few atrocities committed by him or his army. It also emerges that it was among the Romans that Hannibal had a reputation for cruelty. . . . In the day-to-day conduct of operations there are few generals to compare with Hannibal: from his use of Hanno's outflanking force at the crossing of the Rhône, to his retention of his third line as a reserve, and, possibly, his use of cavalry as a decoy, at Zama, he showed a consistent sureness of touch, an ability to assess any situation and to arrive at a solution, often involving a departure from normal methods and considerable boldness. He was clearly a master of what amounted to psychological warfare, and of all of the tricks a general needs to deceive an enemy: it is easy to admit the planning of the ambush at Trasimene, but easy to forget how unique an ambush on such as scale is in the annals of warfare.

References: "Hannibal," in *Command: From Alexander the Great to Zhukov—The Greatest Commanders of World History,* edited by James Lucas (London: Bloomsbury Publishing, 1988), 40–41; Baker, George Pierce, *Hannibal* (New York: Dodd, Mead & Company, 1929); Ross, Thomas, *The Second Punick War between Hannibal, and the Romanes* . . . (London: Tho. Roycroft, 1672); Bradford, Ernle, *Hannibal* (New York: McGraw-Hill, 1981); Bruce, George, "Cannae" and "Ticinus," in *Collins Dictionary of Wars* (Glasgow, Scotland: HarperCollins Publishers, 1995), 49, 247; "Hannibal," in *The Penguin Dictionary of Ancient History,* edited by Graham Speake (London: Penguin Books, 1995), 298–299; Lazenby, J.

F., *Hannibal's War* (Warminster, England: Aris & Phillips, Ltd., 1978).

Harold II (Harold Godwinsson) (ca. 1020–1066)
king of England

Born about 1020 (some sources report 1022) at Bosham, West Sussex, Harold was the second son of Godwin, the earl of Wessex, and his wife Gytha. Earl Godwin had risen in the ranks of Anglo-Saxon England to become one of the most powerful military and political commanders in that nation's early history—even more powerful than the king at the time. Gytha was the sister-in-law of Canute, who had become the Danish king of England in 1016 on the death of EDMUND II IRONSIDE. Canute's death in 1035 set off a fierce struggle among those who wanted to succeed him. Because of Earl Godwin's social and military standing, his son Harold, only about 15 years old, was considered one of the leading candidates. However, another aspirant, Canute's reputed son Harold, nicknamed Harefoot, took power in a shared monarchy with Hardicnut, Canute's half brother. When Harold Harefoot died on 18 June 1040 at age 24, Hardicnut was crowned as the sole ruler of England. Two years later, on 8 June 1042, Hardicnut died, and his older half brother, Edward the Confessor, was crowned king of England. One of Edward's chief supporters was Earl Godwin, who gave his daughter Ealdgyth, Harold Godwinsson's sister, in marriage to the king.

While Edward the Confessor served as king, Earl Godwin continued to push for his son's advancement, gaining for him the earldom of East Anglia in 1045. In 1050, both Godwin and Harold were banished because king Edward feared their growing power, but they were allowed to return in 1052. At the same time, Harold was in conflict with his other brother Sweyn (also spelled Swein). In April 1053, when his father died, Harold succeeded to the earldom of Wessex. After the death of Sweyn on a pilgrimage to Jerusalem, Harold became the leading man in the kingdom. While fighting, supposedly in the name of King Edward, he put down all opposition by force. By 1057, Harold and his brothers held all the English earldoms except for Mercia. In 1064, shipwrecked off the coast of France, Harold was captured by Count Guy and delivered to William of Normandy (later WILLIAM I). Probably under duress to save his life, Harold swore allegiance to William and promised that he would not claim the English throne and would not oppose William's becoming king of England. Historians have long debated whether Harold in fact made this promise under duress or willingly. Whatever the reason, it later came back to haunt him.

When Harold returned to England, Edward, on his deathbed, blessed him as the heir to the English throne, throwing aside his own grandson, Edgar the Ætheling, and disregarding Harold's own alleged promise to William of Normandy. When Edward died on 5 January 1066, Harold moved immediately to become the new king. In a 1705 work, *A New History of the Succession*, it is stated:

> We have quite a different Account of Harold's accession to this Throne from Florentius, who plainly tells us, That upon King Edward's Interment, Harold the Viceroy, son of Duke Godwin, whom the King had elected for his Successor before his death, was chosen to the Royal Dignity by the Grandees of the whole Kingdom; and was accordingly consecrated thereto by Alfred Archbishop of York. William of Malmesbury on the other hand, tho Junior to Florentius, seems to side in his Narrative with that of Ingulphus, telling us, That Harold took the Diadem by force: Altho he adds, that the English affirm That it was granted to Harold by the King; I suppose he means by Edward the Confessor, which notwithstanding that Historian seems not to believe, but judges it urg'd by them in the own Excuse.

Almost immediately, Harold's claim on the throne was challenged by others. An angry William of Normandy assembled an army and sailed across the English Channel. At the same time, Tostig, Harold's own brother, had wanted his close ally, Harald Hardrada, king of Norway, to become king of England, and he joined with Harald to invade northern England in September 1066. Harold assembled an army and met Harald and Tostig on 25 September at Stamford Bridge, near York. The invaders had not expected Harold to raise an army so soon, and when the battle began, they were caught unawares. Harold's forces easily defeated them, and Harald and Tostig were killed. Their forces fled, but Harold followed them, destroying nearly all of their ships before Harald's son Olaf pledged his loyalty to Harold, upon which the Norwegians were allowed to return to Norway.

While Stamford Bridge was a great victory for Harold and the Anglo-Saxons, the battle had badly depleted his forces and material. Three days after the battle ended, William of Normandy and his forces landed at Pevensey, East Sussex (although recent archaeological discoveries show that William probably landed at Hastings), and Harold received the news with dismay. He rushed his forces south while William established his force's position at Hastings and waited for Harold's army to come south. On 3 October, they began their march to Hastings, pausing at Waltham Abbey to pray for divine guidance. On 13 October, they reached the main battle point at Caldbec Hill, assembling at the "hoary apple tree" approximately seven miles from Hastings. On the following day, Harold's 6,000 or 7,000 troops faced about the same number of Normans, who had cavalry and archers. The Anglo-Saxons held their own for a while, defeating the Norman archers and inflicting heavy casualties with battleaxes. When the Normans began an orderly move backward, the English rushed forward, a fatal move that broke their hitherto impregnable close formation—the "shield wall." The Norman archers attacked again, and it was perhaps during this attack that Harold was struck and killed. His brothers Leofwine and Gyrth were also killed, leaving the English without a natural leader.

In his 1869–76 history of the Norman conquest of England, Edward A. Freeman notes that contemporary and later English historians have differed on the manner and timing of Harold's death. Historian Margaret Ashdown, in a 1959 work, claimed that Harold survived the battle of Hastings and moved to Iceland, where he later died. Some modern historians, rereading the writing on the Bayeaux Tapestry, now feel that Harold was not hit by an arrow in the eye but was beheaded. Freeman writes:

While Harold still lived, while the horse and his rider still fell beneath his axe, the heart of England failed not, and the hope of England had not wholly passed away . . . the Duke [William] bade his archers shoot up in the air, that their arrows might, as it were, fall straight from heaven. The effect was immediate and fearful. No other device of the wily Duke that day did such frightful execution. Helmets were pierced; eyes were put out; men strove to guard their heads with their shields, and, in doing so, they were of course less able to wield their axes. . . . As twilight was coming on, a mighty shower of arrows was launched on its deadly errand against the defenders of the Standard [the English flag]. There Harold still fought, his shield bristled with Norman shafts; but he was still unwounded and unwearied. At last another arrow, more charged with destiny than its fellows, went still more truly to its mark. Falling like a bolt from heaven, it pierced the King's right eye; he clutched convulsively at the weapon, he broke it off at the shaft, his axe dropped from his hand, and he sank in agony at the foot of the Standard. Meanwhile twenty knights who had bound themselves to lower or to bear off the English ensigns strove to cut their way to the same spot. Most of the twenty paid for the venture with their lives, but the survivors succeeded in their attempt. Four of them reached the Standard at the very moment when Harold fell. Disabled as he was, the King strove to rise; the four rushed upon him and despatched him with various wounds. . . . [O]ne pierced through the shield of the dying King and stabbed him in the breast; another smote him with the sword just below the fastenings of his helmet. But life was still in him; as he still struggled, a third pierced his body through his lance, and a fourth finished the work by striking off his leg with the sword.

William founded a church on the site of the battle—Battle Abbey—and some believe Harold is buried there. Most historians now agree that his body was taken away and buried at Waltham Abbey, 20 miles north of London. In the 1950s, a church renovation at Battle Abbey found a tomb with a headless body that was also missing a left leg and part of a right—injuries that historians claim Harold sustained on the field. Despite this controversy, Harold's death is considered a turning point in European history. As shown in the Bayeaux Tapestry, it led to the first French king of England, William, duke of Normandy, better known as William the Conqueror, whose descendants still sit on the throne of England.

References: Loyn, H. R., *Harold, Son of Godwin* (Hastings, U.K.: The Hastings and Bexhill Branch of the Historical Association, 1966); Freeman, Edward A., *The History of the Norman Conquest of England, Its Causes and Its Results,* 5 vols. (Oxford, U.K.: Clarendon Press, 1869–76), III:495–497; Lloyd, Alan, *The Making of the*

King 1066 (New York: Holt, Rinehart and Winston, 1966); Greene, Parnell, *On the Banks of the Dee: A Legend of Chester Concerning the Fate of Harold . . .* (London: F. V. White & Company, 1886); Ashdown, Margaret, "An Icelandic Account of the Survival of Harold Godwinson," in *The Anglo-Saxons: Studies in some Aspects of their History and Culture, Presented to Bruce Dickins,* edited by Peter Clemoes (London: Bowes & Bowes, 1959), 122–136.

Hawke, Edward, first baron Hawke of Towton
(1705–1781) *English admiral*

Considered the "founding father" of the modern Royal Navy, Edward Hawke was born in London, England, on 21 February 1705. One early biographer noted that Hawke's family could only be traced through his grandfather, a London merchant, who had settled at Treriven (or Treraven), St. Cleather, Cornwall. His father, Edward Hawke, was a barrister (lawyer) who had studied at Lincoln's Inn, one of the four Inns of Court of English law. In February 1720, when he was only 15 years old, Hawke joined the English navy as a volunteer on board the *Seahorse.* He served for several years, eventually qualifying for a commission as a lieutenant.

In 1739, when Spain declared war on England, Hawke served as the captain of the *Portland,* which sailed in the West Indies looking for Spanish ships to attack. However, the ship was rotten and nearly foundered several times, and while it sailed into Boston in 1741, a gale struck its masts and tore them off. In 1742, it was taken out of commission and destroyed, upon which Hawke took over a new craft, the *Berwick.* He took this ship against the Spanish and their French allies at the Battle of Toulon (11 February 1744), where he attacked several ships, succeeding against overwhelming firepower. He remained at sea for the next 18 months, and in 1745 Sir William Rawley, commander of the English fleet, transferred him to serve on the *Neptune,* which was ordered to return to England. In 1747, Hawke was placed in command of 14 ships to attack a French convoy. On 14 October 1747, he set upon the French fleet at the Bay of Biscay and captured six of the eight ships. Following this action, he returned home to England, where he was elected as a member of Parliament for Portsmouth and promoted to rear admiral, along with Lord George ANSON.

Hawke served in the navy almost continuously until his death, although he did not see action in every year. From 1748 to 1752, he commanded the Home Fleet. In 1755, he was made commander of the Western Fleet of the British navy. In June 1756, he was ordered to the Mediterranean to replace Admiral John Byng following Byng's defeat at Minorca. Hawke immediately sailed for Minorca to see if it could be saved, but, finding it fallen to the Spanish, he sailed for home. Returning to England in January 1757, he was promoted to the rank of full admiral.

By 1759, the French were planning a full-scale invasion of the British Isles. Hawke was sent to Brest to blockade the Bay of Biscay in case any French ships tried to move on England. After sitting in the bay for a period of six months, Hawke was forced to withdraw to Torbay because of strong winds and a storm. This allowed the French admiral, Hubert de Brienne, the comte [count] de Conflans, to try and run the blockade. Conflans moved along the French coast for six days, but on 20 November 1759, Hawke, with 23 ships in his fleet, caught up to the French vessels just west of Belle Isle. Conflans decided to retreat to the safety of Quiberon Bay, which, with its rocky coast, is one of the most dangerous bays in the world. Hawke later wrote:

> All the day we had very fresh gales at N.W. and W.N.W. with heavy squalls. Monsieur Conflans kept going off under such sail as all his squadron could carry and at the same time keep together, while we crowded after him with every sail our ships could bear. After about half-past 2 p.m., the fire beginning ahead, I made the signal for engaging. We were then to the southward of Belle Isle; and the French admiral headmost soon after led round the Cardinals, while his rear was in action. About 4 o'clock the *Formidable* struck, and a little after the *Thésée* and *Superbe* were sunk. About 5 the *Héros* struck and came to an anchor, but it [the wind] blowing hard, no body could be sent on board her. Night was now come, and being on a part of the coast among islands and shoals, of which [we] were totally ignorant, without a pilot, as was the greatest part of the squadron, and blowing hard on a lee shore, I made the signal to anchor.

When the battle was over, Hawke had taken or destroyed only five French ships, but the others ran aground, while the British lost only two vessels. Conflans later wrote, "I had no reason to believe that if I went in first with ships the enemy would dare follow, in spite of his superiority which must anyway restrict his movements."

Quiberon Bay was a landmark clash, ending the French threat of invading Britain. A song was written in honor of Hawke's victory, printed in pamphlets at the time:

> Ere Hawke did bang,
> Mounseer Conflang,
> You sent us beef and beer;
> Now Mounseer's beat,
> We've nought to eat,
> Since you have naught to fear.

Following the Quiberon Bay victory, Hawke served as First Lord of the Admiralty from 1766 to 1771, and in 1776 he was raised to the peerage as Baron Hawke of Towton. He died on 17 October 1781 at Sunbury in Middlesex. In 1904, the biographer Montagu Burrows wrote of Hawke's place in history: "It may be hoped that it is no longer necessary to vindicate the place which has of late years been assigned to Lord Hawke in naval history, that is to say, in the history of Great Britain. It will be seen . . . that he was the parent of the modern Royal Navy in the sense which can be attributed to no one else . . . that he had left behind him a name unrivalled in the maritime records of his country."

References: Burrows, Montagu, *The Life of Edward Lord Hawke, Admiral of the Fleet, Vice-Admiral of Great Britain, and First Lord of the Admiralty from 1766 to 1771* (London: J. J. Keliher & Co., Limited, 1904), 1, 9; *The Secret Expedition impartially disclos'd: Or, an Authentick Faithful Narrative of all Occurrences that Happened to the Fleet and Army Commanded by Sir E. H. [Edward Hawke] and Sir J. M. [John Mordaunt], From its First Sailing to its Return to England . . .* (London: Printed by J. Staples, 1757); Mackay, Ruddock, "Edward, Lord Hawke, 1705–1781," in *Precursors of Nelson: British Admirals of the Eighteenth Century,* edited by Peter Le Fevre and Richard Harding (London: Chatham Publishing, 2000), 201–224; Laughton, John Knox, "Hawke, Edward, Baron Hawke," in *The Dictionary of National Biography,* 22 vols., 8 supps., edited by Sir Leslie Stephen and Sir Sidney Lee, et al. (London: Oxford University Press, 1921–22), IX:192–199; *The Wat'ry God. A Celebrated Song Written on Lord Hawke's Victory over Conflans in 1759* (Dublin: John Lee, 1770).

Hawkins, Sir John (Sir John Hawkyns) (1532– 1595) *English sea captain*

John Hawkins (spelled in some sources as Hawkyns) was born in Plymouth, England, in 1532, the scion of a family of Devon shipowners and sailors. Much of his early life is unknown; it appears that he got his first naval training when he served on ships that stole slaves from Portuguese ships and sold them in the Spanish colonies in the New World. This began about 1562 when Hawkins would have been around 30 years of age. However, when he subsequently set up his own trading venture, two of his vessels were captured by the Spanish. Queen Elizabeth I eventually loaned Hawkins one of her royal ships as a replacement, and he once again went to sea and had two more profitable voyages. Despite the Spanish edict against him, he continued to seize slaves and sell them. For his success, he was granted a coat of arms with the emblem of a slave in chains. In 1567, while he was again searching the Caribbean coasts for slave ships, Hawkins was attacked by a huge Spanish fleet at Veracruz. Although he was defeated, his ship, the *Minion,* and a smaller craft, the *Judith,* piloted by Sir Francis DRAKE, Hawkins's cousin, were able to escape and limp home to England.

For several years after his defeat at Veracruz, Hawkins did not return to the seas, instead using his family's wealth and some of his own to finance privateering missions for slaves. In 1573, he was named as treasurer of the Royal Navy, succeeding his father-in-law, Benjamin Gonson. He later served as controller of the navy, and it was during this time that Hawkins reformed the construction methods and updated the navy's ship purchases, getting rid of old ships that were outmoded and obsolete and replacing them with newer, faster vessels carrying many more guns that could fight far better than the older ships. Although some accused him of corruption and taking bribes, no charges were ever proven, and Hawkins continued with his sterling work in improving England's navy. Indeed, England's great naval victory in this period came because of Hawkins's reforms. In 1588, the Spanish, desiring to invade Protestant England and restore Catholicism there, assembled an enormous fleet—the Spanish Armada—and sailed toward England. The English navy met them in the English Channel (July 1588) and harried them all the way to Gravelines, near Calais. Working closely with the commander of the English navy, Charles HOWARD, second baron Howard of Effingham, Hawkins served as a rear admiral during the battle.

For his service against the Spanish Armada, Hawkins was knighted. Two years later, he was dispatched to the coast of Portugal to attack and seize a Spanish fleet laden with gold and treasure from the New World. However, he missed the ships altogether, and they sailed home safely. Hawkins wrote a lengthy letter to Queen Elizabeth, quoting Scripture: "Paul doth plant, Apollo doth water, but God giveth the increase," to which Elizabeth is allegedly to have exclaimed, "God's death! This fool went out a soldier, and has come home a divine."

In 1595, Hawkins went with his cousin, Sir Francis Drake, on a voyage to the West Indies to hunt for the Spanish treasure fleet, but their mission ended in failure. Hawkins became sick, and he died suddenly on 12 November 1595 off the coast of what is now Puerto Rico. He was buried at sea.

In his 1958 work *Vantage at Sea,* historian Thomas Woodrooffe writes:

> John Hawkins, treasurer of the Navy, was more than any other man responsible for the defeat of the [Spanish] Armada. He was that rare combination in any age, a seaman who was also a good businessman. He himself had made three long voyages, and he knew what was needed to keep a fighting fleet at sea, for months if need be, something his colleagues had never contemplated. He encouraged the building of ships intended not for hand-to-hand fighting but for free maneuver and the rapid discharge of their guns. He was determined not only to have ships of the highest quality but the best men to sail and fight in them, and being a businessman, he knew very well that if he wanted quality, he would have to pay for it. In spite of calculated obstruction and virulent accusations of fraud by other members of the Navy Board, Hawkins went serenely on with his self-imposed task of transforming an old and out-of-date fleet into one that was modern and oceangoing. He seemed impervious to criticism, and it was this bland indifference to those who considered themselves his elders and betters that finally proved too much for old Sir William Winter and made him explode about Hawkins

in a letter to [Lord] Burghley: "He careth not to whom he speaketh, nor what he sayeth, blushe he will not."

References: Williamson, James Alexander, *Sir John Hawkins: The Time and the Man* (Oxford, U.K.: The Clarendon Press, 1927); Kelsey, Harry, *Sir John Hawkins: Queen Elizabeth's Slave Trader* (New Haven, Conn.: Yale University Press, 2003); Walling, Robert Alfred John, *A Sea-dog of Devon: A Life of Sir John Hawkins* (London: Cassell and Company, 1907); Mattingly, Garrett, *The Armada* (Boston: Houghton Mifflin, 1959); Bruce, Anthony, and William Cogar, "Hawkins, Sir John," in *An Encyclopedia of Naval History* (New York: Checkmark Books, 1999), 171–72; Woodroffe, Thomas, *Vantage at Sea: England's Emergence as an Oceanic Power* (New York: St. Martin's Press, 1958).

Henry V (1387–1422) *English king*

Many of the events in Henry's early life depicted in William Shakespeare's *Henry the Fifth* are apocryphal. A descendant of WILLIAM I (the Conqueror), he was born at Monmouth in September 1387, the eldest son of Henry IV (1367–1413) and his wife Mary de Bohun. At his birth, he was styled as Henry Earl of Monmouth, and when his father ascended to the English throne in 1399, he became Prince of Wales. He was raised by his paternal uncle, Henry, duke of Beaufort (ca. 1377–1447), Henry VI's half brother. Historian David Hilliam, in his study of the men and women who have ruled England, writes: "According to Shakespeare, young Prince Hal, as Henry was called while still in his teens, enjoyed a wild lifestyle with an old reprobate of a companion, Sir John Falstaff, and a motley collection of other rogues and thieves. The Boar's Head tavern . . . saw him as a regular tippler." However, when his father died on 20 March 1413, Henry, at 26, gave up his wild ways and took the throne as Henry V.

Henry's reign lasted only nine years, but in that time he became a notable soldier monarch like his ancestor EDWARD III. Almost at once he went to war against France to claim territory through his descent from William the Conqueror. He named his uncle and benefactor Henry, duke of Beaufort, as lord chancellor to act on his behalf while he was away. By 1415, he had raised enough men to invade France.

Henry V, engraving by P. Vanderbanck

In the summer of 1415, Henry, with a force of approximately 10,000 men, landed his fleet in northern France with his first goal being the capture of the town of Harfleur. Finding the French in control there, he laid siege to Harfleur for a period of about one month, from August to September 1415. The French finally capitulated, and Henry marched into the village, victorious. However, it was a Pyrrhic victory, as many of his men were short on food and wracked with illness. Henry had intended next to march on toward Calais, 120 miles away, where he could embark his exhausted army and return to England, but his forces were blocked by the French at Agincourt on 25 October 1415.

Historians continue to write about the significance of the battle of Agincourt both in military history and in the history of Europe. In a small valley near what is now Azincourt, France, Henry led his 6,000 remaining soldiers and 5,000 archers, against some 25,000 French troops, many of them mounted knights in full armor, under the commanders Jean Le Meingre Boucicaut and Charles d'Albret. The day before the battle, the area had been inundated by heavy rains, and the ground was pure mud. This gave Henry, grossly outnumbered, a great advantage he would not have had otherwise. The French knights, weighed down with armor, were easy targets for the English bowmen and sank quickly into the mud. D'Albret was killed during the battle, and Boucicaut was captured by Henry's men and eventually taken back in chains to England, where he would die in 1421.

French casualties, mostly dead, numbered approximately 5,000; the English lost about 200 in total. In this first invasion of France, Henry had lost about 8,000, but the French army of 50,000 was destroyed. The role of the English archers is what makes Agincourt a notable battle: It confirmed the tactics of the Battle of Crécy, demonstrated that good archers on foot could defeat armored knights on horseback, and laid the foundation for the domination of the English army in France for another 30 years.

Henry returned home in triumph and signed an alliance with Sigismund, the Holy Roman Emperor. In 1417, he again invaded France, and for two years, he battled the French forces, defeating them at Rouen (1419) and gaining Normandy for England. The French, desiring an end to the conflict, agreed to the Treaty of Troyes (21 May 1420), in which King Charles VI agreed to marry his daughter, Catherine of Valois, to Henry in exchange for allowing Catherine to corule France with Henry after Charles's death. Henry entered Paris in triumph in 1420, and the following year he returned to England with his new wife. A son, also named Henry, was born in 1421.

Within a year, Henry determined to confirm his claim to the French throne, and despite public opposition to further warfare, he gathered an army and crossed over to France to quell growing resistance there. However, while conducting this campaign, Henry was struck down by dysentery, to which he succumbed on 31 August 1422, age 35. His son, just nine months old, was crowned as Henry VI.

References: Towle, George Makepeace, *The History of Henry the Fifth, King of England, Lord of Ireland, and Heir of France* (New York: D. Appleton and Company, 1866); Goodwin, Thomas, *The History of the Reign of Henry the Fifth, King of England, &c. In Nine Books* (London: Printed by J. D. for S. and J. Sprint, 1704); Allmand, C. T., *Lancastrian Normandy, 1415–1450: The History of a Medieval Occupation* (Oxford, U.K.: The Clarendon Press, 1983); Nicolas, Sir N. Harris, *History of the Battle of Agincourt, and of the Expedition of Henry the Fifth into France, in 1415 . . .* (London: Johnson & Co., 1832), 1–5; Drayton, Michael, *The Ballad of Agincourt. . . .* (Oxford, U.K.: Charles Batey, 1951).

Hindenburg, Paul Ludwig Hans von Beneckendorf und von (1847–1934) *German general*

Born in the village of Posen, Prussia, on 2 October 1847, Paul von Hindenburg was the son of a Prussian military officer. He came from an illustrious background: His family could trace its origins back to the 13th century, with many members serving in the military. Hindenburg continued this tradition when he entered the military cadet school at Wahlstatt in Silesia when he was just 11 years old, advancing after a short period to attend the main military academy in Berlin.

In 1866, upon graduation from the Berlin academy, Hindenburg joined the Prussian military as a member of the 3rd Guards of Foot at Danzig (now part of Poland). He saw service in the Prussian-Austrian War and was wounded on 3 July 1866 at the battle of Sadowa, also known as Königgrätz, while storming an Austrian battery. For his service, he was awarded the Order of the Red Eagle. Hindenburg saw additional action in the Franco-Prussian War (1870–71), winning the Prussian Iron Cross for bravery. In 1871 at Versailles, the Prussian king was declared emperor of Germany, the first time Germany became a unified nation. In the following years, Hindenburg was promoted regularly, rising to the rank of general in the German army. In 1903, he was given the command of the army's II Corps at Magdeburg. However, only eight years later, in 1911, he requested that Kaiser Wilhelm II allow him to retire since a war did not seem to be forthcoming. He retired to the city of Hanover, where he raised a family.

Hindenburg's prediction of there being "no prospect for war" in the near future was shattered when the First World War broke out in the summer of 1914. The assassination in Bosnia of Archduke Franz Ferdinand, of the Austrian royal family, led to a series of treaties being invoked that plunged Europe into war. In late July 1914, Austria declared war on Serbia; Russia came in on Serbia's side, Germany supported Austria, and France had promised to support Russia. Britain had no immediate involvement but had guaranteed Belgian independence, so when the Germans began advancing through Belgium, Britain declared war on Germany on 4 August. At once, Hindenburg asked that he be reinstated in the army, and within three weeks the kaiser had placed him in command of the German Eighth Army in East Prussia. General Erich Ludendorff, was named as Hindenburg's chief of staff. The Eighth Army then marched on Tannenberg, where, on 24–31 August 1914, they attacked the Russians, led by Alexander SAMSONOV, who was woefully unprepared for the battle. Hindenburg's forces surrounded the Russians, who attempted a retreat; only 10,000 were able to escape. More than 100,000 Russian soldiers were slaughtered, and an additional 140,000 were trapped. On 31 August 1914, they surrendered to Hindenburg; Samsonov, disgraced by the disaster, committed suicide.

Hindenburg's masterful victory at Tannenberg shocked the Russian leadership. They were further shocked when he defeated straggling troops led by Samsonov's fellow commander Paul RENNENKAMPF at the first battle of the Masurian Lakes (7–12 September 1914). Hindenburg proceeded to march across the Narev River, but Austro-Hungarian armies were cut down in Galicia and he was forced to change his plans for a direct assault on the Russians, whose forces took Lodz. Hindenburg's divided force could only drive them out but could not pursue them.

Paul von Hindenburg

Hindenburg was then promoted to field marshal and named as commander in chief of all Germans armies on the eastern front. He gathered his armies for a full-scale assault on the Russians but found he did not have the forces needed for such an onslaught; he therefore requested reinforcements from Berlin. This request was refused, as the western front and its trench warfare needed the troops far more than the eastern front did, despite Hindenburg's success in defeating the Russians. Although he appealed to kaiser himself, Hindenburg was still refused further troops; he therefore opposed the offensive by German chief of staff Erich von Falkenhayn to drive the Russians back further. When Falkenhayn, with the assistance of German general August von Mackensen, worked with the Austrians and attacked the Russians in southern Europe, Hindenburg refused to join them; he and Falkenhayn were at odds thereafter. However, he had a very good relationship with Ludendorff from 1914 to 1918, and they worked closely to formulate German strategy. Hindenburg later wrote that the relationship was a "happy marriage."

From 1915 until the end of the war, the German high command saw the war in the east as secondary to the one on the western front. Instead of allowing Hindenburg to keep the forces he had, Falkenhayn stripped him of divisions and moved them to the west. Falkenhayn's offensive at Verdun in 1916 was a dismal failure, and Romania declared war on Germany and Austria. Due to the German losses at Verdun, Kaiser Wilhelm removed Falkenhayn as chief of the German General Staff on 27 August 1916 and named Hindenburg as his replacement. Hindenburg thereupon appointed Ludendorff as first quartermaster general and German army chief of staff. Although some historians claim that Hindenburg improved the German army and raised morale, others point out that his reinstitution of unrestricted submarine warfare against neutral shipping in February 1917 brought about the enmity of the United States and the entry of American forces into the war on the Allied side that year.

The Russian Revolution in February 1917, the role of the Germans (particularly Ludendorff) in getting Russian revolutionary Vladimir Lenin through Eastern Europe into Russia (April 1917), and the Lenin-led overthrow of the government by Bolshevik forces that November resulted in the Treaty of Brest-Litovsk on 3 March 1918 and the removal of Russia from the war. Though Hindenburg was able to move forces in the east to support the western front however, by the time these troops arrived, American troops had joined the Allied armies, giving the Allies stimulus to fight harder. In March 1918, Hindenburg attempted to end the war once and for all with an offensive against the British sector. But the American support of British defenses and a counteroffensive by French marshal Ferdinand FOCH led to extensive German losses. On 8 August, which Hindenburg later called "the black day of the German army," the British attacked German forces near Amiens, forcing them to flee and leading to the capture of thousands of German soldiers. By September, Hindenburg and Ludendorff had realized that the end was near, and they made this clear to the kaiser. Appealing to U.S. president Woodrow Wilson, Hindenburg asked for peace terms, but, angered at the response (which included the kaiser's abdication), he ordered all of his forces to fight to the end. Ludendorff resigned and was replaced by General Wilhelm Groener. On 9 November, Kaiser Wilhelm went into exile in Holland, and two days later the war ended. Defeated, Hindenburg retired to his home in Hanover.

In retirement, Hindenburg wrote his memoirs, published as *Out of My Life* (1920), in which he alleged that the German army had not been beaten on the field of battle but had been "betrayed" by unknown forces in Germany. Historians believe that his accusations led Adolf Hitler to blame the Jews of Germany as the "betrayers."

When German president Friedrich Ebert died in February 1925, German nationalists convinced Hindenburg to run for the German presidency. He was elected over the Socialist candidate Wilhelm Marx and served as president of Germany during its period of hyperinflation and Weimar politics. Historian Timothy Lupfer writes: "He entered politics from a genuine sense of patriotic duty, but his lack of political experience and his old age did not serve him well in the treacherous political climate of Germany during the interwar years." By the late 1920s, Hindenburg was overshadowed by the growing presence of the National Socialist Workers' politician Adolf Hitler, whose putsch, or rebellion, in Munich in 1923 had brought him to national prominence. In 1933, in an attempt to capitalize on Hitler's popularity, Hindenburg named him chancellor of Germany, a move he did not live to regret. Hindenburg died on 2 August 1934 at age 86 and was laid to rest as a national hero. Within five years, Germany would be at war again.

In Paul von Hindenburg's lifetime, the way of fighting wars changed from cavalry on horses to trench warfare and airplanes. His impact on the First World War is incalculable. Historians still argue over what might have happened if he had not been frustrated by Falkenhayn and had been given a freer hand to fight Germany's battles in 1914 and 1915.

References: Wheeler-Bennett, Sir John, *Hindenburg: The Wooden Titan* (London: Macmillan, 1967); Lupfer, Timothy T., "Hindenburg, Paul von," in *Brassey's Encyclopedia of Military History and Biography,* edited by Franklin D. Margiotta (Washington, D.C.: Brassey's, 1994), 427–431; Hindenburg, Gert von, *Hindenburg, 1847–1934: Soldier and Statesman,* translated by Gerald Griffin (London: Hutchinson, 1935); Asprey, Robert B., *The German High Command at War: Hindenburg and Ludendorff Conduct World War I* (New York: William Morrow, 1991); Kitchen, Martin, *The Silent Dictatorship: The Politics of the German High Command under Hindenburg and Ludendorff, 1916–1918* (London: Croom Helm, 1976); Dorpalen, Andreas, *Hindenburg and the Weimar Republic* (Princeton, N.J.: Princeton University Press, 1964).

Holland, Henry Rich, first earl of (first baron Kensington) (1590–1649) *English military commander*

Born in 1590, Henry Holland was the second son of Robert Rich, the first earl of Warwick, and his wife Penelope, the daughter of Walter Devereux, the first earl of Essex. He received his education at Emmanuel College, Cambridge University, and was knighted in 1610. That same year, he was elected to a seat in Parliament from Leicester, serving a second term in 1614.

Rich's military career began about 1610, when he saw action as a volunteer soldier at the siege of Juliers in the war against the Spanish in the Netherlands. For his services in this conflict, he was praised by King James I and named as a gentleman of the bedchamber for James's son Charles, the Prince of Wales. He was promoted to captain of the Yeomen of the Guard on 5 November 1617 and, on 8 March 1623, was raised to the peerage as Baron Kensington after he married Isabel, the daughter of Sir Walter Cope, earl of Kensington. He secured such trust from the royal family that in 1624 James sent him to France with Sir Dudley Carleton to arrange the marriage between James's son Charles and Henrietta Maria, the daughter of the French king Henry IV. That year, he was once raised to the peerage, as earl of Holland. Again, he was trusted with sensitive diplomatic missions, including one to France to end fighting between the government of King Louis XIII and the Huguenot religious minority, and another to the Netherlands with George Villiers, the duke of Buckingham. In 1625, with James I's death, his son succeeded to the throne as Charles I, who named Holland as a Knight of the Garter (KG) on 13 December 1625. Two years later, he was placed in command of the royal fleet to aid Buckingham in an attack on the Isle of Ré, but he could not leave England due to inclement weather and sailed late, only to meet Buckingham returning from a defeat. Buckingham was assassinated soon after, and Holland was selected to succeed him as the chancellor of his alma mater, Cambridge University.

In 1642, following a long and testy relationship between Charles and Parliament, the members of the legislative body refused to accept the king's claims of regal authority, and they challenged him for control of the nation. Although he had served Charles and his father for nearly 20 years, Holland abandoned the royal cause and sided with the Parliamentarians at the outset of the conflict. Historians believe that this move came about because Charles had slighted him by offering the command of the English army to Lord Conway instead of to Holland when the English fought the Scottish in the Second Bishops' War (1640). Whatever the reason, in March 1642, Parliament chose Holland to transmit their official terms to Charles, who dismissed his old friend. In July 1642, Holland was named as a member of the Committee of Safety. When war was declared and a parliamentary army formed, his father's cousin, Robert Devereux, third earl of ESSEX, was named as a commander. Holland met with Essex at Twickenham and convinced him not to fire the first shot against the Royalist forces, even appearing at Turnham Green (13 November 1642) to halt the fighting. When Essex ignored his advice, Holland, returned to the king and asked to join his side in the dispute, but Charles, still furious at his treachery, refused his services. Nevertheless, Holland served as a member of the Royalist army at the siege of Gloucester (10 August–8 September 1643) and at Newbury (20 September 1643). He then again changed sides to support the Parliamentarians. However, instead of fighting, Holland spent his time trying reconcile the two sides; at one point he asked Parliament to recompense him for property he had lost in the war.

In 1648, Holland once again entered the fighting and approached Charles to ask him for a commission; Charles's son, Charles, the Prince of Wales, gave Holland a commission as a general. Holland then took command of a Royalist force at Kingston to march on Colchester and raise the Parliamentary siege of that city. Before he could march, he issued proclamations calling for an end to the struggle against the king, an admission of Charles's royal authority, and a peace treaty to be signed between Charles and the Parliament. These had little effect, and Holland, with 600 men, marched on Kingston. He was defeated there on 7 July 1648 by Sir Michael Livesey, and three days later he was captured at St. Neots. Initially, the House of Commons agreed that Holland and any other Royalist commanders would be banished from their offices, but the army countered by trying Holland; James Hamilton, first duke of Hamilton; and Arthur, Lord Capel. All three were found guilty and sentenced to death. The two houses of Parliament voted 31 to 30 to refuse them clemency, and, on 9 March 1649, all three men were beheaded. Before he was put to death, Holland gave a speech in which he defended his fight for the king. "God be praised, although my blood comes to be shed here, there was scarcely a drop shed in that action I was engaged in." His king, Charles, had suffered the same death by beheading on 30 January 1649.

References: Beatty, John Louis, *Warwick and Holland: Being the Lives of Robert and Henry Rich* (Denver: Alan Swallow, 1965); Doyle, James William Edmund, "Holland," in *The Official Baronage of England, Showing the Succession, Dignities, and Offices of Every Peer from 1066 to 1885, with Sixteen Hundred Illustrations,* 3 vols. (London: Longmans, Green, 1886), II:207; Dalton, Charles, *Life and Times of General Sir Edward Cecil, Viscount Wimbledon, Colonel of an English Regiment in the Dutch Service, 1605–1631, and one of His Majesty's Most Honourable Privy Council, 1628–1638* (London: Sampson Low, Marston, Searle, & Rivington, 1885), I:179; MacCormick, Charles, ed., *The Secret History of the Court and Reign of Charles the Second, by a Member of his Privy Council . . . ,* 2 vols. (London: J. Bew, 1792), I:276.

Hood, Samuel, first viscount Hood (1724–1816) *British admiral*

Samuel Hood was born in Butleigh, Somersetshire, England, on 12 December 1724, the son of Samuel Hood, the village vicar. Hood entered the Royal Navy in 1741 at the age of 16, serving with George Brydges ROD-NEY, later first baron Rodney of Stoke-Rodney, aboard the *Ludlow Castle,* and he was promoted to the rank of lieutenant. He was named as commander of the sloop *Jamaica* in 1754 and, after several additional postings, took temporary command of the 50-gun *Antelope* in 1757. During the Seven Years' War (1756–63), while still only in temporary command, Hood captured a French frigate (1759) and took two privateers (pirate ships carrying contraband). For this service, he was given command of the frigate *Bideford.* He served in the English Channel and in the Mediterranean during the remainder of the war.

Hood was then posted to the North American Station from 1767 to 1770, serving as "commander-in-chief of all the men-of-war of these parts." After returning to England, he was named as commissioner of the dockyard at Portsmouth and as governor of the Naval Academy. In 1780, created a baronet, he was recalled to active duty, promoted to rear admiral, and dispatched to the West Indies to help the English navy against the French in what became the American Revolution.

In early 1781, he took up his post as second in command under his old shipmate, George Rodney. Later that year, he fought an indecisive battle against the French admiral the comte de Grasse in Chesapeake Bay (5 September 1781). In the Battle of the Saints (9–12 April 1782) near the island of Dominica, Rodney and Hood, commanding a fleet of 36 ships, defeated the French under de Grasse with 33 ships. However, due to Rodney's negligence (attributed to his age—he was approximately 64 years old), de Grasse had been able to dock at Fort Royal, Dominica. Rodney returned to England, and for his service, Hood was created Baron Hood of Catherington (an Irish peerage) and given command of the English fleet for the remainder of the war.

In 1784, Hood was elected to a seat in Parliament, but he was forced to relinquish the seat when he was appointed a lord of the Admiralty. Nevertheless, he was elected to this seat again in 1790. In 1793, the outbreak of hostilities after the French Revolution (1789) caused the British government to dispatch Hood to the Mediterranean to serve as commander in chief of English naval forces in that area. From May 1793 until October 1794, he provided important leadership, occupying the city of Toulon when French royalists on the side of King Louis XVI requested his assistance. When the French under NAPOLEON forced him to leave, Hood took his forces to Corsica, occupied it, and transferred his command there.

In October 1794, Hood was recalled to England and thereafter did not serve at sea, being removed from command altogether in 1795. Named as the governor of Greenwich Hospital in 1796, he was styled as Viscount Hood of Whitley that same year. He held this post until his death on 27 January 1816. His brother, Alexander Hood, first viscount of Bridport (1727–1814), was also a noted British naval officer.

Historian Michael Duffy sums up Hood's career and influence:

How did Hood acquire his immense and influential stature with the able officers who commanded the Royal Navy to victory in the Revolutionary and Napoleonic Wars? Unlike his almost equally long-lived brother, Alexander, who rose to the command of the Channel Fleet and to a peerage as Lord Bridport, he did not have chief command in a naval victory. He missed his chance in

1794, and his dismissal in 1795 robbed him of a better opportunity—his friend and successor, Lord Hotham, commanded the Mediterranean Fleet in the actions of 13–14 March and 13 July. Yet Hood's reputation stood far higher than either of these. Some commentators have regarded it as excessively inflated. John Tilley has asserted that "Among eighteenth-century admirals, Sir Samuel Hood was a remarkable character: he made his name one of the most famous in British naval history not by commanding a fleet in a great sea fight, but by convincing the historians that he had been cheated out of his opportunity to do so." But Hood has not simply convinced historians by his letters, he convinced the ablest of his naval contemporaries by his actions. Nelson described him as "the greatest Sea-officer I ever knew."

References: Hood, Dorothy, *The Admirals Hood* (London: Hutchinson & Company, 1942); Duffy, Michael, "Samuel Hood, First Viscount Hood, 1724–1816," in *Precursors of Nelson: British Admirals of the Eighteenth Century,* edited by Peter Le Fevre and Richard Harding (London: Chatham Publishing, 2000), 249–278; Bruce, Anthony, and William Cogar, "Hood, Samuel, First Viscount Hood," in *An Encyclopedia of Naval History* (New York: Checkmark Books, 1999), 181; Rose, John Hollard, *Lord Hood and the Defence of Toulon* (Cambridge, U.K.: The University Press, 1922).

Hooker, Joseph (1814–1879) *American general*

Joseph Hooker was born in Hadley, Massachusetts, on 13 November 1814. He received a local education, then received an appointment to the United States Military Academy at West Point, New York. Commissioned in the 1st U.S. Artillery Regiment in 1837, he saw service in the Mexican War (1846–48), when he served as a staff officer. He was subsequently promoted to the rank of lieutenant colonel, and although his career seemed promising, he left the military in 1853 and purchased a large farm near Sonoma, California, where he intended to retire.

When the Civil War broke out in early 1861, Hooker offered his services to the Union cause. Commissioned as a brigadier general of volunteers, he was

promoted to the rank of major general of volunteers on 5 May 1862. He led troops into battle at Williamsburg, where he served under General George B. MCCLELLAN, and where, despite a Union defeat, he earned the nickname "Fighting Joe" for his heroism in battle. He also saw action at Fair Oaks (31 May–1 June 1862); in the clashes known as the "Seven Days Battle" (26 June–1 July 1862); at Second Manassas, or Second Bull Run (30 August 1862); and in the Maryland campaign of September 1862. As commander of the I Corps of the Army of the Potomac, Hooker led the Union army at Antietam (17 September 1862), where he was severely wounded. For his service, he was promoted to brigadier general in the regular army on 20 September 1862, and upon his return to service, he commanded the center of the Union army at Fredericksburg (13 December 1862).

When General Ambrose Burnside resigned his post in January 1863, Hooker was named to replace him. At Chancellorsville (2–4 May 1863), he moved his troops forward but allowed the forces of Confederate Generals Robert E. LEE and Thomas J. "Stonewall" JACKSON to advance on his flank and force a Union retreat. Six weeks later, as Lee's army crossed the Potomac, advancing into Pennsylvania, Hooker followed him but was relieved by his command and succeeded by General George Meade on 28 June 1863.

He was then sent west to Chattanooga to relieve General William Starke ROSECRANS, who was under siege. Hooker played an important part in the "Battle above the Clouds" at Lookout Mountain (24 November 1863), which led to the Union triumph at Missionary Ridge (24–27 November 1863).

Following these two battles, Hooker remained in the region and played an important part in the battles around Atlanta with General William Tecumseh SHERMAN. However, Hooker and Sherman did not get along, and when General James Birdseye McPherson, commander of the Army of the Tennessee, was killed in action near Atlanta, 22 July 1864, command of his army went not to Hooker, who was in line for it, but, on Sherman's recommendation, to General Oliver Otis Howard. Angered at being passed over, Hooker resigned from his command, retiring from the army completely on 15 October 1868. He spent the remainder of his life on his farm. He was visiting Garden City, Long Island, when he died on 31 October 1879, two weeks before his 65th birthday.

References: Hebert, Walter H., *Fighting Joe Hooker* (Indianapolis: Bobbs-Merrill, 1944); Bruce, George, "Bull Run II," in *Collins Dictionary of Wars* (Glasgow, Scotland: HarperCollins Publishers, 1995), 43; Butterfield, Daniel, *Major-General Joseph Hooker and the Troops from the Army of the Potomac at Wauhatchie, Lookout Mountain and Chattanooga: Together with General Hooker's Military Record from the Files of the War Department, Adjutant-General's Office, U.S.A.* (New York: Exchange Printing, 1896); Tremain, Henry Edwin, *In Memoriam: Major-General Joseph Hooker* (Cincinnati: Robert Clark & Co., 1881).

Hopton, Ralph, first baron Hopton (1596–1651)
English general

Born at Witham Friary in Somerset in 1596, Ralph Hopton was the scion of a family whose fortune had been made through the destruction of monasteries, ordered by King Henry VIII. He received his education at Lincoln College, Oxford University, and was admitted to the Middle Temple, one of the four Inns of Court in English law, in 1614; however, he did not earn a degree from either institution. In 1620, Hopton joined the military mission led by Horace Vere (1565–1635) in an attempt to rescue Elizabeth of Bohemia, daughter of James I of England, after Johann Tserclaes Count von TILLY and his Catholic League marched onto Prague in one of the main battles of the Thirty Years' War. Hopton joined Vere and another young English soldier, William WALLER, to aid Elizabeth in her escape from Prague, successfully bringing her to safety. As a result of this adventure, Hopton began a close friendship with Waller that would last many years.

Although elected to a seat in the House of Commons from Shaftesbury in 1621, Hopton remained in Europe, serving in Sir Charles Rich's Regiment of Foot on the Continent. In 1625, he returned to England, where he was honored with the Knighthood of the Bath (KB), married, and settled down in a home in Somerset. He accepted a seat in the House of Commons in 1625 first representing Bath and then, from 1628 to 1629, representing Wells. From 1629 to 1639, he served in various local offices in Somerset, including deputy lieutenant. In 1639, he served in the First Bishops' War, prompted by King Charles I's attempt to change the Scottish church. With the rank of captain, he served in

a Royalist regiment commanded by Philip Herbert, the fourth earl of Pembroke.

In 1640, Hopton was once again elected to the House of Commons from Wells. This session of Parliament, dubbed the Long Parliament because it stayed in session until 1653, was noted for its opposition to the policies of King Charles I, breaking out in open rebellion and ultimately leading to the English Civil War. Hopton joined Edward Hyde, Lord Clarendon, and Lucius Cary, Viscount Falkland, in opposing the king, and he voted for the bill of attainder against the earl of Strafford, Charles's impeached privy councillor, in 1641. In December 1641, Hopton was one of five members of Parliament to present the Grand Remonstrance—a manifesto or document drawn up by the House of Commons listing reforms drafted by that body—to the king. Nevertheless, he remained loyal to Charles and to the Crown. In January 1642, he backed the king's attempt to arrest five sitting members of the House of Commons. Hopton biographer F. T. R. Edgar writes: "His royalism, always latent, was bound to emerge when the crunch came. It has three roots: first, his non-Laudian high Anglicanism, akin to Falkland's, manifest in Hopton's alignment with the 'Episcopal Party' and his defence of the bishops; second (in common with his colleague Culpeper), a concern for the militia and a recognition of the need on the King's side for a show of strength; and third, it would be hard to deny, a sense of personal loyalty to the throne itself."

Due to his sympathy and support for Charles in the face of growing confrontation, Hopton was imprisoned in the Tower of London for two months in 1642, by order of the House of Commons. After being released, he returned to Somerset and formed an army to implement the King's Commission of Array, an order to raise a fighting force to defend the Crown. As commander of this militia, Hopton marched into Cornwall and, on 19 January 1643, met the 4,000 pro-Parliamentary forces under Lord Ruthven at Braddock Down near Liskeard. He and his fellow Royalist commander Bevil Grenville routed the Parliamentarian troops, forcing them to flee from the battlefield. Because Ruthven's troops were supposed to support the earl of Stamford's army near Cornwall, this rout gave Hopton an advantage in fighting Stamford, who was forced to retreat.

At Stratton, Cornwall (16 May 1643), Hopton won a victory over the Parliamentarian leader Major-General James Chudleigh, who was captured and defected to the

Royalist cause. On 5 July 1643, he won a major triumph over his old friend, Sir William Waller, at Lansdown. The following day, he was injured by the explosion of a wagon full of powder. A week later, at Roundway Down on 13 July 1643, Hopton again faced Waller's forces; the Royalists won a smashing victory and left 1,500 Parliamentarians dead on the battlefield. For this service, he was created Baron Hopton of Stratton.

Hopton spent the winter consolidating his gains and building his army. In March 1644, the Parliamentarians moved on his forces at Cheriton (Arlesford), Hampshire. It was there on 29 March that Waller, with 6,500 men, faced Hopton's force of 3,500 men and 2,500 horse soldiers. Waller's overwhelming advantage of men and arms forced Hopton to retreat, ending the Royalist control of southwest England. In 1646, Charles took over the command of the entire Royalist army, but he was not the military leader or strategist that Hopton was. Moreover, the Royalist cause became hopeless at this point due to growing numbers of Parliamentarian troops. Hopton lost a decisive battle against Thomas, Lord FAIRFAX, at Torrington (16 February 1646), the last major battle of the so-called First Civil War (although the conflict would continue in various forms until 1651). On 14 March 1646, Hopton surrendered to Fairfax at Tresillian Bridge. He later accompanied Prince Charles (later Charles II) in an attempt to prolong the war in the Scilly and Channel Islands, but their efforts were fruitless. He settled in Belgium, dying in Bruges in September 1652.

References: Firth, Charles Harding, "Hopton, Ralph, Lord Hopton," in *The Dictionary of National Biography,* 22 vols., 8 supps., edited by Sir Leslie Stephen and Sir Sidney Lee, et al. (London: Oxford University Press, 1921–22), IX:1241–44; Edgar, Frank Terrell Rhoades, *Sir Ralph Hopton: The King's Man in the West (1642–1652)* (Oxford, U.K.: The Clarendon Press, 1968); Carlin, Norah, *The Causes of the English Civil War* (Oxford, U.K.: Blackwell Publishers, 1999); Reid, Stuart, *All the King's Armies: A Military History of the English Civil War, 1642–1651* (Staplehurst, Kent, U.K.: Spellmount, 1998); Healey, Charles E. H. Chadwyck, *Bellum Civile: Hopton's Narrative of His Campaign in the West (1642–1644) and Other Papers* (London: Harrison & Sons, Printers, 1902); Adair, John, *Cheriton 1644: The Campaign and the Battle* (Kineton, U.K.: The Roundwood Press, 1973).

Howard, Charles, second baron Howard of Effingham and first earl of Nottingham

(1536–1624) *English general and admiral*

The eldest son of William, first baron Howard and his wife Margaret (née Gamage), Charles Howard was born in Norfolk in 1536. His paternal grandfather was Thomas, the second duke of Norfolk, while his maternal grandfather was Sir Thomas Gamage of Coity, in Glamorganshire. His father's sister was the mother of King Henry VIII's second wife, Anne Boleyn. William Howard served as deputy earl marshal to Anne, as well as lord high admiral during the rebellion of Sir Thomas Wyatt in 1554.

Because of his relation to Anne Boleyn and her daughter, who became Queen Elizabeth I, Charles Howard was rewarded by the Crown with various diplomatic missions, including being sent in 1559 to France to congratulate Francis II on his ascension to the French throne. He entered the English military and rose through the ranks, becoming general of the horse under the earl of Warwick in 1569, when he aided in putting down a rebellion in the north of England. In 1563, he was elected to Parliament from Surrey, sitting in that session and in 1572. In 1573, upon his father's death, he succeeded to the title of Baron Howard of Effingham, and three years later he was bestowed with the knight of the garter. He was named as one of the commissioners to try Mary, Queen of Scots, who was an enemy of Queen Elizabeth, in 1586; Mary was eventually found guilty and beheaded.

In late 1587, when war with Spain appeared inevitable, Lord Howard was named as the "lieutenant-general and commander-in-chief of the navy and army prepared to the seas against Spain." He selected the *Ark Royal* as his main flagship, and, with Sir Francis DRAKE, sailed his fleet of some 90 ships from Plymouth. Howard initially proposed a massive attack on the Spanish fleet; however, due to bad weather, he was only able to harry Spain's armada, which, as it transpired, proved a highly successful tactic. His ships followed the armada to Gravelines, near Calais. On 28 July 1588, Howard wrote to Sir Francis Walsingham, on the evening before the battle at Gravelines, about the fleet that he would face the following day, "Ther force is wonderfull gret and strong And yet we ploke ther fethers by lytell and litell. . . ." With the maneuverability of the British ships and the use of fire ships sent into the Spanish in harbor, 16 Spanish galleons were destroyed, and the remainder sailed before a storm up the North Sea and around Scotland before the sad remnants arrived back in Spain.

For the remainder of the war against the Spanish, Howard played a minor role, but his ability to take advice from experienced seamen and his organization of the fleet had led the way to an English victory. He served on only one other military expedition: an attack against the Spanish city of Cádiz in 1596 with Robert Devereux, the second earl of ESSEX, which resulted in the destruction of the Spanish fleet for the second time. That same year, Howard was given the title earl of Nottingham. He was forced to turn on Essex and was instrumental in ending an insurrection when Essex rebelled against Queen Elizabeth in 1601. In 1606, Howard served on one of the courts that tried the conspirators in the Gunpowder Plot to kill King James I. As lord high admiral, he continued to play a managerial role for the remainder of his military career. However, as he aged, he took less and less part in everyday activities, and when fraud was discovered in the lower levels of the naval administration, he was forced to retire in 1618. He died at Haling House, in Croydon, southern London, on 14 December 1624.

Despite the significant role he played in the English victory against the Spanish Armada, Howard has been overshadowed by Sir Francis Drake and Sir John HAWKINS. However, historian Garrett Mattingly, in his 1959 work *The Armada,* has tried to resurrect Howard's reputation. Quoting a work on English military history by historian Thomas Woodroofe, Mattingly writes: "In the past twenty years or so, historians have done Howard more justice. The most recent narrative says roundly, 'It was Howard's battle, and he won it.' It has even been argued that Howard fought the battle the only way it could have been fought—without too much risk—and that no admiral could have done any better." As historians continue to examine the Spanish Armada and evaluate its importance to world and military history, perhaps Howard's reputation will be more enhanced.

References: Southey, Robert, *English Seamen: Howard, Clifford, Hawkins, Drake, Cavendish* (London: Methuen & Co., 1895); Kenny, Robert W., *Elizabeth's Admiral: The Political Career of Charles Howard, Earl of Nottingham, 1536–1624* (Baltimore, Md.: Johns Hopkins Press, 1970); Bruce, Anthony, and William Cogar, "Howard, Charles, Second Lord Howard of Effingham (later Earl of Nottingham)," in *An Encyclopedia of Naval History* (New York: Checkmark Books, 1999), 182–83; *A Discourse Concerninge the Spanish Fleete Invadinge Englande in the Yeare 1588* . . . (London, 1590); Mattingly, Garrett, *The Armada* (Boston: Houghton Mifflin, 1959).

Howard, Thomas *See* NORFOLK, THOMAS HOWARD, SECOND DUKE OF.

Howe, Richard, Earl Howe (1726–1799)
British admiral

Richard Howe was a member of a distinguished English military family. He was born in London on 8 March 1726, the second son of Emanuel Scrope Howe, second Viscount Howe, who served as governor of the Barbadoes (now Barbados) until his death in 1735. Richard Howe attended the prestigious English school Eton about 1735, and in 1740, when he was 14, he entered service in the British navy, and saw action in 1743 and 1746. By 1755, he had risen to the rank of captain, and at the start of the Seven Years' War (1756–63), he was named as captain of the ship *Dunkirk,* serving under Admiral Edward BOSCAWEN in North America. When Howe captured the French ship *Alcide,* it was the first shot fired by English forces in that war. He saw further action during the conflict, with perhaps his most important service coming at the victory of Quiberon Bay (20 November 1759), when, working under Edward HAWKE, his ship, the *Magnanime,* led the attack.

In 1758, Howe's older brother, General George Howe (1724–58), was killed while fighting the French in North America, and because he was the next in line, Richard Howe therefore succeeded to the title of Viscount Howe. In 1762, he was elected a member of Parliament for Dartmouth, and he served from 1763 to 1765 as a member of the Board of Admiralty. He later served from 1765 to 1770 as the treasurer of the navy. He was promoted to rear admiral in 1770 and to vice admiral in 1775.

In 1776, Howe was named as commander of the British fleet off the coast of North America, fighting the insurrection of the formerly British colonies. In secret sympathy with the colonists's aims of breaking away from London's control, he first tried appeasement to mollify them, working with his brother, General Sir William Howe, and one of the leading colonists, Benjamin Franklin. In September 1776, the Howe brothers met with a committee appointed by the Continental Congress, but they were unable to reach a resolution. In 1777, when his brother's forces attacked Philadelphia, Lord Howe backed him with naval support, but when London rebuffed his moves to bring peace, he handed in his resignation. However, before he could sail back to England, France declared war on England and sent a fleet to North America to support the colonists. Howe moved his small fleet off the coast of Long Island, New York, and was able to prevent the French fleet under the comte d'Estaing, from taking Newport, Rhode Island. When Admiral John Byron arrived to succeed him, Howe left the area and returned to England.

In 1782, when the Tory ministry of Lord North fell to the Whig Marquess of Rockingham, who was succeeded that same year by the earl of Shelburne, Howe was selected by the new administration to command British forces in the English Channel and sent to relieve Gibraltar, then under siege by the French and Spanish. Although heavily outnumbered, Howe repulsed his enemies brilliantly and raised the siege. In 1783, he was named as First Lord of the Admiralty, first from January to April and then from December 1783 until 1788, under Prime Minister William Pitt. In 1788, he was created Baron and Earl Howe.

The French Revolution (1789) brought another war between England and France, and in 1790 Howe was again named commander of the fleet in the English Channel. During this conflict, he is noted for his victory at Ushant, also known as the "Glorious First of June" (1 June 1794). Howe, with 25 ships, faced a fleet of 26 ships under the French admiral Louis Villaret de Joyeuse. Historian George Bruce writes: "After four hours' fighting the French were defeated, with a loss of six ships captured and one, the *Vengeur*, sunk. The sinking of this ship was elaborated by the French into a fable, to the effect that she refused to surrender and went down with all hands and colors flying. She had, however, undoubtedly struck her colors, and her captain and over 200 of her crew were rescued by the board of the British fleet. The French admitted a loss of 3,000 men, besides prisoners, while the British lost 922 killed and wounded." In a letter to Howe's sister on the victory at Ushant, King George III of England wrote, "Mrs. Howe's zeal for the great Cause in which this country is engaged, added to her becoming ardor for the Glory of her Family, must make her feel with redoubled joy the glorious news brought by Sir Roger Curtis. She will, I hope, be satisfied now that Earl

Richard has with 25 Sail of the Line attacked 26 of the Enemy, taken six and sunk two; besides, it is not improbable that some of the disabled Ships of the Enemy may not be able to reach their own Shore. I could not refrain from expressing my Sentiments on the Occasion but will not detain Mrs. Howe by adding more."

Howe was made Admiral of the Fleet in 1796 and Knight of the Garter in 1797. His last service was in 1797, when, with the outbreak of a mutiny by British sailors at Spithead, he was called in to negotiate for the government, as he was trusted by the sailors involved. Earl Howe, whose lack of mirth and gaiety had earned him the nickname of "Black Dick," died in London on 5 August 1799 at the age of 73.

References: Knight, Roger, "Richard, Earl Howe, 1726–1799," in *Precursors of Nelson: British Admirals of the Eighteenth Century,* edited by Peter Le Fevre and Richard Harding (London: Chatham Publishing, 2000), 279–300; Bruce, Anthony, and William Cogar, "Howe, Richard, First Earl," in *An Encyclopedia of Naval History* (New York: Checkmark Books, 1999), 183; Gruber, I. D., *The Howe Brothers and the American Revolution* (New York: Atheneum, 1972); Bruce, George, "Ushant," in *Collins Dictionary of Wars* (Glasgow, Scotland: HarperCollins Publishers, 1995), 256; George III of England to Mrs. Howe, 11 June 1794, letter in the private collection of the author.

Hunyadi, János (John Hunyadi, John Huniades, Törökverö) (1387–1456) *Hungarian military leader*

János Hunyadi was born about 1387 in Hunyad, Transylvania (now Hunedoara, Romania), the son of Serba Volk, a farmer. Much of the information on Hunyadi comes from Transylvanian and Romanian stories. He took his name from the estate where he was born, and he became a soldier at an early age. He served Stephan Lazarevic, the prince of northern Serbia, and married the daughter of a nobleman. He then served King Sigismund of Luxembourg, who was Holy Roman Emperor as well as the king of Bohemia and Hungary. When Sigismund led his armies in several wars, including those in Bohemia (1420) and against the Turks, Hunyadi was at his side. In 1437, Hunyadi led troops into battle at Smederovo against the Turks.

Constant invasion by the Islamic Turks threatened southern Europe, and in 1439 the Turks invaded and occupied Serbia. King Albert II had made Hunyadi the *bán* (military governor) of Szörény, a Hungarian province, in 1438. When Albert died in 1439, Hunyadi supported the election of the Polish prince Wladyslaw III as his successor and was rewarded by Wladyslaw with the captaincy of Belgrade and the title of *voivode* (governor) of Transylvania (though he had to share the latter honor). Under Ulászló I, the title taken by Wladyslaw, Hunyadi was able to establish a campaign against the Turks. After raising an army of some 30,000 men, he crossed the Danube River and entered Serbia, beginning what is known in Hungarian history as "The Long Campaign" (1441–44). Hunyadi's army occupied the cities of Nis and Sofia and regained control of much of the Balkans by the following year. This offensive caused the Turks to withdraw, and the Turkish sultan, Murad II, asked for peace. However, Murad soon sent forces across the Dardanelles again to bring war into southern Europe. At Varna on 10 November 1444, the sultan's army slaughtered a Christian force; King Ulászló I was killed in the battle, and Hunyadi escaped with his life. Named as governor to rule during the reign of the new king, young László V, Hunyadi again raised an army to attack Murad, and he met the Turks at Kosovo (17 October 1448). Although they were vastly outnumbered, Hunyadi's army inflicted some 40,000 casualties on the Turks before they were forced to withdraw, having sustained about 17,000 casualties.

With the death of Murad in 1451, MEHMET II came to power as the Turkish sultan. As a consequence of Hunyadi's previous withdrawal, Mehmet marched his forces eastward, and the Turks took Constantinople in 1453. Fresh from this victory, he then turned his armies on Belgrade, presaging a full-scale Turkish attack on Europe as a whole. Consequently, Pope Calixtus III sent a Franciscan monk, John of Capistrano, to Hungary to incite its citizens against the Islamic invaders. Belgrade was ill prepared to fend off the attack but had enough men to force the Turks to besiege the city instead of attacking it. The Hungarian forces, commanded by Hunyadi's brother-in-law and son, numbered only about 60,000–75,000 troops, while Mehmet had approximately 100,000–300,000 men (historians are unsure as to exact numbers). In addition, the Turks had 200 ships stationed in the Danube River as support. Hunyadi, who had gone off to form a new army and fleet, returned and attacked the Turkish fleet, sinking three vessels and capturing four large ships with supplies.

Mehmet ordered an attack on the city's walls on 21 July, but the besieged garrison attacked the Turks with all available materials, including setting the moat around the city on fire. Turks caught in the moat were burned to death, and others were massacred by the Hungarians. The Turks were forced to retreat, but then Hunyadi's land forces arrived and attacked them on 22 July. This led to a massive withdrawal by the Turks, during which Mehmet was wounded.

After 40 days, the siege was broken. It is believed that some 50,000 Turks had been slaughtered in the fighting, while the Hungarians lost about 10,000. The Turks were later attacked by Serb forces, who inflicted an additional 25,000 casualties. Pope Calixtus called Hunyadi "the most outstanding man the world had seen in 300 years." However, Hunyadi's victory was short-lived. During the siege, a plague had swept Belgrade, and he succumbed to the disease on 11 August 1456. On his deathbed, he told his troops, "Defend, my friends, Christendom and Hungary from all enemies. . . . Do not quarrel amongst yourselves. . . . If you should waste your energies in altercations, you will seal your own fate as well as dig the grave of your country." John of Capistrano died of the same disease two months later. Hunyadi's son became the king of Hungary in 1458, taking the throne as Matthias I.

In Eastern Europe, the name of János Hunyadi is still honored as one of the region's saviors. His victory at Belgrade is one of history's great battles, a turning point that caused the Muslim invaders to pause for nearly a century before they attempted another incursion into Europe. Hunyadi is known to Islam as Törökverö, or "Scourge of the Turks."

References: Windrow, Martin, and Francis K. Mason, "Hunyadi, János, Count of Bestercze," in *The Wordsworth Dictionary of Military Biography* (Hertfordshire, U.K.: Wordsworth Editions Ltd., 1997), 139–40; Bak, János M. and Béla K. Király, editors, *Hunyadi to Rákóczi: War and Society in Late Medieval and Early Modern Hungary* (Boulder, Colo.: Social Science Monographs, 1982); Held, Joseph, *Hunyadi: Legend and Reality* (Boulder, Colo.: East European Monographs, 1985); Bruce, George, "Belgrade I," in *Collins Dictionary of Wars* (Glasgow, Scotland: HarperCollins Publishers, 1995), 32; "Hunyadi, Janos," in *Command: From Alexander the Great to Zhukov—The Greatest Commanders of World History*, edited by James Lucas (London: Bloomsbury Publishing, 1988), 41–42.

I

Ivan IV (Ivan the Terrible, Ivan Vasilievich Grozny)
(1530–1584) *czar of Russia*

Ivan Vasilievich Grozny was born on 25 August 1530 in Kolomenskoe, a village near Moscow, the son of Vasili III Ivanovich, whom he succeeded as the grand duke of Moscow upon his father's death when he was only three years old. On 16 January 1547, when he was 16, he was crowned czar of Russia, the first to use that title. Ivan initiated a series of reforms, including updating the law code, and established a standing army for the first time (since previously there had been no army that served during peacetime). He also opened his nation to trade from Europe and set up the Zemsky Sobor, or council of nobles, to advise him.

Despite his introduction of reformist measures and institution of a series of laws that led to the subjugation of serfs for more than 400 years, Ivan is best known for a number of wars that he launched to expand the small duchy of Russia into the empire it later became. Starting in 1552, he initiated hostilities against the Kazan khanate, which his armies conquered after a campaign of six weeks; two years later, he occupied the khanate of Astrakhan. After he annexed the Kazan khanate to Russia, he ordered the construction of St. Basil's Cathedral to honor the addition to his country. The two victories enabled Russia to control the entire length of the highly important Volga River. Starting in 1557, Ivan commenced the long, drawn-out Livonian War in an effort to win a trade port on the Baltic Sea. Russian armies swept across the Baltic, but a series of defeats by the Poles and Swedes forced Ivan to sign the Peace of Zapoli in 1582, shutting off any hope of a Russian trade route through the Baltic.

Historians believe that the deaths of Ivan's wife and son in 1560 drove him insane, and after those events he was no longer a stable ruler. Fearing for his personal safety, he established the *oprichina* (separate estate), by which certain towns and districts became his personal property, controlled only by himself. Privileged residents called the *oprichniki,* were granted far-reaching powers to use force to protect the czar from enemies, real or imagined. History records the intense cruelty and disregard for human rights that the *oprichniki* used, and Ivan was held personally responsible for their actions. In 1570, the *oprichniki* heard that certain elements in the city of Novgorod were conspiring against the czar, and on this rumor alone, Ivan and his armies marched into the city and, in an orgy of murder and destruction, sacked the town and leveled it, leaving perhaps 30,000–40,000 dead. In 1569, when Turks under Selim II invaded Astrakhan to dig a canal from the Don River to the Volga, Ivan sent troops to shore up the Russian garrison, and they routed the Turks. Ivan remarried, but he feared that his wife and her three successors were out to harm him, and in 1580, during an argument, he murdered his own son Ivan.

Ivan's military campaigns and his tyranny left his country, once a prosperous region, a poor and serf-ridden state. His instability led to an illness that caused his death on 18 March 1584, age 53, while he was preparing to play a game of chess. He was succeeded by his crazed son Feodor, who, when he died in 1598, was the last member of the House of Rurik. Despite his cruel regime, Ivan is fondly remembered in Russian history; the Russian filmmaker Sergei Eisenstein made two notable early 20th-century films on Ivan's life.

References: Waliszewski, Kazimierz, *Ivan the Terrible,* translated by Lady Mary Loyd (Philadelphia: J. B. Lippincott Company, 1904); Bobrick, Benson, *Fearful Majesty: The Life and Reign of Ivan the Terrible* (New York: Putnam, 1987); Graham, Stephen, *Ivan the Terrible: The Life of Ivan IV of Russia, Called the Terrible* (London: E. Benn Ltd., 1932); Yanov, Alexander, *The Origins of Autocracy: Ivan the Terrible in Russian History,* translated by Stephen Dunn (Berkeley: University of California Press, 1981); Perrie, Maureen, *The Image of Ivan the Terrible in Russian Folklore* (Cambridge, U.K.: Cambridge University Press, 1987).

Ivanov, Nikolai Yudovich (1851–1919)
Russian general

Nikolai Ivanov was a loyal officer in the regime of Czar Nicholas II who rose through the ranks of the Russian military and saw action in the Russo-Japanese War (1904–05). Afterward, he helped to suppress a revolt of Russian sailors at Kronstadt (1906). He served as commander of the Russian garrison at Kiev from 1908 until the start of the First World War in 1914, when he began by mobilizing Russian forces in the Ukraine. Czar Nicholas then named him as commander of Russian forces in that region on the southwestern front.

Unfortunately for Ivanov, his reluctance to take the offensive against German forces in Galicia and the Carpathian mountains through 1914 and in all of 1915 allowed the Germans to advance. When General Baron Viktor von Dankl of the Austro-Hungarian First Army crossed into Galicia in August 1914, Ivanov quickly withdrew his forces. It was left to Russian forces under Generals Alexander Russki and Alexei BRUSI-

LOV to hold the line against the invading Austro-German force. Despite incredible losses on both sides, the Russians were able to push the Germans and Austrians back.

In April 1915, Ivanov decided to move his troops back into Poland to counter another Austro-German offensive. At Gorlice (also known as Gorlice-Tarnow, 2–12 May 1915), despite commanding numerically superior forces, Ivanov's army was cut down by a combined German-Austrian force commanded by German marshal Paul von HINDENBURG, resulting in some 200,000 Russians taken prisoner. Gorlice and its accompanying towns of Ciezkowice and Przemyśl fell to the Germans on 1 June. Brusilov tried to hold back the German offensive by taking a stand on the Dniester River, but he lost the cities of Lemberg and Warsaw. By the end of August 1915, more than 1 million Russian troops had been killed in this single campaign, leaving the Germans in almost total control of Poland. The czar dismissed Ivanov as commander and replaced him with Brusilov. Historians continued to argue whether it was incompetence or Ivanov's extreme caution in an effort to avoid a grinding battle against the Germans in Poland that cost the Russians so many men. Whatever the reason, Ivanov is almost universally blamed for the military disaster that befell the Russians on the eastern front in the first two years of the First World War.

Despite his responsibility for the disaster at Gorlice, Ivanov was appointed as a senior czarist military adviser, but he was ignored by the Russian army chief of staff, Yevgeni Ivanovich Alekseyev (1843–1918). With the revolt against the czarist regime in February 1917, Ivanov tried to hold the city of Petrograd (now St. Petersburg) for the czar, but he was forced to relinquish his position with the new government's installation. That November, communist forces took control of the country, and Ivanov sided with the anticommunists, or Whites. Although a million men had died under his command, Ivanov was given control over part of the White army. During a clash in the Lower Don Valley in 1919, he was slain in battle by Bolshevik, or Red, forces. Because of his incompetence on the field of battle, Ivanov has been all but forgotten by military and other historians.

References: George Bruce, "Galicia" and "Gorlice," in *Collins Dictionary of Wars* (Glasgow, Scotland: HarperCollins Publishers, 1995), 94, 99–100.

J

Jackson, Andrew (1767–1845) *American general, seventh president of the United States*

Andrew Jackson was born on 15 March 1767 in what was called the Waxhaw Settlement at the borders of the Carolinas, now part of Tennessee, although he considered himself a South Carolinian all his life. Little is known of Jackson's early life. In 1780, when he was 13 years old, his schooling was interrupted when the British invaded the western Carolinas. He was captured sometime the next year and, despite being only 14, taken as a prisoner of war. When he refused to shine the boots of a British officer, Jackson was struck across the face with a sword, leaving a deep scar that remained for the rest of his life. In addition to this, Jackson's own mother and two brothers died as a result of British actions, and it was because of this that he hated the British until his death.

After being released, in 1784 Jackson began to study law, and he was admitted to the North Carolina state bar in 1787. The following year, he was sent to the Cumberland region, now in Tennessee, to serve as prosecuting attorney for the western district of North Carolina. Based in Nashville, Jackson showed fairness in trying cases and collecting debts, and he formed strong bonds, both financial and political, with many of the landowners in the area, making him one of the more important figures in what is now Tennessee. It was at this time that he met and married Mrs. Rachel Robards, the wife of an army officer who later learned that she had failed to get a proper divorce from her first husband before her marriage to Jackson. This was subsequently used by Jackson's political opponents against him, and he later fought a duel with a man who had insulted his wife.

As Tennessee grew both financially and politically, Jackson was in a good position to become a leader in the territory destined to became a new state. While working as an attorney, he also speculated in land, raised horses, farmed cotton, and bought and sold slaves. Gradually he became a wealthy man, and he built a large mansion that he named the Hermitage, near Nashville. He also became involved in the territory's politics, being appointed its solicitor in 1791. In 1796, when Tennessee was admitted to the Union and a convention met to draft a new state constitution, Jackson served as a delegate. He was subsequently elected as Tennessee's first representative to the U.S. House of Representatives on 5 December 1796, serving in the Fourth and Fifth Congresses; however, he left office on 4 March 1797. Historians note Jackson's key moment in the House was his speech denouncing outgoing president George WASHINGTON for the latter's support of the controversial Jay Treaty. He also voted against a House measure sending thanks to the president for his farewell address to the nation.

Andrew Jackson

Political life in Washington had left a bad taste in Jackson's mouth, and he returned to Tennessee after his single term in Congress vowing never to run for political office again. Nevertheless, before the year 1797 had ended, he was elected to a seat in the United States Senate. Jackson saw that his upward climb in Tennessee would be hampered by a refusal to serve. However, after only one year in the Senate, Jackson resigned his seat in April 1798 and again returned to Tennessee, where he was named as a judge on the Superior Court, then the equivalent of a modern state Supreme Court. He remained on this court for six years, resigning in 1804, upon which he returned to his business ventures.

When Congress declared war against the British on 18 June 1812, Jackson was not immediately called to serve because he had sided with former vice president Aaron Burr in his plans for establishing a new state, perhaps a new nation, in Florida or Texas. However, in October 1812, Tennessee governor William Blount was asked to provide troops to help General James Wilkin-

son defend the city of New Orleans against a British invasion. Blount named Jackson as commander of the Tennessee forces, but as Jackson marched toward Louisiana, he became involved instead in the Creek War. On 30 August 1813, a group of Creek Indians under Red Eagle attacked and murdered some 250 white settlers in Alabama. After several battles against the Creek, Jackson defeated them at the Battle of Horseshoe Bend on 27 March 1814.

President James Madison, recognizing Jackson's abilities, promoted him to the rank of major general and commander of the Seventh Military District. Jackson then marched his army to New Orleans, where, in December 1814 and January 1815, he defeated the British in an important American military victory. Historian George Bruce writes: "[The] city, held by a garrison of 6,000 Americans under General Jackson, was attacked in December 1814 by a British force of 6,000 men under General [John] Keane, aided by the fleet. On the 13th the American warships lying in the Mississippi [river] were captured by a boat attack, and by the 21st the whole of the troops were disembarked. After a few skirmishes General Sir Edward Pakenham arrived and took command on the 25th, and by 1 January 1815 a determined attack was made upon the American position. This failed and owing to supply difficulties the British retired. On the 8th they attacked again with 5,300 men but were again repulsed, with a loss of 1,500, including Pakenham. The expedition then withdrew."

The battle was a landmark victory for the American forces, and particularly for Jackson, who was thereafter known as "The Hero of New Orleans." What no one at New Orleans knew was that a ceasefire had been declared days before the battle began, but because of the slowness of communications, word of the peace treaty—signed at Ghent, Belgium, on 24 December 1814—did not arrive in time. Congress nonetheless presented Jackson with a formal vote of thanks and a gold medal on 27 February 1815.

Jackson was then sent south by President James Madison without specific orders, but historians generally believe it was hoped that he would find an excuse to fight Spanish forces and capture what is now Florida for the United States. His troops quickly captured two Spanish forts inside Florida, and he installed one of his commanders as the territory's new military governor. The Spanish lodged a diplomatic protest with Washington, and a heated debate began in the government about what do with Jackson. Secretary of State John Quincy Adams argued that he was fighting on behalf of the United States, saving him from probable censure. Despite Spanish protestations, Florida was made a part of the United States, and Jackson was named as the military governor of the new territory in 1821. He served in this position for a year.

By 1822, with a new presidential election just two years away, many politicians felt that military hero Jackson should be nominated for president. Jackson, a Democrat, accepted first a "nomination" by the Tennessee legislature to have him nominated as president, then election to a U.S. Senate seat, from 4 March 1823 to 14 October 1825. In 1824, he ran for president against John Quincy Adams, former Speaker of the House Henry Clay, and William H. Crawford. Jackson received more votes, but because there was no candidate with a majority, the election was decided by the House of Representatives. There, Clay gave his votes to Adams, who was declared president; Clay was named as secretary of state. Jackson's supporters called this the "corrupt bargain" and denounced the administration throughout its four-year term. Jackson was convinced that the machinations of Clay and Adams had denied him the presidency.

In 1828, Jackson ran for a second time, this time against the incumbent Adams, who had presided over a poor economy. The campaign that year was one of the worst in American history in terms of the insults and slander thrown around, with unsubstantiated charges being made by both sides. However, Jackson scored an easy victory over Adams, in an election in which rural voters, many of whom had not voted before, came out in large numbers for this son of the South. Elected the seventh president of the United States, Jackson's triumph was marred when his beloved wife died, a tragedy that many historians believe was caused by the accusations of bigamy when she had married Jackson.

On 4 March 1829, Jackson took office as a widower. In short order, he became one of the most dominant leaders to serve as president up until that time—so much so that his opponents called him "King Andrew I." He formed his administration by rewarding friends with high positions and punishing those who opposed him. One senator accurately described this form of patronage when he said that "to the victor belongs the spoils." Thus the practice became known as the "spoils system," and it took nearly 50 years to ban it. Opponents also charged that Jackson did not consult or work with Congress suf-

ficiently. When South Carolina refused to acknowledge the government's high protective tariff on textiles made in the state, it precipitated a crisis with Jackson, who warned the movement's leaders that he would hang them if they defied him. Through the intervention of Henry Clay, a compromise was worked out and a potential government and constitutional showdown was avoided. Jackson also opposed the recharter of the Second Bank of the United States as a government-sponsored corporation. Henry Clay and noted orator Daniel Webster joined a chorus of national leaders who voiced outrage that Jackson refused to work with Congress on the matter. Jackson told Martin van Buren, "The bank is trying to kill me, but I will kill it." Jackson vetoed the bank's recharter, and Congress could not muster enough votes to override the veto. Despite his antagonism toward Congress, Jackson remained popular with the American people, and in 1832 he ran for reelection and received 56 percent of the vote.

In his second term, Jackson again faced down opponents over the Bank of the United States, precipitating the "Bank War" that lasted for much of his second term. He also forcefully moved Indian tribes from their ancestral lands in the eastern United States to unpopulated areas in the Midwest. He groomed his vice president, Martin Van Buren, to succeed him, and Van Buren won the election of 1836, following which Jackson retired to the Hermitage. Although an invalid for the last eight years of his life, Jackson remained close to political associates and continued to write on national and local political matters. He died at the Hermitage on 8 June 1845, age 78, and was buried in the garden on the estate next to his beloved wife Rachel.

In a eulogy to Jackson, famed historian George Bancroft said: "In life, his career had been like the blaze of the sun in the fierceness of its noon-day glory; his death was lonely as the mildest sunset of a summer's evening, when the sun goes down in tranquil beauty without a cloud."

References: Jenkins, John Stilwell, ed., *Life and Public Services of Gen. Andrew Jackson, Seventh President of the United States, Including the Most Important of His State Papers. . . .* (Buffalo, N.Y.: G. H. Derby & Company, 1850); Parton, James, *Life of Andrew Jackson*, 3 vols. (New York: Mason Brothers, 1860); Walker, Alexander, *The Life of Andrew Jackson: To which is Added an Authentic Narrative of the Memorable Achievements of the American Army* *at New Orleans, in the Winter of 1814, '15* (Philadelphia: Davis, Porter & Coates, 1866); Owsley, Frank Lawrence, *Struggle for the Gulf Borderlands, the Creek War, and the Battle of New Orleans* (Gainesville: University Presses of Florida, 1981); Albright, Harry, *New Orleans: Battle of the Bayous* (New Orleans: Hippocrene Books, 1990); Bruce, George, "New Orleans I," in *Collins Dictionary of Wars* (Glasgow, Scotland: HarperCollins Publishers, 1995), 176–177; Dusenbery, B. M., comp., *Monument to the Memory of General Andrew Jackson: Containing Twenty-Five Eulogies and Sermons Delivered on Occasion of His Death. . . .* (Philadelphia: Walker & Gillis, 1846).

Jackson, Thomas Jonathan ("Stonewall" Jackson) (1824–1863) *Confederate general*

Thomas Jackson was born in Clarksburg, Virginia (now in West Virginia), on 21 January 1824. Because of his father's early death, he was forced to forego an education in order to support his family. In 1842, he received an appointment to the United States Military Academy at West Point, New York, graduating in 1846 and receiving a commission as a second lieutenant of artillery. When he graduated, the United States was already at war with Mexico, and Jackson rushed south to join his regiment. He served in the Mexican War (1846–48) with great distinction, and in 1851 he was appointed professor of artillery tactics and of natural philosophy at the Virginia Military Institute (VMI). Here he taught military strategy to many men whom he later faced on the battlefield in the Civil War.

When the Civil War erupted in April 1861, Jackson, a Southern sympathizer, resigned his post at VMI and offered his services to his home state. Appointed as a colonel of Virginia volunteers, he was posted to the command of Harper's Ferry, Virginia (now in West Virginia), in the Shenandoah Valley. His unit was merged with that of General Joseph Johnston, and the Confederate forces under General P. G. T. Beaugard attacked the Union forces under General Irvin McDowell at Manassas, or First Bull Run, on 21 July 1861. During the battle, Confederate general Barnard Bee allegedly rode up to Jackson and yelled, "General, they are beating us back!" Jackson's reply was: "Then, sir, we will give them the bayonet." Revitalized by Jackson's strength in the face of withering fire, Bee allegedly went back to his men and shouted, "Look, there is Jackson standing like a stone wall! Rally behind the Virginians!" With this lead, the

Confederates beat back the Union forces, and the name of Thomas "Stonewall" Jackson became symbolic with heroism overnight.

It was not until early 1862 that Union and Confederate forces again clashed in the East. When Union general George B. MCCLELLAN marched his troops to the Yorktown peninsula to move on the Confederate capital of Richmond, Jackson, with 3,000 men, marched to Kernstown, Virginia, to divert Union reinforcements marching to join McClellan. Although Jackson's troops were decisively beaten, his tactical skill on the battlefield forced the Union to deal with him on a different level. McClellan and several other Union armies converged on Richmond, intending to take the rebel capital and end the war quickly. The Southern armies' commander, General Robert E. LEE, saw that Richmond's defense lay in Jackson's hands. Jackson marched up the Shenandoah and defeated one section of the Union army, driving them back into western Virginia on 8 May 1862. He then turned his attention to forces of the Union army headed by General Nathaniel Banks. Attacking and defeating troops under Banks's command, headed by General John R. Kenly, Jackson forced Banks's withdrawal, then fell on his army at Winchester and pushed him back to the Potomac River.

Hitting at Union forces at Cross Keys (8 June 1862) and Port Republic (9 June 1862), Jackson was able to draw Union reinforcements away from Richmond. Lee and Jackson then attacked McClellan's main army, initiating the clash known as the Seven Days Battles (26 June–2 July 1862), which left approximately 20,000 Confederate and 15,000 Union soldiers dead. Although historians mark this engagement as a loss for the South, it relieved Richmond and ended any chance for a quick Union victory.

Quickly following up the battles around Richmond, Lee and Jackson struck at Union forces around Manassas Junction, Virginia, commanded by General John Pope. This battle, known as Second Manassas or Second Bull Run (28 August 1862), led to a complete and total victory for the Southern forces. Jackson moved north, crossing the Potomac River and attacking the federal garrison at Harper's Ferry, which was forced to surrender on 15 September after a two-day siege. He then turned to support Lee's forces under attack at Antietam, Maryland (17 September 1862), an engagement that ended in a draw. Although Lee and Jackson were forced to withdraw back over the Potomac River into Virginia, the Union forces had been ejected from the state and were far from Richmond.

For his services, Jackson was promoted to the rank of lieutenant general and given command of the II Corps of the Army of Northern Virginia. With this force, he was attacked by Union forces under General Ambrose Burnside at Fredericksburg, Virginia (13 December 1862), but the strengthened Confederate army repelled the offensive. The debacle at Fredericksburg left the Union army with horrendous losses and no ground to show for their efforts in a year of fighting. Burnside was replaced by General Joseph HOOKER, who waited until April 1863 to attack Southern positions around the Rappahannock River. Lee, with Jackson as his right-hand man, moved the main portion of his 60,000-man force to Chancellorsville to head off the attack by Hooker's 120,000-troop army. At Chancellorsville (2–4 May 1863), Lee held his main force in reserve while Jackson's forces attacked Hooker's right flank. The Union forces were taken by surprise by the maneuver, and their entire XI Corps was forced to withdraw with massive casualties. However, the victory came at a high price for the Confederacy: That same night, as he led his forces to attack the retreating Union troops, some of his own men mistook him in the dark for a Union officer, and Jackson was mortally wounded in the shoulder. Carried back to the Confederate lines, his left arm was amputated. Lee wrote to him, "I should have wished for the good of the country to be disabled in your stead." Nine days later, on 10 May 1863, Jackson died of pneumonia while recuperating at Guiney's Station, just south of Fredericksburg. After his body lay in state, he was buried with full military honors in Lexington, Virginia.

The impact of the death of Thomas Jackson on the eventual Confederate defeat is immeasurable. Historians agree that without Jackson, Lee and his army did not have the tactical maneuverability which had characterized Lee's army in the past. Whether or not Jackson would have staved off the ultimate end of the war is a matter for argument. Regardless, his stature as "Stonewall" Jackson has remained untouched, even though historians have recently come to believe that his nickname was given to him not because of his heroism but because of a lack of it. It is alleged that when General Barnard Bee was wounded and needed Jackson to take control of the situation, he later claimed that Jackson "stood there like a stone wall" instead of acting. Whether or not this

is true, it might be irrelevant, as Jackson's name and military genius are forever preserved in American history.

References: Arnold, Thomas Jackson, *Early Life and Letters of General Thomas J. Jackson, "Stonewall" Jackson, by His Nephew, Thomas Arnold Jackson* (New York: Fleming H. Revell Company, 1916); Farwell, Byron, *Stonewall: A Biography of General Thomas J. Jackson* (New York: W. W. Norton, 1992); Henderson, George Francis Robert, *Stonewall Jackson and the American Civil War* (London: Longmans, Green and Company, 1898); Kallman, John D., *Jackson, "Thomas Jonathan 'Stonewall,'"* in *Historical Times Illustrated Encyclopedia of the Civil War,* edited by Patricia L. Faust (New York: Harper & Row, Publishers, 1986), 391–392; Windrow, Martin, and Francis K. Mason, "Jackson, Thomas Jonathan," in *The Wordsworth Dictionary of Military Biography* (Hertfordshire, U.K.: Wordsworth Editions Ltd., 1997), 141–142.

Jellicoe, John Rushworth, Earl Jellicoe of Scapa (1859–1935) *British admiral*

Born in Southampton, England, on 5 December 1859, John Rushworth Jellicoe was the son of J. H. Jellicoe, a captain in the mercantile marine. He received his education at Rottingdean, in Sussex, after which he received an appointment as a naval cadet and entered service in the Royal Navy in 1872. He was given a commission as a sublieutenant in 1880 and, two years later, saw action in the war against Egypt. In 1883, he returned to England as a student at HMS *Excellent,* the naval gunnery school where he subsequently became an instructor (1884–85 and 1886–89). Promoted to the rank of commander in 1891, he was appointed to the HMS *Victoria* and was injured when that ship collided with another English vessel, HMS *Camperdown.* He later served under Admiral Sir Michael Culme-Seymour, and in 1897 he was promoted to the rank of captain.

In 1898, Jellicoe was named to serve on the HMS *Centurion* on the China station under Admiral Sir Edward Seymour. Two years later, he saw action at Beijing (then called Peking) during the insurrection by the Chinese rebels in the so-called "Boxer Rebellion" of 1900. While in battle, he was wounded, and for his services he was made a Commander of the Order of the Bath (CB). He then returned to England, where he served in several naval staff positions, including naval assistant to the controller (1902–03), director of naval ordnance

(1905–07), Third Sea Lord and controller of the navy (1908–10), commander of the Atlantic Fleet (1910–11), and Second Sea Lord (1913–14).

Jellicoe was promoted to vice admiral and named commander in chief of the Grand Fleet on 4 August 1914 at the outbreak of the First World War. He spent his first months in command blockading Germany from resupply of commercial and war matériel. He came under some criticism, both from the government and the press, for his "timidity" in not taking on the German fleet. However, he could do little in this respect since the German navy remained in home waters. In May 1916, Jellicoe's advance squadron under David BEATTY detected movement by German ships into the North Sea. This led to the Battle of Jutland. Historian George Bruce writes:

> The German High Seas Fleet under Admiral [Reinhard] Scheer deliberately or by accident met the British Fleet engaged in a sweep of the North Sea. Admiral [Franz] Von Hipper commanded five battle cruisers, while Scheer followed 50 miles behind with 16 new and eight old battleships. There were also 11 light cruisers and 63 destroyers. The British fleet, under Admiral Jellicoe, consisted of the northern group of three battle cruisers and 24 battleships commanded by Jellicoe himself; and the southern fleet, [commanded by] Admiral Beatty, six battle cruisers and four battleships. In addition there were 34 light cruisers and 80 destroyers. Beatty and Hipper sighted each other, and Hipper turned to link up with Scheer, after which the two groups shelled each other. Beatty then turned back to lure the Germans into Jellicoe's hands and in the process lost two of his battleships, but the maneuver accomplished, the entire British fleet soon formed a line east and southeast into which the Germans were sailing as into a net. Just when their destruction seemed certain, the weather closed down and rescued the Germans, who later, under the cover of darkness, skillfully made their escape. The Royal Navy lost three battle cruisers, three light cruisers and eight destroyers; Germany [lost] four cruisers and five destroyers, but the morale of the German Navy had been destroyed. Thenceforward it avoided

battle, for the sailors threatened mutiny at the prospect.

The losses in manpower for each side pointed more to a German victory than a British one: The Germans lost 2,545 men and no prisoners, while the British lost 6,097 men and 177 prisoners. Despite what appeared to be a British "victory" because of the German withdrawal, Jellicoe was savaged by British public opinion, perhaps because only 12 German ships were lost and their casualties were much lighter. Historian James Lucas writes: "What the British public had expected . . . was a Nelson-style victory, not an inconclusive battle. Ships of the Grand Fleet were greeted by boos, while the newspapers, to whom Beatty was a hero through his battle cruiser exploits, accused Jellicoe of bungling the battle. At the subsequent Court of Inquiry, Beatty's statements seemed to substantiate this." However, when, two years later, the German fleet surrendered at Scapa (November 1918), it was clearly Jellicoe's cautious strategy of waiting them out, rather than taking them on and incurring losses, that had won the day.

Writing in his memoir *The Grand Fleet,* Jellicoe explains why he initiated the strategy he did against the German fleet:

> [A] victory is judged not merely by material losses and damage, but by its results. It is profitable to examine the results of the Jutland Battle. With the single exception of a cruise towards the English coast on August 19th, 1916—undertaken, no doubt, by such part of the High Sea Fleet as had been repaired in order to show that it was still capable of going to sea—the High Sea Fleet never again, up to the end of 1917, ventured much outside the "Heligoland triangle," and even on August 19th, 1916, the much reduced Fleet made precipitately for home as soon as it was warned by its Zeppelin scouts of the approach of the Grand Fleet. This is hardly the method of procedure that would be adopted by a Fleet flushed with victory and belonging to a country which was being strangled by the sea blockade.

Historians now agree that not only was Jutland a strategic success for Britain, but it meant the end of the German surface fleet as a factor in the war.

For his services at Jutland, Jellicoe was given the thanks of Parliament and a grant of £50,000. He was named as First Sea Lord (operational head of the navy) at the end of 1916, replacing Sir Henry Jackson, but almost from the start of this command, he desired to be removed from it. On 24 December 1917, Prime Minister David Lloyd George removed Jellicoe, allegedly over his refusal to guard Allied shipping with British escorts. Raised to the peerage as Viscount Jellicoe of Scapa in 1918, he was given the post of governor-general of New Zealand following the end of the war, serving from 1920 to 1924. In his last years, Jellicoe wrote two volumes of memoirs: *The Grand Fleet, 1914–16: Its Creation, Development and Work* (1919) and *The Crisis of the Naval War* (1920). He died in London on 20 November 1935 and was laid to rest with full military honors near Lord Nelson in the crypt of St. Paul's Cathedral in London.

References: Napier, Robert M., *Sir John French and Sir John Jellicoe: Their Lives and Careers* (London: The Patriotic Publishing Company, 1914); Jellicoe, Sir John, *The Grand Fleet, 1914–16: Its Creation, Development and Work* (New York: G. H. Doran, 1919); Terry, C. Sanford, *The Battle of Jutland Bank, May 31–June 1, 1916: The Dispatches of Admiral Sir John Jellicoe and Vice-Admiral Sir David Beatty* (London: Oxford University Press, 1916); Bruce, George, "Jutland," in *Collins Dictionary of Wars* (Glasgow, Scotland: HarperCollins Publishers, 1995), 12–21; "Jellicoe," in *Command: From Alexander the Great to Zhukov—The Greatest Commanders of World History,* edited by James Lucas (London: Bloomsbury Publishing, 1988), 155–156.

Joffre, Joseph-Jacques-Césaire (1852–1931)
French general

Joseph Joffre was born on 12 January 1852 in the village of Rivesaltes, in the province of Pyrénées-Orientales, near the Pyrenees mountains. His family had been Spanish with the name Goffre, but this was changed after his great-grandfather had fled to France. Joffre received his education at the École Polytechnique in Paris, but his studies were interrupted by the outbreak of the Franco-Prussian War in 1870. He served in the French army during the war and was a member of the brigade that defended Paris against German forces. With the end of the war in 1871, he graduated from the Polytechnique and became an engineer in the French army. In 1876, he was promoted to the rank of captain.

Joffre married, but the early death of his wife left him so disconsolate that he asked to be stationed overseas, and he was sent to Indochina, then a colony of France. He served with French forces in the occupation of the island of Formosa (now Taiwan) in 1885, and for three years afterward, he served as engineer in the city of Hanoi, now the capital of Vietnam. He returned to France in 1888 and worked on a series of engineering projects until he was sent to Senegal in Africa in 1892 to build a railway there. However, he was ordered to command a brigade of French forces marching on the city of Timbuktu. After his return to France, he received a series of promotions, rising to become general of brigade in 1900 and general of division in 1905.

In 1910, Joffre was named to the Conseil Supérior de la Guerre, the council of leading generals formed after the disastrous Franco-Prussian War. A year later, the minister of war, Adolphe Messimy, decided to name one general to command the council and serve as chief of staff to the French president. General Joseph Simon Galliéni, recommended his good friend Joffre, who was named to the new position. As chief of staff, he drew up a plan to halt another German invasion of France, a continuing grave threat to France. Plan 17, as it was called, was presented to the Conseil Supérior on 18 April 1913, and thought it covered a possible German invasion through eastern France, Joffre did not anticipate that Germany might attack through Belgium, to the north. This left a gap in France's defenses that would prove to be lethal to the country just a year after the plan was presented.

On 3 August 1914, Germany declared war on France, plunging Europe into a conflict that would last for four years and leave millions dead. With the outbreak of war, Joffre became commander in chief of French forces on 5 August 1914. The authors of *The Wordsworth Dictionary of Military Biography* write:

> Joffre's position in the supreme seat of military power on the outbreak of the First World War was . . . to some extent the result of precautionary administration rather than that of merit. Certainly he had gained little personal distinction on the field of battle, however inapplicable

such experience might have proved later. Like his contemporary and equally inexperienced subordinate, General [Ferdinand] FOCH, Joffre was a believer in in the *offensive à l'outrance*—although, divorced from actual field command, he was not personally responsible for its tactical application. Utterly unprepared for—indeed, utterly unable to conceive the implications of—such an offensives as that outlined in the [German] Schlieffen Plan, Joffre was responsible for launching the French strategic [offensive], a calamitous front attack by waves of infantry over a ground which should have been discarded as suicidal seventy years previously with the invention of the machine gun.

Joseph Joffre (right) talking with André Maginot on Armistice Day, Paris, 1918

While Joffre's offensive did work at first—by September the French had thrown the Germans back to the Aisne River in anticipation of the Battle of the Marne—it led to the disastrous trench warfare that caused the war to grind to a stalemate and bring hundreds of thousands of casualties on both sides.

Criticism of Joffre grew more and more intense, but he was protected by Alexandre Millerand, the French minister of war. On 30 October 1915, Millerand was replaced by General Joseph-Simon Galliéni, who had come to realize that Joffre needed to be replaced as commander. Nevertheless, on 3 December 1915 Joffre was given the command of all the French armies fighting in Europe. In this capacity, he tried to break the stalemate in the trenches on the western front. On 25 February 1916, he named General Henri-Philippe PÉTAIN as chief of the French forces at the Verdun front in an attempt to break the German hold on that area in northeastern France. However, the Verdun front could not be broken, and on 7 March 1916, Minister Galliéni advised the Conseil Supérior that there needed to be a reform of the high command. His advice was dismissed, and Joffre remained in control. Angered, Galliéni resigned on 17 March and was replaced by General Rocques, a close friend of Joffre. Anger over Joffre's mismanagement of the entire Allied campaign continued, and when French general Robert NIVELLE retook the fort of Douaumont, he was seen as a probable successor to Joffre. Finally, on 13 December 1916, after massive French losses at Verdun, continuing failure to break the war's stalemate, and a growing feeling that Joffre was out of his element, Joffre was named as "technical adviser" to the government. Though retaining his title as commander in chief of French forces, he was shunted aside as the operational commander, a role now assigned to General Nivelle.

Joffre's "promotion" was the end of his career, and he was reduced to a ceremonial role. Thirteen days after being removed from command, he was named marshal of France. In 1917, he made a tour of North America, and in 1918 he was named as president of the Conseil Supérior de la Guerre, retiring from the military soon after. He died in Paris on 3 January 1931, and his memoirs were published posthumously in two volumes in 1932.

References: Kahn, Alexander, *Life of General Joffre, Cooper's Son Who Became Commander-in-Chief* (London: W. Heinemann, 1915); Recouly, Raymond, *Joffre* (New

York: D. Appleton & Company, 1931); Recouly, Raymond, *General Joffre and His Battles* (New York: Charles Scribner's Sons, 1917); Windrow, Martin, and Francis K. Mason, "Joffre, Joseph Jacques Césaire," in *The Wordsworth Dictionary of Military Biography* (Hertfordshire, U.K.: Wordsworth Editions Ltd., 1997), 143–144.

John III Sobieski (John Sobieski, Jan Sobieski)
(1624–1696) *Polish general, king of Poland*

John Sobieski was born and brought up in Cracow (modern Krakow) in southern Poland. He was the eldest son of James Sobieski, castellan (captain of the garrison) of Cracow, and Theofila Danillowiczowna, granddaughter of the great Hetman Zolkiewski. After completing his education, Sobieski spent two years touring Europe with his brother Mark and learned French, German, and Italian, which proved extremely advantageous in his later career.

Poland had once been the major power in eastern Europe, but it was now under threat from the Prussians and Swedes on its western borders and from the Austrians, Turks, and Tartars of the Ukraine to the south. After returning from his European tour, Sobieski joined the military and fought against the Ukranian Cossack leader Chmielnicki in the uprising when the Cossacks attacked Poland from the south. He was also at the battles of Beresteczko (1651) and Batoka (1652). Two years later, however, when the Swedes invaded Poland, he joined them and helped them to win back the Prussian provinces in 1655. (These were the coastal territories in northwest Poland that Prussia and Poland had both claimed.) The following year, he changed sides again and fought with the Polish commander in chief Czarniecki to expel the Swedes from the territories they had won in central Poland.

In 1665, in recognition of Sobieski's services against the Tartars and Cossacks, King John Casimir of Poland promoted him to Great Marshal of the Crown. In 1667, Sobieski won another victory over the Cossacks and Tartars at Podhajce. This confirmed his status as Poland's best general, and in 1668 he was appointed Grand Hetman of the Crown and commander in chief of the Polish-Lithuanian army. (Lithuania was then a province of Poland.)

In the election of candidates for the kingship of Poland in 1669, Sobieski accepted large bribes from the French king Louis XIV to support Louis's candidate. When Michael Wisniowiecki was elected, Sobieski and others at once began to plot to bring about his downfall. The plot was discovered, but with the help of the elector of Brandenburg (Prussia), the conspirators escaped punishment. In 1672, at a time of great peril for Poland when the Turks were advancing into southern Poland, the conspirators renewed their attempt to bring down the king. With little support or military forces, King Michael had to sign the humiliating peace of Buczacz (17 October 1672), which ceded the Ukraine as well as Podolia, Poland's southern province, to the Turks.

Sobieski and his army promptly went to war with the Turks, and in a remarkable campaign, he won four victories in 10 days (Krasnobrod, Niemirow, Komarno and Kalusz). The peace of Buczacz was repudiated, and Sobieski's forces won a decisive victory at Khotin in the western Ukraine on 10 November 1673. King Michael died on the same day, and when Sobieski received the news, he immediately left his army in the Ukraine and traveled to Cracow to secure the throne for himself. Although his claim to election was disputed by some, his retinue of 6,000 veterans turned the scale, and he was elected king of Poland on 21 May 1674.

As King John III, Sobieski at once set about strengthening his southern border against the Turkish threat by an offensive in 1674–75 and took the fortresses of Kamienic Podolski, Bar, and Reszkow. In 1675, a Tartar attack in the same region was defeated and a peace treaty was made with them. Although he was still threatened with warfare by the Prussians in the north and the Austrians to the west, Sobieski set about a rapid program of reorganizing and training his army.

While fully conscious of the threat to Poland from his European neighbors, Sobieski realized the greatest danger to Europe was the apparently inexorable advance into Europe of the Ottoman Turks. The rise of Islam had seen the whole of North Africa lost to Arab armies and the conquest of Spain and southern France, until the great victory by CHARLES MARTEL in A.D. 732 pushed Islamic forces back to the Pyrenees. In eastern Europe, the last traces of the Eastern Roman Empire had vanished with the fall of Constantinople in 1453. Over the next 200 years, the Ottoman Turks had moved ever westward, occupying Greece, Bulgaria, Bosnia, Serbia, Rumania, much of the Ukraine, and Hungary. All of southeast Europe was theirs, and they laid siege to Vienna in 1683.

Even though Poland had nothing to gain—and much to lose—Sobieski took the long-term view and realized the Ottoman threat to Europe far outweighed short-term national differences. He therefore allied himself to his erstwhile enemies, Austria and the Holy Roman Emperor Leopold I, and the three armies advanced on Vienna to raise the siege there. Under Sobieski's overall command, some 81,000 men took up their positions for an attack on the Ottomans planned for 13 September 1683. On the 11th, however, Sobieski noticed weaknesses in the Turkish deployment and ordered the attack to begin early on the morning of 12 September. At 4:00 A.M., the allies advanced with the Austrians on the left, the imperial troops in the center, and the Poles on the right. The Turks fell back, then rallied and attacked the imperial forces in the center of the allied line. The Poles pushed hard on the right wing and, early in the afternoon, took the high ground from the Turks. An hour later, Sobieski showed the leadership and judgment that had won him so many victories. He brought 20,000 cavalry, mainly Polish, to the high ground his infantry had won and led them in a charge straight into the middle of the Turkish force. An hour later, the battle was over and Sobieski had become the hero of Europe.

Sobieski's famous victory had been won at great cost to the Polish treasury and resulted in simmering discontent among the Polish nobles, which made his last years unhappy and unsuccessful. He died on 17 June 1696 and was buried in Wawel Castle, Krakow, Poland.

Judged by some historians to be an unscrupulous ambitious adventurer, the same critics agree that Sobieski's military abilities were extraordinary. Poland soon lost much of the territories it had won in battle, and a century later it had ceased to exist as a nation. But Sobieski's victory at Vienna was a turning point in European history. Within 20 years, Hungary was freed from Ottoman domination, followed by south Russia soon afterward. From 1683 onwards, the Ottomans were slowly forced back out of Europe. It would take 200 years, but it was John Sobieski and the cavalry charge he led at Vienna that began the process. If it had not been for him, the history of Europe would have been very different.

References: Sobieski, John, *The Life of King John Sobieski, John the Third of Poland* (Boston: R. G. Badger, 1915); Morton, J. B., *Sobieski, King of Poland* (London: Eyre and Spottiswoode, 1932); Wójcik, Zbigniew, *Jan III Sobieski* (Warsaw: Zamek Królewski Wójcik, 1991); Bellamy,

Christopher, "John III (Jan Sobieski), King of Poland," in *The Oxford Companion to Military History,* edited by Richard Holmes (New York: Oxford University Press, 2001), 467; Windrow, Martin, and Francis K. Mason, "John III, Sobieski," in *The Wordsworth Dictionary of Military Biography* (Hertfordshire, U.K.: Wordsworth Editions Ltd., 1997), 144–146.

John of Austria (Don John of Austria, Don Juan of Austria, Gerónimo) (1547–1578) *German-Spanish general*

Don John of Austria was born in Regensburg, Bavaria, Germany, on 24 February 1545, the illegitimate son of Holy Roman Emperor Charles V and Barbara Blomberg, the daughter of a Regensburg merchant. As a baby, he was given the name Gerónimo (Spanish for "sacred") and put in the care of foster parents in a village near Madrid. At the age of nine, he was transferred to the household of Magdalena da Ulloa, the wife of Don Luis de Quijada, and brought up in their castle near Valladolid, still in ignorance of his parentage.

Charles V died in 1558, and a codicil in his will recognized John as his son and entrusted him to the care of Charles's successor, his legitimate son Philip II of Spain. Philip acknowledged John, brought him to court with the title Don Juan (John) of Austria, and had him educated with the Infante Don Carlos and Alessandro Farnese, prince of Parma. Philip intended him to become a priest, but John made it clear he wanted to become a soldier, a wish to which Philip acceded.

In 1568, at age 23, Don John was given command of a squadron of galleys to fight the Algerian corsairs, pirates who terrorized the western Mediterranean. The following year, he fought against the rebellious Moriscos in Granada, and in 1571 he fought the historic battle for which he is still remembered.

Ever since they had taken Constantinople in 1453, the Ottoman Turks had dominated eastern Europe and had conquered Greece and the territories known today as Rumania and Bulgaria. They had been equally successful at sea, and their taking Cyprus in 1571 had forced the European powers to put aside their differences in the face of this common threat to the eastern Mediterranean. Pope Pius V called for an alliance to combat the Ottomans; Spain and Venice, the major sea powers in the eastern Mediterranean, and others combined their fleets in the common cause.

On 7 October 1571, the combined Christian fleet—with ships from Genoa, Savoy, and the Knights of Malta, as well as Spain and Venice—met the Ottoman Turkish fleet off Lepanto in the Gulf of Corinth in Greece. Two hundred oared galleys faced 220 Turkish galleys, and while the apparent difference in numbers was small, the armor of the 28,000 soldiers on board the Christian fleet and the guns carried by some of their smaller vessels played an important part.

In an encounter that depended on close ship-to-ship battles and men fighting at close range with muskets and bows and arrows, the casualties were appalling. Nevertheless, the tactics set down by Don John to maintain the closest possible formation of his galleons and his measures to ensure his fleet could not be outflanked by the more maneuverable Turkish galleys earned him an overwhelming victory. The Turks lost all but 50 of their ships as well as 35,000 men, while some 15,000 Christian galley slaves were released. The last major sea battle fought between oar-powered galleys, Lepanto saw Turkish domination of the eastern Mediterranean destroyed forever.

Due to dissent among the allies, the victory was not followed up as it should have been, but it roused Don John's military ambitions further. He knew that, being illegitimate, he would never achieve a place among the ruling families of Europe, and he began to entertain ideas of winning a kingdom for himself. He planned to take over the area of Greece south of Lepanto known as the Morea, then occupied by the Ottomans, and from there move north up the Adriatic and establish himself in today's Bosnia. This plan was nullified by the Venetians, who withdrew from the Christian alliance and made a treaty with the Ottoman sultan. Don John then led an expedition in 1573 to take Tunis, a city on the north African coast that he hoped to hold as ruler, but it was soon recaptured. He sought assistance from his half brother, Philip II of Spain, but the latter, while happy to utilize John's military leadership, refused to support his attempts to win a kingdom for himself.

In 1576, Philip appointed John governor-general of the Spanish Netherlands (also called the Provinces). These territories, today's Belgium and the Netherlands, had long rebelled against Habsburg rule, and although the religious divisions among them were great, they were at one in their hatred of Spain. William of Orange ("William the Silent," 1533–84) had become their recognized leader, and when Don John took up his appointment,

he found the Provinces united in opposition. He negotiated without success for months, trying to satisfy the Provinces' demands for a measure of self-rule, including employment of Netherlanders in government service, but was eventually forced to sign a treaty meeting many of their demands on 12 February 1577. On 1 May that same year, he made his official entry into Brussels but soon found that he was governor-general only in name and that William of Orange exercised real authority. In July, Don John moved south to Namur, in the Catholic section of the Provinces, where he hoped to gain more support. The prompt response of William of Orange was to enter Brussels himself and exercise his authority openly there.

The situation came to a head with the arrival of large numbers of troops from Spain, under the command of Alexander Farnese. With these reinforcements, Don John attacked the Provinces' army on 31 January 1578 at Gembloux, 20 miles south of Brussels. The Provincial army under Antony de Goignies fought bravely, but the skill of Alexander Farnese led to a decisive victory for the Spanish forces. Shortage of money and supplies meant that Don John was unable to follow up his victory, and he spent the summer appealing in vain to Philip II in Spain. His health gave way under an attack of fever, and he died on 1 October 1578 at the age of 33.

Like CHARLES MARTEL and JOHN III SOBIESKI, John of Austria is remembered today for a single battle—but a battle that was a decisive victory against an enemy threatening the whole of Europe. Lepanto had shown the mighty Ottoman empire could be defeated, and Don John earned his place in military history.

References: Yeo, Margaret, *Don John of Austria* (New York: Sheed & Ward, Inc., 1934); Petrie, Sir Charles, *Don John of Austria* (London: Eyre & Spottiswoode, 1967); "Don John of Austria," in *Command: From Alexander the Great to Zhukov—The Greatest Commanders of World History,* edited by James Lucas (London: Bloomsbury Publishing, 1988), 42–43; Bruce, George, "Lepanto," in *Collins Dictionary of Wars* (Glasgow, Scotland: Harper-Collins Publishers, 1995), 140; Coloma, Luis, *The Story of Don John of Austria, Told by Padre Luis Colomba and Translated by Lady Moreton* (London: John Lane, 1912); Slocombe, George, *Don Juan of Austria, the Victor of Lepanto (1547–1578)* (London: I. Nicholson and Watson, Limited, 1935).

Jones, John Paul (Paul Jones) (1747–1792)
Scottish-American naval officer

John Paul Jones was born the son of a gardener at Arbigland, near Kirkbean in Kirkcudbrightshire on the Solway Firth, Scotland, on 6 July 1747. He was christened Paul Jones, although during his life he took the names of John Paul, John Jones, Captain Paul, Captain John Paul Jones, and even Kontradmiral Pavel Ivanonich Jones—all names documented by historian Samuel Eliot Morison in his biography of Jones. Apprenticed as a merchant seaman to one John Younger, Jones went to America in 1759 to visit his brother William, a tailor who had moved to the colony of Virginia. When Younger released him from his apprenticeship in 1766, Jones's love of the sea led him to enter the British navy with the rank of midshipman. However, he soon resigned, and records show that he then commanded a slave ship in the waters off Jamaica. After giving up this trade, he returned to Scotland, but during the journey home, the ship's captain died, and Jones, an experienced seaman, took command for the remainder of the voyage. At sea, he was forced to flog the ship's carpenter for some crime, and the man died from his injuries. When he arrived in Scotland, Jones was arrested for murder, but he was allowed to return to Jamaica to obtain proof of his innocence. In Tobago, his crew mutinied, and in a pitched battle he killed the ringleader. With two murder charges now hanging on him, Jones decided not to return to his homeland and, changing his name to John Paul Jones, fled to the English colonies. Historians believe that Jones had met Joseph Hewes, a revolutionary from the colony of North Carolina, who convinced him that freedom from English law could be had by helping the American colonies fight for their independence from England.

Jones's knowledge of the Bahamas proved useful to the revolutionaries when he was sent there in March 1776 to help capture the port of New Providence from British forces. He was made commander of the ship *Alfred,* the lead ship of the fleet that sailed into the Bahamas under the command of Commodore Esek Hopkins. The city was taken with little difficulty, leaving a great supply of ordnance to fall into the colonists' hands. Hopkins then gave command of the sloop *Providence* to Jones, and on 8 August 1776 he was confirmed to the rank of captain by a marine committee in Philadelphia. His main mission was to cruise from Bermuda north to Nova Scotia, Newfoundland, Canada; along the way, he captured eight British ships and sank eight more. Upon returning from this mission in October 1776, he was transferred to the command of the *Alfred* and sent back to the coast off Nova Scotia; again, he attacked and sank a number of British ships.

On 14 June 1777, Jones was named by the Continental Congress to the command of the newly built privateer *Ranger.* He immediately sailed for France on word of the surrender of British general John BURGOYNE at Saratoga, hoping to obtain a large frigate being built in Amsterdam for the colonists. However, Burgoyne had not surrendered, and the Netherlands hastily transferred the frigate to France, which refused to let Jones have her. He received permission from the American legation in Paris to sail up the Irish Sea and attack British shipping, and in the ensuing mission he captured several ships, sank several more, and shelled the town of Whitehaven. On 23 April 1778, he landed on St. Mary's Island in Scotland's Solway Firth, in an attempt to seize Lord Thomas Douglas, earl of Selkirk, and use him as a hostage. Selkirk was away from home, so sailors from Jones's ship snatched a silver plate from his residence, an item that was later returned to Selkirk's wife with Jones's regrets. The following day, off the coast of what is now Northern Ireland, he was attacked by the British ship *Drake,* and in the subsequent clash the Americans inflicted 42 casualties on the British and sailed off in victory. Known as the Battle of Carrickfergus, this was the first defeat of a British warship by an American naval craft. Jones returned to France as a hero, but he was asked to turn over control of his ship to a subordinate and await new orders, which did not come for several months.

In August 1779, Jones sailed from France as the commander of the *Bonhomme Richard,* with a number of smaller ships as part of his battle group, including the *Alliance,* the *Pallas,* and the *Vengeance.* (Jones later wrote that he named his ship in honor of Benjamin Franklin, the writer of *Poor Richard's Almanack,* one of the leading news journals in the colonies.) Several prizes were taken, but an attack on the Scottish port of Leith was abandoned because of bad weather. It was on 23 September 1779 that Jones entered naval and military history. Off Flamborough, England, his fleet intercepted a British flotilla led by the ship *Serapis.* Historian John Shy writes:

> The heavier guns smashed the *Richard* during the first half hour, but Jones seized a moment when *Serapis* lost way in a failing breeze to close in. By 9:00 p.m., both ships were ablaze. The American ship *Alliance,* under the [command of the] eccentric French Captain Landais, appeared and fired several broadsides, doing more damage to *Richard* than to *Serapis*—deliberately so, in the opinion of Jones' chief biographer. But when hand grenades thrown from *Richard* ignited power cartridges on the British gundeck, killing or wounding about fifty seamen, the British captain surrendered. About half of each crew had been killed or wounded. Transferring his flag to the crippled *Serapis* from the sinking *Richard,* Jones and his squadron limped to The Texel, Amsterdam's port, as his orders dictated. His presence there compromised Dutch neutrality, but in Amsterdam, he was a popular hero, as he was in Paris, where he returned in April 1780.

Jones returned to America on the French ship *Ariel,* where he was greeted as a national hero. On 14 April 1780, he was given the official thanks of Congress and assigned to the ship *America.* But the ship was soon sold to France to replace a lost French ship, and Jones was sent to that country to serve as a prize agent, or broker, to sell those ships captured for profit. He returned to the United States in 1787, was awarded a gold medal by Congress for his service to his adopted country, and again sent overseas, this time to Denmark to demand payment for two ships the Danish had given to England that belonged to America. However, while in Copenhagen in 1788, he accepted a commission from Russian czarina Catherine the Great to serve in the Russian navy with the rank of rear admiral. He was immediately dispatched to the Black Sea, where Russia was at war against Turkey, but he soon became disenchanted with his command as his orders were circumvented and victories due him were credited to others.

In March 1789, while in St. Petersburg, Jones was falsely accused of assaulting a young girl, although he was never formally charged. Catherine saw him as a worn-out warrior and offered him a dismissal from the Russian service. He returned to Paris, where his health quickly declined, and he died on 18 July 1792. He was buried in an unmarked grave in a Protestant cemetery which, over the years, became a garbage dump, covered with refuse and the bodies of dead horses.

At the beginning of the 20th century, the American ambassador to France, Horace Porter, angered that Jones, an American hero, lay in an unknown grave without the credit due him, set out to find the missing naval officer. After a lengthy search, Jones's remains were located, and an American warship was dispatched to Paris to bring him back to his adopted nation. With full honors, he was laid to rest in the naval chapel at Annapolis, Maryland, now the home of the U.S. Naval Academy. Historian Victor Hawkins writes of Jones's impact on history: "Jones was a brave, resolute, and brilliant commander; an adventurer-turned-patriot, he gave valuable service to the [American] nation; his tomb at Annapolis reads: 'He gave our navy its earliest traditions of heroism and victory.'"

References: Bowen, Marjorie, *The Life of Rear-Admiral John Paul Jones, Chevalier of the Military Order of Merit and of the Russian Order of the Empress Anne, 1747–1792* (London: H. Jenkins, 1940); Lorenz, Lincoln, *John Paul Jones: Fighter for Freedom and Glory* (Annapolis, Md.: United States Naval Institute, 1943); Morison, Samuel Eliot, *John Paul Jones: A Sailor's Biography* (Boston: Little, Brown, 1959); Thomas, Evan, *John Paul Jones* (New York: Simon & Schuster, 2003); Shy, John, "Jones, John Paul," in *American National Biography,* 24 vols., edited by John A. Garraty and Mark C. Carnes (New York: Oxford University Press, 1999), 12:220; Hawkins, Victor B., "Jones, John Paul," in *The Encyclopedia of Military Biography,* edited by Trevor N. Dupuy, Curt Johnson, and David L. Bongard (London: I. B. Taurus & Co., Ltd., 1992), 381–382.

Junot, Jean-Andoche Alexandre, duc d'Abrantes (1771–1813) *French general*

Jean-Andoche Junot was born at Bussy-le-Grand, on the Côte d'Or, France, on 23 October 1771. In 1790, before he turned 20, he volunteered for service in the French army, rising to the rank of sergeant, and he fought at Toulon in 1793. There, because of his service, he was noticed by NAPOLEON BONAPARTE, who named Junot as his personal secretary. When Napoleon went to fight in Italy, Junot served as his aide-de-camp and, during the French campaign in Egypt, was named as general of brigade. Back in France, Junot fought a duel on Napoleon's behalf and was named as governor of Paris in 1806.

In 1807, Napoleon put Junot in charge of the French invasion of Portugal. That November, he started from Salamanca and moved his forces rapidly through the mountains of Beira. Although he missed a chance to capture the Portuguese royal family at Lisbon, he easily took all of Portugal, for which he received the title duc d'Abrantes and was named as governor of Portugal. Though an efficient soldier, however, Junot was not an administrator, and his government suffered from this lack of experience. In August 1808, Sir Arthur Wellesley, duke of WELLINGTON, attacked his forces at Vimiera in the Peninsular War and, on 30 August, forced him to sign the Convention of Cintra and abandon Portugal to the British and Portuguese forces. Because of this defeat, Napoleon, despite naming Junot a marshal of France, felt betrayed and never fully trusted him again.

Junot subsequently fought with Napoleon's forces at Wagram (5–6 July 1809) and with Marshal André MASSÉNA in the Spanish campaign (1810–11), where he was seriously wounded. He went with Napoleon into Russia but was not given any major command, and his role in that campaign was minor and obscure. Once he returned to France, Napoleon put him in charge of the province of Illyria (now in present-day Balkans), but by this time he was suffering from serious dementia. On 29 July 1813, at his father's home in Montbard, France, he threw himself out a window to his death.

Historian Vincent Hawkins writes of Junot: "[He] was one of Napoleon's most able subordinates, a brave and sometimes headstrong soldier; his plans were hampered by his lack of military education; he was a capable administrator and was completely devoted to Napoleon."

References: Hawkins, Vincent B., "Junot, Jean Andoche, Duke of Abrantes," in *The Encyclopedia of Military Biography,* edited by Trevor N. Dupuy, Curt Johnson, and David L. Bongard (London: I. B. Taurus & Co., Ltd., 1992), 386; "Junot, Gen Andoche, Duc d'Abrantes," in *The Oxford Companion to Military History,* edited by Richard Holmes (New York: Oxford University Press, 2001), 469; *Eight Separate Decrees, 9 January–27 February 1808, issued by General Junot, relating to the administration of the Government of Portugal* (Paris, France: Departments of State and Other Official Bodies, 1809).

K

Kamimura, Hikonojo, Baron Kamimura (1849–1916) *Japanese admiral*

Born in Satsuma Prefecture (later Kagoshima Prefecture), Japan, Hikonojo Kamimura joined the navy in 1871 and, after eight years in the naval academy, was commissioned an ensign in 1879, rising to the rank of commander in the last years of the 19th century. He commanded a series of ships in the First Sino-Japanese War against China (1893–94) and fought at the Battle of the Yalu River (17 September 1894) with distinction. In 1898, he was named as captain of the cruiser *Akitsushima,* and he served in the Second Sino-Japanese War (1898–99). In 1899, he was advanced to the rank of rear admiral, and four years later, he was named as the head of the Educational Bureau of the Japanese Navy.

In the Russo-Japanese War against Russia (1904–05), Kamimura commanded the second Japanese squadron, serving directly under Admiral Heihachiro TOGO. His main task was to blockade and contain the ships of the Russian fleet at Vladivostok so they could not leave to attack the main Japanese forces entering the area; however, the Russian ships slipped out under his watch and easily defeated the Japanese in a series of battles in the Sea of Japan in April and June 1904. This brought about calls for Kamimura's resignation from inside Japan. In his official report to the Japanese government on the initial Japanese attack on Vladivostok on 6 March 1904, Kamimura wrote a cold narrative:

> As pre-arranged, the squadron reached the eastern entrance of Vladivostok on the morning of March 6, after passing through the frozen sea. The enemy's ships were not seen in the outside harbor, and the Japanese vessels approached the batteries on the north-east coast from a point beyond the range of the batteries of the Balzan Promontory and the Bosphorous Strait.
>
> After bombarding the inner harbor for forty minutes from ten minutes to two, the Japanese squadron retired. It is believed that the bombardment effected considerable damage. Soldiers were seen on land, but the Russian batteries did not reply to the Japanese fire.
>
> Black smoke was observed in the eastern entrance about five in the afternoon, and was thought to be from the enemy's ships, but the smoke gradually disappeared. On the morning of the 7th inst. the Japanese squadron reconnoitred America Bay and Strelok Bay, but nothing unusual was seen. The warships again approached the eastern entrance of Vladivostok at noon, but the enemy's ships were not visible, and the batteries did not fire.

The squadron then turned towards Possiet Bay, but seeing nothing of the enemy, retired.

Despite the Japanese losses, Kamimura followed the Russian ships to Ulsan, off the coast of Vladivostok, and during the battle there (14 August 1904), he sank the Russian ship *Rurik* and severely damaged the *Rossiya,* flagship of the Russian admiral Bezobrasov. At Tsushima, the strategic battle of the entire conflict, Kamimura, overseeing a fleet of eight ships from aboard his flagship, the *Idzumo,* backed up Togo, who completed wiped out the Russians; the loss for them was 34 of 37 ships sunk, 4,830 dead, 5,917 captured, and an additional 1,862 held by neutral countries in detention. Japanese losses were light: three torpedo boats sunk, one armored cruiser and two light cruisers damaged, 110 men killed in action, and 590 wounded. Although Togo was the hero of the battle and of the war, Kamimura had made up for his defeat at Vladivostok.

Following the end of the war, Kamimura was made commander of the naval base at Yokosuka, serving from 1905 to 1909, and he was commander in chief of the first fleet (1909–11). He was styled as Baron Kamimura in 1907 and raised to the rank of admiral in 1910. In 1911, he was named councillor of the navy. He died on 8 August 1916 at the age of 66, and in the years since he has been all but forgotten by scholars for his role in the Russo-Japanese War.

References: "Kamimura, Hikonojo," in *Kodansha Encyclopedia of Japan,* 10 vols. (Tokyo, Japan: Kodansha, 1983), 4:127; Chant, Christopher, Richard Holmes, and William Koenig, "Tsushima: 1905," *Two Centuries of Warfare: 23 Decisive Battles that Changed the Course of History* (London: Octopus Books, 1978), 208; Pleshakov, Konstantin, *The Tsar's Last Armada: The Epic Journey to the Battle of Tsushima* (New York: Basic Books, 2002).

Karl XII *See* CHARLES XII.

Khaled ibn al-Walid (Khalid ibn al-Walid, Chaledos) (584–642) *Muslim military leader*
Khaled ibn al-Walid was born in 584 near what is now the holy city of Mecca, in Saudi Arabia, to a clan known as *banu-Quraysh,* or a tribe of the Prophet Muhammad. According to several sources, Khaled's father did not

agree with the burgeoning movement of Islam begun by Muhammad, and his son soon came to accept his father's beliefs. In 625, Muhammad and his Muslim followers fought a major battle with so-called "nonbelievers" at Badr and defeated them. Khaled, taking charge of a group of men from Mecca—also known as "Meccans"—marched to Badr and confronted the Muslims. In a pitched battle, Khaled's army lost, but his military skill and bravery made him a force to be reckoned with.

About 627, after the Truce of Hudaibya, Khaled joined Muhammed and went on to defeat the rival forces holding onto Mecca in 629, again, demonstrating his military genius. Following Muhammed's death in 632, a series of revolts occurred against his successor, the caliph (from "caliphet," literally "successor of the prophet of God") Abu Bakr. In order to reestablish control over the rebels, Abu Bakr initiated a *riddah,* or war, with 11 armies. One of the leading commanders of these armies was Khaled, who displayed such ferocity and lack of compassion for his enemies, slaughtering them at will, that he shocked even Abu Bakr himself. Khaled put down the rebellion led by Mosailima at Akraba (633), the battle that ended the so-called "War of Apostasy."

In the final years of his life, Khaled led a *jihad* (holy war) against border raiders in Mesopotamia, now modern Iraq. In 633, he invaded the city of al-Hira and, in an attempt to head off an invasion of the region by the Byzantine emperor Heraclius, marched from Mesopotamia to the city of Palmyra in just 18 days. In spring 634, his army defeated the Byzantine forces at Marj Rahit, and with the Muslim warrior Amr ibn al-As, Khaled again defeated this army, at Ajnadayn in July 634. In January 635, he captured Fihl, near the Jordan River, and after a six-month siege, he forced the surrender of Damascus, now the capital of Syria, on 4 September 635. Heraclius saw Khaled as a major threat, and he formed an additional army of some 50,000 men to march on Damascus. Khaled retreated from that city to an area now near the Sea of Galilee. The Byzantines, under Theodorus (also known as Theodore), with an army totaling 110,000, marched on them and attacked the Muslims near the River Yarmuk, a tributary of the Jordan River, on 20 August 636. According to historian George Bruce, "The Muslim attack was thrice repulsed, but they returned to the charge and after a long and bloody engagement drove their opponents from the field with enormous loss. The Muslims lost 4,030 killed and went on to attack Jerusalem." The Byzantines left nearly 50,000 dead on the field of battle, and although Khaled was second in command, historians believe that it was he who directed the attack that had culminated in the horrific Byzantine slaughter at the Battle of Yarmuk. Khaled was given the governorship of the new province of Syria, but he died in 642 and was laid to rest in the city of Emesa (now Homs) in Syria. His tomb, still in existence, is a noted site for Muslims to visit.

Historian James Bloom notes: "[K]nown as 'Chaledos' in the Byzantine chronicles, Khalid was an outstanding general, widely regarded as the preeminent war leader of the early Muslim conquests." Nevertheless, Khaled remains largely unknown amongst historians and military scholars.

References: Bloom, James J., "Khalid Ibn al-Walid," in *Brassey's Encyclopedia of Military History and Biography*, edited by Franklin D. Margiotta (Washington, D.C.: Brassey's, 1994), 563–565; Shaban, Muhammad abd al-Hayy Muhammad, *Islamic History: A New Interpretation*, 2 vols. (Cambridge, U.K.: Cambridge University Press, 1971); Bruce, George, "Yarmuk," in *Collins Dictionary of Wars* (Glasgow, Scotland: HarperCollins Publishers, 1995), 272.

Kitchener, Horatio Herbert, first earl Kitchener of Khartoum and Broome (1850–1916) *British general*

Horatio Herbert Kitchener was born at Ballylongford (also spelled Bally Longford), near the town of Listowel, in County Kerry, Ireland, on 24 June 1850, the son of Lieutenant Colonel Horatio Herbert Kitchener. He entered the Royal Military Academy at Woolwich in 1868 (some sources report 1867) and was commissioned a second lieutenant in the Royal Engineers in 1871. While visiting his parents in France, he attached himself to the army of the Loire during the Franco-Prussian War (1870–71) and was injured in action.

In 1874, Kitchener was detached to the Palestine Exploration Fund for survey work in what is now Israel and in Cyprus. In 1883, he was promoted to the rank of captain and seconded to the Egyptian army, beginning a career Africa that made him a major military figure. After taking part in General Wolseley's relief of Khartoum (1885), he was named as governor-general of Eastern Sudan in 1886. Three years later, he commanded a force of cavalry to defeat the dervishes at Gamaizieh

(1888) and Toski (3 August 1889). In 1888, he was promoted to brevet colonel, and he received the award of Companion of the Order of the Bath (CB) in 1889 for his services at Toski.

In 1892, Kitchener succeeded Sir Francis Grenfell as the sirdar, or commander in chief, of the Egyptian army, which was controlled by the British. After reforming and reorganizing this force, he undertook a major military campaign against the Mahdi, the Arabic title ("He who is divinely guided") of Muhammad Ahmad, the Muslim religious leader who led the forces against the British in Sudan. Muhammad had declared himself the Mahdi in 1881, and his initial fight to expel British forces climaxed in the battle of Khartoum (1885) and the death of General Charles "Chinese" GORDON.

The Mahdi died soon after Khartoum was taken, and he was succeeded by Khalifa Addallah. In 1898, Kitchener set out for Khalifa's capital of Omdurman to avenge Gordon's death and secure Sudan for England. The two forces met at Omdurman on 2 September 1898, the British some 23,000 strong, against some 50,000 Mahdists (also called dervishes). Historian George Bruce writes:

The Dervishes attacked the British zareba [a campsite or village protected by an enclosure of thorn bushes or stakes], and were repulsed with heavy loss[es]. Kitchener then advanced to drive the enemy before him into Omdurman and capture the place. In the course of the operation, however, the Egyptian Brigade on the British right, under General [Sir Hector Archibald] Macdonald [1852–1903], became isolated and was attacked in front by the center of the Dervish army, while his flank and rear were threatened by the Dervish left, which had not previously been engaged. The position was crucial, but through the extreme steadiness of the Sudanese, who changed front under fire, the attack was repulsed. The 21st Lancers, among whom was Winston Churchill, made the last full-scale cavalry charge of modern warfare. The British and Egyptian losses were 500 killed and wounded; the Dervishes lost about 15,000.

Omdurman was the turning point for British forces in North Africa as the power of the Mahdists and their Islamic allies was destroyed. Kitchener was then faced with the Fashoda Incident, or Fashoda crisis. Before he left Sudan, he went up the Nile River to the French outpost at Fashoda, where the French had dispatched a small unit from their Equatorial Africa Colony in an attempt to block British control of the Nile. Kitchener, delayed by his victory at Omdurman, arrived at Fashoda on 18 September 1898. The French commander of the fort, Colonel Jean-Baptiste Marchand, at first refused the British entry, but when Kitchener demanded British troops be allowed in, Marchand relented. He also allowed French and British flags to fly over the fort, but war between the two powers looked inevitable. The crisis broke when Theophile Declasse, the French foreign minister, decided to withdraw French claims to Fashoda and allow the British to take over the redoubt. Marchand was ordered to withdraw on 4 November 1898, and warfare was avoided. For his service at Omdurman and at Fashoda, Kitchener was awarded the Knight Grand Cross of the Order of the Bath (GCB) and raised to the peerage as Baron Kitchener of Khartoum. He was 48 years old.

Fresh from his victory against the Mahdists, Kitchener was sent to southern Africa to take on the Boers, a group of Dutch settlers who had colonized the area called the Orange Free State (now part of South Africa). Resisting British expansion into the Orange Free State, the Boers had proved to be brilliant tacticians and guerrilla fighters. Kitchener, who arrived in the midst of the war there, was promoted to the rank of lieutenant general and appointed second in command and chief of staff to Lord ROBERTS, the commander of the British army in southern Africa. Kitchener established the blockhouse system, a strategy of constructing fortifications protecting British troops from surprise attacks by the Boers, and he directed the strategy leading to the battles of Paardeberg (18–27 February 1899), Bloemfontein (31 March 1900), and Pretoria (5 June 1900). Promoted to general in November 1900, he succeeded Roberts as commander, but he was harshly criticized for his methods of fighting the Boers, including destroying their farms and putting women and children into camps.

In June 1902, the war ended with the Peace of Vereeniging. Kitchener was rewarded again for his services to the British nation by being named Viscount Kitchener of Broome. He was then sent to India as commander in chief, where he pushed through important administrative reforms of military organization, command, and control; he also modernized training methods. His

reorganization efforts brought him into conflict with Lord Curzon (1859–1925), the viceroy of India. When Kitchener insisted on raising the dispute to British cabinet level, Prime Minister Arthur Balfour sided with him and dismissed Curzon as viceroy. Kitchener was able to complete the Indian army's reorganization but was not appointed in Curzon's place in order to maintain governmental authority over the military.

In 1909, when Kitchener left India, he was promoted to the rank of field marshal. He was named to succeed the duke of Connaught as commander in chief of British forces in the Mediterranean, but after returning to England in 1910, he refused this assignment, and his place was taken by Sir Ian HAMILTON, who later commanded Allied troops at Gallipoli during the First World War. Kitchener did accept the post of consul general of Egypt and Sudan, taking up his position in September 1911. He was serving in that post and had recently returned to England when the First World War broke out in August 1914. Prime Minister Herbert Asquith immediately named Kitchener to his cabinet as secretary of state for war. Realizing that the British were unprepared, Kitchener warned the government that the conflict would not end quickly, as many believed. He also foresaw that the Russians would achieve little against the Germans because Russia was even more unprepared for war. He quickly began the mobilization and training of 70 British divisions, called "Kitchener's Army." Just as he predicted, the European conflict that became known as World War I bogged down into trench warfare involving the British, French, and their allies against the Germans and Austrians. As tens of thousands and then hundreds of thousands of men were wounded or killed, Kitchener realized that conscription was needed, but because it was politically unpopular, he did not advance the idea. His public image, however, was utilized in the British government's recruitment campaign: The mustachioed Kitchener was seen pointing a finger at the viewer with the words "Your country needs you," inspiring the later American "Uncle Sam" posters that stated, "I want you for U.S. Army."

Kitchener not only organized the equipping and training of troops but also planned strategy and helped mobilize British industry to keep the British economy running. Because he was a loner rather than a "team player," Kitchener was resented by his fellow cabinet members, who saw him as a domineering, over-powerful figure. Despite this opposition, Kitchener continued to direct strategy, though other ministers gradually took over economic matters and armaments production. In 1915, William Louis King wrote a poem in honor of Kitchener entitled "When the War is Done."

In May 1916, Czar Nicholas II of Russia requested that Kitchener visit Russia to confer on military cooperation with the western Allies. Kitchener left England on the HMS *Royal Oak* and met Admiral John JELLICOE before he transferred to the HMS *Hampshire,* which was to take him and his staff to Russia via the Orkney Islands. On 5 June 1916, while sailing near the Orkneys, the *Hampshire* struck a German mine and sank in 10 minutes, taking Kitchener and 642 of the 655 men on board to their deaths. Britain was shocked by the loss of Kitchener, who had become the most important British military leader of the war. The lord mayor of London asked the nation to donate money for a national memorial fund, which still provides university scholarships for the children of servicemen.

Lord Kitchener was a great British military leader, ranking with Lord NELSON and Arthur Wellesley, duke of WELLINGTON. While his public life has been researched extensively, his private life remains a mystery, primarily because that was the way he wanted it. In 1958, the historian Philip Magnus published *Kitchener: Portrait of an Imperialist,* in which he alleged that Kitchener was a closet homosexual who did not allow enemy troops at Omdurman to be treated for their wounds. Recent historical examinations of Kitchener's and his contemporaries' papers reveal these accusations to be untrue. Nearly a century after his tragic death, Lord Kitchener remains a private man whose accomplishments are known more than the man ever will be.

References: Arthur, Sir George, *Life of Lord Kitchener,* 3 vols. (London: Macmillan and Co., 1920); Lanning, Michael Lee, "Horatio Herbert Kitchener," in *The Military 100: A Ranking of the Most Influential Military Leaders of All Time* (New York: Barnes and Noble Books, 1996), 306–309; Holt, Peter Malcolm, *The Mahdist State in the Sudan* (Oxford, U.K.: The Clarendon Press, 1958); Neillands, Robin, *The Dervish Wars: Gordon and Kitchener in the Sudan, 1880–1898* (London: John Murray, 1996); Burleigh, Bennet, *Sirdar and Khalifa; or, the Reconquest of Soudan [sic], 1898* (London: Chapman & Hall, 1898); Ziegler, Philip, *Omdurman* (London: Collins, 1974); Bruce, George, "Omdurman," in *Collins Dictionary of Wars* (Glasgow, Scotland: HarperCollins Publishers,

1995), 183; "Britain's War Ended; The Boers Finally Surrender. Gen. Kitchener Telegraphs, Peaces Terms Concluded," *The New York Herald* (Paris edition), 2 June 1902, 1; Reference to the William Louis King poem in the Papers of Horatio Herbert Kitchener, first earl Kitchener of Khartoum, Public Record Office series PRO 30/57/1, Public Record Office, Kew, England; Wallace, Edgar, *Kitchener: The Man and His Campaigns* (London: George Newnes, 1914); "Kitchener and Staff Perish at Sea; Lost on Cruiser, Perhaps Torpedoed; England Suspects Spies of the Deed," *The New York Times,* 7 June 1916, 1.

Kluge, Hans Günther von   (1882–1944)
German general

Hans Günther von Kluge was born into an aristocratic Prussian family in the village of Posen, Prussia (now Poznan, Poland), on 30 October 1882. Little is known about his early life, except that he entered the German army at an early age, saw action as an artillery officer during the First World War, and was seriously wounded at Verdun. Following the end of that conflict, he remained in the army, becoming a major general in 1933. Dismissed in 1938 because he disapproved of Hitler's war aims, he was recalled at the outbreak of the Second World War in September 1939, commanding the Fourth Army in the German invasion of Poland. In 1940, he commanded an equally successful invasion of France. Promoted to field marshal on 14 July 1940, in 1941 he led the attack on Russia, staying there until he was wounded in battle in October 1943. He returned to his command after recuperation and showed remarkable skill in meeting the massive Russian offensive.

Following the Allied landings on the coast of Normandy in France on 6 June 1944, Hitler replaced the commander of German forces in Western Europe, Field Marshal Gerd von Rundstedt, with Kluge on 3 July 1944. However, Kluge was unable to halt the advance of Allied forces through France, and he came to believe that Hitler needed to be removed from power and peace made with the Allies. Kluge never acted on his beliefs, but a number of men to whom he was close formulated a plan to assassinate Hitler, and they used his name, without his permission, to gain increased acceptance of the plot. The assassination attempt failed on 20 July 1944, and Hitler, who soon came to believe that Kluge had been a part of it, dismissed him as commander on 17 August 1944. Realizing he was about to be arrested and put to death for his alleged role in the conspiracy, Kluge committed suicide on 18 August 1944 near Metz, France. Within a year, Hitler would also take his own life, and Nazi Germany would fall to the Allies.

References: Hoffman, Peter, *The History of the German Resistance, 1939–1945,* translated by Richard Barry (Cambridge, Mass.: MIT Press), 276; Von Dieter, Ose, *Entscheidung im Westen 1944: der Oberbefehlshaber West und die Abwehr der alliierten Invasion* (Stuttgart, Germany: Deutsche Verlags-Anstalt, 1982).

Kublai Khan (Qubilai Khan, Khubilai Khan, Kubla Khan) (1215–1294) *Mongol warlord*

Kublai Khan (also known as Khubilai Khan, Kubla Khan, and several other spellings of his name) was born in 1215, the son of Toluia, a son of Mongol warlord GENGHIS KHAN, and his wife, Sorghaghtani Beki. Kublai was not destined to become a leader until his elder brother Mongke died on the field of battle in 1260; he was then elected a khan, or leader, of a khanate, a province ruled by a warlord. The empire founded by his grandfather Genghis (or Chinggis) Khan covered much of China, western Asia, and southern Russia. Although Genghis Khan was the founder of the khanate that ruled over these areas, it was his grandson Kublai who extended the empire to its greatest boundaries. Even before his rise to power, Kublai Khan was involved in military expeditions to enhance his family's control of the region. Starting in 1251, he became the military governor of China, and seven years later he ordered the Mongol attack on what is now the modern city of Baghdad, Iraq, ending the caliphate there. The following year (1260), he succeeded his brother, and in 1267, he moved the Mongol capital from Karakorum, Mongolia, to Daidu, renamed Khan-Balik (also spelled Cambuluc), now Beijing.

In 1268, Kublai resolved to attack the Song (Sung) Empire in southern China. After five years, the two great cities of Siang-yang and Fen-Cheng fell, and he became ruler of all China in 1276. He was now master of an empire that stretched from the Pacific to Turkestan and the Black Sea.

By 1274, Kublai had assembled a military expedition to invade the islands of Japan. His army—consisting of approximately 40,000 men, including some 8,000 Koreans—sailed on about 800 ships from what

is now South Korea and landed at the islands of Iki and Tsushima (later the scene of the famed battle in the 1904–05 Russo-Japanese War). Taking control of these lands, Kublai's army continued to advance. The Japanese, outmanned with only approximately 10,000 soldiers, fought in small divisions utilizing guerrilla tactics. But their strategy only served as a diversion and not as a defense. What saved them was a typhoon that struck the Mongol fleet, wrecking one third of the ships and forcing the Mongols and their allies to withdraw. This typhoon is known to the Japanese as a *kamikaze,* or "divine wind." Realizing that their defenses were poor and that the Mongols would invade again when they had regained their military strength, the Japanese set out on a major building program, constructing stone walls for defensive measures and building small boats to be used to attack the huge but unwieldy Mongol ships. The second attack came in June 1281, when the Mongol force, 140,000 strong in nearly 5,000 ships, split into two fleets and sailed in part from southern China and the southern Korean Peninsula. The southern Chinese fleet landed first, on the island of Kyushu, and quickly overwhelmed the Japanese defenses. Again, just as it seemed the Mongols would be successful in their assault, another typhoon struck their fleet, killing over 100,000 Mongol soldiers and once again forcing their withdrawal. Following this second defeat, Kublai Khan gave up on his dream of conquering Japan. Additional invasions against what are now Myanmar (Burma), Indonesia, and Vietnam all failed.

Although he was a military leader, Kublai Khan was also the ruler of his people, including those he conquered and controlled. He worked to bring government to China, promoting economic growth and vitality, helping to rebuild the Grand Canal and other internal improvements, introducing paper currency instead of coins, and tolerating all religious activity even though he made Buddhism the state religion. He also sent emissaries to Europe to encourage further trade and commerce.

Much of what is known today of Kublai Khan comes from the journals and writings of an Italian traveler, Marco Polo, who, with his father and uncle, sailed from Europe in 1260 and were caught in a civil war between Mongol warlords only to be rescued and invited to visit Kublai at his capital in Mongolia. During two expeditions to China and related areas, lasting from 1275 until 1292, the Polos served as official advisers to Kublai

Khan and his court, as well as travelers in lands then unknown to Europeans. Polo later wrote a major work of his travels, which was a sensation in Europe when published, and it became a major source of information on the life and work of Kublai Khan. His was also the first major description by a European of Khan's capital city of Khan-Balik in China. The author Samuel Taylor Coleridge's poem *Kubla Khan: or, a Vision in a Dream* published in 1816, named Kublai's summer capital at Shandu (or Shangdu) as "Xanadu."

Kublai Khan, whom the Mongols had called *Set-san Khan,* or "Wise Leader," died in 1294. Although the Mongol Dynasty in China collapsed soon after his death, nonetheless his legacy, both military and economic, transformed China into a nation-state instead of separate regions controlled by warlords. Perhaps the longest-lasting legacy of his time is the term *kamikaze,* the "divine wind" that Japanese felt saved them twice from Mongol invasions—and that became the name given to suicide bombers who plunged themselves into American ships during the Second World War.

References: Rossabi, Morris, *Khubilai Khan: His Life and Times* (Berkeley: University of California Press, 1988); "Khubilai Khan," in *The Oxford Companion to Military History,* edited by Richard Holmes (New York: Oxford University Press, 2001), 476–477; Nicolle, David, *The Mongol Warlords: Genghis Khan, Kublai Khan, Hülegü, Tamerlane* (Poole, U.K.: Firebird Books, 1990); Marshall, Robert, *Storm from the East: From Genghis Khan to Khubilai Khan* (Berkeley: University of California Press, 1993); Komroff, Manuel, *The Travels of Marco Polo* (New York: The Heritage Press, 1934).

Kuropatkin, Alexei Nikolaevich (1848–1925)
Russian general

Born into a noble family in the Kholmskii district of Russia, Alexei Kuropatkin was the son of a retired military official. Because of his father's status, Kuropatkin was able to enter the Cadet Corps of the Russian military, and in 1864 he was admitted to the Pavlovskoe (or Pavlovsk) Military Academy. He graduated two years later, and in 1874 he graduated from the Academy of the General Staff. From 1866 to 1871, and again from 1875 to 1877, Kuropatkin served in the Turkestan Military District, serving with the 1st Turkestan Rifle Battalion. He saw action in the Russo-Turkish War of

1877–78, during which he served as the chief of staff of the 16th Infantry Division. In 1885, he wrote *Lovcha and Plevna,* an account of the war. He later served in the Asiatic Section of the Russian General Staff, and then as commander of the Turkestan Rifle Brigade during the Russian war in Turkestan (1879–83).

During the 1870s and 1880s, Kuropatkin served as an aide to General Mikhail Dmitreyevich Skobelev; he became a major general in 1882. At the end of the 1880s, he served on the General Staff, and from 1890 to 1898 he was chief of the Transcaspian Oblast, or administrative district. On 1 January 1898, he was named by Czar Nicholas II as the czarist minister of war, serving until 7 February 1904. In this position, he was responsible for the growth of the Russian military; however, he felt that perhaps the greatest threat to Russia was in the west and that Japan was militarily too weak to challenge Russian control of the area around what is now North and South Korea. This miscalculation would prove expensive to Russia and to the czar.

Alexei Kuropatkin

On 7 February 1904, Kuropatkin was named as commander of the Russian army in Manchuria, assembling to combat a potential Japanese takeover of the all-important harbor of Port Arthur. Although he was serving under Admiral Evgeni Alexeiev, the czar's viceroy in the Far East, it was Kuropatkin who led some 100,000 Russian soldiers against the Japanese, seven divisions strong led by Marshal Iwao Oyama, at Liaoyang on 25 August 1904. After seven days of horrific fighting, Kuropatkin was forced to withdraw to the north, although he lost only 16,500 dead to Oyama's 25,000.

Historian Douglas Story writes of the battle of Liaoyang (also Liao Yang):

During the night of August 31, General Baron Stakelberg withdrew his headquarters to Liao Yang, as did General Ivanoff. General Mistchenko moved round the town on the west and occupied ground to the north and east whence he might retrieve the position lost by General Orloff, restrain Kuroki's attack, and leave General Kuropatkin's line of retreat open. General Grekov was left to fight a rear-guard action which he maintained throughout September 1.

The defence of those grand old soldiers enabled General Kuropatkin to withdraw his troops and guns, most of his stores, and to destroy whatever could not be carried away, prior to the Japanese entry into Liao Yang. The Japanese who had aimed at cutting off the Russian retreat to the north, of enveloping them in the mud about the Tai-tse-ho, found themselves in possession of a town peopled by Chinese and Cossack stragglers. Those last suffered terribly at the hands of the yellow men. Not one escaped.

While the armies of Oku and Nozu had hammered fruitlessly at the last defences of Liao Yang, General Kuroki had endeavoured to force Kuropatkin's left rear and so obtain the mastery of the railway line and the way of retreat to Mukden. General Orloff, who lay at Yen-tai with more than an army corps of men, broke before the attack and lost General Kuropatkin his entire tactical advantage.

Following the battle of the Shaho (or Sha Ho) River (26 October 1904), the czar removed Alexeiev and replaced him with Kuropatkin as the "Commander of all

Russian forces fighting Japan." On 21 February 1905 at Mukden, now called Shenyang, China, Kuropatkin again faced Oyama, who, backed by 300,000 Japanese troops, faced the Russians with 350,000 men. After 17 days of vicious and deadly fighting, on 10 March Oyama's forces encircled the city, where the Russians were holding out, but he discovered that Kuropatkin had quietly withdrawn some time earlier. Again, the two sides had fought to a draw, but 90,000 Russians lay dead along with 50,000 Japanese. Following this defeat, the czar replaced Kuropatkin with General Nikolai Linievich on 21 March 1905, and Kuropatkin was named as the commander of the First Army in Manchuria. For less than a year, until 16 February 1906, he toiled, unable to lead his army into battle without following the orders of others. He finally retired from the army and returned to Russia, where he wrote his memoirs of the Russo-Japanese War, published in four large volumes in 1906. In *Otchet general-ad"iutanta Kuropatkina* (Report by Adjutant General Kuropatkin, translated into English in 1909), he defended his overall command while admitting many mistakes.

The beginning of the First World War in 1914 saw Kuropatkin being called into action once again. In September 1915, Czar Nicholas II named him to replace Grand Duke Nicholas as supreme commander of Russian forces, and on 22 February 1916, Kuropatkin was made commander of Russian forces on the northern front, conducting a series of offensives, all of which were unsuccessful. In July 1916, he was relieved of his command and became governor-general of Turkestan. Later that year, he suppressed a rebellion in Central Asia.

The end of the czar's regime in February 1917 left Kuropatkin with no allies in St. Petersburg, and he was placed under arrest and taken to the city, renamed Petrograd. He was freed several days later, but his military career was over. He spent the remainder of his life on his estate called Sheshurino near Pskov, where he later worked as a teacher in a local school. He refused offers to lead the White Russian forces fighting the Communist government of Vladimir Lenin after the end of the First World War. Kuropatkin died at Sheshurino on 16 January 1925.

References: "Kuropatkin, Aleksei Nikolaevich," in *The Modern Encyclopedia of Russian and Soviet History*, 55 vols., edited by Joseph L. Wieczynski (Gulf Breeze, Fla.: Academic International Press, 1976–93), 18:191–192; Bruce, George, "Liaoyang" and "Mukden I," in *Collins Diction-*

ary of Wars (Glasgow, Scotland: HarperCollins Publishers, 1995), 142, 170; Kuropatkin, Alexei, *The Russian Army and the Japanese War, Being Historical and Critical Comments on the Military Policy and Power of Russia and on the Campaign in the Far East,* translated by A. B. Lindsay, edited by Major E. D. Swinton (London: John Murray, 1909); Story, Douglas, "The Culminating Battle," in *The Campaign With Kuropatkin* (London: T. Werner Laurie, 1904), 230–241; Davis Paul K., "Mukden," in *100 Decisive Battles From Ancient Times to the Present* (Santa Barbara, California: ABC-Clio, 1999), 343–350.

Kutuzov, Mikhail Illarionovich Golenishchev (Mikhail Golenishchev-Kutuzov, Mikhail Kutusov, Mikhail Kutosov, Prince Kutuzov) (1745–1813)
Russian general

Mikhail Kutuzov, also known as Golenishchev-Kutuzov, was born in the city of St. Petersburg, Russia, on 16 September 1745 (or 5 September 1745 [O.S.]), the son of a noble family. His father, Illarion Matveevich Kutuzov, had served in the Russian army under Peter the Great and in the Russian Senate during the reign of the empress Elizabeth. Tutored privately, Kutuzov entered the Dvoryanskaya Artillery School at the age of 12 in 1757. He graduated as a corporal two years later, and in 1760 he became an instructor in mathematics at the institution. In 1762, advanced to the rank of captain, he was posted to the Astrakhan Infantry Regiment, commanded by Aleksandr Vasilyevich Suvorov. However, after only a year, he left to serve as the aide-de-camp to the military governor of the province of Reval in Estonia.

Kutuzov stayed in Estonia for five years, less a short period serving with the Russian army in Poland (1764–65). In 1768, he left Estonia for good when he again went to Poland to assist in the suppression of an uprising. When Russia went to war against Turkey in 1770, Kutuzov, now a major, was assigned to a force commanded by Count Petr Rumiantsev, which attacked Turkish forces then occupying today's Romania; they took the city of Bucharest in 1773. Named as a member of Rumiantsev's staff, Kutuzov later had a falling out with the count and was sent to the Crimea to serve under a General Dolgorukov. He saw service at the battle of Alushta (1773), where he took a shot to the head, and after a period of recuperation, he was again sent back to the Crimea, where he was assigned to serve under General Suvorov.

Because of his military skill, Kutuzov was promoted several times, reaching the rank of major general by 1784. While fighting in the second Russo-Turkish war (1787–91) in the area of today's Romania where the Danube enters the Black Sea, Kutuzov showed his military proficiency and bravery at the battles of Ochakov (also Oshakov, 17–18 June 1788), Focsani (also Fokshani, 21 July 1789), and Rimnik (also Rimnitz, 11 September 1789), among others. He led Russian forces in the capture of the fortress at Izmail, (also Ismail, 10 December 1790), for which he was awarded the Order of St. George and promoted to lieutenant general. When another Polish insurrection occurred, he was ordered to move his troops into Poland, where he put down the rebellion. When his service in Poland ended in 1793, Kutuzov was named as the Russian minister to Turkey. After this service had ended, he returned to his military career, serving as the commander of Russian forces that invaded and then occupied Finland. In the succeeding years, he served as the Russian minister to Germany and the governor of St. Petersburg. In 1802, after a disagreement with Czar Alexander I, Kutuzov retired to his private estate.

In 1805, when the allies of Europe, known as the Third Coalition, decided to fight NAPOLEON BONAPARTE of France, Kutuzov was recalled to duty and given command of the Russian First Army. He defeated French forces at Ulm on 17 October 1805, but this was before Napoleon's main army could arrive, and Kutusov realized that he had to withdraw to avoid being cut down by the superior French forces. At Dürnstein, Austria on 11 November 1805, he gained an important victory over the French marshal Édouard Mortier. Because of this triumph, Czar Alexander I made him commander of all coalition armies. At Hollabrünn (16 November 1805), Russian forces under General Pyotr Ivanovich BAGRATION fought the French under Marshal Jean LANNES, duc de Montebello, in an effort to allow the main Russian army under Kutuzov to continue its retreat back to Russia. Bagration lost half his forces before he, too, was forced to retreat. This plan of withdrawal to an area where he could more easily confront the French led to one of the most important battles in world history.

Austerlitz (now Slavkov, the Czech Republic) was Napoleon's greatest victory. On 2 December 1805, he was able to lure the Russians under Kutuzov and the Austrians under General Franz von Weyrother to bring their 89,000 troops onto a field where he had only

73,000 French troops at his command. However, Napoleon then brought in a reserve unit under Marshal Louis-Nicolas DAVOUT, which helped to swing the battle for the French. When it was over, the coalition had lost 30,000 dead—more than one third of their entire force—with only 9,000 French killed. This battle is sometimes known as "the battle of the Three Emperors," as it involved Napoleon, Czar Alexander I of Russia, and Holy Roman Emperor Francis II of Austria. Kutuzov's loss—he was wounded during the battle—forced the Russians to withdraw, and on 26 December 1805, the Austrians signed the Treaty of Pressburg with France.

Although he was still considered the premier Russian military leader, Kutuzov was removed from command because of Austerlitz. He served from 1806 to 1811 as military governor of Lithuania and Kiev, now in the Ukraine, and he did command Russian forces in the Third Russo-Turkish War (1806–12). In this conflict, he helped to defeat the entire Ottoman army at Bessarabia, now called Moldova, and for his services, he was given the title of Prince Kutuzov.

Napoleon was still a threat, however, and when the French invaded Russia in 1812, Kutuzov was named to succeed Prince Mikhail BARCLAY DE TOLLY as commander of all Russian forces in Europe. He immediately left the war against Turkey and returned north to aid the resistance to the invasion. It was during this period that he utilized his scheme of delaying withdrawals, forcing the French to fight a series of minor battles that wore them down. After three months of French advances, Kutuzov made a stand at the village of Borodino. It was here, on 7 September 1812, that one of the greatest battles in the Napoleonic Wars occurred.

Russian troops under Kutuzov and French forces under Napoleon met near the small village of Borodino, about 80 miles southwest of Moscow. In using this last stand to halt the French advance into Moscow, Kutuzov had formed a force of approximately 125,000 Russian soldiers who built a series of fortifications and earthworks around the village's fields. Napoleon, commanding his Grand Armeé, composed of approximately 130,000 men, reached Borodino and the Russian defenses on 6 September 1812 and ordered his large guns to soften up the Russians with heavy bombardment. During the battle, Napoleon reportedly suffered a stroke, an event that caused a turn in the war and had great repercussions later. The heavy French cannonade enabled their cavalry to move forward, forcing the Russians to slowly retreat.

This led to the massive battle on 7 September in which Napoleon's forces broke the back of the Russian army and forced Kutuzov's forces to hastily retreat. Borodino's death toll was horrific: 42,000 Russians lay dead, along with 32,000 French—a total of nearly 75,000 dead in just two days of battle. Napoleon, possibly because of the stroke he had suffered, hesitated to follow Kutuzov's retreating troops, although he did eventually march on Moscow and occupied the city. But allowing Kutuzov to escape would be Napoleon's undoing.

The Russians had burned Moscow and anything of value in it, making occupation of the city of little use to the French. Forced to retreat by the cruel Russian winter and a lack of supplies, Napoleon's army soon found itself the subject of a series of guerrilla-style attacks from Russian forces. The French leader tried to fend off these attacks by quickly withdrawing his army southward through the city of Kaluga, but this set up another major land battle. At Maloyaroslavets on 23 October 1812, the Russians under Kutuzov met a French army commanded by General Alexis-Joseph Delzons and Eugène de Beauharnais, Napoleon's son-in-law. Historian George Bruce writes:

On 19 October, Napoleon evacuated Moscow and marched southwest to Kaluga, de Beauharnais leading the advance. Unaware of this, and believing the force sighted at Forminskoie, 40 miles southwest of Moscow, was a foraging party, Kutuzov sent General [Sergeievich] Docturov with 12,000 infantry, 3,000 cavalry, and 84 guns to surprise it. While on the road, Docturov learned this force was the [French] Grand Armeé and decided to hold out until reinforcements came at the road junction and town of Maloyaroslavets, on the Lutza River.

Docturov entered the town from the south and found the French spearhead had seized a bridgehead. Fierce fighting began; the town changed hands five times. General [Nikolai] Raevski arrived with 10,000 more Russians; once more they took the town, though not the bridgehead. De Beauharnais threw in his 15th (Italian) Division, under General [Domenico] Pino, and by evening they had again expelled the Russians. Marshal Kutuzov arrived, decided against a pitched battle with the Grand Armeé next day, and to retire instead to Kaluga. The French claimed a victory, but it was a Russian strategical success, for now wishing to avoid battle, Napoleon changed his line of march to the north, through Mozhaisk and Smolensk, the route of his advance that he had wished to avoid. French casualties were about 5,000, including Delzons who was killed; Russian [casualties] were 6,000.

However, at Krasnoi (17 November 1812), the Russian force under Kutuzov, having inflicted several days of horrific losses on the French, were surprised by a fresh force under Marshal Davout, who defeated them but suffered a loss of some 5,000 French killed. Much of Marshal Peter Ney's army was wiped out in an attempt to shield the main French force from further losses. Russian losses are unknown.

On 27 November 1812, a force of nearly 150,000 Russians held the heights over the Berezina River, forcing the French under General Claude-Victor Perrin, duc de Bellune, to fight their way over a bridge and shield the main French army under Napoleon, enabling them to continue their retreat. In January 1813, Kutuzov led the Russians into Poland and Prussia to harass the French, but he became ill and died on 28 April 1813 at Bunzlau, Germany (now Boleslawiec, Poland), at the age of 68.

Kutuzov's legacy is mixed, as is his record. Although he assisted in driving the hated French out of Russia just prior to his death, leaving tens of thousands of French dead in the snows of retreat, he was responsible for the deaths of an equal number of Russian forces at Austerlitz and Borodino, just two of the battles he commanded. The editors of the *The Wordsworth Dictionary of Military Biography*, write of this mixed legacy:

> Although widely credited, as the Commander-in-Chief of all Russian forces, with the Russian

victory over Napoleon in 1812, Kutusov never won a wholly decisive battle against that legendary conqueror; indeed, one is left to speculate whether he possessed any real qualities as a supreme commander. It is true that he managed his commands skillfully and conserved his armies intact in circumstances of great tribulation before Moscow; but in view of the extreme exhaustion of Napoleon's army, one must doubt whether Kutusov displayed any outstanding generalship when the enemy lay at his mercy. But he occupied high office in the Russian army for twenty years, and will be remembered, if for no other achievements, for his handling of the Turkish campaign.

References: Schweizer, Karl W., "Kutusov, Mikhail Illarionovich," in *The Modern Encyclopedia of Russian and Soviet History*, 55 vols., edited by Joseph L. Wieczynski (Gulf Breeze, Florida: Academic International Press, 1976–93), 18:213–216; Parkinson, Roger, *The Fox of the North: The Life of Kutusov, General of War and Peace* (New York: D. McKay Company, 1976); Bruce, George, "Austerlitz," "Borodino," "Hollabrunn," and "Maloyaroslavets," in *Collins Dictionary of Wars* (Glasgow, Scotland: HarperCollins Publishers, 1995), 25, 39, 111, 152; Holmes, Edward Richard, *Borodino, 1812* (London: C. Knight, 1971); Tarle, Professor Evgenii, *How Kutuzov Defeated Napoleon* (Moscow, USSR: Soviet War News, 1943?); "Kutusov, Mikhail," in *Command: From Alexander the Great to Zhukov—The Greatest Commanders of World History*, edited by James Lucas (London: Bloomsbury Publishing, 1988), 78; Windrow, Martin, and Francis K. Mason, "Kutusov, Prince Mikhal Ilarionovich," in *The Wordsworth Dictionary of Military Biography* (Hertfordshire, U.K.: Wordsworth Editions Ltd., 1997), 155–157.

L

Lafayette, Marie-Joseph-Paul-Yves Roch-Gilbert du Motier, marquis de (1757–1834)
French military officer

Born at the Château of Chavaniac, in Auvergne, France, on 6 September 1757, Marie-Gilbert du Motier was the scion of a distinguished French family. His father's death at the battle of Minden (1759) when Marie-Gilbert was only two, followed by the deaths of his mother and grandfather, left him in his teens with a considerable fortune. Following a family tradition, at an early age he entered the French army, studying at the military academy at Versailles near Paris. In 1771, he became a member of the prestigious King's Musketeers, and he rose to become a member of the Noailles Dragoons in 1773. A protégé of the duc d'Ayen, he married the duc's daughter in 1774 and assumed the title of marquis de Lafayette. In 1775, when he was only 18, he received word of the attempt by the American colonies to break away from the English government in London and instantly decided to go to their aid. In December 1776, he received a commission as a major general in the Continental Army from Silas Deane, the Americans' agent in Paris. In April 1777, he left his native France for Spain and, from there, sailed for America on his private ship, *La Victoire* (the victory).

Lafayette arrived in South Carolina in June 1777, and the following month he met General George WASH-INGTON, who invited him to serve with the American forces in New Jersey. He first saw action at Brandywine (11 September 1777), when the Americans were defeated by the British under Lord William Howe. Lafayette was wounded in the leg, but Washington was so impressed by his service at this single battle that he was given command of the Virginia division of the Continental Army, which he led in a retreat from Barren Hill (28 May 1778) and to an apparent draw at Monmouth Court House (28 June 1778). When the French admiral Jean-Baptiste Charles Henri Hector, comte d'Estaing, sailed the pro-American French fleet of 12 battleships and 14 frigates off the coast of Rhode Island and attacked that of the British under Earl HOWE, driving the British away, Lafayette was the liaison officer between the two forces. In 1779, after returning to France with an official message from the Continental Congress, he convinced his native country to assist the colonies in their fight, and he was present for the birth of his son, whom he named George Washington de Lafayette. He was nominated as the commander of a French army to invade England, but the invasion never came about, and in 1780 he returned to the United States. There he saw action in the campaigns against the British in Virginia, including at the battle of Green Springs (6 July 1781), in which forces under Lafayette bore down on the British on the York peninsula. This campaign ended at

Yorktown with the surrender of British forces under Lord CORNWALLIS (19 October 1781), and Lafayette again returned to France.

Back in his home country, Lafayette was an avid proponent of an alliance with the new nation of the United States. In 1782, he was named as the quarter-master general of a joint Franco-Spanish mission to British Canada, and the following year he was given the rank of *maréchal de camp* (major general). He toured America to large crowds in 1784 and Europe in 1785. In America, where he was welcomed as a hero, he served as a special French representative to the American Indian tribes, participating in a peace conference as well.

Growing political unrest in France led to Lafayette's election to the Assembly of Notables in 1787 and the Estates-General in 1789. He was elected as vice president of the French National Assembly and later named as commander of the militia when the Bastille, the noted French prison, fell to antiroyalist rebels on 14 July 1789, the beginning of the French Revolution. Despite his fame, Lafayette soon became unpopular, especially when he ordered his forces to fire into a crowd to end a riot in 1791. Named commander of an army division to defend the nation against an invasion by Austrian forces, he spent only a short period at the front when he was relieved of his command on suspicion of supporting the royalists and ordered to return to Paris. Sensing that his life was in danger, he instead crossed the border, where he was captured by Austrian forces. It was not until 1797 that he was freed through the efforts of the French general NAPOLEON BONAPARTE. Returning to France two years later, he retired.

Later in life, Lafayette returned to the world of French politics when he was elected to several terms in the Chamber of Deputies starting in 1815, and in 1830 he served as a leader of the moderates during the so-called July Revolution (1830). His leadership led to the installation of Louis Philippe as the king of France that year. He revisited the United States in 1824, when he was welcomed warmly and voted a large cash award by Congress. In 1831, he wrote on and supported revolutions in Poland and Italy.

Lafayette died in Paris on 20 May 1834 at the age of 76. Despite the fact that he was born and had died in France, and that he had spent only a few years in the service of the newly formed United States, he is remembered more in his adopted land than in his own. In 1917, when the American Expeditionary Force landed in France to assist Allied forces in the First World War, the American commander, John PERSHING, said upon his arrival, "Lafayette, we are here." In 2002, the U.S. Congress passed a resolution making the marquis de Lafayette an honorary American citizen.

References: Buckman, Peter, *Lafayette: A Biography* (New York: Paddington Press, 1977); Gottschalk, Louis Reichenthal, *Lafayette between the American and French Revolution* (Chicago: University of Chicago Press, 1950); Adams, John Quincy, *Oration on the Life and Character of Gilbert Motier de Lafayette. . . .* (Washington, D.C.: Printed by Gales and Seaton, 1835); Blanchard, Amos, *American Military Biography, Containing the Lives and Characters of the Officers of the Revolution who were most Distinguished in achieving our National Independence. Also, the life of Gilbert Motier La Fayette* (Cincinnati: E. Duming, 1834); Loveland, Anne C., *Emblem of Liberty: The Image of Lafayette in the American Mind* (Baton Rouge: Louisiana State University Press, 1971).

Lambert, John (1619–1684) *English general*

John Lambert was born the son of the squire at Calton Hall in the small village of Kirkby Malham near Skipton, Yorkshire, England, in 1619. Little is known of his early life, except that he studied the law. When the English Civil War began in 1642, Lambert joined the Yorkshire Parliamentarians as a captain serving under Ferdinando, the second baron Fairfax of Cameron, and his son, Sir Thomas FAIRFAX. He became an important military leader for the Parliamentarians, especially in early battles at Hull (October 1643); Nantwich, Cheshire (25 January 1644); Bradford, Yorkshire (March 1644); and Marston Moor (2 July 1644), a battle that left the forces of Parliament in control of northern England. Lambert showed his compassionate side when he released the head of the garrison at Bradford, who, he discovered, was distantly related to his wife. When Fairfax left his command to lead the so-called New Model Army, Lambert succeeded him as commander of the northern forces. He was later given the command of a regiment of foot, and in 1647 he advanced to the rank of major general.

Long-standing grievances between those in Parliament and the army fighting for them came to a head in 1647. Lambert stepped forward to breach these differences. Working with Henry Ireton (1611–51), a member of Parliament for Appleby, Westmoreland—and also, as some historians believe, with Lords Philip Wharton and William Fiennes, Viscount Saye and Sele—he drew up a manifesto, titled "The Heads of the Proposals [Offered by the Army]," which laid out parliamentary and military reforms. When members of the army resisted the reforms, Ireton issued a paper called the "Representation of the Army," in which he declared, "We are not a mere mercenary army, hired to serve any arbitrary power of a state, but called forth and conjured by the several declarations of Parliament to the defence of our own and the people's just rights and liberties." Further dissent over these reforms forced Lambert to restore order, especially in the northern part of the country.

When the second stage of the Civil War began in 1648, Lambert was named as the commander of all Parliamentary forces in northern England. At first he was able to march quickly against Scottish forces who were siding with King Charles I, but he was eventually forced to withdraw in the face of overwhelming numbers, although he harried and delayed their advance. With the arrival of Oliver CROMWELL and his army, Lambert routed the Scots at Preston, Lancashire (August 1648). Following Charles's execution on 30 January 1649, his son became Charles II, and the Scots took up the new king's fight. Lambert besieged and eventually took Pontefract Castle, Yorkshire (December 1648–March 1649), the last Royalist stronghold in northern England, and he remained in northern England while Cromwell struck at Royalist forces in Ireland. When Cromwell returned, they marched together into Scotland and were victorious at the Battle of Dunbar (3 September 1650). Historians believe it was Lambert's cavalry charge that won a clear and convincing victory.

Cromwell fought the Scots at Stirling but, being pinned down, sent Lambert into Fife to force them into a two-front campaign. This march led to the battle of Inverkeithling (20 July 1651) in eastern Scotland, in which Lambert again won a compelling triumph. This victory forced Charles II to march into northern England, with Lambert pursuing him every step of the way. Finally, the last important battle of the English Civil War took place at Worcester on 3 September 1651. Historian George Bruce writes: "Charles II [commanding the Royalist forces] attacked Cromwell's wing, and was repulsed and driven into Worcester, where he was met by the other wing of the Parliamentary army under Fleetwood. The Royalists were routed and dispersed, losing 3,000 killed and a large number of prisoners, including Lords Derby, Lauderdale, and Kenmure, and five generals. Charles himself escaped with difficulty to France." Cromwell later described the battle as "a crowning mercy."

Following the death of Henry Ireton in January 1652, Lambert was named to succeed him as lord deputy in Ireland, but at the last moment General Charles FLEETWOOD, one of the heroes of Worcester, was named in his place. Lambert remained close to Cromwell, and his dissatisfaction with Parliament has led some historians to suggest that he was behind Cromwell's decision to dissolve the Rump Parliament (also known as the Purged Parliament) in 1653. Lambert was responsible for drafting the documents that became the Instrument of Government under which Cromwell was named as lord protector of England following its adoption on 15 December 1653. A new parliament, the Protectorate Parliament, was summoned, but when this body refused to pass any of Cromwell's measures, he disbanded it in January 1655, maybe on Lambert's advice.

With Cromwell as the head of England, Lambert proposed his idea of a military government, which historians call the "Rule of the Major Generals." Under this rule, the country and Wales would be divided into 12 military districts, each controlled by a military governor, of which Lambert was one. For two years this system governed England until Cromwell summoned the second Protectorate Parliament in September 1656 and, under widespread criticism of the plan, abolished it in January 1657.

When Cromwell died on 3 September 1658, his son Richard Cromwell succeeded him as lord protector, and a third Protectorate Parliament was summoned. Lambert, who was elected to this body representing Pontefract, backed Richard Cromwell against a group of his opponents known as the Grandees. Because of resistance to his policies, Cromwell resigned as lord protector in May 1659 and restored the Rump Parliament. The power of the Grandees was broken, and Lambert was named as commander of the army, which went into battle against a Royalist uprising led by Sir George Booth in Chesire; in August 1659, he defeated the rebels and captured Booth.

The end of Lambert's career came quickly. In September 1659, Sir Arthur Haselrig, a former Member of Parliament who had been a supporter of Oliver Cromwell and served in the English Civil War, accused

Lambert of plotting a coup against the Rump Parliament and demanded his impeachment. Lambert, angered at the accusation, dissolved the Parliament with a threat of violence. Haselrig appealed for aid from the nation's military, and General George MONCK, another Parliamentary veteran of the civil war and the commander in chief of forces in Scotland, sided with Heselrig and reported that he would support the right of Parliament against Lambert. Lambert marched his army north to confront Monck; however, on the way, much of his army deserted him, and he was captured. Monck imprisoned Lambert in the Tower of London and went on to restore Charles II to the throne.

Lambert somehow escaped from the tower in April 1660 and issued a proclamation that all supporters of the anti-Royalist cause should rally to his side at Edgehill, the site of an earlier Civil War battle. However, no support was forthcoming, and he was captured by Colonel Ingoldsby, who had participated in the execution of Charles I and hoped for a pardon from the new monarch. Initially sentenced to death, Lambert was again taken to the Tower of London, then moved to the island of Guernsey and finally to Drakes Island in Plymouth Sound, where he remained for the rest of his life. Following the death of his wife in 1676, Lambert lapsed into insanity. He died in prison in February 1684 at the age of 64, having spent the last 24 years of his life imprisoned. A brilliant painting of him, by artist Robert Walker, is in the National Portrait Gallery in London.

References: Dawson, William Harbutt, *Cromwell's Understudy: The Life and Times of General John Lambert and the Rise and Fall of the Protectorate* (London: W. Hodge and Company, Ltd., 1938); Farr, David, *John Lambert: Parliamentary Soldier and Cromwellian Major-General, 1619–1684* (Rochester, N.Y.: Boydell Press, 2003); Rushworth, John, *Historical Collections of Private Passages of State, Weighty Matters in Law, Remarkable Proceedings in five Parliaments: . . . ,* 8 vols. (London: Printed by Tho. Newcomb for George Thomason, 1659–1701), VII:731; Gardiner, Samuel Rawson, *History of the Great Civil War, 1642–1649,* 4 vols. (London: Longmans, Green & Company, 1893); Bruce, George, "Worcester," in *Collins Dictionary of Wars* (Glasgow, Scotland: HarperCollins Publishers, 1995), 269–270; *The Case of Colonel John Lambert, Prisoner in the Tower of London* (London, 1661).

Lannes, Jean, duc de Montebello (1769–1809)
French general

Jean Lannes was born the son of a stableboy in the village of Lectour, France, on 11 April 1769. Unable to afford an education, he was taught by the village priest to read and write and was later apprenticed to a dyer of materials. He joined the French army in 1792, rising to the rank of *chef de brigade* during the French war with Spain (1793–94). In 1795, a reform of the army ranks lost him his commission. Nevertheless, he enlisted as a volunteer and fought in NAPOLEON's Italian campaign. His bravery at the battle of Dego (14–15 April 1796) brought him to the attention of Napoleon, who took Lannes under his wing and promoted him to the rank of brigadier general in 1797.

Lannes accompanied Napoleon during the Egyptian campaign (1798–99), playing a key role in several engagements, including the battle at Gaza (25 February 1799), the Siege of Acre (19 March–20 May 1799), and the battle of Aboukir (25 July 1799), where he was wounded. After Napoleon returned to France in 1799, Lannes was named as commander of the 9th and 10th French divisions, and he was again at his leader's side when Napoleon undertook the coup d'état of 18 Brumaire and declared himself emperor. Now France's ruler, Napoleon immediately sent Lannes and the French army into Italy, where they defeated the Austrians under Marshal Karl Peter Ott, Freiherr von Batorzek, at Montebello (9 June 1800), the battle from which Lannes later took his title. The French victory at Montebello in northwest Italy contributed to Napoleon's stunning victory against the Austrians under Lieutenant General Michael Melas at nearby Marengo (14 June 1800). With the end of the campaign, Lannes was named by Napoleon as the French minister to Portugal in 1801.

Upon the establishment of the French Empire in 1804, Lannes was made one of its 18 marshals. As commander of the V Corps of the Grand Armée, he played a key role in Napoleonic victories at the battles of Ulm (16 October 1805), Austerlitz (2 December 1805), and Jena (14 October 1806). At Austerlitz, also called the battle of the Three Emperors because the forces fighting represented three empires, he commanded the left wing of Napoleon's army, bringing defeat on France's enemies. At Pultusk, Poland, on 26 December 1806, he commanded the French army to victory over the Russians, with the same result occurring at Friedland in June 1807.

For his services to the French Empire, Lannes was styled as the duc de Montebello (duke of Montebello). Sent to command French forces in Spain, he directed the siege and capture of Saragossa, which fell to the French on 20 February 1809. Shifted back to the main conflict on the continent, Lannes continued to command his forces to victory. At Abensberg, Bavaria, on 20 April 1809, as commander of a joint French-Bavarian force of some 90,000 troops, he confronted the Austrians under Archduke CHARLES, who was forced to withdraw after Lannes's French forces drove back the Austrians. The Austrians lost approximately 7,000 men, while the French-Bavarian force lost 3,000 killed and wounded.

During the battle at Aspern-Esseling near Vienna (21–22 May 1809), however, Lannes was mortally wounded. Gangrene set in, and both of his legs had to be amputated. On 31 May 1809, nine days after being wounded, he died in a hospital in Vienna, Austria. (His death closely resembles that of the American general Thomas J. "Stonewall" JACKSON, who, at the height of his success in the American Civil War, was struck by a rifle bullet and died shortly afterward.)

Jean Lannes was undoubtedly one of Napoleon's greatest generals. Had he not died in 1809, it is possible that the fall of the French emperor would never have occurred just a few years later at Waterloo. The loss of Lannes marked the beginning of the end of the Napoleonic Wars and their impact on the European continent. His role in Napoleon's victories ranks him with André MASSÉNA and Louis-Nicolas DAVOUT. His moral strength, his instinctive use of forces at key moments in battle, and his ability to deploy his troops skillfully made him one of Napoleon's best commanders.

References: Chrisawn, Margaret Scott, *The Emperor's Friend: Marshal Jean Lannes* (Westport, Conn.: Greenwood Press, 2001); Bruce, George, "Aspern," "Austerlitz," and "Montebello I," in *Collins Dictionary of Wars* (Glasgow, Scotland: HarperCollins Publishers, 1995), 23, 25, 164–165.

La Tour d'Auvergne, Henri de   *See* TURENNE, HENRI DE LA TOUR D'AUVERGNE, VICOMTE DE.

Lee, Robert Edward   (1807–1870) *Confederate general*

Robert E. Lee was born into a prestigious Virginia family in Stratford, Virginia, on 19 January 1807. His father, Henry Lee (1756–1818), also known as "Light Horse Harry," served with distinction as a military commander under General George WASHINGTON during the American Revolution (1775–83); Henry Lee's uncles included Francis Lightfoot Lee (1734–97), a signer of the Declaration of Independence; Arthur Lee (1740–92), a noted early American diplomat; and Richard Henry Lee (1732–94), another signer of the Declaration of Independence who was also a member of the Continental Congress. All were descended from Richard Lee, who emigrated from England during the reign of King Charles I and settled in Virginia, where he served as a member of the Privy Council and secretary of state of the Virginia colony.

Robert E. Lee, the fourth son of Henry Lee's second wife, followed his father by entering the U.S. Military Academy at West Point, New York, in 1825, graduating second in his class four years later. Commissioned as a second lieutenant in the Corps of Engineers, in 1831 he married Mary Custis, the great-granddaughter of Martha Washington. The Lees moved into the Custis family estate at Arlington House in northern Virginia, near Washington, D.C.

In 1846, when America went to war with Mexico, Lee—by then a captain—was sent to San Antonio, Texas, to serve under General John E. Wool. He saw action in some of the earliest battles of the conflict and was recognized for his skill and ability at the battle of Buena Vista (22 February 1846). Because of this, Lee was noticed by the commander of American forces, General Winfield SCOTT, who selected the young officer to serve on his staff. Lee took part in the battle at Veracruz (9 March 1847), and he also helped to bring about victories at Cerro Gordo (17–18 April 1847) and Chapultepec (12–13 September 1847), where he was slightly wounded. He returned home in 1848, was promoted to the rank of brevet colonel for his role in the war, and served for four years at Fort Caroll in Baltimore, Maryland. In 1852, he was named as superintendent of West Point and promoted to the rank of colonel of cavalry. In March 1855, Secretary of War Jefferson Davis named him as commander of the 2nd Cavalry in Texas, with the rank of lieutenant colonel. During this period, Lee led a series of engagements against American Indian tribes in the western United States. In 1859, at home in Virginia, he was placed in command of the force that arrested the antislavery raiders who attacked Harper's Ferry, Virginia

Robert E. Lee

bayonets, and in which strife and civil war are to take the place of brotherly love and kindness, has no charms for me. If the Union is dissolved and the Government dispersed I shall return to my native State and share the miseries of my people and, save in defense, will draw my sword no more." Nevertheless, when President Lincoln ordered the American military to put down the insurrection and offered him the command of the army—on the recommendation of his former commander, Winfield SCOTT—Lee sided with Virginia and the South, resigning his commission in the U.S. Army and offering his services to the new Confederate government.

As the war began, Lee set about organizing an army in Virginia. He also served as the military adviser to former secretary of war and now Confederate president Jefferson Davis. At First Bull Run (21 July 1861), the first major battle of the war, the Confederates were commanded by General Pierre Gustave Toutant Beauregard (1818–93). When the Union forces invaded western Virginia, Lee was sent there to combat them, but his soldiers were too inexperienced, and they were defeated in several quick battles. His reputation questioned by those in charge of the Confederacy, Lee was dispatched not to a field command but to help organize the coastal defenses of North and South Carolina against a Union invasion. In March 1862, however, he was called back to Richmond as Davis's military adviser, just as it was becoming clear that the Northern army was prepared to advance south.

In the same month, the Union forces, 180,000 strong, marched into Virginia in an attempt to capture the Confederate capital, Richmond, and end the war with one bold stroke. The South could muster only 80,000 to oppose them. As the Union moved from three different directions, Southern commanders proposed an all-out defense of Richmond. Lee, however, felt that an offense against two of the three Northern wings would save the city and the Confederacy. He advised President Davis to send General Joseph Johnston to hold Union general George Brinton McCLELLAN on the Yorktown Peninsula and to send Thomas "Stonewall" JACKSON to attack Union forces in the Shenandoah Valley. Johnston's offensive, known as the battle of Seven Pines (31 May 1862), split the Union army into two, and Jackson's move prevented reinforcements being sent to McClellan's assistance. Johnson was wounded, however, and Lee took Command of the Army of Northern Virginia. Mc-

(now in West Virginia), including John Brown, who was later executed.

Although he came from a wealthy Virginia family, Lee saw slavery as an evil and had liberated those owned by his family. In 1860, Republican Abraham Lincoln was elected President of the United States and several southern slave states left the American Union to form the Confederate States of America. Lee had previously written, "I can anticipate no greater calamity for the country than the dissolution of the Union. . . . Still a union that can only be maintained by swords and

Clellan was ultimately forced to withdraw to the James River, and Lee's offensive of a smaller force against a larger force broken into two worked. He then dispatched Jackson to attack Union forces under the command of General John Pope. Combined with Jackson, Lee and the Confederates attacked, forcing the battle known as Second Bull Run (29–30 August 1862), and the arrival of General James Longstreet gave the South another clear victory. McClellan then attacked Southern forces at Antietam, Maryland (17 September 1862), where Lee, backed by Jackson, repelled the Union attack, but they were forced to withdraw back into Virginia, ending a Southern chance to threaten the capital of Washington, D.C.

Although Lee defeated the Union forces decisively at the battles of Fredericksburg (13 December 1862) and Chancellorsville (1 May 1863), he had insufficient men or matériel to finish the war. At Chancellorsville, confederate armies defeated Union forces under General Joseph HOOKER. However, during the clash, Thomas "Stonewall" Jackson was wounded in a friendly-fire incident by his own troops, and he died two days later from his wounds, inflicting a grave blow to the Confederates and Lee in particular.

Although his army never recovered from Jackson's loss, Lee planned another attack into the North to destabilize—perhaps even overthrow—the Union and relieve the growing pressure from Ulysses S. GRANT and William Tecumseh SHERMAN in the west. To this end, he marched his army into Pennsylvania, where he attacked Union forces at Gettysburg (1–3 July 1863). Historians claim that Lee's temporary indecisiveness led him to make several mistakes in this three-day campaign, including finally sending a force led by General George E. Pickett in his famed charge uphill against the enormously strong Union center, an action that ended disastrously. After three days of bloodshed, Lee withdrew to the South. Never again would he fight on Northern soil.

Bloody battles through the remainder of 1863 and into 1864 slowly sapped the strength of the Confederate army. At the Wilderness (5–7 May 1864), Spotsylvania Courthouse (7–20 May 1864), and Cold Harbor (also known as Chickahominy, 3 June 1864), Lee caused more than 60,000 casualties for the Union armies, but he lost some 25,000 men, and he could not replace them as the Union did. As 1864 ended, the writing was on the wall for an inevitable Confederate defeat. Lee biog-

rapher Russell Weigley notes that "Lee persisted in the struggle because he believed himself bound by duty." As Grant's army slowly moved south, and Sherman's army advanced from the west, capturing more and more territory, the South's hopes faded away. On 2 April 1865, after a massive Union victory in Virginia, Lee ordered the evacuation of Richmond and Petersburg. Moving his remaining forces toward Appomattox Courthouse on 9 April, he found all avenues of escape blocked. Facing the inevitable, he sent a messenger to his opponent, Union general Ulysses S. Grant, to say that he wished to surrender. The two men met at the Wilmer McLean home at Appomattox Courthouse, and Lee surrendered his army, with his men allowed to take their horses and sidearms and return home without being punished. Although Lee himself was later indicted for treason—and he was not allowed to vote during his lifetime—he was never punished for his role in the war except in one way: His family home in Arlington had been deliberately confiscated and converted into a cemetery for the war dead, now the Arlington National Cemetery.

Lee spent the remainder of his life attempting to reconcile the war-torn nation. In August 1865, he was appointed president of Washington College in Lexington, Virginia, an office he held until his death. Lee suffered a cerebral hemorrhage on 28 September 1870, and died on 12 October at the age of 63. He was buried in the Lee Chapel, now a museum, in Lexington, and in his honor, the name of the institution was changed to Washington and Lee College. Historian Michael Lee Lanning writes of his legacy: "Lee remains a military hero respected and studied for his strategic skills in fighting a larger, better-supplied enemy and his leadership abilities in gaining the respect and adoration of his subordinates. He is the icon of American military dignity. Yet despite the South's romanticized immortalization of their leader, Lee ranks far below the victor Grant in actual long-term influence. Lee left a legacy that makes him a symbol of Southern pride, but the cause he represented so well was truly a lost one."

References: Fowler, Robert H., "Lee, Robert Edward," in *Historical Times Illustrated Encyclopedia of the Civil War,* edited by Patricia L. Faust (New York: Harper & Row, Publishers, 1986), 429–431; Weigley, Russell F., "Lee, Robert E.," in *American National Biography,* 24 vols., edited by John A. Garraty and Mark C. Carnes (New York: Oxford University Press, 1999), 12:392–397; Porter,

Horace, *Campaigning With Grant* (New York: Century, 1897); Lanning, Michael Lee, "Lee, Robert E.," in *The Military 100: A Ranking of the Most Influential Military Leaders of All Time* (New York: Barnes and Noble Books, 1996), 226.

Leicester, earl of *See* MONTFORT, SIMON DE, EARL OF LEICESTER.

Leslie, Alexander, first earl of Leven (ca. 1580–1661) *Scottish military leader*

Alexander Leslie was born about 1580 (although one source of his life reports 1582), the illegitimate son of George Leslie, a captain of Blair Castle in Athol. Little is known of his early life, but in 1605 he was in Sweden, serving in the army of Swedish king GUSTAV II (Gustavus Adolphus). He went on to see extensive action in the Thirty Years' War (1618–48), forcing Albrecht von Wallenstein to raise the siege of Stralsund, Prussia (1628), and he was present at the battle of Lützen (6 November 1632) when Adolphus was killed in action. In 1634, Leslie besieged and took the city of Brandenburg; he was made a field marshal in 1636.

Leslie left Sweden when he was asked to assume command of Scottish forces against King Charles I in the First Bishops' War (1639), and he served in the same capacity in the Second Bishops' War (1640–41). As the Scottish commander, he participated in numerous battles, including the capture of Edinburgh (March 1639), and in 1640 he marched south and invaded England, defeating Charles's forces at Newburn upon Tyne (28 August 1640). Because of this, Charles asked the Scots for peace, and Leslie met the king at Ripon, where a treaty of peace was signed in 1641. In October that same year, Charles made Leslie earl of Leven and Lord Balgonie in an effort to gain support for his side in his growing argument with Parliament. In 1642, the year the English Civil War broke out, Charles sent Leslie into Ireland as commander of Scottish forces, but he gave this up in 1643 when Scotland sided with Charles's opponents.

Lord Leven's command of Scottish forces led to one of the most important battles of the Civil War. In his work on Leslie's life, historian Charles Stanford Terry reproduced a contemporary source note on the battle of Marston Moor, 2 July 1644:

Upon Mundy, July 1 we marched with all our Forces unto Hessammoore (on the South-side of the River Owse) with hope there to meet with Prince RUPERT on his way towards York. . . . But Prince Rupert fax [and] 3 thousand horse fled at once, our horsemen upon that hand stood till they were disordered. . . . [At Marston Moor] God gave a great victorie, more nor we knew there were, by the accounts of these that buried the dead being about 4000 there was of them, many private men; above 1500 prisoners. . . . God did preserve those that stayed marvellouslie; of all our armie there were not ane [one] hundred killed; the most part of them killed running, few of them killed standing; there were 800 hurt, many in running; of the others not so many either hurt or killed.

A description of the battle's consequences was given in a "Letter from Generall Leven," printed in 1644:

The issue was the totall Routing of the Enemies Army, the losse of all their Ordnance, to the number of 20 their Ammunition and Baggage, about 100 Colours, and ten thousand Armes. There were killed upon the place about 3000 of them, whereof many are chief Officers, and 1500 prisoners taken, amongst whom there are above 100.

. . . Our losse, God be praised, is not very great, being onely of one Lieutenant Colonell, some few Captains, and about two or three hundred common Souldiers. The Prince in a great distraction, with a few Horsemen, and almost no Foot [soldiers], marched the next morning from York Northwards. Wee are now lying down again in our old Leaguer before York, which we in hopes in a few dayes to gain, and are resolved to send a great part of our Calvarie after Prince Rupert.

Marston Moor's importance in the English Civil War has been repeatedly debated by historians.

In May 1646, Leslie surrounded Charles's force at Newark and personally supervised the king's surrender before taking him to Newcastle. Despite his opposition to Charles, Leslie tried to reason with him to accept the role of Parliament in the affairs of the English government as well as to recognize the claims of the Scottish Covenanters, a religious sect. When Charles refused, Leslie handed him over to the Parliamentary forces in January 1647, disbanded his army, and returned to Scotland.

Leslie followed Charles's trial, but he argued that the king's execution in January 1649 was wrong, and it forced him to change his mind on the English monarchy. When Charles's son, Charles II, invaded England with Scottish troops in 1650, Leslie participated but did not command pro-Royalist forces; this task was undertaken by his nephew, Sir David LESLIE. Leslie saw action at Dunbar in September 1650, but he was captured at Alyth (August 1651) by an English force. Sent to London in chains, he was imprisoned in the Tower of London but released in 1654 after Queen Christina of Sweden interceded on his behalf. He then returned to Scotland and spent his final years on his estate at Balgonie, in Fife, where he died on 4 April 1661.

Although he was an important commander in the ranks of the Parliamentary army in the first phase of the English Civil War, Leslie's role has been all but forgotten by historians. Nonetheless, he remains a soldier who served both his native and adopted countries with honor and with much courage.

References: Terry, Charles Sanford, *The Life and Campaigns of Alexander Leslie, First Earl of Leven* (London: Longmans, Green & Company, 1899); Stewart, William, Captain, *A Full Relation of the Late Victory Obtained, through Gods providence by the forces under the command of Generall Lesley, the Lord Fairfax, and the Earl of Manchester* . . . (London: Printed by J. F. for L. Blaiklock, 1644); T. M., *A Particular List of Divers of the Commanders and Officers taken Prisoners at Marston Moore neer York (otherwise called Hesham Moore)* . . . (London: Printed for Ralph Rounthwait, 1644); *A Relation of the Good Successe of the Parliaments Forces under the Command of Generall Lesly, the Earl of Manchester, and the Lord Fairfax, against the Forces commanded by Prince Rupert and the Earl of Newcastle on Hesham-Moore, on Tuesday July 2, 1644* . . . (Cambridge, U.K.: Printed by W. F., 1644); Terry, Charles Sanford, *Life of Alexander Leslie, Earl of Leven* (London: Longmans, Green & Company, 1899); *A Letter from Generall Leven, the Lord Fairfax, and the Earle of Manchester, to the Commonwealth of both Kingdoms* . . . (Edinburgh, Scotland: Printed by Evan Tyler, 1644).

Leslie, Sir David, first baron Newark (1601–1682) *Scottish military leader*

Born at Pitcairlie House, his family's ancestral home in Fife, Scotland, sometime in 1601, David Leslie was the fifth son of Sir Patrick Leslie, a longtime Scottish military leader who was created first lord of Lindores in 1600. Like his uncle, Alexander LESLIE, Lord Leven, David Leslie served in the Swedish army, seeing action during the Thirty Years' War (1618–48) and rising to the rank of colonel of horse. However, when the English Civil War broke out in 1642, he returned to Scotland and sided with the forces of the English Parliament against those of King Charles I. Rising to become one of the most important of the Parliamentarian commanders, he was promoted to major general and named as second in command of Scottish forces under his uncle.

The Scottish forces backing the Parliamentary army marched into England, joined up with their English compatriots at Tadcaster on 20 April, and saw action at York (30 June 1644), where the Parliamentarians were defeated by a Royalist force led by Prince RUPERT. Falling back, the Parliamentarians took up a position on the Ouse River, at Marston Moor in Yorkshire. On 2 July 1644, some 18,000 Royalists under Prince Rupert and Sir Charles Lucas met the combined Parliamentary forces of David Leslie, Edward MONTAGU, the earl of Manchester, and Thomas, Lord FAIRFAX. Backed by Leslie's forces, Parliamentary officer, Oliver CROMWELL, charged into the royalist forces and forced them to flight. The Royalists were routed, losing some 4,000 men, and northern England was in Parliamentary hands. Leslie was a hero of the battle, as was Cromwell.

Marston Moor was a fateful battle for King Charles I, as Parliamentary forces moved onto the city of York and quickly captured it. A series of engagements followed, including at Lothian. In memoirs that lay in the collections of the British Museum until the historian Samuel Jefferson published them in 1840, Isaac Tullie, a soldier who marched with the Parliamentarians, wrote:

> Leslie marched with about 800 hors [horses] as farr as Salkeld wthout opposition; but when he came to passe the ford of Eden, which was not very shallow, he found the other side manned wth regiments of hors and foot, wch the Gentrie of Cumberland and Westmorland had raised to oppose him; wch so appalled him, yt he refused to march on, and fell arailing at Barwise, who

had perswaded him yt he should meet wth no ememyes. And needs he would retreat to Newcastle, till great Barwise set himself first into the water; and the rest, following him, so frighted ye fresh water countrie whiggs, yt all of them answered the Motto, *veni, vidi, fugi;* some of the cheif of the Country, whom I will not name, gave occasion to this shamefull flight.

Leslie became one of the most important of the Parliamentarian commanders. With the capture of King Charles in 1645, the "first phase" of the English Civil War came to an end.

Following Charles's capture, the duke of Hamilton tried to mediate between the king and the Scots and offered Leslie the command of a small force to rescue the king if he accepted the Scottish demands. Leslie refused, and Charles was tried and executed in 1649, leaving supporters and even many Parliamentarians outraged at the king's murder. A number of Scottish officers formed an army to fight the English Parliament and named Leslie's uncle, the earl of Leven, as commander, with David Leslie as his second in command. This army marched into England in support of Charles's son (later Charles II). With Lord Leven's resignation, David Leslie took command in the fight against his former ally Oliver Cromwell. The most important battle of this war was on 3 September 1650 at Dunbar, where the Scots under Leslie's command—with his uncle, Lord Leven, present—were routed by Cromwell's Parliamentary force. A pamphlet on the battle by a Parliamentary supporter, entitled *A Brief Narrative of the Great Victorie . . . Near Dunbar,* explains what happened in this clash:

> Our Armie, having long faced the Scot's Armie to the West of Edinburgh, and finding they could not draw them to fight, thought fit to draw off to Dunbar, to refresh themselvs. And being com [come] to their old Quarters at Massleborough, and beginning their march on Saturday night they were pressed upon by the Scot's Armie close after them, so, as they were somtimes within a mile, and somtimes half a mile of their Armie . . .
>
> Our Armie quartered that night at Haddington: Sunday morning our Armie marched to Dunbar, whither wee came on Sunday night. And their whole Armie followed, consisting of eighteen Regiments of Foot, which, together with their Hors [horses], and Dragoons (as themselvs say) were 27000, our Armie about 12000. They there drew up their Armie upon a verie high hill, within a mile of the Town; and ours stood in *battalie* in the Corn-fields, between them and the Town, readie to engage. . . .
>
> That night our Armie, by command, marched as close to the sald ditch as possible as they could, and placed their Field Pieces in everie Regiment. Tuesday morning at four of the clock wee drew down a *Brigade* consisting of three Regiments of Hors, *viz.* Major General *Lambert's,* Commissarie Generall Whalley's, and Colonel Lilborn's; and two Regiments of Foot towards a Pass, that is upon the Road-waie, between Dunbar and Barwick, by which wee might with more eas [easily] pass over to their Armies. And there gave the Enemie an hot Alarm, firing hard at one at another; the dispute lasted there above an hour; the issue was, our men gained the Ground, and possessed the Pass. Then the Enemies Hors charged strongly, beeing most *Lancers,* and coming down the Hill, our Hors gave waie a little; but presently Rallying, and our Foot of that Brigade advancing and charging the Enemie, put them suddainly to the Rout, it being now about six of the Clock in the Morning. . . .
>
> Prisoners of qualitie, brought in before the Messenger came awale, were, S[ir] James Lunsdain, heretofore Governor of New-Castle; and now the Lieutenant General of their Armie; General David *Leslie's* Lieutenant Colonel; which Lieutenant Colonel saith, that hee supposeth *David Leslie* himself is slain.

But Leslie was not slain; instead, with approximately 3,000 dead Scottish left on the field at Dunbar, he and what was left of his army fled to Stirling to regroup. Leslie marched with his army into England again, and at Worcester on 3 September 1651, Cromwell's forces again routed the Scots. Leslie, fleeing to Yorkshire, fell into enemy hands, and he was taken in chains to London and imprisoned in the Tower of London for nine years.

In 1660, following Charles II's ascension to the English throne, Leslie was released. For his service to the Crown, he was created Baron Newark, with a pension of

£500 per year for the remainder of his life and that of his heirs. Charles wrote to him:

> Although we have on all occasions, both abroad and since our happy return, declared ourself fully satisfied with your conduct and loyalty in our service, and although in consideration of the same, we have given you the title and honour of a lord; yet, seeing we are told, that malice and slander do not give over to persecute you, we have thought fit to give you this further testimony, and to declare under our hand, that while you was the lieutenant-general of our army, you did, both in England and Scotland, behave yourself with as much conduct, resolution, and honesty as was possible or could be expected from a person in that trust: and as we told you, so we again repeat it, that if we had occasion to levy an army fit for ourself to command, we would not fail to give you an employment in it fit for your quality.

Leslie lived his last years in Scotland, where he died in 1682.

References: Jefferson, Samuel, ed., *A Narrative of the Siege of Carlisle, in 1644 and 1645, by Isaac Tullie . . .* (Whitehaven, Cumbria, U.K.: Michael Moon's Bookshop, 1988); *Another Victory in Lancashire obtained against the Scots by Major General Harrison, and Collonel Lilburn . . .* (London: Printed by B. A., 1651); *A Letter from Scotland, giving a full and impartiall relation of the scattering of those forces risen against the Parliament . . .* (London, 1649); *A Brief Narrative of the Great Victorie . . . Near Dunbar* (London: Printed by William Dugard, by the Appointment of the Council of State, 1650).

Lincoln, Benjamin (1733–1810) *American general*

Benjamin Lincoln was born in Hingham, Massachusetts, on 29 January 1733, the sixth of eight children of Colonel Benjamin Lincoln, a farmer and maltster (maker of malt), and his wife Elizabeth Thaxter Lincoln. Little is known of Lincoln's early life, except that he received a moderate education in Hingham. In 1754, he was elected as the town constable for Hingham, and in 1755 he was named as the adjutant in his father's colonial militia regiment, the 3rd Regiment of Suffolk County, Massachusetts. Promoted rapidly, he rose to the rank of lieutenant colonel by 1772, and during this period, he held other offices, such as justice of the peace and clerk of the city of Hingham. He was also elected to the colonial legislature.

By the early 1770s, relations between the colonies and the English Parliament in London had become strained, and Lincoln was one of those involved in the movement to make America an independent nation. In 1774, he served as a member of the provincial congress, and when war broke out in Massachusetts in April 1775, he served on the committees of supplies and correspondence. In January 1776, he was promoted to the rank of brigadier general, and the following month he became major general of the Massachusetts militia. He saw action at the Battle of White Plains (28 October 1776), where he was noticed by General George WASHINGTON, leader of the revolutionary forces.

On 19 February 1777, Lincoln was promoted to the rank of major general in the Continental army, and that summer he helped to organize a band of militia in Vermont to head off the invasion of British forces under General John BURGOYNE into what is now the northern part of New York State. As part of this defense, Lincoln commanded the right wing of the revolutionary forces in the battle of Bemis Heights (7 October 1777), near Saratoga, New York, in which 7,200 colonists under the command of General Horatio GATES halted 6,000 British troops under Burgoyne marching toward what is now the city of Albany, New York. During the second day of fighting (8 October 1777), sometimes called Bemis Heights but also known as Freeman's Farm or Stillwater, Lincoln was wounded in the right ankle and forced to leave the army for nearly a year to recuperate. Burgoyne surrendered on 17 October, a serious set back for the British.

On 25 September 1778, Lincoln was named as commander of the southern department of the Continental army. Dispatched to Charles Town (now Charleston), South Carolina, he made initial military movements into Georgia and fought several indecisive actions against the British but was forced back to Charles Town and had to surrender there on 12 May 1780. Held as a prisoner of war, Lincoln was finally exchanged in November 1780, but he did not return to service until the following June, when he served with Washington in New York. By this time the British were nearing defeat in the war, and in August 1781 Washington sent Lincoln to Yorktown, Virginia, to try to destroy the main British army there under Lord CORNWALLIS. When Cornwallis, hemmed in by Colonial forces, finally relented and surrendered his army, it was Lincoln, not Washington, who accepted his sword in a ceremony on 19 October 1781. The war was over.

On 31 October 1781, less than two weeks after the historic victory at Yorktown, the Continental Congress named Lincoln as secretary at war, a post he held until October 1783 (and which, with the enactment of the Constitution in 1787, later became secretary *of* war). Following Lincoln's resignation, he returned to Hingham, where he was elected president of the Massachusetts Society of the Cincinnati, a veterans' organization. He speculated in land in Maine, but when the economy went down, he nearly went into bankruptcy.

In 1787, Lincoln was placed in command of the Massachusetts militia again, this time to put down an internal insurrection. A farmer in Massachusetts, Daniel Shays, had led a group of hundreds of farmers angered by high taxes and foreclosures against their farms into a revolt against the central government. At first, "Shays's Rebellion" was ignored, but when the rebels' forces closed the courts in Springfield, Massachusetts, Lincoln and his 3,200-man militia were sent to put them down. Shays and his troops, hearing that the militia was coming for them, attacked the Springfield arsenal, which was lightly defended; nonetheless, a small force was able to drive Shays's army back. The commander of this force, former congressman William Shepard, sent word to Lincoln to rush his forces to Springfield. Lincoln responded by dispatching first another small force and then the remainder of the militia on 27 January 1787. He then took the battle to the rebellious farmers, defeating them easily and ending the uprising.

Lincoln resigned his commission as head of the militia on 10 June 1787, and he was elected as lieutenant governor of Massachusetts that same year. He served as a member of a 1788 state convention to vote on a new state constitution, and in 1789 he was named as the collector of the port of Boston, a post he held for nearly 20 years. Returning home to Hingham, Lincoln died in the home of his birth on 9 May 1810 at the age of 77. He was buried in the town two days later.

References: Nelson, Paul David, "Lincoln, Benjamin," in *American National Biography,* 24 vols., edited by John A. Garraty and Mark C. Carnes (New York: Oxford University Press, 1999), 13:673–674; Mattern, David Bruce,

A Moderate Revolutionary: The Life of Major General Benjamin Lincoln (Ph.D. dissertation, Columbia University, 1990); Mattern, David Bruce, *Benjamin Lincoln and the American Revolution* (Columbia: University of South Carolina Press, 1995); Cavanagh, John Carroll, *The Military Career of Major General Benjamin Lincoln in the War of the American Revolution, 1775–1781* (Ph.D. dissertation, Duke University, 1969).

Lucan, George Charles Bingham, third earl of
(1800–1888) *British commander*

George Charles Bingham was born in London on 16 April 1800, the eldest son of Richard, the second earl of Lucan, and his wife Elizabeth, the daughter of Henry, the third Earl Fauconberg of Newborough. He was educated at the prestigious Westminster School, and at the age of 16 he entered the English army as an ensign in the 6th Regiment of Foot. Two years later, he was transferred to the 3rd Foot Guards, and in 1820 he was promoted to lieutenant in the 8th Foot. By 1825, he had been promoted to the rank of major and joined the 17th Lancers. He volunteered to fight with the Russians against the Turks in the Balkans (1828–29) and served as a member of Parliament from County Mayo in Ireland from 1826 to 1830.

In 1839, Bingham succeeded his father as the earl of Lucan, and a year later he was elected as a representative peer of Ireland. During his service in Ireland, he worked to improve the lives of tenants on his estates there, although he showed little consideration for their privations during the Irish potato famine.

With the outbreak of the Crimean War (1854–56), Bingham, now the earl of Lucan, wanted to serve, even though he had limited military experience. Regardless, he was given the command of the cavalry division, of which one-half was the Light Brigade, commanded by James Thomas Brudenell, the seventh earl of Cardigan, who was also Lucan's brother-in-law. Despite this tie, both men hated each other, and their military relationship reflected this. Lucan complained on more than one occasion that Cardigan ignored his orders and went past him to the commander of English forces in the Crimea, Lord RAGLAN. At Balaclava on 25 October 1854, Raglan, looking at the battlefield from a high hill, ordered Lucan to capture some guns being moved by a small Russian force off to a flank. Lucan, down in the valley, could only see straight up the valley ahead of him at the guns in the middle of the entire Russian position. Because Raglan's order was in writing, Lucan had to order Lord Cardigan to take his 600 troops "into the Valley of Death." The charge of the Light Brigade, immortalized by Tennyson, was a disaster—albeit a heroic one. Returning to headquarters, Lucan was castigated by Raglan.

Lucan's actions at Balaclava, having led to so many killed in action, were questioned in Great Britain, although William Howard Russell, a correspondent of *The Times* (London) who spent months covering the Crimean War, wrote:

> Lord Lucan with reluctance gave the order to Lord Cardigan to advance upon the guns, conceiving that his orders compelled him to do so. The noble Earl, though he did not shrink, also saw the fearful odds against him. Don Quixote in his tilt against the windmill was not near so rash and reckless as the gallant fellows who prepared without a thought to rush on almost certain death. . . . At ten past eleven our Light Cavalry Brigade rushed to the front . . . The whole brigade scarcely made one effective regiment, according to the numbers of continental armies; and yet it was more than we could spare. As they passed towards the front, the Russians opened on them from the guns in the redoubts on the right, with volleys of musketry and rifles . . .

Angered at this apparent censure, Lucan demanded that Raglan be recalled and asked that he (Lucan) be court-martialed so that he could clear his name. He was recalled but not allowed the military court. However, on 19 March 1855, he was invited to speak before the House of Lords, where he spoke at length about his role at Balaclava:

> Your Lordships are so well acquainted with the details of this charge, and so fully appreciate the extraordinary valour and gallantry displayed by the light cavalry on that occasion, and also the steadiness and bravery of the heavy brigade, more particularly the Scots Grey and Royals, and two regiments most exposed, that I would only add, that the brilliancy of the charge and the gallantry displayed by the whole of the cavalry, were never surpassed at any former period. Your Lordships should be told that the infantry, which I was informed was coming to support me, was composed of two divisions, the 1st commanded by His Royal Highness the Duke of Cambridge, and the 4th by an officer whose death the army and the country so much deplore, both my seniors, and therefore both my commanding officers. In the evening of the action, I saw Lord Raglan; his first remark to me was, "You have lost the light brigade." I at once denied that I had lost the light brigade, as I had only carried out the orders conveyed to me, written and verbal, by Captain Nolan. He then said that I was a lieutenant general, and should, therefore, have exercised my discretion, and not approving of the charge, should not have made it. He subsequently said that I had not moved sufficiently in advance in the previous movement; but he never attempted to show then, or has he ever allowed me to suppose since, until the present time, that he ever intended that No. 4 order was at all to be connected with the preceding order.

Lucan's defense of himself led to all sorts of questions as to his actions. Nevertheless, he received the Legion of Honour and was given a knighthood (KCB) in July 1855. Although promoted to the rank of field marshal in 1887, he never saw battlefield action again. He died at his home in London on 10 November 1888 and was laid to rest in Laleham, Middlesex.

References: Marnham, Patrick, *Trail of Havoc: In the Steps of Lord Lucan* (London: Penguin, 1988); Woodham Smith, Cecil Blanche, *The Reason Why* (London: Constable, 1953); Paget, George, Lord Paget, *The Light Cavalry Brigade in the Crimea: Extracts from the Letters and Journal of General Lord George Paget* (London: John Murray, 1881); "The Battle of Balaclava and the Charge of the Light Brigade," *25 October 1854* in *Eyewitness to History,* edited by John Carey (Cambridge, Mass.: Harvard University Press, 1987), 333–344; Lucan George Charles Bingham, earl of, *Speech of Major Gen. the Earl of Lucan, delivered in the House of Lords on Monday, March 19, 1855, on his Recall from his Command in the Crimea* (London: T. & W. Boone, 1855); Russell, Howard, "Parliamentary Intelligence," *The Times* (London), 7 March 1855, 6.

M

MacArthur, Douglas (1880–1964) *American general*

The son of General Arthur MacArthur (1845–1912), a Civil War veteran who commanded American forces in the Spanish-American War (1898), Douglas MacArthur was born on 26 January 1880 in the army base at Little Rock, Arkansas, where his father was stationed. He attended the U.S. Military Academy at West Point, New York, from which he graduated first in his class in 1903. He was commissioned as an engineer officer, and for the next decade he served in various capacities, including as aide to his father during a tour of the Orient, and as aide to President Theodore Roosevelt.

During the American participation in the fighting in Europe during the First World War, MacArthur, as the commander of the 84th Infantry Battalion, led his troops into action in the St. Mihiel salient in September 1918. As the commander of the 42nd ("Rainbow") Division, he was gassed and wounded in action before the war came to an end in November 1918. In 1919, as a brigadier general, he was named as the superintendent of West Point, serving until 1922. During this period, he revitalized the officer training course and brought new discipline to the academy. In January 1925, he was advanced to the rank of major general, and he was subsequently named as commander of the Department of the Philippines, in which role he served from 1928 to 1930. On 21 November 1930, President Herbert Hoover appointed him chief of staff of the U.S. Army and promoted him to the rank of full general. In 1935, MacArthur retired from the U.S. Army and became a military adviser to the Philippine government; he was named as field marshal of the Philippine army in June 1936. When he wanted to retire in 1937, at age 57, Philippine president Manuel Quezon asked him to stay on as head of all the Filipino military forces.

MacArthur was in the Philippines in 1941 when the United States entered the Second World War. He had already established a plan in July that year to fight a potential Japan invasion of the Philippine islands, at the same time integrating Filipino forces inside the American military structure. When Japan invaded the Philippines in December 1941, President Franklin Delano Roosevelt reappointed MacArthur to the U.S. military with the rank of lieutenant general and put him in complete control of the islands' defenses. Although MacArthur was able to slow down the Japanese march on the city of Manila, he could not hold back their forces, and upon Roosevelt's direct orders he was forced to withdraw himself and his immediate staff to Australia, leaving behind thousands of American and Filipino soldiers who fell into Japanese hands; many were tortured and later executed.

General of the Army Douglas MacArthur on Luzon, the Philippines, 1945

The fall of the Philippines, as well as Bataan and Corregidor, left much of the western Pacific in Japanese hands. MacArthur arrived in Australia on 17 March 1942, where he was named as Southwest Pacific Area commander. Shortly after his arrival, he made his now-famous speech to reporters: "The President of the United States has ordered me to break through the Japanese lines and proceed from Corregidor to Australia for the purpose, as I understand it, of organizing the American offensive against Japan, a primary objective of which is the relief of the Philippines. I came through and I shall return." Working with Admiral Chester W. NIMITZ, MacArthur undertook a series of offensives against Japanese targets in New Guinea, leading to the capture of Leyte Island in 1944 and the eventual recapture of the Philippines, which dragged on from October 1944 to July 1945. Keeping his promise, MacArthur

returned to the Philippines landing on Leyte on October 20, 1944.

MacArthur was promoted to the rank of General of the Army in 1944, only one of a handful of officers to ever hold this title. He was preparing to invade the Japanese islands when atomic bombs were dropped on Hiroshima and Nagasaki, and Japan sued for peace. As supreme commander of the Allied powers in the Pacific Theater of Operations, it was MacArthur who accepted the surrender of the Japanese government on 2 September 1945. Named by President Harry S. Truman as commander of the occupation forces in Japan, he established a democratic government and began instituting a series of political and economic reforms that consequently helped make Japan the democratic and economic giant that it is today. Although MacArthur wished to break all ties with the monarchy, he realized the importance of

Emperor Hirohito in Japanese society and retained him as a figurehead leader.

In June 1950, forces from North Korea invaded South Korea, and MacArthur was named as commander of United Nations forces sent in to repel the invasion. As North Korean forces moved south, he devised a plan to land behind them and attack them from the rear. His landings at the port of Inchon, in what is now northern South Korea, changed the course of the conflict. Devastated, the North Korean forces were forced back behind the 38th parallel border dividing north and south. However, MacArthur decided to pursue the North Koreans toward their border with China, at the Yalu River. Having foreseen that Communist China would become a huge threat to American interests in the Pacific region, he felt that attacking the Chinese troops now reinforcing the Koreans was the only way to counter this growing threat. When President Truman personally warned him not to take action against China, MacArthur, angered, wrote a letter to several congressmen criticizing civilian leaders who refused to let military commanders do their job properly. Truman immediately relieved him of his command on 11 April 1951, replacing him with General Matthew RIDGWAY. MacArthur returned to the United States, where he delivered an address to a joint session of the U.S. Congress eight days later. At the end, he spoke these immortal words:

> I am closing my 52 years of military service. When I joined the Army, even before the turn of the century, it was the fulfillment of all of my boyish hopes and dreams. The world has turned over many times since I took the oath at West Point, and the hopes and dreams have all since vanished, but I still remember the refrain of one of the most popular barracks ballads of that day which proclaimed most proudly that old soldiers never die; they just fade away. And like the old soldier of that ballad, I now close my military career and just fade away, an old soldier who tried to do his duty as God gave him the light to see that duty.

MacArthur toured the nation, where he was met by enormous crowds cheering his every move. Although he had delivered the keynote address to the Republican Convention in Philadelphia in 1948 and was asked to do so again in Chicago in 1952, he was not popular enough to receive the party's presidential nod. He spent

his final years as chairman of the board of the Remington Rand Corporation, later the Sperry-Rand Corporation. Shortly before his death, he published his memoirs. As he lay dying, he was visited by President Lyndon Baines Johnson, whom he had personally warned against getting American forces bogged down in a land war in Vietnam.

Douglas MacArthur died in Washington, D.C., on 5 April 1964 at the age of 84. Historian Michael Schaller writes, "MacArthur left an ambiguous legacy. Admiration for his World War II victories, supervision of occupied Japan, and eloquent rhetoric on the themes of duty, honor, and country must be tempered by his performance during the Korean War. His public challenge of civilian authority and accusations against the Truman administration contributed to the appeal of Senator Joseph McCarthy's charges that Communist subversion undermined American security." Despite this, MacArthur remains one of the most important commanders of the 20th century. He ranks with Dwight D. EISENHOWER, Ulysses S. GRANT, and George WASHINGTON in his leadership and excellent grasp of strategy.

References: Manchester, William Raymond, *American Caesar* (Boston: Little, Brown, 1978); Nicolay, Helen, *MacArthur of Bataan* (New York: D. Appleton-Century Company, 1942); Windrow, Martin, and Francis K. Mason, "MacArthur, Douglas," in *The Wordsworth Dictionary of Military Biography* (Hertfordshire, U.K.: Wordsworth Editions Ltd., 1997), 174–176; Parkinson, Roger, "MacArthur, Douglas," in *The Encyclopedia of Modern War* (New York: Stein & Day, 1977), 103; Schaller, Michael, "MacArthur, Douglas," in *American National Biography*, 24 vols., edited by John A. Garraty and Mark C. Carnes (New York: Oxford University Press, 1999), 14:195–199.

Macbeth (d. 1057) *Scottish king*

Macbeth's exact date of birth is lost to history; he may have been a grandson of the Scottish king Kenneth II, who ruled from 971 to 995, although some sources note that his mother was a daughter of King Malcolm II of Scotland. His life before 1031 is unknown, but in that year he succeeded his father Findlaech as the mormær, or chief, of the province of Moray in northern Scotland. In order to take the throne of the Scots, Macbeth took his people into war against his cousin, King Duncan I.

He formed an alliance with another cousin, Thorfinn, the earl of Orkney, and together the two men defeated Duncan's forces near Elgin in Moray province on 14 August 1040. (In Shakespeare's play *Macbeth*, Duncan is killed in his own bed.)

Solidifying his hold on the Scottish throne, in 1045 Macbeth defeated an army apparently led (sources differ on the leader) by Crinan, the abbot of Dunkeld and father of the murdered Duncan, by Dunkeld near Tayside. A history of Scotland written in the early 19th century reports, "In that battle was slain Crinan, Abbot of Dunkeld, and many with him; namely nine times twenty heroes." A year later, Siward, the earl of Northumbria, invaded Scotland from England to bring Malcolm, a son of the murdered Duncan, to the throne, but he was repulsed by Macbeth at Lothian, where Siward had concentrated his forces. By 1049, Macbeth felt that his kingdom was secure, so much so that he was able to make a pilgrimage to Rome.

In 1054, rebels who opposed Macbeth tried again to overthrow him. This time, Siward was joined by rebels from Denmark, who invaded Scotland and laid siege to Macbeth's army at Dunsinane (27 July 1054). There the king lost a critical battle, and Malcolm, who was at the head of Siward's army, took control of southern Scotland. Macbeth retreated into Moray province, launching a series of raids against the rebels. This led to a crushing defeat by Siward and Malcolm on 15 August 1057 near Lumphanan in Aberdeenshire, Scotland, and Macbeth was killed in battle. The Scottish crown passed from him to his stepson Lulach, nicknamed "the Stupid," who held the throne for less than a year until he was killed on 17 March 1058, when Malcolm again invaded Scotland and took control of the monarchy. Macbeth's body was taken to the island of Iona in the Inner Hebrides, where all Scottish kings had been buried and where he was laid to rest, becoming the last Scottish king to be interred there.

Historian Michael Lynch writes of Macbeth: "Contrary to the image presented by Renaissance writers, there is little evidence that Macbeth was any more tyrannical than the run of early medieval kings and his claim to the kingship was probably as good as that of his predecessor, the young, rather than aged, Duncan. He may even have begun some of the transformation of the kingdom usually credited to Malcolm III."

References: Ellis, Peter Berresford, *MacBeth, High King of Scotland, 1040–57 A.D.* (London: F. Muller, 1980); Turner, John, *Macbeth* (Buckingham, U.K.: Open University Press, 1992); Aitchison, Nick, and Tony Robinson, *Macbeth, Man and Myth* (Stroud, U.K.: Sutton, 2000); Stewart, R. J., *Macbeth: Scotland's Warrior King* (Poole, Dorset, U.K.: Firebird Books, 1988); "Macbeth," in *Collins Encyclopedia of Scotland*, edited by John Keay and Julia Keay (New York: HarperCollins, 1994), 644; "Macbeth," in *The Oxford Companion to Scottish History*, edited by Michael Lynch (Oxford, U.K.: Oxford University Press, 2001), 402.

MacMahon, Marie-Edmé-Patrice-Maurice de, duc de Magenta (1808–1893) *French general*

Marie-Edmé-Patrice-Maurice de MacMahon was born in the village of Sully, in the area of Sâone-et-Loire, France, on 13 July 1808; his family had come from Ireland around 1690 to avoid persecution. After attending the military academy of St. Cyr, MacMahon entered the French army in 1827. He served under French marshal Louis-Auguste Bourmont, comte de Ghaisnes de Bourmont, in the French invasion of Algeria in 1830, seeing action in several battles and serving as the aide-de-camp under a General Achard. In 1832, he was recalled to France and served in the French invasion of Antwerp. He then returned to northern Africa and eventually spent a period of 20 years in Algeria (1834–54), during which he fought a series of engagements with the Bedouin tribes and their leader, Abd-el-Kader, the emir of Mascare. MacMahon earned great praise for his role in the French victory at Constantine (1837), and by 1843 he had risen to the rank of colonel of infantry and appointment as commander of the French Foreign Legion.

In 1854, the Crimean War broke out between England, France, and Russia, and MacMahon was sent to the Crimean peninsula as the commander of an infantry division under General François Canrobert. One of the first major engagements was the French siege of the city of Sebastopol. Several French attacks on the Russian defenses failed, and Canrobert was replaced by General Aimable Pélissier. When the siege stretched into 1855, new strategies were considered for breaking the Russian hold on Sebastopol. MacMahon was ordered to assault the Malakoff works, one of the two strongholds in the city's defense; the other was the Redan works, to be attacked by British forces. MacMahon and his forces launched the so-called battle of Malakoff on 8 September 1855, overwhelming Sebastopol's Russian defenders.

The editors of *The Wordsworth Dictionary of Military Biography* write: "The attack of 8 September was the one perfectly-planned and executed operation by the Allies in the Crimea. With meticulous attention to detail the French columns assaulted the Russian defenses, the critical attack being carried out successfully by the division commanded by MacMahon. After eight hours' fighting the Malakoff was in French hands and, after the failure of the British to take the Redan, MacMahon turned his fire on the Russians there and drove them out also. The following day the Allies occupied Sebastopol."

The fall of Sebastopol led to the quick collapse of the Russians and an eventual end to the war. For his services in the Crimea, MacMahon was offered the post of head of the French army, but he declined, desiring instead to return to Algeria.

In 1859, MacMahon's talents were soon called on again when the newly created king of Italy, Victor Emmanuel II, tried to evict the French and Austrians who had long occupied Northwest and Northeast Italy, respectively. Victor Emmanuel made a secret deal with the French to send forces into Italy to assist in fighting the Austrians. MacMahon's most important victory was at Magenta (4 June 1859) against an Austrian force commanded by the Austrian general Count Franz von Gyulai. Historian George Bruce writes of this battle: "MacMahon crossed the Ticino River, attacked the Austrian position and after hard fighting drove them out of Magenta and totally defeated them with a loss of about 6,000 killed and wounded. The French lost 4,400." In response to this loss, the Austrians advanced along the Mincio River to take on MacMahon's forces, but he evaded them and in the end was able to avoid another major battle. For his brilliant victory at Magenta, MacMahon was made a marshal of France by Emperor Napoleon III, and he was given the title of the duc de Magenta (duke of Magenta).

On 1 September 1864, MacMahon was appointed governor-general of Algeria, a post he held until 1870. In the latter year, he was recalled to France when the Prussians attacked and invaded there. MacMahon was named as the commander of the Alsace division of the French army. However, where he had been brilliant against the Austrians, he was less successful against the Prussians. At Wissembourg (4 August 1870), his front-line advance forces were quickly dispatched by the Prussians, and at Wörth (also called Reischoffen, 6 August 1870) on the Sauer River, he was again beaten and forced to fall back

to the city of Saverne, and then to Toul. Seeing the Prussian advance as a direct threat to Paris, Emperor Napoleon III named MacMahon as supreme commander of all French forces, assembling at Châlons-sur-Marne.

Although he had a force of some 120,000 men, MacMahon was opposed to an operation against the Prussians because of a lack of organization in the French military. Nonetheless, he began to march his troops northeast to Metz to relieve the French Army of the Rhine, trapped there under heavy Prussian bombardment. However, the Prussians cut him off near the Meuse River, where a series of engagements (29–31 August 1870) forced him to fall back to the ancient fortress at Sedan. On 1 September 1870, French forces took on some 200,000 Prussians under General Helmuth von Moltke, but MacMahon was seriously wounded during the fighting, leaving his army without proper guidance. The Prussians hit the French middle with bombardment and then launched a main attack. Within hours, Napoleon III, on the battlefield, was informed that the chances for victory were hopeless, and he surrendered himself and his forces. In one of the worst moments in the history of France, more than 80,000 French soldiers were taken as prisoners of war; more than 3,000 lay dead on the battlefield, with another 15,000 wounded. Although the Prussians lost nearly 10,000 killed and wounded, their loss was less grievous because their army was so much larger. The victorious Prussians marched on Paris, where, just three days after the French defeat at Sedan, a riot overthrew the government of Napoleon III.

In 1871, there was a rising of the revolutionary Commune of Paris after the Prussians left; MacMahon was called upon by the new government to put it down. He was widely praised for his firm suppression of the insurrection, and his services to the nation were rewarded two years later when he was elected by the French National Assembly as president of France, succeeding Adolphe Thiers. Although he had been a monarchist and had resolved to bring back a French king, he nonetheless decided against any measures that would force the issue, and thus a monarchy was not reinstated. A new constitution was promulgated in 1875, and with the resignation of Premier Jules Simon in May 1877 and the election of several nonmonarchist assemblies, MacMahon was forced to drop the matter completely, leaving him a weakened president. He resigned in January 1879, before the end of his term, when he decided not to support a law that outlawed the hiring of those with monarchist leanings; he was succeeded by Jules Grévy.

MacMahon then retired, having never been a politician, as he noted in his memoirs. "I have remained a soldier," he wrote, "and I can conscientiously say that I have not only served one government after another loyally, but, when they fell, have regretted all of them with the single exception of my own." He died at his home in Montcresson, Loiret, on 16 October 1893, and, following a funeral with full military honors, he was laid to rest in the crypt of the Invalides in Paris, where NAPOLEON BONAPARTE had been interred some 80 years before.

References: "M'Mahon, General of France," in *Men of the Time. Biographical Sketches of Eminent Living Characters. Also Biographical Sketches of Celebrated Women of the Time* (London: David Bogue, 1856), 520–522; Windrow, Martin, and Francis K. Mason, "MacMahon, Marie Edmé Patrice Maurice de, Duc de Magenta," in *The Wordsworth Dictionary of Military Biography* (Hertfordshire, U.K.: Wordsworth Editions Ltd., 1997), 177–179; Bruce, George, "Magenta," in *Collins Dictionary of Wars* (Glasgow, Scotland: HarperCollins Publishers, 1995), 149.

Makharoff, Stepan Osipovich
(Stepan Makharov, Stepan Makarov)
(1848/49–1904) *Russian admiral*
Born in the village of Nikolaev in the Ukraine on 27 December 1848 O.S. (or 8 January 1849 [N.S.]), Stepan Makharoff was the son of Osip Makharoff, an officer in the czarist navy. In 1858, he was transferred to the Far East, and his wife and son traveled with him. That same year, only nine years old, Stepan Makharoff was placed in the National Maritime Academy located at Nikolaevsk-na-Amure, where he learned the skills to enter the Russian merchant marine corps. Coming to the attention of some of the commanders in the school, he joined the Russian navy in 1864 and rose rapidly through a series of promotions.

Makharoff saw his first action in the Russo-Turkish War of 1877–78, when he commanded the gunboat *Grand Duke Constantine* in a succession of hit-and-run torpedo-boat attacks on ironclads in several Turkish ports, including Sukhum Kalé. Following the end of the conflict, he was promoted to the rank of captain

and named as an aide-de-camp to Czar Alexander III. In 1880, working under the famed Russian general Mikhail Dmitreyevich Skobelev, Makharoff saw action in Russian Turkestan (now the independent nation of Turkmenistan) and took part in Skobelev's march to the fortress of Geok-Tepe, whose surrender in December 1880 completed the Russian conquest of the region. Another Russian officer who participated in Skobelev's mission was Alexei KUROPATKIN, who, like Makharoff, would figure largely in Russian military history.

In 1881, fresh out of Turkestan, Makharoff was assigned as the commander of the cruiser *Taman,* which protected the Russian legation in the city of Constantinople (now Istanbul, Turkey). His studies of the area included one of the military and naval defenses of the Bosporus Strait. From 1882 to 1886, he served on the staff of Admiral Andrey Popov in the Baltic, eventually traveling around the globe on the ship *Vitiaz* from 1886 to 1889. This voyage led to a book, *The Vitiaz and the Pacific Ocean* (1894), one of 50 books Makharoff wrote. A paper he had written in 1881 on water currents in the Black Sea and Mediterranean earned him a reputation as "the father of Russian oceanography." As an inventor, he conceived an armor-piercing tip for shells, called Makharoff tips. In 1890, he was promoted to admiral, the youngest man in Russian history to be named to that rank. He was subsequently named as commander of the Mediterranean Squadron in 1894, as chief of fleet training in 1895, and as commander of the Baltic Fleet in 1896.

At the end of the 19th century, one of the key areas of Russian interest was the peninsula of Korea. The power struggle between Russia, a longtime military power in the northern Pacific, and Japan centered on control of Korea, which became the focus of world attention by 1904. The previous year, historian Alexander Hume Ford had written that "Korea is the bone of contention over which Russia and Japan are most likely to come to blows. It is equally essential to either country as a guarantee of future peace." Makharoff, as commander of the port of Kronshtadt in the Baltic since 1899, tried to warn his leadership of the need to reinforce the nearby Russian naval port of Port Arthur, but his cries went unheeded.

On the night of 8 February 1904 (or 26 January 1904 [O.S.]), Japanese forces attacked the Russians at Port Arthur, and Makharoff called on St. Petersburg to send torpedo boats via the Trans-Siberian railway as quickly as possible. The Russian government blundered when, instead of supplementing Makharoff's forces, it recalled a squadron of battleships commanded by Admiral A. A. Virenius. On 9 February 1904, Makharoff was named as commander of the Pacific Squadron, replacing Admiral Oskar V. Stark, and he traveled eastward across Asia by rail. Historian Patrick Rollins writes: "There had been no strategic or tactical planning for a war with Japan, but that was a relatively unimportant oversight since the dispirited officers and crews were untrained and unable to navigate, maneuver, or shoot as a unit. Makharoff had only days to overcome years of neglect, and he had no possibility of overcoming the numerical and qualitative superiority of the Japanese navy. Nevertheless, he aggressively addressed the elements he could affect—training and morale—with visible success."

Unfortunately, Makharoff's time was short. Two months after being named as Pacific commander, his flagship, the battleship *Petropavlosk,* hit a mine, newly laid by Japanese forces, on 13 April (or 31 March [O.S.]) and sank in less than two minutes. Approximately 800 sailors went down to their deaths, including Makharoff; only his overcoat was recovered. Mourned in his homeland, his death was quickly forgotten in the horrific military disaster that soon befell the Russians in the Russo-Japanese War. In 1913, a statue of Makharoff was raised at Kronshtadt. Although he only served in the czarist navy, ships were named in his honor in both the czarist and Soviet navies. In 1948, a school for the navigation of the Arctic was founded in Leningrad and named in his honor.

References: Rollins, Patrick J., "Makarov, Stepan Osipovich," in *The Modern Encyclopedia of Russian and Soviet History,* 55 vols., edited by Joseph L. Wieczynski (Gulf Breeze, Florida: Academic International Press, 1976–93), 21:11–14; Ford, Alexander Hume, "The Russification of Manchuria," *The Era Magazine* 12, no. 3 (September 1903): 205; Maxwell, William, *From the Yalu to Port Arthur: A Personal Record* (London: Hutchinson & Company, 1906); Cowen, Thomas, *The Russo-Japanese War from the Outbreak of Hostilities to the Battle of Liaoyang* (London: E. Arnold, 1904).

Manchester, second earl of *See* MONTAGU, EDWARD, SECOND EARL OF MANCHESTER.

Marion, Francis (1732–1795) *American military leader*
Francis Marion was born in Winyaw, near Georgetown, South Carolina, in 1732. A descendant of Huguenots who had been driven out of France and arrived in South Carolina in 1690, he was the youngest of six children of Gabriel and Esther Cordes Marion. A short biography by the 19th-century historian Benson J. Lossing states: "There is scarcely a plantation within thirty miles of the banks of the Congaree and Santee, from Columbia to the sea, that has not some local tradition of the presence of Marion, the great partisan leader in South Carolina during the Revolution." Frail and puny in his childhood, Marion grew strong and hardy during adolescence and developed a passion for the sea. At 16, he embarked on a small vessel sailing to the West Indies, saw the ship wrecked, and spent a week in an open boat before being rescued. He spent the next 11 years assisting his father on the family's small plantation, but upon Gabriel Marion's death in 1759, Francis moved to a plantation at Pond Bluff, near Eutaw, South Carolina.

While some sources state Marion took part in Colonel Montgomery's expedition to the Indian country in 1760, it now seems more likely that he first saw military service the following year when he served as a lieutenant under Colonel Thomas Middleton in his 1761 campaign against the Cherokee. Marion distinguished himself by leading the assault on the main Indian position at Etchoee in mid-June, which was followed by the destruction of 14 Indian villages.

In 1775, Marion was a delegate to the Provincial Congress of South Carolina, which agreed to raise two regiments for the Revolutionary cause. He was commissioned as a captain in the 2nd South Carolina Regiment on 21 June 1775 and took part in the capture of Fort Johnson in Charleston harbor on 14 September. Early in 1776, Marion was promoted to major and played an important part in the training and organization of his regiment. On 28 June 1776, he saw action in the successful defense of Charleston against a British sea-borne attack, and three months later he was promoted to lieutenant colonel and given command of Fort Moultrie on Sullivan's Island.

In September 1779, Marion took part in the disastrous campaign to take Savannah under the command of General Benjamin LINCOLN, who launched an attack in conjunction with the French admiral Comte d'Estaing. The Americans were repulsed with heavy losses (9 October 1779), and Lincoln withdrew to reinforce Charleston, leaving Marion in temporary command of the defeated Revolutionary force. Marion was then appointed to take charge of a training camp at Bacon's Bridge on the Ashley river. It is believed that during this time (April 1780), he was dining with friends in Charleston when the host, determined that his guests should enjoy themselves, locked the door of the dining room, declaring it would not be opened until the wine ran out. Marion was abstemious in his habits but did not wish to cause embarrassment, so he decided to escape though a window. He did so but fell and broke his ankle in the process, and since the British were about to besiege the city, he was evacuated to his home in Eutaw. It was a fortunate escape since Charleston fell to the British on 12 May 1780.

As soon as he was fit to mount a horse, probably in June or July 1780, Marion rode north to meet General Horatio GATES to offer his services. For some reason, Gates refused his cooperation, and Marion returned from North Carolina and began to form a small force, later to be known as "Marion's brigade." On 16 August 1780, Gates was defeated at Camden, and Colonel Thomas Sumter was defeated at Fishing Creek two days later. Marion was now leading the only Revolutionary force in South Carolina. Promoted to the rank of brigadier general by Governor John Rutledge, he began the campaign of harassment and raiding that was to make his name. With a small, highly mobile force of horsemen, he lived off the country, launching attacks on British camps and outposts, cutting their supply lines, and intercepting their messengers. Such raids were followed by rapid withdrawal into the forests and swamps of the area, a tactic that earned Marion the nickname "the Swamp Fox."

On 20 August 1780, at Nelson's Ferry, Marion routed a force of British regulars and released 150 American prisoners taken at Camden. On 4 September 1780, he defeated a Loyalist force at Tarcote and put another to flight at Black Mingo river on 27 September. In October 1780, before the battle of Kings Mountain, his horsemen prevented reinforcements reaching the British, a factor that led to the American victory. In December 1780, Marion made an unsuccessful attempt to take Georgetown and repeated the attempt with Colonel Henry Lee on 12 January 1781. This also failed, though Marion had the consolation of capturing the British commandant and several of his officers.

In April 1781, on the orders of General Nathanael GREENE, Marion and Lee attacked Fort Watson, which fell to them on 23 April, forcing Lord Rawdon to withdraw from Camden to Monk's Corner. Marion then besieged Fort Motte, which fell on 12 May 1781, and launched his third, and this time successful, attempt to take Georgetown. On 17 July 1781, Marion and Sumter, another successful Revolutionary partisan leader known as "the Gamecock," fought an indecisive engagement with Lord Rawdon at Quimby Bridge, and a few weeks later, Marion took part in the major battle of the Eutaw campaign. His remarkable contribution to this campaign had begun on 31 August, when he had led his cavalry on a journey of 200 miles across country, right around the British force, and then destroyed their cavalry wing in a skillfully planned battle at Parker's Ferry. At the Battle of Eutaw Springs (8 September 1781), which ended the campaign, Marion commanded the right wing of the American forces and joined Henry Lee in taking many prisoners after their victory. It was his last major engagement.

In June 1782, Marion put down a small Loyalist insurrection but, elected state senator that year, he spent much of it in the South Carolina state senate at Jacksonborough. In 1784, he married Mary Videau, and as a reward for his services during the war, he was made commandant of Fort Johnson. He was reelected to the state senate until 1790, in which year he helped draw up the state constitution and then retired. He died on 26 or 27 February 1795.

Marion's remarkable success as a partisan leader has been attributed to the loyalty he inspired in his soldiers and the tight control he exercised over them. While guerrilla warfare all too often led to indiscipline and outright theft of supplies of food from farms and villages, Marion's insistence on paying for everything his men needed, or issuing promissory notes to be redeemed later, brought him much popularity and support across South Carolina. Making full use of his knowledge of the terrain, his ability to move his troops rapidly and to elude pursuit from the British troops meant his small force exercised an influence far out of proportion to its size. The British general Banastre Tarleton summed up Marion's skill in his exasperated comment on Sumter and Marion: "Come, boys, let us go back and find the game-cock; as for this damn swamp-fox, the devil himself could not catch him."

References: Weems, Mason Locke, *The Life of Gen. Francis Marion: A Celebrated Partisan Officer in the Revolution War against the British and Tories in South Carolina and Georgia* (Philadelphia: J. Allen, 1834); Lossing, Benson John, *Lives of Celebrated Americans: Comprising Biographies of Three Hundred and Forty Eminent Persons* (Hartford, Conn.: Thomas Belknap, 1869), 184–186; Bass, Robert D., *Swamp Fox: The Life and Campaigns of General Francis Marion* (New York: Holt, 1969).

Marlborough, first duke of *See* CHURCHILL, JOHN, FIRST DUKE OF MARLBOROUGH.

Martel, Charles *See* CHARLES MARTEL.

Masséna, André, duc de Rivoli (Andrea Massena, prince d'Essling) (1758–1817)
French general

André Masséna was born as Andrea Masséna in the village of Leven, near what is now Nice, France (then part of the kingdom of Sardinia), on 6 May 1758. His father was Guilio-Cesare Masséna, whose family had been merchants and farmers in the Nice region for many years. At the age of 17, Masséna entered the Sardinian army and served for a period of 14 years before retiring and settling in Nice, where he married and raised a family.

In 1791, Masséna volunteered in the French revolutionary cause and raised a battalion of volunteers; he was named general of brigade the following year. When NAPOLEON BONAPARTE was sent to fight in Italy, Masséna joined him, and in the two-year campaign (1794–96), he commanded the right wing of the French army. Masséna's victories at Bassano (8 September 1796), in which he defeated the Austrian commander Marshal von Wurmser, as well as his victory at Rivoli (14 January 1797) earned him a reputation as a military strategist. In 1799, he defeated Austrian and Russian armies in Switzerland, an action that saved France from invasion by the allies of the so-called Second Coalition. In addition, Masséna's desperate five-month defense of Genoa against the Austrians enabled Napoleon to win his great victory at Marengo (14 June 1800).

In 1804, as one of Napoleon's most trusted commanders and advisers, Masséna was named as a marshal of the French Empire. The following year, he was given command of all French toops in Italy, and, following the signing of the Peace of Pressburg (26 December 1805) between France and Austria, he took possession of the kingdom of Naples. Starting in 1807, he again ably assisted Napoleon in his conquests across Europe, seeing action in Poland, winning a key victory at Esslingen (also known as Aspern, 21–22 May 1809), when Marshal Jean LANNES, another of Napoleon's key military commanders, was killed in battle. For saving the French from being destroyed, Napoleon titled Masséna as the prince d'Essling, having already named him the duc (duke) de Rivoli in 1808.

Masséna's first failure came during the Peninsular War (1808–14), when Napoleon sent him to Portugal to attack the British commander Arthur Wellesley, the Duke of WELLINGTON. Hampered by Spanish guerrillas who constantly attacked his lines of communication, Masséna forced Wellington back to Torres Vedras, outside Lisbon, but spent a fruitless five months there attempting to break through impregnable British defenses. Because of a lack of supplies and reinforcements, he failed to stop Wellington's advance at Bussaco (27 September 1810) and lost at Fuentes d'Onoro (5 May 1811). Historians have faulted Masséna for this defeat, claiming that he did not work effectively with the other French commanders such as Marshal Michel NEY and Marshal Jean-Andoche JUNOT. Despite this, Wellington wrote at the time that it was Masséna, more than any other French commander, whom he feared and respected on the field of battle.

With Napoleon's fall from power in 1814, Masséna accepted the accession of King Louis XVIII, who made him a French peer. However, when Napoleon escaped from Elba and landed in France in a bid for power, Masséna did not oppose him but refused to fight for him and took no part, either militarily or politically, in Napoleon's "One Hundred Days," which ended at Waterloo (18 June 1815). Masséna died in Paris on 4 April 1817, a month before his 59th birthday. His *Memoires* were published in seven volumes from 1848 to 1850.

The editors of the *The Wordsworth Dictionary of Military Biography* sum up Masséna's record:

> In modern history it is rare to find a military leader whose record commands respect despite his enthusiastic indulgence in both financial greed

and lechery. André Masséna somehow managed to pursue a lifelong and monumental enthusiasm for gold and women, while at the same time achieving an enviable professional reputation. He regarded men and events from the standpoint of a worldly cynicism which, it has been said, was second only to that of Talleyrand among his contemporaries. This merciless realism stood him in good stead on many battlefields. He was capable of the bold stroke, and was tenacious and cool in defense, but the rash grabs at glory of a Murat or a Ney were foreign to him. In the end, he was ruined—professionally—by Wellington, but even this was not unforeseen. The Duke paid him a pretty compliment when they met in Restoration Paris, to the effect that Masséna had made him lie awake at nights—a practice which the Duke made a point of avoiding.

References: Marshall-Cornwall, James, *Marshal Massena* (London: Oxford University Press, 1965); Horward, Donald D., *The Battle of Bussaco: Masséna vs. Wellington* (Tallahassee: Florida State University Press, 1965); Horward, Donald D., *Napoleon and Iberia: The Twin Sieges, Ciudad Rodrigo and Almeida, 1810* (Gainesville: University Presses of Florida, 1984); Windrow, Martin, and Fancis K. Mason, "Masséna, André, Duc de Rivoli, Prince d'Essling," in *The Wordsworth Dictionary of Military Biography* (Hertfordshire, U.K.: Wordsworth Editions Ltd., 1997), 189–191.

Maurice, prince of Orange and count of Nassau (Maurits) (1567–1625) *Dutch general and statesman*

Maurice (Maurits in Dutch) was born at the castle of Dillenburg on 13 November 1567, the second son of William the Silent, prince of the Netherlands, and his second wife, Anna of Saxony. With his father's assassination in 1584 by a French Catholic fanatic, and with his elder brother held hostage in Spain, Maurice became the heir apparent to the title. At this time, he was only 17 and a student at the University of Leiden. Because of his new role, he was removed from school and named as the stadtholder (chief executive) of Holland. The independent states that later became the Netherlands, including Gelderland, Utrecht, and Zeeland, also named Maurice as their stadtholder. These states were all fighting Spain

to keep their independence, and Maurice received the assistance of Robert, earl of Leicester, the powerful English nobleman who had been fighting against Spanish power in the Netherlands.

In 1587, Leicester was recalled to England and Maurice was named as captain-general of the Dutch army. His role was now the organization of Dutch resistance to Spanish rule, and he formed a military triumvirate with his cousin, Willem Lodewijk (William Louis in English), a stadtholder from Friesland, and the Dutch politician Johan van Oldenbarnevelt. Starting in 1590, under Maurice's command, a series of attacks were made against the Spanish and their garrisons were besieged, particularly at Breda (1590), where Maurice and his forces were victorious. More victories followed: at Steenwijk (1592), Geertruidenberg (1593), Turnhout (1597), and Nieuwpoort (1600). Turnhout was the key battle, as a 1597 work reported:

> The Randeuow of the States armie, which met for the defeating of the enemy, was Gertrudenberge a towne in Holland, bordering on [the] Brabant, where at the day appointed, being the twelfth of this moneth, there met Count Morris [Maurice], Counts Hollock and Solms, Sir Robert Sidney, & Sir Frances Vere, chief men beith their commanders, and Mouray with a regiment of Scottes, Brederode and Eregmere with some troupes out of the Garrisones: and besides some companies of the Zealand regiment. . . . But newes was brought him that Sir Robert Sidney and Sir Frances Vere, with maintaining the skirmish, were very far engaged. . . . About an houre after, order came from his Excellencie that the English which staid at Turnehaut should come forward, which we did with al the hast[e] we could. After two or three houres retyring and skirmishing, the enemy entered a faire health, some three English miles from Turnehaut towards Herentals, where they marched in order of battell. . . .

A pamphlet written in 1600, *[The] Battaile Fought Betweene Count Maurice of Nassau, and Albertus Arch-Duke of Austria*, detailed the battle of Flanders:

> The second daie of the siege being Saterdaie the one and twentieth of Iune, intll came that the enemie was come to Oudenborough, which his

excellency supposed to be John de Riuas with the forces of Flaunders: but shortly after advertisement came, that the Archduke was there in person and had taken in Oudenborough by competition, whereupon his excellencie bethought himself, howe he might best hinder his nearer approach: and because he feared least in the pursuite, the enemie might take in the [unknown word] Albertus, and to cut off the passage betweene Newport and Ostend, he sent the Regiment of the Scots on the Sundaie morning, and the Regiment of the Almains under the command of Count Ernesius to hinder the passage by a bridge, which was made by us in a bound land betweene Oudenborough and the [unknown word] Albertus, and so he should put them to march three daies about, before they came on to him, and then also it was in his choice, either to fight or leave them, and returne to Ostend.

But the enemie had passed the Bridge before the Scots could come to make good the place: and so they all fell under the execution of the vanguard of the enemie, being all Spaniards, and the choicest men of the Armie: and were chased to the wals of Ostend.

Maurice was highly regarded for even more than his military prowess. An English writer later described him as being "of great forwardness, good presence and courage, flaxen haired, endued with a singular wit."

Although Maurice fought the Spanish and forced them to keep large armies in the Netherlands, his ally Johan van Oldenbarnevelt, who controlled the nation-state's domestic and foreign affairs, decided to make peace with the Spanish. In 1609, Oldenbarnevelt signed a treaty with them that recognized the Netherlands and called for a 12-year truce, which lasted from 1609 to 1621. A civil war then ensued between these two former allies; van Oldenbarnevelt was arrested in 1618, put on trial for treason, and beheaded the following year. In 1621, war with Spain broke out again, but old age and internal disputes and struggles had taken a toll on Maurice. In 1625, Breda was lost to the Spanish, led by a vigorous new commander, Ambrosio Spinola, who reimposed Spanish control over much of the country.

By that time, Maurice had contracted a liver ailment, and on 23 April 1625 he died of the disease; he was mourned throughout his homeland. In summing up

his legacy, the authors of *The Wordsworth Dictionary of Military Biography* write: "The father of the independent Netherlands, the moving spirit behind the weary struggle for freedom, and the greatest martyr for the cause was William the Silent, Prince of Orange and Count of Nassau. The great military figure of the Netherlands' turbulent childhood was, however, his son Maurice of Nassau. William pointed the way, but it was Maurice who achieved the victories which made success possible. He was one of the ablest generals of his century, and had considerable importance on a level far beyond the Dutch struggle for independence."

References: *The Triumphs of Nassau: or, A description and representation of all the victories both by land and sea, granted by God to the noble, high, and mightie lords, the Estates generall of the united Netherland Provinces Under the conduct and command of his excellencie, Prince Maurice of Nassau,* translated by W. Shute (London: Printed by Adam Islip, 1613); *A True Discourse of the Overthrowe given to the common enemy at Turnhaut, the 14 of January last 1597 by Count Moris of Nassau and the states, assisted with the Englishe forces . . .* (London[?]: Printed by Peter Short, 1597); *The Battaile Fought Betweene Count Maurice of Nassau, and Albertus Arch-Duke of Austria, nere Newport in Flaunders, the xxij of June 1600 . . .* (London: Printed for Andrew Wise, 1600); *An Exact and True Relation in Relieving the Resolute Garrison of Lyme in Dorsetshire, by the Right Honourable, Robert Earle of Warwicke, Lord High Admirall of England . . .* (London: Printed for Mathew Walbanke, 1644); *True Intelligence, and Joyfull Newes from Ludlow, Declaring a Battell fought by his Excellency the Earle of Essex, against Prince Robert, Prince Maurice . . .* (London: Printed for Th. Rider, 1642); Windrow, Martin, and Francis K. Mason, "Maurice, Prince of Orange and Court of Nassau," in *The Wordsworth Dictionary of Military Biography* (Herfordshire, U.K.: Wordsworth, 1997), 191–192.

McClellan, George Brinton (1826–1885)
American general
The son of Dr. George McClellan and Elizabeth Brinton McClellan, George B. McClellan was born in Philadelphia, Pennsylvania, on 3 December 1826. Because of his father's wealth and social standing, he attended the finest prep school in the city and then the University of Pennsylvania (1840–42), but he left when he was given

an appointment to the United States Military Academy at West Point, New York. In 1846, he graduated second in his class and was assigned to an engineering unit that saw some action during the Mexican-American war (1846–48). Awarded three commendations for distinguished service, McClellan was promoted to the rank of captain after the war and returned to West Point, where he served as a professor of military engineering. Before leaving that post in 1851, he wrote a manual on French methods of bayonet training, which the Army adopted in 1852.

McClellan was posted to a various stations around the United States, but in 1855 he was sent to Europe to study military organization and equipment. He witnessed the siege of Sebastopol (the Crimean War), and on his return to the United States he wrote *The Armies of Europe*. He also designed a new saddle, known as "the McClellan," which was used for more than 50 years. In 1857, he retired from the military as a captain and became the chief engineer, and later vice president, of the Illinois Central Railroad before becoming president of the Ohio and Mississippi Railroad in 1860.

With the outbreak of the American Civil War in early 1861, McClellan was recalled to service in the U.S. Army and made major general of the Ohio state volunteers. Just one month later, he was given command of the Department of Ohio, which embraced the states of Ohio, Indiana, and Illinois, later expanded to Virginia and parts of Pennsylvania. Moving his troops east, McClellan secured what is now the state of West Virginia for the Union through a victory against Confederate forces at Rich Mountain, West Virginia (11 July 1861). This major battle came 10 days before the Union defeat at First Bull Run, which many historians consider the first major battle of the war. Because of his quick victory at Rich Mountain, McClellan was summoned to Washington, D.C., and replaced Irvin McDowell as commander of the Union's Army of the Potomac, which was confused from the defeat at First Bull Run. He quickly reorganized the units in his command and restored their morale through training and good administration. Although his men came to think of McClellan as a father figure—he was known to his troops as "The Young Napoleon"—in reality he was a poor general, hesitant of committing his troops and constantly failing to follow up successes on the battlefield.

Nonetheless, when General Winfield SCOTT, an old officer who had fought in the War of 1812, retired on 1 November 1861 following the Union defeat at

Ball's Bluff, McClellan was named as his replacement as commander in chief. McClellan, age 34, immediately decided to change the way Scott had fought the war and shift to a different strategy, a move at odds with the wishes of President Abraham Lincoln, who wanted decisive major engagements against the Confederates to quickly defeat them and end the war. Lincoln was continually frustrated with his general's cautious approach to fighting. Although McClellan won victories against the Confederates at Williamsburg (5 May 1862) and Hanover Court House (27 May 1862), he did not follow these up with offensives. Historian Richard Holmes explains: "His amphibious Jamestown peninsular campaign (March–September 1862), brilliant in conception and potentially war-ending both in terms of the numbers under his command and their location so close to the Confederate capital, was undone by a caution bordering on paralysis. Extending a flank to reach out to a secondary Union advance from the north under McDowell, he was checked at Seven Pines [31 May–1 June 1862], sat still for three weeks, and was then driven back to the water's edge by Lee during the Seven Days' Battles [25 June–1 July 1862], showing a skill in retreat conspicuously absent from his hesitant advance to contact." When General John Pope moved south to preserve the small Union gains, he was easily defeated at Second Bull Run (29–30 August 1862)—all because of McClellan's refusal to advance his troops properly. With Robert E. LEE's invasion of Maryland, McClellan moved from Washington, D.C., to attack the Southerners, meeting at Antietam (17 September 1862), another Union victory. However, when Lee's force retreated over the Potomac, instead of following them and delivering a staggering blow against a fleeing army, McClellan let them slip away, unmolested, as he waited for additional supplies from his rear. Finally, seeing that McClellan would never defeat Lee's army, Lincoln replaced him as general in chief with General Ambrose Burnside and ordered him to Trenton, New Jersey. McClellan's military career was over.

In 1864, the Democrats, realizing that the war's growing number of casualties had made Lincoln unpopular, approached McClellan to be their candidate for president. Although until that time he had been apolitical, he accepted their nomination, with Representative George H. Pendleton (later author of the Pendleton Civil Service Act) as his running mate. For a time, it appeared that McClellan would be victorious, as Northern voters, the only ones allowed to participate in the election, were angered by Union defeats in battle after battle and desired an end of the war. However, a series of battlefield victories, culminating in General William Tecumseh SHERMAN's march into Georgia, swung the country back to Lincoln, and on election day McClellan was defeated by more than 400,000 votes out of some 4 million cast, receiving only 21 electoral votes to Lincoln's 212. After the election, he formally resigned from the army and went abroad, staying overseas until 1868.

Upon his return to the United States, McClellan was named as engineer in charge of the construction of the Stevens floating battery, an innovative warship of the future that was scrapped in 1869 due to lack of funds. In 1870, he was named as chief engineer of the Department of Docks for the City of New York, where he served for two years, afterward serving as the president of the Atlantic and Great Western Railroad. In 1877, as a Democrat, he was elected governor of New Jersey, serving a single three-year term (1878–81) and retiring at the end of this service. He died of heart failure in Orange, New Jersey, on 29 October 1885. George McClellan is known to historians as a man who had great potential, but whose refusal to take chances or sieze opportunities on the battlefield led to his failure.

References: Michie, Peter Smith, *General McClellan* (New York: D. Appleton & Company, 1901); Macartney, Clarence Edward Noble, *Little Mac: The Life of General George B. McClellan* (Philadelphia: Dorrance and Company, 1940); Parkinson, Roger, "McClellan, George Brinton," in *The Encyclopedia of Modern War* (New York: Stein & Day, 1977), 103; Barnard, John Gross, *The Peninsular Campaign and its Antecedents, as Developed by the Report of Maj.-Gen. Geo. B. McClellan, and other Published Documents* (New York: D. Van Nostrand, 1864); Ketchum, Hiram, *General McClellan's Peninsula Campaign: Review of the Report of the Committee on the Conduct of the War Relative to the Peninsula Campaign* (New York, 1864).

Mehmet II (Mehmed II, Kayser-i Rum) (1432–1481) *Ottoman sultan*

The son of Sultan Murad II and a slave girl, Mehmet (also Mehmed) was born in the city of Adrianople (now Edirne) on 30 March 1432. When he was 12, his father abdicated in his favor, but Mehmet was inexperienced, and after only two years Murad took back control until his death, when his son was 19. Although the Ottoman Empire had long since expanded into southeastern Eu-

rope, the vast city of Byzantium, the last bastion of the Eastern Roman Empire, was still unconquered. Nicknamed "Fatih" (the conqueror) by his people, Mehmet made his first objective the capture of Byzantium (formerly called Constantinople and now modern Istanbul) in the name of his empire. The city, which lay on the narrow strait that connected Europe to Asia and had been a citadel for the 2,000-year-old Roman Empire, at last seemed ripe for the picking.

Mehmet marched on Byzantium with upward of 250,000 men. As he moved his army into position on the Bosporus, the Byzantine emperor, Constantine Palaeologus, ordered the gates of the city closed on 21 June 1452. Constantine at best had approximately 7,000–8,000 men defending the city, and Mehmet ordered a massive bombardment. The siege itself began on 6 April 1453 and lasted just a few weeks, until 29 May. A work from 1607, called *The Turkes Secretorie,* features a series of letters between Mehmet and other leaders concerning his battles to take over southern Europe. Regarding the battle for Byzantium, the introduction states:

> The first and fearefullest feate of warre which he did, was the winning of Bizantium the most renowned and Famous Citie of Constantine the Great, which is acknowledged of all, to have beene the glory and beauty of all Christendome. There is no man living . . . that is able to fit with words, and due compassion to expresse so greevous and so great calamities. For then the great and mighty Empire of Greece that was wont to be the wall and bulwark of the Romane Empire, in lesse than two moneths siege was dissolved, and utterly subverted. The Emperour Constantinus Paleologus, a Prince endued [endowed] with all commendable parts of piety, and vertue, seeing his estate was desperate, and thinking to escape with his people at a backe gate, was miserably smothered and killed in the throng: at what time, the bloody and cruell tyrant [Mehmet] caused Proclamation to be made, that no person of what age, sex, or condition soener should be saved or pitied in that common massacre.

Once he had taken Byzantium, Mehmet renamed the city Istanbul and turned it into the capital of the Ottoman Empire; by the start of the 16th century, it had become the largest city in Europe. He turned the large church inside the city into a mosque—the largest in the world—which he renamed the Haghia Sophia. The 15th-century historian Tursun Beg wrote that Mehmet's mosque "not only encompassed all the arts of Haghia Sophia, but modern features constituting a fresh new idiom unequalled in beauty." Utilizing his Janissaries, a corps made up of children captured in battle and then trained as Islamic warriors, Mehmet conquered most of Serbia (1459) as well as Morea (1460) and Anatolia (1461), which took the borders of his empire up to the Danube River, the main trade artery of southeast Europe. Conflict was bound to erupt at this incursion, and this came in 1463, when Albanian peasants rebelled against his authority but were quickly subdued. An attack by the state of Venice occurred in 1479 and was also contained. However, resistance from other quarters, including from the southern areas of what is now the Middle East, such as Syria and Iran, forced him to concentrate on consolidating these territories. For Mehmet, this conflict was part of his grand scheme to bring the world under his rule: He saw himself as another Roman emperor and styled himself Kayser-i Rum (the Roman Caesar).

In 1480, Mehmet began planning a series of actions against the island of Rhodes and southern Italy. However, on 3 May 1481, he suddenly died of unknown causes, and his son took power as Bayezid II. Bayezid, however, did not have his father's grand territorial ambitions, and the plans to conquer southern Europe were postponed.

References: Tursun Beg, *The History of Mehmed the Conqueror,* translated by Halil Inaloik and Rhoads Murphey (Minneapolis, Minn.: Bibliotheca Islamica, 1978); Kritovoulos, *History of Mehmed the Conqueror,* translated by Charles T. Riggs (Westport, Conn.: Greenwood Press, 1970); Finlay, George, *History of the Byzantine and Greek Empires, from 716 to 1453* (Edinburgh, Scotland: W. Blackwood, 1854); Cambini, Andrea, *Two Very Notable Commentaries the one of the Originall of the Turcks and Empire of the house of Ottomanno . . .* (London: [Printed] by Rouland Hall for Humfrey Toye, 1562); *The Turkes Secretorie conteining his Sundrie Letters sent to divers Emperours, Kings, Princes and states . . .* (London: Printed by M[elchisedec] B[radwood] 1607).

Miltiades (ca. 540–ca. 489 B.C.) *Athenian general*

A great-grandson of the Athenian politician Philaïdes, Miltiades was the son of the Athenian statesman Cimon (who, with Aristides, helped to establish the Delian League) and his wife Irodice. Around 524 B.C., Miltiades was trained as an archon, or one of nine chief magistrates of Athens. Upon the death of his uncle about 524 B.C., he inherited the leadership of Chersonese, an Athenian colony in what is now the peninsula of Gallipoli.

In 515 B.C., Miltiades joined King DARIUS I of Persia (now modern Iran) in an expedition against the Scythians. Plutarch, the noted Greek historian whose *Lives* encapsulated small biographies of famous Grecians, wrote of Miltiades' role in this campaign: "At the same time Darius king of Persian having passed all his armie out of Asia into Europe, determined to make war with the Scythians, and made a bridge over [the] Danuby [river] to passé over his troupes: the guard of which in his absence, was committed unto the Lords which he had brought with him out of Ionia and Æolia, and unto every one of the which he had given perpetuall power and goverment ouer their townes. Supposing by this policie, easily to bring into subjection all the Greekes that dwelt in Asia, if he gave the guard of the townes unto their friends and confederates, that could not escape by any meanes if he were oppressed. Miltiades was of the number of the guards of this bridge." Possibly realizing that Darius would one day turn on Greece, Miltiades urged that the bridge over the Danube be destroyed to cut off any retreat by Darius. His request was refused, and when the Scythians forced Darius back over the bridge, he learned of Miltiades' potential betrayal. Miltiades fled to Athens, but he was captured and impeached by his own government on charges of tyranny at Chersonese.

When the Persian invasion of Greece that Miltiades has prophesied went forward, he was released from custody and named one of 10 commanders to defend his homeland. He gathered his forces and decided to make a stand at Marathon, 20 miles northeast of Athens, in September 490 B.C. There he stood with some 10,000 Athenians and approximately 1,000 Plataeans against Darius, commanding some 60,000 men. To all appearances, Darius had complete battlefield supremacy. Historian John Laffin writes: "Early in the afternoon of a September day in the year 490 B.C. an Athenian general, Miltiades, gave to his small but compact army the command to prepare for battle. This was a momentous order, for it led to the shaping of history, and the battle that followed provided a model which many a general would follow in the centuries to come. . . . No battle could better serve as a starting point for a study of the links of leadership, because the victory was the weaker numerically, because he had his opponent at a psychological disadvantage before the battle, because he dared to take the initiative, and because the fruit of victory was the birth of Europe, from where most of the great generals of history were to come."

Historian George Bruce writes: "Being greatly outnumbered, Miltiades altered the usual arrangement of the Greek line, so as to extend his wings across the whole width of the valley in which the battle was fought, and thus escape being outflanked. To effect that he was forced to weaken his center, which was repulsed, but both his wings drove back the invaders, and then fell upon and routed the victorious Persian center. The Persians fled in confusion to their ships, which they succeeded in launching, and escaped with a loss of 6,400 men. The Athenians lost 192 only, and inspired other Greek states to resist [Persian oppression]."

Darius tried to invade Athens itself, but Miltiades and his forces rushed to the city and were able to ward off this secondary assault. According to Plutarch's biography of Miltiades, the hero of Marathon was given "a fleet of threescore and ten gallies . . . to make war upon the Iles which had aided the Persians." One of the islands he attacked, Paros, held out against his invasion, and when he went ashore to visit with Timo, a priestess on Paros, he was seriously wounded and taken back to Athens, where he was impeached by the Greek legislature for some unknown crime, found guilty, and ordered to pay a fine. Before he could do this, however, he succumbed to the wound he suffered on Paros, dying in either 488 or 489 B.C. His son Cimon paid the fine, and Miltiades' name was cleared. In modern histories, his role in defeating the Persians at Marathon and saving the concept of the Greek city-state, from which democracy sprang, is why this remarkable victory is always included in lists of the most important battles in world history.

References: Plutarch, *The Lives of Epaminondas, of Philip of Macedon, of Dionysius the Elder, and of Octavius Cæsar Augustus: Collected out of Good Authors . . . ,* translated by Sir Thomas North (London: Richard Field, 1603), 120–122; Nepos, Cornelius, *The Lives of T. Pomponius Atticus, Miltiades, and Cimon . . . ,* translated by Richardson Pack (London: E. Curll, 1735); Nepos, Cornelius, *Cornelius Nepos' Life of Miltiades,* edited by M. Hughes (London: City of London Book Depot, 1901); Nepos, Cornelius, *Lives of Miltiades and Epaminondas,* edited by J. E. Melluish (London: Blackie & Son, 1901); Ward, George, *A Close Translation of the Lives of Miltiades and Epaminondas* (London: Ralph, Holland & Co., 1901); Laffin, John, "Unorthodoxy at Marathon," in *Links of Leadership: Thirty Centuries of Command* (London: George G. Harrap & Co., Ltd., 1966), 35–50; Bruce, George, "Marathon," in *Collins Dictionary of Wars* (Glasgow, Scotland: HarperCollins Publishers, 1995), 154.

Mohammed Ibn Da'ud *See* ALP-ARSLAN.

Moltke, Helmuth Johannes Ludwig, count von Moltke (1848–1916) *German general*

Born in Gersdorf, Mecklenburg, on 23 May 1848, Helmuth Johannes Ludwig Moltke was the nephew of Helmuth Karl Bernard MOLTKE. He entered the officer's corps in 1870, although he did not see service during his uncle's successful campaign against France, which led to the consolidation of Prussia and other states into modern Germany. In 1902, Moltke was given the command of the 1st Division of the German Guards Corps, followed by his being named as quartermaster general in 1904 and chief of the general staff of the German army two years later, again following in his uncle's footsteps.

At the outbreak of the First World War in August 1914, Moltke, then chief of the General Staff, was in failing health. Despite this, he continued to direct the German strategic plan for the war. His fatal error was the change he made to the plans of his predecessor as chief of the General Staff, General Alfred von Schlieffen. Moltke's uncle's fear following German unification in 1871 was that the nation could face simultaneous attack from France to the west and Russia to the east. In evolving a strategy to deal with this situation, von Schlieffen devised the "Schlieffen Plan," a lightning strike through neutral Belgium into Northern France, bypassing the immensely strong French fortresses at Metz and Verdun, to the south. If done quickly enough, Paris would fall, France would capitulate, and Germany could then turn to the east to fight Russia. However, as von Schlieffen's successor, Moltke modified the plan, moving several divisions from the right wing, advancing (through Belgium) to shore up the left wing marching on Verdun. This modification undermined the entire plan, as an overwhelming right wing was needed to overcome any resistance before Paris was reached. Further, this allowed for less time to mobilize the troops to wheel back east facing the potential Russian threat moving against Germany's eastern border. When the time came, Moltke altered the plan even further, withdrawing six whole divisions from the western attack to concentrate on what he saw as a growing Russian threat. Moltke's changes to the plan were its undoing: Because the right wing's approach through Belgium did not hit French forces strongly enough, the French army rallied some 30 miles east of Paris, forcing them to dig in for the beginning of the horrific trench warfare that left hundreds of thousands dead. Further confusing decisions made by Moltke led to more upheaval, including allowing the German commander General Karl von Bulow, already in command of the German Second Army, to command the First as well when he did not have the experience. Historians blame Moltke's orders directly for the German defeat at the first battle of the Marne (20–24 August 1914).

By 3 November 1914, Moltke's plans for a quick French defeat lay in ruins, and his health was failing. In December, he was replaced as chief of the General Staff by General Erich von Falkenhayn and shifted to chief of the home general staff in Berlin, a tremendous demotion. On 19 June 1916, the 68-year-old Moltke suffered a fatal heart attack while in the Reichstag building in Berlin; he was in the midst of a tribute to a Marshal von der Goltz when he collapsed. Kaiser Wilhelm II stated: "I have just received the overwhelming news of the sudden death [of Moltke]. Words fail me to give full impression to my feelings. I recall with deep emotion his illness at the beginning of this war, the brilliant preparation of which was the object of his untiring activity as Chief of the General Staff of the Army. The Fatherland will not forget his great services. So long as I shall live I shall gratefully remember what this upright and wise man with a character of gold and a warm and loyal heart was to me and the Army." In the years after Moltke's death, two works written by him were posthumously published: *Erinnerungen, Briefe, Dokumente, 1877–1916* (1922) and *Aufzechnungen, Briefe, Schriften, Reden* (1923).

References: "Moltke, Gen Helmuth von, 'the Younger,'" in *The Oxford Companion to Military History*, edited by Richard Holmes (New York: Oxford University Press, 2001), 596; Mombauer, Annika, *Helmuth von Moltke and the Origins of the First World War* (Cambridge, U.K.: Cambridge University Press, 2001); "Von Moltke's Death. A Sudden Heart Seizure," *The Times* (London), 20 June 1916, 8.

Moltke, Helmuth Karl Bernard, count von Moltke (1800–1891) *Prussian general*

Although he was not a field commander, Helmuth Karl Bernard Moltke's contributions to military logistics, equipment, and organization are some of the most important in the field. He is better known to historians and laymen as Helmuth von Moltke the Elder, to distinguish him from his nephew, known as the Younger. Coming from two families of nobility, the elder Moltke was born in Parchim, in the state of Mecklenburg (now in Germany), on 26 October 1800. In 1805, his father took the family from Mecklenburg, emigrating to Holstein, then a possession of Denmark, and they became Danish citizens. Moltke completed his education in Copenhagen with service in the Royal Cadet Corps; after graduating, he joined the Danish infantry. However, in 1821, he visited Berlin, then the capital of Prussia, and immediately transferred to the Prussian army. The following year, he received a commission in the 8th Infantry Regiment with the rank of second lieutenant.

In 1823, Moltke was sent to the General War College in Berlin to augment his military education and training. However, after only two years, ill health, which had plagued him since childhood, forced him to travel to the sanatorium at Bad Salzbrunn to recuperate. There, he attended a gymnasium, or school, where he studied modern languages. In 1826, he returned to Frankfurt, where he took up writing to earn some money; his novel *Die beiden Freunde* (The Two Friends, 1827), was followed by an essay, *Holland and Belgium in their Mutual Relations* (1831) and a more substantial paper, *Darstellung der inner Verhäktnusse und des gesellschaftlichen Zustandes in Polen* (An account of the internal circumstances and social conditions of Poland, 1832). He contracted to translate Edward Gibbons's landmark *Decline and Fall of the Roman Empire* into German for a payment of £75, but he never finished the project. In 1828, he was sent to the Topographical Bureau of the German General Staff located in Berlin.

In 1832, Moltke was attached to the Prussian General Staff, and the following year he was promoted to the rank of first lieutenant. In 1835, when he was promoted to captain, he was given six months' leave, during which he traveled through Constantinople and advised Sultan Mahmud II on the transformation and modernization of the Turkish army. Moltke eventually spent two years in Constantinople, where he learned to speak Turkish and traveled through southern Europe for the Sultan. In

Helmut Karl Bernhard, count von Moltke

1838, Mahmud sent him to Armenia to advise a Turkish general who was preparing his troops to battle against Mehemet Ali of Egypt; however, the frightened general fled in panic at the first sight of the Egyptian forces. Moltke took control of the Turkish artillery at the battle of Nisib (1839), although, again, many of the soldiers were frightened and ran away. Moltke made his way back to Constantinople, and upon learning that Mahmud, his patron, had died, he returned to Germany, where he was allowed to rejoin the Prussian military as a member of the staff of the 4th Prussian Army Corps. In 1841, he published some of his letters from Turkey in *Briefe über Zustände und Begebenheiten in der Türkei* (Letters on conditions and events in Turkey during the years 1835 to 1839), and that same year he maried Mary Burt, an Englishwoman. Other published works resulting from his experiences in the employ of the Turkish sultan include: *What Considerations Should Determine the Choice of the Course of Railways?* (1843); *[The] Russo-Turkish Campaign in Europe, 1828–1829, described in 1845 by Baron von Moltke, Major in the Prussian Staff* (1845); and *Der russisch-türkische Feldzug in der europäischen Türkei 1828–1829* (*The Russians in Bulgaria and Rumelia,* 1854). This latter work is still considered by military strategists and historians as one of the most important of its time. Moltke also published maps of

Asia Minor and a geographical work on Turkey and its region.

In 1845, Moltke was appointed as the personal aide to Prince Henry of Prussia, who lived in Rome, Italy. Henry, an invalid, died the following year, but the time spent in Rome allowed Moltke to again broaden his horizons, and he published a book of maps of Rome and its vicinity in 1852. When he returned to Berlin, he retained his position on the Prussian General Staff, and in 1855 he was became the aide-de-camp to Prince Frederick William, the king of Prussia and later Emperor Frederick III of Germany. During his time with the prince, Moltke jotted down more travel notes, which were published in part as *Briefe aus Russland* (*Letters from Russia,* 1877).

During his years with the Prussian General Staff (becoming chief of staff on 29 October 1857), Moltke worked to build the Prussian army into an efficient military machine that would conquer parts of Europe in the name of Prussia. The first conflict fought following Moltke's doctrine of a strong army was against Denmark in 1864, when a border dispute over Schleswig-Holstein led to war. Moltke drew up plans for an attack on the main Danish flank before they could shore up their positions inside Schleswig or retreat to several Danish islands. When the war began in February, his plan was haphazardly conducted, allowing the Danish to retreat to the fortresses at Düppel and Fredericia and to the islands of Alsen and Fünun. Although a Prussian assault on Düppel ended the threat there, and the Danes abandoned Fredericia, the war dragged on. On Moltke's advice, the Prussians' attack on the Danes on Alsen was undertaken on 29 June and forced the Danish to give up that island. When the Prussians threatened to invade the island of Fünun, the Danes asked for peace terms, and the war ended. Moltke's advice and counsel, working closely with Prince Frederick William, made him a favorite of the Prussian royal family.

Two years after the conflict with Denmark, Prussia went to war against Austria. The Austro-Prussian War, or Seven Weeks' War (1866), demonstrated Moltke's strategic talent and military genius. Relations between the two nations had been tense since at least 1850, when Austria had forced Prussia to accept the Punctuation of Olmütz, a treaty that had halted Prussia's aims of consolidating the Germanic states into one nation. Moltke advised deploying a portion of the Prussian army—nearly 300,000 men—across the frontier shared by Prussia and

Austria. On 5 May 1866, he wrote to Prince Frederick Charles:

> Does not expect the Austrian main attack to be aimed at Silesia, which would not strike the center of the monarchy and would give Prussia the time to bring up the 1st Army to help the 2nd, either north of the Giant Mountains or, by a bolder and more effectual advance, south of them. More probable an advance of all the available Austrian forces against the 1st Army; but not the whole Austrian army would be available; 50,000 men would have to watch the 2nd Army. At the beginning of June, [General Ludwig Ritter von] Benedek could not have more than 130,000 men, the strength of our 1st Army, which on the fourth day will be further strengthened. . . . Against the Saxons VII [Corps] and VIII [Corps] are an ample force, whether they stand at Zeitz or Düben. The concentration of our forces, which at the beginning are separated in consequence of our geographical position, the direction of our railways and by considerations of defense, can be obtained in a few marches if they move forwards; if they remain where they are it will be more difficult.

The war quickly ended when the Prussians won a stunning victory at Königgrätz (also known as Sadowa, 3 July 1866), ending the war after less than two months of fighting. In recognition of his service, Moltke was granted a large award (approximately $50,000), which he used to purchase an estate at Kreisau in the province of Silesia (now in Poland). In 1867, he wrote the official government report on the conflict, *Der Feldzug von 1866 in Deutschland* (*The Campaign of 1866 in Germany*, English translation 1872). Moltke was praised for the innovations he brought to the Prussian military, including the use of railways to shuttle troops and matériel into battle and new technology such as the breech-loading gun. With the support of Otto von Bismarck and Albrecht von Roon, the minister of war from 1859, he brought about a new, effective Prussian army.

Although the Seven Weeks' War had demonstrated Moltke's strategic skill, it was not until the Franco-Prussian war of 1870 that his innovations and theories were fully implemented. Bismarck saw France and its leader, Emperor Napoleon III, as Prussia's rival. In a series of reports, Moltke pointed out to Bismarck how weak France was militarily and how it could be quickly defeated. In July 1870, Bismarck tricked France into declaring war on Prussia, whose troops were already mobilized and in position. Within a few weeks, Moltke's plan succeeded, as the Prussians outmaneuvered the French at Sedan on 1 September 1870. Historian George Bruce writes:

> The French, 20,000 strong, with 564 guns, under Marshal de MACMAHON, who was wounded early in the action, were driven from all of their positions by the 200,000 Germans, with 774 guns, under General von Moltke, and compelled to retire into Sedan where they laid down their arms. The Emperor Napoleon III was among the prisoners, and one of the results of the surrender was his dethronement and the proclamation of a republic in Paris. The battle is remarkable for the desperate charge of the Chasseurs d'Afrique under General Margeuritte. The brigade was cut to pieces and the general killed. The Germans lost in the action 460 officers and 8,500 men; the French 3,000 killed, 14,000 wounded and 21,000 prisoners, while 83,000 subsequently surrendered in Sedan. The Germans took 419 guns, 139 fortress guns and 66,000 rifles, marched on Paris.

Another key Prussian victory came at the fortress of Metz, which fell on 26 October 1870 following a three-month siege. The French defeat led to the end of the Second Empire, and at Versailles on 18 January 1871, the German Empire, a consolidation of the Prussia, its client North German states, and some captured French territory, was declared. Kaiser Wilhelm I made Moltke a count following the declaration, and Moltke continued his service on the General Staff, serving as its chief from 1871 until his retirement in 1888.

As chief of the General Staff, Moltke saw Prussia/Germany as a nation threatened by France in the west and Russia in the east, and he formed plans for what he felt was an inevitable conflict. On his retirement in 1888, he was named chair of the committee for national defense, but by then his patron Wilhelm I was dead, and Wilhelm II did not share his father's faith in Moltke and Bismarck. Moltke served as a member of the German Reichstag, or

Parliament, from 1871 until his death. He published more books, including *Wanderbuch* (Notes on travel, 1879), and died in Berlin on 24 April 1891 at the age of 90.

Moltke was better known for his military strategy and writings rather than field service. Historian Gunther E. Rothenberg writes:

> Moltke may be considered the most incisive and important military European military writer between the Napoleonic Era and the First World War. [Carl von] Clausewitz was a more profound thinker, and equal claims to greatness as tacticians and combat leaders could be advanced for a number of other commanders, but Moltke excelled not only in organization and strategic planning but also in operational command, abilities he combined with an acute awareness of what was and was not possible in war. Moltke had broad cultural interests and has been pictured as "essentially a humanist of the post-Goethe era." Perhaps too much has been made of this. Moltke did indeed share many of the intellectual characteristics of German classicism, but above all he was a soldier and what truly mattered to him was the controlled application of force in the service of the Prussian monarchy.

References: Morris, William O'Connor, *Moltke: A Biographical and Critical Study* (New York: Haskell House, 1893); "Moltke, FM Graf Helmuth Karl Bernhard von, 'the Elder,'" in *The Oxford Companion to Military History,* edited by Richard Holmes (New York: Oxford University Press, 2001), 594–596; Echevarria Antulio J., II, "Moltke and the German Military Tradition: His Theories and Legacies," *Parameters* 26, no. 1 (Spring 1996): 91–99; Hughes, Daniel J., ed., *Moltke on the Art of War,* translated by Harry Bell and Daniel J. Hughes (San Francisco: Presidio Press, 1993); Bruce, George, "Sedan," in *Collins Dictionary of Wars* (Glasgow, Scotland: HarperCollins Publishers, 1995), 223–224; Wilkinson, Spenser, *Moltke's Correspondence during the Campaign of 1866 against Austria* (London: Printed Under the Authority of His Majesty's Stationary Office, 1915), 19; Rothenberg, Gunther E., "Moltke, Schlieffen, and the Doctrine of Strategic Envelopment," in *Makers of Modern Strategy from Machiavelli to the Nuclear Age,* edited by Peter Paret (Princeton, N.J.: Princeton University Press, 1986), 296–325.

Monash, Sir John (1865–1931) *Australian general*

The first major Australian military commander, John Monash was born in Melbourne, Victoria, on 27 June 1865; his family were Prussian Jews who had fled to Australia to escape religious persecution. Monash received his education at Scotch College and the University of Melbourne, where he studied law and engineering. He joined the army reserve in 1884 as a member of the University company of the 4th Battalion, Victorian Rifles and eventually became a member of the Metropolitan Brigade of the Garrison Artillery based in Melbourne. He worked as an engineer on various city projects, including a main railway line, and also went into private business, forming an engineering partnership that built bridges in the Melbourne area. However, he remained in the military reserve, and by 1914 he had risen to the rank of colonel of the 13th Infantry Brigade.

Following the outbreak of the First World War in August 1914, Monash was named commander of the 4th Infantry Brigade of the Australian Imperial Force (AIF), which was sent to Egypt and took part in the ill-fated campaign on the Gallipoli peninsula. After Gallipoli, Monash was promoted to major general and given command of the 3rd Australian Division. Stationed in England, he oversaw the training of the division and then took them to France, where Monash and his men saw action at the battle of Messines (7 June 1917). He eventually fought in the battles of Polygon Wood (26 September 1917) and Passchendaele, also known as the third battle of Ypres (July–November 1917), among others. In May 1918, Monash was made Knight Commander of the Order of the Bath (KCB), promoted to lieutenant general, and named as commander of the entire Australian Corps. He led this corps at Hamel (4 July 1918), where tanks and aircraft were utilized, and at the second battle of Amiens (8 August 1918), all of which contributed to the breach of Germany's Hindenburg Line and the end of the horrendous trench warfare that had lasted since 1914.

With the end of the war, Monash remained in France as director general of the Australian Office of Repatriation and Demobilisation, getting his men back to civilian life and employment. When he returned to Australia in 1919, he was given a hero's welcome in Melbourne. The following year, he went to work as the general manager of the State Electricity Commission of

Victoria, serving in that position until 1931. Under his leadership, the state of Victoria was, for the first time, able to provide cheap electric power and not rely on other Australian states.

Monash died at his home, "Iona," in Toorak, Victoria, on 8 October 1931. His funeral drew a crowd of some 300,000 to Melbourne's Brighton Cemetery, where he was laid to rest. Australian governor-general Sir Isaac Isaacs said, "With all Australia I mourn the loss of one of her ablest, bravest, and noblest sons, a loyal servant of the King and country. He served Australia and the Empire well, and in his passing he has left an example that will be a beacon light of patriotic and unselfish endeavour." Monash University in Melbourne is named in his honor.

Monash was the author of *The Australian Victories in France in 1918,* published in 1920. Historian Peter Nunan writes: "Appalled at the horrific casualties and 'ghastly inefficiency' of World War I combat, Monash . . . adopted the view that the infantry's role was 'not to expend itself upon heroic physical effort,' but 'to advance under the maximum possible array of mechanical resources, in the form of guns, machine guns, tanks, mortars, and aeroplanes . . . to the appointed goal.' Monash became an advocate of the use of combined arms operations, including those that employed tanks."

References: Serle, Geoffrey, *John Monash* (Melbourne, Australia: Melbourne University Press, 1982); Pederson, P. A., *Monash as Military Commander* (Carlton, Victoria: Melbourne University Press, 1985); Nunan, Peter, "Diggers' Fourth of July," *Military History* 17, no. 3 (August 2000): 26; Monash, Sir John, *War Letters of General Monash,* edited by Frederic Morley (Sydney, New South Wales: Angus & Robertson, 1934); Monash, Sir John, *The Australian Victories in France in 1918* (London: Hutchinson, 1920).

Monck, George, duke of Albemarle (George Monk) (1608–1670) *English military and naval commander*

George Monck—also noted as "Monk" in early histories of the English navy—was born in the village of Potheridge, near Torrington in the county of Devon, England, on 6 December 1608. Historian John Charnock wrote in 1794 that "he was the second son of Sir Thomas Monk of Potheridge . . . where his family had,

for many ages, flourished in a knightly degree, and had, by marriages into great and worthy families, continued the same. . . ." His great-grandmother was a daughter of Arthur Plantagenet, son of King Edward IV of England. As a young man, Monck assaulted the under-sheriff of Devonshire, who had come to arrest his father for debt, despite the fact that the family had bribed the official not to go forward with the arrest. To escape a prison sentence, he volunteered for the duke of Buckingham's expedition to Cádiz, Spain, in 1625. Two years later, he participated in Buckingham's mission to the Ile de Ré.

Much of the details of Monck's life are unknown, so dates for some of his accomplishments are guesses and not exact. For instance, it is thought that in 1629 Monck joined the prince of Orange and fought in Holland during the Thirty Years' War and that he distinguished himself at Breda in 1637. When Charles I raised an army to fight the Scottish uprising known as the Second Bishops' War in 1640, Monck was given a commission as a lieutenant colonel and sent to fight. He saw action in several battles, with his most noted service being at Newburn-on-Tyre (1640), when Scottish Covenanters routed the English, but Monck's troops were among the few English units not to flee. Following the end of that war, King Charles I sent Monck to Ireland to fight the rebels there, serving under the earl of Ormonde. In 1643, a year after the Civil War had begun, Monck received a letter in Ireland from John Pym, a member of Parliament who invited Monck to serve with Parliamentary forces. Ormonde discovered the letter's contents and had Monck arrested and sent back in chains to England, where he was imprisoned at Bristol. After Monck appealed personally to Charles that he was still loyal to the Crown, the king released him and gave him command of Irish troops who had come over to fight for the Royalists. At Nantwich in January 1644, Monck was taken prisoner by the Parliamentarians and held for two years.

With his release in November 1646, Monck changed sides and joined the Parliament forces. He was sent to Ireland, where his troops fought both the king's forces under Ormonde and the Irish rebels under Owen O'Neill. Following Charles's capture and execution in 1649, Monck signed a peace treaty with O'Neill and was then summoned back to London, where he was reprimanded for the treaty. In 1650, Oliver CROMWELL, the Parliamentary leader gave him command of two regiments, and Monck went to Scotland when Cromwell invaded there in July. (His unit became the Coldstream Guards, a regiment that remains in existence to this day.)

In 1651, when Cromwell moved south to battle Charles's son (later Charles II), he left Monck in command of forces in Scotland, and in August Monck won victories at Stirling (14 August) and Aberdeen. On 1 September, his forces raided Dundee, looted it, and killed an estimated 500 civilians. Monck later wrote to Cromwell, "The stubbornness of the people enforced the soldiers to plunder the town." An interesting sidenote to this story is that Monck's forces placed the stolen items on a ship that sank in the River Tay in Dundee, taking the booty to the bottom, and it has yet to be found. Some estimate the treasure to be worth about $4 billion today.

In 1652, with Scotland subdued, Monck was appointed one of three generals of the fleet, along with Richard Deane and Robert BLAKE, in the first Anglo-Dutch War. Following Deane's death in a battle off the coast of the Netherlands (2–3 June 1653) and Blake being wounded, Monck became the sole commander of the English fleet. Implementing a blockade, he forced a closure of Holland's ports, and when the Dutch tried to break it, Monck's forces defeated them at Scheveningen (29 & 31 July 1653). During that battle, Dutch commander Maarten TROMP was killed in action.

While Monck was serving in the English navy, Cromwell had taken control of England and dissolved Parliament; Monck, Deane, and Blake had acceded to Cromwell's control in the "Declaration of the Generals at Sea, and the Captains under their command, concerning the late dissolution of the Parliament; and their resolution thereupon. As it was sent to Vice-Admiral Penn, to be communicated to the commanders and officers of the ships under his command." However, in a letter Monck later wrote to Vice Admiral William Goodson, he explained, "When this Parliament was interrupted formerly, I shall answer you that, it was never in my Conscience to go out of Gods way under the pretence of doing Gods work, and you know the the variety of times doth much vary the nature of affaires, and what might then patiently be submitted unto, we being engaged with a forraine [foreign] Enemy in a bloody Warre, cannot be drawn into a precedent at this time; after our Repentance and assurance of Loyalty and Constancy."

In 1654, Monck returned to serve in the army, and he was sent once again into Scotland, this time to suppress the earl of Glencairn's uprising. He replaced Rob-

ert Lilburne as Parliamentary commander and issued an edict calling on all those against him to lay down their arms. He then preceded to march into each town and destroy its food stocks, and after a series of Parliamentary victories, Glencairn sued for peace in August 1654.

Following Oliver Cromwell's death (3 September 1658), Monck advised his successor, Cromwell's son Richard, to reduce the army from two divisions to one. Instead, Richard dissolved Parliament (22 April 1659), which led Monck to oppose him. Monck then became instrumental in helping to recall the dissolved Long Parliament, which had become known as the Rump Parliament. However, because he was not in London, he could not stop John Lambert, another Parliamentarian commander, from dismissing this parliament on 13 October 1659. Once he heard of Lambert's move, Monck determined to retire from the army and wrote a lengthy letter from his station at Dalkeith in Scotland to William Lenthall, the Speaker of the House of Commons:

> I received yours of the 7th Instant, and cannot but with thankfulness Acknowledge the Great Grace and Favour the Parliament are pleased to vouchsafe to me, in taking Notice of my weak and wrothless Endeavours in their Service. I confess such Encouragement is sufficient to Reward the Highest Merits; I hope I shall such Use of It, not only to satisfie me self as the best Recompense for my former poor Services, but as a Motive to Future Obedience and Loyalty to them: I bless the Lord I have a Witness in mine own Heart, That my Designes tend not to any other End than my Countries good, and I shall with more Cheerfulness return the Sword into Your Hands, than ever I received it with, and desire to attend your Pleasure if You shall have no further Use of my Service.

Monck was not dismissed, but Lambert saw him as a threat and marched north to arrest him. At Newcastle, Monck played for time by offering to negotiate, but the weather came to his aid, as inclement conditions forced many of Lambert's forces to desert, leaving him ill-prepared to battle Monck's army. Then, however, the Rump Parliament was restored, and Lambert gave up and headed back to London; Monck followed him, arriving on 3 February 1660. Although he never threatened military action, Monck did advise on 1 May that the murdered king's son be allowed to take the throne as the new monarch.

When Charles II arrived at Dover on 25 May 1660, Monck was there to welcome him. Allegedly, when Charles came ashore, he knelt before Monck and called him "father." In this period, called the Restoration, Monck was styled as the duke of Albemarle and named as captain-general of the army. Although he played a minor role in the fighting in the Second Anglo-Dutch War (1665–67), his career was over, and he never entered the political realm. George Monck died in London on 3 January 1670 and was buried with great ceremony in Westminster Abbey. His *Observations upon Military and Political Affairs,* which he wrote while a prisoner in the Tower of London, was published posthumously in 1671.

References: Warner, Oliver, *Hero of the Restoration: A Life of General George Monck, 1st Duke of Albemarle, K.G.* (London: Jarrolds Publishers, Ltd., 1936); Charnock, John, "Albemarle, George Monk, Duke of," in *Biographia Navalis; or, Impartial Memoirs of the Lives and Characters of Officers of the Navy of Great Britain, From the Year 1660 to the Present Time; . . . ,* 4 vols. (London: Printed for R. Faulder, Bond-Street, 1794–98), I:189–214; Lloyd, David, *Modern Policy Compleated, or, The Publick Actions and Councels both Civill and Military of His Excellency the Lord Generall Monck: Under the Generall Revolutions since 1639, to 1660* (London: Printed by J.B. for Henry Marsh, 1660); Powell, the Rev. J. R., and E. K. Timings, *The Rupert and Monck Letter Book 1666, Together With Supporting Documents* (London: Printed for the Navy Records Society, 1969); "A Letter from General Monck from Dalkeith, 13 October 1659. Directed as Followeth. For the Right Honorable William Lenthal, Esquire, Speaker; to be communicated to the Parliament of the Commonwealth of England, at Westminster" (London, 1659); "A Letter from the Lord General Monck and The Officers Here, to the Several and Respective Regiments and Other Forces in England, Scotland, and Ireland" (London: Printed by John Macock, 1660).

Monmouth, James Scott, duke of (James Walter, James Crofts) (1649–1685)

claimant to the English throne

James Scott was born in Rotterdam on 9 April 1649 as James Walter, the son of Charles II and his mistress Lucy Walter. After James's birth, his mother returned to En-gland, but, upon a warrant sworn out by Lord Protector Oliver CROMWELL, she was arrested and sent to the Tower of London; however, she was soon released and returned to the Netherlands. When she died in 1658, James became the ward of William, Lord Crofts, whose name he took for a time. When Charles was restored to the throne in 1660, he commanded that James, his favorite son, be brought to his royal court. In 1663, James was styled first as duke of Orkney and duke of Monmouth and then was made a Knight of the Garter at Windsor Castle. Upon his marriage to Anne Scott, countess of Buccleuch, he took the name Scott.

As Charles II and his wife, Queen Catherine, did not have any children, it appeared likely that he would name his son James Scott as his heir. Charles's brother, also named James, was not well-liked and was a Roman Catholic, in conflict with most of England. (Because of his father's Protestant religion, Monmouth had been brought up in that faith under the tutelage of Thomas Ross, one of Charles II's close friends.) Therefore a rivalry between the duke of Monmouth and his uncle, the duke of York, took on extreme proportions. During this period, Monmouth served in a series of appointments, including captain of the Life Guards from 1668 and member of the English Privy Council from 1670. During the Second Anglo-Dutch War (1665–67), he served as head of the English armed forces on the European continent, and in April 1674 he succeeded the duke of Buckingham as master of the horse. As captain general of the English army, he led English forces into battle against Scottish troops and won an important victory at Bothwell Bridge on 22 June 1679.

Despite Monmouth's accomplishments, Charles came under increasing pressure not to name his illegitimate son as his successor. On 3 March 1679, he publicly announced that he and Scott's mother had never been married, and he overruled three separate Parliamentary bills to exclude the Catholic James, duke of York, from succeeding to the throne. Angered at this action, Monmouth took part in a conspiracy called the Rye House Plot (1683), an attempt on Charles II's life; when the plot was uncovered, he fled to the Netherlands.

Upon the death of Charles II on 6 February 1685, Monmouth's illegitimacy barred him from succeeding, and Charles's brother became James II. According to historian David Hilliam, "Charles' eldest and favorite bastard, the Duke of Monmouth . . . made a bid to seize the throne by force. His only claim to the throne was that he was a Protestant, but he tried to bolster up his chances by claiming that his parents had actually been married in secret. He landed at Lyme Regis [Dorset], declared his Uncle James to be a usurper, claimed the throne, and gathered an army of about 4,000. In Taunton he was actually proclaimed king, taking the title of James II, loftily disregarding the properly crowned James II. In an odd way, therefore, for a few weeks England had two James IIs."

Monmouth's "rebellion" lasted but a few weeks: The proper James II launched his army against Monmouth, and on 5 July 1685 at Sedgemoor, in Somerset, the entire insurrection came to an abrupt end when some 2,500 Royalist forces under the earl of Faversham took on Monmouth's army of approximately 3,700 troops. Historian George Bruce writes: "Monmouth attempted a night attack on Faversham's camp, but the alarm was given and the Royal troops, falling upon their assailants, put Monmouth's cavalry to flight, and though his infantry made a sturdy resistance they were at length overpowered and routed with heavy loss." Sedgemoor was to be the last battle on English soil.

Monmouth fled from the defeat but was captured days later in a ditch in Dorsetshire while trying to get out of England. Taken back to London, he was quickly found guilty of crimes against the crown. Many of his followers were tried before Lord Jeffreys, and 320 were executed. Although he offered his uncle James his own submission and a change of his religion to Roman Catholic, Monmouth's entreaties were turned down, and he was beheaded on 15 July 1685 at the age of 36. Ironically, because he was of royal blood, his official portrait needed to be painted; in order to do this, his severed head was sewn back onto his body, and a likeness was done. His uncle, James II, was later forced into exile in France when William and Mary of Orange took the throne in the Glorious Revolution of 1688.

References: Watson, J. N. P., *Captain-General and Rebel Chief: The Life of James, Duke of Monmouth* (London: Allen & Unwin, 1979); *An Historical Account of the Heroick Life and Magnanimous Actions of the Most Illustrious Prince, James Duke of Monmouth . . .* (London: Printed for Thomas Malthus, 1683); Roberts, George, *The Life, Progresses, and Rebellion of James, Duke of Monmouth, to his Capture and Execution: with a Full Account of the Bloody Assize, and Copious Biographical Notices*, 2 vols. (London: Longman, Brown, Green and Longmans, 1844); Hilliam, David, "James II," in *Kings, Queens, Bones and Bastards: Who's Who in the English Monarchy from Egbert to Elizabeth II* (Thropp, Stroud, U.K.: Sutton Publishing, 2000), 83–86; Laffin, John, "Sedgemoor," in *Brassey's Battles: 3,500 Years of Conflict, Campaigns and Wars from A–Z* (London: Brassey's Defence Publishers, 1986), 383–384; Bruce, George, "Sedgemoor," in *Collins Dictionary of Wars* (Glasgow, Scotland: HarperCollins Publishers, 1995), 224; *An Account of the Defeat of the Rebels in England and also the taking of the late Duke of Monmouth, the late Lord Gray, &c* (London: Printed by Thomas Newcomb, 1685); *A Faithful and Impartial Account of the Proceedings in the Case of James, Duke of Monmouth* (London: Printed for J. Hayther, 1682).

Montagu, Edward, second earl of Manchester (Edward Montague, Viscount Mandeville) (1602–1671) *English general*

Born in 1602, Edward Montagu (some historians list his name as Montague) was the son of Henry Montagu, later the first earl of Manchester, and was educated at Sidney Sussex College, Cambridge. He served as a member of Parliament for Huntingdon in the House of Commons, and in 1626, when his father was styled as the earl of Manchester, he took the courtesy title of Viscount Mandeville while still in the House of Commons.

With the outbreak of war between Parliament and King Charles I in 1642, Montagu—who succeeded his father as earl of Manchester the same year—was given the command of a regiment of foot, serving under Robert Devereux, earl of ESSEX. One work that mentions his service during the early part of the conflict claims that Montagu was captured and taken back to London, although no other biographical item on him mentions this. In August 1643, he was promoted to the rank of major general and named as commander of forces in the eastern counties of England. In this capacity, he took control of Lincolnshire when he won the battle of Winceby (11 October 1643) and captured the city of Lincoln (6 May 1644). Once this area was under Parliamentian control, he and his forces besieged the city of York and participated in the battle at Marston Moor (2 July 1644), when his forces backed up those of Oliver CROMWELL. Montagu clashed with Cromwell over military strategy and national policy, and when he was ordered to the south to support the forces of Sir William WALLER, he went to London, where he quarreled with the Parliamentarian leader.

Montagu and Waller met the Royalist forces at the second battle of Newbury on 27 October 1644. Although the agreed plan was for Waller to attack and then for Montagu to support him, Montagu brought his forces in late, allowing King Charles I and his troops to escape. Montagu came under heavy criticism for his action, and Parliament enacted the Self Denying Ordinance, which disallowed any member of Parliament from serving as a commander of an army. This meant that members of the House of Commons could resign from Parliament and carry on serving as soldiers, but members of the House of Lords could not do so. Despite the new "law," Cromwell remained a member of the House of Commons, but Montagu, a peer, resigned his commission on 2 April 1645.

With the capture and trial of Charles I, Montagu became even more disillusioned with the Parliamentary stand. He strongly opposed the king's execution, and his antagonism and hostility toward Cromwell deepened when Cromwell took the title of lord protector of England. Montagu withdrew from politics until the restoration of the Stuart dynasty in the form of Charles II, son of the executed king, to the throne in 1660. In the years that followed, Montagu served Charles II as chancellor, privy councillor, and lord chamberlain. In 1667, he returned to military service when he saw limited action during the Second Anglo-Dutch War (1665–67).

Edward Montagu, second earl of Manchester, died at Whitehall in London on 7 May 1671 at the age of 68 or 69.

References: Holmes, Richard, and Peter Young, *The English Civil War: A Military History of Three Civil Wars, 1642–1651* (London: Eyre Mehuen, 1974); Hamblet, John, *A Famous and Joyfull Victory obtained by the Earl of Stamfords forces neere Stratford in Northampton-shire, against Prince Robert [sic] his forces . . .* (London: Printed for H. Blunen, 1642); Montagu, Edward, earl of Manchester, *A Journall, or, a True and Exact Relation of Each Dayes Passage, of that Party of the Right Honourable the Earle of Manchesters army . . .* (London: Printed by Hugh Perry, 1644); *A List of all the Ships and Frigots of England with their number of men, guns, and what rates . . .* (London: Printed by M. Simmons, 1660).

Montcalm de Saint-Véran, Louis-Joseph de Montcalm, marquis de (Louis-Joseph de Montcalm-Gozon, marquis de Montcalm)
(1712–1759) *French general*

Louis-Joseph de Montcalm was born in the village of Candiac, near Nimes, France, on 28 February 1712, the son of a nobleman who had served in the French military. When he turned 15, his father purchased him a commission in the French army as an ensign; he saw active service, and two years later, he was promoted to the rank of captain. When he was 23, he succeeded to his father's title as the marquis de Montcalm, although this did not come with the appropriate wealth for a French nobleman, so he entered into an arranged marriage with a wealthy woman. Montcalm and his wife grew to love each other, and their letters, which survive, show a warm and affectionate relationship.

In 1741, Montcalm first saw military action during the War of the Austrian Succession (1741–48) when, serving under Marshal François Marie, duc de Broglie, his unit moved into Bohemia in central Europe to resist an invasion from Bavarian forces. He later served as aide-de-camp to the marquis Charles de la Fare and distinguished himself during the defense of Prague in 1742. Because of his service, on 7 March 1743 Montcalm was named as the colonel of the Régiment d'Auxerrois. He then served under Marshal Jean-Baptiste-François Desmarets, the duc de Maillebois and performed noble service on 16 June 1746 at Piacenza, Italy, where he was wounded and captured. After he was paroled back to the French, King Louis XV promoted him to brigadier general. Returning to the army, he took part in the battle of Assiette (July 1747) before the end of the war.

Montcalm left the army for several years until, in 1756, he was promoted to major general and given command of the French land forces in New France, in what is now Canada. When he arrived there, he found that his troops were not properly trained, and there was deep antipathy between the French soldiers and the Canadian citizens. In trying to resolve these problems, Montcalm clashed with Govenor-General Philippe de Rigaud, the marquis de Vaudreuil and wrote to Nicholas-René Berryer, a French minister: "Let us beware how we allow the establishment of manufactures in Canada; she would become proud and mutinous like the English. So long as France is a nursery to Canada, let not the Canadians be allowed to trade, but kept to their wandering laborious life with the savages, and to their military services, they will be less wealthy, but more brave and more faithful to us." In reports back to Paris, Montcalm complained bitterly that with limited resources and troops, he and his army were headed for disaster.

Montcalm was ordered to attack a series of British forts, starting with the major fortress at Oswego on Lake Ontario. This attack (July 1756) as well as one against Fort William Henry on Lake George (August 1757) showed that he could use his limited resources to great effect. However, the British recovered from these attacks and in 1758 set out to attack Fort Carillon (Ticonderoga) on Lake Champlain, controlled by Montcalm's forces of 4,000. The British general, James Abercromby, with 17,000 men, attacked Carillon without artillery, a lack that left the British vulnerable and allowed Montcalm to win a decisive victory. French losses were about 400, while Abercromby left some 2,000 dead and wounded behind. Although Montcalm had warded off the far superior English attack, the government in Paris refused to send him any more troops or matériel.

Seeing Montcalm as a threat, the British sent more forces into New France, and he was forced to abandon Ticonderoga when they won a decisive victory at Louisburg (1758) and moved on the main city of Quebec. At first, because of that city's geography, Montcalm concluded that they could not land any troops there. Once they did, he hurriedly moved his army to Quebec. Commanded by General James WOLFE, the British landed some three miles downriver from the city on 26 June 1759. A second force commanded by Brigadier General Robert Monckton captured Port Levis, and both forces laid siege to Quebec, although the high cliffs there did not allow a direct assault. Wolfe ordered that farms near Quebec be burned, so that the occupants would flee into the city and drain supplies from the stores there. When Montcalm did not attack, Wolfe decided on a daring surprise. In a remarkable maneuver, he crossed the river with a body of troops and scaled the steep banks in silence. On the morning of 13 September, Montcalm's army found the British force on high ground above them. With Wolfe's troops holding the advantage of a higher position and surprise, the quickly formed French line was soon broken, and during the battle Montcalm was shot and wounded mortally. He succumbed to his wounds the following day, and that evening his body was buried under the floor of an abandoned Ursuline convent nearby. Wolfe had also been killed in the battle, but he died knowing that he had taken Quebec. On 18 September, the city fell to the British, ending French control of Canada forever.

The authors of *The Wordsworth Dictionary of Military Biography* write: "Montcalm's fame rests on a short career during which he never commanded more than some 4,000 regular troops, and which ended with his death and defeat, and the loss of France's considerable American colonies for all time. It might be thought strange that he should be remembered as one of France's most respected soldiers, yet few dispute his right to the name. The respect is partly due to his extremely attractive personality, and the unusual affection he inspired in his subordinates; and partly to the impressive successes he achieved with indifferent resources in the face of a superior enemy."

References: Lewis, Meriwether Liston, *Montcalm: The Marvelous Marquis* (New York: Vantage Press, 1961); Casgrain, Henri Raymond, *Wolfe and Montcalm* (London: Oxford University Press, 1926); Winsor, Justin, *Note on the Spurious Letters of Montcalm, 1759* (Cambridge, U.K.: John Wilson and Son, 1887); Windrow, Martin, and Francis K. Mason, "Montcalm, Louis-Joseph, Marquis de Montcalm-Gozon de Saint-Véran," in *The Wordsworth Dictionary of Military Biography* (Hertfordshire, U.K.: Wadsworth Editions Ltd., 1997), 196–198; Windrow, Martin, *Montcalm's Army* (Reading, Pa.: Osprey Publishing, 1973); Beatson, Lieutenant-Colonel R. E., *The Plains of Abraham. Notes, Original and Selected* (Gibraltar, Garrison Library Press, 1858).

Montfort, Simon de, earl of Leicester

(ca. 1208–1265) *English military leader*

Simon de Montfort was born about 1208 at his family's castle, Montfort-l'Amauri, in the village of Montfort in the Île de France, near Paris. He was the son of Simon de Montfort l'Amauri, who had suppressed the Albigensians in a crusade in southern France. Because de Montfort's older brother, Amaury de Montfort (ca. 1192–1241), was the heir to family's estate in France, he renounced his right to these lands to claim the Montfort lands in Leicester, England. These had belonged to his grandmother, and his father had been granted them by King John, along with the earldom of Leicester, in 1207. Because de Montfort's father had then sided with the French king against John, he lost the English earldom.

In 1229, Simon de Montfort came to England under the auspices of his cousin Ranulf, the earl of Chester, who had held the lands since the departure of the Montfort family. Montfort met King Henry III and convinced him to regrant the title of earl of Leicester back to him; this was promised in 1231 but not fulfilled until 1239. His rapport with Henry led Montfort to become one of the king's advisers, and in 1238 he married Eleanor of Provence, Henry's sister, thus becoming a member of the royal family. This marriage, however, did not sit well with English noblemen, who felt that Eleanor's vow of chastity, taken after the death of her first husband, should be honored. Henry's own brother Richard, the earl of Cornwall, persuaded Henry to remove Montfort from his council of advisors, and Simon fled to the European continent. Richard soon realized his error, and wrote to Montfort to resolve their differences.

Starting in 1240, Montfort accompanied Richard on a year-long crusade to the Holy Land. He returned to France in 1242 and fought for Henry III in the campaign in Gascony (1242–43). In 1248, Henry sent him back into Gascony to bring some stability to a part of France wracked by internal dissension and rebellion against English invaders. However, Montfort's harsh suppression caused the barons in Gascony to complain to Henry, who recalled him. Montfort subsequently convinced Henry that he could bring order to Gascony, but shortly after he returned to France, he was recalled again so that Henry's son Edward—later King EDWARD I of England—could take control of the region.

Angered by his treatment at the hands of a king he had served so faithfully, Montfort returned to England, where in 1254 he became one of a number of barons who wanted an end to Henry's dictatorial powers. The group eventually forced the king to enact a series of reforms called the Provisions of Oxford, in which they demanded that Henry accept the appointment of a committee of 24 noblemen, half selected by the king, who would meet and draft a number of constitutional reforms. Montfort had been one of the barons who had drawn up the provisions of the plan at Oxford in June 1258. Henry accepted the panel, and a year later their plan, which expanded on the Provisions of Oxford, was presented as the Provisions of Westminster, which called for tax reforms. However, Henry was unhappy with this second code, and, calling on papal intervention in the crisis, received the blessings of Pope Urban IV to renounce the reforms. This rejection of their demands led

to a period of warfare now called the Barons' War, which began in 1263 and lasted until 1267.

As the head of the barons' army, Montfort won a victory at Lewes (1264), took Henry prisoner, and then took control of England. As the country's new leader, he intended to institute the Provisions of Westminster and called Parliament into session, summoning not just knights but representatives from different boroughs. This was the first time such a thing had been done, and it formed the basis of the modern House of Commons. However, Montfort ruled as a dictator and gradually alienated his supporters. Soon after Parliament came into session, another baron, Gilbert de Clare, the eighth earl of Gloucester, defected from Montfort's side and joined Prince Edward. Montfort called on his armies to defend the new government, and the opposing forces met in battle at Evesham on 4 August 1265. Montfort's army was dealt a horrific defeat, and he was killed in the battle.

The monk Matthew Paris, known as Matthew of Westminster, wrote of the battle of Evesham in *Flores Historiarum per Matthaeum Westmonasteriensem Collecti* (The Flowers of History, 1307):

> And when Simon, the son of the aforesaid earl of Leicester, had, with many barons and knights, traversed and plundered all Kent, and the country about Winchester and the other southern districts of England, and then proceeded, to his own misfortune, with great speed to Kenilworth to meet his father, the aforesaid Edward and Gilbert and their armies, being, by the favor of God, forewarned of his approach, attacked his army at dawn on the day of Saint Peter ad Vincula, and took them all prisoners, except Simon and a few with him who escaped into the castle, and put them in chains, and stripped those robbers and plunderers of all their booty, and so celebrated a day of feasting at the New Chains.
>
> The earl of Leicester and his companions, being ignorant of this event, and marching on with all speed, reached the river Severn that very same day, and having examined the proper fords, crossed the river at twilight with the design of meeting and finding the aforesaid Simon and his army, who were coming from England, and having stopped the two next days on the borders of Worcestershire, on the third day they entered

the town of Evesham, and while they were occupying themselves there with refreshing their souls, which had been long fainting under hunger and thirst, with a little food, their scouts brought them word that the lord Edward and his army were not above two miles off. So the earl of Leicester and the barons marching out with their lord the king (whom they took with them by force) to the rising ground of a gentle hill, beheld Edward and his army on the top of a hill, not above a stone's throw from them, and hastening to them. And a wonderful conflict took place, there being slain on the part of the lord Edward only one knight of moderate prowess, and two esquires. On the other side there fell on the field of battle Simon, earl of Leicester, whose head, and hands, and feet were cut off, and Henry, his son, Hugh Despenser, justiciary of England, Peter de Montfort, William de Mandeville, Radulph Basset, Roger St. John, Walter de Despigny, William of York, and Robert Tregos, all very powerful knights and barons, and besides all the guards and warlike cavalry fell in the battle, with the exception of ten or twelve nobles, who were taken prisoners. And the names of the nobles who were wounded and taken prisoners were as follows: Guy de Montfort, son of the earl of Leicester John Fitz-John, Henry de Hastings, Humphrey de Peter de Montfort the younger, Bohun the younger, John de Vescy, and Nicholas de Segrave.

In the end, the Provisions of Westminster that had been rejected were included in another edict, the Statute of Marlborough (1267). Five years later, Henry III died, to be succeeded by Edward I.

References: Prothero, George Walter, *The Life of Simon de Montfort, Earl of Leicester, with Special Reference to the Parliamentary History of His Time* (London: Longmans, Green, and Company, 1877); Maddicott, J. R., *Simon de Montfort* (Cambridge, U.K.: Cambridge University Press, 1996); Hutton, William Holden, ed., *Simon de Montfort & His Cause, 1251–1266: Extracts from the Writings of Robert of Gloucester, Matthew Paris, William Rishanger, Thomas of Wykes, etc.* (London: D. Nutt, 1888); Beamish, Sir Tufton Victor Hamilton, *Battle Royal: A New Account of Simon de Montfort's Struggle against King Henry III* (London: F. Muller, 1965); Treharne, Reginald Francis, *The Personal Role of Simon de Montfort in the Period of Baronial Reform and Rebellion, 1238–65* (London: Cumberlage, 1954); Hutton, the Rev. W. H., *Simon de Montfort & His Cause, 1251–1266* (London: David Nutt, 1888); Matthew of Westminster, *The Flowers of History*, edited by C. D. Yonge II (London: Henry G. Bohn, 1853); "Montfort, Simon de, Earl of Leicester," in *The Oxford Companion to Military History*, edited by Richard Holmes (New York: Oxford University Press, 2001), 598.

Montgomery, Bernard Law, first viscount Montgomery of Alamein (1887–1976)
British field marshal

Bernard Law Montgomery was born in London on 17 November 1887, the fourth of nine children of the Reverend Henry Montgomery and his wife Maude (née Farrar) Montgomery. When Bernard was two, his father was named as the bishop of Tasmania, and that same year the entire family moved to Hobart, New Zealand, where, he later wrote, "Certainly I can say that my own childhood was unhappy." In 1901 the family returned to England, where Bernard finished his education at the private St. Paul's School in London. His elder brother Harold served in the British army, seeing action in the last months of the Boer War, and this may have persuaded Bernard to join the army himself. In January 1907, he entered the Royal Military Academy at Sandhurst, after which he was commissioned into the Royal Warwickshire Regiment, stationed in Peshwar, India.

In 1914, when the First World War began, the Warwickshires were sent to France as part of the British Expeditionary Force (BEF). There Montgomery saw action in several battles, including at Le Cateau (26 August 1914) and at the first battle of Ypres (13 October 1914), where he was wounded. He was awarded the Distinguished Service Order (DSO), promoted to the rank of captain, and, after recovering from his wounds, sent back to France, seeing action at the Somme (January 1916). He served in two staff appointments, with the 33rd Division from January 1917 and with IX Corps from July 1917. In June 1918, he was promoted to brevet major, ending the war with that rank.

After the war, Montgomery attended the Staff College at Camberly in 1920, followed by service in Ireland fighting the organization known as the Irish Republican Army (IRA). In 1926, he returned to the Staff College

Bernard Law Montgomery

as an instructor. He then spent two years (1928–30) in the War Office in London, where he helped to revise the official Infantry Training Manual. In 1931, he was sent to the Middle East, where he commanded the 1st Battalion of the Royal Warwickshire Regiment in what is now Israel. He returned to India in 1934, becoming the chief instructor at the Staff College in Quetta. Upon his return to England in 1938, he served as the commander of the 9th Infantry Brigade in Portsmouth, and in 1939 he was named as the commander of the 3rd Division.

As part of General Alan Brooke's II Corps, Montgomery and his division were sent to France on the outbreak of the Second World War. The 3rd Division defended the city of Louvain, Belgium, but had to withdraw after the Allied force collapsed and made their way back to Dunkirk. Before the Allied retreat from the European continent, Brooke was called back and Montgomery replaced him as commander of II Corps. Returning to England, Montgomery was promoted to lieutenant general, and on 17 November 1940, he was named commander in chief of the South-Eastern Command.

A major area of conflict was North Africa, where the territorial gains of the Axis forces led to a shakeup in the Allied military command. In August 1942, General Claude Auchinleck was removed from command in North Africa and replaced by General Harold ALEXANDER, who chose Montgomery to command the Eighth Army in Egypt. Immediately, Montgomery organized his forces against those of his German rival, General Erwin ROMMEL, to check the Germans at Alam Halfa (31 August–2 September 1942). He knew that desert warfare presented severe problems to the movement of troops and supplies, but he also realized that the Germans, with long sea-lines of communication, had more problems than the Allies. With this in mind, Montgomery, having built up his forces, struck at the Germans at El Alamein (23 October–3 November 1942). Working with American general Dwight D. EISENHOWER, whose forces landed on the west coast in November, Montgomery carried out a campaign that saw thousands of German troops captured or killed. The enemy force was rapidly destroyed, and by May 1943 the German presence in North Africa was ended.

Montgomery then turned his attention to southern Europe, where he was one of the key planners of Operation Husky, the Allied invasion of the island of Sicily (10 July 1943). Historians have noted that Montgomery and the other Allied commanders did not get along, due largely to Montgomery's sometimes arrogant behavior. Nonetheless, the Allied force captured Sicily and moved into Italy, slowly fighting their way north.

In December 1943, Montgomery returned to England, where he was given command of the 21st Army Group prior to the Allied assault on the European continent through France that was set for 1944. Operation Overlord, better known as the D-Day or Normandy landings, took place on 6 July 1944. Gradually, the Allied forces moved out from their beachhead, and Montgomery was given complete command of Operation Goodwood, the breakout from Normandy into northern France, which took several weeks. The escape of German forces from the Allied attacks has been blamed directly on Montgomery. In August 1944, Eisenhower, as previously agreed, was named commander of all ground forces in Europe, ending Montgomery's command role in the theater, although he was promoted to field marshal on 1 September 1944. In the last months of the war, the Allied commanders differed on how to best defeat Germany. Montgomery sided with Generals Omar BRADLEY and George PATTON in hitting Germany with one decisive thrust, while Eisenhower ultimately decided on a steady advance along the entire front. Montgomery's forces marched into Germany, ultimately reaching the city of Lübeck, near the Baltic Sea, when the war ended on 4 May 1945.

On 1 January 1946, Montgomery was styled as Viscount Montgomery of Alamein, and in June that year he was named as chief of the Imperial General Staff (CIGS), where he served until November 1948. In the years that followed, he served as chair of the Western Union Commanders-in-chief Committee (1948–51) and then as deputy supreme allied commander of allied forces in Europe from 1951 until 1958. During this period, he was a driving force behind the formation of the Northern Atlantic Treaty Alliance (NATO). In 1958, he retired after serving for more than 50 years in the British military. He also published his memoirs, in which he criticized many of his contemporaries, including Claude Auchinleck, for errors of command. The book left many embittered toward Montgomery, who wrote numerous articles and spoke out on military matters. Ill for the last three years of his life, he died at his home at Islington Mill, near Alton, Hampshire, on 24 March 1976, age 88.

The editors of *The Wordsworth Dictionary of Military Biography* write of Montgomery's legacy:

Like many other commanders of the Second World War, Montgomery was haunted by the recollection of the appalling casualties suffered in the stagnant warfare of 1914–18, and his battlefield tactics developed accordingly. Never committing himself to offensive risks until possessed of superior strength, and being an ardent believer in "set-piece" warfare, he attracted fairly widespread criticism from other commanders; but one cannot deny that his caution eliminated costly setbacks such as that which occurred in the Ardennes. . . . [H]is achievement in North Africa assures him of a place in any list of outstanding British commanders. Many observers attribute his greatness to his ability to assess changing conditions and make his plans accordingly. He was a rigid disciplinarian, never reluctant to take harsh action against an inefficient subordinate commander, but was much respected by his troops. He had a clear understanding of the importance of morale: prior to his arrival in Egypt the British forces had been "messed about" continually, and he immediately improved their outlook by a number of reforms, including the inculcation of a strong *esprit de corps* within individual divisions. He carefully projected a personal "image" to the troops, which laid him open to charges of theatricality, but paid off in terms of morale. His well-founded self-confidence and rather Olympian manner made him enemies, but his achievements far outweigh the petty criticisms he attracted.

References: Moorehead, Alan, *Montgomery: A Biography* (New York: Coward-McCann, 1946); Montgomery of Alamein, Bernard Law Montgomery, Viscount, *The Memoirs of Field-Marshal the Viscount Montgomery of Alamein* (Cleveland: World Publishing Company, 1958); D'Este, Carlo, *Decision in Normandy: The Unwritten Story of Montgomery and the Allied Campaign* (London: Collins, 1983); Horne, Alistair, *The Lonely Leader: Monty, 1944–45* (London: Macmillan, 1994); "Montgomery, Bernard Law," in *Brassey's Encyclopedia of Military History and Biography,* edited by Franklin D. Margiotta (Washington, D.C.: Brassey's, 1994), 676–681; Windrow, Martin, and Francis K. Mason, "Montgomery, Bernard Law, 1st Viscount Montgomery of Alamein," in *The Wordsworth Dictionary of Military Biography* (Hertfordshire, U.K.: Wordsworth Editions Ltd., 1997), 199–203; "Montgomery, FM Sir Bernard Law, 1st Viscount," in *The Oxford Companion to Military History,* edited by Richard Holmes (New York: Oxford University Press, 2001), 598–599.

Montrose, James Graham, first marquis of
(fifth earl of Montrose) (1612–1650) *Scottish military leader*

Born in Edinburgh, Scotland, in 1612, James Graham was the scion of a famed Scottish family with a long and distinguished history of supporting Scotland's independence. He received his education at St. Andrew's University, then went traveling in Europe. In 1626, he succeeded to the earldom of Montrose upon his father's death.

Following in his family's footsteps, Montrose became a strong advocate for the independence of Scotland and helped to compose the National Covenant, which set out the steps for the acceptance of Scottish Presbyterianism. He served in both of the Bishops' Wars (1638–39) against England and King Charles I, which ended with the Treaty of Berwick. However, his moderate views led to his loyalty being suspect, and Archibald Campbell, the eighth earl of Argyll, had him imprisoned. Once released, Montrose felt slighted enough to go to London and offer his services to his former enemy, Charles I, who did not take him seriously until the English Parliament went to war against the king, and the Scots sided with Parliament. Needing a leading Scot in his command, Charles named Montrose as captain general of the Royalist forces in Scotland. After making a vain attempt to invade Scotland, Montrose slipped into his native land in disguise to recruit troops for the Royalist cause. With this force, he went to war against Argyll and defeated the Scots in several battles, including at Tippermuir (1 September 1644), Inverlochy (2 February 1645), and Kilsyth (16 August 1645). Historians agree that Montrose's victories, utilizing a small force against superior numbers, were due to his superb tactical skill. Had Montrose had the proper backing from the Royalists and Charles I, he may have become far more successful. However, Charles's defeat at Naseby (14 June 1645), as well as his repudiation of Montrose in an attempt to gain Scottish support, left Montrose severely weakened and caused his defeat at Philiphaugh (13 September 1645) at the hands of Sir David LESLIE. He escaped from the battle with a few supporters, and after a few months was able to flee to Europe.

On 30 January 1649, after being tried by Parliament, Charles was beheaded. Siding with Charles's son, who would later be crowned as Charles II, Montrose returned to Scotland to fight for the monarchy. Once again, however, he was betrayed by some of his allies when Charles II disavowed him to gain Scottish support, and his small army was easily defeated at Invercharron (27 April 1650). Montrose himself was captured and taken back to Edinburgh in a cart as his captors yelled, "Here comes James Graham, a traitor to his country." Stripped of his title, he was taken to Edinburgh, where he was hanged before a crowd on 21 May 1650. A contemporary work on his execution stated that "His sentence was, to be hanged upon a Galhouse, 30 foot high three houres, at Edeburgh-crosse, to have his head strucken off, and hang'd upon Edenburgh Towlebooth, and his arms and legs to be hanged up in other publique towns in the Kingdome . . . and his body to be buried, at the common burying place." According to several sources, his last words were, "God have mercy on this afflicted land!" Many cried when he was put to death.

Montrose was only 37 when he was executed. He is remembered today as a Scot first and a Royalist second. A poet as well as a brilliant soldier, he is best known for the lines he wrote:

> He either fears his fate too much,
> Or his deserts are small,
> That dares not put it to the touch
> To gain or lose it all.

References: Wishart, George, *Memoirs of the Most Renowned James Graham, Marquis of Montrose.* . . . (Edinburgh: Printed for A. Constable & Co., 1819); Pryce, Mrs. Hugh, *The Great Marquis of Montrose* (London: Everett & Company, Limited, 1912); Buchan, John, *Montrose: A History* (Boston: Houghton Mifflin Company, 1928); Wishart, George, *De Rebus Auspiciis Serenissimi, & Potentissimi Caroli (The History of the kings majesties affaires in Scotland: under the conduct of the most Honourable James, Marques of Montrose, Earl of Kincardin, &c., and generall governour of the kingdome, in the Years 1644, 1645, & 1646)* (Amsterdam: Privately printed, 1649); H. P., *A Relation of the Execution of James Graham late Marquesse of Montrosse, at Edenburgh, on Tuesday the 21 of May instant.* . . . (London: E. Griffin, 1650); Napier, Mark, *Montrose and the Covenanters, their Characters and Conduct,* . . . , 2 vols. (London: J. Duncan, 1838).

Moore, Sir John (1761–1809)   *British general*

The son and namesake of a physician, John Moore was born in Glasgow, Scotland, on 12 November 1761. According to his biographers, Moore was interested in military life from an early age, and at 15 he was able to get a commission (with the help of the duke of Hamilton) to enter the 51st Foot with the rank of ensign. After two years of training, he was placed in a new regiment under Hamilton's command and sent to the American colonies, where he saw action in the Revolutionary War in 1783. After his return to England, Moore was elected to a seat in Parliament at the age of 23. After three years, though, he tired of politics, and reentered military service. Promoted to the rank of major, he was assigned to the 60th Rifles, but a year later he was transferred back to the 51st Foot. In 1790, he was promoted to lieutenant colonel.

In 1792, Moore was sent to the Mediterranean to serve in the French revolutionary wars. He was involved in operations on the island of Corsica and in the taking of the fort at Mozello, where he was wounded, and Calvi. In 1794, he was appointed adjutant general to succeed General Charles Stuart. Upon his return to England in 1795, he was promoted to brigadier general and was sent to the West Indies under the command of Sir Ralph ABERCROMBY. On the island of Santa Lucia, Moore played a key role in the storming and capture of the cities of Demerara, Vigie, Berbice, and Essequebo, among others. Abercromby became very impressed with his ability and wrote that the young officer was "the admiration of the whole army." When Abercromby returned to England, he named Moore as governor and military commander. However, an attack of yellow fever forced Moore to leave the West Indies and return to England.

In 1798, Moore once again saw action under the command of Abercromby. A rebellion in Ireland had forced England to dispatch troops there, and Abercromby placed Moore in command of the southern part of the country. Fighting off a group of Irish troops at Vinegar Hill (2 June 1798), he helped to save the city of Wexford from the rebels, earning Abercromby's written praise again. Moore was then named to command a brigade invading Helder, in Holland. Landing at Egmont-op-Zee on 2 October 1799, once again Moore showed his propensity for brilliant tactics, although he was wounded in the battle.

Two years later, Moore was sent to Egypt to fight the French, seeing action at Aboukir (21 March 1801), where he was again wounded, and at Alexandria. Back in England, he was named as commander of the force at Shorncliffe, the possible location of an invasion by the French under NAPOLEON. Although the invasion never took place, Moore impressed his superiors with his training of the troops, with the assistance of Colonel (later General) Kenneth Mackenzie, these forces were to become the first light infantry regiments. Sir William Pitt, the prime minister, made Moore a Knight of the Bath (KB). Promoted to lieutenant-general, Moore saw action in the Mediterranean and rose to become commander in chief of British forces in the region.

In 1808, Moore was sent to the Baltic region to offer military assistance to King Gustavus IV of Sweden in his war against Denmark, France, and Russia. When Gustavus rejected all his advice and even arrested him, Moore was forced to escape in a disguise. Returning to England, he was sent to Portugal during the Peninsular War to work under commanders Sir Hew Dalrymple and Sir Harry Burrard. However, when he arrived, he found that Dalrymple had been recalled and Burrard had resigned. Consequently, Moore was named as commander of British forces in Portugal on 25 September 1808. Ordered to proceed into Spain to head off a Napoleonic invasion, he wrote to Lord Castelreagh, "At this instant, the army is without equipments of any kind, either for the carriage of the light baggage of regiments, military stores, commissariat stores, or other appendages of an army, and not a magazine is formed in any of the routes by which we are to march." Nonetheless, he made his way as commanded. He awaited backup forces from Sir David BAIRD, but, with those not coming, he retreated from Salamanca in the face of heavy pressure from the larger French forces. However, in a brilliant move to delay Napoleon, Moore marched north with his force of 15,000 troops, then west to Corunna (also known as La Coruña). Fearing a flank attack, Napoleon stopped his advance into Spain and followed Moore. On 16 January 1809 at the battle of Corunna, Moore was hit in the left side by a large shot, which nearly tore off his left arm and caused a gaping wound on his left side. He refused to loosen his sword to be treated and was carried off the field with a mortal wound, suffering in horrendous agony until he died later that night. Men of the 60th Foot secretly wrapped his body in a blanket and buried him in an unmarked grave.

Sir John Moore's name has become synonymous with gallantry and consideration for the soldiers under his command. He trained officers and men to think for themselves, and this was his finest legacy. The House of Commons posthumously thanked him for his service, and statues were erected in his memory in both St. Paul's Cathedral in London and in Glasgow. Irish poet Charles Wolfe (1791–1823) penned the immortal *The Burial of Sir John Moore,* which was published anonymously in 1817.

Historian D. W. Davies writes: "'Sir John Moore is certainly a most unlucky fellow,' said the Duke of WELLINGTON, and he certainly was. An example of his bad luck is that he was Britain's foremost general immediately before Wellington took over that distinction. Moore's career lay in the trough between Marlborough and Wolfe on the one side and Wellington on the other. . . . Moore has been saved from obscurity first, because he conducted one of the longest retreats in British army history, and second, because a poem was written upon his death."

References: Brownrigg, B., *The Life & Letters of Sir John Moore* (Oxford, U.K.: Blackwell, 1923); "Moore, Sir John," in *The Oxford Companion to Military History,* edited by Richard Holmes (New York: Oxford University Press, 2001), 599; Anderson, J., *Spanish Campaign of Sir John Moore* (London: R. J. Leach, 1990); Small, Harold A., *The Field of His Fame: A Ramble on the Curious History of Charles Wolfe's Poem 'The Burial of Sir John Moore'* (Berkeley: University of California, 1953); Wolfe, Charles, *The Burial of Sir John Moore, and Other Poems* (London: Sidgwick and Jackson, 1909), 59; Davies, D. W., *Sir John Moore's Peninsular Campaign* (The Hague: Martinus Nijoff, 1974).

Murat, Joachim (Prince Murat) (1767–1815)

French cavalry commander, king of Naples

Joachim Murat had a long and distinguished career in the French army, tied mainly to the fate of his friend and brother-in-law, NAPOLEON BONAPARTE. The son of an innkeeper, he was born in the village of La Bastide-Fortunière, in the departement of Lot, France, on 25 March 1767. Although he studied theology and canon law at the University of Toulouse, he decided instead for a career in the military and entered the French army in February 1787. In 1792, he was commissioned an officer, rising to the rank of *chef d'escandron* (chief of squadron) in the 16th Chasseurs in October 1795, when he participated in Napoleon's suppression of the royalist-inspired insurrection of a mob in Paris (3–5 October 1795), known as 13th Vendémiaire. Napoleon was appointed general of the interior, and in 1796, when he became commander of the French army in Italy, he named Murat as his chief aide-de-camp, with the rank of colonel.

In Italy, serving by Napoleon's side, Murat saw action at the battles of Mondovi (21 April 1796), Borghetto (30 May 1796), and Tagliamento (March 1797), as well as at the siege of Mantua (24 August 1796–2 February 1797). Advanced to the rank of brigadier general, he was dispatched by Napoleon to the Congress of Rastadt to arrange a treaty with the Austrians. He then went to serve in the Napoleonic invasion of Egypt, seeing action at Alexandria (2 July 1798) and at the battle of the Pyramids (21 July 1798). In 1799, Murat personally commanded the invasion of what is now Syria. During the battle of Aboukir (25 July 1799), he siezed the Pasha Mustapha and took him prisoner. Wounded during this battle, he was promoted to the rank of major general.

Murat accompanied Napoleon back to France, where he was made a commander of the Consular Guard. In January 1800, he married Caroline, Napoleon's youngest sister. Sent back to Italy he took command of the cavalry wing, leading them against the Austrians at Marengo (14 June 1800). A series of battles then consolidated the French hold on Italy.

In 1804, Napoleon named Murat as governor of Paris and later that year promoted him to rank of marshal of France. In February 1805, Napoleon, by now crowned as emperor of France, bestowed on Murat the title of Prince Murat. Dispatched to fight Austria as the head of the French cavalry, Murat was instrumental in the capture of the city of Ulm (15–20 October 1805). Although Napoleon had ordered him to move against the Austrian and Russian armies that fled from Ulm along the Danube, he instead marched triumphantly into Vienna on 11 November 1805. Napoleon later reprimanded him for this act of insubordination, writing

that Murat had acted "like a bewildered idiot, taking not the least notice of my orders." However, he let Murat, a brilliant cavalry leader, remain in command. Murat again proved his worth at Austerlitz (2 December 1805), a battle in which more than 27,000 Austrians and Russians drowned as they fled across a near-frozen lake. Napoleon rewarded his service in this battle by granting Murat the title of Grand-Duc de Berg et de Clèves.

When England and Prussia joined Austria and Russia in the war against France, Murat's cavalry helped defeat the Prussians at Jena (14 October 1806) and at Lübeck (6 November 1806), where, with the assistance of Marshals Soult and BERNADOTTE, he forced the capitulation of Field Marshal Gebard von BLÜCHER. At Eylau (8 February 1807), Murat personally led a cavalry charge—"the charge of eighty squadrons"—into the midst of the enemy ranks. In 1808, Napoleon named Murat as the king of Naples, and for a time he left the battlefield and worked for his new kingdom, implementing civil reforms that eventually led to disagreements with Napoleon.

In 1812, Napoleon set out to invade and Russia and, once again he called on Murat to serve as his commander of cavalry. Murat led French forces at Borodino (7 September 1812) and avoided being routed at Taroutino (18 October 1812). Napoleon had to retreat from Moscow and left for Paris, placing Murat in control of the French forces in Russia. However, Murat preferred his role of king of Naples, and at Vilna he abandoned his army, fleeing back to Naples in December 1812. Napoleon never berated him for this, instead allowing him to take command of the French armies in southern Europe. However, after Murat suffered a horrible defeat at Leipzig (16–19 October 1813), he again went back to Naples.

In January 1814, without Napoleon's approval, Murat signed a peace treaty with Austria. When Napoleon was sent into exile on the island of St. Helena, and the reinstated Bourbon family reclaimed the throne of Naples, Murat tried to have his title recognized by the victorious allies. When this recognition was refused, he backed Napoleon's flight from Elba and return to power. As soon as Napoleon landed in France, Murat declared war on Austria, moving his army into Rome and Bologna, and issued a declaration calling for the unification of Italy under his control. The Austrians, under the command of General Wilhelm Neipperg, invaded Italy and, on 3 May 1815, confronted Murat at Tolentino, where his forces were overwhelmed. He was forced to flee for France, but Napoleon, in the midst of his famed "100 days" in power which ended in his own defeat at Waterloo, refused to see him. Murat therefore raised a small force and set out for Italy to regain his throne. He landed at Pizzo, but the Austrians were waiting, and he was captured. Quickly tried and found guilty, he was sentenced to death. The judge ordered that he be given "half an hour to receive the solace of religion" before the sentence was carried out. On the morning of 13 October 1815, Murat was taken to a courtyard. Carrying a small engraving of his wife, he shouted to the firing squad, "Save my face . . . aim at my heart . . . fire!" His body was buried in an unmarked grave.

Although Murat is considered one of the better of the French generals during the Napoleonic era, he had serious faults. The writers of the *The Wordsworth Dictionary of Military Biography* note:

> It is unthinkable to exclude Joachim Murat from any list of the great names of the Napoleonic Wars, yet his claims for inclusion are curiously unsatisfactory to the student of military history. In the final analysis Murat stands as the ultimate symbol of a particular type of soldier: the outrageously-uniformed officer of light cavalry, swaggering and dueling and wenching, laughing at danger . . . and quite prepared to start his own wars if his masters were slow to provide him with entertainment. Murat was by no means a great commander; there were several among his subordinates who displayed a far greater mastery of the art of maneuvering large bodies of horse in the field. In keeping with his Gascon heritage, he was extravagantly boastful and vain, and even in an age of conspicuous military glamour his dazzling personally-designed uniforms were considered a trifle ridiculous. Hot-headed to a fault, he often crossed the line which divides a fiery spirit from sheer unthinking stupidity.

References: Perodi, P., *Memoirs of the Reign of Murat . . .* (Boston: West and Richardson, 1818); Espitalier, Albert, *Napoleon and King Murat* (London: John Lane, 1911); Cole, Hubert, *The Betrayers: Joachim and Caroline Murat* (London: Eyre Methuen, 1972); Maceroni, Francis, *Interesting Facts Relating to the Fall and Death of Joachim Murat, King of Naples . . .* (London: Printed for Ridgways, 1817); Windrow, Martin and Francis K. Mason. "Murat, Joachim, Prince Murat," in *The Wordsworth Dictionary of Military Biography* (Hertfordshire, U.K.: Wordsworth Editions Ltd., 1997), 208–210.

N

Napier, Sir Charles (Count Napier de São Vicente) (1786–1860) *English admiral*

Charles Napier was born in his family's residence of Merchiston Hall, near Falkirk, Stirling, Scotland, on 6 March 1786, the son of Charles Napier, a naval officer. The Napiers were a highly successful military family, and his cousins included Sir Charles James NAPIER and Sir William Patrick Napier. He joined the British navy in 1800, when he was just 14, rising to the rank of lieutenant in 1805. He initially saw action in the Mediterranean and the West Indies, and was named commander of his own brig, the *Pultusk,* in 1807. He helped to capture the French ship *Hautpoult* and sailed back to England in 1809. There being no immediate need of his services, he attended the University of Edinburgh but was recalled for duty later in the Napoleonic wars and in the War of 1812 against the United States. Following that conflict, he spent some time in Europe and invested heavily in a steamship company that went bankrupt. In 1827, he was named as captain of the *Galatea.*

In 1831, while still a British naval officer serving in the Azores, Napier became involved in the struggle of Princess Maria da Glória (later Queen Maria II) to suppress a rebellion against the Portuguese throne. Asked to take command of her fleet to fight Dom Miguel, a pretender to the throne, Napier destroyed Miguel's fleet at Cape St. Vincent (5 July 1833). Consequently, the title of Conde (count) Napier de São Vicente was bestowed on him by the Portuguese government. Napier also led Portuguese forces in the defense of Lisbon (1834).

Napier returned to the service of England in 1836, receiving command of the ship *Powerful.* In 1840, he was made second in command in the war against Syria, seeing action during the fight for the cities of Beirut and Acre (October–November), for which he was created Knight Commander of the Order of the Bath (KCB). Returning to England, he was elected as a member of Parliament from Marylebone, serving from 1842 to 1846. In the latter year, he was promoted to the rank of rear admiral and given command of the English Channel fleet from 1847 to 1849. In 1854, with the outbreak of the Crimean War against Russia, Napier was named commander of the Baltic fleet. However, when he was ordered to attack the Russian base at Kronshtadt, he refused, citing insufficient strength, and was relieved of command.

Napier returned to England, never again to hold a naval command. He was elected again to Parliament from Southwark, serving from February 1855 until his death near the village of Catherington, in Hampshire, on 6 November 1860.

References: Napier, Priscilla Hayter, *Black Charlie: A Life of Admiral Sir Charles Napier KCB, 1786–1860* (Wilby, U.K.: Michael Russell, 1995); Williams, Hugh Noel, *The Life and Letters of Admiral Sir Charles Napier, K.C.B.* (London: Hutchinson & Co., 1917); "Napier, Vice-Admiral Sir Charles," in *Men of the Time. Biographical Sketches of Eminent Living Characters. Also Biographical Sketches of Celebrated Women of the Time* (London: David Bogue, Fleet Street, 1856), 578.

Napier, Sir Charles James (1782–1853)
British general

Charles James Napier—not to be confused with Sir Charles NAPIER, who was his cousin—was born in London on 10 August 1782. He was the eldest son and one of three military sons (including Sir William Patrick Napier) of Colonel George Napier and his wife, born Lady Sarah Lennox. Charles James Napier was commissioned into the British army at age 12 and, through the influence of his cousin, General Henry Edward Fox, was advanced to the rank of major by the time he was 24. He saw action in the Napoleonic wars, particularly in Spain, when he served in Sir John MOORE's campaign against the French at Corunna (16 January 1809). Wounded at the battles of Coa and Busaco, he returned to England to recuperate and was then given command of the 102nd Regiment, which was sent to fight the United States in the War of 1812.

In 1819, Napier was posted to Cephalonia, in the Ionian Islands, where over the next decade he implemented much-needed civic reforms and introduced a program of public works, including bridge and road building. In 1837, he was promoted to major general, and in 1838 he was made a Knight Commander of the Order of the Bath (KCB). In 1839, when the Chartists, a group of reformers who demanded expansion of the suffrage, agitated for immediate change, Napier was dispatched to northern England. Sympathizing with their goals, he was able to convince the Chartists not to turn to violence, thus avoiding bloodshed.

In 1841, Napier went to India, where he was given command of the Sind, also known as the Scinde, serving under Edward Law, earl of Ellenborough, governor-general of India. In 1843, Ellenborough signed a treaty with the Sind leaders to build British forts in the area but allowing the Sindhi amirs, or tribal rulers to continue in power as long as they remained peaceful. Napier soon found many of these rulers were breaking their word; he wrote that "barbaric chiefs must be bullied or they think you are afraid: they do not understand benevolence or magnanimity." He was soon forced into warfare, winning victories at Miani (17 February 1843) and Dabo (also Dubba, 24 March 1843) near Haidarabad (now Hyderabad), and was named as governor of the Sind. Lord Ellenborough paid him £50,000 for his conquest of Haiderabad.

As the Sind's governor, Napier formed a new administration, including a police force, built roads, and improved communications. When he departed in 1847, he left behind a peaceful and prosperous region. In 1849, he was sent back to India to replace Lord Gough as commander in chief of British forces there. His time in India was short, and he departed in 1851 following an argument over policy with the governor-general, Lord Dalhousie. He died in Portsmouth, Hampshire, on 29 August 1853, shortly after his 71st birthday. A statue of Napier was later placed in Trafalgar Square in London. The note on the pedestal states: "Erected by Public Subscription, the most numerous Contributors being Private Soldiers."

Although nearly forgotten today, Sir Charles James Napier's legacy as a military commander is solidly placed in military history. Sir William Butler, a Napier biographer, wrote in 1890:

"When the light was made manifest to the world four years after the hero's death, the man who had stood [a] faithful sentinel through so many years over his brother's fame—William Napier—was still left to haul the full-risen beam, and to show to a careless world the length and breadth of that signal vindication. And long before the lower crowd could see the light, it had flashed upon the great solitary summits. 'A lynx-eyed, fiery man, with a spirit of an old knight in him,' wrote Carlyle, one year before the Indian Mutiny. 'More of a hero than any modern I have seen for a long time; a singular veracity one finds in him, not in his words alone, but in his actions, judgments, aims, in all that he thinks, and does, and says, which indeed I have observed is the root of all greatness or real worth in human creatures, and properly the first, and also the earliest, attribute of what we call *genius* among men.'"

References: Vetch, Robert Hamilton, "Napier, Sir Charles James," in *The Dictionary of National Biography,* 22 vols., 8 supps., edited by Sir Leslie Stephen and Sir Sidney Lee, et al. (London: Oxford University Press, 1921–22), XIV:45–54; Bruce, William Napier, *Life of General Sir Charles Napier* (London: John Murray, 1885); Lawrence, Rosamond, Lady Lawrence, *Charles Napier: Friend and Fighter, 1782–1853* (London: John Murray, 1952); Lambrick, H. T., *Sir Charles Napier and Sind* (Oxford, U.K.: Clarendon Press, 1952); Outram, General Sir James, *The Conquest of Scinde: A Commentary* (Edinburgh, Scotland: Blackwoods, 1846); Napier, General Edward Delaval Hungerford Elers, *Life and Correspondence of Admiral Sir Charles Napier, K.C.B. from Personal Recollections, Letters, and Official Documents,* 2 vols. (London: Hurst and Blackett, 1862); Butler, Colonel Sir William, *Sir Charles Napier* (London: Macmillan and Company, 1890), 214–215.

Napoleon Bonaparte (Napoléon I, Napoleon Buonoparte) (1769–1821) *French emperor*

Ironically, Napoleon Bonaparte was not of French parentage: He was born on 15 August 1769 in Ajaccio, Corsica, an island off the southern French coast, into a family whose real name was Buonoparte (the spelling was changed about 1796). His father was Carlo Maria Buonoparte, a moderately wealthy attorney; his mother was named Letizia Ramolino. Napoleon was one of seven children, all of whom would come to dominate Europe. He started his military training early, entering the military academy at Brienne in 1779. He then went into the École Militaire in Paris, graduating in 1785. When he was 16, he was given a commission as a second lieutenant in the French army, and in 1789, when the French Revolution exploded, he became a Jacobin—a member of the opposition to King Louis XVI of France. His command of artillery at the siege of the British garrison at Toulon (1793) gave him credibility among the leaders of the French army, and he was subsequently promoted to brigadier general.

On 5 October 1795, Napoleon swiftly put down a rebellion by proroyalist forces in Paris by clearing the streets with what has been dubbed the "whiff of grapeshot," killing over 100 demonstrators. This action is known as 13 Vendémiaire, the date in the new calendar instituted by the French radicals who had overthrown the king. Napoleon's act in defense of the revolution led to his promotion to commander of Army of the Interior; the next year, he was named commander of the French army of Italy. As he later wrote during his in exile on St. Helena, "Centuries will pass before the unique combination of events which led to my career recur in the case of another."

In March 1796, Napoleon moved toward the Italian frontier with a ragtag army of 30,000 men who were ill prepared for war and had few supplies. He said to them, "You are badly fed and all but naked. . . . I am about to lead you into the most fertile plains in the world. Before you are great cities and rich provinces;

Napoleon Bonaparte

there we shall find honor, glory and riches." In a short period of time, Napoleon turned them into an outstanding fighting force, and on 10 April 1796, the army entered Italy. In a series of lightning-fast skirmishes—at Montenotte (12 April), Millesimo (13 April), and Dego (15 April), his troops captured extensive territory. The Italian leaders fled as their armies collapsed, and Napoleon called on the Italian people to embrace him as their new leader. In May 1796, he forced Sardinia to sign a peace treaty, then turned on the Austrians, whom he saw as a continuing threat to France. He crossed the bridge at Lodi (10 May), entered Milan (14 May), and attacked Mantua (July 1796); then, turning northward, he crossed the Alps and headed toward Vienna. Aware that the Austrians, under the command of the Archduke CHARLES (brother of Holy Roman Emperor Francis II) and General Baron Joseph Alvintzy, were strengthening their forces on the Rhine River, Napoleon decided to utilize the talents of several French generals, most notably Jean-Baptiste BERNADOTTE, and attack Charles's army head on. He mocked the Austrians, whose commanders, "faithful to the old system of warfare, scattered their troops in small detachments before a man who practiced mass-movement." At Rivoli (January 1797), he won a huge victory over the Austrians, leading to negotiations and the truce of Leoben (April 1797), which was solidified by the Treaty of Campo Formio (17 October 1797). The remarkable campaign established his reputation.

Napoleon's dream was to invade England, the French revolutionaries' steadfast enemy, and conquer the British Isles. However, because of Britain's naval superiority, he decided instead to attack British possessions. Starting in Egypt, he moved an army of 40,000 men into Malta, seizing the island before landing at Alexandria on 1 July 1798. He won several battles, but the destruction of the French fleet by Admiral Horatio NELSON at the battle of the Nile (also Aboukir, 1 August 1798) reduced his ability move his army. His attempt to conquer Syria to the north was stopped by the heroic defense of Acre (16 March–20 May 1799) by the British admiral Sidney Smith.

Napoleon's gains in Europe were threatened when French troops in Italy were forced to withdraw before forces of the Second Coalition, composed of Austria, Great Britain, Naples, the Ottoman Empire, Portugal, and Russia. However, on 4–7 June 1799 at Zurich, Archduke Charles was held and then pushed back by French marshal André MASSÉNA. When the Russian general Alexander Vasilyevich Suvorov moved to support Charles's gains, friction and conflict between the Austrians and Russians led to a series of defeats for the anti-Napoleon coalition.

Napoleon returned to France just as the Directory, the haphazard council that was running France, collapsed in the coup of 18 Brumaire (9 November 1799). Named as first consul and de facto ruler of France, Napoleon immediately began a series of military maneuvers to recapture the land lost to the Second Coalition. With Russia out of the confederacy, it became easier for the French to fight on varying fronts, and he moved back into Italy, destroying the Austrians at Marengo (14 June 1800). At Hohenlinden (3 December 1800), Jean Moreau, Peter NEY, and Emmanuel Grouchy set 100,000 French troops against Archduke John's 130,000, cutting down the Austrians, who lost some 18,000 dead and wounded. These two horrendous losses forced Emperor Francis II to sign the Treaty of Lunéville (9 February 1801), which set the Rhine River as France's eastern border.

Returning to France, Napoleon established a government and constitution in 1802 and, in 1804, declared himself emperor of France. His Napoleonic Code codified many laws in the lands he conquered and controlled and established one set of laws—guidelines that would rule Europe for many years after his fall. A series of further codes, dealing with trade and civil and criminal litigation, followed until 1810.

In 1805, Napoleon declared himself king of Italy, and when this move was followed by the annexation of Genoa to France, another alliance, called the Third Coalition, was formed by Austria, Great Britain, Russia, and Sweden. Once again, French forces moved eastward to attack the Austrians; at Ulm on 20 October 1805, Napoleon encircled the 40,000-man Austrian army and forced General Karl Mack to surrender. He occupied Vienna, and at Austerlitz on 2 December 1805, he won a crushing victory over a combined Austrian and Russian force that suffered over 27,000 killed and wounded in a single day. On 26 December 1805, Napoleon forced Austria to sign the Treaty of Pressburg and leave the Third Coalition. The Prussians took their place, but at Jena (14 October 1806), the French again routed their enemy, and Napoleon's forces marched into Berlin. Fighting against Russia was less victorious: At Eylau (8 February 1807), a clash in a horrific snowstorm ended indecisively, but Napoleon followed this up with a major victory at Friedland (14 June 1807), and Russia was forced out of the war. Under the Treaties of Tilsit (July 1807), half of Prussia's territory was given to the French, and Prussian Poland was given its independence.

Napoleon now stood as the conqueror of most of continental Europe. He placed his brother Louis on the throne of Holland, his brother Jerome on the throne of Westphalia, his brother Joseph on the throne of Naples, and, in 1808, made Joseph king of Spain. In 1806, he declared the Holy Roman Empire to be ended. At Aspern-Essling (21–22 May 1809), Napoleon's forces, although not defeated, were forced to withdraw before the Austrians under Archduke Charles, marking Napoleon's first reverse; in this battle, Marshal Jean LANNES was killed by a cannonball. However, Austria failed to defeat Napoleon at Wagram (6 July 1809).

The first real signs of French vulnerability came in the Peninsular War (1808–14), when Napoleon's troops were routed in Spain and Portugal in 1808 and 1809 by British forces. Nevertheless, he decided to invade Russia, following the end of the peace with Russia established under the 1807 Treaties of Tilsit (expanded by the 1808 Congress of Erfurt). When Russia refused to remain in the Continental System, Napoleon's grand scheme for a single economic system in Europe, and continued to trade with Britain, he gathered an army of 500,000 men and marched on Russia in June 1812. As with Adolf Hitler and the Germans 130 years later, Napoleon's forces moved quickly into Russia, forcing General Mikhail KUTUZOV to rapidly withdraw his troops. On 7 September 1812, at Borodino, a small village west of Moscow, the two great armies met in a bloody but indecisive battle: The French lost some 33,000 killed and wounded, while the Russians lost 45,000 men. Kutuzov withdrew further, and Napoleon entered Moscow on 14 September. However, he found a city destroyed by the fleeing Russians; there were no supplies, and the Russian winter was rapidly killing off his army. After trying to arrange for peace with Czar Alexander I of Russia, Napoleon gave up and began a hasty withdrawal back to France. Kutuzov used guerrilla strikes to harrass the French, but he did not dare take them on. When

the French army finally returned to France, Napoleon had just 10,000 soldiers of his original 500,000. The Russian disaster spelled the beginning of the end for his reign.

Sensing Napoleon's vulnerability, the Prussians joined the Russians, British, and Swedish in a fourth coalition. At Leipzig (16–19 October 1813), these combined armies forced the French troops to retreat. An offer was made for Napoleon to retain France's old borders; when he refused, the coalition armies marched into France and took Paris on 31 March 1814. Napoleon abdicated his throne on 11 April and went into exile on the island of Elba, while Louis XVIII was installed on the French throne. The Congress of Vienna was established to redraw the borders of Europe, but as the congress was meeting, Napoleon, backed by some of his generals and followers, escaped from Elba, landed at Cannes, and proceeded to Paris. He entered the city on 20 March 1815 and began a period of rule known as the Hundred Days, during which he reassembled the French army and set out to reestablish the empire he had once ruled over. However, on 18 June 1815, the forces under the command of Arthur Wellesley, duke of WELLINGTON, to face Napoleon at Waterloo. Of this battle, Captain H. W. Powell, a British officer of the 1st Foot Guards, later wrote:

> There ran along this part of the position a cart road, on one side of which was a ditch and bank, in and under which the Brigade sheltered themselves during the cannonade, which might have lasted three-quarters of an hour. Without the protection of this bank every creature must have perished. . . . The Emperor [Napoleon] probably calculated on this effect, for suddenly the firing ceased, and as the smoke cleared away a most superb sight opened on us. A close column of Grenadiers (about seventies in front) of *la Moyenne Garde,* about 6000 strong, led, as we have since heard, by Marshall [Michel] Ney, were seen ascending the rise *au pas de charge* shouting "Vive l'Empereur." They continued to advance till within fifty or sixty paces of our front, when the Brigade were ordered to stand up. Whether it was from the sudden and unexpected appearance of a Corps so near them, which must have

seemed as starting out of the ground, or the tremendously heavy fire we threw into them, *La Garde,* who had never before failed in an attack *suddenly* stopped. Those who from a distance and more on the flank could see the affair, tell us that the effect of our fire seemed to force the head of the Column bodily back.

Napoleon was crushed at Waterloo, and his 100-day rule ended. Once again he was exiled, this time to the island of St. Helena, where he was kept a prisoner and wrote his memoirs as his health declined. Suffering from cancer of the stomach (and possibly, as some historians claim, from severe arsenic poisoning), Napoleon Bonaparte died on St. Helena on 5 May 1821. His remains were first buried there, but in 1840 they were taken back to France and installed in the Invalides in Paris next to his son.

Historian Michael Lee Lanning sums up Napoleon's influence on world history: "As emperor of France, Napoleon Bonaparte dominated European political and military life for more than two decades. His military genius led him to conquer most of the Continent and extend French control into Asia and Africa. Napoleon not only captured massive [amounts of] territory; he also exported his military and political ideas and techniques and influenced armies and governments throughout the world. In doing so, he clearly established himself as one of the most influential military leaders of all times."

Historian Robert Asprey's two-volume work on Napoleon is perhaps one of the greatest on this mysterious and little-understood man. Asprey writes, "Napoleon Bonaparte has been too often remembered as either [a] demi-god or devil incarnate."

References: Asprey, Robert B., *The Rise of Napoleon Bonaparte* (London: Little, Brown and Company, 2000); Palmer, Alan Warwick, *Russia in War and Peace* (London: Weidenfeld and Nicolson, 1972); Shosenberg, James W., "Napoleon's Masterstroke at Rivoli," *Military History* 13, no. 5 (December 1996): 34–40; Petre, F. Loraine, *Napoleon & the Archduke Charles: A History of the Franco-Austrian Campaign in the Valley of the Danube in 1809* (London: Arms & Armour Press, 1976); Keegan, John, *The Face of Battle: A Study of Agincourt, Waterloo and the Somme* (New York: Penguin Books, 1984); "Waterloo," *18 June 1815: Napoleon's Last Throw—Charge of the Imperial Guard, 7 P.M.,* in *Eyewitness to History,* edited by John Carey (Cambridge, Mass.: Harvard University Press, 1987), 291; Smith, Robert Barr, "'A Damned Nice Thing' at Waterloo," *Military History* 12, no. 2 (June 1995): 62–69; Lanning, Michael Lee, "Napoleon I," in *The Military 100: A Ranking of the Most Influential Military Leaders of All Time* (New York: Barnes and Noble Books, 1996), 8–13; Kintz, P., J. P. Goulle, Fornes, P. Ludes, et al. "Letter to the Editor: A New Series of Hair Analyses from Napoleon Confirms Chronic Exposure to Arsenic," *Journal of Analytical Toxicology* 26, no. 8 (2002): 584–585.

Narses (ca. A.D. 478–573) *Byzantine commander*
Little is known of Narses' life; he was apparently born in Armenia about A.D. 478, but he is not mentioned in histories until his entry into the imperial household of Byzantine emperor Justinian I. A eunuch, Narses advanced to become the chamberlain [an officer who manages the household of a monarch] of the imperial court. Justinian, convinced of his abilities after Narses put down the Nika riot of 532, soon named him as the emperor's treasurer. In 538, believing that Narses was completely trustworthy, Justinian sent him to Italy to oversee the movements of his leading commander, BELISARIUS. Although he was recalled in 539, in 551 Narses was sent back and named as Belisarius's successor as the head of the Byzantine army. As the new commander, he defeated the Ostrogoth king Totila (552) and the Franks and the Goths at Capua (554), thus reestablishing Byzantine control over Italy. Historian André Corvisier, who wrote perhaps the longest biography of Narses, describes the victory over Totila:

> At Taginae (552), in central Italy, Narses' Byzantine army of 15,000 encountered the Ostrogothic army of King Totila. The two armies went into line of battle across a shallow valley. Narses formed his heavy infantry into a phalanx to block the foot of the valley, ordering some of his heavy cavalry to dismount and join the infantry. Over 4,000 archers were massed on either flank with the remaining heavy cavalry in their rear. The Ostrogoths placed their heavy cavalry in front of

their infantry and charged. They were unable to break through the Byzantine infantry and stood halted before the infantry line receiving showers of arrows from the flanks. Narses then ordered his infantry to press forward while his heavy cavalry attacked from either wing. The Ostrogothic cavalry retreated but became entangled with their own foot soldier. King Totila was mortally wounded. The victory at Taginae led to the recapture of Rome in 553 and the return of Italy to Byzantine control.

Justinian's death in 565 left Narses without a Byzantine leader who trusted him implicitly, and the emperor's successor, Justin II, recalled him on account of his levying heavy taxes on the Roman peoples. He died in 573. Although now almost forgotten, Narses was an important Byzantine military leader who, together with Belisarius, evoked the ancient glory of the Roman Empire in the West.

References: "Narses," in *A Dictionary of Military History and the Art of War,* edited by André Corvisier (London: Blackwell, 1994), 547–548; Hodgkin, Thomas, *Italy and Her Invaders,* 6 vols. (Oxford, U.K.: The Clarendon Press, 1880–89), IV:220.

Nassau, Maurice, Prince of Orange-Nassau

See MAURICE, PRINCE OF ORANGE AND COUNT OF NASSAU.

Nebuchadnezzar (ca. 630–ca. 561 B.C.)
Babylonian emperor

The son of the Chaldean leader Nabopolassar, who founded a Babylonian dynasty, Nebuchadnezzar was born about 630 B.C. Cuneiform writings found in the Middle East report that his name, from the Akkadian language translation of Nabukudurri-usur, means "O Nabu, protect my boundary stone," which indicates that during his reign Nebuchadnezzar was known for his military might in protection of what he claimed were his nation's borders. Historian William Hinke writes: "Babylonian boundary stones and their inscriptions have long been the subject of study and investigation. Among the

earliest Babylonian monuments which arrived in Europe was the now famous *Caillou de Michaux,* found by the French botanist C. Michaux, at the Tigris, a day's journey below Bagdad, in the ruins of a palace, and brought by him to Paris in the year 1800."

Nebuchadnezzar is first mentioned in historic writings around 610 B.C., when Babylonian histories show him to have entered military service. Cuneiform tablets written about his father further show that he had worked as a laborer on the temple of Marduk (also called Saggil), which idolized the chief Babylonian god. Although he was the son of the leader of Babylon, Nebuchadnezzar nonetheless worked among the people. However, starting about 607 or 606 B.C., he began assisting his father, serving as second in command in a military expedition to the mountains north of Assyria, in what are now the nations of northern Iraq and Syria. When their armies returned to Babylonia, Nebuchadnezzar was placed in charge of all military operations. Following a defeat at the hands of the Egyptians, he opened up an offensive, defeating the Egyptians at Carchemish (605 B.C.), a key crossing at the Euphrates River, and at Hamath (605 B.C.), with these battles culminating in the expulsion of all Egyptian forces from Assyria.

Following Nabopolassar's death in 605 B.C., Nebuchadnezzar returned to Babylon and assumed his father's throne. As the new leader of the Babylonian Empire, he began a campaign of economic and military revival of his nation-state. He instituted a program of building canals for agriculture and rebuilding old canals that had fallen into disrepair. He also created a wall around the main city of Babylon that was 10 miles in length and had one main entry point called the Ishtar Gate. He constructed a port on the Persian Gulf for trade and ordered the assembly of a terrace with brick arches filled with flowers, now known as the Hanging Gardens of Babylon, one of the seven wonders of the ancient world.

Nebuchadnezzar's primary legacy is of a military nature. Starting in 604 B.C., a year after assuming the throne, he marched his armies into what is now Syria and Israel to gain the acceptance—and submission—of local tribesmen. When the city of Ashkelon, now in Israel, refused to cooperate, he captured it, then sought to stretch his influence as his armies pushed south. However, a clash with the Egyptians in what is now southern Israel (601/600 B.C.) led to a defeat, forcing him to return to Babylon to repair his armies and his chariots. A period of peace until late 599 B.C. gave Nebuchadnezzar a chance to restore his army's strength, leading to another campaign that lasted for several years. During this operation, he attacked the nomadic tribes of what is now Saudi Arabia and, in 598, the city of Judah. In 597, he laid siege to the city of Jerusalem, capturing it in March that same year and taking the city's leader, king Jehoiachin, to Babylon.

Fighting again in what is now Syria in 596 and 595 B.C., Nebuchadnezzar marched east to counter a potential invasion from tribes in what is now southwest Iran. He easily put down a rebellion inside Babylon in 594, and in 586 he put down a revolt against Babylonian rule in Jerusalem, destroying that city. Thousands of Jerusalem's occupants were taken as slaves to Babylon, marking a period in history called the Babylonian captivity (586–538 B.C.).

After this period, Nebuchadnezzar's military record is unclear. The Jewish historian Josephus Flavius relates a 13-year siege of the city of Tyre, now in Lebanon, and suggests that Nebuchadnezzar's armies may have invaded Egypt, which is explained in some cuneiform tablets found by archaeologists. One tablet, in the British Museum in London, reads in part, "In the thirty-seventh year of Nebuchadnezzar, king of the country of Babylon, he went to Mitzraim [in Egypt] to make war. Amasis, king of Egypt, collected [his forces] and marched and spread abroad." But Nebuchadnezzar was not only a man of war: He sent perhaps the world's first "ambassador," Nabonidus, to defuse a potential conflict between the Lydians and the Medes in Asia Minor (now Turkey). (Nabonidus later succeeded Nebuchadnezzar as the head of Babylon and was its last leader when the army of CYRUS THE GREAT of Persia invaded and occupied the Babylonian Empire in 539 B.C.)

Nebuchadnezzar died about 561 B.C., approximately 83 or 84 years old. His legacy is mixed, as Hinke explains:

> Where is he to be placed in the dynasty? It is now generally agreed that he did not occupy the first place. A renewed examination . . . seems to have placed that beyond doubt. On the other hand, there is strong and even irresistible evidence to show that he was actively engaged in freeing his country from chaos and disorder such as we know prevailed at the close of the Cassite period. This appears first of all in the remarkable titles that are attributed to him. He is called "the Sun of his land who makes Prosperous His People," "the Protector of Boundary Stones who fixes the Boundaries," [and] "the King of Right who Judges a Righteous Judgment." The last two statements clearly imply previous lawlessness and disorder, which he brought to an end. The titles applied to him in the new inscription from Nippur point even more strongly to a change in dynasty. It is said that "Ellil broke the weapon of his [Ellil's] enemy and laid the Scepter of his enemy into [Nebuchadrezzar's] hand."

References: Budge, Ernest A., *Nebuchadnezzar, King of Babylon. On Recently-discovered Inscriptions of this King* (London: Victoria Institute, 1884); Weisberg, David B., *Texts from the Time of Nebuchadnezzar* (New Haven, Conn.: Yale University Press, 1980); Sack, Ronald Herbert, *Images of Nebuchadnezzar: The Emergence of a Legend* (Selinsgrove, Pa.: Susquehanna University Press, 2004); Hinke, William J., *A New Boundary Stone of Nebuchadrezzar I from Nippur, with a Concordance of Proper Names and a Glossary of the Kuddurru Inscriptions thus far Published* (Philadelphia: University of Pennsylvania, 1907); *Clarke, Samuel, The Life and Death of Nebuchadnezzar, the Great, the First Founder of the Babylonian Empire . . .* (London: Printed for William Miller, 1664).

Nelson, Horatio, Viscount Nelson (1758–1805) *British admiral*

Horatio Nelson was born in the parsonage house in Burnham Thorpe, a village in Norfolk, England, on 29 September 1758, the sixth of 11 children of the rector Edmund Nelson and Catherine Suckling Nelson. His maternal great-grandmother was an elder sister of Sir Robert Walpole, who had served as the first prime minister of England from 1721 to 1742. Perhaps the greatest influence on Nelson was his maternal uncle, Captain Maurice Suckling, who served as the comptroller of the British navy. When Catherine Nelson died, Captain

Painting of Lord Nelson in the cabin of *Victory*

Suckling took in young Horatio and schooled him in the ways of the sea.

Starting in 1771, Nelson went to sea on board the *Raisonnable,* and he soon became an experienced seaman. In 1772, at the age of 14, he served as a member of the crew on a scientific expedition to the Arctic. Later, struck by malaria in the Indian Ocean, he was sent back to England, where he resolved to become a naval leader. In 1777, he passed the examination for lieutenant and was sent to the West Indies. In 1779, at age 20, he was promoted to the rank of post captain and given command of his own frigate, then was sent to Nicaragua, where he attacked Spanish settlements (a consequence of Spain and France having sided with the American colonists in the American Revolution). Although his attacks on San Juan (now in Puerto Rico) were militarily successful, his force caught yellow fever, and Nelson barely escaped with his life. Sent back to En-

gland a second time, he recovered and again was given command of a frigate, which sailed to Quebec and then in the West Indies. While in the West Indies, Nelson met Prince William Henry, who was later to become King William IV of England. William wrote that although he was somewhat shocked at Nelson's youth, he nonetheless "found something irresistibly pleasing in his address and conversation; and an enthusiasm, when speaking on professional subjects, that showed he was no common being."

With the victory of the American colonists and the end of the war, Nelson went back to England. The following year, 1784, he was again named to command a frigate and was sent to the West Indies, where he met Mrs. Frances Nisbet, a widow whom he married in 1787. He subsequently returned to England and settled in his home village, staying there, unemployed, for nearly four years. This state of affairs vexed Nelson, who was so used to a sea career, and at one point he believed that the powers in control of the navy were purposely holding him back from advancement. In a letter, he wrote of "a prejudice of the Admiralty evidently against me, which I can neither guess at, nor in the least account for," and it was perhaps this that prompted his superiors to give him command of the warship *Agamemnon* in 1793.

By this time, France was again Britain's enemy, and Nelson was placed in charge of reinforcing the fort of Toulon against French revolutionary soldiers, including a young officer named NAPOLEON BONAPARTE. While escorting troops sent by King Ferdinand IV of Sicily and Naples to reinforce Toulon, Nelson met Sir William Hamilton, the English minister to Naples and Hamilton's wife Emma, with whom he soon became close friends.

Following the loss of Toulon, Lord Samuel HOOD, first viscount Hood, moved his main base to the island of Corsica. In July 1794, while laying siege to the town of Calvi, on Corsica, a small French attack led to injuries—among them, Nelson, who was hit in the face with fragments from a gunshot, leaving his right eye sightless. Nelson wrote simply to Lord Hood, "I got a little hurt this morning." Hood was replaced in command by Admiral William Hotham, whose lackluster control led to the British abandoning their bases on Corsica. During the attempt to retake the island, Nelson and his men captured the French ship *Ça Ira.* He later wrote, "I wish to be an Admiral and in command of the English Fleet; I should very soon either do much, or be ruined. My disposition cannot bear tame and slow measures. Sure I am, had I commanded our Fleet on the 14th, that either the whole French Fleet would have graced my triumph, or I should have been in a confounded scrape. . . . Now, had we taken ten sail and allowed the eleventh to escape, when it had been possible to have got at her, I could never have called it well done."

Admiral Hotham was replaced by Sir John Jervis, who sailed with Nelson in the Atlantic off Cape St. Vincent. Accosted by Spanish ships, the British fought the battle of Cape St. Vincent on 14 February 1797, in which Nelson's single ship took on several Spanish ships and eventually captured two of them—the *San Nicolas* and the *San Josef*. Following this battle, Nelson was made a Knight of the Bath (KB) and promoted to rear admiral. On 21 July 1797, an attempt to capture a number of Spanish ships filled with treasure at Tenerife led to disaster, and Nelson lost his right arm. After his recovery, he rejoined the fleet in 1798 aboard his flagship, the *Vanguard.*

On 1 August 1798, Nelson attacked the French at Aboukir Bay in Egypt, also known as the Battle of the Nile, one of the most important sea engagements in the wars between England and France. Nelson's fleet destroyed the French ships, leaving Napoleon's army in Egypt isolated and earning Nelson a peerage as Baron Nelson of the Nile.

It was during this period that Nelson, still married, began a love affair with Emma Hamilton, the wife of his friend Sir William Hamilton. Although the two never divorced their respective mates, they eventually had a child together, scandalizing English society. Nelson remained in love with his "darling Emma" until his death.

In the last years of his life, Nelson was one of the commanders who made the British navy the most effective fleet in the world. He aided King Ferdinand's effort to retake control of Naples in 1799 and was given the dukedom of Brontë for his service. Because of disagreement with his superior, Lord Keith, he was recalled to London. Once he returned, he was forgiven for his offense and named as second in command to Admiral Sir Hyde Parker. The threat of a Russian invasion of Denmark led Parker, an aged seaman, to allow Nelson to at-

tack and defeat the Danish fleet at Copenhagen on 2 April 1801. Nelson succeeded Parker as commander in chief and was made a viscount.

On March 1802, the Peace of Amiens brought peace between Britain and France, but on 16 May 1803, Napoleon reopened the war against England. Nelson was given command of the Mediterranean fleet in May 1803, and he launched a blockade of Toulon to prevent the French and Spanish from joining forces. In March 1804, French admiral Pierre Villeneuve broke the blockade and sailed to the West Indies. Nelson set off in pursuit, but Villeneuve managed to return across the Atlantic to safety in Cádiz, Spain. The British blockaded them, waiting for any move, which came on 20 October, when Villeneuve's fleet sailed out to Trafalgar. There, Nelson and his fleet met them, leading to one of the most famous battles in world military history. As the fleets closed, Nelson signaled his ships from his flagship, the *Victory:* "England expects that every man will do his duty." During the fight, when Admiral Cuthbert Collingwood's ship *Royal Sovereign* broke the enemy's lines, Nelson cried out, "See how that noble fellow Collingwood carries his ship into action." Sometime during the engagement, a sniper from the French ship *Redoutable* fired at Nelson, striking him in his chest. He was carried below by his men and examined by the ship's surgeon, who diagnosed the wound as mortal. As Nelson lay dying, reports on the battle were given to him. When news was heard that 15 French ships had been seized, he said, "That is well, but I had bargained for 20." Moments before his death, his flag captain, Thomas Hardy, kissed his forehead, to which Nelson replied, "Now I am satisfied. Thank God, I have done my duty." He died never knowing the full extent of the English victory at Trafalgar, with the combined Franco-Spanish fleet defeated and those ships not destroyed being captured and taken as war booty.

Nelson's body was taken back to England, and his grateful nation mourned him with a full state funeral and burial in St. Paul's Cathedral in London. His ship *Victory* was sent to Portsmouth, where it is still preserved. In 2004, archaeologists found the remains of his ship *Agamemnon,* which had been sunk off the coast of Uruguay in 1809.

Horatio Nelson's legacy is the growth of the British navy and his own mark as its "father." He is remembered for his tactical innovations, brilliant leadership, and ensuring that his captains knew exactly what was expected of them in a battle. This resulted in a series of remarkable naval victories and led to Britain becoming the dominant maritime power in the 19th century.

References: Southey, Robert, *Life of Nelson* (London: Everyman's Library, 1906); Lloyd, Frederick, *An Accurate and Impartial Life of the Late Lord Viscount Nelson, Duke of Bronte in Sicily. Comprehending Authentic and Circumstantial details of his Glorious Achievements: together with private anecdotes* (London: J. Fowler, 1806); Pocock, Tom, *The Terror Before Trafalgar: Nelson, Nap, and the Secret War* (New York: W. W. Norton, 2003); "How Nelson's Memorandum Was Carried Out at Trafalgar," *The Nineteenth Century and After,* 416 (October 1911): 679–704; Beatty, William, *The Death of Lord Nelson* (Birmingham, U.K.: The War Library, 1894); "Funeral of Lord Nelson," *The Times* (London), 10 January 1806, 1; Savill, Richard, "Nelson's Favourite Ship Found at Last," *The Daily Telegraph* (London), 27 March 2004, 8.

Neville, Richard See WARWICK, RICHARD NEVILLE, EARL OF.

Nevsky, Alexander, Saint (Aleksandr Yaroslavich) (ca. 1220–1263) *Russian prince*

Alexander Nevsky was born about 1220 as Aleksandr Yaroslavich, the son of Yaroslav II Vsevolodovich, the grand prince of the Grand Principality of Vladimir. When he was approximately 16, Alexander was elected as a prince of the city of Novgorod, in northern Russia. His first test came in 1240, when the Swedish invaded Russia to prevent them from gaining a sea port. Commanding the armies of Novgorod, he took on the Swedes at the confluence of the Izhore and Neva rivers, and defeated them. A biography written by Soviet historians during the Second World War relates, "On July 15, 1240, a battle took place between the Novgorodites and the Swedes, which is known in history as the Battle of the Neva. The Russians launched a vigorous attack,

driving into the very heart of the Swedish camp. The Swedes resisted, but they were pressed towards the river. Alexander pushed forward to engage [Swedish commander Jarl] Birger in mortal combat and cut him down with a sword. The Swedes were unable to withstand the onslaught and began to retreat to the river pursued by the Russians to prevent them from embarking on their ships. . . . The remnants of the defeated Swedish forces managed to embark and sail back to their country." For his services in defense of his homeland, Alexander was given the name of Nevsky, or "Prince of the Neva." However, when he began to interfere in the city's affairs, a role he felt was due to him, the city fathers expelled him in 1241.

In 1242, Pope Gregory IX urged followers of the Catholic faith to invade northern Russia to "Christianize" the peoples of that region, and the Teutonic Knights of Prussia (north Germany) took up his call. Novgorod, fearing another invasion, invited Nevsky to return to defend them. A series of clashes led to a major battle in April 1242 on a slender body of frozen water between Lakes Chud and Pskov. Alexander lured the Knights onto the icebed and then slaughtered them en masse—"the massacre on the ice." Nevsky also fought a series of battles against the Swedes and the Lithuanians, defeating both.

Another threat to Russia rose from the east: the Mongol hordes of Khan Batu, who were overrunning Russia. Alexander's father was named as an official envoy to go to Khan Batu to negotiate a peace. However, after he returned in September 1246, he was poisoned by unknown persons, leaving his sons Alexander and Andrew in charge of the peace mission. Both men traveled to see Khan Batu, who accepted their overtures since he wanted tribute and allies. He named Alexander as prince of Kiev and Andrew as grand prince of Vladimir, his father's title. Andrew nonetheless planned to fight Khan Batu, but Alexander, knowing armed resistance could lead to catastrophe for Russia, informed the Mongol leader, who overthrew Andrew and installed Alexander as grand prince of Vladimir in 1251.

As the leader of Russia—though only by Mongol permission—Alexander went on a campaign of reform, strengthening and encouraging the church and instituting new laws. He had his son Vasily installed as the prince of Novgorod; when the people of Novgorod expelled Vasily, Nevsky marched on the city and reinstalled him. Working with the Mongols, Nevsky took a census of the people in Russia in 1257. However, five years later, when a rebellion broke out against Muslims taking farmland, Nevsky went to the Mongol leaders to negotiate an end to the crisis. Successful, he returned home but became ill and died on 14 November 1263 in the village of Gorodets. Although Russia remained leaderless for a time thereafter, his nephew Daniel brought the peoples of northern Russia together in a confederation that would later become modern Russia.

Although many considered Nevsky a traitor for collaborating with the Mongols, he realized that opposition to a power that ruled the whole of Asia was impossible and deliberately chose submission. With the support of the Russian Orthodox Church, whom he in turn supported by encouraging the foundation of schools and monasteries, he was able to alleviate the tax burden imposed by the Mongols. Nevsky was canonized in 1547. As a military leader, he defeated the Swedes and Teutonic Knights, but he had the sense not to involve his people in a hopeless struggle against a Mongol empire that stretched to the Pacific Ocean. It was therefore his role as a diplomat that provided his greatest legacy.

References: *Alexander Nevsky* (Moscow, USSR: Foreign Languages Publishing House, 1943); Presniakov, A. E., *The Formation of the Great Russian State: A Study of Russian History in the Thirteenth to Fifteenth Centuries* (Chicago: Triangle Books, 1970); *The Life of St. Alexander Nevsky, . . .* (St. Petersburg, Russia: Aurora Art Publishers, 1992); Waszink, Paul M., *Life, Courage, Ice: A Semiological Study Essay on the old Russian Biography of Aleksandr Nezskij* (München, Germany: Sagner, 1990).

Newcastle, William Cavendish, duke of

(1592–1676) *English military commander*
William Cavendish was born in 1592, the son of Sir Charles Cavendish and his wife Catherine, the daughter of Cuthbert, Lord Ogle. William attended St. John's College, Cambridge University, and was made a Knight of the Order of Bath (KB) in 1610, when Prince Henry became the Prince of Wales. He served as an aide to Sir Henry Wotton, the ambassador to the duke of Savoy, and when he returned to England, he married Elizabeth

Basset, daughter of William Basset of Blore. Cavendish became a close friend of Kings James I and Charles I, and he was ennobled as Viscount Mansfield in 1620 and as earl of Newcastle in 1628. In 1638, he was named as a governor (guardian) of Charles's son, the Prince of Wales, and the following year he was made a privy councillor.

With the outbreak of the English Civil War between King Charles I and Parliament, Newcastle offered his services to the Crown. Charles sent him to take the city of Hull in January 1642, but the city fathers refused him admittance and he was forced to withdraw. He then led raids into the Northern cities and took York in late 1642. His actions were noted in a letter to the House of Commons: "The House of Commons having received a report, concerning the Earle of Newcastle, that the said Earle hath put in about 500 Men in Garrison, and that the said Earle is about to raise a Troope of Horse, and beats the Drum for Volunteers, the Trained Bands refuse to come in, four pieces of Ordnance is gone towards South Sheels, Tinmouth, and there are 300 men in worke making a Sconce, to command all Ships, that in or goe out, the Towne is in greater perplexity then they were the last yeare, Ship-masters refuse to goe in, least their Ships be Staid."

Starting in early 1643, a series of lightning-quick attacks by Newcastle's forces captured the cities of Wakefield, Rotherham, and Sheffield. He defeated Lord FAIRFAX, a Parliamentarian general, at Adwalton Moor on 30 June 1643 and was able to march unmolested into parts of Lincolnshire, including the city of Lincoln. However, a part of his force was defeated by Oliver CROMWELL at Winceby (11 October 1643), and Newcastle retreated to York. Surrounded by Fairfax and Lord Manchester, he was saved by Prince RUPERT, who fought the battle of Marston Moor (2 July 1644) against Newcastle's advice. Rupert's army was devastated in the clash, and Newcastle was so distraught at the loss that he resigned his commission and sailed to Hamburg, Germany, eventually moving to Paris in April 1645. Three years later, he moved to Rotterdam, where he joined a group of those opposed to Parliament's takeover of the English government. He then settled in Antwerp.

In 1650, Newcastle became a member of the Privy Council of Charles II, son of the executed Charles I. When Charles II was restored to the throne in 1660, Newcastle returned to England and was given back some of his lands and titles, although he had spent his entire personal fortune for the Royalist cause. Advanced to the title of duke of Newcastle in 1665, he retired from public life. He died at his home in Welbeck, Nottinghamshire, on 25 December 1676, and was laid to rest in Westminster Abbey. His son Henry succeeded to the dukedom of Newcastle, but upon his death, Henry having had no children, the title became extinct. The duke of Newcastle has since become one of the more obscure of Charles I's commanders in the English Civil War, though he was always the king's loyal supporter.

References: Trease, Geoffrey, *Portrait of a Cavalier: William Cavendish, First Duke of Newcastle* (New York: Taplinger Publishing Company, 1979); Newcastle, Margaret Cavendish, Duchess of Newcastle, *The Life of the Thrice Noble, High and Puissant William Cavendishe, Duke, Marquess, and Earl of Newcastle . . .* (London: Printed by A. Maxwell, 1667); *The Good and Prosperous Success of the Parliaments Forces in York-Shire . . .* (London: Printed for John Wright in the Old Bailey, 1642); *True Newes from Yorke. Consisting of severall Matters of Note, and High Concernment, since the 13 of June, concerning these several heads, viz: Concerning 1. Sir Iohn Meldrum. 2. L. Marq. Hamilton. 3. Earle of Newcastle . . .* (London, 1642).

Ney, Michel, duc d'Elchingen, prince of the Moskowa (1769–1815) *French general*

Michel Ney was born the son of a cooper (a maker of barrels), in the village of Sarrelouis (now Saarlouis) in the Saar Valley in eastern France on 10 January 1769. Although his father wanted him to become a lawyer, apprenticing him to learn the trade, Ney ran away and joined the French military, joining a regiment of Hussars in 1788. Almost from the start of his career, he saw action, fighting the Prussians at Valmy in the Argonne (20 September 1792) and the Austrians at Jemappes, now in Belgium (6 November 1792), before the battle against the Austrians at Hohenlinden (3 December 1800), near present-day Munich, which brought about the collapse of the so-called Second Coalition against the French leader NAPOLEON. Ney became famous for his courage and tactical skill, and he was quickly promoted, rising to the rank of general of division under General Jean Moreau's Army of the Rhine at Hohenlinden.

Ney's actions on the battlefield caught the attention of his superiors, including Napoleon. He became so close to Napoleon's wife, Josephine, that she arranged for Ney to marry one of her maids of honor in 1802. The renewal of a war against England in 1803 resulted in Ney's being given the command of the VI Army Corps. On 19 May 1804, Napoleon made himself emperor of France, and he named 14 generals—including Ney—as marshals of the French Empire. When Napoleon was faced by the Third Coalition of Austria, England, and Russia, Ney attacked the Austrians under General Riesch at Elchingen, near the city of Ülm in what is now Germany, on 14 October 1805. His victory there earned Ney the title of Duc d'Elchingen (duke of Elchingen) in 1808.

On 14 October 1806, Ney led French armies at Jena, also known as Auerstädt, near the city of Leipzig, and though the French sustained heavy losses (14,000 dead and wounded), the ultimate defeat of the Prussians (who lost 40,000 casualties) allowed Napoleon to commence his northern march on Berlin. Ney also led French troops at Eylau, also known as Bagrationovsk (7–8 February 1807), where Napoleon's advance on the Russian frontier was halted; and at Friedland, also known as Pravdinsk (14 June 1807), in which the French scored a major victory over the Russians, leaving thousands of retreating Russians soldiers drowning in the Alle River in Prussia. Napoleon considered Ney to be his most indispensable commander but also found him to be a touchy and temperamental man. When Ney was transferred to Spain in 1808, he refused to listen to the commanders who were fighting there, preferring to take his commands directly from Napoleon himself. In 1811, he was dismissed from the Spanish front and sent back to France in disgrace.

The French invasion of Russia in 1812 forced Ney's return to service, and he was named commander of the III Corps of the Grande Armée. Following the battle of Borodino (7 September 1812), in which the Russians under Field Marshal Mikhail KUTUZOV made a heroic stand against the French but failed to stop Napoleon's advance—the French would enter Moscow seven days later—Napoleon made Ney prince de la Moskowa, or prince of Moscow. However, lack of supplies meant the French were forced to retreat westward back to France. Ney's command of the French rear as they retreated still attracts high praise, despite massive casualties. At Berezina, also known as the battle of Berezina River (26–29 November 1812), his army saved Napoleon from defeat by the Russians, prompting Napoleon to say of Ney, "He is the bravest of the brave." On 12 March 1813, Ney received a dispatch from Napoleon: "I am sure that as soon as you have heard of my arrival in Lyon you will have ordered your troops to hoist again the tricolor flag. Follow the orders you receive from Bertrand and come and join me at Chalon. I shall receive you as I did on the day after the battle of Moskva [Moscow]."

Ney's fortunes changed after the Russian debacle: He defeated his former commander, Jean Moreau, who had switched sides and was serving as the commander of the Russian czar Alexander I's army when he was killed at the battle of Dresden (27 August 1813). But Ney lost an important fight against the Swedes commanded by Prince Charles John, the crown prince, at Dennewitz (6 September 1813). At Liebertwolkwitz, also known as Leipzig (14 October 1813), Ney was wounded and sent back to France to recuperate. In 1814, he was once again in command; however, the tide had turned against the French, and he could see that Napoleon was fighting a losing war. When he refused to march into battle, Napoleon raged, "The army will obey me!" Ney countered, "Sire, the army will obey its generals." Realizing that without Ney he was finished, Napoleon abdicated the throne of France. Ney was rewarded for his change of heart: When the Bourbon king Louis XVII retook the throne, he allowed Ney to keep his titles and his freedom.

On 1 March 1815, Napoleon escaped from his imprisonment on the island of Elba and returned to France to lead another crusade against Europe. Ney was sent to arrest him but then decided to rejoin his old commander. Louis XVII fled Paris, and with Ney at his side, Napoleon reentered the city. Ney was then shunted aside for other officers, and he spend much of the next three months at his county estate. However, on 15 June Napoleon summoned Ney and gave him the command of the French army's left wing. The French forces met the British and their commander, Arthur Wellesley, the duke of WELLINGTON, at Waterloo (18 June 1815), where Ney led several charges on the British squares. Realizing that the battle was a defeat for the French, he told one of his men, "If they catch us now, they'll hang us."

Returning to his estate, Ney gathered up his belongings and tried to escape, but he was recognized in southwestern France, arrested, and put on trial. Arguing his innocence, he refused to acknowledge the tribunal and demanded that he be tried by his peers. Nonetheless, he was found guilty and sentenced to death, and on 7 December 1815 he was taken to the Luxembourg Gardens and shot by a firing squad.

For years rumors have existed that Ney was spirited away by persons unknown before his execution and allowed to escape to America in 1816. There he presumably spent the remainder of his life in North Carolina as a teacher under the name Peter Stewart Ney. One historian compared papers signed by Peter Ney to those of Michel Ney and found the handwriting to be identical. In addition, Michel Ney was known to have been struck in the forehead by a sword, leaving a scar, while Peter Ney combed his hair down low to cover up a scar on his forehead. Peter Ney died in 1846 and was buried in the Third Creek Churchyard in Bowan County, North Carolina. Whether he was Michel Ney is highly suspect.

Michel Ney's legacy is ambiguous. He is remembered by historians as a brilliant tactician whose victories gave France some of its most important triumphs in the Napoleonic wars. Nonetheless, his downfall came from his arrogance, which made relations with his fellow marshals and commanders difficult at best.

References: Atteridge, A. Hilliard, *The Bravest of the Brave* (London: Methuen & Co., Ltd., 1912); Blythe, Legette, *Marshal Ney: A Dual Life* (London: Jarrolds Publishers, 1937); De Ségur, Count Philippe-Paul, *Napoleon's Russian Campaign* (Alexandria, Va.: Time/Life Books, 1980); Keegan, John, *The Face of Battle: A Study of Agincourt, Waterloo and the Somme* (London, England: Jonathan Cape Ltd., 1976), 127; Kurtz, Harold, *The Trial of Marshal Ney, His Last Years and Death* (London: H. Hamilton, 1957); "Marshal Ney in America: Did He Escape Death and Teach School in North Carolina?," *The World* (New York), 11 May 1884, 10; Smoot, J. Edward, *Marshal Ney Before and After Execution* (Charlotte, N.C.: Queen City Printing Company, 1929).

Nimitz, Chester William (1885–1965) *American admiral*

Born in Fredericksburg, Texas, on 24 February 1885, Chester William Nimitz was the son of Chester Bernard Nimitz, who died before his son was born, and was raised by his grandfather, Charles Nimitz, until his mother remarried. Following a common school education, Nimitz entered the U.S. Naval Academy at Annapolis, Maryland, and graduated in 1905 as a midshipman. He then served on a series of warships and submarines until becoming commander of the destroyer *Decatur,* which ran aground in 1908. Nimitz was court-martialed but only received a reprimand, after which he again served on a series of warships.

In 1911, Nimitz was named as commander of the Third Submarine Division of the Atlantic Fleet, and in 1912 he became commander of the Atlantic Submarine Flotilla. During the First World War, he introduced new methods for destroyers to refuel at sea. He went on to

Admiral of the Fleet Chester W. Nimitz

command the flagship of the Asiatic Fleet. In 1939, he was made commander of Task Force Seven, the leading ship task force in the navy, and that same year he was appointed as chief of the Bureau of Navigation of the U.S. Navy.

Following the Japanese attack on Pearl Harbor, Hawaii (7 December 1941), Nimitz—then serving as chief of naval personnel—was named commander in chief of the Pacific Fleet. Historian Vincent Hawkins writes: "Nimitz's first priority in the Pacific was to defend the Hawaiian Islands and Midway [Island] and to protect the lines of communication from the United States to Hawaii and Australia. His second priority was to launch offensive operations against the Japanese in the Central Pacific in an attempt to divert their attention from Singapore and the Dutch East Indies. Facing superior Japanese naval strength, Nimitz resolved to carry out a series of naval hit-and-run actions designed to deplete the enemy's strength. While these operations inflicted only minor losses, they did raise American morale."

Nimitz's first effort to restrain Japanese expansion in the Pacific was at the battle of the Coral Sea (3–9 May 1942), but he saw that the island of Midway, in between Hawaii and Japan, would be the key battle point in the Pacific. Using intelligence sources and his own beliefs, Nimitz transferred all of his resources to Midway, trying to lure the Japanese into a trap. The battle of 3–6 June 1942 was a turning point in the war: The Japanese lost four aircraft carriers against one carrier loss for the Americans. For the remainder of the war, the Japanese were on the defensive at sea and were gradually pushed back towards the Japanese homeland.

Working with General Douglas MACARTHUR, Nimitz attacked the Japanese across the Pacific theater: From the Solomon Islands (August 1942–February 1943) to the Gilbert Islands (20–23 November 1943) to the Marshall Islands (31 January–23 February 1944), the Japanese were rolled back. A series of actions in the Marianas Islands (14 June–10 August 1944) and Leyte Gulf (23–26 October 1944) also furthered the Allied advance. The final battles on the islands of Iwo Jima (19 February–24 March 1945) and Okinawa (1 April–21 June 1945) gave the United States the ability to launch full-scale raids on Japan itself. On 6 and 9 August 1945, two atomic weapons were dropped on Hiroshima and Nagasaki, forcing the Japanese to capitulate on 14 August 1945. Nimitz—who had been promoted to Fleet

Admiral on 19 December 1944—sailed his flagship, the battleship *South Dakota,* into Tokyo Bay and, on board the *Missouri,* signed the papers of Japan's surrender as the official U.S. representative (2 September 1945).

Following the war, Nimitz succeeded Admiral Ernest King as chief of naval operations (CNO). In his two years as CNO, Nimitz tried to remold the United States Navy to adapt to the cold war, away from the Second World War organization. On 15 December 1947, he resigned as CNO and retired to California. In his last 20 years, he wrote *Sea Power: A Naval History* with E. B. Potter (1960). After undergoing surgery in late 1965, he came down with pneumonia and died on 20 February 1966. He was buried with full military honors in Golden Gate National Cemetery in San Francisco, California.

Chester Nimitz is remembered for his leadership during the darkest days of the Second World War for the United States. With limited resources, including those not destroyed by the Japanese at Pearl Harbor, he devised a strategy of resisting and delaying the enemy until the American military could build up forces to take the war to the Japanese and win strategic victories at Midway and in the South Pacific islands. His reliance on aircraft carriers to accomplish this, the first time they had been used to such effect, paved the way for current naval thinking and policy.

References: Potter, Elmer Belmont, *Nimitz* (Annapolis, Md.: Naval Institute Press, 1976); Brink, Randall, *Nimitz: The Man and His Wars* (New York: D. I. Fine Books/Dutton, 1996); "Nimitz, Chester William," in *Brassey's Encyclopedia of Military History and Biography,* edited by Franklin D. Margiotta (Washington, D.C.: Brassey's, 1994), 703–707; Driskill, Frank A., *Admiral of the Hills: Chester W. Nimitz* (Austin, Tex.: Eakin Press, 1983); Hoyt, Edwin Palmer, *How They Won the War in the Pacific: Nimitz and his Admirals* (New York: Weybright and Talley, 1970); North, Bruce, "Nimitz, Chester William," in *Encyclopedia of American War Heroes* (New York: Checkmark Books: 2002), 184–185.

Nivelle, Robert-Georges (1856–1924) *French general*

Robert Nivelle was born in the village of Tulle in Corrèze, France, on 15 October 1856. He entered the Poly-

technic, or special school, in Paris in 1876, but two years later he left to join the French army, where he was assigned to an artillery unit. In 1990, he was sent to China to fight in the Boxer Rebellion, and he subsequently served in the French wars in Algeria.

In 1914, when the First World War broke out, Nivelle was serving as the commander of the 5th French Artillery in Besançon, France. He was named as a general of brigade on 24 October 1914 and saw action on the western front during the horrific early days of the war in 1914 and 1915. In January 1915, he led French forces in the fight to capture Quesnevières. He was promoted to be the head of the III Corps on 23 December 1915, and in March 1916 he was assigned to the defense of the French strong point, the enormous fortress of Verdun. Nivelle impressed Allied commanders with his defense of the citadel, and on 2 May 1916 he was named as the successor to the French Second Army commander, General Henri PÉTAIN. When the Germans launched their main attack on Verdun, Nivelle stated unequivocally, "Ils ne passeront pas." ("They shall not pass.") Successful in holding Verdun, Nivelle was named as commander of all French forces in the north and northeast on 12 December 1916, succeeding Marshal Joseph JOFFRE. In spring 1917, he formulated an Allied plan for a massive offensive, intended to break the deadlock of trench warfare. This plan had the support of the French prime minister, Aristide Briand, but was opposed by other Allied commanders, such as Sir Douglas HAIG and even Pétain. The offensive, also called the Nivelle Offensive or the Second Battle of the Aisne, started on 16 April 1917 and sent more than 1 million French soldiers against the German lines, at a loss of 40,000 men the first day alone. Even though little ground was being made, Nivelle continued to pour tens of thousands of men into the battle. After a period of time, the French attacks let up until they ended on 9 May. In the end, nearly 200,000 French soldiers were killed, with untold thousands more wounded. This was the end for Nivelle: On 15 May 1917, he was replaced by Pétain as the French commander in chief.

Nivelle's career was effectively over, and he was posted to North Africa. Nominated as a member of the Supreme War Council in 1920, he was retired in 1921. He died in Paris on 23 March 1924 at the age of 67.

Robert Nivelle, barely remembered today, is known for sending 200,000 men to their deaths in his attempt to break the German lines after the French had been bled white from the Verdun clashes. His refusal to listen to his colleagues and to see the true picture of the war on the field, led to the debacle of the Nivelle Offensive. Twenty years after his death, Nivelle's memoirs were published; they were translated into English as *And Yet France Smiled.*

References: Spears, Sir Edward Louis, Bart., *Prelude to Victory* (London: Jonathan Cape, 1939); Bongard, David L., "Nivelle, Robert Georges," in *The Encyclopedia of Military Biography,* edited by Trevor N. Dupuy, Curt Johnson, and David L. Bongard (London: I. B. Taurus, 1992), 547–548; Caddick-Adams, Peter, "Nivelle Offensive," in *The Oxford Companion to Military History,* edited by Richard Holmes (New York: Oxford University Press, 2001), 648–649; Bruce, George, "Aisne II" and "Verdun," in *Collins Dictionary of Wars* (Glasgow, Scotland: HarperCollins, 1995), 7, 259.

Nogi, Maresuke, Kiten (Count Maresuke Nogi)
(1849–1912) *Japanese general*

Maresuke Nogi was born in Edo, now Tokyo, in Yamaguchi prefecture, Japan, in 1849. From an early age he was involved in the military, and in 1868 he sided with the new emperor, Mutsuhito, in fighting the shogunate of Tokugawa Yoshinobu. During the reign of Mutsuhito, also known as Meiji (1852–1912; reigned 1867–1912), the old Japanese feudal society was destroyed, and Japan was transformed into a growing world military and economic power. This conflicted with the ideas of those who followed Tokugawa Yoshinobu, and this led to the Boshin War, or the War of the Year of the Dragon (1868–69). Nogi fought in the army under the command of Aritomi Yamagata (1838–1922), a samurai who was fundamental in the restoration of the Meiji emperor. The war ended with Yoshinobu's surrender and the defeat of his forces in September 1868.

Nogi also helped to put down the rebellion led by the samurai Saigo Takamori in 1877, known as the Seinan War. He then went abroad, studying military science in Germany before he returned to Japan and became a farmer. However, in 1894, with the outbreak of the Sino-Japanese War (1894–95), he was recalled to service and saw action in the battles of Song-hwan (1

September 1894) and Ping-yang (15 September 1894). The conflict ended with China signing the humiliating Treaty of Simonoseki (March 1895). Afterward, Nogi was named as a general in the Japanese army, and he served as governor-general of Taiwan from 1895 to 1898.

With the outbreak of the Russo-Japanese war (1904–05), Nogi was named as one of the commanders of Japanese forces, in conjunction with Admiral Heiachiro TOGO, and together they soundly defeated Russian forces at Port Arthur (8 February 1904). However, a closer examination of the battle shows that Nogi's command of the Third Japanese Army was not as competent as often described, and that nearly 60,000 Japanese soldiers were killed in the assault on Port Arthur. It was a last-minute intervention by General Kodama Gentaro that saved Nogi's force. Following the surrender of the Russian general Stoessel, Nogi sent a telegram outlining the points of capitulation: "The plenipotentiaries of both parties concluded their negotiations today at 4:30 o'clock. The Russian Commissioners accepted on the whole the conditions stipulated by us and consented to capitulate. The document has been prepared and signatures are now being affixed. Simultaneously with the conclusion of negotiations both armies suspended hostilities. . . . It is expected that the Japanese Army will enter the City of Port Arthur tomorrow."

Nogi's two sons died during the Battle of Mukden (21 February 1905), now called Shenyang, China. Created a kiten, or count, in 1907, Nogi was named as the director of the Peers' School in Japan, where, writes biographer Mark Peattie, "he fostered a stern regimen of patriotism, austerity, and manly virtue." On 30 July 1912, Emperor Mutsuhito died, ending the Meiji era. Nogi, consumed by grief over the emperor's passing and steadfast in his loyalty to Mutsuhito, decided to end his life as an act of devotion and allegiance. This act, called *junshi* ("to follow one's lord into death"), had been illegal in Japan since the late 18th century and was part of the old customs the emperor had sought to end. Nonetheless, on 13 September 1912, Nogi and his wife committed *jumonji giri,* or ritual suicide by disemboweling themselves with a ceremonial knife.

Although still remembered in Japan for his loyal suicide, Maresuke Nogi has been forgotten by military strategists, even though he took part in the first major

Japanese victory of the 20th century—a century that saw first the rise of Japanese militarism, then the fighting of the Second World War.

References: Peattie, Mark, "Nogi Maresuke," in *Kodansha Encyclopedia of Japan,* 10 vols. (Tokyo, Japan: Kodansha, 1983), VI:31; Frédéric, Louis, "Nogi Kiten," in *Japan Encyclopedia* (Cambridge, Mass.: The Belknap Press of Harvard University Press, 2002), 723; Scherer, James A. B., *Three Meiji Leaders: Ito, Togo, Nogi* (Tokyo: The Hokuseido Press, 1936); "Nogi, Maresuke," in *Command: From Alexander the Great to Zhukov—The Greatest Commanders of World History,* edited by James Lucas (London: Bloomsbury Publishing, 1988), 127–128; Hackett, R. F., *Yamagata Aritomo in the Rise of Modern Japan, 1838–1922* (Cambridge, Mass.: Harvard University Press, 1971); Eastlake, F. Warrington, and Yamada Yoshiaki, *Heroic Japan: A History of the War between China & Japan* (London: Sampson Low, Marston, 1897); "Stoessel, After Long Conference, Surrenders City; Articles of Port Arthur's Capitulation Signed at 4:30 O'Clock Yesterday Afternoon," *The New York Times,* 3 January 1905, 1.

Norfolk, Thomas Howard, second duke of (first earl of Surrey, Earl Marshal) (1443–1524)
English nobleman

Born in 1443, Thomas Howard was the son of Sir John Howard, the first duke of Norfolk, and related to Sir William Howard, a lawyer who was named chief justice of the Court of Common Pleas by King EDWARD I. His father was a supporter of the House of York and fought on their side during the Wars of the Roses, seeing action at Towton (1461) and Barnet (1471). Because of his father's ties to the English royal family, Thomas Howard shared in their fortunes. At Bosworth (22 August 1485), Sir John Howard, in command of the king's forces, was killed along with King RICHARD III. Thomas Howard, then the earl of Surrey, was captured by the forces of Henry Tudor, who marched on London and was crowned as Henry VII.

Howard remained in captivity until January 1489, when he was released and given back his title of earl of Surrey, but his father's title of duke of Norfolk was refused him. However, Henry VII realized that he needed a strong commander to fight the Scots, and he turned

to Howard, who fought the Scots to a bitter draw. To help ensure peace, Howard urged the marriage between Henry's daughter Margaret and James IV, the king of Scotland. When Henry went to France to fight, he left Howard in charge of his kingdom. However, during the king's absence, James IV invaded England. Howard put together an army and rushed north to stem the incursion. In September 1513 at Flodden Field, Northumberland, his forces completely routed the Scots, killing James along with some 10,000 of his men. Henry, impressed with Howard's services, reinstated his title of duke of Norfolk as well as his lands, and named him as Lord High Admiral of England.

Although he had served as Henry's primary commander, Norfolk spent the remaining years peacefully, although he ended a revolt by apprentices in London in 1517. In 1522, Henry named him England's ambassador to the Holy Roman Empire. He died two years later in the castle of Framlingham in Norfolk at the age of 80.

References: "Norfolk, Thomas Howard, 2nd Duke of," in *Encyclopaedia Britannica,* 14th ed., 24 vols. (London: Encyclopaedia Britannica Co., 1929), 488–489; "Howard, Thomas II," in *The Concise Dictionary of National Biography,* 3 vols. (Oxford, U.K.: Oxford University Press, 1992), II:1497; Tucker, Melvin J., *The Life of Thomas Howard, Earl of Surrey and Second Duke of Norfolk, 1443–1524* (The Hague: Mouton & Co., 1964).

Nottingham, Charles Howard, first earl of *See* HOWARD, CHARLES, SECOND BARON HOWARD OF EFFINGHAM AND FIRST EARL OF NOTTINGHAM.

Nur-ad-Din (Nurredin, Nouraddin, Nur-ed-Din) (1117/1118–1174) *Islamic military commander*
Nur-ad-Din—also known as Nurredin, Nouraddin, or Nur-ed-Din—was born in either 1117 or 1118, the second son of Zangi, the *atabeg* (provincial emir or governor) of Aleppo and Mosul Province (now in modern Syria and Iraq). Nur-ad-din's name is loosely translated in English to mean "Light of the Religion." He succeeded his father as the ruler of Syria in 1145.

It was the taking of Edessa (to the east, in today's Kurdistan) in 1144 by Zangi that began the Second

Crusade (1144–87). In 1147, King Louis VIII of France and the Holy Roman Emperor Conrad III sent armies to recapture Edessa. Nur-ad-Din led the campaign against the Crusaders, defeating them at Inab (1149) and taking the city of Damascus (1154).

It was Nurad-al-Din's ambition to unite the Muslim effort against Crusader attacks, and he achieved some success even though several Muslim rulers resisted his approaches. When the Crusaders turned their attention to Egypt and landed there in 1164, Nurad-al-Din sent an army to resist them. By 1169, his army had gained control of Egypt, and he named SALADIN as vizier of the country. With further successes in Syria, it seemed he might at last be able to unify the Islamic struggle, but Saladin made it clear he resented Nurad-al-Din's authority. Nurad-al-Din was assembling an army to face Saladin when he died in 1174.

References: "Nur-ad-Din," in *The Hutchinson Dictionary of Ancient and Medieval Warfare* (Oxford, U.K.: Helicon Publishing, Ltd., 1998), 232; "Nur-ad-Din," in *A Dictionary of Military History and the Art of War,* edited by André Corvisier (London: Blackwell, 1994), 619.

Octavian *See* AUGUSTUS.

Oda Nobunaga (Oda Kippōshi) (1534–1582)
Japanese warrior

Oda Nobunaga was born Oda Kippōshi on 23 June 1534, the son of Oda Nobuhide, a lord and warrior (*Sengoku daimyo*) who was a samurai in Owari province. Nobuhide died in 1549, and Nobunaga inherited his father's estates and titles when he turned 17. Nobunaga became known for his ruthlessness, utilizing his samurai training to capture territory and make other samurai dependent on his leadership; he even had his own younger brother Nobuyuki, whom he suspected of plotting to overthrow him, killed. By 1559, Owari was firmly under Nobunaga's control, and he undertook a series of actions against other overlords. In 1560, he fought his first major battle at Okehazama, in which he defeated the forces of Imagawa Yoshimoto, one of the lords of a neighboring province. While carrying on the fight, he also strengthened his leadership by cementing an alliance with another lord, Tokugawa Ieyasu. Siding with the hereditary governor Ashikaga Yoshiaki, in 1568 Nobunaga marched on the city of Kyoto, at that time the capital of Japan, and installed Yoshiaki as the 15th shogun (ruler). Nobunaga soon quarreled with Yoshiaki,

and in 1573 he again marched on Kyoto and deposed him, ending the rule of the Ashikaga shoguns.

As the leading figure of Japan, Nobunaga instituted a series of economic reforms, including ending the toll-collecting by guilds and introducing free trade across the country. As a military leader, Nobunaga also fought the Buddhist monasteries (whose warriors resisted state control) and destroyed their influence over political affairs. In 1574, he mercilessly put down a rebellion by the Buddhists of Nagashima, killing upward of 20,000 adherents. In 1575, he defeated the Takeda clan at the battle of Nagashino. In 1580, he completed his struggle against the Buddhist forces after a decade of fighting by capturing the monastery of Hogan-ji in Osaka. In 1582, to consolidate all of Japan under his rule, Nobunaga planned a campaign to move against western Japan. However, in June that year, he was assassinated by one of his generals, Akechi Mitsuhide, while he was at the Honno-ji Temple in Kyoto. Historian Michael Cooper writes: "Oda Nobunaga died on June 21, 1582, in the flames of Honno-ji in Kyoto, where he was caught off his guard by the treachery of Akechi Mitsuhide. With Nobunaga disappeared the city of Azuchi, which symbolized his power and dreams . . ."

Although he died before he could unite the Japanese islands, Nobunaga began this movement, and for that reason he is remembered in Japan today. His development of firearms, fortifications, and iron-clad ships make him a significant figure in Japanese military history.

References: "Oda Nobunaga," in *The Hutchinson Dictionary of Ancient and Medieval Warfare* (Oxford, U.K.: Helicon Publishing, Ltd., 1998), 235; Lamers, Jeroen Pieter, *Japonius Tyrannus: The Japanese Warlord Oda Nobunaga Reconsidered* (Leiden, Netherlands: Hotei Publishing, 2000); Sansom, George, "The Road to Unification," in *A History of Japan, 1334–1615* (Stanford, Calif.: Stanford University Press, 1961), 273–290; Cooper, Michael, ed., *The Southern Barbarians: The First Europeans in Japan* (Tokyo, Japan: Kodansha Ltd., 1971).

Oudinot, Nicolas-Charles, duc de Reggio
(1767–1847) *French general*

Nicolas Oudinot was born at Bar-le-duc, France, on 25 April 1767, the son of a farmer. He received a local education, but at age 17 he ran away from home and entered the French military, serving in the regiment of Médoc for three years before his parents convinced him to return home. He was given an honorable discharge in 1787, but in 1792, with the outbreak of war, he returned to service with the rank of lieutenant colonel in the Meuse Volunteers. He saw action at Arlon (June 1793), Saverne (1793), and Gundershofen-Mietesheim (26–27 November 1793) and was promoted to general of brigade on 12 June 1794, following his service at the battle of Kaiserslautern.

During the war against the Swiss in 1799, a part of the War of the Second Coalition, Oudinot served under Marshal André MASSÉNA, who wrote to the French government, "The greatest praise is owed to the *sang froid* and to the talents of this general, the same is owed to his troops whose courage did not waver by the number of the enemy or by the lack of munitions." During the attack on Austrian forces at Schwyz (14 August 1799), Oudinot was shot and wounded. Once he recovered, he returned to service under Masséna, leading the attack on Zurich in September 1799. Masséna later noted, "I owe great praise to General Oudinot, my chief of staff, who knows how to apply his fiery energy to clerical labor, but whom I am always glad to have back on the battlefield. He has followed me in everything, and has made a perfect second-in-command." Oudinot eventually was named as inspector general of infantry for the French military.

NAPOLEON BONAPARTE's rise to power in France led to his taking over much of the command of the French military. Napoleon marched into Italy and defeated the Austrians at Marengo on 14 June 1800. Following this battle, Masséna was replaced by Marshal Guillaume-Marie-Anne Brune as commander of the French Army of Italy, and Oudinot was named as Brune's chief of staff. Following the battle of Hohenlinden (3 December 1800), the Austrians sued for peace, and Oudinot returned home to France.

His stay was short: In 1803, war resumed between France and England, and Oudinot was given the command of the 1st Division under Marshal Louis-Nicolas DAVOUT. By 1805, France was facing an alliance of England, Russia, and Austria, known collectively as the Third Coalition. Oudinot saw action at Wertingen (8 October 1805) and Ulm (17 October 1805). His forces became known as the "Grenadiers Oudinot" and played an important role in the seizure of the bridges into Vienna (13 November 1805); they also provided the critical attack on the Russians at Austerlitz (2 December 1805). French marshal Joachim MURAT wrote to Napoleon: "Oudinot's division covered itself in glory; it withstood, repelled, defeated a corps three times as strong as it [was]." Oudinot was named as commander of the 2nd Foot Guards in 1806, and he participated in the siege of Danzig (18 March–27 May 1807) and the crucial clash at Friedland (14 June 1807). In 1808, he was named as governor of Erfurt in Germany, and in 1810, following the battle of Wagram (6 July 1809), he was made a count of the empire. In 1810, he was named duc de Reggio (duke of Reggio), and he served as the governor of Holland from 1810 to 1812.

Oudinot played a major role in the French invasion of Russia that began in 1812. Commanding the II Corps of the Grand Armeé, he saw action at Polotsk (18 August 1812), where he was wounded, and at Grossbeeren (23 August 1813), near Berlin, where he fought to a draw. Napoleon forced him to defend Polotsk against the Russians under Petr Wittgenstein, even though intelligence had told Oudinot that the Russians vastly outnumbered his own forces. He managed to hold the city but was wounded; it was Marshal Gouvion St. Cyr who completed the defense. Oudinot was finally replaced by Marshal Michel NEY. He was wounded again at Berezina (28 November 1812).

In 1814, Oudinot was named commander of the VIII Corps, seeing action at Brienne (29 January), where he was wounded again, and at La Rothiere (1 February). The fall of Napoleon, and the return of King Louis XVII, did not adversely affect his career as he was named commander of the Corporations Royale de Grenadiers et Chasseurs de France and governor of the 3rd Military Division at Metz. Napoleon's escape from the island of Elba and resumption of power was a key point in French history. Though Napoleon asked for his services again, Oudinot, who had taken an oath to support the new king, refused, the only one of Napoleon's former commanders to do so. He eventually retired to his home in Bor-le-Duc, near Paris.

Napoleon's defeat at Waterloo (18 June 1815) left Oudinot vindicated on his stand. The royal family of the Bourbons considered him an ally and appointed him to important positions. He served as a peer of France and as inspector general of the National Guard of Paris. In 1823, he led an invasion of Spain, and he served for a time as governor of Madrid. Oudinot remained close to the royal family, and after the removal of Charles X in 1830, he retired rather than cooperate with the new government, although he later served as the governor of Les Invalides from 1842 until his death on 13 September 1847 at the age of 80.

Charles Oudinot is perhaps one of the least remembered of Napoleon's marshals. Despite his lengthy career, he did not win the dramatic victories that other marshals accomplished. Nonetheless, he was an efficient and effective commander without whom Napoleon would not have achieved as many military successes as he did.

References: Oudinot, Marie Charlotte Eugénie Julienne, duchess de Reggio, *Memoirs of Marshal Oudinot, Duc de Reggio,* translated by Alexander Teixeira de Mattos (New York: D. Appleton and Company, 1897); De Ségur, Count Philippe-Paul, *Napoleon's Russian Campaign* (Alexandria, Va.: Time/Life Books, 1980).

Oxford, John de Vere, 13th earl of (1442–1513)
English soldier

John de Vere, the second son born of John, the 12th earl of Oxford, was born on 8 September 1442. His older brother, Aubrey, should have become the 13th earl of Oxford. However, Aubrey and his father both fought for the Lancastrians when the Wars of the Roses broke out in 1455, and both were captured and beheaded in 1462 at the order of King Edward IV. The title of earl of Oxford then passed to John because he had been involved with a peaceful reconciliation of the two families. He was also allowed to resume the hereditary de Vere office of lord great chamberlain, even serving in that capacity at the coronation of Elizabeth Woodville, Edward IV's queen. Oxford strengthened his connection to the royal family when he married Margaret, a sister of Richard Neville, earl of WARWICK. Nonetheless, it was alleged he was plotting for the removal of Edward, and in 1468 he was arrested. Although he was sent to the Tower of London, historians believe that his brother-in-law, the earl of Warwick, interceded on his behalf since he was released in 1469. Some historians now believe that Warwick himself was forming a plot against Edward and had made Oxford a part of it.

Free from the Tower, Oxford fled to France and joined Margaret of Anjou, the "queen mother" of the Lancastrian side and the wife of King Henry VI, still imprisoned in the Tower. Once Warwick had also fled to France, the two men formed an alliance against Edward, and they landed in England with their army in September 1470. One of Oxford's first tasks was the capture and execution of John Tiptoft, the earl of Worcester, who had put Oxford's father and brother to death. Worcester was, in turn, put to death by Oxford himself, who took over his office of constable of England when Henry VI was restored to the throne. Andrew Kippis, a famed English historian whose multivolume collection *Biographia Britannica* covers the lives of famed men and women of England prior to the start of the 18th century, writes: "The Earl of Oxford bore the sword in the procession from the Tower (where the King was imprisoned) to St. Paul's Cathedral. Upon the recovery of the Crown, King Henry VI called a parliament, wherein Edward being declared a Traitor and Usurper, the Earl of Oxford, attainted by him, was restored in blood, dignities, and ancient positions. On the 23d of December following he was commissioned, with Richard Earl of Warwick, and others, to levy all persons capable of bearing arms, and to muster and review them as often as occasion should require; and to lead and command them in opposing Henry's enemies . . ."

In 1471, Edward IV, who had fled England on Henry's restoration the year before, returned with his own army at Ravenspur inn Yorkshire to fight the Lancastrians for the throne. Edward sent Oxford a message asking for his support; Oxford's reply to Edward's messenger was, "Go, tell your Duke, that I had rather be an Earl, and always like myself, than a false and perjured Duke; and that e'er my oath shall be falsified (as his apparently is) I will lay down my life at me enemy's foot, which I doubt not shall be bought very dear." Serving as one of Henry's commanders, Oxford fought for the Lancastrians at Barnet (4 April 1471), where the earl of Warwick was killed and the Lancastrians defeated. Oxford fled again from England, this time first to Wales (not Scotland, as many historians have written) and then to France.

In exile a second time, Oxford received monetary aid from King Louis XI of France to conduct raids against English shipping. He now sided with Edward's brother George, duke of Clarence, in his claim to the throne. In 1473, Oxford's forces seized the island of St. Michael's Mount off the coast of Cornwall, which he intended to use as a foothold for a second invasion of England. He waited in vain for additional forces to arrive, and a force sent by Edward captured him. Instead of imprisoning him in England, however, Edward sent him to France, and he was incarcerated in the castle of Hammes, near Calais. Oxford planned an escape, and in 1477, after three years in custody, he jumped over the walls into the moat but was caught.

In 1484, Oxford formed an alliance with Sir James Blount, the governor of Hammes, and Sir John Fortescue. The three men approached Henry Tudor, the earl of Richmond, to form an army and retake the throne of England, to which Henry had a claim through his descent from John of Gaunt, son of EDWARD III. It is written that when Henry heard of the plan "he was ravished with joy incredible." Oxford swore he would not leave Henry's side until the crown was on his head. On 22 August 1485 at Bosworth, Leicestershire, Henry's army met the forces of RICHARD III, who had become king in 1483. Andrew Kippis writes: "Richmond marshaled his army, and appointed this Earl [Oxford] to commander the vanguard, consisting of archers. And he behaved with such great courage in the battle, that when they came to the sword, fearing to be encompassed, he

commanded that no soldier should stir above 10 feet from his colours: and then most valiantly charging the enemy in [the] form of a wedge, put them to the rout, in which he flew many, and thereby became one of the chiefest instruments in obtaining the happy victory that day."

Henry marched on London and was crowned as Henry VII. He restored to Oxford all of his family's titles and possessions and reinstated him as lord great chamberlain, in addition to bestowing the title of lord admiral of England. Oxford later fought at Stoke, Nottinghamshire (16 June 1487), the last battle of the Wars of the Roses, and helped put down the rising of Baron Audley's Cornish troops at Blackheath near London in 1497. He retired thereafter, having served the Lancastrian side of the royal family well.

Oxford's role in the success of the Lancastrian cause cannot be underestimated. Historian Desmond Seward writes: "John de Vere, Earl of Oxford, was as unshakeable Lancastrian as [his brother-in-law Warren] Hastings was Yorkist. He was the head of England's most ancient noble family, a rare example of a great family that stayed loyal to the House of Lancaster throughout the wars. He too was something of a hero, a fine soldier with a shrewd grasp of strategy and tactics." The last de Vere to hold the title of earl of Oxford, Aubrey de Vere (20th earl), died in 1703. Today it is incorporated in the title of earl of Oxford and Asquith, now held by the family of Henry Asquith, prime minister of England from 1908 to 1916.

References: "Vere," in *Biographia Britannica; or, The Lives of the Most Eminent Persons who have flourished in Great Britain and Ireland . . . ,* 6 vols. edited by Andrew Kippis (London: Printed for W. Walthoe, T. Osborne, H. Whitridge [et al.], 1793), VI:4026–4027; Seward, Desmond, *The Wars of the Roses and the Lives of Five Men and Women in the Fifteenth Century* (London: Constable, 1995), 14, 340; Elliot, Henry Lettsom, *On Some Badges and Devices of John de Vere, 13th Earl of Oxford, on the Tower of Castle Hedingham Church* (Colchester, U.K.: Wiles & Son, 1919).

P

Paskevich, Ivan Fedorovich **(count of Erivan, prince of Warsaw)** (1782–1856) *Russian field marshal*

Ivan Paskevich was born in Poltava, Russia (now in the Ukraine), on 19 May 1782; little is known of his early family life, background, and education. At a young age, he served as a page in the court of Czar Paul of Russia (1754–1801), the son of Catherine the Great. Paskevich entered the Russian army in 1800, took part in the Battle of Austerlitz (1805), and fought against the Turks in the Russo-Turkish War of 1806–12. He also participated in the Russian army's resistance to NAPOLEON's advance on Moscow in 1812, fighting at Borodino (7 September 1812).

Serving for a time under General Alexei Yermolov, Paskevich rose to prominence when Russian forces defeated the Persians in the Russo-Persian War of 1826–28. During this conflict, he captured the Armenian fort of Etchmiadzin, and his conquest of the provinces of Erivan and Nakhichevan brought about the Russian victory, concluded with the Peace of Turkmanchai (1828). For his service, he was named the count of Erivan by Czar Nicholas I.

Soon after the Russo-Persian War ended, Paskevich was sent to fight in the Russo-Turkish War of 1828–29. He successfully captured the towns of Erzurum and Kars on the Turkish eastern border, and once again his military bravado earned him glory and acclaim from his country. Following the conflict, he was advanced to the rank of field marshal, and when an uprising against Russian rule in Poland broke out, Paskevich was sent to Warsaw and put down the rebellion in 1831. For this service, Czar Nicholas made him prince of Warsaw and viceroy of Poland. Placed in charge of the Russian puppet government in Poland, he began a brutal regime to "russify" the country, and for nearly 20 years there were no further uprisings in Poland.

In 1849, Paskevich, now nearly 67, was called into action again. When Hungarians revolted against Austrian rule of their country, Austria asked Nicholas I for aid. Nicholas dispatched Paskevich, who led 200,000 Russian and Polish troops to end the insurrection; the Hungarians surrendered at Vilagos on 13 August 1849. In 1854, when the Crimean War broke out in southern Russia, Nicholas sent the 72-year-old Paskevich to the area as head of the Army of Danube. Paskevich marched south, first stopping to besiege the town of Silistra (now in Bulgaria) on 14 April 1854; the town on the Danube was an important center for Turkish commerce. The daguerrotypes of photographer Carol Szathmari highlighted the battle; one is entitled *The Bombardment of Silvistra.* However, Russian guns could not breach the emplacements, and on 8 June 1854 the Russian forces retreated. This first reverse of Paskevich's career was also his last, and he was removed from command. He returned to Warsaw, where he died less than two years later on 13 February 1856. He is one of only four Russian field marshals to have worn all four classes of the Military Order of St. George the Great Martyr and Vanquisher, the most important of Russian military decorations.

References: Czerapowicz, Josephine Mary, *Kingdom of Poland during the Paskevich Viceroyalty, 1832–1856: Erosion of Autonomy* (Master's Thesis, Michigan State University, 1975); Royal, Trevor, *Crimea: The Great Crimean War, 1854–56* (New York: St. Martin's Press, 2000).

Patton, George Smith, Jr. (1885–1945)
American general

George Patton was born in Lake Vineyard Ranch in San Gabriel (now San Marino), California, on 11 November 1885, the son of George Smith Patton Sr. He attended local schools and the Virginia Military Institute, then was admitted to the United States Military Academy at West Point, New York; however, he was forced to leave when he failed several exams. Allowed to reenter, he improved his aptitude and in 1909 graduated 46th out of 103, upon which he was given a commission in the cavalry. A talented athlete, Patton competed in the 1912 Olympic Games in Stockholm, Sweden. In 1916, he was assigned to serve under General John J. PERSHING and saw action in the American invasion of Mexico against the Mexican bandit Pancho Villa. In the First World War, he served on the western front in France, again under Pershing, fighting in the St. Mihiel offensive and the offensive at Meuse-Argonne, where he was wounded. He was eventually named as the commander of the 304th Tank Brigade, one of the first to use tanks in modern combat. In the years after the end of the First World War, he studied the use of tanks in warfare and served in several administrative posts in the U.S. Army.

When the United States entered the Second World War in 1941, the army deployed a strong tank force, due largely to Patton's leadership. (Although budget cuts in the interwar years had hindered research, Patton had worked to keep development of tank studies alive. During this period, he also had become close friends with another rising star in the American military, Dwight D. EISENHOWER.) Patton was made a three-star general and put in command of II Corps in North Africa. In

Lieutenant General George S. Patton, Jr., in 1944

November 1942, a series of battles led to a combined American and British victory against the Germans led by General Erwin ROMMEL. Following the defeat of Nazi forces in northern Africa, the Allies planned to move into southern Europe through Sicily, and Patton was placed in command of the Seventh Army. The combined American and British armies (the latter commanded by General Harold ALEXANDER) landed on 10 July 1943, and Patton's forces quickly took a series of local villages, including Gela, Licata, and Vittoria. Working with the British, the Americans took Niscemi and the Biscani airfield (14 July 1943). An American force under General Omar BRADLEY moved north as Patton's men moved onto Palermo (22 July 1943), and Messina (17 August 1943), the capture of which forced the resignation of Italian dictator Benito Mussolini.

Although considered one of the American army's finest commanders, Patton had a volcanic temperament, which got him in trouble when he hit two soldiers who he felt were evading their duty. In January 1944, he was quietly replaced by General Mark CLARK as commander of the Seventh Army and sent to England, where he replaced General Courtney Hodges as an army commander in the planned Normandy landings in northern France. Once the landings occurred, Patton joined his men on 1 August 1944 and led them through western France. After his forces overran Le Mans (8 August 1944), he told his superiors that he believed a resolute tank attack on a narrow front would end the war quickly. However, General Bradley ordered him into Brittany to eliminate the last German forces there. Finishing this, Patton's forces crossed the Meuse River on 30 August 1944 and headed toward Metz. He found the city well-defended by Nazi forces, and his Third Army took heavy casualties. He was unprepared for the German offensive of 16 December 1944 through the Ardennes; this became known as the Battle of the Bulge. Although the Germans inflicted heavy casualties on the Americans, it was their last major battle on the western front. On 22 March 1945, Patton's forces crossed the Rhine River and pushed through Germany, moving south into Austria and Czechoslovakia before the Soviet Union demanded that he withdraw. Once the Germans had surrendered, he was promoted to the rank of four-star general and named as the governor of Bavaria. He was then given command of the Fifteenth Army.

On 9 December 1945, one day before he was to return to the United States, Patton was involved in a jeep accident in which he suffered horrific injuries. Paralyzed from the neck down, he lingered for nearly two weeks in a hospital near Heidelberg. On 21 December, he died of an embolism that went to his brain. Following a state funeral in Luxembourg Cathedral, he was laid to rest in the U.S. Military Cemetery in Hamm, outside of Luxembourg, Belgium, where some 30,000 American soldiers killed in the Second World War were buried.

George Patton, known as "Old Blood and Guts," kept a diary of his exploits in wartime from July 1942 until 5 December 1945, just four days before he was killed. Later published as *War as I Knew It* in 1947, it contains a letter Patton wrote about what he thought of his own role in the war:

> I can say this, that throughout the campaign in Europe I know of no error I made except that of failing to send a Combat Command to take Hammelburg. Otherwise, my operations were, to me, strictly satisfactory. In every case, practically throughout the campaign, I was under wraps from the Higher Command. This may have

been a good thing, as perhaps I am too impetuous. However, I do not believe I was, and feel that had I been permitted to go all out, the war would have ended sooner and more lives would have been saved. Particularly I think this statement applies to the time when, in the early days of September [1944], we were halted, owing to the desire, or necessity, on the part of General Eisenhower in backing MONTGOMERY's move to the north. At that time there were no question of doubt but that we could have gone through and on across the Rhine within ten days. This would have saved a great many thousand men.

References: Wellard, James Howard, *The Man in a Helmet: The Life of General Patton* (London: Eyre & Spottiswoode, 1947); Mellor, William Bancroft, *Patton: Fighting Man* (New York: Putnam, 1946); Army Times editors, *Warrior: The Story of General George S. Patton* (New York: Putnam, 1967); Ayer, Frederick, *Before the Colors Fade: Portrait of a Soldier, George S. Patton* (Boston: Houghton Mifflin, 1964); Allen, Robert S., *Lucky Forward: The History of Patton's Third U.S. Army* (New York: Vanguard Press, 1947); Farago, Ladislas, *The Last Days of Patton* (New York: McGraw-Hill, 1981); Patton, George S., *War as I Knew It* (Boston: Houghton Mifflin, 1947).

Paullus Macedonicus, Lucius Aemilius
(Lucius Aemilius Paulus) (ca. 229–160 B.C.)
Roman general

Lucius Aemilius Paullus was born about 229 B.C., the son and namesake of a military leader and Roman consul who was killed fighting the Carthaginians at the Battle of Cannæ (216 B.C.), the key clash in the Second Punic War (218–202 B.C.). He was a member of the Aemilii Paullii, a noted Roman family of great wealth and influence in Roman affairs. Paullus served in the Roman military as a tribune before being elected as a *curule aedile* (a civil office similar to mayor) in 193 B.C. Two years later, he was elected as praetor and subsequently went to what is now Spain, where he fought for two years against the Lusitanians, a nomadic tribe. He was elected as a consul for the first time in 182 B.C., and the following year he fought the Ingauni in Liguria in northeast Italy.

In 171 B.C., King Perseus of Macedon defeated the Romans at Callicinus, setting off the Third Macedonian War, which sputtered on for two years without any major battles. In 168 B.C., Paullus was reelected consul, and the Roman Senate appointed him to lead its forces in Macedonia. He fought Perseus at Pydna, a port on the east coast of Macedonia, on 22 June 168 B.C., defeating the Macedonians and taking Perseus captive. To impress his victory on his enemies, he ordered the executions of 500 Macedonians who refused to vow allegiance to the Roman victors.

The victory at Pydna ended the war, Paullus returned to Rome in glory, and the Senate gave him the surname of Macedonicus to herald his victory. He had siezed the Macedonian treasury and returned with enough to allow the Roman government to cease collecting taxes for a period. He was elected as censor in 164 B.C. and died four years later.

Because of the single victory at Pydna, Paullus is remembered for ending the Macedonian war and capturing his opponent. With his death, however, the power of the Aemilii Paullii family ended as well. Nevertheless, one of his sons was adopted by the elder son of SCIPIO AFRICANUS (THE ELDER) and became Scipio Aemilianus, better known as Publius Cornelius Scipio Aemilianus, or Scipio Africanus the Younger.

References: Reiter, William, *Aemilius Paullus: Conqueror of Greece* (London: Croom Helm, 1988); "Paullus," in *The Penguin Dictionary of Ancient History,* edited by Graham Speake (London: Penguin Books, 1995), 471–472; "Paullus, Lucius Aemilius," in *The Hutchinson Dictionary of Ancient and Medieval Warfare* (Oxford, U.K.: Helicon Publishing, Ltd., 1998), 243.

Paulus, Friedrich Wilhelm Ernst (1890–1957)
German general

Born in the village of Breitenau-Gershagen, in Hesse, Germany, on 23 September 1890, Friedrich Paulus received his education at the Wilhelms-Gymnasium in Kassel. In 1909, he completed his school examinations and hoped for a career in the navy. However, the German navy rejected him, and he turned to the study of the law, attending Marburg University from 1909 to 1910. When he heard that the army was recruiting, he signed up and was accepted as a cadet officer in the Markgraf Ludwig Wilhelm Infantry Regiment No. 111, stationed at Rastatt. He saw action with the German army during the First World War.

Following the end of the war, Paulus remained in the military as a member of the Freikorps, the German militia. During the interwar period, he rose in the ranks, and in September 1935 he succeeded Heinz Guderian as head of the German mechanized forces. He became a close friend and confidant of Adolf Hitler, the German leader, and was instrumental in the organization and growth of the Wehrmacht (the German army) and the establishment of a plan for Germany to win the war in Europe that it had lost in 1918.

In 1939, Paulus was named as chief of staff of the Tenth Army, and in September 1940 he became chief of operations for the Wehrmacht. In January 1941, Hitler appointed him commander of the Sixth Army, then readying its march into southern Russia as part of Operation Barbarossa. Paulus had not commanded a unit during the First World War, and he had no leadership experience, but this was not evident at the beginning of the operation. The Sixth Army had already crashed through France, quickly defeating Germany's largest European enemy, and had taken the Low Countries. Then came Barbarossa, the invasion of Russia in June 1941, for which Hitler had long planned. Under the command of Field Marshal Gerd von Rundstedt, the German armies fought their way into the Ukraine and captured its capital, Kiev, also taking some 600,000 Russian soldiers as prisoners. However, the Germans had not planned for the horrific Russian winter, and—like NAPOLEON's French army in 1812—they quickly became bogged down. Von Rundstedt resigned his position after Hitler refused to allow him to retreat from the worsening winter conditions, and he was replaced by General Walther von Reichenau on 5 January 1942. This left Paulus completely responsible for the Sixth army. Paulus biographer Martin Middlebrook states: "The man who had never commanded any unit in war was given direct responsibility for an army of more than a quarter of a million men."

Ordered by Hitler to capture Stalingrad no matter the cost, Paulus marched on the city and took it in September 1942, the high-water mark of German conquest in Russia. The Russians, however, had lured the Germans into a trap, and they quickly surrounded Stalingrad in a siege that began in November 1942. At first, Hitler tried a rescue mission, sending Field Marshal Erich von Manstein and the 4th Panzer Division to Stalingrad. Halted by the Soviets 30 miles from the city, von Manstein ordered Paulus to try to break out of Stalingrad, but the German forces, weak and low on supplies, were in no condition to do so, and Paulus refused. Unable to resupply the German forces there, Hitler abandoned them. After three months of starvation and continual attrition from Russian bombardment, Paulus surrendered his entire Sixth Army on 31 January 1943 to the Russian commander Konstantin ROKOSSOVSKY. Ironically, Hitler had promoted him to the rank of field marshal the day before he surrendered. The whole of the German force was sent to Siberia; of 300,000 men, some 45,000 died during the march to the camps, and only 7,000 survivors emerged from Russia after the war.

Paulus was arrested by the Soviets and initially refused to speak with them. However, when he discovered that several of his military comrades, including Erwin von Witzleben, had been executed for their involvement in the "July Plot" (1944) of German military officers to kill Hitler, Paulus changed his mind, joined the so-called National Free Germany Committee, and began to make anti-Nazi radio broadcasts, which were broadcast inside Germany. Hitler ordered that Paulus's family be imprisoned, but none were physically harmed.

With the end of the war, Paulus was allowed to travel to Nuremberg, where he testified in the war crimes trial against former Nazi officials. He was released from Soviet custody in 1953 and he settled in Dresden, in Communist East Germany, where he became outspoken for his anti-American views. He died of motor neuron disease in Dresden on 1 February 1957.

Paulus is not highly rated by historians. The biographer Martin Middlebrook explains that even his contemporaries did not view him kindly: "History gives a simple and unkind verdict on Friedrich Paulus: gifted Staff officer, uninspired commander, an unquestioning general of the 'orders-are-orders' type. He never questioned Nazism and was willing to do almost anything ordered by Hitler. Finally, when the fate of a quarter of a million men rested in his hands, he 'froze' and did little but let events take their course to the complete destruction of his army and the miserable deaths of most of his soldiers."

References: Goerlitz, Walter, *Paulus and Stalingrad: A Life of Field-Marshal Friedrich Paulus with Notes, Correspondence, and Documents from his Papers* (New York: The Citadel Press, 1963); Middlebrook, Martin, "Field-Marshal Friedrich Paulus," in *Hitler's Generals,* edited by Corelli Barnett (New York: Grove Weidenfeld, 1989), 361–373; Roberts, Geoffrey, *Victory at Stalingrad: The Battle That Changed History* (London: Longman, 2002).

Pembroke, second earl of *See* CLARE, RICHARD, FITZGILBERT DE, SECOND EARL OF PEMBROKE.

Penn, Sir William (1621–1670) *English admiral* Born in Bristol, Gloucestershire, on 23 April 1621, William Penn was the son of Giles Penn, a seaman and merchant from Bristol. At an early age, he began service on the sea at his father's side, although apparently he did not see military action until the English Civil War. When that conflict broke out in 1642 between the forces of King Charles I and those who backed Parliament, Penn sided against the monarch. However, the first phase of the war saw few if any naval clashes, and he mainly spent his time in the Irish Sea commanding a ship in the squadron watching for any invasion by the king's forces. In 1647, he was named by Parliament as rear admiral of the Irish seas, and he maintained his watch there. However, some believed that Penn was in fact working for the king, and in 1648 he was arrested by the Parliamentarians and accused of carrying on a correspondence with Charles I. He was sent to London in chains, but after a quick investigation into the allegation, he was released, and in 1650 he was granted his own warship, the *Assurance,* as part of the Ocean squadron. As commander of this squadron, he chased Prince RUPERT, one of the leading Royalist commanders, who had fled England following the king's capture, trial, and 1649 execution.

Although he had played only a small part in the first phase of the English Civil War, Penn came into his own in the First Anglo-Dutch War (1652–54). Upon the outbreak of this conflict, he was named as vice admiral, serving under Robert BLAKE, who had also participated in the English Civil War. Penn supported Blake at the battle off Kentish Knock (28 September 1652), and in the clash against the Dutch off Portland (February 1653), his "Blue Squadron" ensured victory. Although he fought for the Parliament forces, now controlling England, in 1654 Penn conspired with Charles I's son, later Charles II, offering him control over the entire English fleet. Apparently Charles refused this offer, and Penn remained loyal to the new Parliamentary ruler, Oliver

CROMWELL. Unaware of Penn's treachery, Cromwell gave him command of a fleet sent to the West Indies in 1655. Under Penn, this expedition captured Jamaica in May 1655 but was heavily driven back and defeated at San Domingo. Historians attribute this failure not to Penn's actions but to the panic of his troops ashore. A dejected Penn returned to England, where he was briefly imprisoned in the Tower of London for his performance in the West Indies. When he was released, he retired from the service to an estate he purchased in Munster in Ireland.

Although out of the limelight, Penn continued secret negotiations to return Charles II to the throne. Charles's restoration in 1660 led the monarch to knight Penn and grant him the post of commissioner for the navy. He was named captain of the fleet when the Second Dutch War (1665–67) began, serving as second in command under James, duke of York, who would later become King James II. Penn led ships into battle in the naval engagement at Lowestoft (3 June 1665) and subsequently retired from active service. He died in London on 16 September 1670, at the age of 49, and was laid to rest in the crypt of the church of St. Mary Redcliffe in Bristol. In 1681, 11 years after Penn's death, King Charles II granted land in the American colonies to Penn's son, William; this is now the state of Pennsylvania.

The name of Sir William Penn has long been eclipsed by that of his son. Nonetheless, he played an important role in naval affairs during and after the English Civil War. He was also the author of a series of works on naval tactics, which were eventually printed as *Sailing and Fighting Instructions for His Majesty's Fleet* by his commander, James, duke of York.

References: Penn, Granville, *Memorials of the Professional Life and Times of Sir William Penn from 1644 to 1670* (London: J. Duncan, 1833); Conner, Philip Syng Physick, *Sir William Penn, Knight: Admiral, and General-at-Sea; Great-Captain-Commander in the Fleet: A Memoir* (Philadelphia: J. B. Lippincott, 1876); *Another Great Victorie obtained by Vice-Admiral Penn against the Hollanders . . .* (London: Printed for G. Horton, 1653); Bruce, Anthony, and William Cogar, "Penn, Sir William," in *An Encyclopedia of Naval History* (New York: Checkmark Books, 1999) 282; Street, Lucie, *An Uncommon Sailor: A Portrait of Admiral Sir William Penn* (Bourne End, U.K.: Kensal Press, 1986).

Perry, Oliver Hazard (1785–1819) *American naval officer*

Oliver Hazard Perry was born in South Kingston, Rhode Island, on 23 August 1785, the eldest child of eight children of Christopher Perry, who served in the American Revolution, and Sarah Alexander Perry, whom he had met when returning from being held as a prisoner of war in Ireland. All five sons of the Perrys became military officers, including Oliver and his brother Matthew Calbraith Perry (who led the first American military expedition to Japan, then a closed society, in 1853). Oliver Perry received an appointment as a midshipman in 1799 and saw limited service in the Mediterranean before he served in the "Quasi War" between the United States and France from 1798 to 1800, and in the Tripolitan War (1801–05). At the start of the War of 1812 with the British, Perry was given the task of building a flotilla of warships for the infant U.S. Navy to fight on Lake Erie and end British superiority of the waters there. After 10 ships had been completed, Perry made his base in Sandusky, Ohio, where he launched his fleet to battle the British.

On 10 September 1813, Perry and a force of nine ships sailed into Lake Erie to do battle with six British vessels under the command of Captain Robert Heriot Barclay. Although the two forces were of roughly equal size—the British ships being larger—the Americans had a superior edge in firepower, and Perry used this edge to his advantage. His flagship, the *Lawrence,* was named after his good friend James Lawrence, who had been killed off Boston, Massachusetts, on 1 June 1813, and on its flag were some of Lawrence's last words: "Don't give up the ship." In the battle that ensued, the British were defeated with heavy casualties. Historian George Bruce writes: "The whole British flotilla was destroyed, with a loss of 134 killed and wounded. The Americans lost 27 killed and 96 wounded. The British were obliged to withdraw from Detroit." Following the battle, Perry sent a note to William Henry Harrison (later president of the United States), the commander of American forces waiting to march into Canada: "We have met the enemy, and they are ours. Two ships, two brigs, one schooner, one sloop."

Although this victory made Perry one of the most important military leaders of early American history, never again did he participate in such an important battle. Nonetheless, his career continued: He returned to Newport, Rhode Island, and in 1815 he became the commander of the frigate *Java* and was sent to northern Africa to the area known as the Barbary Coast, where pirates of the Barbary states had been capturing, harassing, and attacking ships. Perry's ship patrolled for two years before he returned home in 1817.

In 1819, Perry was sent by President James Monroe to serve on a diplomatic mission to Venezuela. However, while on the voyage, he contracted yellow fever or malaria (historians differ as to which), and he succumbed to the disease off the coast of Trinidad on his 34th birthday, 23 August 1819. He was buried at Port of Spain, Trinidad, with full military honors. Seven years later, in 1826, his remains were exhumed and returned to Newport, where he was laid to rest.

Oliver Perry's reputation rests on his single victory on Lake Erie. Historian Richard Dillon writes: "He absolutely refused to admit, much less accept, defeat when he was literally beaten on Lake Erie. He was that *rara avis* in our history, the true hero-patriot." In his honor, the class of American frigates known as the Oliver Hazard Perry class, as well as the lead ship of the class, the USS *Oliver Hazard Perry* (FFG-7), were named for him.

References: Mackenzie, Alexander Slidell, *The Life of Commodore Oliver Hazard Perry,* 2 vols. (New York: A. L. Fowle, 1900); Dutton, Charles J., *Oliver Hazard Perry* (New York: Longmans, Green & Company, 1935); Bruce, George, "Lake Erie," in *Collins Dictionary of Wars* (Glasgow, Scotland: HarperCollins Publishers, 1995), 135; Bruce, Anthony, and William Cogar. "Perry, Oliver Hazard," in *An Encyclopedia of Naval History* (New York: Checkmark Books, 1999), 284; Dillon, Richard, *We Have Met the Enemy: Oliver Hazard Perry, Wilderness Commander* (New York: McGraw-Hill, 1978).

Pershing, John Joseph ("Black Jack" Pershing)

(1860–1948) *American general*

John Pershing was born on 13 September 1860 in the town of Laclede, in Linn County, Missouri, the son of John Frederick Pershing, a storekeeper, and Anne Elizabeth Thompson Pershing. He attended the state normal school in Kirksville, Missouri, receiving a degree in teaching, before he received an appointment to the United States Military Academy at West Point, New York, in 1882. He graduated four years later the 30th out of 77 graduates. Assigned to the 6th Cavalry, he saw action against American Indian tribes, including

the Sioux (Lakota, Nakota, Dakota) and Apache, in the American West. One source notes that Pershing was at Wounded Knee, South Dakota, in 1890 when a number of Indians were killed by American troops there, though other historians dispute this claim. In 1891, he received an appointment at the University of Nebraska to teach military science, and he later taught the same course at West Point. In 1893, he earned a law degree from the University of Nebraska law school. Two years later, he was assigned to the 10th Cavalry in Montana, an African-American regiment to which he became so devoted that he was dubbed "Black Jack," a nickname he held for the rest of his life.

Pershing was teaching at West Point in 1898 when the Spanish-American War began. Named as quartermaster of the 10th Cavalry division, he was sent to Cuba and saw action in several battles, including at San Juan Hill, made famous by Theodore Roosevelt's Rough Riders, and at El Carney. However, he contracted malaria and was shipped home to the United States to recuper-

General of the Armies John J. Pershing

ate. He was then attached to the Department of War in Washington, D.C., and in September 1898 he was named chief of insular affairs in the War Department. The following year, after the United States had defeated Spain, Pershing was sent to the Philippines to fight the so-called Moro campaign in Mindanao in the northern part of that country. In 1905, he served as a military attaché in Japan, closely watching the Russo-Japanese War (1905–06). The following year, on 20 September 1906, President Theodore Roosevelt promoted Pershing to brigadier general, passing him over 862 more senior officers. Pershing was named as the brigade commander at Fort McKinley in the Philippines in 1908, and he remained in that country until 1913, when he returned to the United States.

In 1914, Pershing was named as commander of the 8th Infantry Brigade headquartered at the Presidio in San Francisco, California. Tragically, his wife and daughter were killed in a terrible fire, leaving him with no family. In 1916, he was appointed commander of the force to hunt down the Mexican outlaw Pancho Villa, who had crossed into the United States and murdered several innocent Americans in Columbus, New Mexico. Pershing's force invaded Mexican territory but never caught Villa, who remained at large until his assassination in 1923. On 25 September 1916, despite his failure to capture Villa, Pershing was promoted to major general, and then to general on 6 October 1917.

In April 1917, the United States declared war on Germany and her allies, beginning American participation in the First World War. President Woodrow Wilson named Pershing to command the American Expeditionary Force (AEF), the first U.S. troops to land in France and fight for the Allies. In June 1917, Pershing went to France to determine the course the Americans should take. When he returned, he presented the president and the Department of War with a "general organization report," which advocated sending 1 million American troops to Europe by the end of 1918, and a total of 3 million by the end of 1919 if the war was still being fought. Pershing realized that such a force was needed to win the war and overcome three years of a conflict that had cost millions of troops their lives. Britain and France had been, in the words of one historian, "bled white." Germany was barely keeping afloat, although the victory against Russia on the eastern front had allowed it to concentrate all of its firepower against the Allies on the western front,

which had turned into a military stalemate. While the Allies had not counted on such an American response, huge losses during 1917 made it clear they needed U.S. support. Pershing had been told by Wilson that American forces must not be under any foreign command. Although the Supreme War Council of Britain and France asked to have American forces put under British-French command, Pershing held his ground and refused, except when circumstances made it necessary, and he allowed his troops to fight under the command of French marshal Ferdinand FOCH during the German offensives of March and June 1918.

In September 1918, Pershing launched the St.-Mihiel offensive, continuing through what became the Meuse-Argonne offensive in late 1918. It proved slower and costlier than Pershing had thought, but, combined with the British and French advance, it played an important part in the final offensive that led to the armistice ending the conflict on 11 November 1918. Pershing returned to the United States a hero, and on 3 September 1919 he was given the rank of General of the Armies, a position that had been created for George Washington in the American armed forces but never held by the first president.

Although he was now the leading figure in the country, Pershing turned down any political reward and instead decided to remain with the army. On 1 July 1921, he was named chief of staff of the army, an office he held until he formally retired in 1924. During his tenure as chief of staff, he established the War Plans Board, called for a strict program of national preparedness outside of wartime, supported the institution of a course of officer schooling and training throughout the country, and endorsed the full funding of National Guard units in the states. Following his retirement, Pershing wrote his memoirs, which were published as *My Experiences in the World War* in 1931 and won the Pulitzer Prize for history.

Pershing was stricken with a serious illness in 1941, and he moved into Walter Reed Hospital in Maryland, where he spent the last years of his life. He died there in his sleep on 15 July 1948 at the age of 87. He was laid to rest in Arlington National Cemetery in Virginia, buried among the men he had fought with. His marble tombstone bears no special marks and is no larger than those of men of lower rank. This emphasizes what is perhaps most important about John Pershing: Not only was he an important military commander during the First

World War, but he also had an affinity for his men. Part of his legacy concerns African-American troops, starting with his service with the 10th Cavalry in the last decade of the 19th century. When he went to France, he determined that black soldiers, usually relegated to occupations behind the lines, would play a larger part, seeing combat and being treated as equals by their white comrades. In this respect, Pershing was years ahead of his time.

References: Vandiver, Frank Everson, *Black Jack: The Life and Times of John J. Pershing* (College Station: Texas A&M University Press, 1977); Palmer, Frederick, *John J. Pershing, General of the Armies: A Biography* (Harrisburg, Pa.: Military Service Publishing Company, 1948); Braddy, Haldeen, *Pershing's Mission in Mexico* (El Paso: Texas Western Press, 1966); "President Calls the Nation to Arms; Draft Bill Signed; Registration on June 5; Regulars under Pershing to Go to France," *The New York Times,* 19 May 1917, 1; Vandiver, Frank Everson, "Pershing, John Joseph," in *American National Biography* 24 vols., edited by John A. Garraty and Mark C. Carnes (New York: Oxford University Press, 1999), 17:376–379.

Pétain, Henri-Philippe-Benoni-Omer-Joseph
(1856–1951) *French marshal*

Born at Cauchy-à-la-Tour, in northern France, on 24 April 1856, Philippe Pétain was born into a family of farmers and received a local education in local schools. He was admitted to the Saint-Cyr military academy, known as St-Cyr, which had been founded by NAPOLEON BONAPARTE, and was commissioned into the French army in 1878. For a number of years, Pétain served as an instructor in military tactics. Following the Russo-Japanese War (1904–05), he came to believe that a new way of fighting wars was needed for the armies of Europe, although his was a minority view among French military officers. He was promoted to colonel in 1910.

By the time the First World War broke out, Pétain was 58 years old and nearing retirement. However, the French needed every soldier and officer they had to fight the German army, whose invasion of France had brought them to within 30 miles of Paris. Promoted to brigadier general, Pétain led French troops in the offensive known as Artois in the first days of the war. At the start of 1916, he was dispatched to Verdun to command French forces there. Although Verdun was surrounded by the Germans, and the French were hopelessly outnumbered and outgunned, Pétain was able to utilize the artillery to a greater degree and hold off the continual enemy assaults. As a result of his actions, he rose from being an unknown officer to a hero of France in a short period.

Throughout 1916, the British and French armies were "bled white" on the western front as they poured millions of men into a gruesome conflict that left appalling numbers of dead and wounded. By early 1917, French troops were in full mutiny against their commanders, and Robert-Georges NIVELLE, the French commander in chief, was replaced by the more trusted Pétain, who immediately accepted the troops' demands and improved their living conditions (food, shelter, and so on). He also changed fighting conditions by conducting only defensive operations. Discipline in the French troops was quickly returned to normal, which historians believe came about due to Pétain replacing Nivelle.

Pétain coordinated the activities of the French army with the British and other commanders, including the American general John J. PERSHING and the overall commander in chief of the Allied armies, French marshal Ferdinand FOCH. He oversaw the offensive of September 1918, which broke the back of the German army in France and led eventually to the armistice in November 1918. Soon afterward, Pétain was named as a marshal of France. He was appointed to the Supreme War Council, the coordinating committee overseeing the war as a whole, and to the office of inspector general of the French army.

Pétain remained an important leader in the French military in the years after the war, serving as minister of war in 1934. Following the German invasion of France in May 1940, Paul Reynaud, the new prime minister—who had replaced Edouard Daladier in March 1940—named Pétain as vice premier to stabilize the government. On 16 June 1940, Pétain, who was then 84 years old, was asked to form a government to negotiate with the Germans, who had taken Paris and controlled much of France. Reynaud tried to escape the country, but Pétain, now anxious to save France from further punishment, ordered his arrest and turned Reynaud over to the Germans. The French government led by Pétain is known as the Vichy government, or the Régime de Vichy, named after the new capital in the town of Vichy, southeast of Paris. The Vichy government elected Pétain as "chief of state" to deal with the Germans on all matters.

Pétain later said that he headed the Régime de Vichy to try to protect the French people as much as possible from repressive measures by the occupying German forces. However, in areas where the Germans ceded control to his government, he set up an administration which aided in the expulsion of Jews; its slogan was "Work, Family, Fatherland." Despite his compliance with the Nazis, Pétain did try to hinder German ambitions in Europe, including working secretly with General Francisco Franco of Spain and sending messages to Admiral William Leahy, the U.S. ambassador to the Vichy government from 1940 to 1942. Although Pétain argued with Adolf Hitler over policy, he refused to resign, realizing that such a move would allow the Germans to exercise even stricter control over France. In December 1940, he dismissed his vice premier, Pierre Laval, replacing him with Admiral François Darlan, but in April 1942 Hitler forced Pétain to accept Laval's return.

When American forces landed in North Africa in November 1942, Pétain publicly denounced the move but secretly ordered Darlan to order French troops in Africa to aid the Allied forces. However, his playing both sides came back to haunt him. When the Allies invaded France in June 1944 and moved on Paris, he ordered that power be transferred peacefully to the French forces commanded by General Charles de Gaulle. The Germans, angered at his attempt to arrange a peace, arrested him and took him to Germany. At the end of the war, he was handed over to the French and taken back to his homeland to stand trial. Found guilty of collaboration with the enemy, Pétain was sentenced to death in August 1945, although the sentence was eventually commuted to life imprisonment. He was sent to the castle prison on the Île d'Yeu off the coast of Brittany on the Atlantic Ocean, where he died on 23 July 1951 at the age of 95.

Although an energetic military officer who played a key role in the First World War and the subsequent Allied triumph at the end of that conflict, Pétain's reputation was ruined by his acceptance of the Nazis occupation. Historian Sisley Huddleston's 1951 work *Pétain: Patriot or Traitor?* is just one of the works published after the end of the Second World War that sums up the historical quandary over Pétain and his role in history.

References: Griffiths, Richard, *Marshal Pétain* (London: Constable, 1970); Lottman, Herbert R., *Pétain, Hero or Traitor: The Untold Story* (New York: William Morrow, 1985); Pertinax, *The Gravediggers of France: Gamelin, Daladier, Reynaud, Pétain, and Laval; Military Defeat, Armistice, Counter-Revolution* (Garden City, N.Y.: Doubleday, Doran & Company, 1944); Aron, Richard, and Georgette Elgey, *The Vichy Regime, 1940–44* (Boston: The Beacon Press, 1958); Huddleston, Sisley, *Pétain: Patriot or Traitor?* (London: A. Dakers, 1951).

Philip II (Philip-Augustus, Philippe Capet)
(1165–1223) *French king*

Also known as Philippe Capet, Philip-Augustus was born at Gonesse, in Val-d'Oise, France, on 21 August 1165, the son of King Louis VII and his third wife Adèle de Champagne, members of the Capetian dynasty of French royalty. His father had him crowned as joint king at Reims in 1179 when his health declined. The following year, Philip II became the sole king on his father's death, and he married Isabella of Hainault.

Although Philip reorganized the medieval government of France, bringing financial stability and strength for the first time, he is better known for his military campaigns. He participated in the Third Crusade with RICHARD I, THE LION-HEARTED of England and Frederick I Barbarossa, the Holy Roman Emperor, from 1189 to 1192. He went on to win back large areas of France then held by other kings, including Anjou and Brittany as well as Normandy, which were then controlled by England. Over the next 30 years, hindered by rivalry among the French nobility and by the German emperor to the east, Philip slowly recovered town after town, province after province. In the course of these campaigns, perhaps his greatest victory was at Bouvines (27 July 1214) when his forces defeated King John of England and his allies, including Otto (or Otho) IV of Germany. This victory left Philip as the most powerful monarch in continental Europe and challenged not only English military superiority but that of the German emperor as well.

In addition to being a warrior, Philip brought an era of growth in French teaching and culture. He helped to build a stronger Paris as his capital and began the construction of the great Notre Dame de Paris cathedral, destined to become one of the world's great places of worship. He died at his private estate at Nantes on 14 July 1223 and was buried in the Saint Denis Basilica. Philip was succeeded by his son, Louis VIII (1187–1226).

References: Bradbury, Jim, *Philip Augustus: King of France, 1180–1223* (London: Longman, 1998); Baldwin, John W., *The Government of Philip Augustus: Foundations of French Royal Power in the Middle Ages* (Berkeley: University of California Press, 1986); Luchaire, Achille, *Social France at the Time of Philip Augustus* (New York: Henry Holt, 1912).

Philip VI (Philippe the Fortunate) (1293–1350)
French king

Also known as Philippe the Fortunate, Philip was born in 1293, the son of Charles of Valois, the French prince and military leader who fought a series of wars in Europe, and his wife, Margaret of Naples-Sicily. His father's sister, Isabella, married the English king EDWARD II, and their son rose to become King EDWARD III. In 1315, Philip was titled as the count of Le Mans, and upon his father's death, he became the count of Valois and Anjou. In February 1328, when King Charles IV, Philip's cousin, died without issue, Philip and his cousin Edward III both claimed the crown of France. A group of French nobles urged Philip to take the throne, as they refused to accept an English king reigning over France. Philip relied on the Salic law, which forbade any female or the descendants of females to ascend to the throne. On 29 May 1328, he was crowned in the cathedral at Reims.

Almost from the start of his reign, Philip was involved in a number of conflicts, and although historians call attention to his fighting a series of battles that were part of the Hundred Years' War (1337–1453), he was involved in fighting before that war started. For instance, when Louis of Nevers, the count of Flanders, requested his assistance to fight the Flemings, Philip formed an army and defeated them at Cassel on 23 August 1328. But the growing differences between Philip and Edward III came to a head in 1337, when Philip declared that Edward had forfeited his right to the lands he claimed in Guienne in western France. In response, Edward declared that he was the rightful king of France, a move that set off the Hundred Years' War. For the next 116 years, England and France fought for control of the French throne. Starting with the naval battle of L'Ecluse, better known as the battle of Sluys (24 June 1340), in which the French were beaten badly, with a loss of some 30,000 men, Philip incurred defeat after defeat. The English were commanded by Sir Robert Morley and

Richard Fitzalan, and at Morlay (30 September 1342), William de Bohun defeated Charles de Blois.

The numerous clashes between the two powers culminated in a collision at Crécy-en-Ponthieu on 26 August 1346, when a small force under Edward III clashed with Philip's forces of approximately 30,000 men. This was the first major battle in which English archers were used to attack the main French troops. English losses are unknown, but French casualties were about 10,000 regular soldiers, 1,200 knights, and 11 princes killed, which historian George Bruce notes was "a total exceeding the whole English force." The king of Bohemia was among the dead; total casualties were upward of 31,000. With the defeat, Philip retreated to the castle of Labroye. Two years later, France was struck by the bubonic plague (the "Black Death"), which destroyed the national economy.

Philip was struggling with the English army's victories and the plague when he died at Nogent-le-roi on 22 August 1350. He was buried in the Saint Denis Basilica near Paris, and his second wife, Blanche de Navarre, was interred next to him when she died in 1398. He was succeeded as king of France by his son, Jean, from his first marriage. Although almost his entire reign was marked by war, Philip is probably best remembered for his defeat at Crécy, where the long bow demonstrated the vulnerability of armor.

References: Barnie, John, *War in Medieval English Society* (Ithaca, N.Y.: Cornell University Press, 1974); Duby, Georges, *France in the Middle Ages 987–1460* (Paris: Blackwell, 1987); Palmer, John Joseph Norman, *England, France and Christendom* (London: University of North Carolina Press, 1972); Bruce, George, "Crécy," in *Collins Dictionary of Wars* (Glasgow, Scotland: HarperCollins Publishers, 1995), 65.

Phocion (ca. 402–317 B.C.) *Athenian statesman and general*

Little is known of Phocion's life. He was apparently born about 402 B.C. of humble origins and received his education from Plato and Xenocrates. He joined the Athenian military soon thereafter and fought at the Battle of Naxos (376 B.C.) under Chabrias with great distinction. He helped defend Euboea in 348 and 341 B.C., and he resisted Philip of Macedon at Aeschines in 343 and again at Byzantium in 340–339 B.C. After the Athenians were heavily defeated in the Battle of Chaeronea (338

B.C.), he managed to secure lenient terms from Philip of Macedon, now ruling most of Greece.

Realizing the strength of Macedonia, Phocion continually urged the Athenians to avoid going to war, but they ignored his advice repeatedly. Philip's son, ALEXANDER THE GREAT, held him in great esteem and therefore did not attack Athens directly. Nevertheless, the Athenians elected Phocion as a war leader to fight Macedonian incursions into the Athenian colonies.

Phocion's defense of Attica in the Lamian War (322–321 B.C.) against the Macedonian regent once again led the Athenians to make him their leader. However, in 318 he was deposed for preaching peace and forced to flee to Polyperchon. Captured, he was sent back, tried as a criminal, found guilty, and sentenced to death. Plutarch, one of his biographers, writes: "Truly it was not long after [he was executed] that the Athenians found by the untowardnesse of their affaires, that they had him put to death, who onely maintained justice, and honestie at Athens. Whereupon they made his image be set up in brasse, and gave honourable burial to his bones, at the charges of the citie. And for his accusers, they condemned *Agnonides* of treason, and put him to death themselves. The other two, *Epicurus* and *Demophilus* being fled out of the citie, were afterwards met with by his sonne *Phocus,* who was revenged of them."

Phocion was a faithful servant of Athens, and the Athenians who had sentenced him to death soon came to realize what they had done and the greatness of the man they had so cruelly killed.

References: Tritle, Lawrence A., *Phocion the Good* (London: Croom Helm, 1988); Plutarch, "The Life of Phocion," in *The Lives of the Noble Grecians and Romaines, Compared together by that grave learned philosopher and historiographer, Plutarke of Chaeronea,* translated by James Amiot (London: Richard Field, 1603), 751–67; "Phocion," *The Hutchinson Dictionary of Ancient and Medieval Warfare* (Oxford, U.K.: Helicon Publishing, Ltd., 1998), 252.

Plumer of Messines, Herbert Charles Onslow Plumer, first viscount (1857–1932) *British field marshal*

Herbert Plumer was born on 13 March 1857 at his family's estate of Malpas Lodge, Torquay, in Devon, England, the second son of Hall Plumer and his wife Louisa Alice Hudson. According to General Charles Harington, Plumer's primary biographer, his family originally came from Yorkshire, the earliest relation there being Thomas of Bedale in 1638. Plumer received his education at Eton, the prestigious British private school, although he left in 1876 when he received a commission in the 65th Foot (later the York and Lancaster Regiment) with the rank of second lieutenant. When the regiment was sent to Lucknow, India, Plumer went with them. In 1882, he was promoted to the rank of captain, but instead of being sent to fight in Afghanistan, he went to Africa, and it was there that he saw his first fighting. His unit was attached to the various British forces assembled under Sir Gerald Graham to relieve the Egyptian army hemmed in at Tokar. The English were at war against the Muslim extremist leader Muhammad Ahmad ibn Sayyid Abdullah, also known as the Mahdi, the spiritual and military leader of the Sudanese Muslims in a war against the British and Egyptians in 1884. Plumer took part in the battle against the Mahdi's forces at El Teb. On 13 March, he was again in the engagement against the Mahdi's troops, this time at Tamai, where the British lost 91 dead and only 100 wounded against more than 8,000 dead Mahdists. With the Mahdi army all but destroyed, Plumer's unit was rotated back to England.

Plumer entered the Army Staff College at Camberley, where he graduated in 1887. He was sent to Ireland but in 1890 was appointed to the senior staff in Jersey, where he served until 1893. He was then reassigned to his old unit, now the 2nd Battalion, the York and Lancaster Regiment, and sent to Natal in southern Africa. He was eventually appointed as military secretary to Lieutenant General W. H. Goodenough and aided in the raising of a military force to aid white settlers threatened by the Matabele (Zulu warriors). Plumer later wrote *An Irregular Corporations in Matabeleland* (1897), which outlined his experiences. He returned to England for a short vacation with his family but was sent back to southern Africa in 1899, just before the conflict known as the Boer War broke out. There he was named as commander of the Rhodesia Field Force, which saw heavy action during the siege of Mafeking (13 October 1899–17 May 1900) on the Bechuanaland border of the Transvaal.

In August 1900, Plumer was named as the successor to Sir Robert Baden-Powell (later the founder of the Boy Scouts), made a Commander of the Order of the

Field Marshal Lord Plumer

mand of V Corps. As commander of this corps, he oversaw the action at Second Ypres (22 April–25 May 1915). His experience and knowledge during this crucial battle led French to fire Smith-Dorrien and replace him with Plumer (although the official version was that Smith-Dorrien had retired). Plumer remained as head of the Second Army for the remainder of the war, demonstrating his respect for and care of the troops who fought for him and in turn earning their admiration.

In 1916, Plumer began planning an offensive on Messines Ridge, which had been held by the Germans since late 1914. His attack plan opened on 21 May 1917, starting with massive bombardment to soften up the German lines. Then, on 7 June, the British exploded a series of mines which had been secretly placed under the enemy lines, killing some 10,000 German soldiers. Using this attack as a front, Plumer's forces struck the Germans across the entire ridge, occupying the area after just three hours of fighting. Although the Germans launched a counteroffensive on 14 June 1917, the British held the ridge until the end of the war. Reporter Henry Perry Robinson of *The Times* of London wrote of the battle:

> How many mines went up at once I do not exactly know, but it was nearly a score. Many of these mines were made over a year ago, and since then had lain under German feet undiscovered. In all, I believe over 600 tons of high explosives were fired simultaneously. Can you imagine what over 600 tons of explosives in 20 or so blasts along an arc of 10 miles looks like? I cannot describe it for you. Personally, I can only vouch for having seen nine of the great leaping streams of orange flame which shot upwards from that part of the front immediately before me, each one of the nine a huge volcano in itself, with as many volcanoes going off at the same moment beyond them, hidden by their flames and out of sight, and each vast sheet of flame as it leaped roaring upwards threw up dense masses of dust and smoke, which stood like great pillars towering into the sky, all illuminated by the fires below.

Bath (CB), and promoted to brigadier general. In November 1902, he was promoted to major general. After being transferred back to England, he was named as commander of the 4th Infantry Brigade at Aldershot. Knighted in 1906, he served in Ireland, and in 1908 he was promoted to lieutenant general.

In August 1914, following Britain's declaration of war on Germany, Plumer was supposed to be appointed commander of II Corps on the recommendation of Sir John FRENCH. However, General Horatio KITCHENER vetoed Plumer's appointment, instead naming General Horace Smith-Dorrien to that post and then promoting him to command the Second Army in December 1914. Plumer was placed in charge of the Northern Command and then sent to France at the end of 1914 to take com-

Plumer is alleged to have told his men before the battle: "Gentlemen, we may not make history tomorrow, but we shall certainly change the geography."

Plumer biographer George MacMunn writes of how Plumer planned a follow-up to his victory at Messines

Ridge: "Plumer had now shown what he and his staff could arrange and his troops carry out; and he and Sir Hubert Gough were told to continue as soon as possible the attack on the high ground running from near Messines to the far side of Passchendaele, beyond which the Fourth Army under Sir Henry Rawlinson had been collected. The great series of operations which began on 21 July cannot be described here, but the two commanders, acting in perfect unison, fought eight great battles with immense results despite the foulest weather."

Although Plumer had a difficult relationship with Sir Douglas HAIG, the British commander, he nonetheless remained loyal to Haig's every command, and for a time he was considered to be a replacement for Sir John French. On 9 November 1917, he was sent with British troops to Italy to encourage the Italian government to continue fighting the Austrians. Plumer returned to the Second Army on the western front in March 1918 and thereafter commanded a series of offensives that led to the liberation of northern Belgium.

World War I ended in November 1918, and Plumer was created Baron Plumer of Messines and Bilton and promoted to field marshal in 1918. Six months later, he was named as commander of the Army of Occupation on the Rhine River. He was then appointed as governor and commander in chief of Malta, an office he held until May 1924. During his tenure, the first representative government in Malta was established, and the Prince of Wales inaugurated the first legislative assembly. Plumer also served as the British high commissioner in Palestine (now modern Israel) in 1925–28. Created Viscount Plumer of Messines in 1929, he also served in the House of Lords. He died in London on 16 July 1932 and was buried with full military honors in Westminster Abbey. Although he is largely forgotten today, Lord Plumer's services during the First World War assured the Allied victory, especially the triumph at Messines Ridge.

References: Powell, Geoffrey, *Plumer: The Soldiers' General: A Biography of Field-Marshal Viscount Plumer of Messines* (London: Leo Cooper, 1990); Harington, General Sir Charles, *Plumer of Messines* (London: John Murray, 1935); MacMunn, George, "Plumer, Herbert Charles Onslow, First Viscount Plumer," in *The Dictionary of National Biography,* 22 vols., 8 supps., edited by Sir Leslie Stephen and Sir Sidney Lee, et al. (London: Oxford University Press, 1921–22), XV:702–706.

Pompey (Gnaeus Pompeius, Pompey the Great)
(106–48 B.C.) *Roman general*

Pompey was born Gnaeus Pompeius in Rome on 29 September 106 B.C. into an important Roman family whose members had included consuls, including his father, Pompeius Strabo. Strabo sided against the Roman general Cornelius Sulla during the Roman Civil War (88–87 B.C.) between Sulla and his enemy, Gaius Marius. However, following Strabo's death, Pompey turned against the Marians and their ally, Cinna. While Cinna was marching to the Balkans to fight Sulla, he was killed by his own disaffected troops. Historians do not believe that Pompey led the mutiny against Cinna, although he may have been one of its instigators.

In an attempt to retake Rome from the Marians, Pompey offered his and his army's services to Sulla, who married his stepdaughter, Aemilia, to Pompey, although she was pregnant by another man; she died in childbirth soon after the marriage. Sulla demanded that the Roman Senate send Pompey to defeat the Marians in both Sicily and Africa, and in two quick battles (82–81 B.C.) he accomplished these tasks. Pompey showed his merciless side when he ordered the execution of Marian commanders who had surrendered to his forces. But he also saw himself as a future leader of Rome, and when he returned to that city in 81 B.C. and Sulla demanded that he disband his army, Pompey refused, forcing Sulla to back down. Disgraced, Sulla resigned as consul in 79 B.C., and Pompey became a dictator in effect. He backed the candidacy of Sullan Marcus Lepidus to become consul, but when Lepidus took control of Rome, Pompey turned against him as well and fought to have him removed.

Once again, Pompey refused to disperse his army, and he demanded that he be allowed to fight the Marian commander Sertorius in Spain. The Roman Senate, cowed into accepting all of his demands, acceded, and he marched his army to Spain. Once he had Spain under his control (76–71 B.C.), Pompey returned to Rome, where he assisted the new Roman leader, Marcus Licinius CRASSUS, to put down a rebellion led by the slave Spartacus, known as the Servile War. Once this was completed, Pompey and Crassus were elected as consuls in 70 B.C. He continued his military conquests, defeating pirates in the Mediterranean Sea in just three months and conquering ports of Armenia, Pontus, and Syria.

In 67 B.C., the Roman Senate appointed Pompey as the commander of forces to fight Mithradates, starting the third Mithraditic War. He defeated Mithradates' armies in Asia Minor, conquering Syria and taking Jerusalem. Returning to Rome in 61 B.C., Pompey found a city in turmoil. Promising a series of reforms in a city that had become a hotbed of corruption, he decided to work with Crassus and the Roman general Julius CAESAR in a collaboration known to history as the First Triumvirate (60 B.C.). Although the three men were never friends, they did cooperate in controlling Rome for a period of five years. Caesar's ambition, however, led to a strained relations between the three leaders, and the break came in 55 B.C. when Crassus was murdered while fighting in Syria. Pompey asked the Roman Senate to demand that Caesar, then returning from Gaul, disband his army, as was customary when entering Italy. Caesar refused and crossed the Rubicon River in northern Italy with his army, leading the Roman Senate to declare war against him in 49 B.C. Pompey was named as the commander to defend Rome, but his forces were dispersed outside Italy, and he was forced to flee the country.

Caesar marched on Rome and then advanced on the Adriatic to take on the force Pompey had gathered but suffered a defeat when he tried to attack Pompey's camp at Dyrrhachium. When Caesar retreated into Thessaly, Pompey followed him and, with his father-in-law, Scipio Africanus, decided to attack Caesar on the plains of Pharsalus (48 B.C.). English historian Samuel Clarke, a 17th-century writer who was an early biographer of Pompey, writes of this battle:

> Pompey himself led the ring wing of his Battel against *Anthony*. The middle Battle he gave to *Scipio* his Father in Law which was right against *Domitius Calviares:* His left Wing was led by *Lucius Domitius Ænobarbus,* which was guarded by the men at Armes, for all the Horsemen were placed there, to distresse *Casar* [sic] if possibly they could, and to overthrow the tenth Legion, which contained the valiantest Souldiers that *Casar* had; and amongst whom himself always used to fight in Person. *Casar* seeing the left Wing of enemies so strong with the guard of Horsemen, brought six Companys of Foot for a reserve, and placed them behind the tenth Legion, commanding them to stand close, that they might not be discovered by the enemy: and commanded them when the Horsemen should charge upon them, that they should not throw

their darts strait [sic] forward but upward at their faces: For (said he) ['] *These brave Fellows and fine Dancers, will not endure to have their faces marred.* ['] Pompey being on Horseback rode up and down to observe how both Armies were marshalled, and perceiving that his enemies stood still in their ranks, expecting the signall of Battel, and that his Battle waved up and down disorderly, as men unskillful in the Wars, he feared that they would fly before they were charged. Therefore he commanded his Van to stand steadily in their ranks, and to defend themselves in a close fight when the enemy should assault them. But *Casar* disliked this devise [sic]: for thereby (said he) the force of their blowes was lessened, and by withholding them from giving the charge, that courage was taken away which the assailant carrieth with him when he comes on with fury, it made them also more fainthearted in receiving the enemies charge. . . .

> When the signal of Battel was given on either side, and the Trumpets sounded an Alarme, every man began to look to himself. . . . Now when the Fields of *Pharsalia,* were covered over with Horse and men in Armes, after the Signall was given, the first man of *Casars* Army that advanced gave the charge, was *Caius Crassinius,* a Captain of one hundred and twenty and five men: and this he did to make good his promise to *Casar,* who having asked him that morning what he thought of the event of the Battel? he said, ['] Oh, Cæsar! Thine is the Victory, and this day than shalt commend me either alive or dead.['] There upon he brake out of his rank (many others also following him) and ran into the midst of his enemies, making a great slaughter; but as he still pressed forward, one ran him through the neck and slew him. Pompey did not make his left wing to advance over suddenly, but staid [sic] to see what his Horsemen would do, who had already divided themselves, intending to compasse in *Casar*s Horsemen (who were fewer in number) to give back upon his squadron of Foot men, and thereby to disorder them. But on the other side, Casars Horsemen gave back a little and the six Companies of Footmen that he had placed secretly behind them (being three thousand in number) ran suddenly to charge the enemy in the

flank and comming neer to *Pompeys* Horsemen, they threw their Darts (as *Casar* had appointed them) full in their faces. The young Gentlemen, being raw Souldiers, and little expecting such a manner of fight, had not the hearts to defend themselves, not could abide to be hurt in their faces, but turning their heads, and clapping them hands on their faces, they fled shamfully [sic].

Pharsalus was Pompey's first defeat on the field of battle. He was forced to flee with his men and escaped to Egypt, where he sought the backing of Ptolemy XIII, the brother of Caesar's lover Cleopatra. Ptolemy gave Pompey his word that he would be protected in Egypt, but instead, when Pompey came ashore, he was killed by either one of his own soldiers or one of Ptolemy's men. According to Plutarch in his *Lives of the Noble Grecians and Romaines,* Pompey's aide Philip cared for the remains of the Roman general after he was butchered:

Philip his infranchised [sic] bondman remained ever by it, untill such time as the Ægyptians had seen it their bellies full. Then having washed his body with salt water, and wrapped it up in an old shirt of his, because he had no other shirt to lay it in: he fought upon the sands, and found at the length a peece of an old . . . boate, enough to serve to burne his naked bodie with, but not fully out. As he was busie gathering the broken peeces of this boate together, thither came unto him an old ROMAINE, who in his youth had served

under *Pompey,* and said unto him: O friend, what are thou that preparest the funerals of Pompey the Great? Philip answered, that he was a bond-man of his infranchised. Well, said he, thou shalt not have all this honor alone, I pray thee let me accompany thee in so devout a deed, that I may not altogether repent me to have dwelt so long in a strange country.

Plutarch states, "The Romaines seemed to have loved Pompey from his childhood." A brilliant commander who brought much glory to his country, Pompey came to a tragic end as the result of warfare with another general, Caesar, who was a strategist as well as a tactitian.

References: Clarke, Samuel, *The Life and Death of Pompey the Great: With all his Glorious Victories and Triumphs* . . . (London: Printed for William Miller, 1665); Lucan, *Lucan's Pharsalia or the Civill Warres of Rome, betweene Pompey the Great and Julius Caesar. The three first bookes.* (London: J[ohn] N[orton] & A[ugustine] M[athewes], 1626); Broé, Samuel de, *The History of the Triumvirates* . . . , translated by Tho. Ottoway (London: Printed for Charles Brome, 1686), 458–459; Plutarch, "Life of Pompeius," in *The Lives of the Noble Grecians and Romaines* . . . , translated by Sir Thomas North (London: Richard Field for John Norton, 1603), 632–669.

Pontecorvo, Prince de *See* BERNADOTTE, JEAN-BAPTISTE-JULES, PRINCE DE PONTECORVO.

R

Radetzky, Joseph Wenzel Anton Franz Karl, count Radetzky von Radetz (1766–1858)

Austrian general

Joseph Radetzky was born into a family of Hungarian ancestry on 2 November 1766 in Trzebnitz, Bohemia, in what is now the Czech Republic. He joined the Austrian military in 1784 when he was 18 and saw action in the Austrian-Russian war against Turkey (1787–92) as a galloper (messenger) on the staff of Count Franz Moritz Lacy. He was also involved during the opening years of the wars against Revolutionary France, particularly in Italy from 1796 onward. Seeing action against French forces, he took part in Dagobert Wurmser's campaign in Mantua and showed considerable courage in several battles, including at Trebbia (17–19 June 1799) and Novi (15 August 1799); at Marengo (14 June 1800), he was struck by five shots but survived. In 1801, he received the knighthood of the Maria Theresa order.

In 1805, following a series of promotions, Radetzky was made a major general and given command of a brigade of Austrian forces in Italy. Four years later, he fought at Wagram, near Vienna (6 July 1809), when the Austrians were defeated by a French army under NAPOLEON BONAPARTE. Following this battle, Radetzky was named as chief of the Austrian army general staff. In this role, he modernized tactics and implemented a number of reforms, but he resigned when the Austrian treasury refused him the funds needed. Nonetheless, he was able to implement reforms that were extremely effective and improved the Austrian military performance. He also aided in the planning for the Battle of Leipzig (16–18 October 1813), where the former French commander, Jean-Baptiste BERNADOTTE, a Swedish prince, defeated Napoleon himself. Radetzky was one of the key leaders in Napoleon's eventual defeat, and in 1814 he was invited to attend the Congress of Vienna, which met to settle the question of the boundaries of nations that had been overrun by Napoleon. Following the congress, Radetzky returned to the Austrian army. He served as commander in chief of the Austrian army in northern Italy (1831–37), and in 1836 he was promoted to field marshal.

In 1848, agitation by Italian partisans wanting to end Austrian control over their country erupted into war, and Radetzky was placed in charge of Austrian troops to put down the insurrection. Although he was then 82 years old, he skillfully defeated the Italians at Custoza (24 July 1848) and at Novara (23 March 1849). Historian George Bruce writes of the battle at Novara that it was "between 47,000 Piedmontese under Chrzanowski and three Austrian army corporations, 45,000 [strong], under Field Marshal Radetzky. After hard fighting the Piedmontese were completely defeated and driven from the field in disorder. Under the peace treaty the defeated paid a huge indemnity to Austria." Ironically, Radetzky's victory at Novara gave birth to an even larger Italian independence movement, and in 1866 another war broke out that finally expelled Austrian forces from Italy.

From 1849 to 1857, Radetzky was governor-general of the kingdom of Lombardy and Venetia, controlled by Austria. He died on 5 January 1858 in Milan, Italy, at the age of 91. To his troops, he was known as "Vater Radetzky." In 1848, Johann Strauss, the famed Austrian composer, had penned the famed Radetzkymarsch, or Radetzky March, in his honor. Today the march is better known than Radetzky himself.

References: Flagg, Edmund, *Venice: The City of the Sea, From the Invasion by Napoleon in 1797 to the Capitulation to Radetzky in 1849; With a Contemporaneous View of the Peninsula,* 2 vols. (New York: Charles Scribner, 1853); Sked, Alan, *The Survival of the Hapsburg Empire: Radetzky, the Imperial Army, and the Class War, 1848* (London: Longman, 1979); Bruce, George, "Novara II," in *Collins Dictionary of Wars* (Glasgow, Scotland: Harper-Collins Publishers, 1995), 181.

Raglan, FitzRoy James Henry Somerset, first baron (1788–1855) *British general*

Lord FitzRoy Somerset was born at Badminton, England, on 30 September 1788, the eighth son of Henry, the fifth duke of Beaufort, and his wife Elizabeth, the daughter of Admiral Edward BOSCAWEN. His older brother, Lord Robert Edward Henry Somerset (1776–1842), served in the British military and saw action at Waterloo. FitzRoy Somerset received his education at the prestigious Westminster School, and in 1804 he entered the British army. He did not see action in his early years but was given a post with Sir Arthur Paget in the British Mission in Turkey. In 1807, he was posted to serve with Sir Arthur Wellesley, duke of WELLINGTON, during his military expedition to Copenhagen, Denmark. Somerset served with Wellington during the Peninsular War in Spain (1808–14), first as his aide-de-camp and then as his military secretary. He was wounded at the battle of Busaco (27 September 1810), and following the battle of Fuentes de Onoro (3–5 May 1811), he was promoted to the rank of brevet major. He saw additional action at Badajoz (5 April 1812), earning praise for his heroism. In 1814, he married Wellington's niece and served in the British Embassy in Paris as a secretary. With the resump-

tion of the war against Napoleon, Somerset returned to military duty. At Waterloo (18 June 1815), he fought under Wellington but received a horrible wound in his right arm, forcing amputation of the limb. Unable to fight, Somerset became secretary to the British Embassy in Paris. In 1818, he was elected a member of Parliament from Truro, serving until 1820 and again from 1826 to 1829. He served as military secretary from 1827 until Wellington's death in 1852, following which Somerset was created Baron Raglan and named as master general of the ordnance. Two years later, he was promoted to general.

Raglan is best known for his service during the Crimean War (1854–56). The Crimea peninsula on the northern shores of the Black Sea became the focal point of world attention when Russia annexed it in 1783, giving rise to the suspicion that Russia would use it to attack the Ottoman Empire and capture the capital, Constantinople (now Istanbul). Russia pressed for Greek independence from the Ottoman Empire, and war broke out in 1828, leading to the Treaty of Adrianople, allowing for Russian access to the strait of the Dardanelles. Greek independence followed in 1832, but tensions only increased when Russia established a massive naval base at Sebastopol (now Sevastopol) on the Crimean peninsula on the Black Sea, threatening the Ottoman Empire. In 1852, a dispute broke out between Greek Orthodox and Roman Catholic monks over the custody of certain Christian shrines in Jerusalem. In 1853, feelings had grown so strong that the Russian Czar Nicholas I claimed authority over all Orthodox believers in the Ottoman Empire. His claim was rejected, and therefore Russian troops crossed the border into what is now eastern Turkey in June 1853, rapidly taking control of several large pieces of territory. Under pressure from the British, the government in Constantinople did not declare war, instead relying on diplomatic pressure to get the Russians to withdraw. When this failed, the Ottomans declared war on Russia (4 October 1853); England and France also declared war on Russia in March 1854. Raglan was named as commander in chief of British forces sent to the Crimea.

On 14 September 1854, some 25,000 British troops under Lord Raglan landed and occupied the port of Balaklava along with some 50,000 French forces under the command of Marshal Armand J. de Saint-Arnaud. The allied troops advanced toward Sebastopol, home of the czar's Black Sea naval fleet. The immediacy of the threat forced the Russians to scuttle their ships in order to use the cannons against the allies, whom they met at the Alma River on the route to Sebastopol. The Battle of the Alma (20 September 1854) was a victory for the British and French that left the Sebastopol base open to the allies and could, if taken, have ended the war. Nevertheless, because of lack of agreement on strategy between the British and French, the Russians were able to hold off the allied forces. A second encounter led to the Russians' retreat to Sebastopol. Whether it was poor planning or negligence by Raglan, the allies did not follow up the victory at the Alma, and the Russians were able to turn a horrific loss into a draw. Raglan's mistakes lost the chance to take Sebastopol quickly, and further blunders made the situation worse. On 25 October 1854 at Balaklava, Raglan, on a hilltop, sent an order to his main field officer, Lord LUCAN, to attack a small Russian force taking away some guns in front of one flank of the British forces. From Lucan's position in the valley, these guns were hidden behind a rise in the grounds. He therefore ordered his men to attack the only guns he could see—in the middle of the main Russian force in front of him. The Light Brigade, commanded by James Thomas Brudenell, Lord Cardigan, charged straight down the valley under fire from three sides. Of the 700 men sent, only 195 came back. The horrific carnage led Alfred, Lord Tennyson, then England's poet laureate, to pen "The Charge of the Light Brigade," recording their slaughter in heroic and picturesque poetry.

The problems for the English troops in the Crimea were not limited to poor leadership. The government had failed to supply them with sufficient food, clothing, or medical support, and the sufferings of the soldiers were publicized by reporters such as *The Times's* William Howard Russell, who used the pages of his paper to criticize and expose the conditions under which the English troops were fighting. Historians believe that Raglan had tried to address these concerns before the war but had been rebuffed by the government of Lord Aberdeen. Nonetheless, the press accounts blamed him for what had happened, and he was bitterly denounced. In January 1855, an investigation was launched in the House of Commons to demand a full enquiry into the war. Unable to stop the criticism, Aberdeen resigned on 1 February 1855 and was replaced by Lord Palmerston, who appointed Lord Panmure as secretary for war and ordered him to immediately send additional supplies to the Crimea. In the meantime, Raglan had continued

to fight, including the important battle of Inkerman (5 November 1854), following which he was promoted to the rank of field marshal.

The war and the continued criticism in the British press took a toll on the aging Raglan, breaking his spirit. Suffering from dysentery, he followed Palmerston's order to take Sebastopol. On 18 June 1855—the 40th anniversary of the Battle of Waterloo—the attack began. Disastrously, Raglan allowed the French commander to talk him out of breaking the Russian lines with cannon fire, instead sending waves of soldiers against the Russian guns. The result was pure carnage. This final affront to Raglan's military sense was his end; he succumbed to his illnesses on 28 June 1855 at the age of 66. His body was returned to England by ship, and he was buried in Badminton with full military honors.

In 1857, an anonymous writer wrote, "Does any body know who Lord Raglan was? Was he a general under Cornwallis in the Revolutionary war? Or did he fight Napoleon in Spain? Or who was he? It is so long since one heard of him, that perhaps none but very learned persons ought to be expected to remember his history. It is actually twenty months since he died; and twenty months in the present age are as long as twenty years—bah! Two hundred years of olden time." Raglan's troops did not have kind things to say about him: A Captain Cuninghame of the 95th Rifles wrote in a letter home, 19 January 1855:

How bitterly *The Times* and other papers are beginning to abuse poor old Raglan. Man is a regular contrary animal and I suppose it is for that reason that I who abused him myself a little time ago begin to think that he is a little hardly used or at least the newspapers should not be allowed to write in such terms of any man holding the position of Commander-in-Chief especially in the field. There is however a great deal of truth in what they say. He is no doubt a shocking old muff and also very sensitive to the weight of newspaper censure. Since the Article in *The Times* about the invisible Commander-in-Chief he had been riding about the lines in a most frantic way making himself obnoxious in every direction.

Lord Raglan had long served as an efficient staff officer to Wellington and was a master tactician. Unfortunately, by the time of the Crimean War he had not commanded troops in battle for 40 years and lacked both the experience and the intelligence to win battles. The most that can be said of him is that he was an old man who did his best. Unfortunately, his best was not good enough, and thousands of men died needlessly as a result.

References: Lloyd, Ernest Marsh, "Somerset, Lord Fitzroy James Henry, First Baron Raglan," in *The Dictionary of National Biography,* 22 vols. 8 supps., edited by Sir Leslie Stephen and Sir Sidney Lee, et al. (London: Oxford University Press, 1921–22), 18:645; Russell, Sir William Howard, *Complete History of the Russian War, from Its Commencement to Its Close* (New York: J. G. Wells, 1857); Tyrrell, Henry, *The History of the War with Russia: Giving Full Details of the Operations of the Allied Armies* . . . (London: The London Printing and Publishing Company, 1855–58); "The Battle of Balaclava and the Charge of the Light Brigade, 25 October 1854," in *Eyewitness to History,* edited by John Carey (Cambridge, Mass.: Harvard University Press, 1987), 333–344; "Anecdotes of Lord Raglan," *Harper's New Monthly Magazine* 14, no. 83 (April 1857): 631.

Ramses II (Ramesses II, Rameses II, Ramses the Great) (ca. 1314–1224 B.C.) *Egyptian king*

Ramses II, the son of Seti I and grandson of Ramses I, was one of the most important Egyptian kings, serving for a total of 66 years, from the time he was 24 until his death at 90. Sources disagree on the exact dates of his life and reign, which is given variously as 1290–24, 1279–12, and 1304–1237 B.C., as well as other date ranges. (This book prefers a beginning reign date of 1290 B.C. and 1224 B.C. as Ramses' date of death.)

As king of Egypt, Ramses II used his power to launch a great revolution in building. During his reign, the Great Temple of Abu Simbel, known as one of the greatest achievements of mankind, was constructed, and his face is said to be one of the huge statues carved into the structure. Although renowned as a great builder, Ramses is best known as a warrior. In the early years of his reign, he fought the Nubians and Libyans and led expeditions into the area of what is now modern Israel and Syria. His greatest military achievement came just four or five years into his reign when he took on the Hittites at Kadesh (or Qadesh, near today's Beirut) (1285 B.C.). Historian Arthur Ferrill writes:

Although Egypt was well protected by deserts and relatively isolated from the other centers of civilization in Syria-Palestine, Asia Minor, and Mesopotamia, the pharaohs always had an army. Under warlike pharaohs, such as Tuthmosis III and Ramses II, the mobile field army numbered around 20,000. It consisted of light infantry armed with spears, swords, and bows, and of fast, light horse-drawn chariots. At the Battle of Kadesh in 1285 B.C., Ramses II marched several hundred miles out of Egypt into Syria where he fought the king of the Hittites in a major battle. Although the Egyptian army was caught in an ambush as it marched up to Kadesh and was hit hard in the flank, Ramses personally rallied his panic-stricken troops and led them to a tactical victory over the Hittites. They were not able to take the fortified city, however, and the campaign ended in a strategic stalemate.

Historian Robert Collins Suhr, in his landmark 1995 article on Kadesh and its impact on world history, notes:

The Battle of Kadesh holds great interest to scholars of military strategy but, as pointed out by Egyptian press attaché and Egyptologist Ahmed Nouby Moussam, its epilogue was equally historic in the realm of international diplomacy. After a dynastic struggle, Khattusilis III succeeded Muwutallis and subsequently invited Egyptian plenipotentiaries to Hattusas for what would amount to the first summit conference between two equally matched powers. In 1280 B.C., Ramses and Khattusilis signed history's oldest recorded international agreement, establishing a condominium [the joint control of a state's affairs by other states] between the two empires. After 13 years of peace, Ramses sealed the treaty by marrying one of Khattusilis' daughters.

In the seventh or eighth year of his reign, Ramses led his forces in storming the city of Askalon, now in Israel, and the following year he conquered towns and villages in Galilee. In his 10th year, he again fought the Hittites at Katna and Tunip. Ramses came to realize that he could not hold territory he had conquered, leading him to conclude a peace agreement with the Hittites. Although he then warred against the Libyans in northern Africa, historians believe that most of his later years were free of warfare. Married several times, Ramses allegedly had up to 200 children during his lifetime.

Following his death, Ramses was ceremonially mummified and laid to rest in his tomb. His mummy was discovered in Deir-al-Bahari in Egypt in 1881 and was moved to the Egyptian Museum in Cairo, where it remains to this day.

References: Kitchen, Kenneth Anderson, *Pharaoh Triumphant: The Life and Times of Ramesses II, King of Egypt* (Warminster, U.K.: Aris & Phillips, 1983); Lanoye, Ferdinand de, *Rameses the Great; or, Egypt 3300 Years Ago* (New York: Charles Scribner and Company, 1870); Schmidt, John D., *Ramesses II: A Chronological Structure for his Reign* (Baltimore, Md.: Johns Hopkins University Press, 1973); Suhr, Robert Collins, "Ambush at Kadesh," *Military History* 12, no. 3 (August 1995): 46–53; Seele, Keith Cedric, *The Coregency of Ramses II with Seti I and the Date of the Great Hypostyle Hall at Karnak* (Chicago: The University of Chicago Press, 1940); Ferrill, Arthur, "History, Ancient Military," in *Brassey's Encyclopedia of Military History and Biography,* edited by Franklin D. Margiotta (Washington, D.C.: Brassey's, 1994), 432–433; Weeks, Kent R., *The Lost Tomb: The Greatest Discovery at the Valley of the Kings since Tutankhamen* (London: Weidenfeld & Nicolson, 1998).

Reggio, duc de   *See* OUDINOT, NICOLAS CHARLES, DUC DE REGGIO.

Rennenkampf, Pavel-Georges Karlovich von
(1854–1918)   *Russian general*
Born in Estonia on 17 April 1854, the son of a German noble, Pavel-Georges von Rennenkampf received a military education at the Helsingfors Cadet School in what is now Helsinki, Finland. After graduating from the Nikolaevsky Military Academy, St. Petersburg, in 1882, he was appointed to the Russian General Staff. He rose to the rank of colonel in 1890, and in 1900 he became a major general. That same year, he was attached to Russian forces in China and became involved in the revolt to eject foreigners from China, known as the Boxer Rebellion.

Rennenkampf's name was made during the Russo-Japanese War (1904–05), when he served as the commander of the Trans-Baikal Cossack Division. He was promoted to the rank of lieutenant general in July 1904 and saw action in the battles of Liao-Yang (24 August–4 August 1904), the Sha Ho River (9–16 October 1904), and Mukden (21 February 1905). In the latter battle, he replaced Major General Alexiev in control of the Russian left flank. With the war's conclusion, Rennenkampf took control of the III Siberian Corps and assisted in the suppression of several mutinies in Siberia. In the years leading up to the First World War, he was given the command of the III Army Corps and promoted to general.

With the outbreak of the First World War in August 1914, Rennenkampf was given the command of the Russian First Army and took part in the Russian advance into east Prussia—the Tannenberg campaign. On 26–31 August, General Alexander SAMSONOV's army was surrounded and completely destroyed at Tannenberg. The Russian lost 100,000 killed, and Samsonov committed suicide. Rennenkampf should have supported Samsonov but failed to do so and was accused of negligence. He had also lost men at the Battle of Gumbinnen (20 August), and he was decisively beaten by Paul von HINDENBURG at the Battle of Masurian Lakes (9–14 September) and again at Lodz (11–25 November). Rennenkampf was then dismissed from his command and did not see action for the remainder of the war, retiring to his private home on the coast of the Black Sea.

The Bolshevik Revolution in 1917 led to the collapse of the Russian war effort. However, the Bolshevik leaders approached Rennenkampf and offered him the command of the Russian army, which he refused. He was therefore arrested, tried for treason, found guilty, and executed about May 1918 near the city of Taganrog; he was buried in an unmarked grave.

The refusal of the Russian government to adapt to changing military attitudes and ways of fighting, as well as its sending a woefully unprepared army into battle against the Germans at Tannenberg and Masurian Lakes, are not to be blamed on Rennenkampf. But he was certainly culpable for failing to support Samsonov, perhaps because of the strongly held personal enmity between them.

References: Tuchman, Barbara, *The Guns of August* (New York: Macmillan, 1962); Donat, Karl von, *The Russo-*

Japanese War: The Battle on the Scha-Ho (London: Hugh Rees, 1910); Solzhenitsyn, Alexandr Isaevich, *August Chetyrnadtsatogo (August 1914),* translated by Michael Glenny (New York: Farrar, Straus, and Giroux, 1972).

Richard I the Lion-Hearted (Richard Coeur de Lion) (1157–1199) *English king*

Richard I was born on 8 September 1157 at Beaumont Palace, Oxford, the third son of King Henry II and his wife Eleanor of Aquitaine. At the age of 11, he was given his mother's duchy in Aquitaine, France, and in 1172 he was given control of Poitiers. However, although Henry had granted similar titles to all of his children, he had not given any of them any substantive power, and by 1173 Richard was chafing for real control over the duchy. He therefore sided with his elder brother Henry, the heir to the throne, who was upset at his father's infidelity against their mother and launched a revolt, joined by Richard and their brother Geoffrey. King Henry quickly put down their rebellion, and Richard was forced to give up on 21 September 1174 and beg his father for forgiveness. Soon, a war broke out between Richard and his brother Henry in France, and though they eventually made peace, Henry died of an illness on 11 June 1183, making Richard the heir to the throne. Following the death of King Henry II, Richard, now the eldest surviving son, was crowned as king of England at Westminster on 3 September 1189, shortly before his 32nd birthday.

Although Richard came to England to take control there, he concentrated on raising resources to fund a crusade. Two years before, the Muslim warrior SALADIN had captured Jerusalem, and Henry II had tried to arrange a joint expedition with the French to rescue the city, but he was still negotiating the matter when he died. Richard, however, took up the cause with enthusiasm. He named William of Longchamp as chancellor of England (regent), disregarding his brother John, and set out to rescue Jerusalem.

In 1190, taking with him some of England's best knights, Richard left on what has become known as the Third Crusade. He traveled with PHILIP II, the French king, and they spent the winter in Sicily. Early in 1191, the two men separated, and Richard sailed for Rhodes. However, some of his ships were wrecked on Cyprus, and the island's ruler maltreated the crews. Richard sailed back to Cyprus and took the island before resuming his journey. He reached Acre in the Holy Land on 8 June 1191. The city had been under siege by the Crusaders for two years, but they had been kept at bay by the Muslims' using, among other weapons, "Greek fire"—pots of a fiery compound made of sulfur, saltpeter, and naphtha, like an early version of napalm. Richard quickly took control of the assault, and the Crusaders at last breached the walls of Acre, forcing the Muslims to flee. One of Richard's allies, Duke Leopold of Austria, raised his own banner over the city, and Richard angrily tore it down. Leopold pulled out his troops and departed, leaving Richard with no more allies since he had also quarreled with Philip II. He proved to be a merciless conqueror: In taking Acre, he had seized some 3,000 Muslims as prisoners, and he ordered that all be put to death.

On 7 September 1191, Saladin tried to attack Richard's forces near Arsuf, 10 miles from Jaffa along the Galilee coast, but Richard won a brilliant victory in which Saladin suffered some 7,000 casualties, including 32 emirs. Nevertheless, Richard soon realized that even if he took Jerusalem, he could not hold it because of dissent among his Crusading allies. At the same time, he learned that his brother John was taking control of England. He therefore signed a three-year peace with Saladin and departed from the Holy Land, leaving his nephew, Henry I of Champagne, in command of the armies there. Back in Europe, he was taken captive by Duke Leopold, still holding a grudge from the slur at Acre, and then turned over to Henry VI, the Holy Roman Emperor, who demanded a ransom for him. English knights, including Richard's good friend Hubert Walter (later the archbishop of Canterbury), raised a sum of 150,000 marks, which left England financially weak for many years, and Richard was released in 1194. He returned to England, where he was coronated a second time to demonstrate he was still king of England.

In May 1194, intending to take back lands lost to his family in France, Richard departed England again—never to return. He began an armed campaign against Philip II, and during a battle at Gisors (10 October 1198), he allegedly yelled, "Dieu et mon droit!" (God and my right), which is now the motto of English sovereigns. Wounded during a fight at the castle of Chaluz in Aquitaine, France, Richard died there on 6 April 1199 at the age of 42. His remains were laid to rest in the Fontevrault Abbey in Anjou, France, next to both his parents. Sir Richard Baker writes: "The remorse for his undutifulness towards his father, was living in him till he died; for at his death he remembered it with bewail-

Richard I, engraving by George Vertue, 1732

ing, and desired to be buried as near him as might be, perhaps as thinking they should meet the sooner, that he might ask him forgiveness in another world." He left no children or heirs, and his brother John succeeded him as king. (John is best known as the signer of the Magna Carta in 1215.)

Richard only spent six months of his 10 years as king of England in the country he reigned over. His prowess and courage in battle earned him the nickname *Coeur de Lion* (heart of the lion), but the training at his mother's court is revealed in a verse Richard composed during his German captivity:

> No one will tell me the cause of my sorrow
> Why they have made me a prisoner here.
> Wherefore with dolour I now make my moan;
> Friends had I many but help have I none.
> Shameful it is that they leave me to ransom,
> To languish here two winters long.

A statue of Richard, "Cœur De Lion," stands in front of Parliament in London, his right arm lifting a sword into the air.

References: Stubbs, William, ed., *Chronicles and Memorials of the Reign of Richard I. . . .* 2 vols. (London: Longman, Green, Longman, Roberts, and Green, 1864–65); Archer, Thomas Andrew, *The Crusade of Richard I, 1189–92* (New York: G. P. Putnam's Sons, 1889); Hampden, John, *Crusader King: The Adventures of Richard the Lionheart on Crusade, Taken from a Chronicle of the Time* (London: Edmund Ward, Publishers, 1956); Gillingham, John, *Richard I* (New Haven, Conn.: Yale University Press, 2002); "Richard I Massacres Prisoners after Taking Acre, 2–20 August 1191," in *Eyewitness to History,* edited by John Carey (Cambridge, Mass.: Harvard University Press, 1987), 35–37.

Richard III (1452–1485) *English king*

Richard III was born on 2 October 1452 in Fotheringay Castle, Northamptonshire, England, the 11th child of Richard, duke of York, and Cicely Neville. When he was eight years old, his father was killed at the Battle of Wakefield (30 December 1460), which occurred during the Wars of the Roses (1455–85). The king at that time, Henry VI, was a weak ruler who had acceded to the throne as a baby and had been controlled by a suc-

cession of power-hungry barons, of whom the strongest was Richard Neville, earl of WARWICK. Although Warwick had originally supported Henry VI—the Lancastrian cause—he had taken offense at the king's favoring other barons and decided to support the duke of York's claim to act as regent—the Yorkist cause. When the duke of York was killed in battle in 1460, Warwick supported his son Edward, Richard's brother, to become king in 1461.

On his brother's accession as King Edward IV, Richard was given the title duke of Gloucester. When Edward married Elizabeth Woodville in 1464, Warwick, who had wanted Edward to marry a French princess, was infuriated and withdrew his support, determining to restore the deposed Henry VI to the throne. Richard followed his brother when he fled to France in 1470, but came back with him the following year, and they defeated Warwick at the battle of Barnet (14 April 1471), where Warwick was killed. The Lancastrians raised another army, but the Yorkists defeated them again at Tewkesbury (4 May 1471). Edward, now firmly in control, imprisoned Henry VI in the Tower of London, where he was killed the same month. There has been much speculation that Richard was involved in the king's death, and it is recorded that he was in the Tower on 22 May 1471 when Henry was killed.

Richard was granted lands and official honors by his brother the king, and in 1472 he married his cousin Anne Neville, younger daughter of Warwick the Kingmaker, and thus became master of much of Warwick's vast wealth. Another brother of Richard's, the duke of Clarence, had married Warwick's elder daughter, and having to share the Neville wealth led to Clarence's enmity, which grew so bitter that he began to plot against the senior brother, Edward IV. For this, Clarence was impeached and put to death in the Tower on 18 February 1478. (It is now believed that Richard had nothing to do with Clarence's death.)

Richard acted as chief adviser to Edward IV and, on his behalf, invaded Scotland in an attempt to stop the Scots' border incursions; he defeated them at Edinburgh in July 1482. When Edward died on 9 April 1483, he left his two young sons in the care of Richard as regent. Richard named himself as England's lord high protector and had the two princes put in the Tower of London for safety. He then set about reducing the power of the Woodville family, who had gained much wealth and authority from Elizabeth Woodville's marriage to Edward

IV. Richard dealt firmly with opposition and rebellion, and on 22 June 1483 he announced that his brother's children were illegitimate. Shortly thereafter, on 6 July, he was crowned king of England.

By the end of 1483, rumors about the fate of the two young princes began circulating when it was reported that they were no longer in the Tower. Richard's previous loyal supporter, the duke of Buckingham, began to plan a rising to put Henry Tudor on the throne, but his plot was discovered and Buckingham was executed on November 1483.

In 1485, Henry Tudor, a claimant to the throne, raised an army and, supported by the barons envious of Richard's power, defeated him in battle at Bosworth in Leicestershire on 22 August 1485. Abandoned by his leading general, Sir William Stanley, on the battlefield, Richard was killed there, the last English king to die in battle. It was also the last major battle in the Wars of the Roses.

Tudor historians subsequently accused Richard of the murder of Henry VI, his brother Clarence, and the two little princes in the Tower, but some historians now believe he was innocent of these crimes. However, William Shakespeare's portrayal of him in *Richard III* means that history and popular opinion has damned him.

References: Buck, Sir George, *The History and Life and Reigne of Richard the Third, Composed in Five Bookes by Geo. Buck* (London: W. Wilson, 1647); Shakespeare, William, *The Tragedie of King Richard the Third . . .* (London: Thomas Creede, 1612); Fields, Bertram, *Royal Blood: Richard III and the Mystery of the Princes* (New York: Harper Collins, 1998); Gill, Louise, *Richard III and Buckingham's Rebellion* (Stroud, Gloucestershire, U.K.: Sutton Books, 1999); Jesse, John Heneage, *Memoirs of King Richard the Third and Some of His Contemporaries: With an Historical Drama on the Battle of Bosworth,* 2 vols. (New York: F. P. Harper, 1894).

Ridgway, Matthew Bunker (1895–1993)
American general

Matthew Ridgway was born in Fort Monroe, Virginia, on 3 March 1895, the son of Colonel Thomas Ridgway, an artillery officer, and Ruth Bunker Ridgway. He later wrote in his memoirs, published in 1956, that his "earliest memories are of guns and marching men, of rising to the sound of the reveille gun and lying down to sleep at night while the sweet, sad notes of 'Taps' brought the day officially to an end." As the son of an army officer, Ridgway grew up on army bases before he graduated from the English High School in Boston, Massachusetts, in 1912. He tried to enter West Point in 1912, but poor grades forced him to postpone his plans. He succeeded in gaining entry in 1913 and graduated in 1917, described in the academy's yearbook as "beyond doubt, the busiest man in the place." Commissioned with the rank of second lieutenant of infantry as the United States was entering the First World War, he underwent training for service on the western front, but the war ended before he could be sent to France. At the end of 1918, he returned to West Point as an instructor in Spanish as well as an athletics teacher. He was sent to Fort Benning, Georgia, in 1925 and then posted to Tsientsin, China, to command the 15th Infantry, a regiment guarding American installations there.

Because he was fluent in Spanish, Ridgway was sent as a member of the U.S. mission to Nicaragua to monitor elections held there in 1927. This appointment forced him to forego a chance to compete in the 1928 Olympics in Amsterdam. He later served on a military commission examining boundary disputes between Bolivia and Paraguay, and in 1930 he was named as a military adviser to General Theodore Roosevelt, Jr., the governor-general of the Philippines. In 1935, he was posted to the U.S. Army's Command and General Staff School in Fort Leavenworth, Kansas, where he served until 1937. Promoted to major, he became an aide to General George C. Marshall.

With the outbreak of the Second World War in Europe in September 1939, Ridgway was named to the War Plans Division of the General Staff of the Department of War in Washington, D.C. From here he quickly rose in the army ranks, being promoted to brigadier general in August 1942 and given command of the 82nd Infantry Division. When the division was trained to become an airborne formation, Ridgway did likewise and became a paratrooper. In 1943, he helped plan the Allied invasion of Sicily, and his unit was one of the first to drop into Italy when the invasion occurred on 10 July 1943. Although the 82nd suffered serious losses, historians credit Ridgway for taking every precaution he could. He had not jumped at Sicily, but when his men were set to jump in Operation Overlord, the Allied invasion of Normandy, Ridgway demanded that he go with his men—and he did. His commendation for his heroic maneuvers during this battle later noted that "[despite] exposing himself continuously to fire" he "personally directed the operations in [the] important task of securing the bridgehead over the Merderet River."

Ridgway became one of the highest-ranking officers to physically lead his troops into battle against the Germans in the war. A few months later, he was given the command of the 18th Airborne Corps, recently established, and he led this formation to the Rhine River and into Germany. It was Ridgway's forces that met Soviet forces on the Baltic on 2 May 1945. General Marshall later wrote, "General Ridgway has firmly established himself in history as a great battle leader. The advance of his Army corps to the Baltic in the last phase of the war in Europe was sensational to those fully informed of the rapidly moving events of that day." Another contemporary used less-diplomatic words to describe Ridgway: "[He was] a kick-ass man." Ridgway's men called him "Tin-tits" because he went into battle with grenades strapped to his chest. In his memoirs, published in 1956, he explained that this was not showing off but simply an easy way to carry them: "They were purely utilitarian. Many a time in Europe and Korea, men in tight spots blasted their way out with hand grenades."

Following the end of the war, Ridgway was sent to London, where he served as military adviser to General Dwight D. EISENHOWER on the U.S. delegation to the United Nations General Assembly. Ridgway presented the United Nations with a plan to establish an international fighting force, under UN auspices, that could fight in minor conflicts around the world. (Within a few years, such a force would be sent to the Korean peninsula.)

Ridgway was then given command of American forces in the Caribbean. In 1950, he was named as deputy army chief of staff at the Pentagon in Washington, D.C. Following the death of Lieutenant General Walton A. Walker, the commander of U.S. ground forces in Korea, in a jeep accident on 23 December 1950, General Douglas MACARTHUR, commander of UN forces, named Ridgway as Walker's replacement. MacArthur allegedly told Ridgway, "The Eighth Army is yours, Matt. Do what you think best." When Ridgway took command, the American army and its allies were in full retreat from North Korean and Chinese forces pouring over the border at the Yalu River, and were threatened with being expelled from the entire Korean peninsula. Ridgway was able to rally his men to halt the North Korean advance north of the South Korean capital of Seoul, and in early January he was able to open up an offensive that carried American forces into North Korean territory. This offensive inflicted massive casualties on the Chinese and North Koreans, and the attack became known as the "meatgrinder."

On 11 April 1951, only four months after MacArthur was named as the head of U.S. forces in Korea, President Truman relieved him of his command and replaced him with Ridgway. Truman called Ridgway personally, and Colonel Harry Maihafer later noted, "[Army] Secretary [Frank] Pace came over, took the phone call. . . . Then, he and General Ridgway went outside. As I recall, it was raining cats and dogs and a hail storm was going on. And they came back in and General Ridgway looked as though he had the weight of the world on his shoulders." Ridgway continued the fight in Korea, stabilizing the war and leaving it in a deadlock not unlike that on the western front in the First World War. On 3 July 1951, working through the United Nations, he agreed to start cease-fire talks with the North Koreans and the Chinese. In his letter to both parties, he stated, "Since an agreement on armistice terms has to precede the cessation of hostilities, delay in initiating the meeting and reaching agreement will prolong the fighting and increase tension."

In June 1952, Ridgway was promoted to succeed Eisenhower as supreme commander of allied forces in Europe. A year later, Eisenhower, newly elected as U.S. president, named him as army chief of staff. During his two years in this position, Ridgway, who had worked closely with Eisenhower during the Second World War, quarreled with the president over policy and was constantly overruled in favor of Eisenhower's secretary of defense, Charles E. Wilson. Ridgway saw Wilson reducing the postwar military to dangerous levels and tried to prevent it, without any success. Finally, he asked to be allowed to retire. On 28 June 1955, Eisenhower presented him with the Distinguished Service Medal. The president praised him:

> As Supreme Allied Commander, Europe, General Ridgway was charged with the responsibility of welding an effective military structure for the defense of Western Europe. Through dynamic leadership, he furthered the development of the elements of the North Atlantic Treaty Organization into an alert, efficient, fighting team.

He advanced the prestige of the Allied Forces and strengthened the bonds of friendship and cooperation among the many nations serving together in the common defense of democratic principles. In discharging this grave responsibility, he displayed indomitable spirit, inspirational application of military skills, and a sincere concern for the furtherance of the causes of freedom. As Chief of Staff of the United States Army, he continually demonstrated the highest order of leadership, professional competence, astute judgment, and devotion to duty. Under his brilliant direction, the Army was maintained in a state of combat readiness, and fulfilled its world-wide commitments in a manner which contributed significantly to the advancement of the foreign policies of the United States. Ever mindful of the well-being and dignity of the individual soldier, he constantly worked to improve the welfare of the men entrusted to his care. His keen professional ability and great strength of character, displayed in his every action, have been an inspiration to the entire Army. His selfless dedication to the service of his country represents the highest form of patriotism, and merits the gratitude of not only the American people but of free peoples everywhere.

Following his retirement, Ridgway wrote his memoirs, which were published as *Soldier* in 1956. He wrote, "I say in all earnestness and sincerity that throughout my two years as Chief of Staff I felt I was being called upon to tear down, rather than build up, the ultimately decisive element in a properly proportioned fighting force on which the world could rest its hopes for maintaining the peace, or, if the catastrophe of war came, for enforcing its will upon those who broke that peace." In retirement, he remained controversial, disparaging the end of Selective Service and the introduction of women into the military. Nevertheless, in 1986 President Ronald Reagan bestowed on Ridgway the Presidential Medal of Freedom, the nation's highest civil award. The award citation stated, "Heroes come when they are needed. Great men step forward when courage seems in short supply. WWII was such a time, and there was Ridgway." In 1991, he was given the Congressional Gold Medal, presented by General Colin L. Powell (later secretary of state).

Ridgway died of cardiac arrest at his home in Fox Chapel, Pennsylvania, on 26 July 1993 at the age of 98. Because of his service to his nation, he was laid to rest in Arlington National Cemetery in Virginia. At his funeral, Powell—then chairman of the Joint Chiefs of Staff—said, "The legacy of General Ridgway is universal, it's timeless . . . You see a long, devoted service to the nation, of duty, of honor, of country. No soldier knows honor better than this man."

References: Ridgway, Matthew, *Soldier: The Memoirs of Matthew B. Ridgway, as Told to Harold H. Martin* (New York: Harper & Brothers, 1956); Mitchell, George Charles, *Matthew B. Ridgway: Soldier, Statesman, Scholar, Citizen* (Mechanicsburg, Pa.: Stackpole Books, 2002); Blair, Clay, *Ridgway's Paratroopers: The American Airborne in World War II* (Garden City, N.Y.: Dial Press, 1985); Appleman, Roy Edgar, *Ridgway Duels for Korea* (College Station: Texas A&M University Press, 1990); Soffer, Jonathan M., *General Matthew B. Ridgway: From Progressivism to Reaganism, 1895–1983* (Westport, Conn.: Praeger, 1998).

Rivoli, duc de   *See* MASSÉNA, ANDRÉ, DUC DE RIVOLI.

Roberts, Frederick Sleigh, first earl Roberts of Kandahar   (1832–1914)   *British general*

Frederick Sleigh Roberts was born in Cawnpore, India, on 30 September 1832, the second son of British general Sir Abraham Roberts, who was then serving there. He returned to England as a boy, receiving his education at the prestigious Eton College and the Royal Military Training College at Sandhurst. On 12 December 1851, at the age of 19, Roberts joined the army of the British East India Company as a lieutenant in the Bengal artillery. He was sent to serve with a field battery in Peshawar (now in Pakistan), where he served under his father. In 1856, he was appointed deputy quartermaster general, and he served in that capacity during the Sepoy Rebellion (usually known as the Indian Mutiny, 1857–58). Serving under Sir Colin CAMPBELL, Roberts saw action at Lucknow (November 1857) and at Cawnpore (6 December 1857), which culminated in the defeat of the Gwalior fighters near Shinrajpur. The rebels continued their fight into 1858, and Roberts fought against them at Khudaganj (2 January 1858) and Kursi (22 March 1858). He was struck with a sickness, and was sent back to England, where he received the Victoria Cross for his bravery at Khudaganj. He served in staff appointments for the next 22 years, playing a vital part in the logistical support of campaigns in Africa and India. In December 1863, he fought in the "Ambela" campaign north of Peshawar, India, under Major General John Garvock.

In 1867, Roberts was appointed assistant quartermaster general in Abyssinia (now Ethiopia) to Sir Donald Stewart's brigade. He saw limited action during his four months' tour in 1868, returning to India later that year. Afghanistan was then, as now, an unstable land, and this was proven in the Second Afghan War (1878–80) when Roberts, now a major general and the commander of British forces, invaded Afghanistan from India. His Frontier Field Force set out to repair the defeat of Sir Neville Bowles Chamberlain's army in Afghanistan in early 1878. Through a series of battles with the Afghans, including at Spingawi Kotal (2 December 1878) and Hagir Pir (January 1879), he advanced on the city of Kabul, taking it with few losses on 6 October 1879. Although much of the enemy had been routed, Muslim fanatics threatened Roberts and the British mission, and he moved out from Kabul to attack them. He defeated them outside Kabul, but, with the British mission at Sherpur threatened, he moved his forces there and consolidated the mission's defenses. The Muslim army attacked on 23 December 1879 with forces of upward of 100,000 men, but Roberts and the British beat them back, with horrific losses to the Muslims. Roberts then moved his army out of the city, attacked them with great force, and defeated them again.

Roberts recommended that Afghanistan be divided into several regions, and, on 5 May 1880, Sir Donald Stewart's army arrived in Kabul from Kandahar (now Qandahar). On 22 July 1880, under Roberts's command, Abdur Rahman was named as the new amir of Kabul. As Roberts planned to march his army out of Afghanistan back into India, he received word that a British force had been defeated by the Muslims at Maiwand (27 July 1880) and that British troops under Lieutenant General James Primrose were under siege in Kandahar. He departed Kabul with an army of 10,000 soldiers on 9 August and arrived at Kandahar on 31 August, a march of some 310 miles in 22 days. On 1

September, this force took on the besieging Muslim forces, defeating them and relieving Primrose's army. This victory ended the war. Awarded the honor of a baronetcy and Knight Commander of the Order of the Bath (KCB), Roberts sailed home to England for a period of rest before assuming command of the Madras army in India.

While Roberts was in England, however, the British army was defeated at Majuba Hill in South Africa (27 February 1881). Immediately, the British government transferred Roberts from India to South Africa, making him governor of Natal Province and commander in chief of British forces in southern Africa. He sailed to Africa, but when he arrived he learned that peace had been gained between the Boers and the English. He went back to England, declined the post of quartermaster general, and returned to India. In July 1885, he succeeded Sir Donald Stewart as commander in chief of British forces in India, a post he held for seven years. In 1886, he took personal command of the forces of Burma in a campaign there. In 1892, for his service to the Crown, he was styled as Baron Roberts of Kandahar and Waterford. He departed India for the last time in 1893 and was promoted to the rank of field marshal in 1895. That same year, he published *The Rise of Wellington,* and in 1895 he published his memoirs, *Forty-One Years in India.*

In 1899, the Boer War broke out in southern Africa, and after British defeats at Magersfontein and Colenso, where his son was killed, Roberts was given the command of British forces there. He arrived in Cape Town (now in South Africa) on 10 January 1900, and he quickly established a strategy of relieving British forces under siege in the cities of Kimberley and Ladysmith. He concentrated on defeating the main Boer force under the South African commander Piet Cronje, meeting his army at Paardeberg on 27 February 1900 and forcing Cronje's surrender and that of some 5,000 Boer troops on what was the 19th anniversary of the Boer victory at Majuba Hill. Roberts took Bloemfontein on 13 March 1900 and moved on the capital of Pretoria. After relieving the siege of Mafeking (17 May 1900), he took Pretoria with little bloodshed on 5 June 1900.

With much of South Africa now under British control, Roberts stepped down as commander in chief and sailed back to England; he was succeeded by Lord

Horatio KITCHENER. In London, he was named as commander in chief of the British army, succeeding Lord Garnet Wolseley. Given an earldom as Lord Roberts, he also received a grant of £100,000 from Parliament. In 1905, he retired formally to serve as the head of the National Service League, a group advocating a strong national defense. In 1911 he published *Fallacies and Facts,* a work discussing compulsory military service, which he supported.

When the First World War broke out in 1914, Roberts visited the western front to welcome the two Indian divisions to France. It was while touring the front that he caught pneumonia, and he succumbed to it at the age of 82 on 14 November 1914, while in the hospital in St. Omer. He was buried with full honors at St. Paul's Cathedral in London.

Long fondly remembered in the British army, Lord Roberts won impressive victories on two continents. The authors of the *The Wordsworth Dictionary of Military Biography* write: "Roberts was one of the truly respected commanders of the British Army, much loved by his men and adored by the public. From an early age his personal courage was well-known—the evidence was his extraordinary 'chest' of medals, at a time when gallantry decorations were, in general, sparsely awarded. After his early commands in India, his presence alone in charge of British forces was capable of reviving morale and even in his old age his dynamic presence in South Africa quickly brought about the victories which had hitherto escaped the British Army."

References: Jerrold, Walter, *Field-Marshal Earl Roberts, V.C.: The Life Story of a Great Soldier* (London: W.A. Hammond, 1914); James, David, *Lord Roberts* (London: Hollis & Carter, 1954); Roberts, Frederick Sleigh, Earl Roberts, *Roberts in India: The Military Papers of Field Marshal Lord Roberts, 1876–1893,* edited by Brian Robson (Dover, N.H.: Alan Sutton for the Army Records Society, 1993); Windrow, Martin, and Francis K. Mason, "Roberts, Frederick Sleigh, 1st Earl of Kandahar, Pretoria, and Waterford," in *The Wordsworth Dictionary of Military Biography* (Hertfordshire, U.K.: Wordsworth Editions Ltd., 1997), 242–246; Wallace, Edgar, *Britain's Great Men: Lord Roberts: The Man and His Campaigns* (London: George Newnes, 1914); Hannah, W. H., *Bobs, Kipling's General: The Life of Field-Marshal Earl Roberts of Kandahar, V.C.* (London: Lee Cooper, 1972).

Robert the Bruce (Robert Broyss, Robert de Broyss, earl of Carrick, Lord Annandale, Robert I)

(1274–1329) *Scottish king*

Robert the Bruce, whose name may have been Robert de Broyss or Robert Broyss, was born sometime in 1274 in Turnberry, Ayrshire, the son of Robert Broyss, earl of Carrick, and descended from a Norman baron who came with William the Conqueror to England in 1066. In 1292, Robert Broyss was styled as Lord Annandale, and he allowed his son to take the title of earl of Carrick, a title he held until his coronation as king of Scotland in 1306. Unfortunately, details of Robert's early life are uncertain, but it is known that he became Lord Annandale upon his father's death in 1304.

In 1296, along with other Scottish barons, Robert swore his loyalty to King EDWARD I of England, but he betrayed Edward by siding with those who desired Scottish independence. On 25 March 1306, he was crowned as Robert I, king of Scotland. At once, Edward, known as "The Hammer of the Scots," launched a massive attack on the Scottish forces Robert now led. After the Scots were defeated at Methven in Perthshire (19 June 1306), Robert was forced to flee into exile on the island of Rathlin, off the coast of Ireland. Edward confiscated his family's estates and slaughtered or punished his supporters. Robert planned his return, gathering a new army to take on Edward. In 1307, he marched this army into Scotland and defeated the English forces at Loudon Hill, also known as Drumclog (10 May 1307). This battle took place two months before Edward died on 7 July 1307. Robert used Edward's death and the interregnum to defeat Scottish rivals at the battles of Inverurie (May 1308) and Brander (August 1308) and to take several castles at Balvenie and Urquart.

Edward's 23-year-old son, crowned as EDWARD II, did not move against the Scots, and a period of years went by during which the Scots regained control of Scottish lands in the north. However, by 1314 Edward was old enough to take up his father's crusade against the Scots, and the English army was sent north. Edward's attempts to relieve the English garrison at Stirling Castle was cut off by Robert at the famed battle of Bannockburn nearby (23–24 June 1314). In this landmark battle, Robert the Bruce, backed by some 40,000 Scottish troops, took on an immense army of 60,000–80,000 English soldiers commanded by Edward II himself (the exact number is unknown). Historian George Bruce writes: "Bruce's position was partly covered by a marsh, and further strengthened by pitfalls, in which the English cavalry was entrapped, and defeated with great loss." (Pitfalls are deep holes in the ground with spikes placed in the bottom, the pits being camouflaged by grass and foliage.) The numbers remain unknown, but Edward fled the field with only a few thousand men, and Scottish independence was assured.

Although Robert the Bruce lived only 15 years after Bannockburn, he remained a focal point of Scottish independence. In 1315, he invaded Ireland and named his brother Edward Bruce as king of that country. Three years later, Edward Bruce was killed in battle at Dundale, and Robert oversaw the Scottish capture of the city of Berwick in northern England. In 1320, with the threat of Edward II again invading Scotland, a number of Scottish lords and earls met and dispatched a letter to Pope John XXII, claiming Robert as their monarch and asking for papal agreement. This "Declaration of Arbroath" is considered the first formal avowal of Scottish independence. In 1324, the pope recognized Robert the Bruce as the king of an independent Scotland. In 1327, Edward II was removed from the throne, and his son EDWARD III offered peace to the Scottish, signed as the Treaty of Northampton in 1328. By this time, Robert was ill with what many historians consider to be leprosy. He spent his last year at his castle at Cardross, Dunbartonshire, where he died on 7 June 1329 at age 54. His last wish was to have his heart removed, embalmed, and carried by his friend Sir James de Douglas to Jerusalem, where it was to be buried. On his way to Jerusalem, Douglas was killed in battle in Spain. Robert's heart was returned to Scotland and buried in Melrose Abbey in Roxburghshire. His other remains were laid to rest in Dunfermline.

In 1996, an agency of the Scottish government, Historic Scotland, announced that Robert's mummified heart had been found and identified in the grounds of Melrose Abbey, in the southwestern corner of Scotland. Subsequently, 667 years after Robert's death, his heart was given a proper ceremonial burial.

References: Barbour, John, comp., *The Bruce: or, The Book of the Most Excellent and Noble Prince, Robert de Broyss, King of Scots . . .* (Edinburgh: W. Blackwood and Sons, 1894); Barrow, G. W. S., *Robert Bruce and the Community of the Realm of Scotland* (Berkeley: University of California Press, 1965); Mackenzie, Agnes Mure, *Rob-* ert Bruce, King of Scots (London: A. Maclehose & Co., 1934); Scott, Ronald McNair, *Robert the Bruce, King of Scots* (New York: P. Bedrick Books, 1989); "Medieval King's Heart is Found in Scotland," *The New York Times,* 3 September 1996, A4.

Rodney, George Brydges, first baron Rodney of Stoke-Rodney (George Bridges Rodney)
(1719–1792)   British admiral

Rodney was born in London in 1719, the fourth of five children and second son of Henry Rodney, a naval officer, and Mary Newton Rodney. He was the grandson of Anthony Rodney, who had served in the navy of Charles II. The Rodneys were an old, well-established family of England. Rodney biographer David Hannay writes: "From the reign of Henry the Third until far into the seventeenth century [the Rodneys] were established as owners of land in and about Stoke Rodney, at the foot of the Mendips, in the valley of the Axe between Draycott and Wells." George Rodney briefly attended Harrow School, and records show that upon his leaving in 1732, he was given an appointment as "volunteer" in the English navy aboard the *Sunderland.* His service during the next few years was undistinguished; what is known is that in 1739 he was promoted to lieutenant and given the command of the *Dolphin,* then serving in the Mediterranean.

In 1740, the War of the Austrian Succession—a struggle for the Austrian throne following the death of Charles VI, the Holy Roman Emperor—began, and it would last until 1748. It is not known what part Rodney played in the first years of this conflict, but in 1742 he was promoted to the rank of post captain and placed in command of the *Plymouth* and, the following year, of the *Sheerness.* He served under the command of Sir Edward VERNON and then under Sir Edward HAWKE. As the commander of the *Eagle,* a 60-gun ship, he participated with Hawke in the English victory over the French fleet off Finisterre on 14 October 1747. Rodney's service during the battle was later praised by Lord ANSON. For this he was promoted to commodore and named as the governor and commander in chief of Newfoundland in Canada in 1749. He was only 30 years old.

In 1751, back in England, Rodney was elected as a member of Parliament (MP) for Saltish, and two years later he married Jane Compton, the sister of the Seventh earl of Northampton (she would die in childbirth in 1757). When Parliament was dissolved in 1754, he did not have this political seat to fall back on, and he looked for additional work. He was given command of the *Fougueux,* a captured French vessel, which was set to guard the port of Portsmouth, allowing him to remain at home with his family. With the outbreak of the Seven Years' War (1756–63), Rodney was given command first of the *Prince George,* a 90-gun ship, and then the *Dublin,* a 74-gun ship. On the second ship, he helped to transport General Jeffrey AMHERST to Louisbug.

Rodney was promoted to rear admiral of the blue in 1759, seeing action against the armed French transports intended to invade England and sinking several of them off the coast of Normandy. He was elected as an MP representing Okehampton in 1759, but two years later his constituents did not choose him to stand for reelection, and he lost the seat. Instead, he was selected to represent Penryn, and he won in a close election. In October 1761, he was appointed as commander in chief of the Leeward Islands, and within several months he forced the surrender of the French-controlled islands of Martinique, Grenada, and St. Lucia while commanding the 60-gun ship the *Marlborough.* In 1764, he was made a baronet, and from 1765 to 1770, he served as the governor of Greenwich Hospital.

In 1768, Rodney was elected as an MP from Northampton with the help of his former brother-in-law, the earl of Northampton. The election cost Rodney thousands of pounds, and he remained in severe debt for many years. Following a period of service as commander in chief of the Jamaica squadron (1771–74), when he thwarted a Spanish invasion of the Falkland Islands, Rodney was put on half-pay, and he was forced to flee to France to avoid being arrested for his debts. He was not able to return until 1778, when he was named as admiral and again as commander in chief of the Leeward Islands.

This began a period that saw Rodney become one of Britain's most important naval officers. He was involved in fighting several countries that opposed Britain in the American Revolution, including France and Spain. Off Cape Finesterre (8 January 1780), his flotilla captured a large Spanish fleet of 16 ships. A week later, off Cape St. Vincent (16 January 1780), he defeated the famed Spanish admiral Don Juan de Langara, destroying one ship and capturing six others in the "Moonlight Battle," fought under a moonlit sky in the middle of the night. Rodney's fleet sailed to St. Lucia, where they joined other English ships under Rear Admiral Sir Hyde Parker.

Consolidating their armada, they sailed to Martinique, where they faced a French force commanded by Admiral Luc Urbain de Bouexic, comte de Guichen. Parker faced de Guichen on 9 April 1780, and then Rodney fought the Frenchman on 19 May 1780, with both engagements doing little except to force de Guichen's return to France. Rodney then turned his attention to the seizure of the Dutch-controlled island of St. Eustatius, which he accomplished on 3 February 1781. Following this victory, he wrote to his naval superior, Lord George Germain, asking to be placed in charge of the British navy fighting the American colonists, but Germain refused. Rodney therefore continued his successful campaign in the Caribbean, winning the "Battle of the Saints" off the island of Dominica (now the Dominican Republic) on 9 April 1782. Historian George Bruce writes that the battle was "between the British fleet of 36 sail of the line, under Admiral Rodney, with Admiral Lord Hood second in command, and the French fleet of 33 sail under the Comte de Grasse. Rodney departed from the usual tactics of ship-to-ship action, and broke the enemy's line, gaining a complete victory, and capturing or destroying five ships, while two more were captured within the next few days. The British lost 261 killed and 837 wounded. The French losses have been put as high as 15,000, but it is probable that they lost about 3,000 killed and wounded, while 7,980 were taken in the captured ships." Rodney was feted upon his return to England; Parliament thanked him and gave him a barony and a pension of £2,000 a year. This was Rodney's last service. He retired to his home, dying in London on 24 May 1792 at the age of 73.

Historian Kenneth Breen writes:

The esteem in which Rodney was held by his contemporaries may be gauged from remarks made in letters and speeches by supporters as influential as Lord Sandwich and by opponents as articulate as [Charles] Fox and [Thomas Henry] Burke. From the time he entered the navy in 1732, though influence played a part, Rodney had impressed his superiors by his efficiency and his understanding of naval principles; by his vigour, determination and aggression when opposing the enemy; and by those qualities of leadership which led him to care for the welfare of his men. Consequently he had risen to post and then flag rank very much on these merits. . . . [M]any cities honoured Rodney with their Freedom, including Huntingdon, at which ceremony Sandwich made reference to the fact that Rodney's record was unsurpassed in that he had taken or destroyed sixteen ships of the line and capturing the commanding admiral of each of the nations with which England was at war.

References: Hannay, David, *Rodney* (London: Macmillan and Co., 1891); Mundy, Godfrey B, *The Life and Correspondence of Admiral Lord Rodney,* 2 vols. (London: J. Murray, 1830); Charnock, John, "Rodney, George Brydges, 1st Baron Rodney of Stoke-Rodney," in *Biographia Navalis; or, Impartial Memoirs of the Lives and Characters of Officers of the Navy of Great Britain, From the Year 1660 to the Present Time; . . . ,* 6 vols. (London: Printed for R. Faulder, Bond-Street, 1794–98); V:204–228; Breen, Kenneth, "George Bridges, Lord Rodney, 1718?–1792," in *Precursors of Nelson: British Admirals of the Eighteenth Century,* edited by Peter Le Fevre and Richard Harding (London: Chatham Publishing, 2000), 225–248; Bruce, George, "Dominica," in *Collins Dictionary of Wars* (Glasgow, Scotland: HarperCollins Publishers, 1995), 75; "Rodney, George Brydges Rodney, 1st Baron," in *A Dictionary of Military History and the Art of War* edited by André Corvisier (London: Blackwell, 1994), 703.

Rokossovsky, Konstantin Konstantinovich (Konstantin Rokossovskii) (1896–1968)
Soviet general

Little is known of Konstantin Rokossovsky, whose name is also spelled Rokossovskii by some sources. He was born in the village of Velikiye Luki, Russia, on 21 December 1896 (or 9 December 1896 [O.S.]), the son of a railroad engineer. He joined the Russian army as a youth and saw action on the eastern front as a noncommissioned officer during the First World War. In 1917, following the overthrow of the czarist regime, Rokossovsky threw his support behind the new Communist government and served with the Red forces during the Russian civil war. He won a series of promotions through the ranks of the Soviet army.

In 1938, at the height of Joseph Stalin's purges of the Soviet military and society, Rokossovsky, despite his unblemished record, was arrested and accused of anti-Soviet behavior. For some reason—never ascertained—he was released in 1939. Although this system of purges claimed upward of 60 million people, most of whom were never heard from again, Rokossovsky spoke out against his superiors, denouncing the commissar system in 1941. That same year, however, he was spared any further punishment when the Germans invaded the Soviet Union in what was called Operation Barbarossa, and Stalin found himself without many experienced military officers because of his purges. Rokossovsky was placed in command of forces to resist the Germans advancing to attack Moscow. His troops, the Soviet Sixteenth Army, defended the capital city, and his devastating counterattack, which came as his forces were encircled by the Nazi shock troops, led to a much-needed victory just as Soviet forces were being defeated everywhere else in Russia. Rokossovsky's attack was so decisive that he immediately asked his superiors if he could march on Warsaw and take it from the Germans. Instead, he was ordered to withdraw and consolidate his forces.

Although he went on to command forces at Smolensk and Omsk, Rokossovsky is best known for his leadership of Russian forces at Stalingrad (November 1942–February 1943). The German Sixth Army, commanded by Field Marshal Friedrich Wilhelm Ernst PAULUS, had taken this important Russian city, but they had extended themselves far from their supply lines just as winter was setting in. Rokossovsky decided that a siege of the Germans at Stalingrad was the best method of attack. He initially offered Paulus terms of surrender in early January 1943, after the siege had lasted some weeks, but Paulus rejected these conditions. Two days later, under Rokossovsky's command, the Russian offensive began, pounding the German forces inside the city. As he later explained in his memoirs, published in 1985, "The High Command kept pressing on, demanding that we advance [against Stalingrad] in December, later pushing the date back to the end of December. We were not ready yet and remained to be so in early January, too. On January 10th we were more or less prepared to hit out. To cut through the enemy's defenses, we amassed a formidable artillery force there. The might of that initial barrage was absolutely devastating. Our troops followed up on that initial success, dashing whatever hopes the Germans had for any protracted defense in Stalingrad."

On 12 January, at a cost of approximately 26,000 men, the Russian forces captured the western section of the city. On 27 January, Rokossovsky, seeing that the Germans were weakened by lack of supplies and the horrific Russian winter, led a massive full-scale attack, forcing Paulus to surrender; the remainder of the German forces formally capitulated on 2 February 1943. Paulus submitted directly to Rokossovsky, offering the Soviet commander his personal weapon. In total, the Germans had lost approximately 110,000 killed, and nearly 100,000 were taken prisoner when the city fell; of this latter number, only about 5,000 survived the war. Paulus became so disillusioned by Adolf Hitler's lack of aid during the siege that he cooperated with his Soviet captors and helped to make propaganda broadcasts to destroy German morale.

Rokossovsky continued his push against the Nazis, taking part in the famed tank battle at Kursk (3–13 July 1943). He led forces in the capture of Byelorussia in what was called Operation Bagration (1944), where his troops routed the German Ninth Army, and eastern Prussia and Pomerania in the early weeks and months of 1945. For his services to his homeland during this latter period, he was promoted to Marshal of the Soviet Union. His forces crossed into Poland, where he captured Warsaw, and then into Germany, stopping at the city of Wismar when the Germans surrendered on 3 May 1945. The Soviet forces linked up with troops of the British Second Army, and Field Marshal Bernard Law MONTGOMERY, the British commander, invested Rokossovsky as Knight Commander of the Order of the Bath (KCB). Rokossovsky subsequently returned to the Soviet Union, where he was the leader of the Victory Parade held in Moscow's Red Square on 24 July 1945. The Second World War had made him perhaps the most important Soviet military commander aside from Marshal Georgi ZHUKOV.

Following the end of the war, in 1949 Rokossovsky was named as Soviet defense minister as well as deputy chairman of the Council of Ministers. That same year, the Polish nationalist Władysław Gomułka, who was secretary of the Communist Polish Workers' Party, was purged from power as deputy premier of Poland due to his sympathy with the Yugoslav Communist leader Josip Broz, known as Tito, who had differed with control of the Eastern European Communist states from Moscow. In 1950, Rokossovsky was made commander of Soviet forces in Poland, in essence controlling that country, and a series of events followed which led to his downfall. Starting in 1953, with Soviet premier Nikita Khrushchev's denunciation of the Stalinist era, a period of liberalization began in the Eastern European satellite states controlled by the USSR. The following year, Gomulka was released from prison and readmitted to

the Communist Polish Workers' Party, now called the United Workers' Party. That October, he became the first secretary of the party in obvious defiance of Moscow's and Rokossovsky's wishes. Nonetheless, Gomulka's regime was highly popular, instituting a series of economic reforms of which Moscow disapproved. On 28 October 1956, in a move to lessen Soviet control on his country, Gomulka ordered that all Soviet military advisers, including Rokossovsky, leave Poland on the pretext that a pro-Soviet coup was being planned. Rokossovsky, disgraced, returned to Russia, where he was named as deputy minister of defense, serving in that office twice from 1956 to 1962. He died in Moscow on 3 August 1968 at the age of 71.

Although it was his actions that in many ways won victory for the Soviet Union on the eastern front, Rokossovsky is often ranked well below Marshal Georgi Zhukov in terms of military excellence. Nonetheless, he played a vital part in the USSR's defeat of the mighty German army during its invasion of Russia in 1942, and for this he helped to change the course of history.

References: Rokossovsky, Konstantin K., *A Soldier's Duty*, translated by Vladimir Talmy. Edited by Robert Daglish (Moscow, USSR: Progress Publishers, 1970, 1985); Sevruk, Vladimir, comp., *Moscow 1941/42 Stalingrad* (Moscow, USSR: Progress Publishers, 1970); Zhukov, Georgil, et al., *Battles Hitler Lost, and the Soviet Marshals Who Won Them: Marshals Zhukov, Konev, Malinovsky, Rokossovsky, Rotmistrov, Chuikov, and other Commanders* (New York: Richardson & Steirman, 1986); "Rokossovsky, Kontantin," in Windrow, Martin, and Francis K. Mason, "Rokossovsky, Konstantin," in *The Wordsworth Dictionary of Military Biography* (Hertfordshire, U.K.: Wordsworth Editions Ltd., 1997), 249–250.

Rommel, Erwin Johannes Eugen (1891–1944)
German general

Born in the village of Heidenheim, in Württemberg, Germany, on 15 November 1891, Erwin Rommel received his education in Stuttgart before he entered the German army. In 1910, he became an officer cadet in the 124th Infantry Regiment, and in 1912 he received a commission as a second lieutenant. When the First World War broke out, he was sent to the western front in France, seeing action before being transferred to fight against Italy and Romania. He helped in the seizure of the city of Monte Matajur, near Caporetto, Italy, for which he won the Prussian Ordre pour le Mérite, an award usually given to senior officers. He received the Iron Cross for his service on the western front.

Following the end of the war, Rommel attended the University of Tübingen for a short period, then served in a number of regimental commands. He was an instructor at the Dresden Infantry School from 1929 to 1933 and at the Potsdam War Academy from 1935 to 1938. With the rise of Adolf Hitler to power in Germany, he became a member of Hitler's National Socialist, or Nazi, Party, and some historians claim that Rommel served as the head of the hated corps of special Nazi troops called the Schutzstaffel, known as the SS; one source, however, notes that he was probably the head of the Nazis' paramilitary force, the Sturmabsteliung, or SA. In 1938, he was promoted to colonel and named as the commandant of the War Academy at Wiener Neustadt. In mid-1939,

Erwin Rommel

shortly before the Second World War broke out, Rommel was promoted to major general. Following the invasion of Poland on 1 September 1939, he was given command of the 7th Panzer Division, known as the "Ghost Division" because of the speed of its movement, which raced across northern France ("Blitzkrieg"), bypassing all attempts to halt the German advance and leading to France's capitulation. In 1941, Rommel was promoted to lieutenant general and given command of the Afrika Korps, the German forces in northern Africa.

Rommel won a series of brilliant battles, outmaneuvering the British and pushing their Eighth Army back, from Cyrenaica into Egypt to El Alamein, and taking the important port of Tobruk on 20 June 1942. The following day, he was promoted to field marshal. However, although he had forced the British back, Rommel could not defeat them completely, a failure that would eventually cost him and the Germans dearly. Commanding a joint German and Italian force, he raced ahead of his supply lines, and he and his forces were defeated at the critical battle of El Alamein (23–24 October 1942) when the British general Bernard MONTGOMERY stifled his maneuvering room and beat him back with overwhelming tank and air attacks. Rommel's forces turned and fled into Tunisia, where he had to face American forces under Dwight D. EISENHOWER, who had landed in the west, culminating in the battle at Medinine (5 March 1943). Rommel became ill, and he departed for Germany before his forces in Africa were forced to surrender. Although he was not personally blamed for the North Africa defeat, he was in effect demoted when he was placed in command of the Nazi defense lines on the Atlantic coast in France.

Since the start of the war and the forced ejection of Allied forces from the European continent, Hitler and his generals believed that the Allies would attempt a landing somewhere in northern France, and to this end they fortified the entire coastline with machine guns and concrete blockhouses. Under Rommel, these measures were improved even further, and by the beginning of June 1944, he was so confident that an Allied landing would not be attempted that he returned home to Germany to visit his family. He was there when the D-Day landings, known as Operation Overlord, occurred, and he rushed back to command the German defense. On 14 July, though, his car was struck by gunfire from an Allied aircraft, and he was seriously wounded. He was taken back to Germany to convalesce.

While in the hospital, Rommel was apparently contacted by senior German officers who were plotting to kill Hitler and end the war. Although he had been a member of Nazi Party, Rommel now realized Germany's danger if Hitler remained in charge, and he spoke out on the German regime's failings. On 14 October 1944, two German generals investigating a failed attempt on Hitler's life on 20 July (the "Bomb Plot") visited Rommel. Afterward, he told his wife, "I have come to say goodbye. In a quarter of an hour I shall be dead." Whereas Hitler had arrested and executed others implicated in the plot, he had offered Rommel a chance to take his own life rather than suffer the humiliation of arrest, trial, and certain execution. In a car near Ulm, Rommel took a dose of poison and died, a month before his 53rd birthday. The Nazis announced that Rommel had been killed in battle, and Hitler ordered a state funeral for the man he had effectively put to death.

In the introduction to Rommel's edited papers, British historian B. H. Liddell Hart writes: "Until I delved into Rommel's own papers I regarded him as a brilliant tactician and great fighting leader, but I did not realize how deep a sense of strategy he had—or, at any rate, developed in reflection. It was a surprise to find that such a thruster had been so thoughtful, and that his audacity was so shrewdly calculated. In certain cases, his moves may still be criticized as too hazardous, but not as the reckless strokes of a blind and hot-headed gambler. In analysis of the operations it can be seen that some of the strokes which miscarried, with grave results for him, came close to proving graver for his opponents. Moreover, even in failure his strokes made such an impression on them as to assure his army a chance of escape."

References: Young, Desmond, *Rommel: The Desert Fox* (New York: Harper, 1950); Heckmann, Wolf, *Rommel's War in Africa* (New York: Doubleday, 1981); Liddell Hart, B. H., ed., *The Rommel Papers* (London: Hamlyn Paperbacks, 1983); Windrow, Martin, and Francis K. Mason, "Rommel, Erwin," in *The Wordsworth Dictionary of Military Biography* (Hertfordshire, U.K.: Wordsworth Editions Ltd., 1997), 250–251.

Rooke, Sir George (ca. 1650–1709) *English admiral*

George Rooke was born in or about 1650—the exact date is unknown—the son of Sir William Rooke, the sheriff of Kent. Of his early life, few details can be ascertained. Historian John B. Hattendorf writes that "George Rooke was among the category of 'gentlemen' officers. . . . [He was] the second son of Dame Jane Finche Rooke and Colonel Sir William Rooke (1624–1691) of St. Lawrence, Canterbury; [the] sheriff of Kent (1685–1688) and cousin, once removed, of Lawrence Rooke (1622–1662), the astronomer and founder member of the Royal Society."

According to several sources, Rooke went to sea at an early age and first saw naval action during the Second Anglo-Dutch War (1665–67). The historian John Charnock writes: "Having discovered an early propensity to the sea, contrary, it is said, to the wishes of his relations, he entered as a volunteer in the navy, and rendering himself very soon conspicuous as second lieutenant of the *London* in 1672, and of the *Prince* in the following year, was, on the 13th of November 1673, at the early age of twenty-three, appointed to the command of the *Holmes*." Rooke also saw action during the War of the Grand Alliance (1688–97), and perhaps his greatest achievement during this period was his fighting at the Battle of Bantry Bay (11 May 1689), off the coast of Ireland, between the English and French navies.

Rooke was promoted to the rank of rear admiral following Bantry Bay, and he took command of English forces fighting at La Hogue against the Dutch off the northern coast of Normandy, France (19–23 May 1692). His victory there led to his being knighted as Sir George Rooke, and he was given command of the English fleet, which destroyed the French warships aiding in the return of James II to the English throne. Rooke's low point came in 1693. While his fleet was escorting the so-called "Smyrna expedition" to the Levant in what is now Turkey, a French fleet commanded by Anne-Hilarion de Cotentin, comte de Tourville, intercepted and attacked them in Lagos Bay, leaving the English with extreme losses, although Rooke was not blamed for the incident.

Rooke's most important service came during the War of the Spanish Succession (1701–13), but with mixed results, as historians Anthony Bruce and William Cogar explain: "Failure also marked the first two years of his command during the War of the Spanish Succession. His inability to capture Cádiz in September 1702 was only partially redeemed by a successful attack on Vigo [also known as Vigo Bay, 12 October 1702] on the homeward journey. Two years later he was able to seize Barcelona, but on his way back to England he took the opportunity to capture Gibraltar, which fell on 23–24 July 1704. Rooke successfully defended his conquest three weeks later when he fought the French fleet at the battle of Velez Malaga [13 August 1704], and it has remained in English hands ever since."

Rooke's career then came to a sudden end. The Whig government in London was attacked by Tories in the House of Commons who compared Rooke's military record to that of the Whig favorite, John CHURCHILL, the first duke of Marlborough. In order to make Marlborough look better, the government decided to retire Rooke from any further service in February 1705. He never saw any further military action and died in London on 24 January 1709 at the age of approximately 59.

Historian John Hattendorf writes of Rooke's impact on history: "Rooke was a man who seemed to want to avoid the public limelight and political controversy in attending to his duty. Writers such as Daniel Defoe were unwilling to accept this and created quite another image of him. Rooke's death in quiet retirement on 24 January 1709 led to no great public notice, and, indeed, the political attempts of the Tories during Rooke's lifetime to turn him into a popular hero during his active career failed miserably. . . ."

References: Hattendorf, John B., "Sir George Rooke and Sir Cloudsley Shovell, c.1650–1709 and 1650–1707," in *Precursors of Nelson: British Admirals of the Eighteenth Century,* edited by Peter Le Fevre, and Richard Harding (London: Chatham Publishing, 2000), 43–77; Charnock, John, "Rooke, Sir George," in *Biographia Navalis; or, Impartial Memoirs of the Lives and Characters of Officers of the Navy of Great Britain, From the Year 1660 to the Present Time; . . . ,* 4 vols. (London: Printed for R. Faulder, 1794–98), I:402–430; Browning, Oscar, ed., *The Journal of Sir George Rooke, Admiral of the Fleet, 1700–1702* (London: Printed for the Navy Records Society, 1897); Bruce, Anthony, and William Cogar, "Rooke, Sir George," in *An Encyclopedia of Naval History* (New York: Checkmark Books, 1999), 311; *An Account of Sir George Rook's Arrival in the Channel with the Fleet under His Command* (London: Edw. Jones, 1696); *A Narrative of Sir George Rooke's Late Voyage to the Mediterranean, Where He Commanded as Admiral of the Confederate Fleet . . .* (London: Printed for Benj. Tooke, 1704).

Rosecrans, William Starke (1819–1898)

American general

Born in Kingston, Ohio, on 6 September 1819, William Rosecrans received a local education and then entered the United States Military Academy at West Point, New York, in 1838. He graduated in 1842 and joined the American army that same year as a second lieutenant of engineers. Two years later, he returned to West Point, where he was an assistant professor of engineering. After three years of teaching, Rosecrans served as superintendent of the repair of harbors along the eastern coast of the United States, specifically in Virginia, a position he held until 1854. However, not seeing any further advancement in the army, he resigned his commission and retired to private life in Cincinnati, Ohio, where he went to work as an engineering consultant.

The onset of the American Civil War in 1861 saw Rosecrans reenter the military, and in May 1861 he was made a brigadier general and given a command under Generals George B. MCCLELLAN and John Pope. At first, Rosecrans was given the task of raising troops in Ohio, but in June he was given command of three brigades in the fight for Virginia. He oversaw several Union victories, most notably at Rich Mountain (11 July 1861) and Carnifax Ferry, West Virginia (10 September 1861). Following these victories, he succeeded Pope as commander of the Army of the Mississippi. In 1862, Rosecrans led the Union forces under his command to victory at Iuka (September 1862) and Corinth (October 1862), both in Mississippi. He then took command of the Army of the Cumberland, succeeding Don Carlos Buell, and won an important victory at Stones River, also known as Murfreesboro (31 December 1862–2 January 1863), defeating the Confederate general Braxton Bragg. In this, known as the Chattanooga campaign, Rosecrans deftly outmaneuvered Bragg and pursued him with part of his army, leading to the most crucial battle of his career.

The battle of Chickamauga Creek (19–20 September 1863) was a classic engagement between two armies: Approximately 55,000 Union forces, led by Rosecrans, took on a much-larger army of some 70,000 led by Bragg. Historian George Bruce writes: "On the 19th the Confederates attacked along the whole line and drove back their opponents, cutting them off from the river, and forcing them to bivouac for the night in a waterless country. On the 20th the attack was renewed, and although Bragg's right was repulsed, he was else-where successful, and by nightfall Rosecrans was in full retreat. Bragg, however, failed to follow up his victory, and allowed Rosecrans to retire on Chattanooga unmolested. The Federals lost 16,351 men killed, wounded or missing, and 36 guns; the Confederates lost about 12,000." Although Chickamauga was no different from many of the other battles in which thousands of men died, in this encounter Rosecrans was blamed by his superiors for pursuing Bragg with only a small portion of his army, and he was relieved of his command. He was posted to the Department of the Missouri, where there was little fighting, and ended the war in this position.

Following the war, Rosecrans waited until 1867 before he resigned his commission. He served as the U.S. minister to Mexico (1868–69) under President Andrew Johnson, and in 1880 he was elected to a seat in the U.S. House of Representatives, where he served two terms. In 1885, the year he left Congress, he was named as register of the U.S. Treasury, and he served in that post until 1893. Shortly before his death, Rosecrans was restored to the list of brigadier generals in the United States Army. He died in Redondo Beach, California, on 11 March 1898 at the age of 77. Fort Rosecrans in California was named in his honor.

William Rosecrans's legacy is an ambiguous one. While he was known in the early part of the Civil War as a tactician, his impetuosity and severe defeat at Chickamauga ruined his military career. Perhaps it is because of this that most Civil War histories mention his name only in connection with this battle.

References: Lamers, William M., *The Edge of Glory: A Biography of General William S. Rosecrans, U.S.A.* (New York: Harcourt, Brace, 1961); Van Horne, Thomas Budd, *History of the Army of the Cumberland: Its Organization, Campaigns, and Battles, Written at the Request of Major-General George H. Thomas chiefly from his private Military Journal and official and other Documents furnished by him,* 3 vols. (Cincinnati, Ohio: R. Clarke & Co., 1875); Bickham, William Denison, *Rosecrans' Campaign with the Fourteenth Army Corps, or, the Army of the Cumberland: A Narrative of Personal Observations with Official Reports of the Battle of Stone River* (Cincinnati, Ohio: Moore, Wilstach, Keys & Co., 1863); George Bruce, "Chickamauga," in *Collins Dictionary of Wars* (Glasgow, Scotland: HarperCollins Publishers, 1995), 58.

Rupert, Prince (duke of Cumberland, earl of Holderness, "Rupert of the Rhine") (1619–1682)
English Civil War military leader

Prince Rupert was born in Prague, Bohemia (now capital of the Czech Republic), on 17 December 1619 (or 7 December 1619 [O.S.]), the son of Frederick V, king of Bohemia, and his wife Elizabeth Stuart, the daughter of James I of England; her brother Charles later became King Charles I of England. Historian Patrick Morrah explains: "This third son and fourth child, born to a queen in her husband's capital city, was given an imperial name, Rupert, after his ancestor Rupert III, the one member of the Palatine family who had worn the crown of the Holy Roman Empire. Great rejoicings followed his birth. A month later the news reached London, and King James, though he officially denied the royal title to his son-in-law, 'joyfully asked for a large beaker of wine and drank to the health of the new born prince in Bohemia and of the new king and the queen his daughter.'" Rupert served as a soldier from his 14th birthday, seeing action at the siege of Rheinberg (1633) under the tutelage of William, the Prince of Orange, and at Breda (1637). Captured at the battle of Vlotho (17 October 1638) during the invasion of Westphalia, which was part of the Thirty Years' War (1618–48), he was imprisoned in Linz, Austria, for a period of more than three years. Released for good behavior in 1641 if he promised never to fight against the Holy Roman Emperor (i.e., Austria) again, he joined his mother in the Netherlands.

In 1642, Rupert went to England, where his uncle, Charles I, was in deep trouble. Years of fighting Parliament for control of England's financial resources led to a break between the monarch and the legislature, finally becoming a civil war in 1642. Rupert offered to assist Charles, as historian John Charnock writes: "As the nephew of King Charles [I], at the commencement of that monarch's troubles, [Rupert] came over to England, together with his brother Maurice, and offered the only means of service in his power—his sword." Rupert was appointed general of the horse and given the title of baron of Kendal. Charles also directed that Rupert be allowed to act independently from Lord Lindsey, the commander in chief of the Royalist forces. Given this freedom, he led the king's army to its finest period in the early months of the war. Forces on both sides admired Rupert's boldness and dubbed him the "Mad Cavalier." He defeated the Parliamentarians at Edgehill (23 October 1642) and took the city of Bristol after a siege (15–24 July 1643). In June 1644, he was given the titles earl of Holderness and duke of Cumberland.

Rupert was not defeated until the famed battle of Marston Moor (2 July 1644), where he and 9,000 men took on Lord Thomas FAIRFAX and some 13,000 Parliamentarian troops. Historian George Bruce notes that "Prince Rupert's first charge broke the Parliamentary left wing, but as usual the pursuit was carried too far, and before the cavalry returned, [Oliver] CROMWELL on the right had turned the scale, and the battle was over. The Royalist infantry, overwhelmed by superior numbers, were almost annihilated, 5,000 prisoners and all the artillery being captured." One general wrote to the marquis of Ormonde on that battle:

> In the fire, smoke and confusion of that day, the runaways on both sides were so many, so breathless, so speechless, and so full of fears, that I should not have taken them for men; both armies being mingled, both horse and foot; no side keeping their own posts.
>
> In this horrible distraction did I coast the country; here meeting with a shoal of Scots crying out 'Weys us, we are all undone'; and so full of lamentation and mourning, as if their day of doom had overtaken, and from which they knew not whither to fly: and anon I met with a ragged troop reduced to four and a Cornet; by and by with a little foot officer without hat, band, sword, or indeed anything but feet and so much tongue as would serve to enquire the way to the next garrisons, which (to say the truth) were well filled with the stragglers on both sides within a few hours, though they lay distant from the place of the fight 20 or 30 miles.
>
> I shall now give your Excellence the short of the action. The armies faced one another upon Hessam-Moor, three miles from York, about 12 of the clock, and there continued within the play of the enemy's cannon until 5 at night; during all which time the Prince and the Marquis of NEW-CASTLE were playing the orators to the soldiers in York, (being in a raging mutiny in the town for their pay) to draw them forth to join with the Prince's foot; which was at last effected, but with much unwillingness. The enemy perceiving the advance of that addition to the Prince's army, instantly charged our horse, and mingled with

very great execution on both sides. On the left wing the enemy had the better of us, and on the right wing, where the Prince charged, we had infinitely the better of the enemy; so that in truth the battle was very doubtful, as in the number of the slain as well as the success of the day. This, my Lord, is what can be punctually said of this encounter; each side being retired with a broken wing and gone to the bone-setter.

> The horse of P. Rupert and Lord Byron were totally routed; all their cannon taken; the Marquis of Newcastle fled unto Scarborough, and some say unto France; P. Rupert's forces of foot destroyed; yet he keeps the field with 5000 horse and 2000 foot, but will shortly march to Chester. The fault is laid wholly upon the Marquis of Newcastle.

Despite this defeat, Rupert was named General of the King's Army. Although Charles trusted him implicitly, the king's counsellors did not, and some went over Charles's head to support Rupert's fellow commanders instead. This internal dissent led to shortages in troops and supplies, and finally to the disastrous battle at Naseby (14 June 1645), where Charles was defeated. Rupert was forced to surrender to Lord Fairfax at Bristol (September 1645). Charles, on the run at the time, was so angered with Rupert's surrender that he dismissed him and his younger brother Maurice from royal service.

After demanding a court-martial (at which he was acquitted), Rupert was allowed by Parliament to leave England in 1646. He returned to the European continent, where he joined French forces in fighting the new government of Oliver Cromwell. He took up command of naval forces against the English, and in what has been called the Second English Civil War, he took on three important English admirals: Robert BLAKE, Richard Deane, and Edward Popham. He lost to Blake off Kinsale, Ireland, on 30 January 1649—coincidentally, the same day that his uncle, Charles I, was put to death—forcing Rupert to flee to Portugal, where he was given the protection of the Portuguese king. Blake followed him there and waited until Rupert made a dash to escape, then cornered him at Cartagena, off the coast of Spain, where Blake annihilated the Royalist fleet (6 November 1650).

Rupert cruised the West Indies for several years, acting more as a pirate than a soldier and taking the booty of ships he captured. He returned to France in 1653 but, after arguing with the English Royalists there, left for Germany, where he spent several years. Following the restoration of Charles I's son, Charles II, to the English throne in 1660, Rupert returned to England and settled there. Charles gave him a subsidy and made him a member of his privy council. Rupert saw limited action as a naval commander during the Second (1665–67) and Third (1672–74) Anglo-Dutch Wars, rising to become First Lord of the Admiralty (1673–79). He retired from fighting in 1674, spending his final years in scientific research; he is credited with the discovery of mezzotint, and a type of gunmetal is called "Prince's metal" in his honor. He served as the first governor of the Hudson's Bay Company, and for his services, the city of Prince Rupert, British Columbia, was named in his honor following his death.

Prince Rupert died in Spring Gardens, Westminster, on 29 November 1682, three weeks before his 63rd birthday. Historian Peter Young sums up Rupert's service and impact:

An intelligent and experienced professional soldier, [Rupert] had proven an excellent General of the Horse, able to train his men as well as lead them. He had achieved remarkable successes at Powick Bridge, Cirencester, Lichfield, Chalgrove Field, Bristol, Newark and Bolton and had shown himself as adept as laying a siege, as leading a cavalry charge. . . . His defeat at Marston Moor, when he had offered battle to a superior army, in the mistaken belief that he had no alternative, had probably eroded his self-confidence, though not his matchless valour. Rupert was certainly the most versatile of the Civil War generals. Unfortunately he was of a somewhat rough and proud nature, and at the age of 25 he had not yet learned to suffer fools gladly.

References: Morrah, Patrick, *Prince Rupert of the Rhine* (London: Constable, 1976); Charnock, John, "Rupert, Prince," in *Biographia Navalis; or, Impartial Memoirs of the Lives and Characters of Officers of the Navy of Great Britain, From the Year 1660 to the Present Time . . .* , 4 vols. (London: Printed for R. Faulder, 1794–98), I:124–135; Kitson, Frank, *Prince Rupert: Admiral and General-at-Sea* (London: Constable, 1998); Thomson, George Malcolm, *Warrior Prince: Prince Rupert of the Rhine* (London: Secker & Warburg, 1976); Wilkinson, Clennell, *Prince Rupert the Cavalier* (Philadelphia: J. B. Lippincott & Company, 1935); *A Copie of the Articles Agreed Upon at the Surrender of the City of Bristol, Betweene Colonell Nathaniel Fiennes, Governour of the Said City, on the one Party, and Colonell Charles Gerrard, and Captain William Teringham, for, and on the Behalfe of, Prince Rupert, on the other Party, the 26 of July, 1643 . . .* (London: Printed for Henry Overton, 1643); Carte, Thomas, *A Collection of Original Letters and Papers, Concerning the Affairs of England, from the Year 1641 to 1660: Found Among the Duke of Ormonde's Papers*, 2 vols. (London: Printed by James Bettenham at the Expence of the Society for the Encouragement of Learning, 1739), I:56; *An Exact Relation of the Several Engagements and Actions of His Majesties Fleet, Under the Command of His Highnesse Prince Rupert . . .* (London, 1673); Young, Peter, *Naseby 1645: The Campaign and the Battle* (London: Century Publishing, 1985), 30–31; Blumberg, Arnold, "Bohemian Prince Rupert fought for the Crown against Parliament in England's Civil War," *Military Heritage* 5, no. 1 (August 2003): 12–15, 89; *A More Exact Relation of the Late Battell neer York; fought by the English and Scotch forces, against Prince Rupert and the Marquess of Newcastle . . .* (London: Printed by M. Simmons, 1644).

S

Saladin (Salah Ad-Din Yusuf Ibn Ayyub, Al-Malik An-Nasir Salah Ad-Din Yusuf I) (ca. 1137/38–1193) *Muslim king and warrior*

In full, Saladin's name was Salah Ad-Din Yusuf Ibn Ayyub ("Righteousness of the Faith, Joseph, Son of Job"), but he was also known as Al-Malik An-Nasir Salah Ad-Din Yusuf I. Born about 1137 or 1138 in Tikrit, Mesopotamia (now in modern Iraq and coincidentally the same village where the Iraqi tyrant Saddam Hussein would later be born), he was a member of a prominent and influential Kurdish family from that area. Soon after Saladin's birth, his father moved the entire family to Aleppo, now in modern Syria, and entered the service of 'Imad ad-Din Zangi ibn Aq Sonqur, the governor of northern Syria. Thus, Saladin grew up in what is now Syria, where his main studies focused on the religion of Islam. This changed when he became an aide to his uncle, Asad ad-Din Shirkuh, who served as the military commander for NUR-AD-DIN, the emir of Syria. Shirkuh commanded four military expeditions south into Egypt (1164 and 1167–69) to fight local rulers who were resisting Syria's overlordship with the help of Crusaders in the Holy Land also fearful of Syria's overlords. Shirkuh also had to deal with political matters, and he became the enemy of Amalric I, the king of Jerusalem, as well as Shawar, the caliph of Egypt. Shirkuh ordered Shawar's assassination, which was carried out after Shirkuh's own untimely death (1169). His passing gave his nephew, Saladin, the chance to become the head of Syrian forces in Egypt when he was just 31 years old. In 1171, just two years later, Saladin abolished the Fatamid caliphate in Egypt, which was of Shi'ite religious backing, and replaced it with one of Sunni Muslim control.

When Nur-ad-Din died in 1174, Saladin declared himself sultan of Egypt and Syria. Working from Egypt, he began his campaign to conquer the region that became the Middle East. He was able to bring together a small but devoted army of followers who marched into what is now Syria to take control of that land. He went on to bring together the states of Egypt, Mesopotamia, Syria, and others under a Muslim regime headed by him. Saladin saw this union as one that would extend the influence of Islam to the rest of the world, and he earned great respect from his fellow Muslims. When he could not convince the leaders of Damascus to submit to his rule, he invaded Syria and conquered that city. The following year, 1175, the Syrian leader Rashideddin tried twice to assassinate Saladin, who mustered an army to invade Syria and destroy him. However, although his army laid siege to Rashideddin's fortress at Masyaf, he suddenly withdrew permanently, a move that still puzzles historians. He nonetheless continued his military expansion by taking the city of Aleppo in northern

Syria (1183), and he took control of the Kurdish city of Mosul, now in modern Iraq in 1186.

Saladin's unification of Muslim nations encircling Jerusalem aroused fears in Europe, where his rise was seen as a threat to the Holy Land, and European religious and political leaders moved to counter and fight him. This began what is known as the Third Crusade, which led to the clash between two of the greatest generals of the age: Saladin and RICHARD I THE LION-HEARTED, also known as Richard Coeur de Lion. In 1187, Guy de Lusignan, who held Jerusalem for the Christians, led his army out to meet Saladin but was defeated, first at Tiberias (2 July 1187) and then at Hattin (4 July 1187), where his forces were destroyed by Saladin. Although Guy escaped with some of his men, he had to leave behind the bulk of his army, which was put to death *en masse* by Saladin's army. Having fled to the city of Tyre (now in Lebanon), Guy called on his fellow Christians to send more forces to the Holy Land. Three months after their victory at Hattin, Saladin's forces took the cities of Acre, Beirut, Nazareth, and Jaffa. On 2 October 1187, he occupied Jerusalem, the first time in nearly a century it was held by anyone but Christians.

It was left to Richard I and his forces to fight Saladin. A series of battles began soon after Richard's arrival at Acre on 8 June 1191. He soon took the city and ordered that all 3,000 Muslim prisoners taken at Acre be put to death. Richard then moved south to Jaffa, but Saladin blocked his route. On 7 September 1191, Richard's forces entered Arsuf, where they met Saladin's forces in one of the greatest battles of the 12th century. Saladin sent wave after wave of light infantry against Richard's forces, but the Crusaders held their ground. When the Muslims' line broke, they panicked and fled the field. Marching to Jaffa, Richard arrived at the city on 10 September 1191 and found that Saladin had ordered it destroyed. Although Richard had a clear path to retake Jerusalem, he realized he would have to hold the city from Muslim attacks, and he did not have the supplies for such control, so he withdrew to Jaffa.

Saladin launched a surprise attack on Jaffa, but again the Crusader line held. Tiring of the battle and concerned by reports of rebellion in England, Richard sought an accommodation with his enemy. On 2 September 1192, following a series of talks, Saladin and Richard signed the Peace of Ramla (1192), which left Jerusalem in the hands of the Muslims while securing Jaffa and some cities along the Mediterranean coast

for Christianity. Richard left the area on 29 September 1192, having fought the Third Crusade to a draw, and Saladin withdrew to Damascus. The following year, on 4 March 1193, Saladin died following a short illness. He was buried in a magnificent tomb in Damascus, which contains the saying, "Oh mighty God, let his soul be acceptable to thee. . . ."

References: Ehrenkreutz, Andrew S., *Saladin* (Albany: State University of New York Press, 1972); Lane-Poole, Stanley, *Saladin and the Fall of the Kingdom of Jerusalem* (New York: G. P. Putnam's Sons, 1906); Brundage, James A., *The Crusades: A Documentary Survey* (Milwaukee: Marquette University Press, 1962); Regan, Geoffrey, *Saladin and the Fall of Jerusalem* (London: Croom Helm, 1987); "Saladin," in *Command: From Alexander the Great to Zhukov—The Greatest Commanders of World History,* edited by James Lucas (London: Bloomsbury Publishing, 1988), 44–45.

Samsonov, Alexander Vasilyevich (1859–1914) *Russian general*

Born in Russia in 1859, Alexander Samsonov joined the Russian army at the age of 18 and served honorably during the Russo-Turkish War (1877–78). Following the end of that conflict, he went to the Nikolaevsky Military Academy in St. Petersburg, where he specialized in cavalry tactics. After serving on the general staff, he was posted to command the cavalry school. Returning to active service in the Russian army, he saw action in China during the Boxer Rebellion (1900), was promoted to general in 1902, and served in the Russo-Japanese War (1904–05). In 1909, he commanded the forces in Turkestan.

Samsonov's big moment came when the First World War began. Following the assassination of Archduke Franz Ferdinand in Sarajevo, Bosnia, on 28 June 1914, all of the powers of Europe implemented their numerous alliances and moved toward all-out conflict on the European continent. Believing Serbia had backed the assassination, Austria made demands that Serbia could not accept. Russia, fearful of Austrian expansion, supported Serbia, while Germany, eager for war, allied itself to Austria. This brought in France, which had signed a defense treaty with Russia. Britain was dragged in because it had guaranteed the independence of Belgium back in 1839; when Germany advanced through Belgium, Britain also went to war.

As the various forces mobilized, Samsonov was named as one of the commanders of the antiquated and ill-equipped Russian army. The war quickly broke down to two fronts: the western front, in eastern France, where the Allies of Britain and France quickly became bogged down against the Germans; and the eastern front, where Russia fought a series of bloody battles with Germany. In an attempt to force more German troops to the eastern front to relieve the Allied forces on the western front, Samsonov pushed his army into eastern Prussia. There, his unprepared forces were confronted by the far superior German forces led by Paul von HINDENBURG at Tannenberg (24–31 August 1914), about 110 miles northwest of present-day Warsaw. Historian George Bruce writes of this battle:

> The Russians invaded East Prussia in August 1914 at the request of the French, and drove the Germans from Gumbinnen and Insterburg, in the north. General Heinrich von Prittwitz was superceded by General Hindenburg. Meantime, a gap had grown between General [Paul] REN-NENKAMPF's 1st Russian Army in the north and General Samsonov's in the south. The Germans moved their force southwest by rail to exploit this by attacking General Samsonov's force, whose exact dispositions they had learned through uncoded radio messages. General [Hermann] von François encircled the Russian left on August 28, [Karl] von Bülow defeated the open flank at Allenstein and [August] von Mackensen attacked Samsonov's VI Corps. The sole escape for the Russians was through a narrow strip of land between the marshes leading to Ortelsburg and here they were decimated. Some 30,000 were killed or wounded, over 90,000 prisoners taken.

Faced with this horrific disaster in his first major field command, Samsonov took his own life as his army retreated, shooting himself in the head on 29 August.

Samsonov's massive inexperience—until World War I, he had served mainly as a bureaucrat, never holding a command appointment before Tannenberg—and his nation's failure to prepare for war led to the debacle at Tannenberg, and he can be only partially blamed for the defeat. The rout gave the Germans the ability to quickly defeat the Russian forces commanded by Rennenkampf at Masurian Lakes (9–14 September 1914), leaving the eastern front dominated by the Germans and allowing them to increase their effort on the western front.

References: Solzhenitsyn, Alexander, *August 1914* (New York: Farrar, Straus, and Giroux, 1972); Bruce, George, "Tannenberg," in *Collins Dictionary of Wars* (Glasgow, Scotland: HarperCollins Publishers, 1995), 243; Bongard, David L., "Samsonov, Aleksandr Vasilievich," in *The Encyclopedia of Military Biography,* edited by Trevor N. Dupuy, Curt Johnson, and David L. Bongard (London: I. B. Taurus, 1992), 655–656.

Santa Anna, Antonio López de (1794–1876)
Mexican general and president

Antonio López de Santa Anna was born in Jalapa, in Veracruz (also known as Vera Cruz), Mexico, on 21 February 1794, the son of a minor civil service official. Spain then controlled Mexico (until 1822), and Santa Anna began his military career as a cadet in the Spanish colonial army starting in 1810, when he was just 16. He spent much of the next several years on the northern border, fighting Indians and so-called "border ruffians" who invaded Mexico for thievery. In 1813, following the Battle of Medina (in what is now the U.S. state of Texas), he was cited for bravery in battle.

In 1821, Santa Anna rose to a leadership position when he supported the "Plan de Iguala," which set out a course for Mexican independence. He was also a supporter of the Mexican politician Agustín de Iturbide, one of the leaders of the independence movement. When Mexico became independent of Spain in May 1822, however, Iturbide declared himself emperor, and Santa Anna soon turned against him and announced his "Plan of Casa Mata," which called for a Mexican republic. He served for a short period as the military governor of Yucatán, then as the civil governor of Veracruz, his home province. In 1823, after just two years in power, Iturbide was forcibly removed as emperor of Mexico by an insurrection that Santa Anna had assisted. As a leading military officer, Santa Anna tried to install a pro-Mexican government in Cuba, then controlled by Spain, by launching an ill-fated revolution from the Yucatan peninsula. In 1828, he backed Vincente Guerrero as president of Mexico but within a year tired of him and once again forced a change in administrations. That same year, 1829, a Spanish army invaded Mexico, and Santa Anna was placed in charge of blocking the incur-

Antonio López de Santa Anna

sion. He marched his army to Tampico, where he defeated the Spanish, earning him the appellation "Victor of Tampico" and making him a hero in Mexico.

Although he retired from the army soon after Tampico, in 1833 Santa Anna reemerged to run for the presidency. His program was based on liberal principles and opposition to the power of the Catholic Church, and he was elected on 1 April. A year into his administration, however, he renounced his principles and advocated a centralization of power in Mexico City, the capital. He clashed with his liberal vice president, Valentin Gomez Farias, over the direction of the government. When the liberals of the Zacatecas province denied his authority to centralize the government in 1833, Santa Anna marched on the rebels, crushing them with exacting brutality and instituting a campaign of repression unseen even under Spanish rule. This backfired on him and led to a chaotic period in Mexican history that saw 36 different administrations in 20 years, with Santa Anna playing a leading part in 11 of them. He was forced out of the presidency in 1834, but a year later he led his own rebellion when reforms proposed by the president were approved by the Church.

Santa Anna's biggest problem, however, was not internal but external. For a number of years, the Mexican government had encouraged American settlers to move into the area now known as the U.S. state of Texas. By 1835, their numbers had grown so much that Mexico sought to end its liberal immigration policy, but the Americans in Texas resisted the move, and on 3 November 1835 they declared themselves an independent nation. Considering the settlers and their leaders to be traitors, Santa Anna marched an army of some 6,000 men north to fight. He met his first real resistance on 6 March 1836 at an old mission known as the Alamo in what is now the city of San Antonio. There he found a small band of approximately 200 American fighters, led by William Travis, Davy Crockett, and Jim Bowie, who refused to surrender to the vastly superior Mexican force. Instead of bypassing the small, militarily insignificant mission, Santa Anna decided to attack it. Although the Americans put up a brave fight, they were quickly overwhelmed and killed, although Santa Anna ordered that women and children found inside were not to be harmed.

This was a tactical victory for the Mexicans, but also a strategic mistake as it stirred the Texans to rise up to avenge the slaughter. With shouts of "Remember the Alamo," a Texan army led by Sam Houston marched quickly on Santa Anna's force, which had crossed the Brazos River to capture the Texas government in the city of Harrisburg.

Realizing he was being pursued by the Americans, Santa Anna turned back and met the Houston force at San Jacinto on the San Jacinto River (21 April 1836). The Americans destroyed a bridge which the Mexicans could have used to escape; Texan troops then attacked the Mexican front line, killing some 700 Mexican soldiers and forcing another 700 to surrender in just a half hour. A monument at the site of the battle reads: "Measured by its results, San Jacinto was one of the decisive battles of the world. The freedom of Texas from Mexico won here led to annexation and to the Mexican War, resulting in the acquisition by the United States of the States of Texas, New Mexico, Arizona, Nevada, California, Utah, and parts of Colorado, Wyoming, Kansas and Oklahoma. Almost one-third of the present area of the American nation, nearly a million square miles of territory, changed sovereignty."

Santa Anna was captured by the Americans and taken back to Washington, D.C., where he could have stood trial. Instead, in exchange for his release he signed a treaty recognizing Texas's independence. However, upon his return to Mexico, the government there rejected the treaty. Humiliated at home and abroad, Santa Anna retired to his home at Manga de Clavo. Two years later, he returned to public service again when the French began what historians call the "Pastry War" (1838), demanding compensation for their property destroyed during Mexico's fight for independence in 1822. When Mexico refused, the French blockaded the harbor at Veracruz and then attacked the Mexican emplacements there. President Anastasio Bustamante called Santa Anna back to command the military against the invading French forces. Santa Anna was able to force a French retreat, but a cannonball struck him in the leg, which had to be amputated.

Santa Anna again retired to his estate, but in 1839 a rebellion rose up against President Bustamante, who called on Santa Anna to crush the rebellion; this was done in May 1839. Two years later, he became embroiled in a disagreement with the government and helped to engineer Bustamante's downfall. On 10 October 1841, Santa Anna took control of the government as president. Serving for a period of three years, he ruled as a military dictator, raising taxes on the wealthy and the Church. During this period, Mexico's economy rapidly deteriorated, and with it went Santa Anna's popularity. On 2 December 1844, the Mexican Congress passed a no-confidence vote, ending his presidency. He was allowed to keep the extensive properties he had accumulated and part of his general's salary if he relinquished all future claims to the presidency and leave the country for exile in Venezuela. He accepted this deal but instead left for Cuba, where he remained a close observer of Mexican affairs. He watched as several men tried to manage the economy, with poor results. Meanwhile, in 1845, outgoing U.S. president John Tyler signed a congressional resolution annexing Texas and making it a part of the Union. Mexico, which still believed Texas to be Mexican territory, protested and made it clear they would fight. Incoming president James K. Polk therefore sent an army commanded by General Zachary TAYLOR to the border. At the same time, he sent an emissary to offer $40 million in exchange for Mexico dropping its claims on Texas.

On 29 December 1845, Texas was formally admitted to the American union. In March 1846, the force led by Taylor secured its base along the Rio Grande River, the natural border between Texas and Mexico. Mexico sent a force of some 1,600 troops to the Rio Grande and attacked American outposts on 24 April. The following month, the United States declared a state of war with Mexico. Santa Anna, still in Cuba, contacted the Polk administration and offered to end the crisis if the United States helped him return to Mexico. Polk agreed, and with American assistance Santa Anna sailed to Veracruz. However, as soon as he landed on 16 August 1846, he proclaimed himself the head of the Mexican army and offered to go to the border to fight the Americans.

This betrayal was to be Santa Anna's downfall. As soon as it became known that he would command the Mexicans, the Americans sent an invasion force to land at Veracruz. To head off Taylor's invasion of northern Mexico, Santa Anna raised a force of some 20,000 soldiers and marched to fight the American general. The two armies met at Buena Vista on 22–23 February 1847. Although the Mexicans held their own, by the second day Taylor's superior army overwhelmed them, and Santa Anna was forced to fall back toward Mexico City. Moving south, he encountered the American army led by Winfield SCOTT—which had landed at Veracruz—at Cerro Gordo (17–18 April 1847). The Mexican forces, tired from the battle against Taylor at Buena Vista and the march south, were no match for the fresh American army. Attacked on three sides, Santa Anna's army collapsed: 1,130 Mexicans were killed, with only 63 Americans dying in the battle, and Santa Anna was forced to flee. He tried to defend Mexico City but did not have the forces to do it, and the city fell on 14 September 1847, ending the war. On 2 February 1848, the Treaty of Guadalupe Hidalgo was signed, giving the United States control not only over Texas but areas spanning what is now the entire American southwest, including New Mexico, Arizona, Nevada, Utah, and California. In exchange, Mexico was paid $15 million.

Santa Anna was forced into exile a second time. For a number of years he desired to return, working with the French and even his old enemy the United States to try to make a comeback. He purchased a boat and attempted an "invasion," but Mexican authorities arrested him and exiled him again. He moved around the Caribbean, settling in Cuba and the Dominican Republic. Finally, the Mexican economy once again called him home, and in March 1853 the Conservatives asked him to take the reins of the country. On 20 April 1853, he was sworn in as president for the fifth time. However, he was only allowed to serve for a single year, with the Conservative politician Lucas Alamán serving as Secretary of State. Initially, Santa Anna carried out the Conservatives' agenda, lowering taxes and pushing for a centralized government. However, the whole program collapsed on 2 June 1852 when Alamán died, leaving Santa Anna in complete control of the government. He named several cronies to important positions and, on 16 December 1853, officially named himself as dictator, to serve in perpetuity. The economy was still in bad condition, and to help defray growing expenses he sold off the Mesilla Valley in northern Mexico to the United States, known as the Gadsden Purchase. This set off a wave of opposition by liberals, and on 1 March 1854, the "Plan of Ayutla" was unveiled, calling for an end to the Santa Anna regime and the adoption of a liberal constitution. Santa Anna gathered another army to march on the liberals at Acapulco. Along the way, his men attacked villages sympathetic with the rebellion and slaughtered civilians, but when they tried to attack the liberal positions, they were repulsed. Forced to return to Mexico City in disgrace, Santa Anna realized that his regime was finished. On 9 August 1855, he and his family sailed into exile for the third time. He spent much of the remainder of his life trying to return. At last, penniless and blind with his health slowly deteriorating, he was allowed to return home in 1874. He died in Mexico City on 21 June 1876 at the age of 82 and was buried near Guadalupe Hidalgo.

Antonio López de Santa Anna is remembered by many for his attack on the Alamo. In Mexico, however, he is remembered for his ruthless crackdowns on dissent and his numerous administrations that gave corruption a home in the Mexican government.

References: Callcott, Wilfred Hardy, *Santa Anna* (Hamden, Conn.: Archon Books, 1964); Jones, Oakah L., *Santa Anna* (New York: Twayne Publishers, 1968); Olivera, Ruth R., *Life in Mexico under Santa Anna, 1822–1855* (Norman: University of Oklahoma Press, 1991); Johnson, Richard A., *The Mexican Revolution of Ayutla, 1854–55: An Analysis of the Evolution and Destruction of Santa Anna's Last Dictatorship* (Rock Island, Ill.: Augustana College Library, 1939).

Sargon II (Sharru-kin) (ca. 763–705 B.C.)
Assyrian king

Sargon II was born around 763 B.C., although his place of birth is unknown. Historians believe (though are not certain) that his father was the Assyrian king Tiglathpilesar III. Another name by which he was known is Sharru-

kin, meaning "the throne is legitimate." The name *Sargon* first appeared in the Bible, in Isaiah 20:1, which states: "In the year that Tartan came unto Ashdod (when Sargon the king of Assyria sent him), and fought against Ashdod, and took it. . . ." It is probable that Sargon took his name from Sargon of Akkad (ca. 2334–2279 B.C.), leader of a Mesopotamian dynasty, although its true origins are now lost to history. If he was a true son of Tiglathpilesar III, then his brother, Shalmaneser IV, served as king of Assyria prior to him, but Shalmaneser either died or was removed from office and replaced by Sargon in 722 B.C. At once, Sargon was forced to deal with Marduk-apla-Iddin (known in the Bible as Merodach-Balaban), a chief in Chaldea whose allies he sought to win over by granting the towns of Assur and Haran exemption from taxation. There were instances of unrest in Armenia and Syria, lands that had been conquered by Tiglathpilesar III, but Sargon's first major task was to begin construction of his royal palace at Dur-Sharrukin (now modern Khorsobad, Iran), a project that would continue to the end of his reign.

In 721 B.C., Marduk-apla-Iddin, in open defiance of Sargon, marched his troops into Babylon (now in modern Iraq) and made a pact with the Elamite king Ummanigash to become king of Babylon. Sargon turned first on Ummanigash, who defeated him at Der in 720 B.C. The *Babylonian Chronicle* notes: "The second year of Merodach-Balaban: Humban-Nikash, king of Elam, did battle against Sargon, king of Assyria, in the district of Der, effected an Assyrian retreat, [and] inflicted a major defeat on them. Merodach-Balaban and his army, who had gone to the aid of the king of Elam, did not reach the battle [so] he withdrew." Later that same year, Sargon took on a coalition from the cities of Hamath, Damascus, and other Syrian towns at Karkara (now Tell Qarqar, in modern Syria), and defeated them, annexing Hamath and Damascus. Consolidating his power in the region, he attacked the numerous towns and villages who opposed him, taking on first Ekron and Gaza, now in modern Israel (720 B.C.). He forced King Ahaz of Judah to pay a tribute for his area's freedom, then moved north to lay siege to the city of Tyre (now in modern Lebanon), finally forcing that city to capitulate. He moved south, taking Carchemish, on the Euphrates (717 B.C.), and defeating the Egyptians at Raphia (today's Gaza) in 716 B.C.

In 714 B.C., Sargon invaded Urartu, now modern eastern Turkey. For several years, the Urartans had been fomenting rebellion among numerous towns under Sargon's control, and he decided to end this uprising. His army attacked the Urartan army in a mountain pass, and a source later wrote that Urartan "blood run [sic] down the ravines like a river." Unstoppable, Sargon's army neared the Urartan capital of Tushpa, forcing the Urartan king, Rusas I (also known as Ursa I), to flee. The Assyrian troops looted Urartu, which allegedly contained some 334,000 precious objects, including more than 1 ton of gold. Accounts of this period of warfare history come from Sargon himself, who penned a lengthy "letter" about his military expeditions—in fact, a clay tablet later found by archaeologists in the town of Assur and now in the Louvre in France—to the god Ashur. It is known as the "8th campaign" of Sargon, and in it Sargon claims that he lost only six troops in the entire Urartan campaign.

Sargon's forces moved back to the west, conquering the city of Ashdod (now in modern Israel) and annexing the city of Philistia. It was during this period (ca. 710 B.C.) that Sargon moved against his old enemy Marduk-apla-Iddin, besieging Babylon and forcing the leader to flee and go into exile in Elam. Babylon capitulated to Sargon, and he was proclaimed as its king in 710 B.C. For the next five years he held the emperorships of Assyria and Babylon.

Sargon's final campaign was against the Cimmerians, a nomadic tribe from Russia who were rampaging westward. Historians believe that Sargon was killed during the Cimmerian invasion of Assyria (705 B.C.), although this cannot be verified. A written chronicle from the period states that "the king was killed [and] the camp of the king of Assyria [was defeated]." Sargon's son, Sin-ahhe-eriba (also known as Sennacherib), became the leader of Assyria in 704 B.C.

Historian James Orr writes of Sargon: "Ancient writers knew nothing of him. He was a mystery: some did not hesitate to deny that he ever existed." Nonetheless, evidence of his existence does survive, including his letter to Ashur and a stele (descriptive column) found at Ashdod, Israel, and now in an Israeli museum dedicated at some early period to Sargon's defeat of Ashdod.

References: Lie, A. G., *The Inscriptions of Sargon II of Assyria* (Paris, France: Librarie Orientaliste P. Guenther, 1929); Luckenbill, Daniel David, *Ancient Records of Assyria and Babylonia,* 2 vols. (New York: Greenwood Press, 1968); Olmstead, Albert Ten Eyck, *History of Assyria* (New York: Charles Scribner's Sons, 1923); Orr, James, *The Problem of the Old Testament Considered with Reference to Recent Criticism* (New York: Charles Scribner's Sons, 1906), 399.

Saxe, Hermann Maurice, comte de (Maurice de Saxe, Mauritz de Saxe, Moritz-Hermann de Saxe) (1696–1750) *German-born military commander*

Maurice de Saxe was born in Goslar, Saxony (now in Germany), on 28 October 1696, the illegitimate son of the elector Frederick Augustus I of Saxony (later King Augustus II of Poland) and his mistress Maria Aurora von Königsmark. Saxe biographer Jon Manchip White writes:

> The birth of Maurice de Saxe occurred in circumstances wholly cut out of key with the brilliant role which he was to play in later life. The illegitimate son of a great German prince and a high-born Swedish adventuress, the prodigy, who was to become one of the outstanding generals of his age, was brought into the world in secrecy, shame, and anguish. . . . In the autumn of 1696 the Lutheran pastor of the city of Goslar, an obscure town in northern Germany, recorded in his parish register that: "Today, October 28, a male child was born to a noble and high-born lady in the house of Heinrich Christoph Winkel, and was christened Mauritz." The boy appears to have been given the dual Christian name of Moritz-Hermann, and it was under the appropriately bastard style of "Arminius-Maurice de Saxe" that his name was to be entered forty-seven years later in the proud roll of the Marshals of France.

About 1709, when Saxe was 13, his father sent him to Flanders, Belgium, to serve in the army under Prince EUGÈNE of Savoy against the French. There he saw action in several battles, including at Malplaquet (11 September 1709). In 1711, after two years of military service, Saxe was given the title of graf von Sachsen (count of Saxony; comte de Saxe in French) by his father, whom he subsequently joined in a war in Pomerania, taking part in the siege of Stralsund (1712). Five years later, his father purchased an entire regiment of German mercenary troops and gave its command to Saxe, who introduced new methods of training, including the use of muskets. In 1719, he went to Paris to study mathematics, and the following year he was granted a commission in the French army.

While Saxe was in Courland, a Baltic province (now in both Poland and Russia), he became good friends with Anna Ivanovna, the dowager duchess of the state and later Empress Anna of Russia. They allegedly became romantically involved, and a marriage was considered, but in 1727 Saxe was expelled by Russian authorities who considered the union unsuitable. He then returned to France, where he wrote a work on military science, *Mes Rêveries* (My daydreams), which was finished in 1732 but not published until 1756 and 1757 in two volumes.

The death of Saxe's father, King Augustus II of Poland, on 1 February 1733 set off a race to succeed him among a number of candidates. These included the former King Stanislaus I, who had originally been installed to power by CHARLES XII of Sweden but had been removed from the throne in 1709; and Frederick Augustus II, the elector of Saxony, who was the son of the late Polish king and Saxe's half brother. Stanislaus was supported by his father-in-law, Louis XV of France, while Russia and Austria backed Frederick Augustus. When Stanislaus took power again as king, a conflict broke out, known as the War of the Polish Succession (1733–35), in which Russia invaded Poland, captured the city of Warsaw, and installed Frederick Augustus as Augustus III. Saxe sided with the French, serving under General James FitzJames, duke of BERWICK, and seeing action at Philipsbourg (12 June 1734) near the city of Württemberg, now in Germany. During this battle, Berwick was struck by a cannonball and killed; Saxe then took command and led the French forces to victory. He was rewarded by the French general Marshal Adrien Maurice, comte de Noailles, with the rank of lieutenant general.

The War of the Austrian Succession (1740–48) soon followed. This conflict was caused by the succession of Maria Theresa of Austria to the throne left vacant by the death in 1740 of her father, Charles VI, the Holy Roman Emperor. Saxe was given the command of a division of French forces sent to invade Austria, and he led them in the siege and subsequent capture of Prague (now in the Czech Republic) on 19 November 1741. He also led the taking of the castle at Eger on 19 April 1742.

For these services, Saxe was made a marshal of France on 26 March 1743.

In January 1744, the French king Louis XV made Saxe commander of an army to be sent to England to support Charles Edward Stuart, known to history as the "Young Pretender," in his fight to win the English throne from George II. A naval armada was formed at Dunkirk in France but was destroyed by a storm in March 1744, before it could sail. Louis XV declared war on England and also began a conflict on the European continent, invading the Austrian Netherlands. Saxe was given complete control over the French forces, and once again he used his military skill to besiege Tournai, but when a combined Anglo-Dutch-Hanoverian army under William Augustus, duke of Cumberland, advanced to relieve the siege, Saxe's forces defeated them at Fontenoy (11 May 1745). Historian George Bruce writes: "[The battle] was between 50,000 British, Dutch and Austrian troops, under the Duke of Cumberland, and 70,000 French under Marshal Saxe. The Duke endeavored to relieve Tournai, which the French were besieging, and the British troops captured the heights on which the French were posted. The Prince of Waldeck, however, who commanded the Dutch, failed to support the Duke, and the French being reinforced, the trenches were retaken, and the Allies beaten back, losing 6,500 men. Tournai fell shortly afterwards."

Following Saxe's victory at Fontenoy, Louis XV gave him the royal chateau at Chambord, in Loir-et-Cher, for his life, and in April 1746 Saxe was made a French citizen. He continued to fight in the Netherlands, seeing action at Rocourt, near Liège (1746) and Lawfeldt, also known as Val (1747). On 10 January 1747, he was given the title of Marshal-General of France, a title previously held only by Henri de la Tour d'Averne, Vicomte Turenne and Claude-Louis-Hector Villars. He finished by capturing the city of Maastricht (May 1748), ending the war and forcing a peace, although the last battle he participated in was Lauffield (2 July 1747). Following the Peace of Aix-la-Chapelle, which officially ended the War of the Austrian Succession, Saxe retired to Chambord, where he died of natural causes on 30 November 1750. However, rumors for many years held that he was killed in a duel with Louis François de Bourbon, prince de Conti. Although married, Saxe, like his father, had a number of mistresses, including the French stage actress Adrienne Lecouvreur. His great-granddaughter was the

French novelist Amandine Aurore Lucie Dupin, whose *nom de plume* was George Sand.

The record of Maurice, comte de Saxe, is one of notable military success. Rising from small beginnings, he became one of France's most important military leaders, serving his adopted country through two major European wars. His skill in maneuvering and tactics led to victory in many battles, and his two-volume work on military strategy, published posthumously, was studied for a century after his death.

References: White, Jon Manchip, *Marshal of France: The Life and Times of Maurice, Comte de Saxe [1696–1750]* (London: Hamish Hamilton, 1962); "Saxe: 'My Reveries Upon the Art of War,'" in *Roots of Strategy: A Collection of Military Classics,* edited by Thomas R. Phillips (London: John Lane the Bodley Head, 1943); Bruce, George, "Fontenoy," in *Collins Dictionary of Wars* (Glasgow, Scotland: HarperCollins Publishers, 1995), 90.

Scheer, Reinhard (Arthur Scheer) (1863–1928)
German admiral

Born as Arthur Scheer in the village of Oberkirchen, Hanover (Germany), on 30 September 1863, Reinhard Scheer was a minister's son who began his service in the German navy in 1879 as a cadet. Over the next 20 years, he rose in rank, being promoted to oberleutnant zur see (lieutenant) in 1885 and kapitänleutnant (lieutenant) in 1893. He served in Cameroon, East Africa, and became commander of the 1st Torpedo Division in 1903. In 1910, he was raised to konteradmiral (rear admiral, two-star) and named as chief of staff of the German High Seas Fleet under Admiral Henning von Holtzendorff. Three years later, he became commander of a battle squadron with the rank of vice admiral.

During his naval career, Scheer continually advocated the use of submarines as a strategic weapon, and when the First World War began, he recommended that they hunt and sink Allied ships off the coast of England. On 24 January 1916, nearly a year and a half into the war, Scheer was named as commander of the German High Seas Fleet. Almost immediately, he was involved in a historic sea engagement: the Battle of Jutland (31 May–1 June 1916), the only major conflict between fleets in the First World War. As historians Anthony Bruce and William Cogar explain:

It originated in a plan developed by Admiral Reinhard Scheer, commander of the High Seas Fleet since January 1916, to lure the British Grand Fleet from its base in order to bring it to battle. Early in 31 May 1916 the High Seas Fleet left the Jade Estuary and moved into the North Sea parallel to the west coast of Denmark. Admiral Franz von Hipper, commander of the German scouting forces, led the way toward the Skaggerak with five battle cruisers and 35 other fast ships at his disposal. The main German fleet, consisting of 59 vessels, including 22 battleships (of which 16 were dreadnoughts), was a long way behind. Radio messages intercepted by the British Admiralty had warned of the German sortie, and the Grand Fleet was ordered to sail immediately. The main British fleet, under Admiral John JELLICOE, left its base at Scapa Flow in the Orkney Islands on 30 May. It comprised 99 ships, of which 24 were dreadnoughts. Sixty miles (96 km) ahead of Jellicoe was Admiral David BEATTY's scouting force, which had left the Firth of Forth on the same day. It consisted of 52 ships, including six battle cruisers and an associated squadron of four super-dreadnoughts.

Historian George Bruce writes: "Beatty and Hipper sighted each other, and Hipper turned to link up with Scheer, after which the two groups shelled each other. Beatty then turned back to lure the Germans into Jellicoe's hands and in the process lost two of his battleships, but the manoeuvre accomplished, the entire British fleet soon formed a line east and southeast into which the Germans were sailing into a net. Just when their destruction seemed certain, the weather closed down and rescued the Germans, who later, under the cover of darkness, skillfully made their escape. The Royal Navy lost three battle cruisers, three light cruisers and eight destroyers; Germany [lost] four cruisers and five destroyers, but the morale of the German navy had been destroyed."

Scheer was credited with the maneuver that led to the Germans being saved by their escape, raised to the rank of full admiral, and awarded the Order of Pour le Mérite for his service. Nonetheless, Jutland was a critical defeat for the Germans, whose High Seas Fleet never ventured out again, as Jellicoe said. Whereas previously they had been able to dispute control of the seas in the northern Atlantic and harass civilian ships, after Jutland the German navy was rendered almost impotent. Mutinies broke out among sailors who refused to serve on any further missions, and the navy reached its nadir. The British Navy, also criticized for not following up on their "victory" at Jutland, went on to blockade Germany, denying it necessary food and supplies. For the remainder of the war, Scheer's strategies could not be implemented. Instead, he was given the unenviable task of punishing mutineering sailors, sentencing many to serve lengthy prison sentences.

On 8 August 1918, Scheer succeeded Admiral Henning von Holtzendorff as chief of the German Admiralty Staff, but he only served in this position for five months until he retired in January 1919. He never held a military post again. All too overlooked, however, is his successful submarine strategy, which caused the Allies many problems until the end of the war.

In his final years, Scheer penned his master work, *Deutschlands Hochseeflotte im Weltkrieg* (*Germany's High Sea Fleet in the World War,* published in Germany in 1919 and in England and the United States in 1920), a critical examination of the German side of the Battle of the Jutland. He died in Marktredwitz, Germany, on 26 November 1928 and was buried in Weimar.

References: Scheer, Reinhard, *Germany's High Sea Fleet in the World War* (London: Cassell & Company, Ltd., 1920); Rasor, Eugene L., *The Battle of Jutland: A Bibliography* (New York: Greenwood Press, 1992); Tarrant, V. E., *Jutland: The German Perspective: A New View of the Great Battle, 31 May 1916* (London: Arms and Armour, 1995); Bruce, Anthony, and William Cogar, "Jutland, Battle of," in *An Encyclopedia of Naval History* (New York: Checkmark Books, 1999), 204–205; Bruce, George, "Jutland," in *Collins Dictionary of Wars* (Glasgow, Scotland: HarperCollins Publishers, 1995), 120–121.

Schwarzkopf, H. Norman (Herbert Norman Schwarzkopf, Jr.) (1934–   ) *American general*

Norman Schwarzkopf was born in Trenton, New Jersey, on 22 August 1934, the son and namesake of Herbert Norman Schwarzkopf, Sr. His father was a career military officer who served as the head of the New Jersey State Police (when he was in charge of the criminal investigation into the kidnapping of the child of famed aviator Charles A. Lindbergh), in the Office of Strate-

gic Services (OSS) during World War II, and in Iran in the 1950s. The younger Schwarzkopf, whose mother was a nurse, did not wish to use his father's name and was known simply as H. Norman. He attended local schools, but from the age of 12 he traveled with his father overseas, not returning to the United States until 1951. The following year, he gained an appointment to the United States Military Academy at West Point, New York, graduating in 1956, 43rd out of a class of 480. Commissioned as a second lieutenant in the U.S. Army that same year, Schwarzkopf was stationed initially at Fort Benning, Georgia, and thereafter at Fort Campbell, Kentucky. In 1963, he enrolled in the University of Southern California at Los Angeles, where he earned a Master's degree in mechanical and aerospace engineering in 1964. He was then assigned to West Point to serve for three years as a professor in the academy's Department of Engineering Mechanics.

In 1965, after only two years, Schwarzkopf asked to be sent to Vietnam, where a communist insurrection had led to a destabilization of the pro-Western government in the southern section of that Asian country. Schwarzkopf was promoted to major during his tour of duty there (1965–66) and later wrote, "We fought almost every day of every month for thirteen months." When he returned to the United States in 1966, he was sent back to West Point to finish his tour there. In 1968, he was promoted to the rank of lieutenant colonel and posted to the Command and General Staff College. In December 1969, he was sent back to Vietnam for a second tour, this time in command of the 1st Battalion, 198th Infantry Brigade. During his two tours in Vietnam, Schwarzkopf won three Silver Stars for bravery, the final one for crossing a minefield to rescue a wounded American soldier. He later wrote in his memoirs of his pride in having served on the front lines rather than in the rear with other officers: "I hated it in the rear. It was a cesspool. I went out to my battalion and I never went back to the rear except when ordered, maybe one time, to division headquarters. There you saw the worst: the commander was living in luxury, his focus was on things like the reenlistment rate. When I took over my battalion, it was totally unprepared for battle, yet it had been in battle. All they were doing was taking casualties, [not] inflicting them. It was a nightmare."

In addition to his Silver Stars, Schwarzkopf was decorated with three Bronze Stars, two Purple Hearts, and the Legion of Merit, among other medals. But he also came home from his tours in Vietnam with the feeling that the American government was not serious about winning the war in Vietnam, and that the U.S. news media—particularly television—were portraying the American soldiers in Vietnam not as heroes but as brutes who were committing war crimes on a daily basis. These feelings led Schwarzkopf to later handle his command of the Persian Gulf War in a very different way to ensure more favorable news coverage.

Following his return from Vietnam in 1970, Schwarzkopf was given a series of postings, starting with command of the 172nd Light Infantry Brigade at Fort Greeley, Arkansas. Eventually he became assistant division commander of the 8th Infantry Mechanized Division in Germany, part of the U.S. Army in Europe

General H. Norman Schwarzkopf

(USAEUR). In 1983, he was sent to Fort Stewart, Georgia, where he was given command of the 24th Infantry Mechanized Division with the rank of major general.

In October 1983, a revolution on the small Caribbean island nation of Grenada had culminated with the overthrow of the Marxist and pro-Cuban government of Maurice Bishop; the new government was even more radical. President Ronald Reagan dispatched American forces to the island to save several hundred American medical students studying on the island; at the same time, Reagan wanted to end the Cuban-inspired revolution on the island. Schwarzkopf served as the deputy commander of the American invasion of Grenada, which ended with the termination of the pro-Cuban regime and the installation of a pro-American democracy. In 1988, he was named to the chairmanship of the U.S. Central Command (USCENTCOM), a strategic planning headquarters in Florida. Two years later, he became a worldwide celebrity.

On 2 August 1990, Iraqi troops invaded the Middle Eastern country of Kuwait, crushing its small army. The Iraqi forces threatened the main Saudi Arabian oil fields to the south, a major oil supply source for the Western world. President George H. W. Bush, in the second year of his presidency, was faced with a serious public threat, and he immediately swung into action, securing a coalition of nations that demanded Iraq withdraw immediately from Kuwait. Iraqi president Saddam Hussein, a dictator known for funding terrorism in the Middle East, refused, claiming that Kuwait was a "lost" part of Iraq and declaring the invasion legal. Bush called upon Schwarzkopf, as head of USCENTCOM, to plan the deployment of American and other forces and then a campaign strategy to eject Iraqi forces from Kuwait. Operation Desert Shield, as it was called, had two goals: to plan up for an invasion of Kuwait if Iraq did not withdraw, and to "shield" the Saudi oil fields if the Iraqis intended to take those as well. Numerous war strategists believed that Schwarzkopf would employ a direct hit on the Iraqi troops from Saudi Arabia in the south. This appeared to be confirmed when the coalition nations assembled an army of some 750,000 American, British, European, and Arab troops in Saudi Arabia in a period of only four months. Further strategy appeared to include an invasion of Kuwait from the Persian Gulf to the east.

On 16 January 1991, after months of warnings that an attack was imminent, President Bush authorized the start of Operation Desert Storm, a period of attacks from aircraft and missiles on hundreds of Iraqi targets inside Kuwait and Iraq. This operation lasted for six full weeks with the intention of forcing the Iraqis to withdraw. When they did not, Schwarzkopf's plan to invade Kuwait was put into motion on 24 February 1991. Using a "left hook," he brilliantly avoided the main Iraqi forces in southern Kuwait and a difficult sea landing by sending the coalition forces into northern Saudi Arabia before crossing into southwestern Kuwait. The six-week bombing campaign had done its job, however: As the coalition forces attacked on land, the Iraqi army broke and made a mad dash back into Iraq, pursued by coalition forces along the way, with massive Iraqi casualties.

Operation Desert Storm's land invasion campaign lasted just 100 hours before President Bush ended it on 29 February 1991. The coalition forces had stormed into Kuwait and cut the enemy forces into ribbons, resulting in perhaps 100,000 Iraqis killed but with only minimal coalition casualties. Kuwait City, capital of the defeated nation, had fallen quickly to American troops. Schwarzkopf was hailed for his leadership of the war planning and operation. Throughout the war, he had held numerous press conferences, announcing successive coalition victories. His demeanor during these sessions led to his being nicknamed "Stormin' Norman." However, he sustained some condemnation after the war when Iraqis rose up against the regime of Saddam Hussein, who brutally suppressed the insurrection. For political reasons, Schwarzkopf did not help the rebels, for which both he and Bush were criticized.

General H. Norman Schwarzkopf stepped down as the head of USCENTCOM and formally retired from active service in August 1991. The following year, his autobiography, *It Doesn't Take a Hero,* was published. To many Americans, he was and still is a hero all the same. He was given a specific task, had to cooperate with the allied forces of many nations, and completed the campaign in Kuwait efficiently and effectively, with very few casualties—a heroic accomplishment.

References: Schwarzkopf, H. Norman, *It Doesn't Take a Hero: General H. Norman Schwarzkopf, the Autobiography* (New York: Bantam Books, 1992); Cohen, Roger, *In the Eye of the Storm: The Life of General H. Norman Schwarzkopf* (New York: Farrar, Straus, and Giroux, 1991); Darwish, Adel, *Unholy Babylon: The Secret History of Saddam's War* (London: Victor Gollancz, 1991); North, Bruce, "Schwarzkopf, H. Norman," in *Encyclopedia of American War Heroes* (New York: Checkmark Books, 2002), 215–216.

Scipio Africanus (the Elder) (Publius Cornelius Scipio, Scipio Africanus Major) (236–184/183 B.C.) *Roman general*

Scipio Africanus was born in 236 B.C. as Publius Cornelius Scipio, the son, grandson, and great-grandson of famed Roman consuls. His father, also named Publius Scipio, was a military leader; legend has it that when, at a battle on the Ticinus River, the elder Scipio was wounded and surrounded, his son rode through enemy lines and saved his father from death. The younger Scipio married the daughter of Consul Aemilius Paullus and had two sons with her.

It is apparent that from his youth that Publius Scipio was aiming for a military career; histories first mention him fighting as a tribune at the Battle of Cannae in 216 B.C. This battle was a horrific disaster for Rome, and Scipio was forced to flee with some 4,000 survivors to Canusium, where he rallied the remaining Roman troops. Three years later, in 213 B.C., he returned to Rome, where he was elected as a curile aedile (a civic official equivalent to a mayor). Despite being underage to hold such an office, Scipio is reported to have stated that "if all the Roman people want to make me aedile, I am old enough."

After Scipio was elected as an aedile, his father and uncle were killed in Spain fighting the Carthaginians. In 211 B.C., the Roman Senate voted to send troops to fight in Spain, but when no general offered to lead the troops, Scipio stepped forward and volunteered, probably to avenge the deaths of his father and uncle. A year later, from his headquarters at Tarraco, he launched a land and sea assault on the Carthaginian command center at Carthago Nova (now Cartagena in southern Spain). Leading his troops, Scipio himself stormed the walls of the city, leading many of his men to believe he was supported by the gods. In 208 B.C., he met the Carthaginian commander Hasdrubal Barca at Baecula (Bailen), in Baetica, and by dividing his troops and attacking both flanks of the enemy, he forced the Carthaginians to flee. Instead of chasing his quarry, however, Scipio remained in Spain, and from 208 to 206 B.C., he led Roman troops in crushing the Carthaginians, including the famous battles of Ilipa (now Alcalá del Río, near Seville) in 206 B.C.; and Gades (now Cádiz), which gave control of the Spanish peninsula to Rome. Returning to Rome, Scipio became a consul in 205 B.C., and was given control of Sicily as his province in recognition of his victories.

Deciding not to take on his old foe Hasdrubal, Scipio headed to Africa to attack the Carthage homeland. Starting in 204 B.C., he began a conflict of plunder and conquest so complete and overwhelming that when he took Tunis, the city neighboring Carthage, the Carthaginians recalled HANNIBAL, their greatest general, from Italy, to help sue for peace. Instead, Hannibal decided to fight Scipio, setting off a renewed conflict that ended at the Battle of Zama in 202 B.C. There, Scipio received support from Masinissa, the Numidian prince, whose cavalry troops provided significant support to the Roman forces. While Roman troops hit the front of Hannibal's army, the Numidians attacked the rear, destroying the Carthaginians and leading to a Roman victory. Historians have calculated that the battle was fought at the area called Naraggara (now Saqiyat Sidi, Tunis). The Second Punic War had ended in complete victory for Rome and Publius Scipio, and for this he received the surname *Africanus* (conqueror of Africa). He has since been known to history as Scipio Africanus Major, or Scipio Africanus the Elder, as distinct from his grandson, Publius Cornelius Scipio Aemilianus, known as Scipio Africanus the Younger.

After Zama, Scipio continued to play a part in his country's affairs. In 199 B.C., he was made a censor and given the office of *princeps senatus* (head of the Roman Senate); he was reelected as a censor in 194 B.C. When his brother Lucius led the Roman war against King Antiochus III the Great of Syria (reigned 223–187 B.C.), Scipio served as a legate (staff officer), aiding in military strategy. His planning led to the Roman defeat of Antiochus's forces at Magnesia in Asia Minor (189 B.C.). For this victory, Lucius was named Asiagenus.

When Scipio and Lucius returned in victory to Rome, they found that their political enemies had accused them of taking bribes from Antiochus. The evidence is murky; historians cannot say whether or not the charge is true, but it was certainly pursued by Scipio's political enemies in the Roman Senate who disagreed with his foreign policy. Shaken by the accusations, he retired to his estate, Liternum, in Campania. A recluse in his final years, he died on his estate in either 184 or 183 B.C., an exile from the nation he had served so well.

Allegedly he was so angered at how the Roman Senate had treated him that he asked that his body be interred in Liternum instead of in glory in Rome.

References: Liddell Hart, Basil H., *A Greater Than Napoleon: Scipio Africanus* (London: W. Blackwood & Sons, Ltd., 1926); Haywood, Richard M., *Studies on Scipio Africanus* (Baltimore, Md.: Johns Hopkins University Press, 1933); Fonner, D. Kent, "After Avidly Studying the Tactics of Hannibal, Scipio Africanus Eventually Bested his Carthaginian Adversary," *Military History* 12, no. 7 (March 1996): 10–12, 16; "Scipio Africanus," in *Command: From Alexander the Great to Zhukov—The Greatest Commanders of World History,* edited by James Lucas (London: Bloomsbury Publishing, 1988), 45–46; Ross, Thomas, *The Second Punick War between Hannibal, and the Romanes . . . With a Continuation from the Triumph of Scipio, to the Death of Hannibal* (London: Tho. Roycroft, 1672); Scullard, Howard W., *Scipio Africanus in the Second Punic War* (Oxford, U.K.: Oxford University Press, 1930).

Scott, Winfield (1786–1866) *American general*

Winfield Scott was born on his family's estate near Petersburg, Virginia, on 13 June 1786. His paternal grandfather, James Scott, had seen military action at Culloden Moor (16 April 1746), in which the Jacobite Scottish rebellion ended in disaster with Bonnie Prince Charlie defeated by the duke of Cumberland. James Scott fled to the American colonies, where he settled and founded an estate near Petersburg, Virginia. Winfield Scott attended the College of William and Mary in 1805, where he studied the law, but after two years he left that institution and moved to Charleston, South Carolina, where he worked in the law office of a David Robinson. By this time (1808), the United States had reached a stage of serious tension with Great Britain, soon to break out into the conflict known as the War of 1812. Scott left South Carolina for Washington, D.C., where he offered his services to the Department of War. Commissioned as a captain of artillery, he was given the task of raising a company of soldiers in Richmond and Petersburg, both in Virginia. Following the completion of this mission, Scott was ordered to move his troops to New Orleans, where he was given the rank of captain in the U.S. Army and served on the staff of General Wade Hampton.

Scott's service in the War of 1812, which began in July 1812, is heralded by his biographers. In October that year, he was promoted to lieutenant colonel and saw action at the Niagara front against British forces. He fought at Queenston Heights (13 October 1812), a failed American offensive in Ontario, British Canada, where he was taken prisoner. Exchanged back to the American lines in January 1813, he then took part in the fight at Fort George (26 May 1813). In March 1814, he was promoted to brigadier general, and he participated in battles at Chippewa (5 July 1814) and Lundy's Lane, also known as Bridgewater or the Battle of the Niagara (25 July 1814). The latter engagement is considered the fiercest land battle of the War of 1812. Scott's leadership of 1,200 American forces against some 4,500 British at Lundy's Lane, west of Niagara Falls, almost led to a disaster until his troops were reinforced by an army led by General Jacob Brown, commanding some 1,700 men. Although outnumbered two to one, the Americans refused to retreat, holding their lines even though several of their leading officers were wounded, including Scott. The British were eventually forced to withdraw; their casualties numbered 86 killed and 559 wounded, while American casualties amounted to 171 killed and 571 wounded. Despite their heavier losses, the battle marked a turning point for the Americans, who showed steadfast courage in standing against numerical odds. For his valor at Lundy's Lane, Scott was brevetted a major general in July 1814, awarded a gold medal by the U.S. Congress, and given a ceremonial sword by the state of Virginia.

For the remainder of the war, Scott's chief responsibility was to oversee and administer the first U.S. Army program of devising standard drill instruction and regulations. Following the end of the war in 1815, he oversaw a board that decided on the retention of officers to the army. Later that year, he traveled to continental Europe, where he spent two years studying the armed forces of various European nations, most notably that of the French. After his return to the United States in 1816, he took up the command of the Division of the North and served as president of the Board of Tactics. In 1828, Scott was passed over for promotion, and he angrily resigned his commission, but this was refused. Instead, he was given command of the Eastern Department in 1829.

Scott served as commander of American forces in the Black Hawk War (1832), begun by the Sac and Fox Indian leader Black Hawk in an attempt to retain tribal lands that had been taken from his people by devious means. Initially, the Indians won a series of victories against the American forces, which ended when they were defeated by troops under General James D. Henry at the Wisconsin River (28 July 1832). Scott then took over from Henry and pushed Black Hawk's forces toward the Mississippi River. He confronted the Indians at Bad Axe River (2 August 1832), where they were slaughtered by the numerically superior American forces, ending the war and forcing Black Hawk to flee. (He was eventually captured by the Winnebago and handed over to the Americans, who held him for a year but then released him under an amnesty.)

Scott was put in charge of negotiating treaties with several of the tribes in conflict with the United States, including the Sac, Fox, Menominee, and Sioux (Lakota, Nakota, Dakota). In the following years, he served as the army's emissary to inspect and strengthen the sea fortifications in South Carolina and to monitor the nullification crisis there. He also served as the commander of a short expedition against the Seminole Indians in Florida (1836), and he oversaw the forcible removal of Cherokee Indians from Georgia, Alabama, North Carolina, and Tennessee to other points in the American West in 1838. The following year, he helped settle a dispute between settlers and British officers on San Juan Island in Puget Sound in what is now Washington State and also restored peace in a dispute along the Aroostook River in Maine. In June 1841, Scott was promoted to the rank of major general, and on 5 July, he was named commanding general of the United States Army, a post he held until November 1861.

Scott served as commander of American forces during the Mexican War of 1846–48. This conflict centered on land claimed by American settlers in what is now the southwestern United States, specifically Texas. In 1846, American forces invaded Mexico, with General Zachary TAYLOR, hand-picked by Scott, as the commander in the field. When Taylor's troops slowed, Scott led an American force in a seaborne invasion of the city of Veracruz, also known as Veracruz (29 March 1847). Moving inland toward Mexico City, he then led his troops in winning two important victories. In the first, at Cerro Gordo (17–18 April 1847), Scott's men defeated the Mexicans under General Antonio Lopez de SANTA ANNA at the Cerro Gordo mountain pass, and in the second, at Contreras-Churubusco (20 August 1847), they again routed Santa Anna. This final battle allowed Scott to march almost unmolested on Mexico City, which fell on 14 September 1847. At the same time, Generals Stephen Kearney and John Fremont took control of New Mexico and California respectively, all under Scott's direction. When Scott returned to the United States, he received the official thanks of the U.S. Congress. At this point, he was the most popular military officer in America since George WASHINGTON.

When the Whigs met in convention in Baltimore in June 1852, their party, although in control of the White House, was deeply divided over several issues, mostly dealing with slavery—so divided that the party's two wings could not agree on a presidential candidate. The southerns, proslavery wing agreed to support the incumbent president, Millard Fillmore, who had succeeded to the office in 1850 upon the death of President Zachary Taylor. The antislavery northerners, however, were angry with Fillmore, a New Yorker, for his support of the Compromise of 1850, and they turned to Scott—ironically, a southerner from Virginia—because he did not support the controversial compromise. After a prolonged process in which Fillmore and Scott became deadlocked and Senator Daniel Webster was brought in as a compromise candidate, a group of delegates committed to Fillmore broke to Scott, giving him the nomination. Secretary of the Navy William Alexander Graham was selected as his running mate.

Slavery was the dominant election issue: The Democrats, who nominated Senator Franklin Pierce of New Hampshire, supported the rights of slave owners and the Compromise of 1850, while Scott and the Whigs were against the compromise but did not advocate an end to slavery. Scott might have won had not the abolitionist Free Soil Party entered the race with its candidate, New Hampshire senator John P. Hale. In numerous northern states crucial to Scott's election chances, Hale's ticket took away vital votes, giving those states to Pierce, who defeated Scott, 254 electoral votes to 42. Scott won only the four states of Kentucky, Massachusetts, Tennessee, and Vermont; Hale won no electoral votes, but his 155,210 votes caused the balance of power to tip to the Democrats.

Three years later, Pierce nominated Scott to the brevet rank of lieutenant general, making Scott the first man to hold that post since George Washington. On 28 February 1855, the president sent a message to the U.S. Senate: "For eminent services in the late war with Mexico, I nominate Major General Winfield Scott, of

the army of the United States, to be Lieutenant General by brevet in the same, to take rank, as such, from March 29, 1847, the day on which the United States forces, under his command, captured Veracruz and the castle of San Juan de Ulua. Franklin Pierce."

Six years after attaining this high rank, Scott was once again called on to serve his country when, following the election of Republican Abraham Lincoln to the presidency, a number of southern slave states seceded from the Union, a step that led to civil war. Unlike his fellow Virginian, General Robert E. LEE, who resigned his commission to serve the new Confederate States Army, Scott—then 74 years old and still commander in chief—chose to support the Union cause. Weighing nearly 300 pounds, suffering from severe bouts of gout, and unable to mount his horse, he was known as "Old Fuss and Feathers." Scott knew his limitations and asked President Lincoln to name a field commander under him. Lincoln turned to George B. MCCLELLAN, who resented having Scott as his superior and disparaged the military hero whenever he could. Through no fault of his, Scott became more unpopular as the Union army lost several early battles, most notably at the Bull Run (21 July 1861). He believed the war would not be won quickly, a view most Union commanders found ridiculous, and recommended that the Confederate States be blockaded from the sea, to cut off the southern states' supplies of matériel.

The end for Scott came after the Union defeat at Ball's Bluff (21 October 1861). On 1 November 1861, he offered President Lincoln his resignation, which was accepted; that same day, Lincoln gave his command to McClellan. Scott retired, writing his memoirs and spending a year in Europe. Meanwhile, as he had predicted, the war dragged on for four long years. It ended only when Ulysses S. GRANT and William Tecumseh SHERMAN followed Scott's plan of blockading the South, slowly tightening the Union grip on its borders and leading to the inevitable Confederacy defeat.

Scott lived to see the end of the war, dying at West Point, New York, on 29 May 1866, two week before his 80th birthday. Although he had not attended the United States Military Academy at West Point, he was buried there. Having served his country in three important conflicts, Scott is probably best remembered for his brilliant Mexican campaign. A skilled diplomat in peacetime and a farsighted strategist and tactician in war, he lived to see his foresighted strategic advice justified in the war that had split his country. The authors of the *The Wordsworth Dictionary of Military Biography* write: "Winfield Scott was an associate of every American president from Jefferson to Lincoln, and carried out important missions for most of them. His life spanned the most formative years of the U.S. Army, from the inefficiency and indecision of the immediate post-Revolutionary years to the peak of disciplined strength achieved at the end of the Civil War. His own part in that progression was not inconsiderable."

References: Eisenhower, John S. D., *Agent of Destiny: The Life and Times of General Winfield Scott* (New York: The Free Press, 1997); information on the 1852 election in *Congressional Quarterly's Guide to U.S. Elections* (Washington, D.C.: Congressional Quarterly, Inc., 1985), 39–41, 280, 333; *Nomination of Winfield Scott. Executive Proceedings of the Senate of the United States . . .* (Washington: Beverley Tucker, Printer, 1854); Hymel, Kevin M., "Winfield Scott's Long and Illustrious Career was Tarnished by Incessant Political Infighting," *Military History* 16, no. 2 (June 1999): 70–72; Windrow, Martin, and Francis K. Mason, "Scott, Winfield," in *The Wordsworth Dictionary of Military Biography* (Hertfordshire, U.K.: Wordsworth Editions Ltd., 1997), 263–264.

Sheridan, Philip Henry (1831–1888) *American general*

Born on 6 March 1831, Philip Sheridan was the son of John and Mary Sheridan, immigrants from Ireland. There is doubt about Sheridan's place of birth; he claimed it was Albany, New York, though others believe it was somewhere in Ireland or on a ship en route to America. After a tempestuous boyhood, he entered the United States Military Academy at West Point in 1848 but was suspended for a year for fighting. He graduated in 1853 and served in garrisons in Texas and Oregon. A captain at the beginning of the Civil War, he served in a staff appointment until May 1862. He was then given command of a cavalry regiment, which fought bravely at Boonville, Missouri (1 July 1862), after which he was promoted to brigadier general.

When General Braxton Bragg led a Confederate invasion of Kentucky, General Don Carlos Buell's Union force met and defeated him decisively at the battle of Perryville (or Chaplin Hills), Kentucky, on 8 October 1862; the Union win was largely due to Sheridan's ef-

forts. Buell followed Bragg back to Murfreesboro (Stone's River) and fought him again there (31 December 1862–2 January 1863), with Sheridan again playing a leading role in holding the first Confederate attack until his men ran out of ammunition. He was promoted to major general of volunteers in December 1862 and commanded the 2 Division, IV Corps.

Sheridan commanded a corps at Chickamauga (19–20 September 1863) and led the assault at Missionary Ridge (25 November 1863). When Ulysses S. GRANT was called east to command all the Union forces in March 1864, he took Sheridan with him to command the cavalry of the Army of the Potomac. Under Sheridan's leadership, the Northern cavalry improved rapidly and lost the sense of inferiority it had long suffered in comparison to the daring exploits of Confederate general Jeb Stuart's Southern cavalrymen. Sheridan fought in the Battle of the Wilderness (5–7 May 1864) and carried out a cavalry raid toward Richmond that met stubborn resistance but resulted in Stuart's death when the two forces met at Yellow Tavern (11 May 1864).

In August 1864, Sheridan was given command of the newly created Army of the Shenandoah. Ever since the beginning of the war, the Shenandoah Valley had enabled Confederate forces to march north, protected by the Blue Ridge Mountains and living off the crops and cattle of the valley while they did so. In summer 1864, as Grant waged a war of attrition against Robert E. LEE in the area around Richmond, the Southern general Jubal EARLY took his army up the valley and, after swinging east, threatened Washington itself on 11 July 1864. Determined to eliminate this constant threat to his flank, Grant ordered Sheridan to destroy Early's force and take control of the valley.

On 29 September 1864, Sheridan attacked Early at Winchester and drove him south to Fisher's Hill, where Sheridan attacked him again, forcing him further southward. This left the northern section of the valley in Sheridan's hands, and he promptly began a scorched-earth policy to ensure the area would never again become a supply source for the South. In October, there were clashes between Sheridan's and Early's cavalry at Fisher's Hill (9 October) and Strasburg (14 October). Sheridan then traveled to Washington for a conference, and Early, learning of his departure, decided to launch a surprise attack in his absence.

On the morning of 19 October 1864, Early attacked Sheridan's army at Cedar Creek and drove them north in disarray. Sheridan, who was on his way back from Washington and had reached Winchester, heard the distant gunfire, mounted his horse, and galloped to meet his troops fleeing in disarray. In a remarkable display of personal leadership, he rallied them, took them back the way they had come, made contact with his subordinate commanders, gave out his orders, and swept down on Early's troops, who had paused to loot the Union camp, driving them from the field. It was the last major engagement in the Shenandoah Valley, and Sheridan's gallop from Winchester to rally his troops was immortalized in the poem 'Sheridan's Ride' by Thomas Buchanan Read.

During the next few months, Sheridan tightened his hold on the Shenandoah Valley, destroying crops and confiscating cattle and any supplies of use to the South. He mopped up the remainder of Early's forces in February 1865 and then took his troops east to join Grant in the final push on Lee. In March, Grant sent Sheridan south and west to cover any chance of Lee's army escaping. When Lee's army at last marched west from Richmond, they met Sheridan's strong cavalry formation in front of them and, behind Sheridan, advancing columns of Union infantry. The next day, Lee surrendered at Appomattox Court House.

After the Civil War, Sheridan served as military governor of Texas and Louisiana, where his harsh measures led to charges of brutality. From 1867 to 1870, he commanded the Department of the Missouri and was engaged in the Indian Wars. In 1870, he went to Europe to observe the Franco-Prussian war. In 1883, he was made commander in chief, replacing William Tecumseh SHERMAN and serving in that post until his death. He was promoted to full general on 1 June 1888, only the third officer to hold that rank, after Grant and Sherman. He died on 5 August 1888 and was buried in Arlington National Cemetery.

While he may not have been the master tactician that Lee was or a master strategist like Grant, Philip Sheridan was a superb field commander who knew his duty and whose gift of leadership and courage played a major part in the Union victory.

References: Wittenberg, Eric J., *Little Phil: A Reassessment of the Civil War Leadership of General Philip H. Sheridan* (Washington, D.C.: Brassey's 2002); Morris, Roy, Jr., *Sheridan: The Life and Wars of General Phil Sheridan* (New York: Vintage Books, 1993); Hutton,

Paul Andrew, *Phil Sheridan and His Army* (Lincoln: University of Nebraska Press, 1985); Bichens, Hugh, "Sheridan, Gen Phil H.," in *The Oxford Companion to Military History,* edited by Richard Holmes (New York: Oxford University Press, 2001), 828–829; Windrow, Martin, and Francis K. Mason, "Sheridan, Philip Henry," in *The Wordsworth Dictionary of Military Biography* (Hertfordshire, U.K.: Wordsworth Editions Ltd., 1997), 269–270; Sheridan, P. H., *Personal Memoirs of P. H. Sheridan, General United States Army* (New York: Da Capo Press, 1992).

Sherman, William Tecumseh (1820–1891)
American general

William Tecumseh Sherman—initially named Tecumseh Sherman after the Shawnee chieftain Tecumseh—was born in Lancaster, Ohio, on 8 February 1820, one of eight children born to Judge Charles R. Sherman, who died when his son was nine. Judge Sherman's widow could not provide for all her children, and Tecumseh was sent to live with Thomas Ewing, a friend of the family who served as a U.S. senator from Ohio. Ewing later adopted the boy, who kept his own name, although he also retained the name of William that his adoptive mother had given him. When William was 16, Ewing used his political connections to gain him an appointment to the United States Military Academy at West Point, New York; Sherman graduated in 1840 near the top of his class.

When Sherman left West Point, the war against the Seminole Indians in what is now the state of Florida was in progress. Sherman was sent south and saw action against the Seminole for a short period before being sent to Fort Moultrie in South Carolina. He saw no action during the Mexican War (1846–48), spending his service as an administrative officer in California. In 1850, he married his adoptive sister, Ellen Ewing, Thomas Ewing's natural daughter, and three years later, he resigned from the army and took a position with a St. Louis banking firm at its San Francisco branch. The economic crash of 1857 left him bankrupt, and he only survived with the help of two old West Point friends, Braxton Bragg and Pierre Beauregard, who secured him a position as superintendent of a military academy in Louisiana in 1859. Ironically, Bragg and Beauregard later joined the Confederacy in the Civil War, and Sherman fought against them.

After the election of Abraham Lincoln to the presidency in 1860, the southern slave states seceded from the American Union, a process that began in February 1861. When Louisiana seceded that same month, Sherman resigned his post and moved to St. Louis, which he considered his second home. Although he was a unionist, he felt the slavery issue was not worth fighting for. However, when the Civil War began, his brother, Ohio senator John Sherman, got him an appointment as a colonel in the United States Army. He was given the command of a brigade of troops in the army of General Irvin McDowell, and he immediately saw action at Bull Run (21 July 1861). Although the battle was a disaster for the Union, Sherman's service earned him a promotion to brigadier general of volunteers. However, when the army tried to give him his own command, he sent a letter to President Lincoln stating that he did not feel ready for such a position. Despite this, Lincoln did name him to a command, serving in Kentucky under General Robert Anderson, the former Union commander at Fort Sumter, South Carolina. In October 1861, Anderson stepped down, making Sherman the new commander

William Tecumseh Sherman

of this army; however, he was removed due to his nervousness about making a mistake. Nevertheless, through the backing of General Henry Halleck, he was given a command in February 1862 under General Ulysses S. GRANT.

It was Grant's steadfast confidence in him that allowed Sherman to blossom into the commander he eventually became. Under Grant, he saw major action at Shiloh, also known as Pittsburg Landing (6–7 April 1862), and was promoted to the rank of major general. He continued to serve with Grant, especially through the Vicksburg campaign (1862–63), which brought the Mississippi River under Union control. He suffered a defeat at Chickasaw Bluffs, also known as Chickasaw Bayou (26–29 December 1862), where Sherman had a 5-to-1 numerical advantage in forces but lost 1,800 men in the battle. However, he was able to reestablish his reputation when he won a victory at Fort Hindman, Arkansas (9–11 January 1863), and took control of the fortification.

Following the fall of Vicksburg to Grant's forces, Sherman was promoted to brigadier general. Although he was unable to relieve the city of Chattanooga, Grant thought well enough of him to dispatch him to Knoxville to aid General Ambrose Burnside. When Grant was promoted to become the commander of the Union armies in the West (October 1863), Sherman was promoted to Grant's old position as commander of the Army of the Tennessee. A few months later, when Grant was given the full command of all Union forces in March 1864, Sherman was given control over the armies in the West. He and Grant then decided on a plan of action: Sherman, with 100,000 troops, would invade the Southern states and march to Atlanta, Georgia. Sherman opened this campaign near Chattanooga, Tennessee, in May 1864. The Confederates ahead of him, led by General Joseph E. Johnston, tried to block his way but were forced to slowly retreat south. Although Sherman lost the crucial battle of Kennesaw Mountain (27 June 1864), he continued his march to Atlanta almost without any resistance because the Confederates had been denied vital goods by a Union blockade. Sherman's forces tore through South Carolina and northern Georgia, leaving a trail of pillage and destruction—not for revenge, as some think, but to reduce the Confederates' ability to fight. On 2 September 1864, Sherman's troops took Atlanta, the nucleus of the Confederacy's railway system in the South. This Union victory, coming just two months before the American presidential election, gave Lincoln's campaign a boost and led to his reelection, which just weeks earlier had been precarious. Sherman then led more than 60,000 of his men in what historians call "Sherman's March to the Sea," an advance in which his men tore up railroads and destroyed civilian and military buildings and supplies in an attempt to destroy the Confederate infrastructure. On 22 December 1864, Sherman sent a telegram to President Lincoln from Savannah, Georgia: "Via Ft. Monroe Va Dec. 25. I beg to present you as a Christmas gift the City of Savannah with 150 heavy guns & plenty of ammunition & also about 25.000 bales of cotton." The war in the South was essentially over.

Moving north, Sherman's troops marched into the Carolinas and reached Virginia just as the Confederate commander, General Robert E. LEE, was surrendering to Grant at Appomattox Courthouse in Virginia on 9 April 1865. General Joseph Johnston, the commander against whom Sherman fought in the last months of the war, surrendered to him on 26 April near Durham, North Carolina.

Sherman's career during the Civil War had been connected with that of Grant, and this continued with the peace thereafter. In 1866, Grant was promoted to full general, while Sherman was promoted to lieutenant general. Two years later, Grant was elected the 18th president of the United States, and he named Sherman as the commander of the American army, a post he held until 1884. For many years, Sherman was urged to run for political office, but he refused. He died in New York City on 14 February 1891, a week after his 71st birthday. Although born in Ohio, he was buried in his adoptive hometown of St. Louis.

William Tecumseh Sherman is best known for two things: his "March to the Sea," which cut the Confederacy in two, and his statement that "war is hell"—his view of warfare as a brutal and horrible affair, not the glorious pastime some young men believe it to be.

References: Lewis, Lloyd, *Sherman: Fighting Prophet* (New York: Harcourt, Brace & Company, 1932); Merrill, James M., *William Tecumseh Sherman* (Chicago: Rand McNally, 1971); Miers, Earl Schenck, *The General Who Marched to Hell: William Tecumseh Sherman and His March to Fame and Infamy* (New York: Alfred A. Knopf, 1951); Wheeler, Richard, *Sherman's March* (New York: Crowell, 1978); Liddell Hart, B. H., "Sherman—Modern Warrior," *American Heritage* 12, no. 5 (August 1962): 20–23, 102–106; Sherman to Lincoln, 22 December 1864, Abraham Lincoln Papers, Library of Congress, Washington, D.C.; North, Bruce, "Sherman, William Tecumseh," in *Encyclopedia of American War Heroes* (New York: Checkmark Books, 2002), 221–223.

Slim, William Joseph, Viscount Slim (1891–1970) *British general*

William Slim was born in the village of Bishopston, near Bristol, England, on 6 August 1891, the son of John Slim, a hardware salesman, and Charlotte Tucker Slim. In 1903, when William was 12, the family moved to the city of Birmingham, where John Slim tried to restart his failing hardware business. William Slim received his education at St. Philips Catholic School in Edgbaston and King Edward's School in Birmingham, joining the Officers Training Corps (OTC) at the latter institution.

Slim had always wanted to join the army, but his father could not afford to send him to Sandhurst, the British military academy. For a time after leaving school, he worked as a teacher, then joined the engineering concern of Stewarts and Lloyds, for which he was working as a clerk when the First World War began in August 1914. He volunteered and was commissioned in the Royal Warwickshire Regiment. Sent to Gallipoli, the regiment saw heavy action in the battle of Sari Bair Ridge (August 1915), and Slim was wounded during the action. He returned to England to recuperate, and it was not until 1916 that he was able to serve again. He was sent to Mesopotamia in the Middle East, where, despite still not being completely recovered, he saw action in several battles, leading to his winning the Military Cross and participating in the capture of the city of Baghdad. Wounded again, he was sent to India to recuperate.

When he was well enough, Slim was assigned to British army headquarters in November 1917, promoted to the rank of captain, and then transferred to the Indian army in May 1919 following the end of the war. He served at army headquarters, being posted to the 1st Battalion, 6th Gurkha Rifles, in March 1920. Serving in this unit until 1925, he was able to apply some of the lessons he learned at Gallipoli and in Mesopotamia to the Indian army. In 1925, he attended the Indian Staff College in what is now Quetta, Pakistan, studying under the tank warfare specialist Colonel

Percy Hobart. He served for an additional four years at the army headquarters in India before being sent to the Staff College at Camberley, England, where he served as the Indian army instructor from 1934 to 1936. He was later sent to the Imperial Defence College in London and promoted to lieutenant colonel. Although he was now highly thought of and extremely well qualified, there seemed little opportunity for advancement, and Slim later wrote that it was at this time that he considered retirement from the military. However, he returned to India, and after attending the Senior Officers School in Belgaum, he was given command of the 2nd Battalion, 7th Gurkha Rifles, in 1937. He then returned to Belgaum as the commandant, serving until the start of the Second World War.

When the war broke out in September 1939, Slim was named as commander of the 10th Indian Infantry Brigade, which was stationed at Jhansi, India. His first major assignment was to train the troops in this brigade to invade Sudan and to assault the Italian forces holed up in what is now Eritrea. In November 1940, after a full year of training, Slim's contingent was ordered to invade and take the city of Gallabat. Although the troops took the city with ease, they were not prepared for the bombardment from the Italian air force, which inflicted heavy casualties. Slim ultimately decided to abandon the hard-won target; he later wrote of the decision, "When two courses of action were open to me, I had not chosen, as a good commander should, the bolder. I had taken counsel of my fears." Nonetheless, in 1941 he was promoted to major general and given command of the 10th Indian Division. His division was sent to Syria and Iraq, where Slim helped to put down an insurrection by Iraqis in Baghdad and then participated in the British invasion of Syria.

The Japanese invasion of Burma on 16 January 1942 changed Slim from the commander of a division to the leader of the British fight against the Japanese attack in Southeast Asia. The British War Office selected him to be commander of the Burma Corps, the British military force formed to fight the Japanese. This force consisted of the 1st Burma Division and the 17th Indian Division. Slim's first objective was to secure Rangoon, the main access for supplies being sent to China to fight the Japanese there. However, by the time he reached Burma, Rangoon had fallen to the Japanese, and he was forced to oversee the retreat and withdrawal of British forces into India. In June 1942, based on his

skill in conducting this move, Slim was named as commander of the newly formed XV Corps, whose first goal was to secure the area of Burma known as the Arakan, near the Bay of Bengal. The campaign to take this small coastal area became mired down in March 1943, and he was forced to a stalemate. In February 1944, he tried once again, beginning with a two-front offensive: one to take Arakan, the second to halt any Japanese invasion of India. By June 1944, the India operation had succeeded, and this part of the Fourteenth Army, to which Slim had been named as commander in October 1943, moved on to Burma and retook it in a long, bitter struggle known as Operation Capital. The Japanese, under Lieutenant General Mutagachi Renya, suffered some 55,000 casualties out of an army of 80,000. Slim wrote about this victory in his diaries: "Some of what we owed we had paid back. . . . Now we were going on to pay back the rest with interest." He was knighted by the viceroy of India in December 1944.

On 10 August 1945, near the end of the war, Slim was named as commander in chief of the Allied land forces, Southeast Asia (ALFSEA), succeeding Sir Oliver Leese. He stayed in this post for a year following the end of the war, and in 1946 he returned to England, where he served as commandant of the Imperial Defence College for two years. He retired from active duty in late 1947 but returned to service in November 1948 when Prime Minister Clement Atlee promoted him to field marshal and selected him to succeed Bernard Law MONTGOMERY as chief of the Imperial General Staff, a post Slim held until 1952. He was then asked to take the position of governor-general of Australia, and he served in that post for eight years. During this period, he wrote two volumes of war memoirs, *Defeat into Victory* (1956) and *Unofficial History* (1959), the latter work a collection of papers on military science. In 1960, he was raised to the peerage as Viscount Slim.

William Slim died in London on 14 December 1970 at the age of 79. Given an official funeral at St. George's Chapel, Windsor Castle, he was cremated, and his son John succeeded him as viscount. The author George Macdonald Fraser writes: "Slim was . . . the only man I've ever seen who had a force that came out of him. British soldiers don't love their commanders. [The] Fourteenth Army trusted Slim and thought of him as one of themselves, and perhaps his real secret was that the feeling was mutual." Slim biographer Harold E. Raugh, Jr., reinforces this positive view: "One of the most charismatic and dynamic soldiers of the twentieth-century Indian army was William Joseph Slim, later Field Marshal the Viscount Slim. His adventure-filled military career started with his receipt of one of the first commissions in Lord Horatio Kitchener's New Army in 1914. Slim rose to the position of army commander in Southeast Asia in 1945, along the way commanding at every echelon from platoon to corps, all of them, with the exception of battalion, in combat. The culmination of Slim's military career was his appointment in 1948 as chief of the Imperial General Staff, the first Indian army officer ever to serve as the professional head of the British army."

References: Lewin, Ronald, *Slim: The Standardbearer* (London: Leo Cooper, 1976); Slim, William Joseph, Viscount Slim, *Unofficial History* (London: Cassell, 1959); Slim, William Joseph, Field Marshal Viscount Slim, *Defeat into Victory* (New York: David McKay, 1961); Smurthwaite, David, ed., *The Forgotten War: The British Army in the Far East, 1941–1945* (London: National Army Museum, 1992); Fraser, George Macdonald, *Quartered Safe Out Here* (London: HarperCollins, 1992), 35–36; Raugh, Harold E., Jr., "Slim, William Joseph [Viscount]," in *Brassey's Encyclopedia of Military History and Biography*, edited by Franklin D. Margiotta (Washington, D.C.: Brassey's, 1994), 885–87.

Sobieski, John   *See* JOHN III SOBIESKI.

Somerset, Lord Fitzroy James Henry   *See* RAGLAN, LORD FITZROY JAMES HENRY SOMERSET, FIRST BARON RAGLAN.

Strongbow, Richard   *See* CLARE, RICHARD FITZGILBERT DE, SECOND EARL OF PEMBROKE.

Suchet, Louis-Gabriel, duc d'Albufera da Valencia   (1770–1826)   *French general, marshal of France*

Born and educated in Lyon, France, on 2 March 1770, Louis-Gabriel Suchet was the son of Jean-Pierre Suchet, a silk manufacturer. When he finished school, he entered his father's business, and it appeared that he would become, like his father, a wealthy businessman, but the French Revolution intervened (1789).

In 1792, with France at war, he volunteered for service in the cavalry of the National Guard at Lyon, rising to become a member of the free company of Ardèche with the rank of captain and the title *chief de bataillon*. In 1793, he served at Toulon when it was under siege by the British, and he personally captured the British general Charles O'Hara, who was exchanged two years later for the French general the comte de Rochambeau. In 1794, Suchet was sent to Italy, where he saw action in several battles, including at Vado and St-Jacques. At Loano (22–23 November 1795), he helped to capture three divisions of enemy forces, following which he was transferred to the command of Marshal André MASSÉNA, one of NAPOLEON's leading commanders. Under Masséna, Suchet saw action at the battles of Castiglione (5 August 1796), Bassano (8 September 1796), and Cerea (11 October 1796), where he was severely wounded. He was sent back to France highly commended by Masséna for his bravery and conduct during battle. After returning to service, he was again wounded fighting the Austrians at Neumark (2 April 1797), and for his service he was given command of the 18th Brigade. Following the peace of Campo Formio (17 October 1797), the end of the war in Italy, he was sent to Switzerland.

Fighting in the Army of Helvetia in Switzerland in 1798, Suchet served under Marshal Guillaume Brune. When Brune left for the campaign in Egypt, Suchet then served in Italy under Barthélemy Joubert, who made him his chief of staff. On 10 July 1799, he was promoted to general of division. Following Joubert's death on 15 August 1799, Suchet took control of his army, serving under the command of Marshal Jean-Victor Moreau. He remained at the head of this army under General Jean Étienne Championnet, who came to relieve Moreau. However, Championnet, who had been accused of brutality to civilians, was quickly transferred to the Army of the Alps and was succeeded by Masséna, who made Suchet commander of the left flank of his force. They marched on Friuli, where they met the Austrians, led by Michael Melas (22–26 May 1800). Suchet helped to secure a French victory by pushing the Austrians back to the Var River. This aided Napoleon's crossing of the Alps, leading to the French victory at Marengo (14 June 1800). Rejoining Masséna, Suchet aided General Dupont at Pozzolo before the end of the war came with the armistice of Treviso (18 January 1801). Suchet was named as the governor of Padua until the Peace of Lunéville (9 February 1801), after which he returned to France to serve the inspector general of infantry. In October 1803, he was appointed commander of the 4th Division of the Grand Armeé at St. Omer.

Although France had renewed the war against Britain in 1803, it was 1805 that saw a renewal of the fighting in Europe. Suchet took the 4th Division, against the Austrians and Russians at Ulm (20 October), Michelsberg (15 October), Hollabrunn (16 November), and Austerlitz (2 December). In 1806, he was granted the Grand Cordon of the Legion of Honour for his bravery in combat. He led his forces at Saalfeld at the side of Marshal Jean LANNES, capturing Landgrafenberg on 11 October 1806, three days before the main battle at Jena, where Napoleon was able to secure a critical and crucial victory against the Prussians. Following Jena, Suchet moved on to capture Closwitz and Vierzehnheiligen, then marched on Weimar, where he joined Lannes. Crossing the Elbe River, the French followed the Prussian general Gerhard BLÜCHER to Prentzlow, but when Blücher hit the French, led by Jean Lannes, at Pultusk (26 December 1806), Suchet was able to strike him and aid in the French victory.

Following the battle at Ostrolenka (now Ostroienka, Poland, on the Narew River), Suchet was promoted to commander of the 1st Division of V Corps of the Grande Armeé. At Eylau on 8 February 1807, he was seriously wounded, but following the end of the conflict, he was given the title of count on 19 March 1808 and sent to Spain, where French forces were fighting the British. First as commander of the III Corps of the Grande Armeé and then as the commander in chief of the Armeé d'Aragon, Suchet led his forces to victory over the British at Maria (14 June 1809) and Lerida (22 April 1810). French victories at Wagram (6 July 1809) and the British retreat from Walcheren allowed Napoleon to pour thousands of troops into Spain. This contributed to several victories by Suchet—who was promoted to marshal in July 1811—in the province of Valencia, allowing him to capture that area for Spain in 1812. For these services, he was bestowed in 1812 with the title duc d'Albufera da Valencia.

Suchet's capture of Valencia was the last major victory for the French in Spain. Although he served as the governor of Catalonia, in late 1813 he replaced Jean-Baptiste Bessières as colonel-general of the French Imperial Guard. In 1814, he was named as commander in chief of the Army of the South, and in this role he led French forces at Molins del Rey (16 January 1814). By this time, Napoleon's hold on power in France was slipping, eventually leading to his abdication and exile to the island of Elba. Suchet, despite his closeness to Napoleon, was accepted by the ruling royal family, the Bourbons, now restored to power. However, when Napoleon escaped from exile and returned to France, Suchet offered his services to his former commander. To the surprise of many, including the historians who have studied this period, Napoleon did not give Suchet an important command in the 100 days of his campaign, instead relegating the marshal to serve as commander of the small Army of the Alps. Suchet saw limited action against the Austrians in Savoy and southern France in June and July 1815 and arranged an armistice with the Austrians after Napoleon's defeat at Waterloo. The Bourbons did not turn on him as they did other Napoleonic commanders, although it was not until 1819 that his peerage was restored to him. Thereafter, Suchet retired, living on his small estate until his death near Marseille on 3 January 1826 at the age of 55. His two-volume *Mémoires,* edited by Baron St. Cyr-Nogues, who had served under Suchet, were published in 1829.

Suchet was highly regarded by Napoleon, who wrote in 1812: "There is no one there [in Spain] but Suchet who does well with his tasks. If I had two commanding generals like him to lead my troops in Spain, this war would already be finished; but there each [of his commanding officers] wants to complete his own projects and not mine." Even in exile on the island of St.-Helena, Napoleon still had kind words for his former subordinate, stating, "It was the pillaging which made me lose Spain, with the exception always of Suchet, whose conduct was exemplary."

References: Windrow, Martin, and Francis K. Mason, "Suchet, Louis-Gabriel," in *The Wordsworth Dictionary of Military Biography* (Hertfordshire, U.K.: Wordsworth Editions Ltd., 1997), 285–286; Bergerot, Bernard, *Le Maréchal Suchet, duc d'Albuféra* (Paris: Tallandier, 1986); Suchet, Louis-Gabriel, duc d'Albuféra, *Memoirs of the War in Spain from 1808 to 1814* (London: H. Colburn, 1829).

T

Tamerlane *See* TIMUR.

Taylor, Zachary (1784–1850) *American general, 12th president of the United States*
Zachary Taylor—a second cousin to future president James Madison—was born in Orange County, Virginia, on 24 November 1784, the son of Colonel Richard Taylor, who served under George WASHINGTON during the Revolutionary War and afterwards held a series of minor government offices. Soon after the birth of his son Zachary, Colonel Taylor moved his family to Kentucky, where he became a wealthy landowner; by the turn of the 19th century, he owned large tracts of land and many slaves.

Zachary Taylor decided from an early age to follow a military career. In 1808, he was given a commission in the United States Army as a first lieutenant in the 7th Infantry and was named commander of Fort Pickering, now on the site of the city of Memphis, Tennessee. In the next several years, he was given a number of garrison assignments, and in 1810 he married the daughter of a well-known Maryland family. He was sent then to Louisiana, where he was given command of a fort near Baton Rouge. When the War of 1812 began, Taylor was promoted to captain and sent to fight the American Indian allies of Great Britain. He earned distinction when he staved off a massive Indian attack against American

forces at Fort Harrison, Indiana; for this service, he was brevetted as a major. In May 1814, he was given a regular commission as a major; nevertheless, when the war ended in 1815 and the military was demobilized for peacetime, he was reduced in rank to captain. Taylor decided at this point to leave the military and enter civilian life as a farmer near Louisville, Kentucky, his home. Within a year, however, he had tired of farming and returned to the army, accepting the rank of major in the 3rd Regiment in 1816. Three years later, he was promoted to lieutenant colonel, and for the next 13 years he was sent to various postings around the country.

In 1832, when the Black Hawk War broke out, Taylor was given the command of the 1st Regiment. This conflict was rooted in expanding tensions between American settlers moving west onto Indian lands and the Native Americans who wished to preserve their way of life but whose lands were being taken from them. Due to the overwhelming superiority of the U.S. Army, the war soon ended at the battle of Bad Axe River (2 August 1832) when an Illinois militia force defeated a combined army of Sac and Fox Indians in southwestern Wisconsin.

Indian uprisings continued across the United States, and Taylor was sent to Florida to suppress a revolt by the Seminole in 1837. In a letter written on 20 July 1837 to General R. Jones, adjutant general of the army,

Zachary Taylor

Taylor explained the operations in the area: "With a view to compel the emigration of the Appalache Indians who had engaged to leave the country on 20th Octr [1837], and who had made some objections to a removal, I left Tampa on or about the 2th Octr for their towns on the Appalachicola River which I reached on the morning of the 12th with two companies [of] mounted men (one Dragoons and one Infantry) the whole under command of Captain E. Barkus, and found on my arrival a portion of the 6th Infantry under Major Noel." On 25 December 1837, Taylor fought the Seminole at Okeechobee and won a decisive victory. Brevetted as a brigadier general, he remained in Florida, acting against the Seminole until 1841. When he left Florida, he was given the command of the First Department of the U.S. Army in the South, with his headquarters at Fort Jessup, Louisiana.

The move by Texans for independence from Mexico, culminating in the acceptance of Texas as a U.S. state in 1845, set off a conflict with Mexico that had been long in coming. When Mexico disputed the border between the new state and their country, President James

K. Polk ordered Taylor and his forces to the area on 30 July 1845 to, as Polk explained, "to occupy, protect and defend Texas." Taylor was also ordered to fight any Mexican units crossing the disputed Rio Grande River border region. Following a period of consolidating his units in southern Texas, Taylor marched to the Rio Grande from the city of Corpus Christi on 11 March 1846. When his forces arrived there on 28 March, Taylor ordered the construction of a garrison, which he dubbed Fort Texas. Angered by this, the Mexicans demanded that Taylor withdraw. When he refused, a group of Mexican fighters ambushed an American dragoon force on 24 April. Taylor sent word to Polk, and the president asked Congress for a declaration of war against Mexico, stating that "Mexico has passed the boundary of the United States, has invaded our territory and shed American blood upon American soil." Polk ordered Taylor to attack the Mexicans at the Rio Grande, and Taylor met them at Palo Alto (8 May), where his force of some 2,200 troops defeated a numerically superior force of some 4,500 men under Mariano Arista. The Mexicans lost about 1,700 men, while American casualties were less than 200. This first battle of the Mexican War made Taylor a national hero in the United States, and, five days after it was fought, the U.S. Congress declared war on Mexico. Taylor followed it up with a victory at Resaca de la Palma (9 May), but he could not continue the fight into Mexico.

Despite the declaration of war, Polk did not like Taylor personally, and the president waited three full months before sending reinforcements to aid his force. In August, Taylor was able to cross the Rio Grande and establish a base at Camargo. Starting in late September, the American force initiated a series of small clashes to capture the city of Monterey. When the Mexicans, after considerable losses, asked to withdraw and keep their guns, Taylor acceded to their request, a move criticized by the Polk administration. Taylor felt he was being attacked by Polk's cabinet, especially Secretary of War William Learned Marcy. He wrote a letter to General Edmund Gaines criticizing Polk and Marcy that was leaked to the press and became a headline in many of the nation's newspapers. In the meantime, he gathered up his forces and moved onto the town of Saltillo, taking it on 16 November 1846.

Taylor received a note from General Winfield SCOTT, a War of 1812 veteran whom Polk had named as commander in chief of American forces in Mexico. Scott reported that he would be coming to Mexico and that Taylor was to hand over all of his troops to serve under Scott in a great offensive in Mexico. Instead of complying with this order, Taylor marched away from where he had been ordered to meet Scott and headed toward the city of Victoria. Scott demanded Taylor return a majority of his troops, which he did unwillingly. Scott then ordered Taylor's now-diminished force to march on Veracruz (also Veracruz). It was at this time that Taylor received word that Mexican general Antonio Lopez de SANTA ANNA was marching to fight his army with some 20,000 troops—more than four times Taylor's force. The two armies met at Buena Vista (22–23 February 1847), south of Saltillo, and despite the numerical disadvantage, Taylor was able to win an important victory. American newspapers editorialized that Taylor had almost been sacrificed by a jealous administration and an incompetent general—Scott—who had removed some of Taylor's finest fighters for his own. Despite the support of the American people, Taylor's unwillingness to follow Scott's direct orders cost him, and after Buena Vista his military career was over.

In 1844, the Whigs had lost an important election to James Polk; four years later, they strove to find a candidate who could appeal to a national audience against the Democrats' candidate, former Michigan governor Lewis Cass. Although Taylor had never expressed political views, "Taylor for President" clubs sprang up after his victories in Mexico. Despite the fact that the Whigs were moving to an antislavery position by 1848, Taylor was a wealthy slave owner. The southern Whigs hoped that as president, Taylor would support the right of slaveholders to move their slaves into new American territories to be carved out of lands taken from Mexico following the end of the war. The northern Whigs hoped that despite his ownership of slaves, he would not do anything to force a breakup of the Union. In fact, Taylor was against both the spread of slavery and the threat of secession from slave states. At the Whig convention in Philadelphia, he was nominated for president, and Millard Fillmore, a former congressman who had been the chair of the House Ways and Means Committee, was named as the candidate for vice president. A faction of antislavery Democrats broke from Cass to support former president Martin Van Buren, who polled enough votes in New York to throw the state and its electoral votes to Taylor. In the end, Taylor won 1,360,099 votes to Cass's 1,220,544, with 291,616 votes going to Van Buren; the electoral vote count was 163-127.

Inaugurated as the 12th president of the United States on 4 March 1849, Taylor was challenged by the split in the nation over the issue of slavery. Proslavery advocates demanded that he support their right to move their slaves into new territories; antislavery supporters wanted those people in the new territories of California and New Mexico to decide for themselves whether or not slavery should be legal there. Taylor sided with the antislavery side, and southerners called for a vote on secession from the Union. Taylor decried any talk of leaving the Union, threatening with death anyone who attempted such a move. In Congress, a number of leaders fashioned a settlement to placate the South and end the crisis. Their work, which allowed for a stronger Fugitive Slave Act to capture and ship escaped slaves from northern free states back to southern slave states, became the Compromise of 1850. It was a short-term fix and lasted only a decade. The compromise permitted slavery in the new territory of New Mexico but made California free, thus leaving the number of free and slave states numerically even. Although this issue dominated his presidency, Taylor did not participate in congressional debates over the compromise, instead allowing the legislative branch to cobble the deal together.

On 4 July 1850, Taylor attended Fourth of July celebrations in Washington, D.C. He drank cold milk and ate cherries, but later in the day he became violently ill with an apparent stomach flu. He lingered for five days until he succumbed on 9 July at the age of 65. His funeral was attended by some 100,000 mourners who lined the route along which his casket was taken. He was laid to rest in what is now called Zachary Taylor National Cemetery in Louisville, Kentucky. Known as "Old Rough and Ready" for his fights against the Seminole in Florida, Zachary Taylor was a notable soldier of the 19th century. Rumors that his death had been caused by poison were disproved in 1991.

References: Bauer, Karl Jack, *Zachary Taylor: Soldier, Planter, Statesman of the Old Southwest* (Baton Rouge: Louisiana State University Press, 1985); Letter on Florida operations, Taylor to General R. Jones, 20 July 1839, RG 94, Records of the Adjutant General's Office, ca. 1775–ca. 1928, National Archives, Washington, D.C.; Lavender, David Sievert, *Climax at Buena Vista: The American Campaigns in Northeastern Mexico, 1846–47* (Philadelphia: Lippincott, 1966); Eisenhower, John S. D., *So Far From God: The U.S. War with Mexico, 1846–48* (New York:

Random House, 1989); Smith, Elbert B., *The Presidencies of Zachary Taylor and Millard Fillmore* (Lawrence: University Press of Kansas, 1988).

Theodoric the Great (ca. 454–526) *king of the Ostrogoths*

With the exception of ATTILA THE HUN, Theodoric was one of the most successful tribal military leaders in European history. He was born about 454, the illegitimate son of Theodomir (also spelled Theudemir), the leader of the Ostrogothic family of Amali and one of three brothers who controlled the eastern Goths in what is now Austria. When he was eight, Theodoric was taken to the court of Leo, the Holy Roman Emperor of the East, in the city of Constantinople, where he received a first-class education. (Some sources note that Theodoric was taken as a "hostage" to Constantinople.) Ten years later, he returned to his people and immediately led an invasion eastward into Sarmatia (today's Romania) and took control of the city of Singidunum (now modern Belgrade). Theodoric then marched south into Moesia and Macedonia, where the Goths settled for a short period. His father Theodomir died in 474, and for the next 14 years Theodoric fought a series of wars against the forces of the Eastern Roman Emperor Zeno as well as those of another Gothic tribal chief, also named Theodoric, the son of Triarius. In 488, with the agreement of Emperor Zeno, Theodoric began a war against Odoacer, also known as Odavacar, the German who was then the ruler of what is now Italy. Theodoric crossed the Sontius (now the Isonzo) River in northern Italy, and the two sides clashed there on 28 August 489, with Theodoric winning an important victory. He followed Odoacer's fleeing army and defeated them again at Verona on 30 September 489. Odoacer fled to Ravenna, but Theodoric's forces blockaded the city for more than three years.

Following the surrender of Odoacer and his army, Theodoric personally killed Odoacer on 15 March 493. He then took control of all Italy. His reign, 493–526, was a period of peace and prosperity for the Italian people as he lowered taxes and encouraged building programs. When two competing bishops, Anastasius and Symmachus, claimed the papacy, Theodoric was asked to adjudicate; he selected Anastasius. Two years later, when Anastasius died, Theodoric successfully pushed for the selection of Symmachus.

Because Theodoric followed Arian religious beliefs, there was a constant campaign against him among the remnants of the old senatorial faction in Rome. They persistently called on the Eastern Roman Emperor in Constantinople to depose Theodoric, even though his rule was supported by the majority of Italy. He executed the philosopher Boethius and Boethius's father-in-law, the leader of the party urging rebellion against him, and some historians maintain that it was remorse for this that brought on Theodoric's final illness and his death on 30 August 526. He was buried in a grand mausoleum in Ravenna and was succeeded by his grandson, Athalaric. He had brought peace and prosperity to Italy for 30 years at a time when the rest of Europe was riven by anarchy and tribal warfare.

References: Hodgkin, Thomas, *Theodoric the Goth: The Barbarian Champion of Civilization* (New York: G. P. Putnam's Sons, 1900); Hodgkin, Thomas, *Italy and Her Invaders,* 6 vols. (Oxford, U.K.: The Clarendon Press, 1880–99), III:30–50; Burns, Thomas S., *A History of the Ostro-Goths* (Bloomington: Indiana University Press, 1984); Moorhead, John, *Theodoric in Italy* (Oxford, U.K.: Clarendon Press, 1992).

Tilly, Johann Tserclaes, Count von (Johann T'serclaes, Jean Tilly, Jean Tserclaes) (1559–1632) *Belgian military commander*

Johann Tilly was born as Johann (or Jean) Tserclaes (some sources list the name as T'serclaes) in the chateau of Tilly, Brabant, in what is now Belgium sometime in 1559. He originally intended to enter the priesthood and studied at a Jesuit institution. However, in 1574, when he was only 15, he left the Jesuits to volunteer for service as a foot soldier in a Spanish regiment. During a period when he served in the army of Alessandro Farnese, duke of Parma, in several clashes, he rose through the ranks to become the commander of a company. He distinguished himself at the Spanish army's siege of Antwerp in 1585 and was given the governorships of the provinces of Dun and Villefranche, which he held from 1590 to 1594. In the latter year, Tilly left to enter the army of Rudolf II, the Holy Roman Emperor, in his war against the Turks. This conflict lasted for many years, during which Tilly raised an army of Walloon (ethnic Belgians) infantry, which he commanded in the empire's assault on the city of Budapest, now the capital of modern Hungary.

He rose in the ranks of the Imperial Army, becoming a field marshal in 1605. In 1609, when Rudolf proposed a controversial and unpopular law to allow freedom of worship, Tilly remained by his side, but when Rudolf was overthrown by his brother Matthias in 1612, Tilly was removed as a leading commander. He then went to serve Maximilian of Bavaria, who headed the Catholic League, and for the next decade he worked to establish a Bavarian army.

In 1620, Tilly was named as a lieutenant general in the Catholic League's army, and he served as commander in chief of its forces in the Thirty Years' War (1618–48). A European conflict arising from religious differences (Catholic/Protestant), the war pitted Austria, France, and Spain against Italy, the Germans, and the Dutch, although alliances often changed. At Bílá Hora (better known as White Mountain), outside of Prague, on 8 November 1620, Tilly first led some 20,000 men into battle and won a victory against some 15,000 Bohemians led by Christian I of Anhalt-Bernberg. He was defeated at Wiesloch (25 April 1622) by Ernst, count von Mansfield, but scored a triumph at Wimpfen (6 May 1622) over Georg Frederick of Baden-Durlach. Following his victory at Höchst (20 June 1622) in which he defeated the forces of Christian of Brunswick trying to cross the Main River, Tilly was given the title of Count Tilly. He took the city of Heidelberg (19 September 1622), and again defeated Christian at Stadtlohn (6 August 1623) near the border with the Netherlands.

The Danes, under King Christian IV of Denmark, entered the war against the Catholic League by invading Germany from the north, and Tilly teamed with Count Albrecht von Wallenstein to fight them. At Lutter am Barenberge (27 August 1626), Wallenstein aided Tilly in achieving a decisive victory in which nearly half of the Danish army was killed or wounded.

In 1630, GUSTAVUS II, the Swedish warrior king, came into the conflict. In order to stop him, Tilly surrounded the city of Magdeburg, which he intended to use as a base. The siege of the city was short, ending on 20 May 1631, but Tilly's plans to use the city were disturbed when his own army sacked Magdeburg and slaughtered its inhabitants, earning him the undeserved reputation of "Butcher of Magdeburg." Adolphus, because of logistical problems, could not arrive in time to save the situation and left his army at nearby Werben. Twice Tilly sent his forces to attack the Swedes, and in both battles, at Breitenfeld, approximately six miles from

Leipzig (17 September 1631), and Rain (15 April 1632), he was defeated. The former encounter, also known as the battle of Leipzig, was key to Tilly's overall defeat. Historian George Bruce writes that the battle was

> between 40,000 Swedes and an equal force of Saxons, under Gustavus Adolphus, and John George, Elector of Saxony, and 32,000 Imperialists, under Field Marshal the Count of Tilly. The Imperialist right totally routed the Saxons, who fled from the field, headed by the Elector. Meanwhile the Swedes had completely defeated the left of the Imperialists, under [Gottfried Heinrich, count von] Pappenheim, and repulsed the center under Tilly, and on the return of the right from pursuing the Saxons, they were attacked by the Swedish left and driven from the field, only four regiments holding their ground in a wood until nightfall. The Imperialists lost 8,000 killed and wounded and 5,000 prisoners; the allies [lost] 2,700, of whom only 700 were Swedes. Gustavus captured the whole of Tilly's artillery, and his victory was the salvation of the Protestant cause, which was trembling in the balance.

Historians believe that Pappenheim, an inexperienced officer, gave Tilly bad intelligence on the Swedes, leading to the defeat. Following the second defeat at Rain, Tilly tried to block Adolphus from crossing the Lech River. Adolphus moved his forces across the river in boats and, on 15 April 1632, attacked Tilly's army before it was ready. During the clash, Tilly was wounded seriously and taken to the city of Ingolstadt. Maximilian I, elector of Bavaria, took control of the army but could not stop Adolphus's forces and was compelled to withdraw, leaving most of the army's supplies and artillery on the field of battle. Tilly lingered for two weeks, finally succumbing to his wounds on 30 April 1632 at the age of about 73.

Historians studying the 17th century and warfare in Europe consider Tilly one of the more successful military leaders of his time. He never lost a battle in which he had the proper resources, and he lost the most important, Breitenfeld, because he had bad intelligence.

References: Windrow, Martin, and Francis K. Mason, "Tilly, Johann Tserclaes, Graf von," in *The Wordsworth Dictionary of Military Biography* (Hertfordshire, U.K.:

Wordsworth Editions Ltd., 1997), 291–292; *A Letter Sent from Maynhem Concerning the late Defeate given the Duke of Brunswicke by Monsieur Tilly: . . .* (London: Printed by Bernard Alsop for Nathaniel Butter, 1622); Watts, William, *The Swedish Intelligencer. Wherein out of the Truest and Choysest Informations are the famous actions of that warlike Prince historically led along, from the Norimberg Leaguer, unto the day of his death at the victory of Lutzen . . .* (London: Printed by I.L. for Nath. Butter and Nicholas Bourne, 1633); Watts, William, *The Swedish Intelligencer. Wherein out of the Truest and Choysest Informations are the famous actions of that warlike Prince historically led along, from His Majesties first entring into the empire, untill his great Victory over the Generall Tilly at the battle of Leipsith . . .* (London: Printed for Nath. Butter and Nicholas Bourne, 1634); *March 14. Numb. 23. The Continuation of our Weekly Newes, from the 18 of February to this 14 of March Containing, amongst other things, these Particulars following: the good Success of the king of Sweden in the land of Meckelburgh, with the names of the townes he hath lately taken. With divers particulars concerning Monsieur Tilly his preparation and strength to oppose the said King of Sweden. . . .* (London: Printed for Nath. Butter and Nicholas Bourne, 1631); Bruce, George, "Leipzig," *Collins Dictionary of Wars* (Glasgow, Scotland: HarperCollins Publishers, 1995), 139.

Timur (Tamerlane, Timur-I-Lenk) (1336–1405)
Tartar warrior

Timur (Persian for "Iron")—known by Asians as Timur-I-Lenk and by Europeans as Tamerlane—was born sometime in the year 1336 at Kesh, the valley of Samarkand (also Samarqand), now in modern Uzbekistan. He was a direct descendant of the famed Mongol warrior GENGHIS KHAN, but he was an ethnic Tartar and not a Mongol. In 1653, historian Samuel Clarke wrote one of the first biographies of Tamerlane in which he notes that "Tamerlane was born at Samercand [sic], the Chief City of the Zain-Cham, or, as others will, Og, Prince of the Zagatajans, of the country Sachithay (sometimes part of the famous Kingdom of Parthia), third in descent from Zingis the Great, and successful Captain of the Tartars, which Og being a Prince of a peaceable nature (accounting it no less honour quietly to keep the Countries left him by his father, then with much trouble and no less hazard to seek how to enlarge the same) long lived in most happy peace with his Subjects, no less

happy therein then himself; not so much seeking after the hoording [sic] of gold and silver . . . as contenting himself with the encrease [sic] and profit of his sheep and herds of cattel [sic]." According to the Arabic historian Ali Sharaf ad-Din, Timur stole sheep as a youth and, sometime in his 20s, was wounded during a theft, suffering wounds in his leg and arm that left him lame for the remainder of his life. It is because of this that he was known as "Timur the Lame," and this nickname became corrupted over the centuries to the current "Tamerlane." However, as the editors of *The Wordsworth Dictionary of Military Biography* note, "Such biographical material as survives appears to be commissioned and distinctly suspect."

Little is known of Timur's early life, or when he first began his military conquests. However, historians believe that sometime about 1365, he took control of a band of nomadic warriors situated between the Oxus and Jaxartes Rivers. From there, over a period of more than 30 years, he led this band in conquering vast areas of territory across Asia. Timur capitalized on the fracturing of the empire of his ancestor Genghis Khan, who had amassed great territories but whose successors could not match his power and influence. Timur traveled constantly, and historians believe he never had a permanent home at any time during his life. For 24 years from 1370, he fought in the Central Asian provinces of Khwareszm (also called Khorezm) and Jatah, and in 1380 he occupied the city of Kashgar. In 1381, the city of Herat—now in Afghanistan—was seized by his horsemen, and four years later all of eastern Persia, now modern Iran, was taken as well. Within two more years, Timur's bands of nomadic horsemen had driven across most of what is now the Middle East, sweeping across Babylon (modern Iraq), Azerbaijan, and Armenia.

Just as Timur conquered Armenia (1386), a group of Mongols headed by the warrior Toktamish invaded Azerbaijan and defeated one wing of Timur's army. Timur quickly moved on the Mongols and defeated them. However, he did not pursue Toktamish, and the Mongol turned to invade Samarkand. Marching approximately 50 miles per day, Timur's army arrived back in Samarkand, where they were able to beat back Toktamish's forces. Timur then decided to invade his enemy's homeland, the Mongol khanate in what is now eastern Russia and northern China. Gathering a force of some 100,000 men, he invaded Russia in 1390, but it was not until the following year that the two forces collided at the Battle of the Steppes, also known as the Battle of Lake Kerguel (July 1391), which historians believe took place east of the Volga River and south of the Kama River. Historian George Bruce writes: "[The battle was] between 300,000 Russians, under Toktamish, and an equal force of Tartars, under Timur. The battle began at daybreak, and by midday the Russians were totally routed, and fled in disorder, leaving the camp in the hands of Timur." It is estimated that 30,000 Mongols died on the battlefield. However, because his own army had taken severe casualties, Timur decided not to pursue Toktamish, instead falling back to Central Asia.

A series of uprisings against Timur's rule began in 1392, and he spent the next several years putting them down. He invaded India, and at Delhi (17 December 1398), his force was attacked by the army of the Delhi Muslims, commanded by Mahmud Tughlak. Utilizing the river nearby to cross and confuse the Muslims, Timur forced them to withdraw back into the city, which he besieged, forcing its surrender; his army then plundered it. At Aleppo (11 November 1400), Timur's forces met those of the Turks under the Syrian emirs. He conquered them quickly, and his army sacked the city. He conquered Damascus (25 January 1401) and then stormed Baghdad, now in modern Iraq (23 July 1401), razing it and massacring thousands of people. At Angora (today's Anatolia, 30 June 1402), Timur's army, estimated at 800,000 men, struck the Turks, commanded by Bazajet I. Timur won a resounding victory, taking Bazajet and one of his sons captive while another was killed.

In 1404, Timur returned to Samarkand and prepared for what he believed would be the ultimate military expedition: a war against the Ming Dynasty in China. He gathered every soldier, horseman, and archer he could find and set out for China, but within months he became ill. In February 1405, near the city of Chimkent in Turkestan, he died, possibly from a fever brought on by excessive drinking. His body was carried back to Samarkand, where he was laid to rest; his tomb, a national monument, is known as the Gur-Amir. In 1941, more than five centuries later, his body was exhumed by a Russian scientist, M. M. Gerasimov, who found that Timur was 5 foot 8 inches tall and excessively lame. Taking measurements of the skull, Gerasimov sketched what Timur might have looked like.

The "myth" of Tamerlane has grown in the six centuries since his death, with historians such as Samuel Clarke and others writing of him. The English playwright Christopher Marlowe penned an ode in the form of his 1587 play *Tamburlaine the Great.*

References: Clarke, Samuel, *The Life of Tamerlane the Great with his Wars against the Great Duke of Moso, the King of China, Bazajet the Great Turk, the Sultan of Egypt, the King of Persia, and Some Others, Carried on with a Continued Series of Success from the First to the Last . . .* (London, 1653); Windrow, Martin, and Francis K. Mason, "Timur-i-Leng," in *The Wordsworth Dictionary of Military Biography* (Hertfordshire, U.K.: Wordsworth Editions Ltd., 1997), 293; Manz, Beatrice Forbes, *The Rise and Rule of Tamerlane* (Cambridge, U.K.: Cambridge University Press, 1989); Bruce, George, "Lake Kerguel," in *Collins Dictionary of Wars* (Glasgow, Scotland: Harper-Collins Publishers, 1995), 135; Craig, Simon, "Battle of Ankara: Collision of Empires," *Military History* 19, no. 3 (August 2002): 58–65.

Togo, Heihachiro, Count (1847–1934) *Japanese admiral*

Heihachiro Togo was born in Kagoshima, Japan, on 27 January 1847 (some sources report the date as being 1848) into a family that included members of the samurai class. He received only a moderate education before he joined the Japanese Imperial Navy in 1866 (some sources report the year as being 1863). He was assigned to the Japanese ship *Kwaiten* in 1871. That same year, he was sent to England, where he spent seven years studying naval science and navigation and training with the Royal Navy at Portsmouth and Greenwich. After he returned to Japan in 1878, this experience helped him to rise in the ranks of the Japanese navy, and by 1888 he had been promoted to captain and given command of his own ship, the cruiser *Naniwa.* In 1893, when native Japanese in the Hawaiian islands complained to their homeland of maltreatment at the hands of the Hawaiians, Togo sailed to the islands and was there when American businessmen and planters staged a coup against Hawaiian queen Liliuoikalani. He nearly became involved in an incident when the captain of the American ship *Boston* demanded his withdrawal; the captain later apologized to him.

In 1894, Togo's cruiser was the first ship to fire in the Sino-Japanese War (1894–95), caused by Japanese concerns over Chinese control of the Korean peninsula.

On 25 July 1894, Togo's ship, *Naniwa,* sank the transport ship *Kowshing,* chartered from the British and carrying Chinese soldiers to fortify Chinese forces in Korea; Togo ordered his men to rescue the British members of the ship but left the Chinese to drown. The sinking caused an international incident, which did not bother Togo. A memoir on his life published in 1937 by one of the men who served under him describes the incident: "On that day, the flag-ship *Yoshino,* the *Akirsushima* and the *Naniwa,* of the First Flying Squadron, were cruising in the Yellow Sea . . . the three vessels which were at sea came across two Chinese men-of-war off Feng-tao, and the latter opened fire on us. Rear-admiral [Kozo] Tsuboi, commanding, gave the command 'fire' at once; and after twenty minutes of engagement, we were able to repulse the enemy. . . . Even in this country [Japan], Captain Togo was the target of reverse criticism. But in due course of time that measure taken by him was judged to be right, which won its author distinction; and the world came to know that there was a man of the name of Heihachiro Togo in the Japanese navy." Togo spent much of the war patrolling the waters off Korea, and following the conflict he was promoted to the rank of rear admiral (1895).

In the remaining years of the 19th century, Togo occupied several posts, including chief of the Japanese Naval Technical Council (1896). In 1900, when the Boxer Rebellion broke out in China, he commanded ships sent to China to keep in check the rampages of the nationalist groups known as Boxers.

In 1904, Japanese ambitions in the Pacific again resulted in conflict. The Russo-Japanese War, caused by Japan's desire to control portions of Manchuria then ruled by czarist Russia, was the first real indication of the growing Japanese military strength. In 1904, however, Japan was considered a second-rate power, especially compared to Russia. In battleships alone, Russia outnumbered Japan two to one. Togo realized that the only chance of a Japanese victory was a preemptive strike on the Russian fleet at Port Arthur, the Russian base neighboring northwest Korea. Before a declaration of war was made, Togo struck at the Russian Pacific fleet on 7 February 1904. While he did destroy part of the fleet at Port Arthur, he did not inflict the scale of damage upon the Russians that the Japanese later dealt to the American fleet at Pearl Harbor on 7 December 1941. However, his attack forced the Russians to find shelter in the harbor at Port Arthur and take precautions against further at-

tack. Assaults against the Russian fleet continued on 23 June 1904 and 10 August 1904 (the Battle of Shantung), when Japanese forces sank most of the Russian fleet in the Yellow Sea. While Togo attacked the remaining ships of the Russian fleet, Japanese land forces moved in and captured Port Arthur.

Togo now concentrated his attacks on the Russian Baltic fleet, which had sailed all the way around the world from Europe. Although Togo's fleet was about the same size as the Russian armada, the Russians had been sailing for more than seven months and the crews were tired. The two forces faced each other at Tsushima Straits, between what is now Japan and Korea, on 27 May 1905 in a battle that lasted two days and is ranked by most historians as one of the most decisive in world history. Historian Eric Grove writes: "Sir Julian Corbett in his confidential Staff History of the battle, called Tsushima 'perhaps the most decisive and complete naval victory in history.' No major Japanese unit had been seriously damaged and only three torpedo-boats sunk: 117 Japanese officers and men had been killed and 583 wounded. On the Russian side twelve major units, four destroyers and three auxiliaries had been sunk or scuttled after being disabled, and four major units and a destroyer captured. Of all Rozhestvensky's motley, but imposing array only one armed yacht and two destroyers got through to their destination. The toll in casualties was terrible, in the worst Russian tradition: 4,830 killed, 5,907 prisoners, 1,862 interned." For his services in the war, Togo was given the title of koshaku, or count, in 1907. He was also named as a member of the British Order of Merit in 1906.

Togo died on 30 May 1934 of throat cancer after an illness of several months. Historian Michael Lee Lanning writes: "Togo received a state funeral, but his death did not end his influence. His belief in a large navy and his example of surprise attack in an undeclared conflict emerged as the Japanese strategy in World War II. Togo brought Japan from the status of isolation and little influence to the rank of world power. As winner of one of history's most significant naval battles, Togo remains a Japanese hero and one of the world's great admirals, ranking behind only Horatio NELSON, Chester William NIMITZ, Alfred Thayer Mahan, and John Arbuthnot FISHER."

References: Bodley, Ronald Victor Courtenay, *Admiral Togo: the Authorized Life of Admiral of the Fleet, Marquis*

Heihachiro Togo (London: Jarrolds, 1935); Nakamura, Koya, comp., *Admiral Togo: A Memoir* (Tokyo, Japan: The Togo Gensui Publishing Company, 1937); Falk, Edwin Albert, *Togo and the Rise of Japanese Naval Power* (New York: Longmans & Company, 1936); Hoyt, Edwin P., *Three Military Leaders: Heihachiro Togo, Isoroku Yamamoto, Tomoyuki Yamashita* (Tokyo, Japan: Kodansha International, 1994), 19–75; Busch, Noel Fairchild, *The Emperor's Sword: Japan vs. Russia in the Battle of Tsushima* (New York: Funk & Wagnall's, 1969); Vail, Jason, "Shocking Triumph at Sea," *Great Battles* 7, no. 7 (September 1994), 50–57; Grove, Eric, *Fleet to Fleet Encounters: Tsushima, Jutland, Philippine Sea* (London: Arms and Armour, 1991), 45; Falk, Edwin Albert, *Togo and the Rise of Japanese Naval Power* (New York: Longmans & Company, 1936); Lanning, Michael Lee, "Heihachiro Togo," in *The Military 100: A Ranking of the Most Influential Military Leaders of All Time* (New York: Barnes and Noble Books, 1996), 252–254; "Togo, Heihachiro," in *Command: From Alexander the Great to Zhukov—The Greatest Commanders of World History,* edited by James Lucas (London: Bloomsbury Publishing, 1988), 132; Muir, Malcolm, Jr., "Togo, Heihachiro," in *Brassey's Encyclopedia of Military History and Biography,* edited by Franklin D. Margiotta (Washington, D.C.: Brassey's, 1994), 988–991.

Tromp, Cornelis Maartenszoon Van (1629–1691) *Dutch admiral*

Cornelis Maartenszoon Van Tromp was born in Rotterdam, Holland, on 9 September 1629, the second son of Maarten Harpertszoon TROMP, also a famous Dutch admiral. An anonymous history, printed in 1697, says of him:

> . . . I venture to Compose the History of one of those Hero's [sic], who without tarnishing the glory of the others may be said to have been one of the greatest and most Renowned Commanders that ever appeared on the Ocean, a Hero whose very name was a terror to his Enemies; That was descended of a Father who had been present in above Fifty Sea Battles in which he either Commanded in chief, or had at least one of the principal Posts of Authority, whose good Conduct and undaunted courage had much contributed to make Holland one of the Richest and most flourishing States of Europe; and who at

last after gaining so many Triumphs and Victories, died with Sword in hand for the advantage of his Country; a Hero, in sine [sic], that always followed the glorious foot steps of his Illustrious Father, who was as much beloved by his own Seamen and peoples, as he was dreaded by his Enemies, and who in a supreme degree possest [sic] all the virtues [sic] of a great and accomplish'd Captain.

Little is known of Tromp's early life, but in 1645, when he was about 16, he served as an aide to his father at sea, and four years later he became a full captain in the Dutch navy. He then took part in a series of engagements against pirates in the Mediterranean Sea, starting in 1650, followed by the First Anglo-Dutch War (1652–54) against England. In Italy, Tromp led Dutch forces at the Battle of Leghorn (31 March 1653), when six English ships under the command of Commodore Henry Appleton were destroyed by the Dutch; Tromp's ship, the *Maan,* did not sustain any damage. Following this victory, he was advanced to the rank of rear admiral. He then went to fight the Algerian pirates off the coast of northern Africa, and in 1655, after being named as a commander of the Dutch fleet, he was sent to the Baltic region, where the Dutch fought Sweden in the First Northern War (1655–60) between Poland and Sweden.

With the outbreak of the Second Anglo-Dutch War (1665–67), Tromp was recalled to fight for Holland. Serving under his fellow Dutch commander, Admiral Michiel de Ruyter, Tromp saw action in the major battles of this conflict, most notably at Orfordness (25–26 July 1666). However, as historians Anthony Bruce and William Cogar note, "in this concluding battle Tromp operated independently without de Ruyter's agreement, and his failure to cooperate with his commander contributed to the Dutch defeat." Complaints from de Ruyter led to Tromp's unceremonious dismissal, and for nearly a decade, he did not serve in any military function.

It was not until William III of Orange became stadtholder of the Netherlands in 1672 that Tromp was reinstated to a command with the outbreak of the Third Anglo-Dutch War (1672–74). He played a leading role in one of that conflict's most important engagements, the inconclusive Battle of the Texel (11 August 1673). Reconciled with de Ruyter, Tromp fought by his side, winning the battles of Schooneveld and Kijkduin, both in 1673. The war ended with the Treaty of Westminster (1674), whose terms permitted Tromp to patrol the English Channel. When he sailed into the Mediterranean, against orders, he was censured by the Dutch admiralty.

In 1676, Tromp was made commander in chief of a joint Dutch-Danish fleet when Denmark went to war against Sweden. In this fight, he once again distinguished himself, winning the battle of Öland (1 June 1676), after which he was made a nobleman of Denmark. He also saw action at Götland and at Rügen, both in 1676, and remained in the service until 1678.

Following the end of the war against Sweden, Tromp, nearly 60 years old, returned to the Netherlands. In 1691, he was given command of the Dutch fleet to fight the French in the War of the Grand Alliance (1688–97), but before he could take command, he was struck by illness. On 29 May 1691, he died in Amsterdam at the age of 61. While he was, like his father, an important military officer whose victories outnumbered his defeats, Cornelis Van Tromp did not oversee any military reforms or innovations. Nevertheless, he was a dominant naval commander of his time.

References: Tromp, Kornelis, Admiral, *The Life of Cornelius Van Tromp, Lieutenant-Admiral of Holland and West-friesland: Containing Many Remarkable Passages relating to the War between England and Holland. As also the Sea-Fights, and Other Memorable Actions of this Great Man, from the Year 1650, to the Time of his Death* (London, 1697); Bruce, Anthony, and William Cogar, "Tromp, Cornelis Maartenszoon," in *An Encyclopedia of Naval History* (New York: Checkmark Books, 1999), 376.

Tromp, Maarten Harpertszoon (1597–1653)
Dutch admiral

Born in Breille, South Holland, on 23 April 1598, Maarten Tromp was the son of Harpert Maartenszoon, a captain in the Dutch navy. When he was eight, Maarten sailed with his father to the East Indies, where, in 1611, the two were attacked by a British ship and Harpert Maartenszoon was killed. Maarten was taken prisoner and held by the British for two years, forced to serve on their ships as a ship's boy. He finally escaped and returned to the Netherlands, where he joined the Dutch navy in 1617, seeing his first military service against Algerian pirates in the Mediterranean Sea. During the fighting, he was taken captive by the pirates and held for

a year before being released. He again returned to the Netherlands, where he rejoined the navy with the rank of lieutenant.

In 1621, the Netherlands went to war with Spain, and Tromp was commissioned as a captain in 1624. He was given command of the flagship of Dutch admiral Piet Heyn, who was killed in 1629 during a battle with pirates. Tromp was then sent to continue Heyn's mission: to blockade the Spanish privateer sanctuary at Duinkerken (modern Dunkirk, on the French coast). He did so, and his success kept the Spanish privateers inactive for five years. However, the tedious blockade duty led him to resign his commission in 1634.

Four years later, Tromp was induced to return to the navy, and he returned to Duinkerken to take up his command. While there, he clashed with a Spanish fleet commanded by Admiral Antonio Oquendo at the battle of the Downs (15 September 1639). Historians Anthony Bruce and William Cogar write:

> During a short initial artillery duel, Oquendo's flagship, the *Santiago,* was damaged and, despite their numerical superiority the Spanish were forced to retreat toward the English coast. They anchored off Dover, where they were monitored by an English squadron under the command of Sir John Pennington who was under orders to protect English neutrality. There they carried out repairs and replenished their supplies. Meanwhile Tromp, who now blockaded the enemy, delayed a further attack until reinforcements had arrived from Holland. Within a month his fleet had expanded to 100 ships. Tromp now outnumbered the Spanish, and, on October 21, with a favorable wind, he decided to attack. His fleet was divided into six squadrons, one of which was used to keep the English squadron under observation. The Spanish fleet, still anchored in the Downs, was taken by surprise. It had not expected the Dutch to attack with the English in such close proximity, and was unable to respond effectively in time. Eleven Dutch fireships found a number of victims while others were captured or run aground. However, 13 enemy vessels, including the *Santiago* (and Oquendo himself) managed to escape. Over 7,000 Spaniards were killed or wounded and nearly 2,000 captured. In contrast, the Dutch lost 500 men and just a single

Maarten Harpertszoon Tromp

ship. The Battle of the Downs marked the end of Spanish supremacy in northern Europe.

Tromp's victory was one of the most important of the period.

Tromp again left the service, only to return in 1652 with the outbreak of the First Anglo-Dutch War (1652–54) between the Netherlands and England. Immediately he sailed to Dover to attack the English fleet, which was commanded by Robert BLAKE. The English were inferior in numbers, and with this in mind Tromp initiated an immediate attack. The battle of Dover (19 May 1652) had no victor, but Tromp was forced to withdraw. That October, he returned to again take on Blake's fleet, but Blake was not there, and he had to return home empty-handed. The Dutch admiralty relieved him of his command, and replaced him with Admiral Witte Corneliszoon de Witt. De Witt sailed to England, where he fought the English off Kentish Knock (26 September 1652) and was defeated, upon which Tromp was quickly reinstated as commander. He sailed back to England and defeated the English under Blake at Dungeness (30 November 1652), then attempted to follow up the victory when he met Blake off Portland (18–20 February 1653), but the English commander won an easy triumph.

Tromp took additional losses when Blake beat him at the battle of the Gabbard (2–3 June 1653), an engagement that led to a blockade of the Dutch coast by English forces. Tromp used his fleet to draw off some of the English ships in the cordon, allowing a number of Admiral de Witt's ships to escape. These ships joined Tromp's main fleet to take on the English at Terheijde, near Scheveningen off the coast of Holland (29 July 1653). During the battle, a soldier on one of Sir William PENN's ships shot Tromp in the heart, killing him instantly. Despite the loss of their commander, the Dutch won when the English had to withdraw for additional supplies. Tromp's body was returned to his homeland, and he was buried with full military honors in the city of Delft, where a memorial now stands in his honor.

The death of Maarten Tromp at the age of 56 was a huge blow for the Dutch government. It has been argued that Tromp's loss caused the Dutch to sue for peace, which ended the war with the Treaty of Westminster (1654). His son, Cornelis Von TROMP, followed in his father's steps and became one of the Netherlands' most important naval commanders of the 17th century.

References: Boxer, C. R., ed. and trans., *The Journal of Maarten Harperszoon Tromp, Anno 1639* (Cambridge, U.K.: Cambridge University Press, 1930); Vere, Francis, *Salt in Their Blood: The Lives of the Famous Dutch Admirals* (London: Cassel & Company, Ltd., 1955); Bruce, Anthony, and William Cogar, "Tromp, Maarten Harpertszoon" and "Downs, Battle of the," in *An Encyclopedia of Naval History* (New York: Checkmark Books, 1999), 114, 376; Mets, James Andrew, *Naval Heroes of Holland* (New York: The Abbey Press, 1902); Waddam, Henry, Sir, *The Danes Plot Discovered against this Kingdome . . .* (London: Printed for Andrew Coe and Marmaduke Boat, 1642); Lawson, John, Sir, *A Great and Bloudy Fight at Sea between the Parliaments Navy, under the command of General Blake, and the Dutch fleet, commanded by the Lord Admiral Van-Trump* (London: Printed for J. Fielding, 1652); *The Common-wealths Great Ship commonly called the Soveraigne of the Seas, built in the yeare, 1637 . . .* (London: M. Simmons, 1653).

Tserclaes, Jean *See* TILLY, JOHANN TSERCLAES, COUNT VON.

Turenne, Henri de La Tour d'Auvergne, vicomte de (Henri Turenne) (1611–1675)

French military commander

Henri Turenne was born at Sedan, France, sometime in 1611, the second son of Henri de La Tour d'Auvergne, duc de Bouillon and prince of Sedan (France), and his second wife, Elizabeth of Nassau, the daughter of William I of Orange (the Silent). Turenne's father was a major military commander, serving the French kings Charles IX and Henry IV in numerous battles. Following his father's death in 1623 Turenne studied military arts under his maternal uncle, MAURICE of Nassau, and entered the service of the Netherlands as an aide to Maurice during the Eighty Years' War, or war for Dutch Independence (1568–1648) from Spanish authority.

In 1625, Maurice was succeeded as the head of the Dutch forces by his brother, Frederick Henry (also known as Fredrik Henrik) of Nassau, and Turenne continued in service with him. The following year, he was advanced to the rank of captain. He served with great distinction under Frederick, seeing action at the battle of S'Hertogenbosch (1629). However, in 1630, he left the Netherlands and entered the service of the French army. Cardinal Richelieu, chief minister to King Louis XIII, gave him the rank of colonel and the command of a regiment of infantry, but he did not see action until 1634, when he led the assault on the city of La Motte in Lorraine in 1634. For his services in this battle, Turenne was promoted to the rank of *maréchal de camp* (major general). In 1635, he began his participation in the Thirty Years' War (1618–48) when France declared war against Spain; he was at Mainz when the French lifted the Spanish siege there, but his forces were forced to retreat to Metz when they ran short of rations and supplies. In 1636, he led the French in the capture of the French Alsatian city of Saverne, where he was seriously wounded. The following year, he rejoined his unit, fighting at the capture of the city of Landrecies (26 July 1637). While serving under Duke Bernhard of Saxe-Weimer, a German commander, Turenne led the attack on the fortress at Breisach and forced its surrender (17 December 1638).

In 1639, Turenne's battlefield exploits led Cardinal Richelieu to send him to Italy to fight under Henri of Lorraine (1601–66), duc d'Harcourt. D'Harcourt moved from the city of Carignano to Casale, sending Turenne to fight Prince Thomas of Savoy at Turin. In 1640, d'Harcourt met Prince Thomas's forces at Turin, forcing Thomas's surrender on 17 September 1640. This action, mainly due to Turenne's services, led to further battles in 1641, most notably at Mondovi, Coni (also Cuneo), and Ceva. In 1641, Turenne, as second in command of French forces, besieged the city of Roussillon.

On 19 December 1643, Turenne was given the command of French forces in Germany, and he was promoted to the rank of marshal. Dispatched to the province of Alsace, he was given command of "the Army of Weimar," the forces that had fought under Duke Bernhard of Saxe-Weimar and suffered the disastrous defeat at Tuttlingen (24–25 November 1643). Within a year, he had reorganized these remaining troops into an effective fighting force and, as second in command to the duc d'Enghien, marched them across the Rhine River into Germany in June 1644. He was the victor in a series of battles, including at Freiburg (also known as the Three Days' Battle, 3, 5, and 9 August 1644), but he was badly beaten at Mergentheim (also known as Marienthal, 2 May 1645) and Nördlingen (also known as Allerheim, 3 August 1645). Nevertheless, he continued to command the French army, capturing Trier (Trèves) and forcing

the elector of Bavaria to sign a peace treaty at Ulm (14 March 1647). Marching into Luxembourg, Turenne was forced to turn back when the Bavarians repudiated the treaty, but he defeated them at Zusmarshausen (17 May 1648), destroying the city. This final defeat of the anti-French alliance forced the signing of the Peace of Westphalia (1648) and an end to the war.

A civil war broke out in France that same year, and at first Turenne sided with the revolutionaries. However, he soon returned to the royalist fold, supporting and leading the forces of King Louis XIV. In 1651, his former superior, the duc d'Enghien, now duc de CONDÉ, sided with the rebels, and the two men then became opponents. Several years of minor and indecisive battles culminated in the battle at Rethel (15 December 1650), where Turenne was defeated; however, at the battle of the Dunes near what is now Dunkirk (14 June 1658), he defeated Condé, who was forced to leave France, and ended the war.

In 1660, Cardinal Mazarin, who had governed France as regent for the young King Louis XIV, died, and Louis took control of the throne. One of his first moves was to name Turenne—now elevated to vicomte de Turenne—as "marshall-general of the camps and armies of the King." In 1672, when Louis XIV fought the Dutch, Turenne's forces overran the Dutch provinces as far as the city of Amsterdam. Instead of surrendering to the French army, however, the Dutch opened the city's dikes and flooded its plains, forcing Turenne to forego an assault. This setback encouraged others to take up arms against France. In January 1673, taking the initiative, Turenne marched into Germany, forcing the elector of Brandeburg to sue for peace. Outmaneuvered by the Italian commander Raimondo Montecuccoli, conte di Montecuccoli, leading European imperial forces, he had to abandon attacking the city of Bonn. In June 1674, he won a victory at Sinzheim, but he was checked at Enzheim (4 October 1674). He lured the imperialists to Turkheim, in the French Rhineland, and won a massive victory on 5 January 1675. He then marched into Alsace and took it back from Montecuccoli's forces, pursuing the Italian commander until they met at Sassbach on 27 July 1675. At the very start of the battle, a bullet struck Turenne, killing him instantly. Mourned by the nation, his body was returned to France and buried in the church of St. Denis in Paris. In 1800, upon an order of NAPOLEON, his remains were exhumed and placed in the church of Les Invalides in Paris.

Henri d'Auvergne, vicomte de Turenne, was one of France's most important military commanders of the late 17th century. A sermon from his funeral, published in 1677, stated: "And the King lamented, and said, Died he as a Fool dieth? Know ye not that there is a Prince and a Great Man fallen this day in Israel?" His impact on helping France to win the Thirty Years War and to consolidate its gains in Europe cannot be underestimated.

References: Du Buisson, Premiere Capitaine [Gatien Courtilz de Sandras], *The History of the Life and Actions of the Great Captain of his Age the Viscount de Turenne . . . ,* translated by Ferrand Spence (London: Printed by J.B. for Dorman Newman & R. Bentley, 1686); Longueville, Thomas, *Marshall Turenne . . .* (London: Longmans, Green and Company, 1907); Cust, Edward, *Lives of the Warriors of the Civil Wars of France and England. Warriors of the Seventeenth Century,* 2 vols. (London: J. Murray, 1867–69); *A True Relation of the Successes & Advantages obtained by the Most Christian King's army, Commanded by the Viscount de Turenne . . .* (London: Tho. Newcomb, 1675); *A Great and Bloudy fight in France between the Kings army, commanded by General Turenne, the Duke of York, and the Lord Digby . . .* (London: Imprinted for Geo. Horton, 1652); Francis, Claude, "A Sermon at the Funeral of the High and Mighty Prince, Henry De La Tour D'Auvergne, Vicount of Turenne, Mareschal General of France; Colonel General of the Light Horse, and Governour of the Upper and Lower Limosin. Preach'd December 15, 1675 . . ." (London, 1677).

Vere, John de *See* OXFORD, JOHN DE VERE, 13TH EARL OF.

Vernon, Edward (1684–1757) *British admiral*
Edward Vernon was born at Westminster on 12 November 1684, the son of James Vernon, who served as secretary of state to King William III from 1698 to 1702, and his wife Mary, daughter of Sir John Buck of Lincolnshire. He joined the English navy in 1700 just prior to the War of the Spanish Succession (1701–14), and in 1704 he took part in the British capture of Gibraltar. Following the end of the war, he was elected to a seat in the House of Commons, serving from 1722 to 1734. During this time, fearful of Spanish intentions, he demanded that action be taken against Spain. He also called for naval reform and increasing training in strategy.

In 1739, Spain threatened Britain's interests in the Caribbean, and Vernon declared he would take Porto Bello (now Portobello, Panama) with six ships. He was given the ships, sailed west, and took Porto Bello on 23 October 1739, losing only seven men in the quick victory. However, in 1740, during the War of Jenkins' Ear (1739–43), he was ordered to attack—against his will—the city of Cartagena (in today's Colombia). This attack fell short, and Vernon was forced to withdraw his fleet to Jamaica. The following year, he tried to take Santiago de Cuba (Cuba), but again he was rebuffed by the Spanish, and he was forced to return to England.

Back in Britain, Vernon was named a vice admiral of the red, but he was also retired for a period—against his wishes, according to a letter written to Thomas Cobbett, at that time the Secretary to the Board of the Admiralty, in which Vernon complained:

> Though . . . promotions are said to be made by their lordship's orders, yet we all know the communication of his majesty's pleasure must come from the first lord in commission, from whom principally his majesty is supposed to receive his information on which his royal orders are founded; and as it is a known maxim of our law, that the king can do no wrong, founded, as I apprehend, on the persuasion that the crown never does so but from the misinformation of those whose respective provinces are to inform his majesty of the particular affairs under their care. . . . The first suggestion that naturally occurs to any officer, that has the fullest testimonies in his custody, of having happily served his majesty on the command he was intrusted with to his royal approbation, is, that your first commissioner must either informed his majesty that I was dead, or have laid something to my charge, rendering me unfit to rise in my

rank in the royal navy, of which, being insensible myself, I desire their lordships would be pleased to inform me in what it consists, having both in action and advice, always, to the best of my judgment, endeavoured to serve our royal master with a zeal and activity becoming a faithful and loyal subject, and having hitherto received the public approbation of your board.

Vernon's career in the navy was essentially over because of his two defeats. Elected as a member of Parliament for Ipswich in 1741, he took his seat in the Commons, but his fortunes changed in 1745 when the British Admiralty named him commander of the North Sea fleet. However, he resigned before taking control because his demand that he be named commander in chief was refused. He was disciplined, removed from command, and struck off the list of flag officers. This time, his career really was over.

Vernon died early in the morning of 28 October 1757 after he told his servant of lingering chest pains. Historian Cyril Hartmann, who studied the last years of Vernon's life, writes: "Admiral Vernon was buried in a vault he had made in the churchyard at Nacton. The entry in the Parish Register reads: 'Edward Vernon, Esq. Buried Nov 7th in linen.' To be buried in linen had become the privilege of the upper classes, since, in an attempt to revive the languishing woolen industry, Parliament had enacted that shrouds for the dead were henceforth to be woven of wool. But this was the sole mark of distinction according to the Admiral at his funeral, for he himself had left instructions in his will that he was to be buried 'in a Christian manner without any unnecessary pomp or vain pageantry.'"

Historians Anthony Bruce and William Cogar write that Vernon may be best be known for his introduction of "grog" into the English vernacular: "Vernon himself had been nicknamed 'Old Grog' because he normally wore a grogram coat—a silk and wool mixture—when on board ship." In 1740, Vernon had ordered that the ration of rum given to each sailor be watered down to save money and supplies, and perhaps because of the anger over this order, the new mixture became known as "grog." One other historical sidenote is that, in the 1740 fight at Cartagena, one of Vernon's officers was Lawrence Washington, eldest brother of the future General George WASHINGTON. When he left the service of the British navy, Lawrence Washington went to the American colonies and built an estate there which he named in honor of his former commander, calling it Mount Vernon.

References: Bruce, Anthony, and William Cogar, "Vernon, Edward," in *An Encyclopedia of Naval History* (New York: Checkmark Books, 1999), 387; Charnock, John, *Biographia Navalis; or, Impartial Memoirs of the Lives and Characters of Officers of the Navy of Great Britain, From the Year 1660 to the Present Time . . .* , 4 vols. (London: Printed for R. Faulder, 1794–98), III:349–374; Ford, Douglas, *Admiral Vernon and the Navy: A Memoir and Vindication* (London: T. Fisher Unwin, 1907); Harding, Richard, "Edward Vernon, 1684–1757," in *Precursors of Nelson: British Admirals of the Eighteenth Century,* edited by Peter Le Fevre and Richard Harding (London: Chatham Publishing, 2000), 151–176; Hartmann, Cyril Hughes, *The Angry Admiral: The Later Career of Edward Vernon, Admiral of the White* (Melbourne, New South Wales, Australia: William Heinemann Ltd., 1953).

Wallace, Sir William (ca. 1270–1305)

Scottish revolutionary

William Wallace was born about 1270 in the Scottish area of Renfrewshire; he is believed to be the second son of Sir Malcolm Wallace of Elderslie and Auchinbothie. Because there are few records of this period, much of the story of Wallace's early life comes from a history written by a 15th-century monk named Blind Harry, who combined legends about Wallace with other anecdotes handed down from generation to generation. Wallace grew up in the village of Dunipace, in Stirlingshire, Scotland, where he lived with an uncle. While attending school, he met John Blair, who became one of his closest friends as well as his personal chaplain. Blind Harry's work claimed his account was based on a 13th-century work by Blair, but Blair's work is lost, and Harry's claims cannot be substantiated.

Although many biographies have depicted Wallace rallying against the English because of their rule over Scotland, some historians believe that his murder of an Englishman named Selby, who had insulted him, led to the English authorities turning Wallace into a outlaw and making him a rebel against the hated English. Steadily, he assembled a band of fellow Scots who hated English rule and were determined to throw off English domination. Many of these men included some of the most important noblemen in Scotland, including Doug-las the Hardy, Sir John de Graham, Sir Andrew Moray, Robert Wishart (bishop of Glasgow), and several others. The first action this group took was to attack the court being conducted by William de Ormsby, the English judge in Scotland. Although Ormsby escaped, many of

William Wallace

his aides, clerks, and supporters were brutally murdered by Wallace's troops. The English sought revenge by murdering Wallace's uncle, Sir Ronald Crawford, and several other Scottish nobles. Wallace's forces then struck back, burning down the Barns of Ayr, where English troops in Scotland were garrisoned.

The burning of the Barns of Ayr forced the English government to react: King EDWARD I dispatched an army under the command of Sir Henry Percy and Sir Robert Clifford to hunt down Wallace and his allies. The English met Wallace's forces at Irvine, and all of his men but Sir Andrew Moray abandoned him and made a peace with the English. Wallace, with Moray, fled north, and even though most of the barons and nobles had turned on him, many Scots began to join his army. With this force, Wallace marched south and took possession of nearly all of the areas north of the Firth of Forth. He was besieging the city of Dundee when he received intelligence that the English under John de Warenne, the earl of Surrey, were approaching from the south.

To head off Surrey, Wallace marched his forces to Stirling, camped his men near the Abbey Craig, now a national monument, and waited. Surrey offered him a surrender, but when Wallace refused, Surrey crossed the bridge over the river Forth (11 September 1297). Wallace waited until half of Surrey's army had crossed—then he attacked. The assault came with such precision that most of this first half of the English army were slain and their bodies thrown into the river. The rest of the army, unable to help because of the narrowness of the bridge, panicked and fled, with Wallace attacking their rear until the city of Berwick. During this latter part of the battle, Sir Andrew Moray was killed.

Wallace's victory at Stirling forced the English to pull their troops from Scotland and reorganize them. However, Wallace invaded northern England and began a systematic campaign of looting in Northumberland, which eventually led him to the city of Newcastle. He soon retreated back to Scotland, where the citizenry elected him by acclamation as the "guardian of the realm" in March 1298. Wallace was, in effect, in control of all of Scotland.

Edward I, who became known as "The Hammer of the Scots," decided once and for all to end Wallace's rebellion. Once again he sent an army led by the earl of Surrey, which captured Roxburgh castle. Edward then commanded the army himself and marched to Falkirk. There, on 22 July 1298, he attacked Wallace's forces with a largely superior force, including some 3,000 cavalry and many archers, easily defeating the Scots. During the battle, Wallace's close friend Sir John de Graham was killed, leaving him without one of his most important advisers. Blind Harry's account of Wallace's grief is considered one of the eloquent of the passages in his story. Moving north to escape the English, Wallace resigned his position as guardian of the realm and prepared for an all-out war against Edward and the English. Allegedly, he visited several countries on the European continent, and presumably met the French king, although this is only speculation from historians and not based on any solid facts. What is fact is that in 1303, Edward exacted from the Scottish nobles an agreement to submit to his rule, but he specifically excluded Wallace, on whose head he placed a bounty.

When Wallace returned to Scotland in 1305, he was betrayed almost immediately and handed over to the English on 4 August 1305. Removed to London in chains, he was taken to Westminster Hall, now part of the Palace of Westminster (the Houses of Parliament), where he was tried, found guilty of treason, and sentenced to death by Sir Peter Mallorie, the king's justice. That same day, he was taken and tortured with extreme brutality and cruelty; his head was cut off, and his body sent to four different sections of England as a warning to those who might fight the Crown.

On 24 June 1861, 556 years after Wallace was executed, a crowd of some 100,000 people formed in Stirling, the site of the famous 1297 battle, to dedicate a 300-foot high National Monument to Wallace and his fight for Scottish independence. The Academy Award-winning film by Mel Gibson, *Braveheart,* exaggerated many details of Wallace's life but nonetheless brought his story to modern audiences nearly seven centuries after his execution.

References: Henry the Minstrel, *The Actis and Deidis of the Illustere and Vailoeand Campioun Schir William Wallace, Knicht of Ellerslie, by Henry the Minstrel, Commonly known as Blind Harry,* edited by James Moir (Edinburgh, Scotland: W. Blackwood and Sons, 1889); Murison, Alexander Falconer, *Sir William Wallace* (Edinburgh, Scotland: Oliphant, Anderson & Ferrier, 1898); Fisher, Andrew, *William Wallace* (Edinburgh: J. Donald, 1986); Morton, Graeme, *William Wallace: Man and Myth* (Stroud, Gloucestershire, U.K.: Sutton, 2001).

Waller, Sir William (1597–1668) *English Parliamentary commander*

The son and one of three children of Sir Thomas Waller, lieutenant of Dover Castle, William Waller was born at Knole House, Groombridge, in Kent, England, on 3 December 1597 (some sources report the date as 1598). He received his education at Magdalen Hall, Oxford University, after which he traveled to the European continent and entered military service in the Venetian army. He saw action against the Austrians during the campaigns of the Thirty Years' War (1618–48) and was a member of Sir Horace Vere's 1620 expedition to rescue Elizabeth of Bohemia from being captured. During this latter mission, he became close friends with another English military officer, Sir Ralph HOPTON, who, like Waller, would play a key role in the English Civil War. In 1622, King James I of England knighted Waller for his services.

Following his knighthood, the events of Waller's life are obscure until 1640, when he was elected as a member of Parliament for Andover. He served in what was called the Long Parliament, which had been called by Charles I following his defeat in the Second Bishops' War (1639–40) and remained in session from 1640 until 1660. It was during this Parliament that numerous grievances against Charles I—long-standing criticisms and objections to royal rule—came to a head amongst the Parliamentarians. Waller became one of Parliament's leaders against Charles, and the break between the king and his subjects led to civil war in 1642. Waller was named as a colonel in the Parliamentary army when war broke out, and one of his first moves was to march against the city of Portsmouth, capturing it in September 1642. He went on to take Farnham, Winchester, and other towns, earning him the nickname "William the Conqueror."

Perhaps the most critical of the engagements Waller fought in the last months of 1642 was at Edgehill (23 October), the first major battle of the conflict. Along with Robert Devereux, the third earl of ESSEX, Waller commanded a force of some 14,000 infantry and cavalry against the Royalist forces directly commanded by Charles I at Edgehill, northwest of the town of Banbury. Charles's troops initially successfully broke the Parliamentary army's lines but became trapped in trying to pursue them, and both forces were forced to retire, although historians give a "victory" to Charles because the army of Waller and Essex withdrew. Nonetheless, the battle showed Charles that Parliament's troops were a force to be reckoned with, and that it would be a long war.

Parliament's army was split into different divisions, with one commanded by Waller. This division marched toward the Welsh border, capturing the vital port of Bristol in early 1643 and forcing the Welsh Royalists under Lord Herbert to surrender when they were surrounded. Waller captured the towns of Monmouth and Chepstow but encountered Prince Maurice, the Royalist commander, at Ripple Field (April 1643), where his forces suffered a serious defeat and had to withdraw. Waller again marched on various cities, but he was dogged by his former comrade, Sir Ralph Hopton, fighting for the Royalists. In a series of battles, Waller and Hopton met head-on, culminating in the battles at Lansdown (5 July 1643), near Bath, and Roundway Down (13 July 1643), where Hopton defeated Waller's forces; Waller later wrote that the latter battle was his most "dismal defeat." Despite the antagonism between the two, Waller still considered Hopton his friend and sent him letters detailing his own personal grief over the conflict dividing them. "That great God," Waller wrote in one missive, "who is the searcher of my heart knows with what a sad sense I go upon this service, and with what a perfect hatred I detest this war without an enemy; but I look upon it as sent from God . . . in his good time send us the blessing of peace[,] and in the meantime assist us to receive it! We are both upon the stage and must act such parts as are assigned us in this tragedy, let us do it in a way of honour and without personal animosities."

In October 1643, despite his losses, Waller was named as commander of Parliament's Southern Association. At Alton (13 December 1643), he surprised a Royalist force of 900 with an army of 3,000. The Royalist commander, only identified as a Colonel Bolle, realized he was surrounded and withdrew to a church, barricading his refuge with dead horses. The Roundhead infantry forces under Waller pulled down the church walls with their pikes and hacked to death some 500 Royalists inside, taking around 400 others prisoner. When Charles got word that Bolle had been killed, he is said to have stated, "I have lost one of the best commanders in this kingdom." Waller lost only 100 men in the slaughter. He laid siege to Basing House near Basingstoke but abandoned this when Hopton moved through Hampshire toward London. Waller then took the town and castle of Arundel (January 1644) and met Hopton at Cheriton (29 March 1644), near Arlesford in Hampshire. There, Waller's 6,500 men attacked Hopton's army of 3,500 infantry and 2,500 horse soldiers. Waller's plan of attack and numerical advantage forced Hopton to retreat, leaving southeastern England in Parliamentary hands. This was also Parliament's first major victory in the war. Essex then ordered Waller to follow the king's army while he moved west in what turned out to be a disastrous move, as Charles turned on Waller and defeated him at Copredy Bridge (29 June 1644).

Waller's final major engagement was the second battle at Newbury (October 1644). Angered that Essex was controlling his forces, Waller wrote an impassioned letter to Parliament that the antiroyal army should be organized based on a national rather than a regional basis, noting that "an army compounded of these men will never go through with your service, and till you have an army merely your own that you may command, it is in a manner impossible to do anything of importance." This letter led to the creation of the so-called "New Model Army" in 1645, with Waller named as one of its commanders. However, while he was marching to relieve Taunton, Parliament enacted the Self-Denying Ordinance, which forced all members of Parliament to relinquish their military commands. Because of this, in early 1645 Waller relinquished his commission as a general, and his military career came to an end. He returned to his seat in Parliament, where he became a leader of the Presbyterian faction. An outspoken member, he was threatened with impeachment, along with 10 others, in June 1647 when his enemies accused him of intolerance to those not in sympathy with his ideas.

Waller subsequently became one of 40 Parliamentarians arrested in "Pride's Purge," initiated by Thomas Pride. In December 1648, as the first phase of the Civil War drew to a close, Pride demanded that Parliament not make any deals with the king. To ensure there was no arrangement or agreement to end the war, he ordered that soldiers prevent any pro-agreement members from taking their seats, and 40 of them, including Waller, were arrested. (Pride was later one of those who signed Charles's execution warrant in January 1649.) Waller, who refused to accede to Pride's demands, was imprisoned until 1652. He played no role in the English government presided over by Oliver CROMWELL, though he was again imprisoned on suspicion of treason in 1659.

In April 1660, Waller was elected to the Convention Parliament, which met to clear the way for the restoration of Charles II, son of the executed king, to the throne. He helped to welcome Charles back to England and retired soon after the new king's return to his home at Osterley. He died in London on 19 September 1668, two months before his 70th birthday. He had been one of the more important of the Parliamentary commanders in the English Civil War, but, because other commanders such as Cromwell played more important roles, Sir William Waller's name has been forgotten, except by historians.

References: Adair, John, *Roundhead General: A Military Biography of Sir William Waller* (London: Macdonald & Co., 1969); *A True Relation of the Fortunate S. William Waller, Collonel Under His Excellency the Earle of Essex, . . .* (London, 1643); *A True Relation of the Late Fight betweene Sr William Wallers forces and those sent from Oxford . . .* (London: G. Dexter, 1643); *A Great Over-throw: Given to Sir Ralph Hopton's whole Army by Sir William Waller neere Farnham . . .* (London: Printed for John Hammon, 1643); *A Fuller Relation of the Great Victory Obtained (Through God's Providence) at Alsford, on Friday the 28. of March, 1644. By the Parliaments Forces, under the Command of Sir William Waller, Sir William Balfore, and Major Generall Browne . . .* (London: Printed for Laurance Blaiklock, 1644); *A Famous Victorie Obtained by Sir William Waller, against the Lord Herbert and the Welch Cavaliers in the Forrest of Deane in the County of Gloucester . . .* (London: Printed for Robert Wood, 1643); Ash, Simeon, *A True Relation, of the most Chiefe Occurrences at, and since the late Battell at Newbery, untill the disjunction of the three Armies, of the Lord Generall, the Earl of Manchester, and Sir William Waller, together with the London Brigade, under the Commander of Sir James Harrington . . .* (London: Printed by G.M. for Edward Brewster, 1643); *The Souldiers Report concerning Sir William Wallers Fight against Basing-house on Sunday last November the 12, 1643 . . .* (London: John Hammond, 1643); *The Battle of Acton: An Account of the Famous Battle in 1643 during England's Civil War* (Alton, U.K.: Peter Canfield Associates, 1999); Adair, John, *Cheriton 1644: The Campaign and the Battle* (Kineton, U.K.: The Roundwood Press, 1973).

Warwick, Richard Neville, earl of (Warwick the Kingmaker) (1428–1471)

English military leader

Richard Neville was born on 22 November 1428, the eldest son of Richard Neville, earl of Salisbury, and was betrothed as a boy to the daughter of the earl of Warwick. When his father-in-law died in 1449, the 21-year-old Neville succeeded to the Warwick title. This made him the most powerful noble in the country, with vast estates and large numbers of fighting men under his command at a time when there was a struggle for supremacy among the great barons over the governance of England. The nominal ruler was Henry VI, who had succeeded to the throne as a baby in 1422. During Henry's childhood, the regents Humphrey of Gloucester and Richard, earl of Warwick (later Neville's father-in-law), had governed England in his name. Others were jealous of the regents' power, and Henry, an indecisive and weak king, found himself constantly embroiled in power struggles among the barons, all using him as a figurehead. The result was the 30-year conflict known as the Wars of the Roses (1455–85), in which those who supported Henry VI were known as Lancastrians, while those who supported Richard, duke of York (who wanted to be appointed regent), were known as Yorkists.

In 1453, Neville—now earl of Warwick—sided with Richard, his brother-in-law, and fought with him in the Yorkist victory of St. Albans in 1455. As a result, Warwick was named captain of Calais, an English-held city in France. He remained in that post for five years and won a victory at sea against the Spanish. In 1458, as trouble from other claimants to power flared up again in England, he took a small force there but was defeated at Ludlow and managed to escape back to France with only a handful of followers. In 1460, he again came to England with an army, this time gaining an easy victory for the Yorkists at Northampton (10 July 1460), seizing Henry VI as prisoner and taking him back to London. Later that year, though, the Lancastrians rallied, and Richard of York—who was now claiming the throne—was killed at Wakefield on 30 December 1460.

The Lancastrians won a second victory, again at St. Albans, on 17 February 1461, but the defeat was not enough to make Warwick flee. He now took up the cause of Richard's son Edward, who had a claim to the throne though his descent from Henry III. Warwick brought Edward to London, had him proclaimed king (Edward IV), and marched north to defeat the Lancastrians at the battle of Towton (29 March 1461).

For nearly four years, with Edward's agreement, Warwick was virtual ruler of England, but Edward offended him by secretly marrying Elizabeth Woodville in 1464, when Warwick was eager for the king to marry a French princess. Further, Edward immediately favored his wife's family and gave them positions of power, which Warwick viewed as both a personal insult and a reduction of his authority. He then withdrew from court, but in 1467 he agreed to go to France to conclude a treaty with that country on Edward's behalf. He returned to find that, swayed by his wife, Edward now favored France's Burgundian rivals.

Infuriated by this sign of the Woodvilles' growing influence, Warwick went back to Calais and instigated a revolt against Edward. When Edward marched north to deal with it, Warwick brought a small army across from France, and Edward was defeated and captured at the battle of Northampton in 1469. However, Warwick was soon obliged to release him, and a rebellion in Lincolnshire in March 1470 gave Edward the chance to gather an army of his own. He put down a rebellion at Stamford, but the rebel leader's admission that Warwick had been involved meant that Warwick once again had to flee to France. Changing sides, he made an agreement with the Lancastrians, gathered more forces, and returned to England. He then marched on London and proclaimed Henry VI (who had been kept a prisoner in the Tower of London) as king in September 1470. Edward fled abroad, and for six months Warwick governed England on Henry's behalf. However, in March 1471 Edward returned and, on 14 April 1471, met Warwick in battle at Barnet, outside London. Here the Lancastrians were defeated—and Warwick was killed. He was buried in the family mausoleum in Bisham Abbey, Berkshire.

Though Warwick had been the most powerful man in England and made no claim the throne himself, he was never content to share power with anybody else. In the end, this proved to be his undoing.

References: Oman, Sir Charles William Chadwick, *Warwick, the Kingmaker* (London: Macmillan, 1891); Young, Charles R., *The Making of the Neville Family in England, 1166–1400* (Woodbridge, U.K.: Boydell Press, 1996); Richardson, Geoffrey, *The Lordly Ones: A History of the Neville Family and Their Part in the Wars of the Roses* (Shipley, U.K.: Baildon Books, 1998); Hallam, Elizabeth, ed., *The Chronicles of The Wars of the Roses* (Surrey, U.K.: Bramley Books, 1996).

Washington, George (1732–1792) *American general, first president of the United States*

George Washington was born at Bridges Creek, near Fredericksburg, Virginia, on 22 February 1732, the son of Augustine Washington, who owned a number of plantations in Virginia. Washington's great-grandfather had left Northamptonshire, England, in 1657, settled in Virginia, and become a member of the Virginia House of Burgesses. His grandson Augustine had become wealthy and purchased several estates, including Bridges Creek, where George was brought up.

Little detail is known of Washington's earliest years, and it is now accepted that the famous story in which the young George admitted chopping down a cherry tree was an invention of one of his early biographers, Mason Weems. Washington attended a small local school where he studied some Latin, and his notes from that time on "Rules of Civility" have been preserved. He appears to have been self-taught in many areas and spent much of his time with his father, seeing how a plantation was run and learning about the iron and smelting business the family owned. He was put in charge of the Hunting Creek estate, where he learned to grow tobacco and oversaw a large number of slaves. He also learned the science of surveying and soon became expert in that profession.

In 1743, when Washington was only 11, his father died and he was left in the care of his older half brother Lawrence. He lived with Lawrence and another half brother, Augustine, on the Hunting Creek estate, whose name Lawrence changed to Mount Vernon in memory of the English admiral Edward VERNON, under whom he had served. Washington applied himself to surveying, and in 1748 he surveyed the extensive Virginia estates of Thomas, Lord Fairfax, keeping a detailed diary of his experiences that has given later historians valuable insight into his thinking at that time. The following year, with Lord Fairfax's assistance, he was named as official sur-

Engraving of General George Washington at the Battle of Trenton, 26 December 1776

veyor of Culpeper County; he also worked in Augusta and Frederick Counties.

In 1751, Washington's brother Lawrence became ill with tuberculosis and went to Barbados to recover. Washington accompanied him and caught smallpox there, which left him with scars for the rest of his life. The brothers returned home, and Lawrence died in July 1752, whereupon George became executor and residuary legatee to his estate. At the age of 20, he was in charge of a flourishing plantation, and he devoted himself to its improvement and enlargement so successfully that, by 1757, he was looking after more than 4,000 acres. He wrote to a friend in England: "No estate in United America is more pleasantly situated than this."

Washington's military experience began in 1752 when he was appointed adjutant of one of Virginia's military districts. Though a salary of £100 a year went with the post, the duties were light, but this changed in 1753 when Governor Robert Dinwiddie became alarmed at French incursions into the Ohio valley. He appointed Washington to take a small party to deliver a formal written ultimatum to the French at Fort Le Boeuf, where the city of Waterford, Pennsylvania, now stands. The party were received with formal courtesy by the French, who told Washington that they intended to occupy the Ohio valley by any means necessary; this was confirmed in a letter to be taken back to Governor Dinwiddie. On the return journey, Washington's party was attacked by Indians, but they reached home safely and Dinwiddie immediately wrote to London to warn them of the French intentions. Rather than wait for guidance from England, Dinwiddie decided the matter needed prompt action, appointed Washington as lieutenant colonel in command of a provincial regiment under Colonel Joshua Fry, and ordered them to attack the French posts in the Ohio valley.

Washington's force marched on what had been a small British fort that the French had occupied and renamed Fort Duquesne (on the site of today's Pittsburgh). Some distance from the French fort, Washington erected a temporary fortification in Great Meadows, called Fort Necessity, and launched a surprise attack on a French detachment on 28 May 1754. The attack, the first engagement of the French and Indian Wars (1754–1763), was successful; the French commander, Colonel Joumonville, was killed and the remainder were taken prisoner. The clash promptly brought about a counterattack from the main French force, which pursued Washington and

his men back to Fort Necessity, besieged them there, and forced their surrender. The French commander showed leniency and allowed Washington to take his soldiers back to Virginia once he had agreed that there would be no English forts built in the Ohio valley for a year and had acknowledged responsibility for the death of Colonel Joumonville. On his return to Virginia, Washington received the thanks of the House of Burgesses and was promoted to colonel, though he resigned his commission later that year (1754) in protest at the poor pay of provincial officers.

When General Edward Braddock and his force arrived in Virginia to resume the campaign against Fort Duquesne in 1755, he asked Washington to accompany him as aide-de-camp, an offer Washington eagerly accepted. He was at Braddock's side when his force was ambushed by a French and Indian force on the Monongahela River on 9 July 1755 and played a major role in rallying the survivors and bringing them back to safety. For his services, he was appointed commander of the Virginia provincial force with the rank of colonel. The appointment was a difficult one since he had only about 700 soldiers to defend a border 400 miles long. Although he had the satisfaction of commanding the advance guard of General John Forbes when he captured Fort Duquesne in 1758, Washington resigned his commission soon afterwards. He was then elected to the House of Burgesses, and on 6 January 1759 he married Martha Custis, a wealthy widow.

For the next 15 years, Washington occupied himself in improving his estates and fulfilling his duties in the House of Burgesses. Though he was opposed to the call for the colonies' independence, he was firm in defending the rights of the colonists against what he saw as undue British repression. He was one of Virginia's delegation to the First and Second Continental Congresses of 1774 and 1775, and on 15 June 1775 he was unanimously chosen as commander in chief of the Continental Army.

Washington arrived at Boston, where the British were besieged, on 3 July 1775, and for the next eight months he brought discipline to the army, settled disputes among his subordinate commanders, and enforced the siege. When he had acquired sufficient guns and equipment, he forced the British to surrender Boston by seizing the Dorchester heights overlooking the harbor and placing cannon there on the night of 4 March 1776. On 17 March, the British evacuated the city. Washington then transferred his army to New York and met Sir William Howe at the Battle of Long Island on 27 August 1776. He erred badly in drawing up his force of 18,000 men in the open where, in a regular, set-piece engagement, they were badly mauled; however, because Howe was reluctant to follow up his victory, Washington was able to withdraw his forces across the East River to Manhattan. Faced with growing British reinforcements arriving in New York (which remained in British hands throughout the war), Washington decided to withdraw north up the Hudson river. Instead of following him, though, Howe took his force south toward New Jersey and threatened an advance on Philadelphia late in 1776.

Washington saw the danger to the American cause if Philadelphia fell. He therefore split his army into three and took one part, about 5,000 men, south around New York to the Raritan River at New Brunswick, reaching it on 1 December 1776. On 7–8 December, his army crossed the Delaware river further south, and he ensured their safety by capturing or destroying all the boats on the northern bank to prevent Howe crossing behind him. Washington's last troops embarked from Trenton as the first British troops entered the town. Howe, unable to pursue him and reluctant to campaign in the winter, dispersed his troops in garrisons across New Jersey and decided to wait for the spring. Washington had other ideas, and on the evening of 25 December 1776, he took a force back across the river and attacked the camp of Hessians at Trenton. In what was an almost bloodless victory, he captured over 900 prisoners plus weapons and cannon. The battle immediately brought the British general Lord CORNWALLIS south with 8,000 men, determined to destroy the American army, but at Princeton in a skillful night maneuver (2 January 1777), Washington marched his men around Cornwallis's force and routed the British by attacking from their rear.

In August 1777, a British force landed south of Washington's force and marched north to try again to take Philadelphia. At the Battle of the Brandywine (11 September 1777), Cornwallis brought in forces from a flank, and Washington's army, badly defeated, was lucky to escape annihilation. The British then marched on and captured Philadelphia unopposed on 26 September 1777.

Forced to withdraw with his hungry and exhausted army to Valley Forge, west of Philadelphia, Washington spent the winter of 1777–78 in restoring the morale

and equipment of his army and fending off conspiracies against him in Congress and from other generals, including Horatio GATES. Vital assistance to the American cause came when France entered the war in February 1778. When the British forces in Pennsylvania and New Jersey began to move back to New York in the spring because of the threat of a French blockade of the Delaware river, Washington marched his forces quickly eastward to cut them off and met Sir Henry Clinton's army at Monmouth (June 28 1778). However, a certain American victory was ruined by the actions of General Charles Lee, who suddenly ordered his troops to withdraw. Washington hurried forward and personally restored the American lines, but the opportunity was lost and the British were able to continue their march to Sandy Hook while Washington was forced to withdraw to New Brunswick. Nevertheless, the arrival of the French fleet off New York isolated the British forces there, and Washington placed some of his forces around the city and established his main base at West Point on the Hudson.

There was then a period of stalemate. Without a navy, Washington was unable to take New York, and the British were reluctant to move outside the city. There was fighting in the Carolinas to the south, but not until 1781 did Washington fight another major engagement. In August that year, he agreed with the French admiral François-Joseph de Grasse that the French fleet would land troops to put pressure on Cornwallis to the south. After elaborate precautions of secrecy and making an ostentatious pretense of preparing to attack Clinton in New York, Washington hurried his soldiers south through New Jersey, embarked them in Delaware Bay, and landed at Williamsburg, Virginia. Cornwallis, who had marched north from the Carolinas, entrenched himself and his army at Yorktown and was promptly besieged by Washington, who, supported by the soldiers from the French fleet, forced the British general to surrender on 21 October 1781. With the exception of some minor skirmishes, the war was over. Washington was present when Clinton evacuated New York on 25 November 1783, took his leave of his staff on 4 December, and tendered his resignation to the Continental Congress on 23 December.

Despite his desire to retire from public affairs and to concentrate on administering his estates, Washington was unhappy with the political confusion that followed the war and urged that some radical reform was needed to the Articles of Confederation of 1777. He reluctantly agreed to act as a delegate to the Constitutional Convention in May 1787 and was unanimously chosen to preside over it. He carried out this task punctiliously, making his views clear on what was needed and, once the Constitution had been drafted, throwing his influence and reputation behind it to ensure its acceptance. He was elected the first president of the United States in 1789 and served two four-year terms until March 1797, when he retired into private life at the age of 65.

In 1798, Washingon was once again appointed as commander in chief by President John Adams when war with France threatened, but this did not come about and Washington was able, at last, to spend his remaining days in peace. In December 1799, he became ill after riding around his estate in a heavy storm, and he died on 14 December. After a period of national mourning, he was buried in the grounds of Mount Vernon.

All too often, Washington's skillful leadership in battle has tended to obscure his success in another, more difficult area. He was facing experienced British generals leading trained regular troops, while his own forces initially comprised inexperienced and untrained volunteers. Further, although fighting for a national cause, many American soldiers saw the security of their own state as their primary aim and were reluctant to serve outside it, while his choice of commanders often led to resentment. Washington's achievement in forming these disparate bodies of soldiers into an efficient and successful fighting force was nothing less than remarkable. Historian Michael Lee Lanning writes:

> While his stature today results more from his role as president than as general, Washington was nevertheless an accomplished military leader. He simultaneously maintained an army in the field against a far superior force, kept a divisive Congress and population satisfied, and solicited military support from other countries. . . . Although other military leaders such as Napoleon, Alexander the Great, and Genghis Khan, directly accomplished more on the battlefield, none left a legacy of influence equaling that of George Washington. Without Washington there would have been no Continental army; without the Continental army there would have been no United States. The American colonies would have remained a part of the British Empire and faced a powerless fate similar to that of other col-

onies. Washington established the standard for America that is today the world's longest-surviving democracy and its single most influential nation. George Washington more than earned the honored title "Father of His Country."

References: Bellamy, Francis F., *Private Life of George Washington* (New York: Crowell, 1951); Bell, William Gardner, *Commanding Generals and Chiefs of Staff, 1775–1995: Portraits & Biographical Sketches of the United States Army's Senior Officers* (Washington, D.C.: United States Army, Center of Military History, 1997), 48, 62; Brookhiser, Richard, *Founding Father: Rediscovering George Washington* (New York: The Free Press, 1996); Cunliffe, Marcus, *George Washington: Man and Monument* (Boston: Little, Brown, 1958); Jackson, Donald, ed., *The Diaries of George Washington,* 6 vols. (Charlottesville, Va.: University Press of Virginia, 1976–79); Lanning, Michael Lee, "George Washington," in *The Military 100: A Ranking of the Most Influential Military Leaders of All Time* (New York: Barnes and Noble Books, 1996), 3–7.

Wellington, Arthur Wellesley, first duke of (Arthur Wesley, Baron Douro of Wellesley) (1769–1852) *British general, prime minister*

Arthur Wellesley was born Arthur Wesley (he changed the name in 1798) in Dublin, Ireland, on 29 April 1769, the fourth son of Garret Wesley, first earl of Mornington, and his wife Anne Hill, daughter of the first viscount Dungannon. Wellesley attended school in Chelsea and went briefly to Eton, the famed British private school, in 1781. He later studied at a private military academy in Angers, France, for a short period, finishing his education in 1786. A year later, in 1787, he entered service in the British army, receiving a commission in the 73rd Regiment of Foot. From 1787 to 1793, he served as aide-de-camp to two lords lieutenant of Ireland, the earl of Westmoreland and Earl Fitzwilliam. In 1790, he was elected to the Irish parliament from Trim.

In 1794, with the rank of colonel, Wellesley saw his first military action when, as the commander of the 33rd Regiment of Foot, he fought the French army in Holland with the duke of York. In 1796, he was sent to India and spent time in the area of the city of Mysore. He again saw action here, fighting Tipu (or Tippoo) Sahib, the sultan of Mysore. Wellesley distinguished himself at the second battle of Seringapatam (6 April 1799) in the fourth British-Mysore War, a victory that, as historian George Bruce writes, "gave the British supremacy in southern India." Tipu Sahib was killed, and Sir David BAIRD, who had more seniority than Wellesley (having been in India since 1779), fully expected to be named as commander of British forces in India. When London chose Wellesley instead, Baird quit. Wellesley served as commander during the Second Anglo-Mahratta War of 1803–05, when he distinguished himself particularly well at the battles of Assaye (23 September 1803) and Argaon (also Argaum, 29 November 1803). It was at Assaye that Wellesley, with just 9,000 men—of whom only 1,800 were British—defeated over 40,000 of the enemy. The war ended with the surrender of the Sindhia and the raja of Berar. Wellesley was made a Knight Companion of the Order of the Bath (KCB) for his services.

In 1805, now as Sir Arthur Wellesley, he returned to England and was recalled into service almost immediately, serving in an abortive expedition to relieve Hanover, Germany. The following year, he was elected as a member of Parliament for Rye—later, for Mitchell (1807), and for Newport (1807–09). In 1807, he was named as chief secretary of Ireland. Later that year, when Britain went to war against Denmark, Wellesley commanded the English Division, composed of the 43rd and 52nd light infantry, the 92nd Highlanders, and the 95th Rifles, winning the only battle of that conflict at Kioge (29 October 1807). For his service in the Danish war, he was promoted to lieutenant general.

In 1808, Wellesley was sent to Portugal to fight the French in Spain, the campaign known as the Peninsular War (1808–14). He commanded a force of some 17,500 men and saw action at Rolica (17 August 1808), when he won a decisive victory, and at Vimeiro (21 August 1808), when the French, under Jean-Andoche JUNOT, were routed. However, following Vimeiro, the British, commanded first by General Burrard and then by General Sir Hew Dalrymple, refused to chase the French, and the ultimate value of the victory was lost. Dalrymple then signed—and forced Wellesley to sign—the Convention of Cintra, which ended the campaign. This "treaty" allowed Junot and his army to return home with all their arms and loot and to be transported by the British fleet. The public outrage at this led to a court of inquiry in London that censured Dalrymple but commended Wellesley for his actions.

In 1809, Wellesley was sent back to counter a French invasion of Spain under General Nicolas Jean

Soult. With some 23,000 men, he moved from Lisbon to Oporto, where Soult had stationed a huge portion of his army of 20,000. Wellesley dispatched some of his force eastward to hold off reinforcements to Soult from General Claude-Victor Perrin, duc de Bellune, while he inflicted a defeat on Soult at the River Douro at Oporto (12 May 1809). A week later, another defeat forced Soult to withdraw, and Wellesley then concentrated on capturing Madrid. At Talavera (27–28 July 1809), he defeated a French force backed by King Joseph, but his forces were threatened by Soult advancing on his lines of communication, and he retreated into Portugal to regroup. He was then created Baron Douro of Wellesley and Viscount Wellington of Talavera.

Knowing that NAPOLEON had made peace with Austria and would now reinforce Spain, Lord Wellington prepared for a second French invasion of Portugal. He established a series of defensive fortifications—called the Lines of Torres Vedras—across the peninsula on which Lisbon stands. He realized that the combined British and Spanish forces were no match for the overwhelming French army, but he felt that, with their long, vulnerable lines of communication, a defensive war rather than an offensive one would eliminate the French advantage. Wellington was right: Marshal André MASSÉNA moved into Portugal to attack the British but was halted at the defensive line at Busaco on 27 September 1810. After a lengthy siege, Masséna was forced to withdraw back to Spain in April 1811. He invaded again in May 1811 to attack the Portuguese garrison at Almeida, but Wellington attacked him at Fuentes de Oñoro on 5 May 1811. Two separate French attacks were repulsed at a loss of some 2,250 killed on the French side; British losses were about 1,400. When Masséna's forces moved to attack a second time, Wellington attacked the French garrison at Ciudad Rodrigo (19 January 1812). The quick British victory was followed by Wellington's attack on Badajoz (17 March 1812), in which his troops laid siege to the French garrison, leaving 3,500 French and over 5,000 British dead. The fortress fell to Wellington's forces on 6 April 1812, but he looked on with horror as his men ransacked the fortress and town for two days before order could be restored. The final major battle of the year was at Salamanca on 22 July 1812, when Wellington, with more than 67,000 troops, including 14,000 Portuguese and 3,000 Spaniards, defeated French general Marshal Auguste Marmont's 49,000 men; French losses were estimated to be over 15,000, while the British and their allies suffered about 5,000 dead. In August, Wellington's forces entered Madrid, and for his service he was created a marquess. Historian Michael Lee Lanning writes: "Wellesley accomplished his victories in Portugal and Spain through a variety of tactics and strategies. His most successful proved to be a shift back and forth between defense and offence, combined with a scorched-earth policy. Always aware of the limited available replacements and his own personal aversion to sustaining useless casualties, Wellesley planned in great detail and proceeded methodically. His tactics were, in fact, fairly simple: He achieved victory by concentrating superior firepower and overwhelming his enemy with a greater number of better-trained and more highly motivated soldiers."

Learning that Soult was once again advancing, Wellington went back to Portugal, but on 25 February 1813, he wrote to Major General Campbell: "The foreign troops are so much addicted to desertion that they are very unfit for our armies, of which they necessarily form too large a proportion to the native troops. The evil is aggravated by the practice which prevails of enlisting prisoners as well as deserters, and Frenchmen as well as other foreigners, notwithstanding the repeated orders of government upon the subject. The consequence is therefore that a foreign regiment cannot be placed in a situation in which the soldiers can desert from it, that they do not go off in hundreds; and in the Peninsula they convey to the enemy the only intelligence which he can acquire." That spring, he once again advanced out of Portugal and chased retreating French forces, defeating them at Vittoria in northern Spain on 21 June. At San Sebastian (10 July–31 August 1813), Wellington besieged a French garrison; although his initial attack was repulsed, his blockade forced the surrender of the French troops after two months. The British troops then crossed into France and fought at Toulouse (10 April 1814), forcing a French withdrawal. The following day, Napoleon abdicated, ending the war.

Wellington returned to London in triumph and was created duke of Wellington in 1814. He was also named as the British ambassador to the court of King Louis XVIII, now restored to the French throne. In 1815, when the Congress of Vienna met to fix the borders of the nations that Napoleon had invaded, Wellington attended as a member of the British delegation. During the congress, Napoleon escaped from his exile in Elba and returned to France to renew his fight to conquer Europe. Wellington therefore moved to lead the British army and, with the aid of Prussian field marshal Gerhard von BLÜCHER, met Napoleon at Waterloo in Belgium (18 June 1815). In one of the most momentous battles in world history, Wellington decisively defeated Napoleon, forcing the end of the French emperor's "Hundred Days" campaign and his second abdication, this time for good. The noted military historian John Keegan writes: "The Duke of Wellington strongly disapproved of all attempts to turn the battle of Waterloo either into literature or history. His own account of it in his official dispatch was almost dismissive and he advised a correspondent who had requested his help in writing a narrative to 'leave the battle of Waterloo as it is.' The Duke's attitude rested in part on his disdain for sensationalism, in part on a well-founded doubt about the feasibility of establishing a chain of cause and effect to explain its outcome."

Wellington again returned to England a hero. In 1818, Prime Minister Robert Jenkinson, Lord Liverpool, invited him to join the government as master general of the ordnance. In 1827, he was appointed commander in chief, and in January 1828, when Frederick Robinson, Viscount Goderich, resigned as prime minister, Wellington was chosen to replace him. His short tenure was marked by a fight for the emancipation of Catholics in Ireland. In 1829, Home Minister Robert Peel asked Wellington for his support in forming the London Metropolitan Police force. A deteriorating economy and high unemployment led to a loss in a vote of confidence in Parliament on 15 November 1830, and Wellington was replaced as prime minister by Earl Grey. He remained in public life until 1846, although in 1848 he helped to organize troops in case of a Chartist rising. Four years later, on 14 September 1852, he died and was buried with full military honors in St. Paul's Cathedral, London. His huge monument reads simply "Arthur, Duke of Wellington."

References: Weller, Jac, *On Wellington: the Duke and His Art of War,* edited by Andrew Uffindell (London: Greenhill Books, 1998); Keegan, John, "Wellington: the Anti-Hero," in *The Mask of Command* (Viking/Elisabeth Sifton Books, 1987), 92–163; Bruce, George, "Seringapatam II," in *Collins Dictionary of Wars* (Glasgow, Scotland: HarperCollins Publishers, 1995), 225; Lanning, Michael Lee, "Arthur Wellesley (First Duke of Wellington)," *The Military 100: A Ranking of the Most Influential Military*

Leaders of All Time (New York: Barnes and Noble Books, 1996), 88–91; Holmes, Richard, "Wellington, Arthur Wellesley, Duke of," in *The Oxford Companion to Military History* (New York: Oxford University Press), 989–991; Napier, W. F. P., "Wellington to Campbell, 25 February 1813," in *History of the War in the Peninsula and in the South of France from the Year 1807 to the Year 1814,* 6 vols. (London: Thomas & William Boone, 1836), VI:616; Keegan, John, *The Face of Battle: A Study of Agincourt, Waterloo and the Somme* (New York: Penguin Books, 1984).

Wet, Christiaan Rudolf de (1854–1922)
Boer general and guerrilla fighter

Christiaan de Wet, the sixth of 14 children, was born in Leeuwkop, the Orange Free State, in what is now South Africa, on 7 October 1854. His ancestor Jacobus de Wet emigrated from Amsterdam to southern Africa in 1693; his father, a farmer, moved to what was called the Orange Free State—composed of "Orange," or European-descended farmers—settling in a village called Dewetsdorp, named after the family. Christiaan de Wet was 11 when he joined his father in guarding Orange farms from Basuto natives, a conflict that culminated in open warfare in 1865. In 1868, de Wet's mother died, and, owing to his having to help support his family on the farm, he never received a formal education and only learned how to read and write.

In 1880, de Wet was one of the leaders resisting British interference in the Orange Free State. When conflict broke out with Britain (the Anglo-Boer War of 1880–81), de Wet led Orange forces into the battles of Bronkhorstspruit (20 December 1880), Laingsnek (or Laing's Neck, 28 January 1881), and Amajuba (also Majuba, 26–27 February 1881), among others. Following the war (which ended in a stalemate), he was elected to the Volksraad, or Orange parliament, in 1885. Although he served only a single parliamentary session, he was strongly opposed to the policies of the Orange president Stephanas Johannes Paulus (Paul) Kruger. In 1889, he was again elected to the Volksraad, serving until 1898.

Starting in October 1899, in what is usually called the Boer War—also the second Anglo-Boer War—de Wet left his farm to take a leadership role in defending his homeland. Serving first as a commander in the province of Natal and later with the rank of general under Piet Cronjé in the western part of the Orange Free State, he conducted a remarkable mobile war against British forces. At Ladysmith on 30 October 1899, he and a small force of only 300 men besieged British forces of over 1,000 and took more than 800 prisoners. For this single battlefield victory, he was promoted to field general. He tried to get Cronjé to attack the main British force, but Cronjé held back, leaving de Wet and his men exposed at Paardeburg, where they were attacked on 16 December 1899. De Wet's army slipped away before they could be defeated, but Cronjé was forced to surrender on 27 February 1900.

Cronjé's removal as the leading military officer of the Boer forces forced de Wet to take command of the Orange Free State army. His main goal was to halt Lord ROBERTS's march on the Free State's capital, Bloemfontaine. Several small skirmishes occurred at Abrahamskraal and Reitfontein, but the overwhelming British presence forced de Wet and his men to abandon Bloemfontaine, which fell to the British on 13 March 1900.

Despite the loss of their capital, de Wet's forces continued their warfare, taking the military post known as Sannapos or Sanna's Post (31 March 1900), a battle in which some 500 British were killed and wounded and an equal number taken prisoner. At Mostertshoek (4 April 1900), he attacked a British force under General William Forbes Gatacre, again winning a stunning victory, and he fought to a standoff at Jammersbergdrif (7 April 1900). Nevertheless, de Wet realized that the Free State's chances of victory were becoming slimmer as more British troops flooded into the area. His forces took up guerilla tactics, hitting supply lines, communications stations, and transportation sectors such as bridges in a vain attempt to slow the British advance. One of these was a massive attack on the Rooiwal train station (7 June 1900), in which a huge amount of British ammunition and supplies was destroyed. This latter attack forced Lord Roberts to change his tactics from seeking a major land battle to cutting off the separate detachments of Free State forces. Although Roberts encircled a major Boer force at the Brandwater Basin in July 1900, de Wet and some of his men managed to escape. However, General Michael Prinsloo and 3,000 Boer fighters surrendered, and de Wet's brother, Piet de Wet, went over to the British side and aided them in containing the Free State army. Utilizing Piet de Wet's information, Roberts tracked the Boer general to the Vaal River and encircled him again with a force of some 50,000 men. Again, de Wet escaped with his force (11 August 1900), and he moved to an area north of the Free State to recuperate. By the end of the year, de Wet had moved his men south to fight the British presence in the eastern part of the Free State near what was called the Cape Colony. Lured into a battle with General C. E. Knox at Sprinkaansnek on 14 December 1900, de Wet again managed to escape. Knox pursued him until the British lines could not support any further marches, and de Wet still evaded his pursuers.

Despite de Wet's remarkable success at harassing the British and forcing them to split their resources to fight him, by the end of 1900 the Boer cause was plainly lost. De Wet opposed the negotiations to end the war that began in May 1901. At Groenkop on 25 December 1901, he defeated a vastly superior British force. However, seeing the inevitable end of the conflict, he decided to join peace negotiations and, serving as acting president of the Orange Free State for a single day, signed the Peace of Vereeniging on 31 May 1902. He had managed to elude every effort the British made to capture him, and at war's end he remained a free man. He subsequently wrote his memoirs of the conflict, published in 1902 as *Three Years' War.*

In November 1907, de Wet was elected as a member of the first legislative assembly of the Orange River Colony and appointed minister of agriculture. In 1912, he backed the policies of South African president General James B. M. Hertzog against those of Prime Minister Louis Botha, especially regarding separation of the races. Angered when his South African Party did not support his stand, he left the party and formed the Nationalist Party in 1914. The split grew larger when, with the start of the First World War, de Wet opposed Botha's decision to invade and conquer German South West Africa (now modern Namibia). He organized a rebellion against Botha's government, for which he was arrested on charges of treason in December 1914 and sent to prison for six years. He served only a year before being released due to his age, upon which he returned to his farm to live out the remainder of his life.

Christiaan de Wet died at his home on 3 February 1922 at the age of 67. Although forgotten by many outside South Africa, his name is still revered in his native land, and the British army still respects him as a brilliant tactician whom they were never able to defeat.

References: Rosenthal, Eric, *General De Wet: A Biography* (Cape Town, South Africa: Simondium Publishers, 1968); De Wet, Christiaan Rudolf, *Three Years' War (October 1899–June 1902)* (Westminster, U.K.: A. Constable, 1902); Pretorius, Fransjohan, *The Great Escape of the Boer Pimpernel, Christiaan De Wet: The Making of a Legend,* translated by Stephan Hofstätter (Pietermaritzburg, South Africa: University of Natal Press, 2001); "De Wet, General Christiaan Rudolf," in *Southern African Dictionary of National Biography,* compiled by Eric Rosenthal (London: Frederick Warne, 1966), 96–97.

William I (the Conqueror) (William, duke of Normandy) (ca. 1028–1087) *French commander, king of England*

From 1066, British monarchs can trace their descent back to the Norman ruler known as William the Conqueror. He was born about 1028, the son and eldest of two children of Robert I (also known as Robert the Devil), duke of Normandy, and his mistress Arlette (also called Herleva), the daughter of a wealthy burgher from Falaise. Because of this, William has been called "William the Bastard" by some historians. In 1035, when his son was either seven or eight, Robert was killed in Asia Minor (now Turkey) while returning from a pilgrimage to Jerusalem, and William, although still a child and under the care of several guardians, succeeded to his father's dukedom; even King Henry I of France accepted William as the duke of Normandy. During his minority, anarchy reigned, and three of his four guardians and his tutor were murdered. Despite this, William consolidated his authority in Normandy, and he worked closely with his mother's husband, Herliun of Conteville, a Norman lord, to protect his interests. In 1042, when he became 15, William was knighted.

Gathering an army to protect his estate, William launched a series of wars against rival barons that lasted from 1046 until 1055. He joined with the French king Henry I, and at Val-ès-Dunes (1047), near Caen, the two men defeated an alliance of Normans who had opposed William's rule. These wars aided in making William a disciplined military commander, but he also became a religious man, taking an interest in the welfare of the church in Norman society. He pushed to have his half brother Odo named as bishop of Bayeux in 1049, and he played host to numerous monks and other religious figures to Normandy in the years he lived there. Historian Christopher Tyerman writes:

> William's subsequent consolidation of control over both church and magnates depended crucially upon military successes and his consequent ability to reward loyalty, attract support and punish opposition. Northern France, a patchwork of competing lordships and conflicting claims of allegiance, offered considerable scope for a vigorous and well-organized power. Between 1054 and 1064 William extended his influence and authority to Ponthieu, the Norman Vexin, Brittany and Maine. A Flemish alliance was achieved by his marriage (ca. 1051) to Matilda (d. 1083) the diminutive but forceful daughter of Baldwin V, count of Flanders. William also allied with the counts of Boulogne. This network of alliances proved vital when William planned his invasion of England.

Mathilda would bear William nine children, including four boys. Among these would be his successor as king of England, William Rufus, later to become William II. Another son, Robert, succeeded his father as duke of Normandy.

William coveted the throne of England, which he claimed through his great-grandfather's sister, Emma, who had married Ethelred II of England. In 1051, King Edward the Confessor named William as his heir, based on this relationship. When Edward died in January 1066, his brother-in-law, HAROLD II, earl of Wessex, immediately took the crown and shut William out. William set out to challenge Harold for the throne, assembling a fleet of ships to carry his Norman army to the shores of the English island. However, he was not the first invader to confront Harold: In September 1066, Harold Hardrada, the king of Norway, invaded England, and Harold II marched north and defeated him at the Battle of Stamford Bridge (25 September). William had allied himself to Harold Hardrada, and two days after Stamford Bridge, he and his fleet sailed from France and landed at Pevensey on the south coast of England on 28 September. Harold and his army of Saxons marched south, and the two forces met at Hastings on 14 October 1066. Harold had easily defeated Harold Hardrada's forces, but his soldiers were exhausted after their forced march from the north. During the battle, Harold was killed, allegedly by an arrow in the eye, and much of the Anglo-Saxon nobility fighting with him were also slain. In the end, as with all battles, the victor wrote the history, and the Normans displayed their great victory at Hastings on the Bayeux Tapestry, a lengthy textile (231 feet) containing 72 scenes depicting William crossing the English Channel and the battle itself. Today Battle Abbey marks the site of the French triumph.

William was crowned king of England on Christmas Day, 1066. He linked the English nation with his own French dukedom and set out to consolidate his gains firmly. One of his decisions was to take inventory of everything in the nation he had just acquired. This account has become known as the Domesday (dooms-day) Book (1085–86), which in fact was two books that listed all the landholdings, animals, homes, and businesses in England. The Domesday Book became the basis of government taxation.

William reigned as king for 20 years, suppressing rebellions and invasions by the Scots and leaving the country only when his Norman duchy was threatened by rebellion. In 1081, he was forced to return to France to fight a series of uprisings there, and these took up the next several years of his life. In 1087, William and his army took the city of Mantes, during which he suffered a serious injury, supposedly the result of fall from his horse. He was removed to the city of Rouen, where he lay for five weeks before succumbing to his wounds on 9 September 1087. As William lay dying, English author Hilaire Belloc writes,

> when he found death very near he was still able to make dispositions for what was to follow. To Robert, as of hereditary right, as to one also to whom the feudatories had done homage, he left the hereditary Continental land. To his younger son, who had been born in England, Henry, now twenty years old, he left a store of silver . . . and presumably certain lands for his endowment as well. But the arrangement he made in the matter of England is strange and provokes our thought. He had no doubt whatsoever on his right—he was King of England by a rightful claim and the favour of God who had confirmed that claim in ordeal by battle—it was his right, without question, to found a new dynasty in that realm. He would not unite it with Robert's Duchy, he did not even actually appoint, what he said was that

he dared not dispose, and that, as in the matter of that "last quarter of an hour" at Hastings, God must decide—which meant in effect the Priest upon whose wisdom and authority he had so long and profoundly relied, the great Lanfranc, still towering above all contemporaries there at Canterbury, in his eightieth year.

William's son, William Rufus, succeeded him as King William II.

Dead more than a millennium, William the Conqueror has nonetheless shaped English history, through his defeat of the ruling family of England and the composition of the Domesday books. *The Anglo-Saxon Chronicles,* one of the Middle Age's most important literary documents, states of William: "He was a very wise man, and very powerful and more worshipful and stronger than any previous king had been. He was gentle to the good men who loved God, [but] stern beyond all measure to those who resisted his will. The good security he made in this country is not easily to be forgotten, so that any honest man could travel over his kingdom [in safety] with a bosom full of gold." Historian James Harvey Robinson, in a 1904 work, utilizes a contemporary document to demonstrate William's character: "King William, about whom we speak, was a very wise man, and very powerful, more dignified and strong than any of his predecessors were. He was mild to the good men who loved God, and beyond all measure severe to the men who gainsaid his will. . . . He was also very dignified; thrice every year he wore his crown, as oft as he was in England. At Easter he wore it in Winchester; at Pentecost, in Westminster; at Midwinter, in Gloucester. And then were with him all the great men over all England, archbishops and suffragan bishops, abbots and earls, thanes and knights."

References: Henderson, Andrew, *The Life of William the Conqueror, Duke of Normandy, and King of England* (London: Printed for the Author, 1764); Hayward, Sir John, *The Lives of the III Normans, Kings of England: William the first, William the seconde, Henrie the first* (London, 1613); Clarke, Samuel, *The Life & Death of William, Surnamed the Conqueror: King of England, and Duke of Normandy. Who dyed Anno Christi, 1087* (London: Printed for Simon Miller, 1671); Tyerman, Christopher, "William I," in *Who's Who in Early Medieval England, 1066–1272* (Mechanicsburg, Pa.: Stackpole Books, 1996), 2; Tait, James, "An Alleged Charter of William the Conqueror," in *Essays in History Presented to Reginald Lane Poole,* edited by H. W. C. David (Oxford: Clarendon Press, 1927); 151–167; Belloc, Hilaire, *William the Conqueror* (London: Peter Davies Limited, 1933); Robinson, James Harvey, ed., *Readings in European History,* 2 vols. (Boston: Ginn, 1904), 1:229–231.

Wolfe, James (1727–1759) *British general*

Born on 2 January 1727 at Westerham, Kent, James Wolfe came from a distinguished family: His grandfather, Edward Wolfe, served in the English army under William III, Anne, and George I, attaining the rank of major; and his father Edward served with distinction under John CHURCHILL, duke of Marlborough, seeing action at Flanders. Wolfe himself entered the service of the British army in 1740, when he was 14, and he saw action in the War of the Austrian Succession (1740–47) in Flanders, Belgium, and Germany. He also took part in the campaign against the pretender to the English throne, Charles Edward Stuart, in Scotland in 1745.

In 1757, Wolfe was appointed quartermaster general of English forces in Ireland. The following year, Secretary of State William Pitt named Wolfe, then just 30 years old, as second in command of English forces in North America under the command of Major General Jeffrey AMHERST. He was put in charge of a brigade of soldiers sent to fight and capture the French garrison at Louisbourg, now in the Canadian province of Nova Scotia. Wolfe's experienced and skilled command during the clash, which led to the capture of the fortress, earned him a promotion to the rank of major general on his return to England and, ultimately, the task of taking the French stronghold of Québec, Canada.

In June 1759, Wolfe and his forces, some 9,000 strong, sailed up the St. Lawrence River and set up their encampment in the hills above the city. Wolfe waited for an expected French attack, but it never came, so he decided to attack on his own, launching his assault on 31 July. The attack was repulsed, and Wolfe retreated back to his original position to await a more advantageous time for another offensive. This came on 12 September, when he secretly moved some 5,000 forces downstream of the St. Lawrence to a point southwest of Québec. The British troops scaled a high cliff to reach a position above the French. The following morning, the surprised French, led by Louis-Joseph de MONTCALM, came out to do battle, but the accuracy of English musketry destroyed them. Nevertheless, Wolfe was fatally injured. Historian Robert Wright writes:

> Before the smoke cleared away the English had reloaded, when Wolfe, placing himself at the head of the Louisbourg Grenadiers and the 28th, led them on so far as to make the enemy feel bullets and bayonets almost at the same moment. He had already been shot in the wrist but, wrapping his handkerchief round the wound, continued to lead on and cheer his followers. His bright uniform rendering him the more conspicuous while he exposed himself in front of the Grenadiers, some Canadian marksmen on the enemy's left singled him out for destruction. He had just given the order for the whole British line to charge, when he was again dangerously wounded; but, acting up to his own words—'while a man is able to do his duty, and can stand and hold his arms, it is infamous to retire'—in spite of pain and weakness, he still persevered. . . . Not long after Wolfe had received a third and mortal wound in the breast. When no longer able to stand, his only concern was lest his men should be disheartened by his fall. "Support me," he whispered to an officer near him, "let not my brave soldiers see me drop. The day is ours . . . keep it!" He was then carried to the rear.

Wolfe succumbed to his wounds soon after this happened. Told that the battle had been won by the British, his last words, according to witnesses, were, "Now God be praised . . . I die in peace!" He was only 32. (Montcalm was also fatally wounded and died the next day.) Wolfe's body was returned to England and given a funeral with full military honors. An impressive monument to his life and service was erected in Westminster Abbey in London.

James Wolfe gave his life to secure British control over Canada and end French power in North America. His death, captured on canvas by famed artist Benjamin West, has become one of the most famous battle scenes in history.

References: J. P., *The Life of General James Wolfe, The Conqueror of Canada: Or, the Elogium of that Renowned Here, Attempted According to the Rules of Eloquence. . . .* (London: Printed for G. Kearsley, 1760); Wright, Robert, *The Life of Major-General James Wolfe, Founded on Original Documents and Illustrated by His Correspondence, Including Numerous Unpublished Letters contributed from the Family papers of Noblemen and Gentlemen, Descendants of his Companions* (London: Chapman and Hall, 1864); *A Short and Authentic Account of the Expedition against Quebec, in the Year 1759, under Command of Major-General James Wolfe. By a Volunteer Upon the Expedition* (Québec: Printed by Middleton & Dawson, 1872); Warner, Oliver, *With Wolfe to Quebec* (Toronto: Collins, 1972).

X

Xerxes (Khshayarsha, Ahasuerus) (ca. 519–465 B.C.) *king of Persia*

Xerxes—whose Persian name is Khshayarsha and who is referred to in the Bible as Ahasuerus—was born about the year 519 B.C., the son of King DARIUS I of Persia and his second wife Atossa, who herself was the daughter of CYRUS THE GREAT. Although Xerxes had an older brother, Artabazanes, his father passed him over to make Xerxes his heir apparent. However, it was not until 485 B.C., when Darius died, that Xerxes became the king of Persia at the age of about 35. He had served as the governor of the province of Babylonia and now ruled the Persian empire, then at the height of its power. His first action was to suppress a revolt in Egypt and install his brother Achaemenes as ruler there, and he successfully put down two more rebellions in Babylonia in 484 and 479 B.C. After doing so, he began his preparations to conquer Greece. In 490 B.C., his father had conducted a similar invasion but was defeated at Marathon. Now, a decade later, Darius's son Xerxes planned to avenge him.

Xerxes crossed the Hellespont (the Dardanelles) using a pontoon bridge made from a large armada of boats and constructed a canal through the isthmus of Athos. He then marched through Thrace and Macedonia but was checked by the Spartans at the narrow defile of Thermopylae (480 B.C.). In the most heroic action in the history of warfare, some 300 Spartans and 1,000 Thespians and Thebans, led by Leonidas, fought to the death to resist an army 50 times their size to give the Greeks time to gather an army behind them. Xerxes was now free to march on Athens, which he sacked, but as his enormous fleet sailed in to support him, the Greeks defeated them at Salamis (29 September 480 B.C.). With 370 ships commanded by their general Themistocles, the Greeks were assaulted by a numerically superior Persian force of 1,200 ships, but they had lured the Persians into fighting in a narrow bay where they were unable to maneuver. As historian George Bruce explains, "an Athenian trireme [a war galley with three banks of oars] commanded by Aminias dashed in, followed by the rest of the Athenians and the Æginetans in good order, and the Persians were, after a hard struggle, totally defeated with the loss of more than half their fleet. Xerxes and his army witnessed the rout from the shores of Salamis."

Humiliated by the defeat, Xerxes left Greece and returned to his palace at Persepolis. His land forces, commanded by his general Mardonius, were soon quickly conquered by the Grecians at Plataea (479 B.C.), and Xerxes' dreams of vengeance on the Greeks were destroyed. Herodotus writes in his history of the period that Xerxes thereafter concentrated on "the intrigues of the harem." In 465 B.C., he was murdered by one of his palace bodyguards, initiated by his minister, Artabanus. He was succeeded by his son, Artaxerxes I, who some historians believe may have been involved in Xerxes' murder. Although remembered for the historic battles at Thermopylae and Salamis, Xerxes' reign as a whole is forgotten despite his governance of one of the great empires of the world.

References: Olmstead, Albert Ten Eyck, *History of the Persian Empire* (Chicago: University of Chicago Press, 1948); Green, Peter, *The Greco-Persian Wars* (Berkeley: University of California Press, 1996); Hignett, Charles, *Xerxes' Invasion of Greece* (Oxford, U.K.: Clarendon Press, 1963); Green, Peter, *Xerxes at Salamis* (New York: Praeger, 1970); George Bruce, "Salamis I," in *Collins Dictionary of Wars* (Glasgow, Scotland: HarperCollins Publishers, 1995), 219.

Y

Yamamoto, Isoroku (Isoroku Takano) (1884–1943) *Japanese admiral*

The son of a schoolmaster, Isoroku Yamamoto was born Isoroku Takano in the city of Nagaoka, Niigata prefecture, Japan on 4 April 1884. Perhaps because his father was of the samurai class, Yamamoto took up a military career. In 1901, he entered the Naval Academy at Etajima, Hiroshima, and graduated three years later. He saw action and was wounded during the Russo-Japanese War (1904–05), when he served on the Japanese cruiser *Nisshin* at the battle of Tsushima (27 May 1905), the overwhelming Japanese naval victory against the Russians.

Following the war, Yamamoto continued in the navy and was sent to the Naval Staff College at Tsukiji in 1913. In 1914, he was formally adopted by the wealthy Yamamoto family and took their name as his own. He graduated from the Naval Staff College three years later and was appointed to the general staff of the Second Battle Squadron. At this time, Japan enjoyed good relations with the United States, and Yamamoto attended Harvard University. In 1921, he returned to Japan, where he was promoted to the rank of commander and given a teaching position at the Naval Staff College for three years. In 1924, he was assigned to the air training center at Kasumigaura as its executive officer. Two years later, he was posted back to the United States to serve as the naval attaché to the Japanese Embassy in Washington, D.C. During his two-year tenure, he traveled across the country and studied American ways and customs. Appointed to the Naval Affairs Bureau in Tokyo, he returned to Japan and was promoted to rear admiral. In the next decade, he was involved in the buildup of the Japanese navy and the construction of many of the aircraft carriers Japan would use in the Second World War. In 1935, he was named as head of the Naval Aviation Bureau.

During this time, Japan saw the rise of militarism among politicians who realized how important military strength was to Japanese political influence. Yamamoto, named in December 1936 as vice minister of the Japanese navy, opposed these ideas but did call for the increase of aircraft in the navy. He opposed the Japanese invasion of Manchuria in China in 1937, and when the Japanese attacked the USS *Panay,* an American gunboat, in China in December 1937, Yamamoto personally apologized to the United States for the incident. Because of this, he was the object of promilitarist hatred, and to avoid assassination he was guarded constantly. Nonetheless, he encouraged the building of the aircraft carriers *Shokuku* and *Zuikaku.* On 30 August 1939, he was promoted to admiral and given the command of the Japanese fleet.

When the Second World War started in Europe, Japanese leaders realized that the United States, sooner or later, would come in on the side of the Allies, Britain and France. However, because he had visited the United States and saw firsthand the overwhelming strategic superiority that nation would have over Japan, Yamamoto warned his superiors that such a war would be the death knell for Japan, even if it could win early victories. He believed that the only way his country could have an advantage would be to strike the United States' naval and air forces before it could strike Japan. He conceived a plan that not only included an attack on America but the quick capture of numerous islands in the Pacific Ocean to use as barriers to fend off the expected counterattack against the Japanese homeland. When the American government froze Japanese assets in the United States in July 1941, Japan's leaders approved Yamamoto's plan and authorized the dispatch of the Japanese fleet east to the coast of Hawaii. On 7 December 1941, some 350 Japanese aircraft commanded by Admiral Chuichi Nagumo attacked the main American naval base at Pearl Harbor, Hawaii, sinking or disabling 18 American warships and killing some 3,000 American sailors. Yamamoto had directed that a second wave of planes be sent to bomb the remaining American ships and completely destroy any chance of an American counterattack, but Nagumo ignored this order and ended the attack after one wave, a mistake that would lead to Japan's eventual defeat. Yamamoto knew that the remaining American ships could be repaired and sent to attack, and he recognized that Japan had now challenged the United States' strength when it could least afford to, as it was pinned down fighting in China. He sent Nagumo's fleet to Java at once, and there, at the Battle of Java Sea (27–28 February 1942), the Japanese defeated a combined American and British fleet to take the islands.

Yamamoto expanded his original strategy of "island-hopping" to include an island he felt would allow Japan to control the Pacific: Midway. Situated, as its name implies, midway between Hawaii and Japan, it was seen as crucial to Japan's efforts to meet the American counterattack. Sending all of his naval forces to the area, which included six battle carriers—more than 200 ships in total—Yamamoto conceived a plan to entrap the American forces near the island and destroy them. However, what he did not know was that the United States had broken the secret Japanese naval code and knew what his plan was.

When the Japanese first attacked the American base on Midway on 4 June 1942, it was lightly defended to make them think the United States had been taken by surprise. Then the American carriers sent off wave after wave of aircraft, with bombs and torpedoes, to attack the Japanese, who were themselves caught by surprise. In a massive two-day battle, the Japanese lost four carriers—*Akagi, Soryu, Kaga,* and *Hirpu*—and some 3,500 killed, to one American carrier lost—the USS *Yorktown*—and about 300 American dead. Yamamoto was forced to order his forces to retreat. The Battle of Midway was a turning point in the war: From then on, Japan was on the defensive against American attacks in the Pacific.

The American victory at Midway allowed them to attack the 15,000 Japanese forces at Guadalcanal in the Solomon Islands, landing on 7 August 1942. In October 1942, Yamamoto attempted to land troops at Guadalcanal, but American navy ships kept the Japanese at bay. The Americans then launched an attack on the Japanese on the island; the subsequent battle (12–14 November 1942) ended any hope of keeping this vital island out of the hands of the United States, and in January 1943 Yamamoto ordered the evacuation of all remaining Japanese forces; the island was cleared on 9 February 1943. As he had feared, the American force now began its counterattack. Next on their agenda were the islands of Bougainville, in what is now Papua New Guinea, and Yamamoto decided to visit the Japanese troops there, first to boost their morale and second to plan its defense against an American invasion. He sent out his itinerary with the same radio code the United States had cracked to get the Japanese plans for Midway, and again the information fell into American hands. Admiral Chester NIMITZ ordered that Yamamoto's plane be intercepted and shot down. On 18 April 1943, Yamamoto's G4M "Betty" transport plane was flying over Kahili in Bougainville when an American fleet of 16 P-38 "Lightning" aircraft, led by Major John W. Mitchell, intercepted it and blew it out of the air, crashing into the jungle below.

Yamamoto was just 59 when he was killed. The Japanese government did not announce his death until 21 May 1943, quietly replacing him as commander in chief of the Japanese fleet with Admiral Mineichi Koga. His remains were eventually discovered and buried in the Tama Reien cemetery in Harjuku Ward in Tokyo. Historians Anthony Bruce and William Cogar write: "Yamamoto's loss was a severe blow to Japanese morale and damaged the faltering Japanese strategy against the Allies. He had launched a brilliant campaign in the Pacific but was unable to sustain the momentum against the Americans, who exploited fully their interception of Japanese naval codes."

Isoroku Yamamoto is remembered chiefly for his successful attack plan against Pearl Harbor and his failure to defeat the United States at Midway. In summing up his impact, historian Edwin Hoyt writes:

> Admiral Yamamoto left a great military legacy to Japan. His strategic concept of the war was followed after his death until the sea battle of the Marianas [June 1944], after which the Combined Fleet was so diminished that its name was dropped and the fleet was called the Mobile Force. At the Battle of Leyte Gulf [October 1944] it was almost completely destroyed. . . . [T]actically and technologically, most of Yamamoto's contributions have been surpassed by weapons development and time. But some of them persist. Yamamoto believed in strict discipline at sea and maximum effort in making the best use of the weapons and facilities at hand. His Combined Fleet had the best discipline of any naval fighting force in the world, and was particularly competent in night fighting at every level, not just destroyers. Those legacies have been retained.

References: Agawa, Hiroyuki, *The Reluctant Admiral,* translated by John Bester (Tokyo, Japan: Kodansha International, 1979); Potter, John Deane, *Yamamoto: The Man Who Menaced America* (New York: Viking, 1965); Hoyt, Edwin P., *Yamamoto: The Man Who Planned Pearl Harbor* (New York: McGraw-Hill, 1990); Hoyt, Edwin P., *Three Military Leaders: Heihachiro Togo, Isoroku Yamamoto, Tomoyuki Yamashita* (Tokyo, Japan: Kodansha International, 1994); Hall, R. Cargill, ed., *Lightning over Bougainville* (Washington, D.C.: Smithsonian Institution Press, 1991); Bruce, Anthony, and William Cogar, "Yamamoto, Isoroku," in *An Encyclopedia of Naval History* (New York: Checkmark Books, 1999), 408–409.

Yaroslavich, Aleksandr *See* NEVSKY, ALEXANDER, SAINT.

Z

Zhukov, Georgi Konstantinovich (Georgii Konstantinovich Zhukov) (1896–1974) *Russian general*

The son of a peasant family, Georgi Zhukov was born in Strelkova, in the Kaluga Oblast about 100 miles southwest of Moscow, on 1 December 1896 (or 19 November 1896 [O.S.]). His father worked as a shoemaker; however, both of Zhukov's parents died before he was 11, and he was raised by his grandfather, who worked as a metallurgist in Moscow. Leaving school when he was 13, he worked a series of jobs, including as a leather tanner and furrier. In 1915, however, when he was 19, he quit these trades and decided to enter the Russian czarist army. Zhukov started his service as a private but only received cursory training before being sent to the front in the First World War. The war was going badly for the Russians, who were heavily defeated by the Germans in battles in Poland. Assigned to the Tenth Novgorod Dragoon Regiment, Zhukov rose quickly through the ranks and by 1917 had reached the highest noncommissioned grade. He was twice awarded the Cross of St. George for bravery.

Zhukov joined the Soviets after the October 1917 revolution, and he was elected as the regiment's chair of the Communist Council. Starting in October 1918, he played a part in the organization and formation of the Red Army, the Soviet Union's main military force. From 1919 until the end of his life, he was a member of the Communist Party. He sided with the Soviets in their struggle against the former czarist supporters, known as Whites, in the civil war that rent Russia for several years and led to nationwide death and destruction. Zhukov's unit saw action against the White commander Anton DENIKIN, and he became the commander of the Soviet First Cavalry Army, seeing action at Tsaritsyn. Wounded, he recuperated in time to participate in the short war against Poland in 1920. For his services, the Soviet government awarded him the Order of the Red Banner, its highest military award.

With the end of the Russian civil war and victory by the Communists, Zhukov decided to remain in the military. He attended training courses for cavalry officers in 1925, and in 1928 he entered the Frunze Military Academy in Moscow, where he received specialized training in armored military operations. For the remainder of the period, until the start of the Second World War, he served as the commander of various brigades and divisions, as assistant inspector of cavalry of the Workers' and Peasants' Red Army, and as deputy commander of the Belorussian Special Military District.

In 1939, Zhukov was given command of the First East Army Group and sent to the Mongolian People's Republic to fight the Japanese invasion of that area. Under his leadership, the Japanese were driven back over the Khalkhin-Gol River into Manchuria in China, suffering

Georgi Zhukov

some 61,000 casualties. On 29 August 1939, Zhukov was awarded the Golden Star by the Presidium of the Supreme Soviet of the Union of Soviet Socialist Republics and given the title of Hero of the Soviet Union. Despite this, he was not given a command in the short-lived Russo-Finnish War (1939–40) until late in the conflict when, in January 1940, he was named as chief-of-staff of the Soviet force. It was during this period that the Soviet leader Joseph Stalin purged the ranks of the Red Army, executing thousands of the military's best commanders and soldiers. Zhukov survived the purges, and in May 1940, he was promoted to general of the Red Army and placed in command of the Kiev Special Military District. In February 1941, he was named as chief of the general staff of the Red Army, and deputy people's commissar of the defense of the USSR, serving as the second highest military officer in the nation under General Semyon Timoshenko, the minister of defense.

On 22 June 1941, Nazi Germany launched Operation Barbarossa, its all-out invasion of the Soviet Union. Although many of Stalin's military officers had warned him that such an attack was likely, he had chosen to ignore this advice and allowed the purges of the ranks to continue unabated. When the invasion began, he panicked and ordered Zhukov to take on the nation's defense as the Nazis headed eastward. Despite evidence that the German forces were moving toward Moscow to take the Soviet capital, Stalin sent Zhukov south to Kiev, believing that the Germans wanted to seize the Ukrainian oil fields first. In October 1941, Stalin replaced Timoshenko with Zhukov to serve as commander of the entire western front, which was being hammered by the German onslaught. Zhukov built up lines of defense in front of Moscow as the Germans moved on that city; his resistance to the Nazis saved the city and made Zhukov a national hero. Historian William J. Spahr writes: "Even before Moscow, he had demonstrated the leadership style and skills that he applied throughout the war. Iron will and determination, the uncanny ability to anticipate the enemy's future course of action and to skillfully apply all available assets, and the courage to withstand [Stalin's] ire when making contrary recommendations made him a tower of strength in a crisis. But in combination with his own vanity, these qualities would also earn him numerous enemies, not only among Stalin's supporters and sycophants but also within the senior military leadership."

Following the Russian victory at Moscow, Zhukov helped to save the city of Stalingrad from falling to the Germans. Encircling the German Sixth Army, he was able to hit the surrounded troops with massive firepower and eventually force a surrender that left over half a million Germans dead or captured. He also led the way in preparations for the defense of Leningrad in the north (now once again named St. Petersburg), which held out for more than three years against the German siege; and the defense of the Caucasus region, setting the stage for the massive tank battle at Kursk (5–13 July 1943), which was won by the Soviets. Zhukov then planned offensives against the demoralized German army as they were pushed back out of Russia and across Eastern Europe. He prepared the strategy that resulted in the drive on Berlin (May 1945), culminating in the collapse of Nazi Germany and the end of the Second World War in Europe. On 8 May 1945, he went to Berlin to accept the surrender of the remnants of the collapsed Nazi regime from Field Marshal Wilhelm Keitel.

Zhukov had been named as first deputy people's minister of defense of the Soviet Union in August 1942, and on 18 January 1943, he was made marshal of the Soviet Union. Twice—in 1944 and 1945—he was named as a Hero of the Soviet Union. When the victorious Allies divided Germany into four sections, to be managed by the United States, the Soviet Union, the United Kingdom, and France, Zhukov was named as commander of the Soviet sector.

In January 1946, Zhukov was relieved of his duties in Germany and recalled back to the Soviet Union, where he was given the posts of deputy minister of defense and commander in chief of Soviet ground forces in the USSR. However, the new posts were actually a demotion, as Stalin saw Zhukov as a growing threat to his own power. After a few months, when the Soviet leader felt that he had destroyed any chance Zhukov might have of eclipsing him, he dismissed the war hero and sent him to Odessa to serve as commander of the Odessa Military District, and later to the Ural Military District. In postwar Soviet histories of "The Great Patriotic War," as the Second World War was called in the USSR, Zhukov's name was barely mentioned.

Following Stalin's death in March 1953, Zhukov was rehabilitated and named as deputy minister of defense; two years later, he became minister of defense. In this position he accompanied Soviet general secretary Nikita Khrushchev to the July 1955 summit in Geneva with U.S. president Dwight D. EISENHOWER. In 1957, when the Presidium tried to oust Khrushchev from power, Zhukov stepped in and gave him his support, ending any threat to Khrushchev's rule. For this service, Zhukov was elected as a full member of the Presidium, becoming the first military officer to be named to the panel. However, his push to reform the military and remove Communist Party control over key facets of national defense led to a falling out with Khrushchev, and on 26 October 1957 he was dismissed as minister of defense and removed from the Presidium. Once again, Zhukov entered a period of being a "nonperson," refused the slightest recognition of his services to his nation's survival. For several years he remained in limbo.

It was not until Khrushchev's removal from power in 1964 that Zhukov was hailed as a hero, although his career in the military and government was long over. He appeared at the national parade in Red Square in 1965 to celebrate the 20th anniversary of the defeat of Nazi Germany and was allowed to stand atop Stalin's tomb with other Soviet leaders. His memoirs, *Toward Berlin,* were published in the Soviet Union in 1969 and published in the west as *The Memoirs of Marshal Zhukov* (1971). He died in Moscow on 18 June 1974 at the age of 77 and was buried with full military honors.

Without the strategic skills and leadership of Georgi Zhukov, the Soviet Union would probably have been defeated in the Second World War, allowing Nazi Germany to throw the world into decades of darkness. His abilities led to victory in the great defensive battles of that conflict (Moscow, Leningrad, and Stalingrad), halting the German advance and causing the loss of vast numbers of their troops. His reforms of the Red Army, ignored before the war, led to its greatest glories, to the battle for Berlin in May 1945, and to the end of Nazi Germany itself. Historian Michael Lee Lanning writes: "Although arrogant, ruthless, and often crude, Zhukov earned the title of the Soviet Union's greatest general. As such, he ranks near the top of all World War II commanders for his tenacious, well-coordinated offense that drove the Germans from interior Russia back to Berlin. That he survived the many purges of Stalin and his successors and died a peaceful death at age 77 is alone sufficient proof of his abilities."

References: Nutsch, James G., "Zhukov, Georgii Konstantinovich," in *The Modern Encyclopedia of Russian and Soviet History,* 55 vols., edited by Joseph L. Wieczynski (Gulf Breeze, Fla.: Academic International Press, 1976–93), 46:62–66; Paxton, John, "Zhukov, Georgy Konstantinovich," in *Encyclopedia of Russian History: From the Christianization of Kiev to the Break-up of the U.S.S.R.* (Santa Barbara, Calif.: ABC-Clio, 1993), 450–451; Spahr, William J., "Zhukov, Georgii Konstantinovich," in *Brassey's Encyclopedia of Military History and Biography,* edited by Franklin D. Margiotta (Washington, D.C.: Brassey's, 1994), 1115–1119; Lanning, Michael Lee, "Georgi Konstantinovich Zhukov," in *The Military 100: A Ranking of the Most Influential Military Leaders of All Time* (New York: Barnes and Noble Books, 1996), 259–262; Zhukov, Georgii, et al., *Battles Hitler Lost, and the Soviet Marshals Who Won Them: Marshals Zhukov, Konev, Malinovsky, Rotmistrov, Chuikov, and Other Commanders* (New York: Richardson and Steirman, 1986).

BIBLIOGRAPHY

BOOKS AND ARTICLES

Abbott, Frank Frost. *A History and Description of Roman Political Institutions.* Boston: Ginn & Company, 1907.

Abbott, Jacob. *Cyrus the Great.* New York: Harper & Brothers, 1900.

———. *History of Darius the Great.* London: Thomas Allman, 1850.

An Account of Sir George Rooke's Arrival in the Channel with the Fleet under His Command. London: Printed by Edw. Jones, 1696.

An Account of the Defeat of the Rebels in England as also the taking of the late Duke of Monmouth, the late Lord Gray, &c. London: Printed by Thomas Newcomb, 1685.

Adair, John Eric. *Cheriton 1644: The Campaign and the Battle.* Kineton, U.K.: The Roundwood Press, 1973.

———. *Roundhead General: A Military Biography of Sir William Waller.* London: Macdonald & Co., 1969.

Adams, John Quincy. *Oration on the Life and Character of Gilbert Motier de Lafayette. Delivered at the Request of both Houses of the Congress of the United States, before them, in the House of Representatives at Washington, on the 31st December, 1834.* Washington: Printed by Gales and Seaton, 1835.

Adams, William Henry Davenport, and William Pairman. *Great Generals: Charlemagne, Edward the Third, Gustavus Adolphus, the Duke of Marlborough, the Duke of Wellington, Earl Roberts.* London: Gall and Inglis, 1905.

Agawa, Hiroyuki. *The Reluctant Admiral.* Translated by John Bester. Tokyo, Japan: Kodansha International, 1979.

Aitchison, Nick, and Tony Robinson. *Macbeth, Man and Myth.* Stroud, U.K.: Sutton, 2000.

Albright, Harry. *New Orleans: Battle of the Bayous.* New York: Hippocrene Books, 1990.

Alexander, Harold Rupert Leofric George Alexander, Earl Alexander of Tunis. *The Alexander Memoirs, 1940–1945.* Edited by John North. London: Cassell, 1962.

———. *The Battle of Tunis.* Sheffield, U.K.: J. W. Northend, 1957.

Alexander Nevsky. Moscow, USSR: Foreign Languages Publishing House, 1943.

Allen, Bernard Meredith. *Gordon.* London: Duckworth, 1935.

Allen, Robert S. *Lucky Forward: The History of Patton's Third U.S. Army.* New York: Vanguard Press, 1947.

Allen, Sir Thomas. *A True Relation of the Victory and Happy Success of a Squadron of His Majesties fleet in the Mediterranean, against the Pyrates of Algiers taken as well out of letters from Sir Thomas Allen, His Majesties admiral in those seas, and from Sir Wil. Godolphin, His Majesties Envoye extraordinary to the court of Spain, as also, from a relation made by the Heer van Ghent, the admiral of the Dutch fleet, who assisted in that Action.* London: Printed by T. Newcomb, 1670.

Allmand, C. T. *Lancastrian Normandy, 1415–1450: The History of a Medieval Occupation.* Oxford, U.K.: Clarendon Press, 1983.

Altchscul, Michael. *A Baronial Family in Medieval England: The Clares, 1217–1314.* Baltimore, Md.: The Johns Hopkins Press, 1965.

Ambrose, Stephen E. *Duty, Honor, Country: A History of West Point.* Baltimore, Md.: Johns Hopkins Press, 1966.

Anderson, J. *Spanish Campaign of Sir John Moore.* London: R. J. Leach, 1990.

Anderson, Jack. *Stormin' Norman: An American Hero.* New York: Kensington Publishing Company, 1991.

Anderson, John Kinloch. *Military Theory and Practice in the Age of Xenophon.* Berkeley: University of California Press, 1970.

"Anecdotes of Lord Raglan." *Harper's New Monthly Magazine* 14, no. 83 (April 1857): 631.

Another Great Victorie Obtained by Vice-Admiral Pen against the Hollanders, since the last great and terrible engagement between both fleets; with the full particulars thereof, advertised by letters from the generals at sea, to the Parliament and Councel of State: together with a list of the names of the ships taken, and brought to Dover, laden with bars of silver, cocheneal, wines, sugar, salt, and tobacco: the landing of seven hundred prisoners; and the number of ships sunk, burnt, taken, and dispursed. Likewise, a narrative of the great loss on the Parl. side. Whereunto is annexed, the answer and remonstrance of the officers and souldiers in Scotland, to the late letter of the Lord Gen. Cromwel, and the Conncel of Officers in England, for the chusing of a new Parliament, to remove the heavy burdens, and to set the oppressed free. Brought by the last post, Sunday, Feb. 26. and published (according to order) to undeceive the people. London: Printed for G. Horton, 1653.

Another Great Victory obtained by the Lord Lambert against Sir George Booth, on Sunday Morning Last with the Manner of his Taking the City of Chester and throwing open the Gates, the Taking of the Five Hundred Prisoners and Divers eminent Commanders, viz, Maj. Gen. Egerton, the Lord Kilmurrey, Col. Brooks and Sir Wil. Neal: as also another Desperate fight at Leverpool, the taking of the Town, the Beating and Pursuing of the Enemy toward Wales, and the Escape of Sir George

Booth with 200 Horse to Cherk Castle. London: Printed for Edw. Horton, 1659.

Another Victory in Lancashire obtained against the Scots by Major General Harrison, and Collonel Lilburn. With, the taking of Lieut. Gen. David Lesly, Maj. Gen. Middleton, and other eminent officers and commanders, with six hundred private souldiers, Horse and Arms; and a list of the Particulars. Also, the death of Maj. Gen. Massey and Duke Hamilton, and the Scots Kings going with Hind the great robber. Together, with the manner of my Lord General Cromwels comming up, and noble reception by the City of London; and an account of the Scots prisoners which marched through the City on Saturday last. London: Printed by B.A., 1651.

The Annual Register, Or a View of the History, Politicks, and Literature, Of the Year 1758. London: Printed for R. and J. Dodsley, 1759.

Anson, Walter Vernon. *The Life of Admiral Lord Anson, the Father of the British Navy, 1697–1762.* London: John Murray, 1912.

Appleman, Roy Edgar. *Ridgway Duels for Korea.* College Station: Texas A&M University Press, 1990.

Archer, Thomas Andrew. *The Crusade of Richard I, 1189–92.* New York: G. P. Putnam's Sons, 1889.

Army Times editors. Warrior: The Story of General George S. Patton. New York: Putnam, 1967.

Arnold, Thomas Jackson. *Early Life and Letters of General Thomas J. Jackson, "Stonewall" Jackson, by His Nephew, Thomas Arnold Jackson.* New York: Fleming H. Revell Company, 1916.

Aron, Richard, and Georgette Elgey. *The Vichy Regime, 1940–44.* Boston: The Beacon Press, 1958.

The Arraignment and Impeachment of Major Generall Massie, Sir William Waller, Col. Poyntz, Sir Philip Stapleton, Sir John Maynard, Ant. Nichols, and one Cheisly, the Scotch Secretary, (lately taken at sea by the Vice-Admirall) with dives [sic] other surreptitious members of the Commons in Parliament, the Court of Aldermen, and Common Councell of the City of London; as namely Col. Sutton, Major Banes, Cap. Cox, now in safe custody, and other citizens of meaner ranke and quality of the Presbyterian faction. With a fresh discovery of their late treasonous plots, and horrid designes against the Parliament, the army, the famous City of London, and consequently of the whole kingdome, engaging them in a second cruell and bloudy warre . . . Also a thankfull remembrance of the late successe it hath pleased the Almighty to confer upon our ever renowned generall, Sir Thomas Fairfax, and his Councell of War, against that viperous brood of rigid Presbyters. London, 1647.

Arthur, Sir George. *Life of Lord Kitchener,* 3 vols. London: Macmillan and Co., 1920.

Ash, Simeon. *A True Relation, of the most Chiefe Occurrences at, and since the late Battell at Newbery, untill the disjunction of the three Armies, of the Lord Generall, the Earl of Manchester, and Sir William Waller, together with the London Brigade, under the Commander of Sir James Harrington. Published upon necessity, both to undeceive the mistaken multitude, and to vindicate the Earle of Manchester, From many undeserved aspersions commonly cast upon him, either through ignorance or prejudice.* London: Printed by G.M. for Edward Brewster, 1643.

Aspinall, Arthur. *Cornwallis in Bengal: The Administrative and Judicial Reforms of Lord Cornwallis in Bengal, Together with Accounts of the Commercial Expansion of the East India Company, 1786–1793, and of the Founding of Penang, 1786–1793.* Manchester, U.K.: Manchester University Press, 1931.

Asprey, Robert B. *The German High Command at War: Hindenburg and Ludendorff Conduct World War I.* New York: William Morrow, 1991.

———. *The Rise of Napoleon Bonaparte.* London: Little, Brown and Company, 2000.

Aston, Major-General Sir George. *The Biography of the late Marshal Foch.* London: Hutchinson & Company, 1929.

Attenborough, F. L., ed., transl. *The Laws of the Earliest English Kings.* New York: Russell & Russell, 1963.

Atteridge, A. Hilliard. *The Bravest of the Brave.* London: Methuen & Co., Ltd., 1912.

Auchmuty, Arthur Compton. *Poems of English Heroism. From Brunanburh to Lucknow and Athelstan to Albert.* London: Kegan Paul, Trench & Co., 1882.

Ayer, Frederick. *Before the Colors Fade: Portrait of a Soldier, George S. Patton.* Boston: Houghton Mifflin, 1964.

Ayton, Andrew. *Knights and Warhorses: Military Service and the English Aristocracy under Edward III.* Woodbridge, Suffolk, U.K.: Boydell Press, 1994.

Bak, János M., and Béla K. Király, eds. *Hunyadi to Rákóczi: War and Society in Late Medieval and Early Modern Hungary.* Boulder, Colo.: Social Science Monographs, 1982.

Baker, George Pierce. *Augustus: The Golden Age of Rome.* New York: Dodd, Mead & Company, 1937.

———. *Hannibal.* New York: Dodd, Mead & Company, 1929.

Baker, Sir Richard. *A Chronicle of the Kings of England from the Time of the Romans Government unto the Death of King James: Containing all Passages of State and Church with all other Observations proper for a Chronicle: Faithfully collected out of Authors Ancient and Modern, and digested into a new Method. By Sir R. Baker, Knight; Whereunto is now added in this Third Edition the Reign of King Charles I, with a Continuation of the Chronicle to the end of the Year MDCLVIII: Being a Full Narrative of the Affaires of England, Scotland, and Ireland, more especially Relating unto the Transactions of Charles, crowned King of the Scots at Scone on the first day of January, 1650.* London: Printed by E. Cotes, 1660.

Baldwin, John W. *The Government of Philip Augustus: Foundations of French Royal Power in the Middle Ages.* Berkeley: University of California Press, 1986.

Balsdon, John Percy Vyvian Dacre. *Julius Caesar: A Political Biography.* New York: Atheneum, 1967.

Barbour, John, comp. *The Bruce: or, The Book of the Most Excellent and Noble Prince, Robert de Broyss, King of Scots.* Edinburgh: W. Blackwood and Sons, 1894.

Barnard, Francis Pierrepont. *Strongbow's Conquest of Ireland.* New York: G. P. Putnam's Sons, 1888.

Barnard, John Gross. *The Peninsular Campaign and its Antecedents, as Developed by the Report of Maj.-Gen. Geo. B. McClellan, and other Published Documents.* New York: D. Van Nostrand, 1864.

Barnes, Joshua. *The History of that Most Victorious monarch Edward III.d King of England and France, and Lord of Ireland, being a Full and Exact Account of the Life and Death of the said king, Together with that of his most Renowned son Edward, Prince of Wales and of Aquitain[e], sirnamed the Black Prince, Collected from the Best and Most Antient [sic] authors, Printed Books, Manuscripts and Records.* Cambridge, England: Printed by J. Hayes for the Author, 1688.

Barnett, Corelli. *The Desert Generals.* London: W. Kimber, 1960.

Barnett, Corelli, ed. *Hitler's Generals.* New York: Grove Weidenfeld, 1989.

Barrett, C. R. B. "The Missing Fifteen Years (1625–1640) in the Life of Robert Blake, Admiral and General at

Sea." *The Journal of the Royal United Science Institution* 62 (1917): 98–110.

Barrow, G. W. S. *Robert Bruce and the Community of the Realm of Scotland.* Berkeley: University of California Press, 1965.

Barrow, Sir John. *The Life of George, Lord Anson, Admiral of the Fleet, Vice-Admiral of Great Britain, and First Lord Commissioner of the Admiralty, Previous to, and During, the Seven Years' War.* London: John Murray, 1839.

Barton, Sir Dunbar Plunkett. *The Amazing Career of Bernadotte, 1763–1844.* London: John Murray, 1929.

Bass, Robert D. *Swamp Fox: The Life and Campaigns of General Francis Marion.* New York: Holt, 1969.

Bates, F. A., comp. *Graves Memoirs of the Civil War, Compiled from Seventeenth Century Records.* Edinburgh and London: William Blackwood & Sons, 1927.

The Battaile Fought Betweene Count Maurice of Nassau, and Albertus Arch-Duke of Austria, nere Newport in Flaunders, the xxij. of June 1600 with the names of such men of accomp[lishmen]t as have been either Slaine, Hurt, or Taken Prisoners by Either Part. Written by a Gentleman imploied in the Said Service. London: Printed for Andrew Wise, 1600.

The Battle of Acton: An Account of the Famous Battle in 1643 during England's Civil War. Alton, U.K.: Peter Canfield Associates, 1999.

Bauer, Karl Jack. *Zachary Taylor: Soldier, Planter, Statesman of the Old Southwest.* Baton Rouge: Louisiana State University Press, 1985.

Beadon, Roger. *Robert Blake: Sometime Commanding All the Fleets and Naval Forces of England.* London: Edward Arnold & Co., 1935.

Beamish, Sir Tufton Victor Hamilton. *Battle Royal: A New Account of Simon de Montfort's Struggle against King Henry III.* London: F. Muller, 1965.

Beatson, Lieutenant-Colonel R. E. *The Plains of Abraham. Notes, Original and Selected.* Gibraltar, Garrison Library Press, 1858.

Beatty, John Louis. *Warwick and Holland: Being the Lives of Robert and Henry Rich.* Denver: Alan Swallow, 1965.

Beatty, William. *The Death of Lord Nelson.* Birmingham, U.K.: The War Library, 1894.

Bell, Douglas Herbert. *Drake.* London: Duckworth, 1935.

Bell, William Gardner. *Commanding Generals and Chiefs of Staff, 1775–1995: Portraits & Biographical Sketches of the United States Army's Senior Officer.* Washington, D.C.: United States Army, Center of Military History, 1997.

Bellamy, Francis F. *Private Life of George Washington.* New York: Crowell, 1951.

Belloc, Hilaire. *William the Conqueror.* London: Peter Davies Limited, 1933.

Bengtsson, Frans Gunnar. *The Sword Does Not Jest: The Heroic Life of King Charles XII of Sweden.* New York: St. Martin's Press, 1960.

Bennett, Martyn. *The English Civil War.* London: Longman, 1995.

———. *Historical Dictionary of the British and Irish Civil Wars, 1637–1660.* Chicago: Fitzroy Dearborn Publishers, 2000.

Berwick, James Fitzjames, duke of Berwick. *Memoirs of the Marshal Duke of Berwick. Written by Himself. With a Summary Continuation from the Year 1716, to his Death in 1734. To this Work is Prefixed a Sketch of an Historical Panegyric of the Marshal, by the President Montesquieu, and Explanatory Notes, and Original Letters Relating to the Campaign in Flanders, in 1708, are Subjoined.* London: T. Cadell, 1779.

Bickham, William Denison. *Rosecrans' Campaign with the Fourteenth Army Corps, or, the Army of the Cumberland: A Narrative of Personal Observations with Official Reports of the Battle of Stone River.* Cincinnati, Ohio: Moore, Wilstach, Keys & Co., 1863.

Bigelow, Poultney. *Genseric: King of the Vandals and First Prussian Kaiser.* New York: G. P. Putnam's Sons, 1918.

Birdwood, Field Marshal Lord Birdwood of Anzac and Totnes. *In My Time: Recollections and Anecdotes.* London: Skeffington & Son, Ltd., 1946.

Bishop, M. C., and Coulston, J. C. N. *Roman Military Equipment: From the Punic Wars to the Fall of Rome.* London: Batsford, 1993.

Blair, Clay. *Ridgway's Paratroopers: The American Airborne in World War II.* Garden City, N.Y.: Dial Press, 1985.

Blake, Martin Joseph. "Field-Marshal Sir John French." *The Journal of the Galway Archaeological and Historical Society* 8, no. 4 (1915): 247–251.

Blanchard, Amos. *American Military Biography, Containing the Lives and Characters of the Officers of the Revolution who were most Distinguished in achieving our National Independence. Also, the life of Gilbert Motier La Fayette.* Cincinnati: E. Deming, 1834.

Blumberg, Arnold. "Bohemian Prince Rupert Fought for the Crown against Parliament in England's Civil War." *Military Heritage* 5, no. 1 (August 2003): 12–15, 89.

Blumenson, Martin. *Mark Clark*. New York: Congdon & Weed, 1984.

Blythe, Legette. *Marshal Ney: A Dual Life*. London: Jarrolds Publishers, 1937.

Bobrick, Benson. *Fearful Majesty: The Life and Reign of Ivan the Terrible*. New York: Putnam, 1987.

Bodley, Ronald Victor Courtenay. *Admiral Togo: The Authorized Life of Admiral of the Fleet, Marquis Heihachiro Togo*. London: Jarrolds, 1935.

Booth, John. *The Battle of Waterloo, Containing the Accounts Published by Authority, British and Foreign and Other Relative Documents, with Circumstantial Details Previous and After the Battle. To which is added an Alphabetical List of the Officers Killed and Wounded, from 15th to 26 June, 1815*. London: John Booth, T. Edgerton, 1815.

Boscobel: Or, the Compleat History of His Sacred Majesties Most Miraculous Preservation After the Battle of Worcester, 3 Sept. 1651, Introduced by an Exact Relation of that Battle; and Illustrated with a Map of the City. London: Printed by M. Clark, 1680.

Boswell, E., ed. *Edmond Ironside; or, War Hath made All Friends*. London: Oxford University Press, 1928.

Bosworth, C. E., E. Van Donzel, W. P. Heinrichs, and G. LeComte, eds. *The Encyclopedia of Islam*, 10 vols. Leiden, The Netherlands: Brill, 1960–2003.

Bowen, Marjorie. *The Life of Rear-Admiral John Paul Jones, Chevalier of the Military Order of Merit and of the Russian Order of the Empress Anne, 1747–1792*. London: H. Jenkins, 1940.

Boxer, C. R., ed. and trans. *The Journal of Maarten Harperszoon Tromp, Anno 1639*. Cambridge, U.K.: University Press, 1930.

Bradbury, Jim. *Philip Augustus: King of France, 1180–1223*. London: Longman, 1998.

Braddy, Haldeen. *Pershing's Mission in Mexico*. El Paso: Texas Western Press, 1966.

Bradford, Ernle. *Hannibal*. New York: McGraw-Hill, 1981.

Bradlaugh, Charles. *John Churchill, Duke of Marlborough*. London: Freethought Publishing Company, 1884.

Bradley, Henry. *The Story of the Goths, from the Earliest Times to the End of the Gothic Dominion in Spain*. New York: G. P. Putnam's Sons, 1888.

Bradley, Omar Nelson. *A General's Life: An Autobiography*. New York: Simon and Schuster, 1983.

Brereton, Sir William. *The Letter Books of Sir William Brereton*, 2 vols. Edited by R. N. Dore. Chester, U.K.: Record Society of Lancashire and Chesire, 1984–90.

A Brief History of the Life of Mary, Queen of Scots, and the occasions that brought her and Thomas, Duke of Norfolk, to their tragical ends shewing the hopes the Papists then had of a Popish successor in England, and their plots to accomplish them: with a full account of the tryals of that Queen, and of the said Duke, as also the trial of Philip Howard, Earl of Arundel: From the papers of a Secretary of Sir Francis Walsingham. Now published by a person of Quality. London: Printed for Tho. Cockerill, 1681.

A Brief Narrative of the Great Victorie, which it hath Pleased God to give to the Armie of this Common-wealth against the Scots Armie, near Dunbar, in Scotland, on Tuesdaie morning, the third of this instant September, related to the Council of State by an express Messenger of the Lord General, sent from the Armie which Messenger was present at the Action. London: Printed by William Dugard, by the Appointment of the Council of State, 1650.

A Brief Relation of the Taking of Bridgewater by the Parliaments Forces under the Command of Sir Tho. Fairfax, and therein, all the Lord Gorings Train, 36 Pieces of Ordnance, 2000 Prisoners, 800 Horse, with great Store of Oxen. Sent in a Letter to the Committee of Both Kingdoms: Together with a Letter Concerning the delivering up of Pontefract Castle by Treaty or the Use of the Parliament, with all the Things therein. Also, hopes of reducing Scarbrough by Treaty. Sent to the Honorable, William Lenthall, Esq., Speaker to the House of Commons. London: Printed for Edw. Husband, Printer to the Honorable House of Commons, 1645.

Brink, Randall. *Nimitz: The Man and His Wars*. New York: D. I. Fine Books/Dutton, 1996.

Brion, Marcel. *Alaric the Goth*. Translated by Frederick H. Martens. London: Thornton Butterworth Limited, 1932.

Brock, Sir Isaac. *The Life and Correspondence of Major-General Sir Isaac Brock, K.B. interspersed with Notices of the Celebrated Indian chief, Tecumseh, and comprising Brief Memoirs of Daniel De Lisle Brock, Esq., Lieutenant E. W. Tupper, R.N., and Colonel W. De Vic*

Tupper. Edited by Ferdinand Brock Tupper. London: Simpkin, Marshall, 1845.

Broé, Samuel de. *The History of the Triumvirates. The First that of Julius Caesar, Pompey and Crassus. The Second that of Augustus, Anthony and Lepidus. Being a Faithfull Collection from the best Historians, and other Authours; Concerning that Revolution of the Roman Government which happened under their Authority.* Translated by Tho. Orway. London: Printed for Charles Brome, 1686.

Brookhiser, Richard. *Founding Father: Rediscovering George Washington.* New York: The Free Press, 1996.

Browning, Oscar, ed. *The Journal of Sir George Rooke, Admiral of the Fleet, 1700–1702.* London: Printed for the Navy Records Society, 1897.

Brownrigg, B. *The Life & Letters of Sir John Moore.* Oxford, U.K.: Blackwell, 1923.

Bruce, Anthony, and William Cogar. *An Encyclopedia of Naval History.* New York: Checkmark Books, 1999.

Bruce, George. *Collins Dictionary of Wars.* Glasgow, Scotland: HarperCollins Publishers, 1995.

Bruce, William Napier. *Life of General Sir Charles Napier.* London: John Murray, 1885.

Brundage, James A. *The Crusades: A Documentary Survey.* Milwaukee: Marquette University Press, 1962.

Brusilov, Aleksei Alekseevich. *A Soldier's Note-Book, 1914–1918.* Westport, Conn.: Greenwood Press, 1971.

Bryant, Arthur. *The Turn of the Tide, 1939–1943: A Study Based on the Diaries and Autobiographical Notes of Field Marshal the Viscount Alanbrooke.* New York: Collins, 1957.

Buchan, John. *Augustus.* Boston: Houghton Mifflin, 1937.

———. *Gordon at Khartoum.* London: P. Davies, Ltd., 1934.

———. *Montrose: A History.* Boston: Houghton Mifflin, 1928.

Buck, Sir George. *The History and Life and Reigne of Richard the Third, Composed in Five Bookes by Geo. Buck.* London: Printed by W. Wilson, 1647.

Budenny, Semyon Mikhailovich. *Proidennyi Put* (The Path of Valour). Moscow: Progress Publishers, 1972.

Budge, Ernest A. *Nebuchadnezzar, King of Babylon. On Recently-discovered Inscriptions of this King.* London: Victoria Institute, 1884.

Buller, Sir Redvers Henry. *The Life and Campaigns of Sir Redvers H. Buller, V.C.* London: George Newnes Limited, 1900.

Burleigh, Bennet. *Sirdar and Khalifa; or, the Reconquest of Soudan, 1898.* London: Chapman & Hall, 1898.

Burns, Thomas S. *A History of the Ostro-Goths.* Bloomington: Indiana University Press, 1984.

Burrows, Montagu. *The Life of Edward Lord Hawke, Admiral of the Fleet, Vice-Admiral of Great Britain, and First Lord of the Admiralty from 1766 to 1771.* London: J. J. Keliher & Co., Limited, 1904.

Bury, John B. "The European Expedition of Darius." *The Classical Review,* 11, no. 6 (July 1897): 277–282.

———. *A History of the Later Roman Empire from Arcadius to Irene (395 A.D. to 800 A.D.),* 2 vols. London: Macmillan, 1898.

———. *History of the Later Roman Empire from the Death of Theodosius I to the Death of Justinian,* 2 vols. London: Macmillan, 1923.

Bury, John B., S. A. Cook, and F. E. Adcock, eds. *The Cambridge Ancient History: VI: Macedon, 401–301 B.C.* Cambridge, U.K.: University Press, 1933.

Busch, Noel Fairchild. *The Emperor's Sword: Japan vs. Russia in the Battle of Tsushima.* New York: Funk & Wagnall's, 1969.

Bushong, Millard Kessler. *Old Jube: A Biography of General Jubal A. Early.* Boyce, Va.: Carr Publishing Company, 1955.

Butler, Colonel Sir William. *Sir Charles Napier.* London: Macmillan and Company, 1890.

Butterfield, Daniel. *Major-General Joseph Hooker and the Troops from the Army of the Potomac at Wauhatchie, Lookout Mountain and Chattanooga: Together with General Hooker's Military Record from the Files of the War Department, Adjutant-General's Office, U.S.A.* New York: Exchange Printing, 1896.

Caesar, Julius Gaius. *The Commentaries of C. Julius Cæsar, of his Wars in Gallia, and the Civil Wars betwixt him and Pompey.* Translated by Clement Edmonds. London: Printed by Tho. Newcomb for Jonathan Edwin, 1677.

Callcott, Wilfred Hardy. *Santa Anna.* Hamden, Conn.: Archon Books, 1964.

Cambini, Andrea. *Two Very Notable Commentaries the one of the Originall of the Turcks and Empire of the house of Ottomanno, written by Andrewe Cambine, and thother of the warres of the Turcke against George Scanderbeg, prince of Epiro, and of the great victories obteyned by the sayd George, aswell against the Emperour of Turkie, as other princes, and of his other rare force and vertues, worthye of memorye.* Translated by John Shute. London, 1562.

Cambrensis, Giraldus. *Expugnatio Hibernica: The Conquest of Ireland by Giraldus Cambrensis.* Translated by A. B. Scott and F. X. Martin. Dublin, Ireland: The Royal Irish Academy, 1978.

Campbell, Sir Colin. *Memorandum of the Part Taken by the Third Division of the Army of the Punjaub at the Battle of Chillianwala.* London: James Ridgway, Piccadilly, 1851.

Campbell, John. *Lives of the Admirals, and Other Eminent British Seamen: Containing Their Personal Histories, and a Detail of All Their Public Services: Including a New and Accurate History from the Earliest Account of Time; and, Clearly Proving by a Continued Series of Facts, Our Interrupted Claims to, and Enjoyment of the Dominion of Our Seas: the Whole Supported Throughout by Proper Authorities,* 4 vols. London: Printed by John Applebee for J. and H. Pemberton and T. Waller, 1744.

Caoursin, Guillaume. *The History of the Turkish War with the Rhodians, Venetians, Egyptians, Persians, and other nations being a compact series of the memorable battels, sieges, and progress of the Ottoman armies in Europe, Asia, and Africa, for near an hundred years, with their various success by sea and land: but a relation more particularly of the first bloody siege of Rhodes in the reign of Mahomet the Great . . . and the last under the command of Solyman the Magnificent, who, at the expense of an 100000 Lives, totally subdued that famous City and Island, defended by the Valour of the Renowned Peter Aubusson, Grant Master of Rhodes, and the Christian Knights of the Order of St. John, against the whole Power of the Ottoman Empire, for 230 Years. With a Pathetick Account of many other remarkable Passages.* London: Printed for Will. Whitwood, 1683.

Caraccioli, Charles. *The Life of Robert Lord Clive, Baron Plassey. Wherein are Delineated His Military Talents in the Field; His Maxims of Government in the Cabinet, During the Last Two Wars in the East Indies. With Anecdotes of His Private Life, and the Particular Circumstances of His Death, Etc.,* 4 vols. London: T. Bell, ca. 1775.

Carey, John, ed. *Eyewitness to History.* Cambridge, Mass.: Harvard University Press, 1987.

Carlin, Norah. *The Causes of the English Civil War.* Oxford, U.K.: Blackwell Publishers, 1999.

Carte, Thomas. *A Collection of Original Letters and Papers, Concerning the Affairs of England, from the Year 1641 to 1660: Found Among the Duke of Ormonde's Papers,* 2 vols. London: Printed by James Bettenham, 1739.

Cary, Earnest, trans. *Dio's Roman History,* 9 vols. London: William Heinemann, 1914.

Caryl, Joseph. *Memorable Dayes and Workes of God, in the Yeare Past, 1645. A Catalogue of the Cities, Castles, Townes, and Forts that have beene taken by the Parliaments Forces since January Last.* London: Printed for J. Bartlett, 1646.

The Case of Colonel John Lambert, Prisoner in the Tower of London. London, 1661.

Casgrain, Henri Raymond. *Wolfe and Montcalm.* London: Oxford University Press, 1926.

Cassar, George H. *The Tragedy of Sir John French.* Newark: University of Delaware Press, 1985.

A Catalogue of the Earles, Lords, Knights, Generalls, Collonels, Lieutenant Collonels, Majors, Captains, and Gentlemen of Worth and Quality Slain on the Parliament and Kings side, since the beginning of our uncivil civil Warrs; with the number of common soldiers slain on both sides: as also a list of those that have fled out of the kingdome. London: Printed for John Hancock, 1647.

Cawkwell, George L. "Epaminondas and Thebes." *Classical Quarterly* 66 (1972): 254–278.

Chalmers, William Scott. *The Life and Letters of David, Earl Beatty, Admiral of the Fleet, Viscount Borodale of Wexford, Baron Beatty of the North Sea and of Brooksby, P.C., G.C.B., O.M., G.C.V.O., D.S.O., D.C.L., LL.D.* London: Hodder and Stoughton, 1951.

Chandler, David G. *Marlborough as Military Commander.* London: Batsford, 1973.

Chandler, David G., ed. *Great Battles of the British Army as Commemorated in the Sandhurst Companies.* London: Arms and Armour, 1993.

Chant, Christopher, Richard Holmes, and William Koenig. *Two Centuries of Warfare: 23 Decisive Battles that Changed the Course of History.* London: Octopus Books, 1978.

Charanis, Peter. *The Monastic Properties and the State in the Byzantine Empire.* London: Dumbarton Oaks Papers No. 4, 1948.

Charlesworth, Martin Percival. *Five Men: Character Studies from the Roman Empire.* Cambridge, Mass.: Harvard University Press, 1936.

Charnock, John. *Biographia Navalis; or, Impartial Memoirs of the Lives and Characters of Officers of the Navy of Great Britain, From the Year 1660 to the Present Time; Drawn from the Most Authentic Sources, and Disposed in a Chronological Arrangement,* 4 vols. London: Printed for R. Faulder, 1794–98.

Chrisawn, Margaret Scott. *The Emperor's Friend: Marshal Jean Lannes.* Westport, Conn.: Greenwood Press, 2001.

Churchill, Winston. *The Boer War: London to Ladysmith via Pretoria: Ian Hamilton's March.* London: Longmans, Green, 1900.

Clark, Mark W. *Calculated Risk.* New York: Harper, 1950.

Clarke, Samuel. *The Life and Death of Julius Cæsar, the first Founder of the Roman Empire: As Also, The Life and Death of Augustus Cæsar, in whose Raign Our Blessed Lord and Saviour Jesus Chrit [sic] was Borne.* London: Printed for William Miller, 1665.

———. *The Life and Death of Nebuchadnezzar, the Great, the First Founder of the Babylonian Empire, represented by the Golden Head of that Image, Dan. 2.32, and by the Lion with Eagles Wings, Dan. 7.4.: As also of Cyrus, the Great, the first Founder of the Empire of Medes and Persians, Represented by the Breast, and Arms of Silver in that Image, Dan 2.32, and by a Bear, Dan 7.* London: Printed for William Miller, 1664.

———. *The Life and Death of Pompey the Great: With all his Glorious Victories and Triumphs: As also the Life and Death of Artaxerxes Mnemon, of the great Persian Emperours.* London: Printed for William Miller, 1665.

———. *The Life and Death of William, Surnamed the Conqueror: King of England, and Duke of Normandy. Who dyed Anno Christi, 1087.* London: Printed for Simon Miller, 1671.

———. *The Life of Tamerlane the Great with his Wars against the great Duke of Moso, the King of China, Bazajet the Great Turk, the Sultan of Egypt, the King of Persia, and Some Others, Carried on with a Continued Series of Success from the First to the last. Wherein are Rare Examples of Heathenish Piety, Prudence, Magnaminity, Mercy, Liberality, Humility, Justice, Temperance, and Valour.* London, 1653.

Clemoes, Peter, ed. *The Anglo-Saxons: Studies in Some Aspects of their History and Culture, Presented to Bruce Dickins.* London: Bowes & Bowes, 1959.

Clinton, Sir Henry. *The American Rebellion: Sir Henry Clinton's Narrative of His Campaigns, 1775–1782, with an Appendix of Original Documents.* Edited by William B. Willcox. New Haven: Yale University Press, 1954.

———. *The Narrative of Lieutenant-General Sir Henry Clinton, K.B., Relative to His Conduct During Part of His Command of the King's Troops in North America, Particularly to That which Respects the unfortunate issue of the campaign of 1781, with an Appendix, Containing Copies and Extracts of Those Parts of His Correspondence with Lord George Germain, Earl Cornwallis, Rear Admiral Graves, &c., which are referred to therein.* London: Printed for J. Debrett, 1783.

Clowes, William Laird. *The Royal Navy: A History From the Earliest Times to the Present,* 7 vols. London: Sampson Low, Marston and Company, 1897–1903.

Codrington, Robert. *The Life and Death of the Illustrious Robert Earle of Essex, &c. Containing at large the Wars he Managed, and the Commands he had in Holland, the Palatinate, and in England.* London: [Printed by] F. Leach for L. Chapman, 1646.

Cohen, Roger. *In the Eye of the Storm: The Life of General H. Norman Schwarzkopf.* New York: Farrar, Straus, and Giroux, 1991.

Cole, Hubert. *The Betrayers: Joachim and Caroline Murat.* London: Eyre Methuen, 1972.

A Collection of Several Letters and Declarations, Sent by General Monck Unto the Lord Lambert, the Lord Fleetwood, and the rest of the General Council of Officers in the Army, As Also, That part of the Parliament, called the Rump, the Committee of Safety, so called, The Lord Mayor and Common Council of the City of London, The Congregated Churches in and about London. London, 1660.

A Collection of State Tracts, Publish'd on Occasion of the Late Revolution in 1688. And during the Reign of King William III. To which is Prefix'd, The History of the Dutch War of 1672, Translated from the French Copy Printed at Paris in 1682, which was Suppresst at the Instance of the English Embassador, because of the Discoveries it made of the League betwixt the Kings of France and England for enslaving Europe, and introducing the Popish Religion into These Kingdoms, and the United Provinces. With a Table of the Several Tracts in this Volume, and an Alphabetical Index of Matters, 3 vols. London: Privately printed, 1705–07.

Coloma, Luis. *The Story of Don John of Austria.* Translated by Lady Moreton. London: John Lane, 1912.

The Common-wealths Great Ship commonly called the Soveraigne of the Seas, built in the yeare, 1637. With a true and exact Dimension of her bulk and burden, and those Decorements which beautifie and adorne her . . . With all the fights wee have had with the Hollander, since the engagement of Lieutenant-Admirall Trompe neere Dover, against the English fleet under the command of Generall Blake, at the same time that three of their embassadours were here treating of peace. With a perfect rehearsall of an act for encrease of shipping, and encouragement of the navigation of this nation, which so much displeaseth the Hollander. London: Printed by M. Simmons for T. Jenner, 1653.

Congressional Quarterly's Guide to U.S. Elections. Washington, D.C.: Congressional Quarterly, Inc., 1985.

Conner, Philip Syng Physick. Sir William Penn, Knight: Admiral, and General-at-Sea; Great-Captain-Commander in the Fleet: A Memoir. Philadelphia: J. B. Lippincott, 1876.

Conroy, Robert. The Battle of Manila Bay: The Spanish-American War in the Philippines. New York: The Macmillan Company, 1968.

Cooper, Michael, ed. The Southern Barbarians: The First Europeans in Japan. Tokyo, Japan: Kodansha Ltd., 1971.

A Copie of the Articles Agreed Upon at the Surrender of the City of Bristol, Betweene Colonell Nathaniel Fienes, Governour of the Said City, on the one Party, and Colonell Charles Gerrard, and Captain William Teringham, for, and on the Behalfe of, Prince Rupert, on the other Party, the 26 of July, 1643. With a Letter hereunto added, in which his Copie of Articles was Inclosed: Wherein is Manifested how well those persidious Cavaliers have kept the said Articles; and may serve as a warning to the whole Kingdome, how to trust againe the whole of such Cavaliers. London: Printed for Henry Overton, 1643.

Coppée, Henry. Grant and His Campaigns: A Military Biography. New York: C. B. Richardson, 1866.

Corbett, Sir Julian Stafford. Drake and the Tudor Navy; With a History of the Rise of England as a Maritime Power. London: Longmans, Green, 1898.

Correspondence, between the late Commodore Stephen Decatur and Commodore James Barron, which led to the Unfortunate Meeting of the Twenty Second of March. Boston: Russell & Gardner, 1820.

Corvisier, André, ed. A Dictionary of Military History and the Art of War. London: Blackwell, 1994.

Cowen, Thomas. The Russo-Japanese War from the Outbreak of Hostilities to the Battle of Liaoyang. London: E. Arnold, 1904.

Coxe, William. Memoirs of John Duke of Marlborough; With His Original Correspondence: Collected From the Family Records at Blenheim, and other Authentic Sources, 3 vols. London: Printed for Longman, Hurst, Rees, Orme, and Brown, 1818–19.

Crabites, Pierre. Gordon, the Sudan and Slavery. London: G. Routledge and Sons, Ltd., 1933.

Craig, Simon. "Battle of Ankara: Collision of Empires." Military History 19, no. 3 (August 2002): 58–65.

Creasy, Edward Shepherd. Decisive Battles of the World. London: The Colonial Press, 1899.

Croly, George. The Year of Liberation: A Journal of the Defence of Hamburgh against the French Army under Marshal Davoust [sic], in 1813, 2 vols. London: James Duncan, 1832.

Cunliffe, Marcus. George Washington: Man and Monument. Boston: Little, Brown, 1958.

Curley, Sister Mary Mildred. The Conflict Between Pope Boniface VIII and King Philip IV, the Fair. Washington, D.C.: The Catholic University of America, 1927.

Cust, Edward. The Campaigns of the Great Condé (1621–1686). Tonbridge, U.K.: G. Simon, 1990.

———. Lives of the Warriors of the Civil Wars of France and England. Warriors of the Seventeenth Century, 2 vols. London: J. Murray, 1867–69.

Czerapowicz, Josephine Mary. Kingdom of Poland during the Paskevich Viceroyalty, 1832–1856: Erosion of Autonomy. Master's thesis, Michigan State University, 1975.

Dalton, Charles. Life and Times of General Sir Edward Cecil, Viscount Wimbledon, Colonel of an English Regiment in the Dutch Service, 1605–1631, and one of His Majesty's Most Honourable Privy Council, 1628–1638, 2 vols. London: Sampson Low, Marston, Searle, & Rivington, 1885.

David, H. W. C., ed. Essays in History Presented to Reginald Lane Poole. Oxford: Clarendon Press, 1927.

Davies, D. W. Sir John Moore's Peninsular Campaign. The Hague: Martinus Nijoff, 1974.

Davies, Godfrey. "Documents Illustrating the First Civil War, 1642–45." The Journal of Modern History 3, no. 1 (March 1931): 64–71.

———. "The Parliamentary Army under the Earl of Essex, 1642–5." English Historical Review 49 (January 1934): 32–46.

———. The Restoration of Charles II. San Marino, Cal.: The Huntington Library, 1955.

Davis, Paul K. 100 Decisive Battles from Ancient Times to the Present. Santa Barbara, Cal.: ABC-Clio, 1999.

Davis, William Stearns. *Readings in Ancient History: Illustrative Extracts from the Sources,* 2 vols. Boston: Allyn and Bacon, 1912–13.

Dawson, William Harbutt. *Cromwell's Understudy: The Life and Times of General John Lambert and the Rise and Fall of the Protectorate.* London: W. Hodge and Company, Ltd., 1938.

Dayan, Moshe. *Moshe Dayan: Story of My Life.* New York: Morrow, 1976.

A Declaration or Representation From His Excellency, Sir Thomas Fairfax, And the Army under his Command, Humbly Tendred to the Parliament, Concerning the Just and Fundamentall Rights and Liberties of themselves and the Kingdome. With Some Humble Proposals and Desire. London, 1647.

Delbrück, Hans. *Warfare in Antiquity: History of the Art of War,* volume 1. Lincoln: University of Nebraska Press, 1990.

Del Mar, Alexander. *The Worship of Augustus Caesar, Derived from a Study of old Coins, Monuments, Calendars, Aeras, and Astronomical and Astrological Cycles, the whole Establishing a new Chronology and Survey of History and Religion.* New York: Cambridge University Press, 1900.

Denikin, Anton Ivanovich. *The Career of a Tsarist Officer: Memoirs, 1872–1916.* Translated by Margaret Patoski. Minneapolis: University of Minneapolis Press, 1975.

———. *The White Army.* Translated by Catherine Zvegintzov. Westport, Conn.: Hyperion Press, 1973.

Denton, Jeffrey Howard. *Philip the Fair and the Ecclesiastical Assemblies of 1294–1295.* Philadelphia: American Philosophical Society, 1991.

De Ségur, Count Philippe-Paul. *Napoleon's Russian Campaign.* Alexandria, Va.: Time/Life Books, 1980.

D'Este, Carlo. *Decision in Normandy: The Unwritten Story of Montgomery and the Allied Campaign.* London: Collins, 1983.

———. *Fatal Decision: Anzio and the Battle for Rome.* New York: HarperCollins, 1991.

Devereux, Walter Bourchier. *Lives and Letters of the Devereux, Earls of Essex, 1540–1646,* 2 vols. London: John Murray, 1853.

De Wet, Christiaan Rudolf. *Three Years War (October 1899–June 1902).* Westminster, U.K.: A. Constable, 1902.

Dillon, Richard. *We Have Met the Enemy: Oliver Hazard Perry, Wilderness Commander.* New York: McGraw-Hill, 1978.

A Discourse Concerning the Spanish Fleete Invadinge Englande in the Yeare 1588, and Overthrowne by Her Maiesties Navie Under the Conduction of the Right-Honourable the Lord Charles Howarde Highe Admirall of England: Written in Italian by Petruccio Ubaldino Citizen of Florence, and Translated for A. Ryther: Unto the Discourse are Annexed Certaine Tables Expressing the Severall Exploites, and Conflictes Had With the Said Fleet. London, 1590.

Dodge, Theodore Ayrault. *Cæsar: A History of the Art of War Among the Romans Down to the End of the Roman Empire.* Boston: Houghton, Mifflin and Company, 1892.

Donat, Karl von. *The Russo-Japanese War: The Battle on the Scha-Ho.* London: Hugh Rees, 1910.

Dorpalen, Andreas. *Hindenburg and the Weimar Republic.* Princeton, N.J.: Princeton University Press, 1964.

Doyle, James William Edmund. *The Official Baronage of England, Showing the Succession, Dignities, and Offices of Every Peer from 1066 to 1885, with Sixteen Hundred Illustrations,* 3 vols. London: Longmans, Green, 1886.

Drake, Sir Francis, Bart. *The World Encompassed by Sir Francis Drake, being his next voyage to that to Nombre de Dios formerly imprinted; carefully collected out of the notes of Master Francis Fletcher, Preacher in this employment, and divers others his followers in the same, etc.* London: Printed for Nicholas Bourne, 1628.

Drayton, Michael. *The Ballad of Agincourt. Reprinted with the Additional Stanza from Richard Butcher's Copy of the 1619 folio edition of the Poems which was Presented to him by Drayton at the Deuell & St. Dunston in the Poets Hall called Apollo the 30th of November 1620.* Oxford, U.K.: [Printed by] Charles Batey, 1951.

———. *The Battaile of Agincourt Fought by Henry the fift of that name, King of England, against the whole power of the French: under the raigne of their Charles the sixt, anno Dom. 1415. The miseries of Queene Margarite, the infortunate wife, of that most infortunate King Henry the sixt. Nimphidia, the court of Fayrie. The quest of Cinthia. The shepheards Sirena. The moone-calfe. Elegies upon sundry occasions.* London: Printed [by Augustine Mathewes] for William Lee, 1627.

Driskill, Frank A. *Admiral of the Hills: Chester W. Nimitz.* Austin, Tex.: Eakin Press, 1983.

Du Buisson, Premiere Capitaine [Gatien Courtilz de Sandras]. *The History of the Life and Actions of the Great Captain of his Age the Viscount de Turenne.* Translated by Ferrand Spence. London: Printed by J.B. for Dorman Newman & R. Bentley, 1686.

Duffy, Christopher. *Frederick the Great: A Military Life.* London: Routledge, 1988.

Duiker, William J. *Historical Dictionary of Vietnam.* Metuchen, N.J.: The Scarecrow Press, 1989.

Dumville, David N. *Wessex and England from Alfred to Edgar: Six Essays on Political, Cultural, and Ecclesiastical Revival.* Woodbridge, U.K.: Boydell Press, 1992.

Dunfermline, James Abercromby, Lord. *Lieutenant-General Sir Ralph Abercromby, K.B., 1793–1801: a Memoir by his son James Lord Dunfermline.* Edinburgh, Scotland: Edmonston and Douglas, 1861.

Dunne, William M. P. "Pistols and Honor: The James Barron-Stephen Decatur Conflict, 1798–1807." *American Neptune* 50, no. 4 (1990): 245–259.

Dupuy, Trevor N., Curt Johnson, and David L. Bongard. *The Encyclopedia of Military Biography.* London: I. B. Taurus, 1992.

Durant, Will, and Ariel Durant. *The Age of Napoleon: A History of European Civilization from 1789 to 1815.* New York: Simon and Schuster, 1975.

Dusenbery, B. M., comp. *Monument to the Memory of General Andrew Jackson: Containing Twenty-Five Eulogies and Sermons Delivered on Occasion of His Death. To which is Added an Appendix, Containing General Jackson's Proclamation, His Farewell Address, and a Certified Copy of His Last Will. The Whole Preceded by a Short Sketch of His Life.* Philadelphia: Walker & Gillis, 1846.

Dutch, Oswald. *Hitler's 12 Apostles.* New York: R. M. McBride & Company, 1940.

Dutton, Charles J. *Oliver Hazard Perry.* New York: Longmans, Green & Company, 1935.

Early, Jubal. *Jubal Early's Memoirs: Autobiographical Sketch and Narrative of the War Between the States.* Baltimore, Md.: Nautical & Aviation Publishing Company of America, 1989.

Eastlake, F. Warrington, and Yamada Yoshi-aki. *Heroic Japan: A History of the War between China & Japan.* London: Sampson Low, Marston, 1897.

Eayrs, Hugh S. *Sir Isaac Brock.* Toronto: The Macmillan Company of Canada, 1918.

Echevarria, Antulio J., II. "Moltke and the German Military Tradition: His Theories and Legacies." *Parameters* 26, no. 1 (Spring 1996): 91–99.

Edgar, Frank Terrell Rhoades. *Sir Ralph Hopton: the King's Man in the West (1642–1652).* Oxford, U.K.: The Clarendon Press, 1968.

Edwardes, Michael. *Clive: The Heaven-Born General.* London: Hart-Davis, MacGibbon, 1977.

Edwards, Mike. "Genghis: Lord of the Mongols." *National Geographic* 190, no. 6 (December 1996): 2–37.

Ehrenkreutz, Andrew S. *Saladin.* Albany: State University of New York Press, 1972.

Ehrman, John. *The Navy in the War of William III, 1689–1697.* Cambridge, U.K.: University Press, 1953.

"Eight Separate Decrees, 9 January–27 February 1808, issued by General Junot, relating to the administration of the Government of Portugal." Paris, France: Departments of State and Other Official Bodies, 1809.

Eisenhower, John S. D. *Agent of Destiny: The Life and Times of General Winfield Scott.* New York: The Free Press, 1997.

———. *So Far From God: The U.S. War with Mexico, 1846–48.* New York: Random House, 1989.

Elliot, Henry Lettsom. *On Some Badges and Devices of John de Vere, 13th Earl of Oxford, on the Tower of Castle Hedingham Church.* Colchester, U.K.: Wiles & Son, 1919.

Ellis, Edward Sylvester. *Dewey and Other Naval Commanders.* New York: Hovendon & Company, 1899.

Ellis, Peter Berresford. *MacBeth, High King of Scotland, 1040–57 A.D.* London: F. Muller, 1980.

The English Hero: Or, Sir Fran. Drake Reviv'd. Being a Full Account of the Dangerous Voyages, Admirable Adventures, Notable Discoveries, and Magnanimous Achievements of that valiant and Renowned Commander. . . . London: Printed for N. Crouch, 1698.

The English Mercurie. Published by Authoritie. For the Prevention of False Reportes. London: Printed by C. Barker, 1588.

Equitable and Necessary Considerations and Resolutions for Association of Arms Throughout The Counties of the kingdom of England, and principality of Wales: Against the now professed combination of Paists, and other Enemies of the Protestant Religion, and English Rights and Liberties. To be presented to the Gentry and Commonalty of the County of Middlesex, at their meeting at Hix-Hall the 26. of December, 1642. And no lesse conducing to the safety of other Counties, especially of York-shire, Lancashite, and Cheshire, where the Malignant Commissioners of Array have been most rampant. London: Printed for Thomas Undergill, 1642.

Espitalier, Albert. Napoleon and King Murat. London: John Lane, 1911.

Everett, Edward. Eulogy on Lafayette, Delivered in Faneuil Hall, at the request of the young men of Boston, September 6, 1834. Boston: N. Hale, 1834.

An Exact and True Relation in Relieving the resolute Garrison of Lyme in Dorset-shire, by the Right Honourable, Robert Earle of Warwicke, Lord High Admirall of England. Besieged by Prince Maurice, the Lord Inchiquin, and his Irish rogues, together with the Lord Pawlet. As also the particular passages in many gallant sallyes and assaults betwixt the enemy and themselves, with the brave courage of many female souldiers: as also the taking two ships of great value, that were comming to relieve the enemy: and the present condition in which the town at this instant is, with other remarkable mews fron Exceter. As it was sent by a speciall and faithfull hand, from His Majesties ship called the James, riding now at anchor before Lyme, dated June the first. London: Printed for Mathew Walbanke, 1644.

An Exact Journal of the Victorious Expedition of the Confederate Fleet the Last Year, under the Command of the Right Honourable Admiral Russel giving an Account of his relieving Barcellona, and the Taking of a great Number of Prizes from the French: with a Copy of a Letter sent by the Algerines to congratulate the English Admiral's arrival in the Mediterranean: to which is added a relation of the engagement between Catp. Killegrew, and the two French Men of War that were taken in the fare of Messina. London: Printed for J. Whitlock, 1695.

An Exact Relation of the Several Engagements and Actions of His Majesties Fleet, Under the Command of His Highnesse Prince Rupert. And of all Circumstances concerning this Somers Expedition, Anno 1673. Written by a Person in Command in the Fleet. London, 1673.

"Extract of a Letter from General Gates, dated camp at Saratoga, October 18, 1777: 'Sir, I have the Satisfaction to Present your Excellency with the Convention of Saratoga, by which His Excellency Lieutenant General Butgoyne has Surrendered Himself.'" Lancaster, Pa.: Printed by Francis Bailey, 1777.

Eysturlid, Lee. The Formative Influences, Theories, and Campaigns of the Archduke Carl of Austria. Westport, Conn.: Greenwood Press, 2000.

A Faithful and Impartial Account of the Proceedings in the Case of James, Duke of Monmouth. London: Printed for J. Hayther, 1682.

Falk, Edwin Albert. Togo and the Rise of Japanese Naval Power. New York: Longmans & Company, 1936.

A Famous Victorie Obtained by Sir William Waller, against the Lord Herbert and the Welch Cavaliers in the Forrest of Deane in the County of Gloucester, where six hundred of the Welchmen were slaine, and a thousand taken prisoners by the Parliaments Forces, the said Lord Herbery Generall of South-Wales being slain. Also, A True Relation of the whole Proceedings of the said Sir William Waller in that County, shewing in what manner he faced Cicester, and what stratagem he and Colonell Maffey (who is Governour of Gloucester) used when they obtained this victory against the Welch, with the number of men which have been lost by Sir William Waller, an what strength he hath. London: Printed for Robert Wood, 1643.

Farago, Ladislas. The Last Days of Patton. New York: McGraw-Hill, 1981.

Farr, David. John Lambert: Parliamentary Soldier and Cromwellian Major-General, 1619–1684. Rochester, New York: Boydell Press, 2003.

Farrow, Edward S. Farrow's Military Encyclopedia: A Dictionary of Military Knowledge, Illustrated with Maps and about Three Thousand Wood Engravings, 3 vols. New York: Published by the Author, 1885.

Farwell, Byron. Stonewall: A Biography of General Thomas J. Jackson. New York: W. W. Norton, 1992.

Faust, Patricia L., ed. Historical Times Illustrated Encyclopedia of the Civil War. New York: Harper & Row, Publishers, 1986.

Fields, Bertram. Royal Blood: Richard III and the Mystery of the Princes. New York: Harper Collins, 1998.

Finlay, George. History of the Byzantine and Greek Empires, from 716 to 1453. Edinburgh, Scotland: W. Blackwood, 1854.

Firth, C. H. Cromwell's Army: A History of the English Soldier During the Civil Wars, the Commonwealth, and the Protectorate. Being the Ford Lectures Delivered in the University of Oxford in 1900–1. London: Methuen & Co., 1902.

Fisher, Andrew. *William Wallace*. Edinburgh: J. Donald, 1986.

Fisher, John Arbuthnot, Baron Fisher. *Memories and Records, by Admiral of the Fleet, Lord Fisher,* 2 vols. New York: George H. Doran Company, 1920.

Fissel, Mark Charles. *The Bishops' Wars: Charles I's Campaigns Against Scotland, 1638–1640.* Cambridge, U.K.: Cambridge University Press, 1994.

Fitzjames Stuart y Falcó, Jacobo Maria Carlos Manuel, duke de Bervick y de Alba. *The Great Duke of Alba as a Public Servant.* London: G. Cumberlege, 1947.

Flagg, Edmund. *Venice: The City of the Sea, From the Invasion by Napoleon in 1797 to the Capitulation to Radetzky in 1849; With a Contemporaneous View of the Peninsula,* 2 vols. New York: Charles Scribner, 1853.

Fletcher, C. R. L. *Gustavus Adolphus and the Thirty Years War.* New York: Capricorn Books, 1963.

Foch, Ferdinand. *The Principles of War.* Translated by Hilaire Belloc. London: Chapman & Hall, 1918.

Fonner, D. Kent. "After Avidly Studying the Tactics of Hannibal, Scipio Africanus Eventually Bested his Carthaginian Adversary." *Military History* 12, no. 7 (March 1996): 10–12, 16.

Fouracre, Paul. *The Age of Charles Martel.* New York: Longman, 2000.

Fox, Frank. *Great Ships: The Battlefleet of King Charles II.* Greenwich, U.K.: Conway Maritime Press, 1980.

France, John. *Victory in the East: A Military History of the First Crusade.* Cambridge, U.K.: Cambridge University Press, 1994.

Francis, Claude. "A Sermon at the Funeral of the High and Mighty Prince, Henry De La Tour D'Auvergne, Vicount of Turenne, Mareschal General of France; Colonel General of the Light Horse, and Governour of the Upper and Lower Limosin. Preach'd December 15, 1675. By Claude Francis, Ministrier. Englished out of French." London, 1677.

Frédéric, Louis. *Japan Encyclopedia.* Cambridge, Mass.: The Belknap Press of Harvard University Press, 2002.

Freeman, Edward A. *The History of the Norman Conquest of England, Its Causes and Its Results,* 5 vols. Oxford, U.K.: Clarendon Press, 1869–76.

French, Gerald. *The Life of Field-Marshal Sir John French, First Earl of Ypres, K.P., G.C.B., O.M., G.C.V.O., K.C.M.G., by his Son, Major the Hon. Gerald French, D.S.O.* London: Cassell and Company, Limited, 1931.

French, John Denton Pinkstone. *Some War Diaries, Addresses, and Correspondence of Field Marshal the Right Honorable. The Earl of Ypres.* Edited by Gerald French. London: H. Jenkins, 1937.

Friendly, Alfred. *The Dreadful Day: The Battle of Manzikert, 1071.* London: Hutchinson, 1981.

Frost, F. J. "The Athenian Military before Cleisthenes." *Historia* 33 (1984): 283–294.

Fryde, Natalie. *The Tyranny and Fall of Edward II.* Cambridge, U.K.: Cambridge University Press, 1979.

Fuller, John Frederick Charles. *Julius Caesar: Man, Soldier, and Tyrant.* New Brunswick, N.J.: Rutgers University Press, 1965.

A Fuller Relation of the Great Victory Obtained (Through God's Providence) at Alsford, on Friday the 28. of March, 1644. By the Parliaments Forces, under the Command of Sir William Waller, Sir William Balfore, and Major Generall Browne, against the forces commanded by the Earl of Forth, the L[ord] Hopton, Commissary Wilmot, and Others. Together with the Names of the chief Commanders slaine and taken prisoners on both sides. Also a Relation of the Death of the Earle of Forth the Kings Generall. As it was presented to the Right Honourable the Lord Maior and the Committee of the Militia for the City of London, by an eye witness. London: Printed for Laurance Blaiklock, 1644.

A Full Relation of The Great Victory Obtained by the Parliaments Forces under the Command of Lieut. Gen. Cromwel Against The Whole Army of the Scots, under the Conduct of Duke Hamilton. With the Numbers Slaine and taken Prisoners. Sent in a Letter under the Lieut. Generals owne hand: Which was read in both Houses of Parliament upon Wednesday the 23 of Aug. 1648. With an Order of Parliament for a Thanksgiving for the Same. London: Imprinted for John Wright, 1648.

Gallagher, Gary W. *Jubal A. Early, the Lost Cause, and Civil War History: A Persistent Legacy.* Milwaukee, Wis.: Marquette University Press, 1995.

Gallaher, John G. *The Iron Marshal: A Biography of Louis N. Davout.* Edwardsville: Southern Illinois University Press, 1976.

Gambone, A. M. *Hancock at Gettysburg: And Beyond.* Baltimore: Butternut and Blue, 1997.

Gardiner, Samuel Rawson. *History of the Great Civil War, 1642–1649,* 4 vols. London: Longmans, Green, and Co., 1893.

Garnett, James Mercer. *Elene; Judith; Æthelstan, or, The Fight at Brunanburh; Byrthnoth, or, The Fight at Mal-*

don; and *The Dream of the Rood: Anglo-Saxon Poems.* Translated by James Mercer Garnett. Boston: Ginn & Company, 1901.

Garraty, John A., and Mark C. Carnes, eds. *American National Biography,* 24 vols. New York: Oxford University Press, 1999.

General Gordon's Mission to the Soudan. Speech Delivered by the Right Hon. The Marquis of Hartington, M.P., in the House of Commons, on Tuesday, the 13th May 1884, on the Proposed Vote of Censure moved by Sir Michael Edward Hicks Beach, Bart., with a Sketch Map, Shewing Obstacles to the Navigation of the Nile, and Route Distances. London: The National Press Agency, Ltd., 1884.

Gilbert, Martin. *First World War.* London: Weidenfeld & Nicolson, 1994.

Gill, Louise. *Richard III and Buckingham's Rebellion.* Stroud, Gloucestshire, U.K.: Sutton Books, 1999.

Gillingham, John. *Richard I.* New Haven, Conn.: Yale University Press, 2002.

Girling, Richard. "Et Tu Julius? A New Investigation Has Yielded a Starting Verdict on History's Most Infamous Murder. It States that Julius Caesar Staged His Own Death. But Why Would He Have Wanted to Die?" *The Sunday Times Magazine* (London) 9 March 2003, 48–55.

Goerlitz, Walter. *Paulus and Stalingrad: A Life of Field-Marshal Friedrich Paulus with Notes, Correspondence, and Documents from his Papers.* New York: The Citadel Press, 1963.

Goldman, Charles Sydney. *With General French and the Cavalry in South Africa.* London: Macmillan and Co., Limited, 1902.

Goltz, Colmar Freiherr von der. *The Conduct of War: A Short Treatise on its Most Important Branches and Guiding Rules.* Translated by Major G. F. Leverson. London: Kegan Paul, Trench, Trübner & Co., Ltd., 1899.

Golubov, Sergei Nikolaevich. *No Easy Victories: A Novel of General Bagration and the Campaign of 1812.* Translated by J. Fineberg. London: Hutchinson International Authors Ltd., 1945.

The Good and Prosperous Success of the Parliaments Forces in York-Shire: Against the Earle of New-Castle and his Popish Adherents. As it was sent in a Letter from the Right Honourable the Lord Fairfax, and read in both Houses of Parliament, on Monday, Jan. 30, 1642. With some Observations of the Lords and Commons upon the said happy Proceedings, as so many Answers from Heaven, which God hath given to the Prayers of his Servants. Published, that their Mouths and Hearts may be as much enlarged in Praises, as they have been in Prayers. London: Printed for John Wright in the Old Bailey, 1642.

Goodwin, Thomas. *The History of the Reign of Henry the Fifth, King of England, &c. In Nine Books.* London: Printed by J.D. for S. and J. Sprint, 1704.

Gordon, Colin Douglas. *The Age of Attila: Fifth-Century Byzantium and the Barbarians.* Ann Arbor: University of Michigan Press, 1960.

Gordon, Henry William. *Events in the Life of Charles George Gordon From Its Beginning to Its End.* London: Kegan Paul, Trench, 1886.

Gore, Montague. *Character of Sir David Baird.* London: James Ridgway, 1833.

Grace, F. R. *The Life and Career of Thomas Howard, Third Duke of Norfolk (1473–1554).* Master's thesis, University of Nottingham (United Kingdom), 1961.

Graham, Stephen. *Ivan the Terrible: The Life of Ivan IV of Russia, Called the Terrible.* London: E. Benn Ltd., 1932.

A Great and Bloudy fight in France between the Kings army, commanded by General Turenne, the Duke of York, and the Lord Digby; against fifteen thousand horse & foot under the command of the Prince of Conde, the Duke of Wittenburgh, and the Duke of Guise. With the particulars of this memorable and desperate engagement; the manner how the said Duke of York led on the Forlorn-Hope, and gave the onset of the day with 2000 horse, against Chevalier de Guise; and after a gallant charge routed him, and beat him up to the main-body. Also, the number killed and taken prisoners; the regaining of all the ordnance and train of artillery; the retreating of the Prince of Conde; and the D. of Lorain's coming into the field with 5000 to behold this bloudy tragedy, fighting neither for King nor Parliament. With a letter from Amsterdam, comprising the affairs and designe now on foot in Holland. London: Imprinted for Geo. Horton, 1652.

A Great Over-throw: Given to Sir Ralph Hopton's whole Army by Sir William Waller neere Farnham, with onely six Troope of Horse, and some Foote, the rest of his Army being stated in severall quarters in other places. With many Remarkable Passages, which deserve everlasting memory. London: Printed for John Hammon, 1643.

A Great Victory Obtained by His Excellency the Lord General Blake, Commander in Chief of the Parliament[']s Navy at Sea; Against the lord Admiral Van Trump, Lieutenant-General for the States of Holland. With the Manner of Their Engagement; the Particulars of the Fight on Sunday last [27 June 1652] upon the Dutch coast. Likewise, the Dutch-mens New Oath and Protestations to Fight it out to the last Man, etc. London: Printed for George Horton, 1652.

Green, Peter. *Alexander to Actium; The Historical Evolution of the Hellenistic Age.* Berkeley: The University of California Press, 1990.

———. *The Greco-Persian Wars.* Berkeley: University of California Press, 1996.

———. *Xerxes at Salamis.* New York: Praeger, 1970.

Greene, Francis Vinton. *Report on the Russian Army and Its Campaigns in Turkey in 1877–1878.* New York: D. Appleton and Company, 1879.

Greene, George W. *Life of Nathanael Greene,* 3 vols. New York: G. P. Putnam and Son, 1867–71.

Greene, Parnell. *On the Banks of the Dee: A Legend of Chester Concerning the Fate of Harold. Preserved in the Harleian MS, British Museum.* London: F. V. White & Company, 1886.

Griffiths, Richard. *Marshal Pétain.* London: Constable, 1970.

Grove, Eric. *Fleet to Fleet Encounters: Tsushima, Jutland, Philippine Sea.* London: Arms and Armour, 1991.

Gruber, I. D. *The Howe Brothers and the American Revolution.* New York: Atheneum, 1972.

Grundy, George Beardoe. *The Great Persian War and its Preliminaries: A Study of the Evidence, Literary and Topographical.* New York: Scribner, 1901.

Guedalla, Philip. *The Two Marshals: Bazaine, Pétain.* New York: Reynal & Hitchcock, 1943.

Gwatkin, H. M., et al., ed. *The Cambridge Mediaeval History,* 8 vols. Cambridge, U.K.: Cambridge University Press, 1911–36.

Hackett, R. F. *Yamagata Aritomo in the Rise of Modern Japan, 1838–1922.* Cambridge, Mass.: Harvard University Press, 1971.

Hall, R. Cargill, ed. *Lightning over Bougainville.* Washington, D.C.: Smithsonian Institution Press, 1991.

Hallam, Elizabeth, ed. *The Chronicles of The Wars of the Roses.* Surrey, U.K.: Bramley Books, 1996.

Halliday, Sir Andrew. *Observations on the Present State of the Portuguese Army.* London: Printed for J. Murray, 1811.

Hamblet, John. *A Famous and Joyfull Victory obtained by the Earl of Stamfords forces neere Stratford in Northampton-shire, against Prince Robert [sic] his forces, who assaulted them at one of the clock at night where they were billetted, declaring the manner of the fight, and how the Earl of Stamfords forces took 50. of them prisoners, putting the rest to flight. Also another happy victory obtained by the Lord Brooks, September the 8. against divers Kentish cavaleers that were going to the standard at Nottingham, with the taking of the Lord Montague prisoner. who was brought to London, Sep. 9. Signified to the Honourable House of Commons.* London: Printed for H. Blunen, 1642.

Hamilton, Sir Ian. *Listening for the Drums.* London: Faber and Faber, 1944.

Hamilton, Ian Bogle Montieth. *The Happy Warrior: A Life of General Sir Ian Hamilton.* London: Cassell, 1966.

Hampden, John. *Crusader King: The Adventures of Richard the Lionheart on Crusade, Taken From a Chronicle of the Time.* London: Edmund Ward, Publishers, 1956.

Handel, Michael I. *Masters of War: Sun Tzu, Clausewitz and Jomini.* London: Frank Cass, 1992.

Hannah, W. H. *Bobs, Kipling's General: The Life of Field-Marshal Earl Roberts of Kandahar, V.C.* London: Lee Cooper, 1972.

Hannay, David. *Rodney.* London: Macmillan and Co., 1891.

Hanson, W. S. *Agricola and the Conquest of the North.* Totowa, N.J.: Barnes and Noble, 1987.

Harington, General Sir Charles. *Plumer of Messines.* London: John Murray, 1935.

Hart, W. E. *Hitler's Generals.* Garden City, New York: Doubleday, Doran & Co., 1944.

Hartmann, Cyril Hughes. *The Angry Admiral: The Later Career of Edward Vernon, Admiral of the White.* Melbourne, New South Wales, Australia: William Heinemann Ltd., 1953.

Haskins, George L. "A Chronicle of the Civil Wars of Edward II." *Speculum: A Journal of Mediaeval Studies,* 14, no. 1 (January 1959): 73–75.

Hatch, Alden. *General Ike: A Biography of Dwight D. Eisenhower.* New York: Henry Holt and Company, 1944.

Hatton, Ragnhild Marie. *Charles XII of Sweden.* New York: Weybright and Talley, 1968.

Hayward, Sir John. *The Lives of the III Normans, Kings of England: William the first, William the seconde, Henrie the first.* London, 1613.

Haywood, John. *Encyclopedia of the Viking Age.* New York: Thames & Hudson, 2000.

Haywood, Richard Mansfield. *Studies on Scipio Africanus.* Baltimore, Md.: Johns Hopkins University Studies in Historical and Political Science, 1933.

Hazlitt, William. *The Classical Gazetteer: A Dictionary of Ancient Geography, Sacred and Profane.* London: Whittaker & Son, 1851.

Head, David M. *The Ebbs and Flows of Fortune: The Life of Thomas Howard, Third Duke of Norfolk.* Athens: University of Georgia Press, 1995.

Healey, Charles E. H. Chadwyck. *Bellum Civile: Hopton's Narrative of His Campaign in the West (1642–1644) and Other Papers.* London: Harrison & Sons, Printers, 1902.

Hebert, Walter H. *Fighting Joe Hooker.* Indianapolis: Bobbs-Merrill, 1944.

Heckmann, Wolf. *Rommel's War in Africa.* New York: Doubleday, 1981.

Heckstall-Smith, Anthony. *Tobruk: The Story of a Siege.* New York: Norton, 1960.

Held, Joseph. *Hunyadi: Legend and Reality.* Boulder, Colo.: East European Monographs, 1985.

Henderson, Andrew. *The Life of William the Conqueror, Duke of Normandy, and King of England.* London: Printed for the Author, 1764.

Henderson, Ernest F. *Blücher and the Uprising of Prussia against Napoleon, 1806–16.* New York: G. P. Putnam's Sons, 1911.

Henderson, George Francis Robert. *Stonewall Jackson and the American Civil War.* London: Longmans, Green and Company, 1898.

Henderson, Sir Nicholas. *Prince Eugen of Savoy.* London: Weidenfeld and Nicolson, 1964.

Henry the Minstrel. *The Actis and Deidis of the Illustere and Vailoeand Campioun Schir William Wallace, Knicht of Ellerslie, by Henry the Minstrel, Commonly known as Blind Harry.* Edited by James Moir. Edinburgh, Scotland: W. Blackwood and Sons, 1889.

Herbert, William. *Attila, King of the Huns.* London: H. G. Bohn, 1838.

Hewitt, H. J. *The Organization of War under Edward III, 1338–62.* Manchester, U.K.: Manchester University Press, 1966.

Hignett, Charles. *Xerxes' Invasion of Greece.* Oxford, U.K.: Clarendon Press, 1963.

Hilliam, David. *Kings, Queens, Bones and Bastards: Who's Who in the English Monarchy from Egbert to Elizabeth II.* Thrupp, Stroud, Gloucestershire, U.K.: Sutton Publishing Limited, 1998.

Hindenburg, Gert von. *Hindenberg, 1847–1934: Soldier and Statesman.* Translated by Gerald Griffin. London: Hutchinson, 1935.

Hingley, Richard. *Boudica: Iron Age Warrior Queen.* London: Hambledon, 2005.

Hinke, William J. *A New Boundary Stone of Nebuchadnezzar I from Nippur, with a Concordance of Proper Names and a Glossary of the Kuddurru Inscriptions thus far Published.* Philadelphia: University of Pennsylvania, 1907.

An Historical Account of the Heroick Life and Magnanimous Actions of the Most Illustrious Prince, James Duke of Monmouth. Containing an Account of his Birth, Education, Places and Titles: With his Great and Martial Achievements in Flanders and Scotland. His Disgrace and Departure both from Court and Kingdom; with the most Material Circumstances that has Occurred since his Return. London: Printed for Thomas Malthus, 1683.

Historical Collections, or, A Brief Account of the most Remarkable Transactions of the two last Parliaments consisting of I. The Speeches, Votes, Accusations, Addresses, and Article of Impeachment, &c., II. The Bills of Association, Exclusion, and Repeal of 35 Eliz. &c., III. The Several Informations, Messages, Narratives, Orders, Petitions, Protestation of the Lords, and Resolves of both Houses, etc., IV. The Tryal [sic] and Sentence of William Howard Lord Viscount of Stafford in Westminster Hall, his Speech and Execution on the Scaffold at Tower Hill with many other Memorable Passages and Proceedings of the two last Parliaments, Held and Dissolved at Westminster and Oxford, V. A perfect list of each Parliament, VI. His Majesty's declaration, shewing the Causes and Reasons that moved him to dissolve the two last Parliaments. London: Printed for Simon Neal, 1682.

Hodgkin, Thomas. *Italy and Her Invaders,* 6 vols. Oxford, U.K.: Clarendon Press, 1880–89.

———. *Theodoric the Goth: The Barbarian Champion of Civilization.* New York: G. P. Putnam's Sons, 1900.

Hodgson, John Ernest. *With Denikin's Armies: Being a Description of the Cossack Counter-Revolution in South Russia, 1918–1920.* London: L. Williams, Temple Bar Publishing Company, 1932.

Hogarth, David George. *Philip and Alexander of Macedon. Two Essays in Biography.* London: J. Murray, 1897.

Holborn, Hajo. "The Prusso-German School: Moltke and the Rise of the General Staff," in *Makers of Modern Strategy from Machiavelli to the Nuclear Age,* edited by Peter Paret. Princeton, N.J.: Princeton University Press, 1986, pp. 281–325.

Holland, Matthew F. *Eisenhower Between the Wars: The Making of a General and a Statesman.* Westport, Conn.: Praeger, 2001.

Holmes, Edward Richard. *Borodino, 1812.* London: C. Knight, 1971.

Holmes, Richard. *The Little Field Marshal: Sir John French.* London: Jonathan Cape, 1981.

Holmes, Richard, ed. *The Oxford Companion to Military History.* New York: Oxford University Press, 2001.

Holmes, Richard, and Peter Young. *The English Civil War.* London: Eyre Methuen, 1974.

Holt, Peter Malcolm. *The Mahdist State in the Sudan.* Oxford, U.K.: The Clarendon Press, 1958.

Hood, Dorothy. *The Admirals Hood.* London: Hutchinson & Company, 1942.

Horn, D. B., and Mary Ransome, eds. *English Historical Documents, 1714–1783.* London: Eyre and Spottiswoode, 1957.

Horne, Alistair. *The Lonely Leader: Monty, 1944–45.* London: Macmillan, 1994.

Horward, Donald D. *The Battle of Bussaco: Masséna vs. Wellington.* Tallahassee: Florida State University Press, 1965.

———. *Napoleon and Iberia: The Twin Sieges, Ciudad Rodrigo and Almeida, 1810.* Gainesville: University Presses of Florida, 1984.

Hough, Richard Alexander. *Admiral of the Fleet: The Life of John Fisher.* New York: Macmillan, 1970.

Howarth, Patrick, *Attila. King of the Huns: Man and Myth.* London: Constable, 1994.

"How Nelson's Memorandum Was Carried Out at Trafalgar." *The Nineteenth Century and After* 416 (October 1911): 679–704.

Howson, Gerald. *Burgoyne of Saratoga: A Biography.* New York: Times Books, 1979.

Hoyt, Edwin Palmer. *How They Won the War in the Pacific: Nimitz and his Admirals.* New York: Weybright and Talley, 1970.

———. *199 Days: The Battle for Stalingard.* New York: Tor Books, 1993.

———. *Three Military Leaders: Heihachiro Togo, Isoroku Yamamoto, Tomoyuki Yamashita.* Tokyo, Japan: Kodansha International, 1994.

———. *Yamamoto: The Man Who Planned Pearl Harbor.* New York: McGraw-Hill, 1990.

H.P. *A Relation of the Execution of James Graham late Marquesse of Montrosse, at Edenburgh, on Tuesday the 21 of May instant. With his last speech, carriage, and most remarkable passages upon the scaffold. Also, a letter out of Ireland, more fully concerning the taking of Clonmell.* London: Printed by E. Griffin, 1650.

Huddleston, Sisley. *Pétain, Patriot or Traitor?* London: A. Dakers, 1951.

Hughes, Daniel J., ed. *Moltke on the Art of War.* Translated by Harry Bell and Daniel J. Hughes. Novato, Calif.: Presidio Press, 1993.

Hughes, Matthew D. *General Allenby and the campaign of the E.E.F. in Palestine, 1917–18.* Ph.D. dissertation, University of London, 1995.

Hummel, Arthur W., ed. *Eminent Chinese of the Ch'ing Period (1644–1912),* 2 vols. Washington, D.C.: Government Printing Office, 1943.

Hunter, Francis T. *Beatty, Jellicoe, Sims and Rodman: Yankee Gobs and British Tars as Seen by an "Anglomanic."* Garden City, N.Y.: Doubleday, Page & Company, 1919.

Hutchins, Frank W. *Washington and the Lafayettes.* New York: Longmans, Green and Company, 1939.

The Hutchinson Dictionary of Ancient and Medieval Warfare. Oxford, U.K.: Helicon Publishing, Ltd., 1998.

Hutton, The Rev William Holden, ed. *Simon de Montfort & His Cause, 1251–1266: Extracts from the Writings of Robert of Gloucester, Matthew Paris, William Rishanger, Thomas of Wykes, etc.* London: David Nutt, 1888.

Huzar, Eleanor Goltz. *Mark Antony: A Biography.* London: Croon Helm, 1978.

Hymel, Kevin M. "Winfield Scott's Long and Illustrious Career was Tarnished by Incessant Political Infighting." *Military History* 16, no. 2 (June 1999): 70–72.

Jackson, Donald, ed. *The Diaries of George Washington,* 6 vols. Charlottesville: University Press of Virginia, 1976–79.

Jackson, William Godfrey Fothergill. *Alexander of Tunis as Military Commander.* London: Batsford, 1971.

James, David. *Lord Roberts.* London: Hollis & Carter, 1954.

Jefferson, Samuel. *A Narrative of the Siege of Carlisle, in 1644 and 1645, by Isaac Tullie. Now First Printed from a MS. in the British Museum. To Which are Added, A Preface, an Historical Account of Carlisle*

During the Civil War; and Biographical, Historical, and Explanatory Notes. Whitehaven, Cumbria, U.K.: Michael Moon's Bookshop, 1988.

Jellicoe, Sir John. *The Grand Fleet, 1914–16: Its Creation, Development and Work.* New York: G. H. Doran, 1919.

Jenkins, John Stilwell, ed. *Life and Public Services of Gen. Andrew Jackson, Seventh President of the United States, Including the Most Important of His State Papers. Edited by John S. Jenkins, with the Eulogy, Delivered at Washington City, June 21, 1845, by Hon. George Bancroft.* Buffalo, N.Y.: G. H. Derby & Company, 1850.

Jerrold, Walter. *Field-Marshal Earl Roberts, V.C.: The Life Story of a Great Soldier.* London: W. A. Hammond, 1914.

Jesse, John Heneage. *Memoirs of King Richard the Third and Some of His Contemporaries: With an Historical Drama on the Battle of Bosworth,* 2 vols. New York: F. P. Harper, 1894.

Johnson, Richard A. *The Mexican Revolution of Ayutla, 1854–55: An Analysis of the Evolution and Destruction of Santa Anna's Last Dictatorship.* Rock Island, Ill.: Augustana College Library, 1939.

Johnson, Samuel. *The Vanity of Human Wishes. The Tenth Satire of Juvenal, Imitated by Samuel Johnson.* London: R. Dodsley, 1748.

Jones, Oakah L. *Santa Anna.* New York: Twayne Publishers, 1968.

Jordan, David M. *Winfield Scott Hancock: A Soldier's Life.* Bloomington: Indiana University Press, 1988.

Josselson, Michael. *The Commander: A Life of Barclay de Tolly.* Oxford, U.K.: Oxford University Press, 1980.

Kahn, Alexander. *Life of General Joffré, Cooper's Son Who Became Commander-in-Chief.* London: W. Heinemann, 1915.

Keay, John, and Julia Keay, eds. *Collins Encyclopedia of Scotland.* New York: HarperCollins, 1994.

Keegan, John. *The Face of Battle: A Study of Agincourt, Waterloo and the Somme.* London, England: Jonathan Cape Ltd., 1976; reprint, New York: Penguin Books, 1984.

———. *History of Warfare.* London: Hutchinson, 1992.

———. *The Mask of Command.* New York: Viking/Elisabeth Sifton Books, 1987.

Keegan, John, and Andrew Wheatcroft. *Who's Who in Military History from 1453 to the Present Day.* London: Routledge, 1996.

Kelsey, Harry. *Sir John Hawkins: Queen Elizabeth's Slave Trader.* New Haven, Conn.: Yale University Press, 2003.

Kenny, Robert W. *Elizabeth's Admiral: The Political Career of Charles Howard, Earl of Nottingham, 1536–1624.* Baltimore, Md.: Johns Hopkins Press, 1970.

Ketchum, Hiram. *General McClellan's Peninsula Campaign: Review of the Report of the Committee on the Conduct of the War Relative to the Peninsula Campaign.* New York, 1864.

Ketchum, Richard M. "'The Decisive Day Is Come,'" *American Heritage* 13, no. 5 (August 1962): 80–93.

Keynes, Simon, and Michael Lapidge, trans. *Alfred the Great: Asser's Life of King Alfred and Other Contemporary Sources.* London: Penguin Books, 1983.

Kibler, William, and Zinn, Grover A., eds. *Medieval France: An Encyclopedia.* New York: Garland Publishing, 1995.

King, Nicholas. "The Siege of Mafeking." *History Today* 6, no. 1 (January 1956): 21–27.

Kinnard, Douglas. *Eisenhower: Soldier-Statesman of the American Century.* Washington, D.C.: Brassey's, 2002.

Kintz, P., J. Goulle, P. Fornes, P. Ludes, et al. "Letter to the Editor: A New Series of Hair Analyses from Napoleon Confirms Chronic Exposure to Arsenic." *Journal of Analytical Toxicology* 26, no. 8 (2002): 584–585.

Kippis, Andrew, ed. *Biographia Britannica; or, The Lives of the Most Eminent Persons who have flourished in Great Britain and Ireland, from the earliest Ages, down to the present Times; Collected from the best Authorities, both Printed and Manuscript, And digested in the Manner of Mr. Bayle's Historical and Critical Dictionary,* 6 vols. London: Printed for W. Walthoe, T. Osborne, H. Whitridge [et al.], 1793.

Kitchen, Kenneth Anderson. *Pharaoh Triumphant: The Life and Times of Ramesses II, King of Egypt.* Warminster, U.K.: Aris & Phillips, 1983.

Kitchen, Martin. *The Silent Dictatorship: The Politics of the German High Command under Hindenburg and Ludendorff, 1916–1918.* London: Croom Helm, 1976.

Kitson, Frank. *Prince Rupert: Admiral and General-at-Sea.* London: Constable, 1998.

Knowles, Elizabeth, ed. *The Oxford Dictionary of Quotations.* Oxford, U.K.: Oxford University Press, 1999.

Kodansha Encyclopedia of Japan, 10 vols. Tokyo, Japan: Kodansha, 1983.

Komroff, Manuel. *The Travels of Marco Polo.* New York: The Heritage Press, 1934.

Kopperman, Paul E. *Braddock at the Monongahela.* Pittsburgh: University of Pittsburgh Press, 1977.

Kritovoulos. *History of Mehmed the Conqueror.* Translated by Charles T. Riggs. Westport, Conn.: Greenwood Press, 1970.

Kuropatkin, Aleksei Nikolaevich. *The Russian Army and the Japanese War, Being Historical and Critical Comments on the Military Policy and Power of Russia and on the Campaign in the Far East,* translated by A. B. Lindsay. Edited by Major E. D. Swinton. London: John Murray, 1909.

Kurtz, Harold. *The Trial of Marshal Ney, His Last Years and Death.* London: H. Hamilton, 1957.

La Colonie, Jean-Martin de. *Chronicles of an Old Campaigner, 1692–1717.* Translated by Walter C. Horsley. London: John Murray, 1904.

Laffin, John. *Brassey's Battles: 3,500 Years of Conflict, Campaigns and Wars from A–Z.* London: Brassey's Defence Publishers, 1986.

———. *Links of Leadership: Thirty Centuries of Command.* London: George G. Harrap & Co., Ltd., 1966.

Lambrick, H. T. *Sir Charles Napier and Sind.* Oxford, U.K.: Clarendon Press, 1952.

Lamers, Jeroen Pieter. *Japonius Tyrannus: the Japanese Warlord Oda Nobunaga Reconsidered.* Leiden, Netherlands: Hotei Publishing, 2000.

Lamers, William M. *The Edge of Glory: A Biography of General William S. Rosecrans, U.S.A.* New York: Harcourt, Brace, 1961.

Lane-Poole, Stanley. *Saladin and the Fall of the Kingdom of Jerusalem.* New York: G. P. Putnam's Sons, 1906.

Lanning, Michael Lee. *The Military 100: A Ranking of the Most Influential Military Leaders of All Time.* New York: Barnes and Noble Books, 1996.

Lanoye, Ferdinand de. *Rameses the Great; or, Egypt 3300 Years Ago.* New York: Charles Scribner and Company, 1870.

The Last Newes from the King of Scots, concerning his uniting with the Lord Belcarris, and Advansing towards the Marquesses of Argile and Huntley, who are raising a new Army of Redshanks in the north of Scotland, about the Isles of Orkney and the Highlands. Also, the remonstrance and declaration of 11000. Scots, touching their King, and the Parl. of England; and the declaration of

James Stuart, (second son to the late King of England) to the English in France. With a great overthrowe given to Prince Ruperts fleet at sea by Captain Pen, Vice-Admiral for the Parliament of England, and the number of ships sunk and taken. London, 1651.

Latimer, Jon. "Storm of Snow and Steel at Narva." *Military History* 17, no. 5 (December 2000): 58–64.

Lau-Lavie, Naphtali. *Moshe Dayan: A Biography.* London: Vallentine, Mitchell, 1968.

Lavender, David Sievert. *Climax at Buena Vista: The American Campaigns in Northeastern Mexico, 1846–47.* Philadelphia: Lippincott, 1966.

Lawrence, Rosamond (Lady Lawrence). *Charles Napier: Friend and Fighter, 1782–1853.* London: John Murray, 1952.

Lawson, Sir John. *A Great and Bloudy Fight at Sea between the Parliaments Navy, under the command of General Blake, and the Dutch fleet, commanded by the Lord Admiral Van-Trump.* London: Printed for J. Fielding, 1652.

Lazenby, J. F. *Hannibal's War.* Warminster, U.K.: Aris & Phillips, Ltd., 1978.

Lee, John. *A Soldier's Life: General Sir Ian Hamilton, 1853–1947.* London: Macmillan, 2000.

Le Fevre, Peter, and Richard Harding, eds. *Precursors of Nelson: British Admirals of the Eighteenth Century.* London: Chatham Publishing, 2000.

Lehovich, Dimitri V. *White Against Red: The Life of General Anton Deniken.* New York: Norton, 1974.

Lerski, George J. *Historical Dictionary of Poland, 966–1945.* Westport, Conn.: Greenwood Press, 1996.

"A Letter from Generall Leven, the Lord Fairfax, and the Earle of Manchester, to the Commonwealth of both Kingdoms: And by them communicated to the Parliament, concerning the great Victory it has pleased God to give them, over the Forces under the Command of Prince Rupert, and the Marquess of Newcastle, at Marston-Moor, near York, July the Second, 1644." Edinburgh, Scotland: Printed by Evan Tyler, 1644.

"A Letter from General Monck from Dalkeith, 13 October 1659. Directed as Followeth. For the Right Honorable William Lenthal, Esquire, Speaker; to be communicated to the Parliament of the Commonwealth of England, at Westminster." London, 1659.

A Letter from Scotland, giving a full and impartiall relation of the scattering of those forces risen against the Parliament; being all taken prisoners by Lieutenant-Generall

David Lesly, and now remaining in his hands at mercy. With an true accompt of all those officers of stat removed which had a hand in the late engagement against England: with the names of those placed in their roomes by the Parliament of Scotland. London, 1649.

Letter from Sir Joseph de Cancy, Knight of the Hospital of St. John of Jerusalem, to King Edward I. (1281), and Letter from King Edward I. to Sir Joseph (1282). Communicated to the Palestine Pilgrims' Text Society by William Basevi Sanders, Esq. London: The Palestine Pilgrims' Text Society, 1890.

"A Letter from the Lord General Monck and The Officers Here, to the Several and Respective Regiments and Other Forxes in England, Scotland, and Ireland." London: Printed by John Macock, 1660.

"A Letter from the Nobility, Barons and Commons of Scotland, in the Year 1320, yet Extant under all the Seals of the Nobility: Directed to Pope John, Wherein they declare their firm Resolutions, to adhere to their King Robert the Bruce, as the Restorer of their Safety, and Liberties of the People, and as Having the true right of Succession: But Without, They notwithstanding Declare, That if the King should offer to subvert their Civil Liberties, they will disown him as an Enemy, and choose another King for their own Defence. Translated from the Original, in Latine, as it is insert by St. George McKenzie of Rosebaugh, in his Observations on Precedency, &c." Edinburgh: Privately published, 1689.

"A Letter Sent from Maynhem (Marnheim) concerning the late defeate given the Duke of Brunswicke by Monsieur Tilly: Whereunto is Added a Couranto of other Newes from Vienna, Prague, the Palatinate and other Places this 20. of June. 1622." London: Printed by Bernard Alsop for Nathaniel Butter, 1622.

Letters of and Relating to Thomas Pelham-Holles, 1st Duke of Newcastle under Lynn. Newcastle, U.K.: University of Nottingham Library, 1725–1771.

Lewin, Ronald. *Rommel as Military Commander.* London: Batsford, 1968.

———. *Slim: The Standard Bearer.* London: Cooper, 1976.

Lewis, Charles Lee. *Famous Old-World Sea Fighters.* London: G. G. Harrap, 1929.

———. *The Romantic Decatur.* Philadelphia: University of Pennsylvania Press, 1937.

Lewis, Lloyd. *Sherman: Fighting Prophet.* New York: Harcourt, Brace & Company, 1932.

Lewis, Meriwether Liston. *Montcalm: The Marvelous Marquis.* New York: Vantage Press, 1961.

Liddell Hart, Basil H. *Foch: Man of Orléans,* 2 vols. London: Penguin, 1937.

———. *A Greater Than Napoleon: Scipio Africanus.* London: W. Blackwood & Sons, Ltd., 1926.

———. "Sherman—Modern Warrior." *American Heritage* 12, no. 5 (August 1962): 20–23, 102–06.

Liddell Hart, Basil H., ed. *The Other Side of the Hill: Germany's Generals with their Own Account of Military Events, 1939–45.* London: Cassell, 1948.

———. *The Rommel Papers.* London: Hamlyn Paperbacks, 1983.

Lie, A. G. *The Inscriptions of Sargon II of Assyria: Transliterated and Translated with notes by A. G. Lie.* Paris, France: Librarie Orientaliste P. Guenther, 1929.

The Life and Military Actions of His Royal Highness Prince Eugene, of Savoy. With an Account of his Death and Funeral. London, 1739.

The Life of Cornelius Van Tromp, Lieutenant-Admiral of Holland and Westfriesland: Containing Many Remarkable Passages relating to the War between England and Holland. As also the Sea-Fights, and Other Memorable Actions of this Great Man, from the Year 1650, to the Time of his Death. London, 1697.

The Life of St. Alexander Nevsky, from a Sixteenth-Century Russian Illuminated Codex, [from] the Saltykov-Schedrin Public Library, St. Petersburg. St. Petersburg, Russia: Aurora Art Publishers, 1992.

Lind, John. "Early Russian Swedish Rivalry: The Clenches and Birger Magnusson's Second Crusade to Tavastia into the Neva in 1240." *Scandinavian Journal of History* 16 (1991): 269–295.

A List of all the Ships and Frigots of England with their number of men, guns, and of what rates. Also, the names of all the commanders in their expedition in May, 1653, against the Dutch, with the number of men and guns which every ship carryed at that memorable fight on the 2d and 3d of June, 1653. In which through Gods blessing on the said fleet, they took and destroyed between 20 and 30. Dutch men of war, and tooke 1350 prisoners, and pursued the Dutch to their own harbours: the ships taken are marked with the letter P. in the margent. Moreover, the fleet sent to the Sound under the conduct of the Right honourable, Generall Edward Lord Montague Admirall, William Goodson Vice Admirall, and Sr Richard Stayner Rear Admirall; with the number of ships, men, and guns, and the names of all the captaines, 1658. London: Printed by M. Simmons, 1660.

Lloyd, Alan. *The Making of the King 1066.* New York: Holt, Rinehart and Winston, 1966.

Lloyd, David. *Modern Policy Compleated, or, The Publick Actions and Councels both Civill and Military of His Excellency the Lord Generall Monck: Under the Generall Revolutions since 1639, to 1660.* London: Printed by J. B. for Henry Marsh, 1660.

Lloyd, Frederick. *An Accurate and Impartial Life of the late Lord Viscount Nelson, Duke of Bronte in Sicily. Comprehending Authentic and Circumstantial details of this Glorious Achievements: together with private anecdotes.* London: J. Fowler, 1806.

Long, John Cuthbert. *Lord Jeffery Amherst: A Soldier of the King.* New York: Macmillan, 1933.

Longman, William. *The History of the Life and Times of Edward the Third.* London: Longmans, Green and Co., 1869.

Longueville, Thomas. *Marshall Turenne.* London: Longmans, Green and Company, 1907.

Lorenz, Lincoln. *John Paul Jones: Fighter for Freedom and Glory.* Annapolis, Md.: United States Naval Institute, 1943.

Lossing, Benson John. *Lives of Celebrated Americans: Comprising Biographies of Three Hundred and Forty Eminent Persons.* Hartford, Conn.: Thomas Belknap, 1869.

Lottman, Herbert R. *Pétain, Hero or Traitor: the Untold Story.* New York: William Morrow, 1985.

Loyn, H. R. *Harold, Son of Godwin.* Hastings, U.K.: The Hastings and Bexhill Branch of the Historical Association, 1966.

Lucan, George Charles Bingham, earl of. *Speech of Major Gen. the Earl of Lucan, delivered in the House of Lords on Monday, March 19, 1855, on his Recall from his Command in the Crimea.* London: T. & W. Boone, 1855.

Lucan's Pharsalia: Or the Civill Warres of Rome, betweene Pompey the Great, and Julius Cæsar. The three first bookes. Translated into English by T.M. London: Printed by J[ohn] N[orton] & A[ugustine] M[athewes], 1626.

Lucas, James, gen. ed. *Command: From Alexander the Great to Zhukov—The Greatest Commanders of World History.* London: Bloomsbury Publishing, 1988.

Luchaire, Achille. *Social France at the Time of Philip Augustus.* New York: Henry Holt, 1912.

Luckenbill, Daniel David. *Ancient Records of Assyria and Babylonia,* 2 vols. New York: Greenwood Press, 1968.

Lugne, Charles Joseph, Prince de Ligne. *The Life of Prince Eugene, of Savoy. From his Original Manuscript, translated from the French, and now Published with Additions and Corrections.* London: Printed by and for J. Davis, 1812.

Lynch, Michael, ed. *The Oxford Companion to Scottish History.* Oxford, U.K.: Oxford University Press, 2001.

Maalouf, Amin. *The Crusades through Arab Eyes by Amin Maalouf.* London: Saqi Books, 1985.

Macartney, Clarence Edward Noble. *Little Mac: The Life of General George B. McClellan.* Philadelphia: Dorrance and Company, 1940.

MacCormick, Charles, ed. *The Secret History of the Court and Reign of Charles the Second, by a Member of his Privy Council: To which are added Introductory Sketches of the Preceding Period from the Accession of James I. With notes, and a Supplement, Continuing the Narrative in a Summary Manner to the Revolution: by the Editor, etc.,* 2 vols. London: J. Bew, 1792.

Maceroni, Francis. *Interesting Facts Relating to the Fall and Death of Joachim Murat, king of Naples: The Capitulation of Paris in 1815, and the second Restoration of the Bourbons. Original Letters from King Joachim to the Author, with some Account of the Author, and of his Persecution by the French government.* London: Printed for Ridgways, 1817.

Mackay, Ruddock F. *Fisher of Kilverstone.* Oxford, U.K.: The Clarendon Press, 1973.

Mackenzie, Agnes Mure. *Robert Bruce, King of Scots.* London: A. Maclehose & Co., 1934.

Mackenzie, Alexander Slidell. *The Life of Commodore Oliver Hazard Perry,* 2 vols. New York: A. L. Fowle, 1900.

———. *Life of Decatur, a Commodore in the Navy of the United States.* Boston: C. C. Little and J. Brown, 1846.

Mackinnon, James. *The History of Edward the Third (1327–1377).* London: Longmans, Green, 1900.

Maclear, Michael. *The Ten Thousand Day War: Vietnam: 1945–1975.* New York: Avon Books, 1981.

MacMunn, Sir George Fletcher. *Prince Eugene, Twin Marshal with Marlborough.* London: S. Low, Marston, 1934.

Macrae-Gibson, O. D. "How Historical Is the Battle of Maldon?" *Medium Ævum* 39, no. 2 (1970): 89–107.

Maddicott, J. R. *Simon de Montfort*. Cambridge, U.K.: Cambridge University Press, 1996.

Mahon, Lord. *The Life of Belisarius*. 2d ed. London: John Murray, Albemarle Street, 1848.

Mahr, Theodore C. *The Battle of Cedar Creek: Showdown in the Shenandoah, October 1–30, 1864: Early's Valley Campaign*. Lynchburg, Va.: H. E. Howard, 1992.

Maltby, William S. *Alba: A Biography of Fernando Alvarez de Toledo, Third Duke of Alba, 1507–1582*. Berkeley: University of California Press, 1983.

Manchester, William Raymond. *American Caesar*. Boston: Little, Brown, 1978.

Manz, Beatrice Forbes. *The Rise and Rule of Tamerlane*. Cambridge, U.K.: Cambridge University Press, 1989.

March 14. Numb. 23. The Continuation of our Weekly Newes, from the 18 of February to this 14 of March Containing, amongst other things, these Particulars following: the good Successe of the king of Sweden in the land of Meckelburgh, with the names of the townes he hath lately taken. With divers particulars concerning Monsieur Tilly his preparation and strength to oppose the said King of Sweden. The French Kings letter to the court of Parliament of Normandy, concerning the restraint of the Queene Mother, and other of the nobility of France. In French and English. London: Printed for Nath. Butter and Nicholas Bourne, 1631.

Marder, Arthur Jacob. *From the Dreadnought to Scapa Flow: The Royal Navy in the Fisher Era, 1904–1919*, 5 vols. London: Oxford University Press, 1961–70.

Margiotta, Col. Franklin D., exec. ed. *Brassey's Encyclopedia of Military History and Biography*. Washington, D.C.: Brassey's, 1994.

Markham, Sir Clements Roberts. *A Life of the Great Lord Fairfax, Commander-in-Chief of the Army of the Parliament of England*. London: Macmillan and Company, 1870.

Marmontel, Jean François. *The History of Belisarius, The Heroick and Humane Roman general: A Man who Possessed the Most Immoveable Fidelity, and Practised the most Disinterested Patriotism, in the Court of a Weak Emperor, Surrounded by a Junto of as Corrupt and Abandoned Ministers, as ever Enslaved and Disgraced Humanity; whose Malice and Envy remained unsatiated, till by Misrepresentation and Perjury they accomplished the Downfall of this Greatest and most Excellent of all Human Beings, . . .* Philadelphia: Printed by J. Crukshank, 1770.

Marnham, Patrick. *Trail of Havoc: In the Steps of Lord Lucan*. London: Penguin, 1988.

Marshall, J. A. *The "Godly Praetorian": The Political Life and Activities of Lieutenant-General Charles Fleetwood in the Destruction of Richard Cromwell's Protectorate and the Demise of the English Republic, September 1658–December 1659*. Master's thesis, University of Lancaster (U.K.), 1985.

Marshall, Robert. *Marshal Massena*. London: Oxford University Press, 1965.

———. *Storm from the East: From Genghis Khan to Khubilai Khan*. Berkeley: University of California Press, 1993.

Marshall-Cornwall, Sir James Handyside. *Foch as Military Commander*. London: Batsford, 1972.

———. *Grant as Commander*. London: Batsford, 1970.

Martin, Christopher. *Damn the Torpedoes! The Story of America's First Admiral: David Glasgow Farragut*. London and New York: Abelard-Schuman, 1970.

Mathews, Sidney T. *General Clark's Decision to Drive to Rome*. Washington, D.C.: Department of the Army, Office of Military History, 1960, 1990.

Matthew of Westminster. *The Flowers of History*. Edited by C. D. Yonge II. London: Henry G. Bohn, 1853.

Mattingly, Garrett. *The Armada*. Boston: Houghton Mifflin Company, 1959.

Maxwell, William. *From the Yalu to Port Arthur: A Personal Record*. London: Hutchinson & Company, 1906.

Maynarde, Thomas. *Sir Francis Drake his Voyage, 1595. Together with the Spanish account of Drake's attack on Puerto Rico*. Edited by W[illiam] D[esborough] Cooley. London: Hakluyt Society, 1849.

Mayo, Lawrence Shaw. *Jeffrey Amherst: A Biography*. New York: Longmans, Green & Co., 1916.

McCardell, Lee. *Ill-Starred General: Braddock of the Coldstream Guards*. Pittsburgh: University of Pittsburgh Press, 1958.

McFeeley, William S. *Grant: A Biography*. New York: Norton, 1981.

McKay, Derek. *Prince Eugène of Savoy*. London: Thames and Hudson, 1977.

McNeal, Robert Hatch. *Tsar and Cossack, 1855–1914*. London: Macmillan in association with St. Anthony's College, Oxford, 1987.

Mellor, William Bancroft. *Patton: Fighting Man*. New York: Putnam, 1946.

Menning, Bruce W. *Bayonets Before Bullets: The Imperial Russian Army, 1861–1914*. Bloomington: Indiana University Press, 1992.

Men of the Time. Biographical Sketches of Eminent Living Characters. Also Biographical Sketches of Celebrated Women of the Time. London: David Bogue, Fleet Street, 1856.

"The Men Who Are Winning the Race to Germany." *Picture Post* 24, no. 5 (29 July 1944): 7–9.

Merrill, James M. *William Tecumseh Sherman*. Chicago: Rand McNally, 1971.

A Message sent to the L. Admiral Vantrump from the High and Mighty Lords the States General of the united Provinces, touching hostile acts toward all English ships, whether merchants of others. With the burning and consuming of the state-house and bank of money at Amsterdam, and the firing of a gallant ship in the harbour; and the debates of the states at the Hague, touchin their constituting the young Pr. of Orange, Governor of the United Provinces. Likewise, a full and perfect relation of the late transactions betwixt the two fleets under the command of Sir Geo. Ascue, and Admiral Vantrump upon the Downs; with Vantrumps design to have surprised our ships in the hope; his sailing westward, and his design therein. Also a bloudy fight at sea, and the taking of divers Dutch ships by his excellency General Blake in the Northern seas. London: Printed by E.C., 1652.

Mets, James Andrew. *Naval Heroes of Holland*. New York: The Abbey Press, 1902.

Michie, Peter Smith. *General McClellan*. New York: D. Appleton & Company, 1901.

Miers, Earl Schenck. *The General Who Marched to Hell: William Tecumseh Sherman and His March to Fame and Infamy*. New York: Alfred A. Knopf, 1951.

Mintz, Max M. *The Generals of Saratoga: John Burgoyne and Horatio Gates*. New Haven, Conn.: Yale University Press, 1990.

A Miraculous Victory Obtained by the Right Honorable, Ferdinando Lord Fairfax, Against the army under the Command of the Earl of Newcastle at Wakefield in York-shire of the enemy there was taken prisoners, Generall Goring, Sir Thomas Bland, 2 colonells, Sergeant Major Car, 13 captains, 1500 souldiers, 27 colours of foot, 3 cornets of horse, 4 lieutenants, 15 ensignes, and 1 cornet, 4 peeces of ordnance, all their ammunition, and a great Number of Armes, with the loss of 7 Common souldiers: sent in Two Letters to the Honorable, W. Lenthall, Esq., speaker in the House of Commons: also a Letter of Great Consequence, which was found in Generall Gorings Chamber, which was sent to him by his father the Lord Goring. London: Printed for Edw. Husband, 1643.

Mitchell, George Charles. *Matthew B. Ridgway: Soldier, Statesman, Scholar, Citizen*. Mechanicsburg, Pa.: Stackpole Books, 2002.

Mócsy, András. *Pannonia and Upper Moesia: A History of the Middle Danube Provinces of the Roman Empire*. London: Routledge & K. Paul, 1974.

Mombauer, Annika. *Helmuth von Moltke and the Origins of the First World War*. Cambridge, U.K.: Cambridge University Press, 2001.

Monash, Sir John. *The Australian Victories in France in 1918*. London: Hutchinson, 1920.

———. *War Letters of General Monash*. Edited by Frederic Morley. Sydney, New South Wales: Angus & Robertson, 1934.

Monshi, Eskandar Beg. *History of Shah 'Abbas the Great—Tarike 'alam ar aye 'Abbas I*. Translated by Roger M. Savory. Boulder, Colorado: Westview Press, 1978.

Montagu, Edward, Earl of Manchester. *A Journall, or, a True and Exact Relation of Each Dayes Passage, of that Party of the Right Honourable the Earle of Manchesters army, under the Commander of the Ever Honoured Maior Generall Craford, from the first of August to the end of the same month. Wherein there is truly related the taking of severall places, with the conditions and articles of the same, etc*. London: Printed by Hugh Perry, 1644.

Montgomery, Field Marshal Bernard Law. *Alamein and the Desert War*. London: Sphere Books in Association with the Sunday Times, 1967.

———. *El Alamein to the River Sangro*. New York: E. P. Dutton, 1949.

———. *The Memoirs of Field-Marshal the Viscount Montgomery of Alamein*. Cleveland: World Publishing Company, 1958.

Montross, Lynn. *War Through the Ages*. New York: Harper & Brothers, 1946.

Moorehead, Alan. *Montgomery: A Biography*. New York: Coward-McCann, 1946.

Moorhead, John. *Theoderic in Italy*. Oxford, U.K.: The Clarendon Press, 1992.

A More Exact Relation of the Late Battell neer York; fought by the English and Scotch forces, against Prince Rupert and the Marquess of Newcastle. Wherein the passages thereof are more particularly set down, presented to the view of those who desire better satisfaction therin. Published for the more inlargement of our hearts to Almighty God on our day of Thanksgiving, commanded by authority for the great victory obtained. Allowed to be printed according to order. London: Printed by M. Simmons, 1644.

Morison, Samuel Eliot. *John Paul Jones: A Sailor's Biography.* Boston: Little, Brown, 1959.

Morrah, Patrick. *Prince Rupert of the Rhine.* London: Constable, 1976.

Morris, John E. *The Welsh Wars of Edward I: A Contribution to Mediaeval Military History, Based upon Original Documents.* Oxford, U.K.: Clarendon Press, 1901.

Morris, Roy, Jr. *Sheridan: The Life and Wars of General Phil Sheridan.* New York: Vintage Books, 1993.

Morris, William O'Connor. *Moltke: A Biographical and Critical Study.* New York: Haskell House, 1893.

Morton, Graeme. *William Wallace: Man and Myth.* Stroud, Gloucestershire, U.K.: Sutton, 2001.

Morton, J. B. *Sobieski, King of Poland.* London: Eyre and Spottiswoode, 1932.

Mossman, Samuel, ed. *General Gordon's Private Diary of His Exploits in China.* London: S. Low, Marton, Searle, & Rivington, 1885.

Mundy, Godfrey B. *The Life and Correspondence of Admiral Lord Rodney,* 2 vols. London: J. Murray, 1830.

Murison, Alexander Falconer. *Sir William Wallace.* Edinburgh, Scotland: Oliphant, Anderson & Ferrier, 1898.

Murray, G. E. Patrick. *Eisenhower versus Montgomery: The Continuing Debate.* Westport, Conn.: Praeger, 1996.

Nakamura, Koya, comp. *Admiral Togo: A Memoir.* Tokyo, Japan: The Togo Gensui Publishing Company, 1937.

Napier, Edward Delaval Hungerford Elers. *Life and Correspondence of Admiral Sir Charles Napier, K.C.B. from Personal Recollections, Letters, and Official Documents,* 2 vols. London: Hurst and Blackett, 1862.

Napier, Mark. *Montrose and the Covenanters, their Characters and Conduct, Illustrated from Private Letters and other Original Documents Hitherto Unpublished, Embracing the Times of Charles the First, from the Rise of the Troubles in Scotland, to the Death of Montrose,* 2 vols. London: J. Duncan, 1838.

Napier, Priscilla Hayter. *Black Charlie: A Life of Admiral Sir Charles Napier KCB, 1786–1860.* Wilby, U.K.: Michael Russell, 1995.

Napier, Robert M. *Sir John French and Sir John Jellicoe: Their Lives and Careers.* London: The Patriotic Publishing Company, 1914.

Napier, W. F. P. *History of the War in the Peninsula and in the South of France from the Year 1807 to the Year 1814,* 6 vols. London: Thomas & William Boone, 1836.

A Narrative of Sir George Rooke's Late Voyage to the Mediterranean, Where He Commanded as Admiral of the Confederate Fleet. With a Description of Gibraltar; and Observations on the Usefulness and Importance of that Place; which was Attack'd and Taken by the Said Fleet, and Now Remains in the Possession of the Allies. An Account also of the Naval Battel Fought Betwixt the Confederates and French King's Fleets: With a Judgment of the Event. In a Letter to a Person of Quality. London: Printed for Benj. Tooke, 1704.

Neillands, Robin. *Attrition! The Great War on the Western Front—1916.* London: Robson, 2001.

———. *The Dervish Wars: Gordon and Kitchener in the Sudan, 1880–1898.* London: John Murray, 1996.

Nelson, Paul David. *General Horatio Gates: A Biography.* Baton Rouge: Louisiana State University Press, 1976.

Nepos, Cornelius. *Cornelius Nepos' Life of Miltiades. . . . With Maps, Notes, Full Translation and Vocabulary.* Edited by M. Hughes. London: City of London Book Depot, 1901.

———. *Lives of Miltiades and Epaminondas.* Edited by J. E. Melluish. London: Blackie & Son, 1901.

———. *The Lives of T. Pomponius Atticus, Miltiades, and Cimon. . . . The Second Edition, to which is added L'abbe Bellegarde's Treatise on Fashions, With an Essay on Entertainments.* Translated by Richardson Pack. London: E. Curll, 1735.

Newby, Percy Howard. *Saladin in His Time.* London: Faber and Faber, 1983.

Newcastle, Margaret Cavendish, Duchess of Newcastle. *The Life of the Thrice Noble, High and Puissant William Cavendishe, Duke, Marquess, and Earl of Newcastle; Earl of Ogle, Viscount Mansfield; and Baron Bolsover, of Ogle, Bothal and Hepple: Gentleman of His Majesties Bed-chamber; one of His Majesties most Honourable Privy-Councel; Knight of the most Noble Order of the Garter; His Majesties Lieutenant of the*

County and Town of Nottingham; and Justice in Ayre Trent-North; who had the honour to be Governour to our most Glorious King, and Gracious Soveraign, in his Youth, when He was Prince of Wales; and soon after was made Captain General of all the Provinces beyond the River of Trent, and other Parts of the Kingdom of England, with Power, by a Special Commission, to make Knights. Written by the thrice Noble, Illustrious, and Excellent Princess, Margaret, Duchess of Newcastle, His Wife. London: Printed by A. Maxwell, 1667.

New Propositions from the Armie, Propounded by Cornet Joyce (who lately guarded His Majesties Person from Holmby), to all Free Commoners within the Kingdome of England and Dominion of Wales. Wherein it more fully set forth, Their further Resolution and Proceedings, concerning the Kings Majesties Royall Person, the preservation of this Nation, and touching every member that challenges an interest in this Kingdome. Whereunto is annexed, The Copy of another Letter sent from the Kings most Excellent Majesty, and read in the High and Honourable Court of Parliament. Printed for the Use and Satisfaction of the Whole Kingdome. London: Printed for Robert Ellson, 1647.

Nicholson, Dennis Dewitt. *A History of the Citadel: The Years of Summerall and Clark.* Charleston, S.C.: The Citadel, 1994.

Nicholson, Ranald. *Edward III and the Scots: The Formative Years of a Military Career, 1327–1335.* Oxford, U.K.: Oxford University Press, 1965.

Nicolas, Sir N. Harris. *History of the Battle of Agincourt, and of the Expedition of Henry the Fifth into France, in 1415; To Which is Added, the Roll of the Men at Arms, in the English Army.* London: Published by Johnson & Co., 1832.

Nicolay, Helen. *MacArthur of Bataan.* New York: D. Appleton-Century Company, 1942.

Nicolle, David. *Lake Peipus 1242: Battle of the Ice.* London: Osprey Military, 1996.

———. *The Mongol Warlords: Genghis Khan, Kublai Khan, Hülegü, Tamerlane.* Poole, U.K.: Firebird Books, 1990.

Nicolson, Nigel. *Alex: The Life of Field Marshal Earl Alexander of Tunis.* London: Weidenfeld and Nicholson, 1973.

North, Bruce. *Encyclopedia of American War Heroes.* New York: Checkmark Books, 2002.

Nunan, Peter. "Diggers' Fourth of July." *Military History* 17, no. 3 (August 2000): 26.

Nursey, Walter R. *The Story of Isaac Brock, Hero, Defender and Saviour of Upper Canada, 1812.* Toronto: William Briggs, 1908.

Oldmixon, John. *The Life and History of Belisarius, Who Conquer'd Africa and Italy; With an Account of His Disgrace, the Ingratitude of the Romans, and a Parallel Between Him and a Modern Heroe.* London: Printed by A. Baldwin, 1713.

Olivera, Ruth R. *Life in Mexico under Santa Anna, 1822–1855.* Norman: University of Oklahoma Press, 1991.

Ollier, Edmund. *Cassell's Illustrated History of the Russo-Turkish War,* 2 vols. London: Cassell and Company, 1896.

Olmstead, Albert Ten Eyck. *History of Assyria.* New York: Charles Scribner's Sons, 1923.

———. *History of the Persian Empire.* Chicago: University of Chicago Press, 1948.

Oman, Sir Charles William Chadwick. *Warwick, the Kingmaker.* London: Macmillan, 1891.

Orr, James. *The Problem of the Old Testament Considered with Reference to Recent Criticism.* New York: Charles Scribner's Sons, 1906.

Ostrogorsky, George. *History of the Byzantine State.* Translated by Joan Hussey. New Brunswick, N.J.: Rutgers University Press, 1969.

Oudinot, Marie Charlotte Eugénie Julienne, duchess de Reggio. *Memoirs of Marshal Oudinot, Duc de Reggio.* Translated by Alexander Teixeira de Mattos. New York: D. Appleton and Company, 1897.

An Outcry after the Late Lieutenant General Fleetwood. London: Printed by Hen. Mason, 1660.

Outram, General Sir James. *The Conquest of Scinde: A Commentary.* Edinburgh, Scotland: Blackwoods, 1846.

The Overthrow of the Scottish Army: Or, a Letter Sent from Lieutenant General Cromwell, to the Committee of Lancashire sitting at Manchester, shewing the utter Routing of the Scottish Forces. London: Printed for John Bellamy, 1648.

Owsley, Frank Lawrence. *Struggle for the Gulf Borderlands, the Creek War, and the Battle of New Orleans.* Gainesville: University Presses of Florida, 1981.

Paget, George, Lord Paget. *The Light Cavalry Brigade in the Crimea: Extracts from the Letters and Journal of General Lord George Paget.* London: John Murray, 1881.

Palmer, Alan Warwick. *Bernadotte: Napoleon's Marshal, Sweden's King.* London: John Murray, 1990.

———. *Napoleon in Russia.* New York: Simon and Schuster, 1967.

———. *Russia in War and Peace.* London: Weidenfeld and Nicolson, 1972.

Palmer, Frederick. *John J. Pershing, General of the Armies: A Biography.* Harrisburg, Pa.: Military Service Publishing Company, 1948.

Paret, Peter, ed. *Makers of Modern Strategy from Machiavelli to the Nuclear Age.* Princeton, N.J.: Princeton University Press, 1986.

Parkinson, Roger. *The Encyclopedia of Modern War.* New York: Stein & Day, 1977.

———. *The Fox of the North: The Life of Kutusov, General of War and Peace.* New York: D. McKay Company, 1976.

The Parliaments Determination, Concerning The Levies of Horse, Armes, and Monies, which is now rays'd for this present Designe. Also a remarkable Passage concerning the Earle of New-Castle, with the Substance of the Letter sent from Sir John Hotham to Mr. Pym. Whereunto is added, A True Declaration for the silencing all false Reports concerning Sir John Hotham's Letter sent to Mr. Pym, for the sending of 300 Men to Hull for to strengthen the said Towne. London, 1641.

Parmet, Herbert S. *Eisenhower and the American Crusades.* New York: The Macmillan Company, 1972.

Parton, James. *Life of Andrew Jackson,* 3 vols. New York: Mason Brothers, 1860.

Patterson, J. *State of the Troops, British and German, under the Command of Lieutenant-General Sir Henry Clinton, at New-York, and Posts Depending, October 1, 1777.* New York(?), 1777.

Patterson, Samuel White. *Horatio Gates: Defender of American Liberties.* New York: Columbia University Press, 1941.

Patton, George S. *War as I Knew It.* Boston: Houghton Mifflin, 1947.

Paxton, John. *Encyclopedia of Russian History: From the Christianization of Kiev to the Break-up of the U.S.S.R.* Santa Barbara, Cal.: ABC-Clio, 1993.

Peddie, John. *Alfred: Warrior King.* Phoenix Mill, Thrupp, Stroud, Gloucestershire, U.K.: Sutton Publishing, 1999.

Pederson, P. A. *Monash as Military Commander.* Carlton, Victoria, Australia: Melbourne University Press, 1985.

Pelling, C. B. R. *Life of Antony.* Cambridge, U.K.: Cambridge University Press, 1988.

Penn, Granville. *Memorials of the Professional Life and Times of Sir William Penn from 1644 to 1670.* London: J. Duncan, 1833.

Perodi, P. *Memoirs of the Reign of Murat: In which the Circumstances of the Confiscation of the American Vessels, his Last Campaign and Death, and the Character of his Generals and Courtiers, are Fully Displayed.* Boston: West and Richardson, 1818.

Perrie, Maureen. *The Image of Ivan the Terrible in Russian Folklore.* Cambridge, U.K.: Cambridge University Press, 1987.

Pertinax. *The Gravediggers of France: Gamelin, Daladier, Reynaud, Pétain, and Laval; Military Defeat, Armistice, Counter-Revolution.* Garden City, N.Y.: Doubleday, Doran & Company, 1944.

Petre, F. Loraine. *Napoleon & the Archduke Charles: A History of the Franco-Austrian Campaign in the Valley of the Danube in 1809.* London: Arms & Armour Press, 1976.

Petrie, Sir Charles. *Don John of Austria.* London: Eyre & Spottiswoode, 1967.

———. *The Marshal Duke of Berwick: The Picture of an Age.* London: Eyre & Spottiswoode, 1953.

Phillips, E. D. *The Mongols.* London: Thames and Hudson, 1969.

Phillips, Samuel. *Essays from the London Times: A Collection of Personal and Historical Sketches.* New York: D. Appleton & Company, 1852.

Phillips, Thomas R., ed. *Roots of Strategy: A Collection of Military Classics.* London: John Lane the Bodley Head, 1943.

Philpotts, Robert. *What Happened at Maldon? The Story of the Battle of Maldon, August 991.* London: Blackwater Books, 1991.

Phinney, Elias. *History of the Battle of Lexington, on the Morning of 19th April, 1775.* Boston: Printed by Phelps and Farnham, 1825.

Pick, Daniel. *War Machine: the Rationalization of Slaughter in the Modern Age.* New Haven, Conn.: Yale University Press, 1993.

Pleshakov, Konstantin. *The Tsar's Last Armada: The Epic Journey to the Battle of Tsushima.* New York: Basic Books, 2002.

Plutarch. *The Lives of Epaminondas, of Philip of Macedon, of Dionysius the Elder, and of Octavius Cæsar Augustus: Collected out of Good Authors. Also the Lives of Nine Excellent Chieftaines of Warre, taken out of Latine from Emylius Probus, by S.G.S. By who also are added the*

Lives of Plutarch and of Seneca: Gathered Together, disposed, and enriched as the Others. Translated by Sir Thomas North, Knight. London: Richard Field, 1603.

Pocock, Tom. *The Terror Before Trafalgar: Nelson, Nap, and the Secret War.* New York: W. W. Norton, 2003.

Porter, Horace. *Campaigning With Grant.* New York: Century, 1897.

Porter, Pamela. *Medieval Warfare in Manuscripts.* London, England: The British Library, 1992.

Potter, Elmer Belmont. *Bull Halsey: A Biography.* Annapolis, Md.: United States Naval Institute Press, 1985.

———. *Nimitz.* Annapolis, Md.: Naval Institute Press, 1976.

Potter, John Deane. *Yamamoto: The Man Who Menaced America.* New York: Viking, 1965.

Powell, Geoffrey. *Buller—A Scapegoat?: A Life of General Sir Redvers Buller, 1839–1908.* London: Leo Cooper, 1994.

———. *Plumer: The Soldiers' General: A Biography of Field-Marshal Viscount Plumer of Messines.* London: Leo Cooper, 1990.

Powell, J. R. *The Navy in the English Civil War.* Hamden, U.K.: Archon Books, 1962.

Powell, The Rev. J. R., and E. K. Timings. *The Rupert and Monck Letter Book 1666, Together With Supporting Documents.* London: Printed for the Navy Records Society, 1969.

Powicke, Sir Frederick, et al. *The Battle of Lewes, 1264.* Lewes, U.K.: Friends of Lewes Society, 1964.

Presniakov, A. E. *The Formation of the Great Russian State: A Study of Russian History in the Thirteenth to Fifteenth Centuries.* Chicago: Triangle Books, 1970.

Pretorius, Fransjohan. *The Great Escape of the Boer Pimpernel, Christiaan De Wet: The Making of a Legend.* Translated by Stephan Hofstätter. Pietermaritzburg, South Africa: University of Natal Press, 2001.

Procopius. *History of the Wars, Books I and II,* 7 vols. Translated by Henry Bronson Deweing. London: W. Heinemann Ltd., 1914.

Prothero, George Walter. *The Life of Simon de Montfort, Earl of Leicester, with Special Reference to the Parliamentary History of His Time.* London: Longmans, Green, and Company, 1877.

Pryce, Mrs. Hugh. *The Great Marquis of Montrose.* London: Everett & Company, Limited, 1912.

Pyle, Richard. *Schwarzkopf: The Man, the Mission, the Triumph.* New York: Signet, 1991.

Rasor, Eugene L. *The Battle of Jutland: A Bibliography.* New York: Greenwood Press, 1992.

Rawson, Edward Kirk. *Twenty Famous Naval Battles, Salamis to Santiago.* New York: T. Y. Crowell & Company, 1899.

Rawson, Geoffrey. *Earl Beatty: Admiral of the Fleet: Viscount Borodale and Baron Beatty of the North Sea and of Brooksby.* London: Jarrolds, 1930.

Read, David Breakinridge. *Life and Times of Major-General Sir Isaac Brock.* Toronto: William Briggs, 1894.

Recouly, Raymond. *General Joffré and His Battles.* New York: Charles Scribner's Sons, 1917.

———. *Joffré.* New York: D. Appleton & Company, 1931.

Redford, Donald B., ed. *The Oxford Encyclopedia of Ancient Egypt,* 3 vols. Oxford, U.K.: Oxford University Press, 2001.

Reese, George Henkle, comp. *The Cornwallis Papers,* 2 vols. Charlottesville: University of Virginia Press, 1970.

Regan, Geoffrey. *Geoffrey Regan's Book of Military Blunders.* London: André Deutsch, 2001.

———. *Saladin and the Fall of Jerusalem.* London: Croom Helm, 1987.

Reid, Stuart. *All the King's Armies: A Military History of the English Civil War, 1642–1651.* Staplehurst, Kent, U.K.: Spellmount, 1998.

Reinhold, Meyer. *Marcus Agrippa: A Biography.* Geneva, N.Y.: The W. F. Humphrey Press, 1933.

Reiter, William. *Aemilius Paullus: Conqueror of Greece.* London: Croom Helm, 1988.

A Relation of the Battel fought between Keynton and Edgehill, by His Majesty's Army and that of the Rebels. Oxford, U.K.: Leonard Lichfield, 1642.

A Relation of the Good Successe of the Parliaments Forces under the Command of Generall Lesly, the Earl of Manchester, and the Lord Fairfax, against the Forces commanded by Prince Rupert and the Earl of Newcastle on Hesham-Moore, on Tuesday July 2, 1644[,] sent by Way of Letter from a Captain there Present to a friend in London. Cambridge, U.K.: Printed by W. F., 1644.

Reston, James, Jr. *Warriors of God: Richard the Lionheart and Saladin in the Third Crusade.* New York: Doubleday, 2001.

Rich, John, and Graham Shipley, eds. *War and Society in the Greek World.* London: Routledge, 1993.

Richardson, Geoffrey. *The Lordly Ones: A History of the Neville Family and Their Part in the Wars of the Roses.* Shipley, U.K.: Baildon Books, 1998.

Ridgway, Matthew. *Soldier: The Memoirs of Matthew B. Ridgway, as Told to Harold H. Martin.* New York: Harper & Brothers, 1956.

Riley-Smith, Jonathan. *The Oxford Illustrated History of the Crusades.* Oxford, U.K.: Oxford University Press, 2001.

Roberts, Frederick Sleigh, Earl Roberts. *Roberts in India: The Military Papers of Field Marshal Lord Roberts, 1876–1893.* Edited by Brian Robson. Dover, N.H.: Alan Sutton for the Army Records Society, 1993.

Roberts, Geoffrey. *Victory at Stalingrad: The Battle That Changed History.* London: Longman, 2002.

Roberts, George. *The Life, Progresses, and Rebellion of James, Duke of Monmouth, to his Capture and Execution: with a Full Account of the Bloody Assize, and Copious Biographical Notices,* 2 vols. London: Longman, Brown, Green and Longmans, 1844.

Robinson, James Harvey, ed. *Readings in European History,* 2 vols. Boston: Ginn, 1904.

Rokossovsky, Konstantin K. *A Soldier's Duty.* Translated by Vladimir Talmy. Edited by Robert Doglish. Moscow, USSR: Progress Publishers, 1970, 1985.

Rooney, David. *Military Mavericks: Extraordinary Men of Battle.* London: Cassell & Co., 1999.

Rose, John Hollard. *Lord Hood and the Defence of Toulon.* Cambridge, U.K.: The University Press, 1922.

Rosenberg, Hans. *Bureaucracy, Aristocracy and Autocracy: The Prussian Experience, 1660–1815.* Cambridge, Mass.: Harvard University Press, 1958.

Rosenberg, William G. *A. I. Denikin and the anti-Bolshevik Movement in South Russia.* Amherst, Mass.: Amherst College Press, 1961.

Rosenthal, Eric. *General De Wet: A Biography.* Cape Town, South Africa: Simondium Publishers, 1968.

Rosenthal, Eric, comp. *Southern African Dictionary of National Biography.* London: Frederick Warne, 1966.

Ross, Charles, ed. *Correspondence of Charles, First Marquis Cornwallis,* 3 vols. London: John Murray, 1859.

Ross, Thomas. *The Second Punick War between Hannibal, and the Romanes: The Whole Seventeen Books, Englished from the Latine of Silius Italicus: With a Continuation from the Triumph of Scipio, to the Death of Hannibal.* London: Printed by Tho. Roycroft, 1672.

Rossabi, Morris. *Khubilai Khan: His Life and Times.* Berkeley: University of California Press, 1988.

Rosskill, Stephen Wentworth. *Admiral of the Fleet Earl Beatty: The Last Naval Hero: An Intimate Biography.* London: Collins, 1980.

Rothenberg, Gunther Erich. *Napoleon's Great Adversaries: The Archduke Charles and the Austrian Army, 1792–1814.* London: Batsford, 1982.

Rough, Sir William. *Lines on the Death of the Late Sir Ralph Abercromby. By the Author of The Conspiracy of Gowrie.* London: J. Bell, 1801.

Royal, Trevor. *Crimea: The Great Crimean War, 1854–56.* New York: St. Martin's Press, 2000.

Rushworth, John. *Historical Collections of Private Passages of State, Weighty Matters in Law, Remarkable Proceedings in five Parliaments: Beginning the Sixteenth year of King James. Anno 1618, and ending the fifth year of King Charls [sic], Anno 1629/. . . ,* 8 vols. London: Printed by Tho. Newcomb for George Thomason, 1659–1701.

Russell, Sir William Howard. *Complete History of the Russian War, from its Commencement to its Close.* New York: J. G. Wells, 1857.

Sack, Ronald Herbert. *Images of Nebuchadnezzar: The Emergence of a Legend.* Selinsgrove, Pennsylvania: Susquehanna University Press, 2004.

Salerno. Washington, D.C.: Historical Division, War Department, for the American Forces in Action series, 1944.

Salzman, Louis Francis. *Edward I.* London: Praeger, 1968.

Sansom, George. *A History of Japan, 1334–1615.* Stanford, Calif.: Stanford University Press, 1961.

Scheer, Reinhard. *Germany's High Sea Fleet in the World War.* London: Cassell & Company, Ltd., 1920.

Scherer, James A. B. *Three Meiji Leaders: Ito, Togo, Nogi.* Tokyo: The Hokuseido Press, 1936.

Schmidt, John D. *Ramesses II: A Chronological Structure for his Reign.* Baltimore, Md.: Johns Hopkins University Press, 1973.

Schneller, Robert John, Jr. *Farragut: America's First Admiral.* Washington, D.C.: Brassey's, 2002.

Scott, Ronald McNair. *Robert the Bruce, King of Scots.* New York: P. Bedrick Books, 1989.

Scullard, Howard W. *Scipio Africanus in the Second Punic War.* Oxford, U.K.: Oxford University Press, 1930.

The Secret Expedition impartially disclos'd: Or, an Authentick Faithful Narrative of all Occurrences that Happened to the Fleet and Army Commanded by Sir E. H. [Edward Hawke] and Sir J. M. [John Mordaunt],

From its First Sailing to its Return to England. By a Commissioned Officer on Board the Fleet. London: Printed by J. Staples, 1757.

Seele, Keith Cedric. *The Coregency of Ramses II with Seti I and the Date of the Great Hypostyle Hall at Karnak.* Chicago: The University of Chicago Press, 1940.

Seeley, Robert Benton. *The Life and Reign of Edward I.* London: Seeley, Jackson & Halliday, 1872.

Serle, Geoffrey. *John Monash.* Melbourne, Australia: Melbourne University Press, 1982.

Seton-Kerr, Walter Scott. *The Marquess Cornwallis.* Oxford, U.K.: Clarendon Press, 1890.

Several Letters to the Honorable William Lenthal Esq; Speaker to the Honorable House of Commons. Concerning the gallant Proceedings of Sir Tho. Fairfax Army in the West. Viz. [,] the Surrendering up of Exeter on this present Monday: the taking of 80 prisoners, with the works and line about Pendennis Castle by Col. Hamond; the taking of 60 prisoners of the Mount, which is the greater part of that Garrison; and the probability of the delivery up of Barnstable. Also very good news from Ireland. London: Printed for Edw. Husband, 1646.

Sevruk, Vladimir, comp. *Moscow 1941/42 Stalingrad.* Moscow, USSR: Progress Publishers, 1970.

Seward, Desmond. *The Wars of the Roses and the Lives of Five Men and Women in the Fifteenth Century.* London: Constable, 1995.

S. H. *Funerall Elegies. Or the Sad Muses in Sables, singing the Epicediums of his Highness Prince Maurice, Count Palatine of the Rhine, Duke of Bavaria, &c. James Duke of Lenox and Richmond. John Earl of Rivers. John Cleveland, the much-cry'd up Poet.* London: Printed by Tho. Wilson, 1658.

Shaban, Muhammad abd al-Hayy Muhammad. *Islamic History: A New Interpretation,* 2 vols. Cambridge, U.K.: Cambridge University Press, 1971.

Shadwell, Lieutenant-General [Lawrence]. *The Life of Colin Campbell, Lord Clyde, Illustrated by Extracts From His Diary and Correspondence.* Edinburgh and London: William Blackwood and Sons, 1881.

Shakespeare, William. *The tragedie of King Richard the Third: Containing his Treacherous Plots against his brother Clarence: the pittifull murther of his innocent Nephewes: his tyrannicall usurpation: with the whole course of his detested life, and most deserved death. As it hath beene lately acted by the Kings Majesties Servants. Newly augmented, by William Shake-speare.* London: Printed by Thomas Creede, 1612.

Shand, Alexander Innes. *Wellington's Lieutenants.* London: Smith, Elder, & Co., 1902.

Sheppard, Eric William. *Coote Bahadur: A Life of Lieutenant-General Sir Eyre Coote.* London: W. Laurie, 1956.

Sheridan, P. H. *Personal Memoirs of P. H. Sheridan, General United States Army.* New York: Da Capo Press, 1992.

Sherley, Sir Anthony. *His Relation of his travels into Persia: The dangers, and distresses, which befell him in his passage, both by sea and land, and his strange and unexpected deliverances. . . .* London: Printed [by Nicholas Okes] for Nathaniell Butter, and Joseph Bagfet, 1613.

Shipley, Frederick W. *Agrippa's Building Activities in Rome.* St. Louis, Mo.: Washington University Press, 1933.

Shores, Christopher F. *Pictorial History of the Mediterranean Air War,* 3 vols. London: Ian Allen, 1973.

Shosenberg, James W. "Napoleon's Masterstroke at Rivoli." *Military History* 13, no. 5 (December 1996): 34–40.

Shuckburgh, Evelyn S. *A History of Rome to the Battle of Actium.* New York: Macmillan and Company, 1894.

Sked, Alan. *The Survival of the Hapsburg Empire: Radetzky, the Imperial Army, and the Class War, 1848.* London: Longman, 1979.

Slater, Robert. *Warrior Statesman: The Life of Moshe Dayan.* New York: St. Martin's Press, 1991.

Slocombe, George. *Don Juan of Austria, the Victor of Lepanto (1547–1578).* London: I. Nicholson and Watson, 1935.

Small, Harold A. *The Field of His Fame: A Ramble on the Curious History of Charles Wolfe's Poem "The Burial of Sir John Moore."* Berkeley: University of California, 1953.

Smith, Elbert B. *The Presidencies of Zachary Taylor and Millard Fillmore.* Lawrence: University Press of Kansas, 1988.

Smith, Robert Barr. "'A Damned Nice Thing' at Waterloo." *Military History* 12, no. 2 (June 1995): 62–69.

Smith, William, ed. *Dictionary of Greek and Roman Biography and Mythology,* 3 vols. London: Taylor and Walton, 1844.

Smoot, J. Edward. *Marshal Ney Before and After Execution.* Charlotte, N.C.: Queen City Printing Company, 1929.

Snow, Vernon F. *Essex the Rebel: The Life of Robert Devereux, the Third Earl of Essex, 1591–1646.* Lincoln: University of Nebraska Press, 1970.

Sobieski, John. *The Life of King John Sobieski, John the Third of Poland.* Boston: R. G. Badger, 1915.

Soffer, Jonathan M. *General Matthew B. Ridgway: From Progressivism to Reaganism, 1895–1983.* Westport, Conn.: Praeger, 1998.

Solzhenitsyn, Alexander. *August 1914.* New York: Farrar, Straus, and Giroux, 1972.

"Some New Spanish Documents Dealing with Drake." *The English Historical Review* 193 (January 1934): 14–31.

The Souldiers Report concerning Sir William Wallers Fight against Basing-house on Sunday last November the 12, 1643. To give satisfaction to the whole Kingdome concerning that designe where are these particulars, viz: 1. How Considerable a thing it would be in case it could be taken. 2. How strongly it is fortified both upon the walls and the house. 3. Sir William Wallers onset and the manner of the fight. 4. The reason of the retreat. 5. The sending up of some prisoners taken by Sir William Waller namely one Lord one Popish Priest, &c. London: Printed by John Hammond, 1643.

Southey, Robert. *English Seamen: Howard, Clifford, Hawkins, Drake, Cavendish.* London: Methuen & Co., 1895.

———. *Life of Nelson.* London: Everyman's Library, 1906.

Spach, John Thom. "Allenby and the Last Crusade." *Military History* 12, no. 7 (March 1996): 26–32.

Speake, Graham, ed. *The Penguin Dictionary of Ancient History.* London: Penguin Books, 1995.

Spears, Sir Edward Louis, Bart. *Prelude to Victory.* London: Jonathan Cape, 1939.

Spector, Ronald H. *Admiral of the New Empire: The Life and Career of George Dewey.* Baton Rouge: Louisiana State University Press, 1974.

Sprigge, Joshua. *Anglia Rediviva: England's Recovery, by Joshua Sprigge.* London: Printed by R. W. for John Partridge, 1647.

Stephen, Sir Leslie, and Sir Sidney Lee, et al., eds. *The Dictionary of National Biography,* 22 vols., 8 supps. London: Oxford University Press, 1921–22.

Stewart, R. J. *Macbeth: Scotland's Warrior King.* Poole, Dorset, U.K.: Firebird Books, 1988.

Stewart, William, Captain. *A Full Relation of the Late Victory Obtained, through Gods providence by the forces under the command of Generall Lesley, the Lord Fairfax, and the Earl of Manchester being about twenty seven thousand Horse and Foot: against His Majesties forces under the command of Prince Rupert and the Earl of Newcastle, being much about the same Number: Fought on Marstam-Moor within 5 miles of York, on the second of July, 1644: With a relation of Prince Ruperts march towards Lancashire, and of the forces sent in pursuit after him, as also of the E[arl] of Newcastle and Gen: Kings taking ship for Holland: with the weak condition that York is now in, having quit their great fort, there not being 500 souldiers in the town besides citizens: together with a list of the cornets and ensignes with their severall motto's: sent by the three generals to the Parliament.* London: Printed by J. F. for L. Blaiklock, 1644.

Stirling, William Alexander, earl of Stirling. *The Tragedie of Darius.* Edinburgh: Printed by Robert Waldegraue, 1603.

Story, Douglas. *The Campaign With Kuropatkin.* London: T. Werner Laurie, 1904.

Stoye, John. *English Travellers Abroad, 1604–1667: Their Influence in English Society and Politics.* London: Jonathan Cape, 1952.

Strayer, Joseph Reese. *The Reign of Philip the Fair.* Princeton, N.J.: Princeton University Press, 1980.

Sugden, John. *Sir Francis Drake.* New York: Holt, 1990.

Suhr, Robert Collins. "Ambush at Kadesh." *Military History* 12, no. 3 (August 1995): 46–53.

Swett, S. *Who was the Commander at Bunker Hill? With Remarks of Frothingham's History of the Battle. With an Appendix.* Boston: Printed by John Wilson, 1850.

Symons, John. *The Battle of Queenston Heights: Being a Narrative of the Opening of the War of 1812, with Notices of the life of Major-General Sir Isaac Brock, K. B., and a Description of the Monument Erected to his Memory.* Toronto: Thompson & Co., Printers, 1859.

Tacitus, Cornelius. *The Agricola.* Edited by Duane Reed Stuart. New York: Macmillan, 1924.

Tallett, Frank. *War and Society in Early Modern Europe, 1495–1715.* London: Routledge, 1992.

Tarle, Professor Evgenii. *How Kutuzov Defeated Napoleon.* Moscow, USSR: Soviet War News, ca. 1943?

Tarrant, V. E. *Jutland: The German Perspective: A New View of the Great Battle, 31 May 1916.* London: Arms and Armour, 1995.

Taylor, Frank. *The Wars of Marlborough, 1702–1709.* Oxford, U.K.: B. Blackwell, 1921.

Terry, Charles Sanford. *The Battle of Jutland Bank, May 31–June 1, 1916: The Dispatches of Admiral Sir John*

Jellicoe and Vice-Admiral Sir David Beatty. London: Oxford University Press, 1916.

———. *The Life and Campaigns of Alexander Leslie, First Earl of Leven.* London: Longmans, Green & Company, 1899.

Thomas, Alastair H., and Stewart P. Oakley. *Historical Dictionary of Denmark.* Lanham, Md.: The Scarecrow Press, 1998.

Thomas, Evan. *John Paul Jones.* New York: Simon & Schuster, 2003.

Thompson, E. A. *A History of Attila and the Huns.* Oxford, U.K.: Clarendon Press, 1948.

Thompson, Henry Yates. *An Englishman in the American Civil War: The Diaries of Henry Yates Thompson, 1863.* Edited by Sir Christopher Chancellor. London: Sedgwick and Jackson, 1971.

Thompson, William. *Montrosse Totally Routed at Tividale in Scotland by Lieut. Gen. Lesly.* London, 1645.

Thomson, George Malcolm. *Warrior Prince: Prince Rupert of the Rhine.* London: Secker & Warburg, 1976.

T.M. *A Particular List of Divers of the Commanders and Officers taken Prisoners at Marston Moore neer York (otherwise called Hesham Moore)[;] also a Relation of Some Remarkable Passages in the Fight: as it is Sent up in a Letter from Hull, Dated the Sixth of July, 1644.* London: Printed for Ralph Rounthwait, 1644.

Towle, George Makepeace. *The History of Henry the Fifth, King of England, Lord of Ireland, and Heir of France.* New York: D. Appleton and Company, 1866.

Trease, Geoffrey. *Portrait of a Cavalier: William Cavendish, First Duke of Newcastle.* New York: Taplinger Publishing Company, 1979.

Treharne, Reginald Francis. *The Personal Role of Simon de Montfort in the Period of Baronial Reform and Rebellion, 1238–65.* London: Cumberlage, 1954.

Tremain, Henry Edwin. *In Memoriam: Major-General Joseph Hooker.* Cincinnati: Robert Clark & Co., 1881.

Tritle, Lawrence A. *Phocion the Good.* London: Croom Helm, 1988.

The Triumphs of Nassau: or, A description and representation of all the victories both by land and sea, granted by God to the noble, high, and mightie lords, the Estates generall of the united Netherland Provinces Under the conduct and command of his excellencie, Prince Maurice of Nassau. Translated by W. Shute. London: Printed by Adam Islip, 1613.

A True and Fuller Relation of the Battell [sic] Fought at Stow in the Would [sic], March 21. 1645. Between the Forces under Sir William Brereton, Coll: Morgan, and the Lord Ashley. With a Catalogue of the Prisoners, &c. Sent by a Gentleman of Crédit under Sir William Brereton to some Members of the Honorable House of Commons, and by them Desired to be Published. London: Printed for Tho. Underhill, 1646.

A True Discourse of the Overthrowe given to the common enemy at Turnhaut, the 14. of January last 1597. by Count Moris of Nassaw and the states, assisted with the Englishe forces. Sent from a gentleman of account, that was present at the service, to a friend of his in England. London[?]: Printed by Peter Short, 1597.

True Intelligence, and Joyfull Newes from Ludlow, Declaring a Battell fought by his Excellency the Earle of Essex, against Prince Robert, Prince Maurice, and the rest of the cavaliers, neere Ludlow, October 1[,] 1642. Also the manner of the Earle of Essex his obtaining the victory, and putting the cavaliers to flight, and how he hath gained the castle, and strongly fortified the town of Ludlow. Together with the names of those that are taken prisoners, and the number of those that are slain. London: Printed for Th. Rider, 1642.

True Newes from Yorke. Consisting of severall Matters of Note, and High Concernment, since the 13 of June, concerning these several heads, viz: Concerning 1. Sir John Meldrum. 2. L. Marq. Hamilton. 3. Earle of Newcastle. 4. Earle of Warwick. 5. Lord Willoughby. 6. Duke of Richmond. 7. L. Marq Hersford. 8. Earle of Bristoll. 9. Lord Paget. Whereunto is added Newes from Ireland. viz. Concerning 1. E. of Antrime. 2. E. of Castlehaven. 3. Lord Conway. 4. Lord Digby. With a Catalogue of the Names of the Lords that Subscribed to Levie Horse to assist his Maiestie in defense of his Royall person, the two Houses of Parliament, and the Protestant Religion. London, 1642.

A True Relation of a Great Victory obtained by the Right Honourable the Lord Willoughby of Parham, Lieutenant of the county of Lincoln, Against divers Forces of the Earle of New-Castle, infesting the said County, As it was delivered to the High Court of Parliament by speedy Posts from the said Lord Willoughby of Parnam. London: Printed for Thomas Johnson, 1643.

A True Relation of the Fortunate S. William Waller, Collonel Under His Excellency the Earle of Essex, Concerning, The manner of the beseeging and taking of Chichester, Together with the Names of all Such Commanders and others taken Prisoners there and brought up to London. London, 1643.

A True Relation of the Great Victory Obtained by the Christian Army Over the Turks, Near the Mountain Harsan, in the Neighbourhood of Syclos, from the camp of Electorial Highness of Barnowar, the 14th of August, 1687. London: Printed for Samuel Carr, 1687.

A True Relation of the Late Fight betweene Sr William Wallers forces and those sent from Oxford. With the manner of Sir William Wallers retreat to Bristoll, and the condition of his army at this present. Sent from a Colonell in that army now in Bristoll to a friend of his in London. London: Printed by G. Dexter for R. Dunscum, 1643.

A True Relation of the Successes and Advantages obtained by the Most Christian King's army, Commanded by the Viscount de Turenne translated out of French. London: Printed by Tho. Newcomb, 1675.

Tuchman, Barbara. *The Guns of August.* New York: Macmillan, 1962.

Tucker, Glenn. *Hancock the Superb.* Indianapolis, Ind.: Bobbs-Merrill, 1960.

Tullie, Isaac. *A Narrative of the Siege of Carlisle, in 1644 and 1645. . . . To Which are Added, a Preface, an Historical Account of Carlisle During the Civil War; and Biographical, Historical, and Explanatory Notes: by Samuel Jefferson.* Carlisle, U.K.: Published by Samuel Jefferson, 1840.

The Turkes Secretorie conteining his Sundrie Letters sent to divers Emperours, Kings, Princes and states, full of proud bragges, and bloody threatnings: with severall answers to the same, both pithie and peremptorie. London: Printed by M[elchisedec] B[radwood], 1607.

Turner, John. *Macbeth.* Buckingham, U.K.: Open University Press, 1992.

Turner, Ralph V., and Richard R. Heiser. *The Reign of Richard Lionheart: Ruler of the Angevin Empire, 1189–1199.* London: Longman, 2000.

Tursun Beg. *The History of Mehmed the Conqueror.* Translated by Halil Inaloik and Rhoads Murphey. Minneapolis, Minn.: Bibliotheca Islamica, 1978.

Tyerman, Christopher. *Who's Who in British History: Early Medieval England, 1066–1272.* Mechanicsburg, Pa.: Stackpole Books, 1996.

———. *Who's Who in Early Medieval England, 1066–1272.* Mechanicsburg, Pa.: Stackpole Books, 1996.

Tyrrell, Henry. *The History of the War with Russia: Giving Full Details of the Operations of the Allied Armies.* London: The London Printing and Publishing Company, 1855–58.

Vail, Jason. "Shocking Triumph at Sea." *Great Battles* 7, no. 7 (September 1994): 50–57.

Vandiver, Frank Everson. *Black Jack: The Life and Times of John J. Pershing.* College Station: Texas A&M University Press, 1977.

Van Horne, Thomas Budd. *History of the Army of the Cumberland: Its Organization, Campaigns, and Battles, Written at the Request of Major-General George H. Thomas chiefly from his private Military Journal and official and other Documents furnished by him,* 3 vols. Cincinnati, Ohio: R. Clarke & Co., 1875.

Vere, Francis. *Salt in Their Blood: The Lives of the Famous Dutch Admirals.* London: Cassell & Company, Ltd., 1955.

The Very Interesting Life of the Famous Oliver Cromwell, With Accounts of the Civil Wars in Those Kingdoms, to Which are Added, Memoirs of Major Desborough, and Henry Ireton. 3d ed. Manchester, U.K.: William Wills, 1840.

A Vindication of His Majesty and The Army. As Also, the Grounds and Reasons of the Armies guarding the preservation of His Majesties Person. Authorized by Speciall Command. London: Printed for John Benson, 1647.

Waddam, Sir Henry. *The Danes Plot Discovered against this Kingdome: with the meeting of Van Trump, Dutch admirall at sea with them, upon the English coast neer Hull, wherein is related their Battell, flight, and Apprehension of two of their ships at Plympton Maries, in the county of Devond, which was sent to the Lord Burrowes and divers other the peers now assembled in Parliament.* London: Printed for Andrew Coe and Marmaduke Boat, 1642.

Waliszewski, Kazimierz. *Ivan the Terrible.* Translated by Lady Mary Loyd. Philadelphia: J. B. Lippincott Company, 1904.

Walker, Alexander. *The Life of Andrew Jackson: To which is Added an Authentic Narrative of the Memorable Achievements of the American Army at New Orleans, in the Winter of 1814, '15.* Philadelphia: Davis, Porter & Coates, 1866.

Walker, Francis Amasa. *Hancock in the War of Rebellion.* New York: The Press of G. J. Little & Company, 1891.

Wallace, Edgar. *Britain's Great Men: Field Marshal Sir John French and His Campaigns.* London: George Newnes, 1914.

———. *Britain's Great Men: Lord Roberts: The Man and His Campaigns.* London: George Newnes, 1914.

———. *Kitchener: The Man and His Campaigns.* London: George Newnes, 1914.

Walling, Robert Alfred John. *A Sea-dog of Devon: A Life of Sir John Hawkins.* London: Cassell and Company, 1907.

Warburton, Rev. William. *Edward III.* New York: Scribner, 1887.

Ward, George. *A Close Translation of the Lives of Miltiades and Epaminondas.* London: Ralph, Holland & Co., 1901.

Warmington, Brian Herbert. *Carthage.* Harmondsworth, U.K.: Penguin Books, 1969.

Warner, Oliver. *Hero of the Restoration: A Life of General George Monck, 1st Duke of Albemarle, K.G.* London: Jarrolds Publishers, Ltd., 1936.

Waszink, Paul M. *Life, Courage, Ice: A Semiological Study Essay on the Old Russian Biography of Aleksandr Nezskij.* Munich, Germany: Sagner, 1990.

The Wat'ry God. A Celebrated Song Written on Lord Hawke's Victory over Conflans in 1759. Dublin: John Lee, ca. 1770.

Watson, J. N. P. *Captain-General and Rebel Chief: The Life of James, Duke of Monmouth.* London: Allen & Unwin, 1979.

Watts, William. *The Swedish Intelligencer. Wherein out of the Truest and Choysest Informations are the famous actions of that warlike Prince historically led along, from the Norimberg Leaguer, unto the day of his death at the victory of Lutzen: with the Election of the Young Queene of Sweden, and the diet of Heilbrun: the Times and Places of every action being so sufficiently Observed and Described that the Reader may finde both Truth and Reason in it: Unto which is added the Fourth Part, wherein the chiefest of those military actions of other Swedish generalls be related, wherein the king Himselfe was not personally with the Army.* London: Printed for Nath. Butter and Nicholas Bourne, 1633.

———. *The Swedish Intelligencer. Wherein out of the Truest and Choysest Informations are the famous actions of that warlike Prince historically led along, from His Majesties first entring into the empire, untill his great Victory over the Generall Tilly at the battle of Leipsith: the Times and Places of every action being so sufficiently Observed and Described that the Reader may finde both Truth and Reason in it.* London: Printed for Nath. Butter and Nicholas Bourne, 1634.

Wawro, Geoffrey. *The Austro-Prussian War: Austria's War with Prussia and Italy in 1866.* Cambridge, U.K.: Cambridge University Press, 1996.

Webster, Graham. *Boudicca: The British Revolt against Rome A.D. 60.* Rev. ed. London: Batsford, 1993.

Weeks, Kent R. *The Lost Tomb: The Greatest Discovery at the Valley of the Kings since Tutankhamen.* London: Weidenfeld & Nicolson, 1998.

Weems, Mason Locke. *The Life of Gen. Francis Marion: A Celebrated Partisan Officer in the Revolution War against the British and Tories in South Carolina and Georgia.* Philadelphia: J. Allen, 1834.

Weigley, Russell F. *The American Way of War: A History of United States Military Strategy and Policy. The Wars of the United States.* New York: Macmillan Co., 1973.

———. *History of the United States Army. The Wars of the United States.* New York: Macmillan Co., 1967.

Weisberg, David B. *Texts from the Time of Nebuchadnezzar.* New Haven, Conn.: Yale University Press, 1980.

Wellard, James Howard. *The Man in a Helmet: The Life of General Patton.* London: Eyre & Spottiswoode, 1947.

Weller, Jac. *On Wellington: The Duke and His Art of War.* London: Greenhill Books, 1998.

Wencker, Friedrich. *Bernadotte, A Biography.* Translated by Kenneth Kirkness. London: Jarrolds, 1936.

Wenckstern, Father Friedrich von. *Bibliography of the Japanese Empire. Being a Classified List of the Literature in European Languages Relating to Dai Nihon [Great Japan],* 2 vols. London: Edward Goldston, 1907.

West, Richard S. *Admirals of American Empire: The Combined Story of George Dewey, Alfred Thayer Mahan, Winfield Scott Schley, and William Thomas Sampson.* Indianapolis, Ind.: Bobbs-Merrill, 1948.

Wheeler, Richard. *Sherman's March.* New York: Crowell, 1978.

Wheeler-Bennett, Sir John Wheeler. *Hindenburg: The Wooden Titan.* London: Macmillan, 1967.

Where His Majesty, in consideration of the Great Merit and Faithful Services of Sir William Penn, Deceased. London: Printed by the John Bill, Thomas Newcomb, and Henry Hills, 1681.

White, Colin. *The Nelson Encyclopedia.* Mechanicsburg, Pa.: Stackpole Books, 2002.

White, Jon Manchip. *Marshal of France: The Life and Times of Maurice, Comte de Saxe [1696–1750].* London: Hamish Hamilton, 1962.

Whitelock, Dorothy, ed. *English Historical Documents, c. 500–1042.* London: Eyre & Spottiswoode, 1955.

Whitlock, Brand. *La Fayette,* 2 vols. New York: D. Appleton and Company, 1929.

Wickwire, Franklin B., and Mary Wickwire. *Cornwallis: The American Adventure.* Boston: Houghton Mifflin, 1970.

Wieczynski, Joseph L., ed. *The Modern Encyclopedia of Russian and Soviet History,* 55 vols. Gulf Breeze, Fla.: Academic International Press, 1976–93.

Wilkin, Walter Harold. The Life of Sir David Baird. London: George Allen & Co., 1912.

Wilkinson, Clennell. *Prince Rupert the Cavalier.* Philadelphia: J. B. Lippincott & Company, 1935.

Wilkinson, Spenser. *Moltke's Correspondence During the Campaign of 1866 Against Austria.* London: Printed Under the Authority of His Majesty's Stationary Office, 1915.

———. *Moltke's Military Correspondence, 1870–71: Published by the Prussian General Staff Department for Military History.* Oxford, U.K.: Printed for Private Circulation, 1922.

Wilks, Mark. *Historical Sketches of the South of India, in an Attempt to Trace the History of Mysoor; From the Origin of the Hindoo government of that State, to the Extinction of the Mohammedan Dynasty in 1799,* 3 vols. London: Longman, Hurst, Rees, and Orme, 1810–17.

Willcox, William B. *Portrait of a General: Sir Henry Clinton in the War of Independence.* New York: Alfred A. Knopf, 1964.

Williams, Hugh Noel. *The Life and Letters of Admiral Sir Charles Napier, K.C.B.* London: Hutchinson & Co., 1917.

Williams, T. Harry. *Americans at War: The Development of the American Military System.* Baton Rouge: Louisiana State University Press, 1960.

———. *McClellan, Sherman, and Grant. The 1962 Brown and Haley Lectures.* New Brunswick, N.J.: Rutgers University Press, 1962.

Williamson, James Alexander. *Sir John Hawkins: The Time and the Man.* Oxford, U.K.: Clarendon Press, 1927.

Wilson, Derek A. *In the Lion's Court: Power, Ambition, and Sudden Death in the Court of Henry VIII.* London: Hutchinson, 2001.

Windrow, Martin. *Montcalm's Army.* Reading, Pa.: Osprey Publishing, 1973.

Windrow, Martin, and Francis K. Mason. *The Wordsworth Dictionary of Military Biography.* Hertfordshire, U.K.: Wordsworth Editions Ltd., 1997.

Winser, Andrew. "Lieut. General Sir Eyre Coote, 1726–1783." *The Hatcher Review* 2, no. 15 (1983): 218–227.

Winsor, Justin. *Note on the Spurious Letters of Montcalm, 1759.* Cambridge, U.K.: John Wilson and Son, 1887.

Wishart, George. *De Rebus Auspiciis Serenissimi, & Potentissimi Caroli (The History of the Kings Majesties Affaires in Scotland: Under the Conduct of the most Honourable James, Marques of Montrose, Earl of Kincardin, &c., and Generall Governour of the Kingdome, in the Years 1644, 1645, & 1646).* Amsterdam: Privately printed, 1649.

———. *Memoirs of the Most Renowned James Graham, Marquis of Montrose. Translated from the Latin of the Rev. Dr. George Wishart. To which are added, Sundry Original Letters, Never Before Published.* Edinburgh: Printed for A. Constable & Co., 1819.

Wolfe, Charles. *The Burial of Sir John Moore, and Other Poems.* London: Sidgwick and Jackson, 1909.

Wolff, Leon. *In Flanders Fields: The 1917 Campaign.* New York: Time-Life Books, 1958.

Wolfram, Herwig. *History of the Goths.* Berkeley: University of California Press, 1988.

Woodham Smith, Cecil Blanche. *The Reason Why.* London: Constable, 1953.

Woodrooffe, Thomas. *Vantage at Sea: England's Emergence as an Oceanic Power.* New York: St. Martin's Press, 1958.

Wright, Frederick Adam. *Marcus Agrippa: Organizer of Victory.* London: G. Routledge & Sons, 1937.

Wrottesley, George. *Crécy and Calais, From the Original Records in the Public Record Office.* London: Harrison and Sons, St. Martin's Lane, 1898.

Wylly, Harold Carmichael. *The Campaign of Magenta and Solferino, 1859.* London: Swan Sonnenschein & Co., 1907.

———. *A Life of Lieutenant-General Sir Eyre Coote, K.B., compiled by Colonel H.C. Wylly, C.B., with an introduction by General Sir Charles Monro, bart.* Oxford, U.K.: Clarendon Press, 1922.

Xenophon. *The Story of Cyrus, Adapted from Xenophon's Cyropaedia.* Translated by Clarence W. Gleason. New York: American Book Company, 1900.

Yanov, Alexander. *The Origins of Autocracy: Ivan the Terrible in Russian History.* Translated by Stephen Dunn. Berkeley: University of California Press, 1981.

Yeo, Margaret. *Don John of Austria.* New York: Sheed & Ward, Inc., 1934.

Yonge, C. D. *The Roman History of Ammianus Marcellinus, During the Reigns of the Emperors Constantius, Julian, Jovianus, Valentinian, and Valens.* London: George Bell & Sons, 1887.

Young, Charles R. *The Making of the Neville Family in England, 1166–1400.* Woodbridge, U.K.: Boydell Press, 1996.

Young, Desmond. *Rommel: The Desert Fox.* New York: Harper, 1950.

Young, Peter. *Naseby 1645: The Campaign and the Battle.* London: Century Publishing, 1985.

Zhukov, Georgii, et al. *Battles Hitler Lost, and the Soviet Marshals Who Won Them: Marshals Zhukov, Konev, Malinovsky, Rokossovsky, Rotmistrov, Chuikov, and other Commanders.* New York: Richardson & Steirman, 1986.

Ziegler, Philip. *Omdurman.* London: Collins, 1974.

NEWSPAPERS

The Daily Mirror [London, England]
The Daily Telegraph [London, England]
The New York Herald [Paris edition]
The New York Times
The Times [London, England]
The Washington Post
The World [New York]

MANUSCRIPT COLLECTIONS

Adjutant General's Office Papers: RG 94. Records of the Adjutant General's Office, ca. 1775–ca. 1928. National Archives, Washington, D.C.

The George Washington Papers, 1741–1799, Series 4: General Correspondence, 1697–1799. Library of Congress, Washington, D.C.

Letters of and Relating to Thomas Pelham-Holles, 1st Duke of Newcastle under Lyne (1725–1771). University of Nottingham Library, Newcastle, U.K.

The Papers of Abraham Lincoln. Library of Congress, Washington, D.C.

The Papers of Horatio Herbert Kitchener, 1st Earl Kitchener of Khartoum. Public Record Office series PRO 30/57/1. Public Record Office, Kew, U.K.

GOVERNMENT DOCUMENTS

United Kingdom. Public Record Office. *Chronicles and Memorials of the Reign of Richard I. Published by the Authority of the Lords Commissioners of Her Majesty's Treasury, under the Direction of the Master of the Rolls.* 2 vols. Edited by William Stubbs. London: Longman, Green, Longman, Roberts, and Green, 1864–65.

U.S. Congress. *Joint Resolution Conferring Honorary Citizenship of the United States Posthumously on Marie Joseph Paul Yves Roche Gilbert du Motier, the Marquis de Lafayette.* Washington, D.C.: Government Printing Office, 2002.

U.S. Senate. "Nomination of Winfield Scott. Executive Proceedings of the Senate of the United States, From which the Injunction of Secrecy Has Been Removed, During the Second Session of the Thirty-third Congress, Commencing on Monday, the Fourth Day of December, 1854, and Terminating Third March, 1855." In *Journal of the Senate of the United States of America, Being the Second Session of the Thirty-third Congress, Begun and Held at the City of Washington, December 4, 1854; and in the Seventy-ninth Year of the Independence of the United States.* Washington: Beverley Tucker, Printer, 1854.

INDEX

Boldface numbers indicate main entries.
Italic numbers indicate photographs.